# THE

# THEOSOPHICAL GLOSSARY

# Theosophy Trust Books

- *Theosophical Astrology*
by Helen Valborg, WQ Judge, HP Blavatsky, Raghavan Iyer

- *The Bhagavad-Gita and Notes on the Gita*
by WQ Judge, Robert Crosbie, Raghavan Iyer, HP Blavatsky

- *Theosophy ~ The Wisdom Religion*
by the Editorial Board of Theosophy Trust

- *Self-Actualization and Spiritual Self-Regeneration*
- *Mahatma Gandhi and Buddha's Path to Enlightenment*
- *The Yoga Sutras of Patanjali*
- *Meditation and Self-Study*
- *Wisdom in Action*
- *The Dawning of Wisdom*
by Raghavan Iyer

- *The Theosophical Glossary*
- *The Secret Doctrine*, Vols. I and II
- *Isis Unveiled*, Vols. I and II
- *The Key to Theosophy*
- *The Voice of the Silence*
- *The Origins of Self-Consciousness
in The Secret Doctrine*
- *Evolution and Intelligent Design
in The Secret Doctrine*
by H.P. Blavatsky

- *The Ocean of Theosophy*
by William Q. Judge

- *Teachers of the Eternal Doctrine*
by Elton Hall

- *Symbols of the Eternal Doctrine*
by Helen Valborg

# The

# Theosophical Glossary

By

H. P. Blavatsky

Author Of "Isis Unveiled", "The Secret Doctrine",
"The Key To Theosophy"

London:
THE THEOSOPHICAL PUBLISHING SOCIETY,
7, DUKE STREET, ADELPHI, W.C.
The Path Office: 132, NASSAU STREET, NEW YORK, U.S.A.
The Theosophist Office: ADYAR, MADRAS, INDIA.
1892

———

THEOSOPHY TRUST BOOKS
NORFOLK, VA

# The Theosophical Glossary

Theosophy Trust books may be ordered through Amazon.com, CreateSpace.com, and other retail outlets, or by visiting:

http://www.theosophytrust.org/online_books.php

ISBN-13: 978-0-9992382-4-0
ISBN-10: 0-9992382-4-8

Library of Congress Control Number: 2018953926

Printed in the United States of America

Dedicated to Theosophists everywhere
Who strive to comprehend the
Depths of the Wisdom Religion

The central tenets of *Theosophia* are not derived from any ancient or modern sect but represent the accumulated wisdom of the ages, the unrecorded inheritance of humanity. Its vast scheme of cosmic and human evolution furnishes all true seekers with the symbolic alphabet necessary to interpret their recurrent visions as well as the universal framework and metaphysical vocabulary, drawn from many mystics and seers, which enable them to communicate their own intuitive perceptions. All authentic mystical writings are enriched by the alchemical flavour of Theosophical thought. Theosophy is an integrated system of fundamental verities taught by Initiates and Adepts across millennia. It is the *Philosophia Perennis*, the philosophy of human perfectibility, the science of spirituality and the religion of responsibility. It is the primeval fount of myriad religious systems as well as the hidden essence and esoteric wisdom of each. Man, an immortal monad, has been able to preserve this sacred heritage through the sacrificial efforts of enlightened and compassionate individuals, or *Bodhisattvas*, who constitute an ancient Brotherhood. They quietly assist in the ethical evolution and spiritual development of the whole of humanity. *Theosophia* is Divine Wisdom, transmitted and verified over aeons by the sages who belong to this secret Brotherhood.

*Spritual Evolution*
*Hermes*, August 1979
Raghavan Iyer

# PUBLISHER'S PREFACE

*The Theosophical Glossary* was H. P. Blavatsky's last publication; in fact, it was not published in full until after her death in 1891. That is not to say she did not write nearly all of it, nor that she did not see any of it published before her death. Many of the entries in this *Glossary* were written by her in one or another of her many articles and books, most notably *The Key to Theosophy*, which contains the embryonic form of this *Glossary* at the end of the book.

The online article "Authorship of the Theosophical Glossary" [1] from the Blavatsky Theosophy Group UK puts the matter succinctly:

> The reason it was "an almost entirely posthumous work" was because only a small portion of its contents had been published while HPB was still alive, such as in the sixty page Glossary she included at the end of the second edition of her book "*The Key to Theosophy*," at the conclusion of which she wrote, "Readers requiring fuller information about any particular term should consult THE THEOSOPHICAL GLOSSARY now in preparation.

A careful and comprehensive study of the entire contents of the *Theosophical Glossary* will show that many of the entries are derived from the books and articles written and published by H.P.B. during her lifetime and are here collated topically and alphabetically for the easy reference of the student of Theosophy; others are reproduced from the Glossary included at the end of *The Key to Theosophy*, whilst numerous other entries can be found nowhere else in the Theosophical literature. These go into such profound depths on esoteric subjects – and in the customary style and language of H.P.B. – that their value and authorship cannot be legitimately questioned.

As H.P.B. wrote in the Introduction to *The Secret Doctrine*, her work "is written for the instruction of students of Occultism, and *not* for the benefit of philologists."

The reader may rest assured all of the entries in this work are those of H.P.B., except those clearly marked as [w.w.w.], which were contributed

---

[1] See https://blavatskytheosophy.com/authorship-of-the-theosophical-glossary/ for the full text of the article.

at the special request of H.P.B. by W. W. Westcott, who was then Secretary General of the Rosicrucian Society. Those entries deal almost exclusively with topics of the *Kabbalah*, or Rosicrucian or Hermetic doctrines.

The original version of this *Glossary* also notes that "H.P.B. desired also to express her special indebtedness, as far as the tabulation of facts is concerned, to the *Sanskrit-Chinese Dictionary* of Eitel, *The Hindu Classical Dictionary* of Dowson, *The Vishnu Purâna* of Wilson, and the *Royal Masonic Cyclopædia* of Kenneth Mackenzie."

The *Glossary* provides meanings and context to the wealth of Sanskrit, Greek, Latin, Tibetan, Chaldean, Persian, Scandinavian, Hebrew, Kabalistic, Gnostic, and Occult terms found in the many works of Theosophical literature: the two volumes each of *Isis Unveiled* and *The Secret Doctrine*, *The Key to Theosophy*, *The Ocean of Theosophy*, the journals *Theosophist*, *Lucifer* and *The Path*, and other publications of the 19th Century Theosophical Society. Directly following each entry, the reader will find a key to the linguistic origins of the terms in the parentheses: (*San.*), (*Heb.*), (*Grk.*), etc. The abbreviation (*S.D.*) of course means *The Secret Doctrine*. Also note, the Tibetan transliterations into English are the 19th century conventions and do not always follow more recent conventions for transliterating Tibetan into English letters. In the original edition, Sanskrit words beginning with the letters Tch were misplaced under 'T', along with a note that they should appear under 'C'; this edition retains those words and note as in the original, and also places them under their rightful heading, 'C'.

Finally, students of Theosophy will find great value in referring to the *Glossary* in their research work, as H.P.B. sometimes provides insight into the primary terms used throughout the literature that can be found nowhere else. For those intent upon uncovering as many threads connected to a given term or phrase as possible, an online and fully searchable version of this work can be found at the Theosophy Trust website at
https://www.theosophytrust.org/Online_Books/Theosophical_Glossary_V 2.4.pdf

Theosophy is the *Sanatana Dharma*, the eternal wisdom of *theosophia*, the knowledge and wisdom which underlie the universe, and which cannot be wholly expressed in discursive thought or words. What the Elder Brothers of Humanity have given to the world as Theosophy aims to help the intuitive student to enter the depths of that wisdom to the degree to which he or she is capable. So, even though there is no obvious theme running throughout the vast universe of terms in the *Glossary*, there is, indeed, an undercurrent of eternal wisdom that knits together all of the comments made, an undercurrent of precise, ordered thought that forms the structure of the Theosophical philosophy, which reaches back, as the term *Sanatana Dharma* implies, into the very origins of thinking Humanity upon this globe. This volume will surely assist all those who approach it from that lofty vantage point.

Editor, Theosophy Trust

https://www.theosophytrust.org/

# THEOSOPHICAL
# GLOSSARY

# A

**A.**—The first letter in all the world-alphabets save a few, such for instance as the Mongolian, the Japanese, the Tibetan, the Ethiopian, etc. It is a letter of great mystic power and "magic virtue" with those who have adopted it, and with whom its numerical value is one. It is the *Aleph* of the Hebrews, symbolized by the Ox or Bull; the *Alpha* of the Greeks, the one and the first the *Az* of the Slavonians, signifying the pronoun "I" (referring to the "I am that I am"). Even in Astrology, Taurus (the Ox or Bull or the *Aleph*) is the first of the Zodiacal signs, its colour being white and yellow. The sacred *Aleph* acquires a still more marked sanctity with the Christian Kabalists when they learn that this letter typifies the Trinity in Unity, as it is composed of two Yods, one upright, the other reversed with a slanting bar or nexus, thus—א. Kenneth R. H. Mackenzie states that "the St. Andrew cross is occultly connected therewith". The divine name, the first in the series corresponding with *Aleph*, is AêHêIêH or *Ahih* when vowelless, and this is a Sanskrit root.

**Aahla** (*Eg.*). One of the divisions of the *Kerneter* or infernal regions, or Amenti; the word means the "Field of Peace".

**Aanroo** (*Eg.*). The second division of Amenti. The celestial field of Aanroo is encircled by an iron wall. The field is covered with wheat, and the "Defunct" are represented gleaning it, for the "Master of Eternity"; some stalks being three, others five, and the highest seven cubits high. Those who reached the last two numbers entered the state of bliss (which is called in Theosophy Devachan); the disembodied spirits whose harvest was but three cubits high went into lower regions (*Kâmaloka*). Wheat was with the Egyptians the symbol of the *Law of retribution* or *Karma*. The cubits had reference to the seven, five and three human "principles".

**Aaron** (*Heb.*). The elder brother of Moses and the *first Initiate* of the Hebrew Lawgiver. The name means the *Illuminated*, or the *Enlightened*. Aaron thus heads the line, or Hierarchy, of the initiated *Nabim*, or Seers.

**Ab** (*Heb.*). The eleventh month of the Hebrew civil year; the fifth of the sacred year beginning in July. [w.w.w.]

**Abaddon** (*Heb.*). An angel of Hell, corresponding to the Greek Apollyon.

**Abatur** (*Gn.*). In the Nazarene system the "Ancient of Days", *Antiquus Altus*, the Father of the Demiurgus of the Universe, is called the *Third Life* or "Abatur". He corresponds to the *Third* "Logos" in the *Secret Doctrine*. (See *Codex Nazaræus*)

**Abba Amona** (*Heb.*). *Lit.*, "Father-Mother"; the occult names of the two higher Sephiroth, *Chokmah* and *Binah*, of the upper triad, the apex of which is Sephira or Kether. From this triad issues the lower septenary of the Sephirothal Tree.

**Abhâmsi** (*Sk.*). A mystic name of the "four orders of beings" which are, Gods, Demons, Pitris and Men. Orientalists somehow connect the name with "waters", but esoteric philosophy connects its symbolism with *Akâsa*—the ethereal "waters of space", since it is on the bosom and on the seven planes of "space" that the "four orders of (lower) beings" and the three higher Orders of Spiritual Beings are born. (See *Secret Doctrine* [*S. D.*] I. p. 458, and "Ambhâmsi".)

**Abhâsvaras** (*Sk.*). The Devas or "Gods" of *Light and Sound*, the highest of the upper three celestial regions (planes) of the second *Dhyâna* (*q.v.*) A class of gods *sixty-four* in number, representing a certain cycle and an occult number.

**Abhâva** (*Sk.*). Negation, or non-being of individual objects; the *noumenal* substance, or abstract objectivity.

**Abhaya** (*Sk.*). "Fearlessness"—a son of Dharma; and also a religious life of duty. As an adjective, "Fearless," Abhaya is an epithet given to every Buddha,

**Abhayagiri** (*Sk.*). *Lit.*, "Mount Fearless" in Ceylon. It has an ancient *Vihâra* or Monastery in which the well-known Chinese traveller Fa-hien found 5,000 Buddhist priests and ascetics in the year 400 of our era, and a School called *Abhayagiri Vâsinah*,, "School of the Secret Forest". This philosophical school was regarded as heretical, as the ascetics studied the doctrines of both the "greater" and the "smaller" vehicles—or the *Mahâyâna* and the *Hinayâna* systems and *Triyâna* or the three successive degrees of Yoga; just as a certain Brotherhood does now beyond the Himalayas. This proves that the "disciples of Kâtyâyana were and are as *unsectarian* as their humble admirers the Theosophists are now. (See "Sthâvirâh" School.) This was the most mystical of all the schools, and renowned for the number of Arhats it produced. The Brotherhood of *Abhayagiri* called themselves the disciples of Kâtyâyana, the favourite Chela of Gautama, the Buddha.

Tradition says that owing to bigoted intolerance and persecution, they left Ceylon and passed beyond the Himalayas, where they have remained ever since.

**Abhidharma** (*Sk.*). The metaphysical (third) part of *Tripitaka*, a very philosophical Buddhist work by Kâtyâyana.

**Abhijñâ** (*Sk.*). Six phenomenal (or "supernatural") gifts which Sâkyamuni Buddha acquired in the night on which he reached Buddhaship. This is the "fourth" degree of Dhyâna (the seventh in esoteric teachings) which has to be attained by every true Arhat. In China, the initiated Buddhist ascetics reckon six such powers, but in Ceylon they reckon only five. The first Abhijñâ is *Divyachakchus*, the instantaneous view of anything one wills to see; the second, is *Divyasrotra*, the power of comprehending any sound whatever, etc., etc.

**Abhimânim** (*Sk.*). The name of Agni (fire) the "eldest son of Brahmâ", in other words, the first element or Force produced in the universe at its evolution (the fire of creative desire). By his wife Swâhâ, Abhimânim had three sons (the fires) Pâvaka, Pavamâna and Suchi, and these had "forty-five sons, who, with the original son of Brahmâ and his three descendants, constitute the *forty-nine fires*" of Occultism.

**Abhimanyu** (*Sk.*). A son of Arjuna. He killed Lakshmana,in the great battle of the Mahâbhârata on its second day, but was himself killed on the thirteenth.

**Abhûtarajasas** (*Sk.*). A class of gods or *Devas*, during the period of the fifth Manvantara.

**Abib** (*Heb.*) The first Jewish sacred month, begins in March; is also called *Nisan*.

**Abiegnus Mons** (*Lat.*). A mystic name, from whence as from a certain mountain, Rosicrucian documents are often found to be issued—"Monte Abiegno". There is a connection with Mount Meru, and other sacred hills. [w.w.w.]

**Ab-i-hayat** (*Pers.*). Water of immortality. Supposed to give eternal youth and sempiternal life to him who drinks of it.

**Abiri** (*Gr.*). See Kabiri, also written Kabeiri, the Mighty Ones, celestials, sons of Zedec the just one, a group of deities worshipped in Phœnicia: they seem to be identical with the Titans, Corybantes, Curetes, Telchines and Dii Magni of Virgil. [w.w.w.]

**Ablanathanalba** (*Gn.*). A term similar to "Abracadabra". It is said by C. W.

King to have meant "thou art a father to us"; it reads the same from either end and was used as a charm in Egypt.

(See "Abracadabra".)

**Abracadabra** (*Gn.*). This symbolic word first occurs in a medical treatise in verse by Samonicus, who flourished in the reign of the Emperor Septimus Seveus. Godfrey Higgins says it is from *Abra* or *Abar* "God", in Celtic, and cad "holy"; it was used as a charm, and engraved on *Kameas* as an amulet. [w.w.w.]

Godfrey Higgins was nearly right, as the word "Abracadabra" is a later corruption of the sacred Gnostic term "Abrasax", the latter itself being a still earlier corruption of a sacred and ancient Coptic or Egyptian word: a magic formula which meant in its symbolism "Hurt me not", and addressed the deity in its hieroglyphics as "Father". It was generally attached to an amulet or charm and worn as a Tat (*q.v.*), on the breast under the garments.

**Abraxas or Abrasax** (*Gn.*). Mystic words which have been traced as far back as Basilides, the Pythagorean, of Alexandria, AD. 90. He uses Abraxas as a title for Divinity, the supreme of Seven, and as having 365 virtues. In Greek numeration, a. 1, b. 2, r. 100, a. I, x 60, a. I, s. 200 = 365 days of the year, solar year, a cycle of divine action. C. W. King, author of The Gnostics, considers the word similar to the Hebrew *Shemhamphorasch*, a holy word, the extended name of God. An Abraxas Gem usually shows a man's body with the head of a cock, one arm with a shield, the other with a whip. [w.w.w.]

Abraxas is the counterpart of the Hindu Abhimânim (*q.v.*) and Brahmâ combined. It is these compound and mystic qualities which caused Oliver, the great Masonic authority, to connect the name of Abraxas with that of Abraham. This was unwarrantable; the virtues and attributes of Abraxas, which are 365 in number, ought to have shown him that the deity was connected with the Sun and solar division of the year—nay, that Abraxas is the antitype, and the Sun, the type.

**Absoluteness**. When predicated of the UNIVERSAL PRINCIPLE, it denotes an abstract noun, which is more correct and logical than to apply the adjective "absolute" to that which has neither attributes nor limitations, nor can IT have any.

**Ab-Soo** (*Chald.*). The mystic name for Space, meaning the dwelling of *Ab* the "Father", or the head of the source of the Waters of Knowledge. The lore of the latter is concealed in the invisible space or akasic regions.

**Acacia** (*Gr.*). Innocence; and also a plant used in Freemasonry as a symbol of initiation, immortality, and purity; the tree furnished the sacred Shittim wood of the Hebrews. [w.w.w.]

**Achamôth** (*Gn.*). The name of the second, the inferior Sophia. Esoterically and with the Gnostics, the elder Sophia was the Holy Spirit (female Holy Ghost) or the *Sakti* of the Unknown, and the *Divine* Spirit; while Sophia Achamôth is but the personification of the female aspect of the creative male Force in nature; also the Astral Light.

**Achar** (*Heb.*). The Gods over whom (according to the Jews) Jehovah is the God.

**Âchâra** (*Sk.*). Personal and social (religious) obligations.

**Âchârya** (*Sk.*). Spiritual teacher, Guru; as Sankar-*âchârya*, lit., a "teacher of ethics". A name generally given to Initiates, etc., and meaning "Master".

**Achath** (*Heb.*). The *one*, the first, feminine; *achad* being masculine. A Talmudic word applied to Jehovah. It is worthy of note that the Sanskrit term *ak* means one, *ekata* being "unity", Brahmâ being called *âk*, or *eka*, the one, the first, whence the Hebrew word and application.

**Acher** (*Heb.*). The Talmudic name of the Apostle Paul. The Talmud narrates the story of the four *Tanaim*, who entered the *Garden of Delight*, i.e., came to he initiated; Ben Asai, who looked and lost his sight; Ben Zoma, who looked and lost his reason; Acher, who made depredations in the garden and failed; and Rabbi Akiba, who alone succeeded. The Kabalists say that Acher is Paul.

**Acheron** (*Gr.*). One of the rivers of Hades in Greek mythology.

**Achit** (*Sk.*). Absolute non-intelligence; as *Chit* is—in contrast—absolute intelligence.

**Achyuta** (*Sk.*). That which is not subject to change or fall; the opposite to *Chyuta,* "fallen". A title of Vishnu.

**Acosmism** (*Gr.*). The precreative period, when there was no Kosmos but Chaos alone.

**Ad** (*Assyr.*). *Ad,* "the Father". In Aramean *ad* means one, and *ad-ad* "the only one".

**Adah** (Assyr.). Borrowed by the Hebrews for the name of their Adah, father of Jubal, etc. But Adah meaning the first, the one, is universal property. There are reasons to think that *Ak-ad,* means the *first*-born or Son of *Ad. Adon* was the first "Lord" of Syria. (See *Isis Unv.* II., pp. 452, 453.)

**Adam** (*Heb.*). In the *Kabalah* Adam is the "only-begotten", and means also "red earth". (See "Adam-Adami" in the *S.D.* II p. 452.) It is almost identical with *Athamas* or *Thomas*, and is rendered into Greek by *Didumos*, the "twin"—Adam, "the first", in chap. 1 of *Genesis*, being shown, "male-female."

**Adam Kadmon** *(Heb)*. Archetypal Man; Humanity. The "Heavenly Man" not fallen into sin; Kabalists refer it to the Ten Sephiroth on the plane of human perception. [w.w.w.]

In the *Kabalah* Adam Kadmon is the manifested Logos corresponding to our *Third* Logos; the Unmanifested being the first paradigmic ideal Man, and symbolizing the Universe in *abscondito*, or in its "privation" in the Aristotelean sense. The First Logos is the "Light of the World", the Second and the Third—its gradually deepening shadows.

**Adamic Earth** *(Alch.)*. Called the "true oil of gold" or the "primal element" in Alchemy. It is but one remove from the pure homogeneous element.

**Adbhuta Brâhmana** *(Sk.)*. The Brâhmana of miracles; treats of marvels, auguries, and various phenomena.

**Adbhuta Dharma** *(Sk.)*. The "law" of things never heard before. A class of Buddhist works on miraculous or phenomenal events.

**Adept** *(Lat.)*. *Adeptus*, "He who has obtained." In Occultism one who has reached the stage of Initiation, and become a Master in the science of Esoteric philosophy.

**Adharma** *(Sk.)*. Unrighteousness, vice, the opposite of Dharma.

**Adhi** *(Sk.)*. Supreme, paramount.

**Adhi-bhautika duhkha** *(Sk.)*. The second of the three kinds of pain; *lit.*, "Evil proceeding from external things or beings".

**Adhi-daivika duhkha** *(Sk.)*. The third of the three kinds of pain. "Evil proceeding from divine causes, or a just Karmic punishment".

**Adhishtânam** *(Sk.)*. Basis; a principle in which some other principle inheres.

**Adhyâtmika duhkha** *(Sk.)*. The first of the three kinds of pain; lit., "Evil proceeding from Self", an induced or a generated evil by Self, or man himself.

**Adhyâtma Vidyâ** *(Sk.)*. Lit., "the esoteric luminary". One of the Pancha Vidyâ Sastras, or the Scriptures of the Five Sciences.

**Âdi** *(Sk.)* The First, the primeval.

**Âdi** (the Sons of). In Esoteric philosophy the "Sons of Adi" are called the

"Sons of the Fire-mist". A term used of certain adepts.

**Âdi-bhûta** (*Sk.*). The first Being; also primordial element. *Adbhuta* is a title of Vishnu, the "first Element" containing all elements, "the *unfathomable* deity".

**Âdi-Buddha** (*Sk.*). The First and Supreme Buddha—not recognised in the Southern Church. The Eternal Light.

**Âdi-budhi** (*Sk.*). Primeval Intelligence or Wisdom; the eternal Budhi or Universal Mind. Used of *Divine Ideation*, "Mahâbuddhi" being synonymous with MAHAT.

**Âdikrit** (*Sk.*). Lit., the "first produced" or made. The creative Force eternal and uncreate, but manifesting periodically. Applied to Vishnu slumbering on the "waters of space" during "pralaya" (*q.v.*).

**Âdi-nâtha** (*Sk.*). The "first" Lord"—*Âdi* "first" (masc.), *nâtha* "Lord".

**Âdi-nidâna** (*Sk.*). First and Supreme Causality, from *Âdi*, the first, and *Nidâna* the principal cause (or the concatenation of cause and effect).

**Âdi-Sakti** (*Sk.*). Primeval, divine Force; the female creative power, and aspect in and of every male god. The *Sakti* in the Hindu Pantheon is always the spouse of some god.

**Âdi-Sanat** (*Sk.*). Lit., "First Ancient". The term corresponds to the Kabalistic "ancient of days", since it is a title of Brahmâ—called in the *Zohar* the *Atteekah d'Atteekeen,* or "the Ancient of the Ancients", *etc.*

**Âditi** (*Sk.*). The Vedic name for the *Mûlaprakriti* of the Vedantists; the abstract aspect of Parabrahman, though both unmanifested and unknowable. In the *Vedas* Âditi is the "Mother-Goddess", her terrestrial symbol being infinite and shoreless space.

**Âditi-Gæa.** A compound term, Sanskrit and Latin, meaning dual, nature in theosophical writings—spiritual and physical, as Gæa is the goddess of the earth and of objective nature.

**Âditya** (*Sk.*). A name of the Sun; as Mârttânda he is the Son of Aditi.

**Âdityas** (*Sk.*). The seven sons of Âditi; the seven planetary gods.

**Âdi Varsha** (*Sk.*). The first land; the primordial country in which dwelt the first races.

**Adonai** (*Heb.*). The same as Adonis. Commonly translated "Lord". Astronomically—the Sun. When a Hebrew in reading came to the name IHVH, which is called Jehovah, he paused and substituted the word "Adonai", (Adni); but when written with the points of Alhim, he called it

"Elohim". [w.w.w.]

**Adonim-Adonai, Adon**. The ancient Chaldeo-Hebrew names for the Elohim or creative terrestrial forces, synthesized by Jehovah.

**Adwaita** (*Sk.*). A Vedânta sect. The non-dualistic (A-dwaita) school of Vedântic philosophy founded by Sankarâchârya, the greatest of the historical Brahmin sages. The two other schools are the Dwaita (dualistic) and the Visishtadwaita; all the three call themselves Vedântic.

**Adwaitin** (*Sk.*). A follower of the said school.

**Adytum** (*Gr.*). The Holy of Holies in the pagan temples. A name for the secret and sacred precincts or the inner chamber, into which no profane could enter; it corresponds to the sanctuary of the altars of Christian Churches.

**Æbel-Zivo** (*Gn.*). The Metatron or anointed spirit with the Nazarene Gnostics; the same as the angel Gabriel.

**Æolus** (*Gr.*). The god who, according to Hesiod, binds and looses the winds; the king of storms and winds. A king of Æolia, the inventor of sails and a great astronomer, and therefore deified by posterity.

**Æon** or **Æons** (*Gr.*). Periods of time; emanations proceeding from the divine essence, and celestial beings; genii and angels with the Gnostics.

**Æsir** (*Scand.*). The same as *Ases*, the creative Forces personified. The gods who created the black dwarfs or the *Elves of Darkness* in Asgard. The divine Æsir, the Ases are the Elves of Light. An allegory bringing together darkness which comes from light, and matter born of spirit.

**Æther** (*Gr.*). With the ancients the divine luminiferous substance which pervades the whole universe, the "garment" of the Supreme Deity, Zeus, or Jupiter. With the moderns, Ether, for the meaning of which in physics and chemistry see Webster's *Dictionary* or any other. In esotericism Æther is the third principle of the Kosmic Septenary; the Earth being the lowest, then the Astral light, Ether and Âkâsa (phonetically Âkâsha) the highest.

**Æthrobacy** (*Gr.*). Lit., walking on, or being lifted into the air with no visible agent at work; "levitation". It may be conscious or unconscious; in the one case it is magic, in the other either disease or a power which requires a few words of elucidation. We know that the earth is a magnetic body; in fact, as some scientists have found, and as Paracelsus affirmed some 300 years ago, it is one vast magnet. It is charged with one form of electricity—let us call it positive—which it evolves continuously by spontaneous action, in its interior or centre of motion. Human bodies, in common with all other forms of matter, are charged with the opposite form of electricity, the negative. That is to say, organic or inorganic bodies, if left to themselves will constantly and involuntarily charge themselves with and evolve the form of electricity opposite to that of the earth itself. Now, what is weight? Simply the attraction of the earth. "Without the attraction of the earth you would have no weight", says Professor Stewart; "and if you had an earth twice as heavy as this, you would have double the attraction". How then, can we get rid of this attraction? According to the electrical law above stated, there is an attraction between our planet and the organisms upon it, which keeps them upon the surface of the globe. But the law of gravitation has been counteracted in many instances, by levitation of persons and inanimate objects. How account for this? The condition of our physical systems, say theurgic philosophers, is largely dependent upon the action of our will. If well-regulated, it can produce "miracles"; among others a change of this electrical polarity from negative to positive; the man's relations with the earth-magnet would then become repellent, and "gravity"for him would have ceased to exist. It would then be as natural for him to rush into the air until the repellent force had exhausted itself, as, before, it had been for him to remain upon the ground. The altitude of his levitation would be measured by his ability, greater or less, to charge his body with positive electricity. This control over the physical forces once obtained, alteration of his levity or gravity would be as easy as breathing. (See *Isis Unveiled*, Vol. I., page xxiii.)

**Afrits** (*Arab.*). A name for native spirits regarded as devils by Mussulmen. Elementals much dreaded in Egypt.

**Agapæ** (*Gr.*). Love Feasts; the early Christians kept such festivals in token of sympathy, love and mutual benevolence. It became necessary to abolish them as an institution, because of great abuse; Paul in his First Epistle to the Corinthians complains of misconduct at the feasts of the Christians. [w.w.w.].

**Agastya** (*Sk.*). The name of a great Rishi, much revered in Southern India; the reputed author of hymns in the *Rig Veda*, and a great hero in the *Râmâyana*. In Tamil literature he is credited with having been the first instructor of the Dravidians in science, religion and philosophy. It is also the name of the star "Canopus".

**Agathodæmon** (*Gr.*). The beneficent, good Spirit as contrasted with the bad one, Kakodæmon. The "Brazen Serpent" of the Bible is the former; the flying serpents of fire are an aspect of Kakodæmon. The Ophites called Agathodæmon the Logos and Divine Wisdom, which in the Bacchanalian

Mysteries was represented by a serpent erect on a pole.

**Agathon** (*Gr.*). Plato's Supreme Deity. Lit., "The Good", our ALAYA, or "Universal Soul".

**Aged** (*Kab.*). One of the Kabbalistic names for Sephira, called also the Crown, or *Kether.*

**Agla** (*Heb.*). This Kabbalistic word is a talisman composed of the initals of the four words "Ateh Gibor Leolam Adonai", meaning "Thou art mighty for ever 0 Lord". MacGregor Mathers explains it thus "**A**, the first; **A**, the last; **G**, the trinity in unity; **L**, the completion of the great work". [w.w.w.]

**Agneyastra** (*Sk.*). The fiery missiles or weapons used by the Gods in the exoteric *Purânas* and the *Mahâbhârata* the magic weapons said to have been wielded by the adept-race (the fourth), the Atlanteans. This "weapon of fire" was given by Bharadwâja to Agnivesa, the son of Agni, and by him to Drona, though the *Vishnu Purâna* contradicts this, saying that it was given by the sage Aurva to King Sagara, his chela. They are frequently mentioned in the *Mahâbhârata* and the *Râmâyana.*

**Agni** (*Sk.*). The God of Fire in the Veda; the oldest and the most revered of Gods in India. He is one of the three great deities: Agni, Vâyu and Sûrya, and also all the three, as he is the triple aspect of fire; in heaven as the Sun; in the atmosphere or air (Vâyu), as Lightning; on. earth, as ordinary Fire. Agni belonged to the earlier Vedic *Trimûrti* before Vishnu was given a place of honour and before Brahmâ and Siva were invented.

**Agni Bâhu** (*Sk.*). An ascetic son of Manu Swâyambhuva, the "Self-born".

**Agni Bhuvah** (*Sk.*). Lit., "born of fire", the term is applied to the four races of *Kshatriyas* (the second or warrior caste) whose ancestors are said to have sprung from fire. Agni Bhuvah is the son of Agni, the God of Fire; Agni Bhuvah being the same as Kartti-keya, the God of War. (See *S. D.*, Vol. II., p. 550.)

**Agni Dhätu Samâdhi** (*Sk.*). A kind of contemplation in Yoga practice, when Kundalini is raised to the extreme and the infinitude appears as one sheet of fire. An ecstatic condition.

**Agni Hotri** (*Sk.*). The priests who served the Fire-God in Aryan antiquity. The term Agni Hotri is one that denotes oblation.

**Agni-ratha** (*Sk.*). A "Fiery Vehicle" literally. A kind of flying machine. Spoken of in ancient works of magic in India and in the epic poems.

**Agnishwattas** (*Sk.*). A class of Pitris, the creators of the first ethereal race of men. Our solar ancestors as contrasted with the *Barhishads*, the "lunar"

Pitris or ancestors, though otherwise explained in the *Purânas.*

**Agnoia** (*Gr.*). "Divested of reason", lit., "irrationality", when speaking of the animal Soul. According to Plutarch, Pythagoras and Plato divided the human soul into two parts (the higher and lower manas)—the rational or *noëtic* and the irrational, or *agnoia,* sometimes written "annoia".

**Agnostic** (*Gr.*). A word claimed by Mr. Huxley to have been coined by him to indicate one who believes nothing which can not be demonstrated by the senses. The later schools of Agnosticism give more philosophical definitions of the term.

**Agra-Sandhânî** (*Sk.*). The "Assessors" or *Recorders* who read at the judgment of a disembodied Soul the record of its life in the heart of that "Soul". The same almost as the *Lipikas* of the *Secret Doctrine.* (See *S. D.,* Vol. I., p. 105.)

**Agruerus**; A very ancient Phœnician god. The same as Saturn.

**Aham** (*Sk.*). "I"—the basis of *Ahankâra,* Self-hood.

**Ahan** (*Sk.*). "Day";the Body of Brahmâ, in the *Purânas.*

**Ahankâra** (*Sk.*). The conception of "I", Self-consciousness or Self-identity; the "I", the egotistical and *mâyâvic* principle in man, due to our ignorance which separates our "I" from the Universal ONE-SELF Personality, Egoism.

**Aheie** (*Heb.*). Existence. He who exists; corresponds to Kether and Macroprosopus.

**Ah-hi** (*Sensar*), **Ahi** (*Sk.*), or Serpents. Dhyân Chohans. "Wise Serpents" or Dragons of Wisdom.

**Ahi** (*Sk.*). A serpent. A name of Vritra, the Vedic demon of drought.

**Ahti** (*Scand.*). The "Dragon" in the *Eddas.*

**Ahu** (*Scand.*). "One" and the First.

**Ahum** (*Zend*). The first three principles of septenary man in the *Avesta;* the gross living man and his vital and astral principles.

**Ahura** (*Zend.*). The same as *Asura,* the holy, the Breath-like. Ahura Mazda, the Ormuzd of the Zoroastrians or Parsis, is the Lord who bestows light and intelligence, whose symbol is the Sun (See "Ahura Mazda"), and of whom Ahriman, a European form of "Angra Mainyu" (*q.v.*), is the dark aspect.

**Ahura Mazda** (*Zend*). The personified deity, the Principle of Universal Divine Light of the Parsis. From Ahura or *Asura,* breath, "spiritual, divine" in the oldest *Rig Veda,* degraded by the orthodox Brahmans into *A -sura,* "no gods", just as the Mazdeans have degraded the Hindu Devas (Gods) into Dæva (Devils).

**Aidoneus** (*Gr.*). The God and King of the Nether World; Pluto or Dionysos Chthonios (subterranean).

**Aij Talon**. The supreme deity of the *Yakoot,* a tribe in Northern Siberia.

**Ain-Aior** (*Chald.*). The only "Self-existent" a mystic name for divine substance. [w.w.w.]

**Ain** (*Heb.*). The negatively existent; deity in repose, and absolutely passive. [w.w.w.]

**Aindrî** (*Sk.*). Wife of Indra.

**Aindriya** (*Sk.*). Or *Indrânî,* Indriya; *Sakti.* The female aspect or "wife" of Indra.

**Ain Soph** (*Heb.*). The "Boundless" or Limitless; Deity emanating and extending. [w.w.w.]

Ain Soph is also written *En Soph* and *Ain Suph,* no one, not even Rabbis, being sure of their vowels. In the religious metaphysics of the old Hebrew philosophers, the ONE Principle was an abstraction, like Parabrahmam, though modern Kabbalists have succeeded now, by dint of mere sophistry and paradoxes, in making a "Supreme God" of it and nothing higher. But with the early Chaldean Kabbalists Ain Soph is "without form or being", having "no likeness with anything else" (Franck, *Die Kabbala,* p. 126). That Ain Soph has never been considered as the "Creator" is proved by even such an orthodox Jew as Philo calling the "Creator" the *Logos,* who stands next the "Limitless One", and the "Second God". "The Second God is its (Ain Soph's) wisdom", says Philo *(Quaest. et Solut.).* Deity is NO-THING; it is nameless, and therefore called Ain Soph; the word *Ain* meaning NOTHING. (See Franck's *Kabbala,* p. 153 ff.)

**Ain Soph Aur** (*Heb.*). The Boundless Light which concentrates into the First and highest Sephira or Kether, the Crown. [w. w. w.]

**Airyamen Yaêgo** (*Zend*). Or *Airyana Vaêgo;* the primeval land of bliss referred to in the *Vendîdâd,* where Ahura Mazda delivered his laws to Zoroaster (Spitama Zarathustra).

**Airyana-ishejô** (*Zend*). The name of a prayer to the "holy Airyamen", the divine aspect of Ahriman before the latter became a dark opposing power, a Satan. For Ahriman is of the same essence with Ahura Mazda, just as Typhon-Seth is of the same essence with Osiris (*q.v.*).

**Aish** (*Heb.*). The word for "Man".

**Aisvarikas** (*Sk.*). A theistic school of Nepaul, which sets up Âdi Buddha as a supreme god ( Îsvara ), instead of seeing in the name that of a principle, an abstract philosophical symbol.

**Aitareya** (*Sk.*). The name of an Aranyaka (Brâhmana) and a Upanishad of the *Rig Veda.* Some of its portions are purely Vedântic.

**Aith-ur** (*Chald.*). Solar fire, divine Æther.

**Aja** (*Sk.*). "Unborn", uncreated; an epithet belonging to many of the primordial gods, but especially to the first *Logos*—a radiation of the Absolute on the plane of illusion.

**Ajitas** (*Sk.*). One of the Occult names of the twelve great gods incarnating in each Manvantara. The Occultists identify them with the Kumâras. They are called Jnâna (or Gnâna) Devas. Also, a form of Vishnu in the second Manvantara. Called also *Jayas.*

**Ajnâna** (*Sk.*) or **Agyana** (*Bengali*). Non-knowledge; absence of knowledge rather than "ignorance" as generally translated. An *Ajnâni* means a "profane".

**Akar** (*Eg.*). The proper name of that division of the Ker-neter infernal regions, which may be called Hell. [w. w. w.].

**Akâsa** (*Sk.*). The subtle, supersensuous spiritual essence which pervades all space; the primordial substance erroneously identified with Ether. But it is to Ether what Spirit is to Matter, or *Âtmâ* to *Kâma-rûpa.* It is, in fact, the Universal Space in which lies inherent the eternal Ideation of the Universe in its ever-changing aspects on the planes of matter and objectivity, and from which radiates the *First Logos*, or expressed thought. This is why it is stated in the *Purânas* that Âkâsa has but one attribute, namely sound, for sound is but the translated symbol of Logos—"Speech" in its mystic sense. In the same sacrifice (*the Jyotishtoma Agnishtoma*) it is called the "God Âkâsa". In these sacrificial mysteries Âkâsa is the all-directing 'and omnipotent Deva who plays the part of Sadasya, the superintendent over the magical effects of the religious performance, and it had its own appointed Hotri (priest) in days of old, who took its name. The Âkâsa is the indispensable agent of every *Krityâ* (magical performance) religious or profane. The expression "to stir up the Brahmâ", means to stir up the power which lies latent at the bottom of every magical operation, Vedic sacrifices being in fact nothing if not ceremonial magic. This power is the Âkâsa—in another aspect, *Kundalini*—occult electricity, the alkahest of the alchemists in one sense, or the universal solvent, the same *anima mundi* on the higher plane as the *astral light* is on the lower. "At the moment of the sacrifice the priest becomes imbued with the spirit of Brahmâ, is, for the time being, Brahmâ himself". (*Isis Unveiled*).

**Akbar.** The great Mogul Emperor of India, the famous patron of religions, arts, and sciences, the most liberal of all the Mussulman sovereigns. There has never been a more tolerant or enlightened ruler than the Emperor Akbar, either in India or in any other Mahometan country.

**Akiba** (*Heb.*). The only one of the four *Tanaim* (initiated prophets) who entering the *Garden of Delight* (of the occult sciences) succeeded in getting himself initiated while all the others failed. (See the Kabbalistic Rabbis).

**Akshara** (*Sk.*). Supreme Deity; lit., "indestructible", ever perfect.

**Akta** (*Sk.*). Anointed: a title of Twashtri or Visvakarman, the highest "Creator" and Logos in the *Rig -Veda*. He is called the "Father of the Gods" and "Father of the sacred Fire" (*See note S. D., II, p 101*).

**Akûpâra** (*Sk.*). The Tortoise, the symbolical turtle on which the earth is said to rest.

**Al or El** (*Heb.*). This deity-name is commonly translated "God', meaning mighty, supreme. The plural is Elohim, also translated in the Bible by the word God, in the singular. [w.w.w.]

**Al-ait** (*Phœn.*). The God of Fire, an ancient and very mystic name in Koptic Occultism.

**Alaparus** (*Chald.*). The second *divine* king of Babylonia who reigned.. "three Sari". The first king of the divine Dynasty was Alorus according to Berosus. He was "the appointed Shepherd of the people" and reigned *ten* Sari (or 36,000 years, a *Saros* being 3,600 years).

**Alaya** (*Sk.*). The Universal Soul (See *S. D.* Vol. I. pp. 47 *et seq.*). The name belongs to the Tibetan system of the contemplative *Mahâyâna* School. Identical with *Âkâsa* in its mystic sense, and with *Mulâprâkriti*, in its essence, as it is the basis or root of all things.

**Alba Petra** (*Lat.*). The white stone of Initiation. The "white cornelian" mentioned in St. John's *Revelation.*

**Al-Chazari** (*Arab.*). A Prince-Philosopher and Occultist. (See Book *Al-Chazari.*)

**Alchemists;** From *Al* and **Chemi**, fire, or the god and patriarch, *Kham*, also, the name of Egypt. The Rosicrucians of the middle ages, such as Robertus de Fluctibus (Robert Fludd), Paracelsus, Thomas Vaughan (Eugenius Philalethes), Van Helmont, and others, were all alchemists, who sought for the *hidden spirit* in every inorganic matter. Some people—nay, the great majority—have accused alchemists of charlatanry and false pretending. Surely such men as Roger Bacon, Agrippa, Henry Khunrath, and the Arabian Geber (the first to introduce into Europe some of the secrets of chemistry), can hardly he treated as impostors—least of all as fools. Scientists who are reforming the science of physics upon the basis of the atomic theory of Democritus, as restated by John Dalton, conveniently forget that Democritus, of Abdera, was an alchemist, and that the mind that was capable of penetrating so far into the secret operations of nature in one direction must have had good reasons to study and become a Hermetic philosopher. Olaus Borrichius says that the cradle of alchemy is to be sought in the most distant times. (*Isis Unveiled*).

**Alchemy**; in Arabic *Ul-Khemi*, is, as the name suggests, the chemistry of nature. *Ui-Khemi* or *Al-Kimia*, however, is only an Arabianized word, taken from the Greek χημεία, *(chemeia)* from χυμός—"juice", sap extracted from a plant. Says Dr. Wynn Westcott: "The earliest use of the actual term 'alchemy' is found in the works of Julius Firmicus Maternus, who lived in the days of Constantine the Great. The Imperial Library in Paris contains the oldest-extant alchemic treatise known in Europe; it was written by Zosimus the Panopolite about 400 A.D. in the Greek language, the next oldest is by Æneas Gazeus, 480 A.D." It deals with the finer forces of nature and the various conditions in which they are found to operate. Seeking under the veil of language, more or less artificial, to convey to the uninitiated so much of the *mysterium magnum* as is safe in the hands of a selfish world, the alchemist postulates as his first principle the existence of a certain Universal Solvent by which all composite bodies are resolved into the homogeneous substance from which they are evolved, which substance he calls pure gold, or *summa materia*. This solvent, also called *menstvuum universale*, possesses the power of removing all the seeds of disease from the human body, of renewing youth and prolonging life. Such is the *lapis philosophorum* (philosopher's stone). Alchemy first penetrated into Europe through Geber, the great Arabian sage and philosopher, in the eighth century of our era; but it was known and practised long ages ago in China and in Egypt, numerous papyri on alchemy and other proofs of its being the favourite study of kings and priests having been exhumed and preserved under the generic name of Hermetic treatises. (See "Tabula Smaragdina"). Alchemy is studied under three distinct aspects, which admit of many different interpretations, viz.: the Cosmic, Human, and Terrestrial. These three methods were typified under the three alchemical properties—sulphur, mercury, and salt. Different writers have stated that there are three, seven, ten, and twelve processes respectively; but they are all agreed that there is but one object in alchemy, which is to transmute gross metals into pure gold. What that gold, however, really is, very few people understand correctly. No doubt that there is such a thing in nature as transmutation of the baser metals into the nobler, or gold. But this is only one aspect of alchemy, the terrestrial or purely material, for we sense logically the same process taking place in the bowels of the earth. Yet, besides and beyond this interpretation, there is in alchemy a symbolical meaning, purely psychic and spiritual. While the Kabbalist-Alchemist seeks for the realization of the former, the Occultist-Alchemist, spurning the gold of the mines, gives all his attention and directs his efforts only towards the transmutation of the baser *quaternary* into the divine upper *trinity* of man, which when finally blended are one. The spiritual, mental, psychic, and physical planes of human existence are in alchemy compared to the four elements, fire, air, water and earth, and are each capable of a threefold constitution, i.e., fixed, mutable and volatile. Little or nothing is known by the word concerning the origin of this archaic branch of philosophy; but it is certain that it antedates the construction of any known Zodiac, and, as dealing with the personified forces of nature, probably also any of the mythologies of the world; nor is there any doubt that the true secret of transmutation (on the physical plane) was known in days of old, and lost before the dawn of the so-called historical period. Modern chemistry owes its best fundamental discoveries to alchemy, but regardless of the undeniable truism of the latter that there is but one element in the universe, chemistry has placed metals in the class of elements and is only now beginning to find out its gross mistake. Even sonic Encyclopædists are now forced to confess that if most of the accounts of transmutations are fraud or delusion, "yet some of them are accompanied by testimony *which renders them probable. . .* By means of the galvanic battery even the alkalis have been discovered to have a metallic base. The possibility of obtaining metal from other substances which contain the ingredients composing it, and *of changing one metal into another . . .* must therefore be left undecided. Nor are all alchemists to be considered impostors. Many have laboured under the conviction of obtaining their object, with indefatigable patience and purity of heart, which is earnestly recommended by sound alchemists as the principal requisite for the success of their labours." (*Pop. Encyclop.*)

**Alcyone** (*Gr.*), or Halcyone, daughter of Æolus, and wife of Ceyx, who was drowned as he was journeying to consult the oracle, upon which she threw herself into the sea. Accordingly both were changed, through the mercy of the gods, into king-fishers. The female is said to lay her eggs *on the sea and keep it calm* during the seven days before and seven days after the winter solstice. It has a very occult significance in ornithomancy.

**Alectromancy** (*Gr.*). Divination by means of a cock, or other bird; a circle was drawn and divided into spaces, each one allotted to a letter; corn was spread over these places and note was taken of the successive lettered divisions from which the bird took grains of corn. [w.w.w.]

**Alethæ** (*Phœn.*) "Fire worshippers" from *Al-alt*, the God of Fire. The same as the Kabiri or *divine* Titans. As the seven emanations of Agruerus (Saturn) they are connected with all the fire, solar and" storm gods (*Maruts*).

**Aletheia** (Gr.). Truth; also Alethia, one of Apollo's nurses.

**Alexandrian School** (of Philosophers). This famous school arose in Alexandria (Egypt) which was for several centuries the great seat of learning and philosophy. Famous for its library, which bears the name of "Alexandrian", founded by Ptolemy Soter, who died in 283 B.C., at the very beginning of his reign; that library which once boasted of 700,000 rolls or volumes (Aulus Gellius); for its museum, the first real academy of sciences and arts; for its world-famous scholars, such as Euclid (the father of scientific geometry), Apollonius of Perga (the author of the still extant work on conic sections), Nicomachus (the arithmetician); astronomers, natural philosophers, anatomists such as Herophilus and Erasistratus, physicians, musicians, artists, etc., etc.; it became still more famous for its Eclectic, or the New Platonic school, founded in 193 A.D., by Ammonius Saccas, whose disciples were Origen, Plotinus, and many others now famous in history. The most celebrated schools of Gnostics had their origin in Alexandria. Philo Judæus Josephus, Iamblichus, Porphyry, Clement of Alexandria, Eratosthenes the astronomer, Hypatia the virgin philosopher, and numberless other stars of second magnitude, all belonged at various times to these great schools, and helped to make Alexandria one of the most justly renowned seats of learning that the world has ever produced.

**Alhim** (*Heb.*). See "Elohim".

**Alkahest** (*Arab.*). The universal solvent in Alchemy (see "Alchemy "); but in mysticism, the Higher Self, the union with which makes of matter (lead), gold, and restores all compound things such as the human body and its attributes to their primæval essence.

**Almadel**; the Book. A treatise on Theurgia or White Magic by an unknown mediæval European author; it is not infrequently found in volumes of MSS. called *Keys of Solomon*. [w.w.w.]

**Almeh** (*Arab.*). Dancing girls; the same as the Indian *nautchies*, the temple and public dancers.

**Alpha Polaris** (*Lat.*). The same as *Dhruva*, the pole-star of 31,105 years ago.

**Alswider** (*Scand.*). "All-swift", the name of the horse of the moon, in the *Eddas*.

**Altruism** (*Lat.*). From alter = other. A quality opposed to egoism. Actions tending to do good to others, regardless of self.

**Aize, Liber**; de Lapide Philosophico. An alchemic treatise by an unknown German author; dated 1677. It is to be found reprinted in the Hermetic Museum; in it is the well known design of a man with legs extended and his body hidden by a seven pointed star. Eliphaz Lévi has copied it. [w.w.w.]

**Ama** (*Heb.*)., **Amia**, (*Chald.*). Mother. A title of Sephira Binah, whose "divine name is Jehovah" and who is called "Supernal Mother".

**Amânasa** (*Sk.*). The "Mindless", the early races of this planet; also certain Hindu gods.

**Amara-Kosha** (*Sk.*). The "immortal vocabulary". The oldest dictionary known in the world and the most perfect vocabulary of classical Sanskrit; by Amara Sinha, a sage of the second century.

**Ambâ** (*Sk.*). The name of the eldest of the seven *Pleiades*, the heavenly sisters married each to a Rishi belonging to the *Saptariksha* or the seven Rishis of the constellation known as the Great Bear.

**Ambhâmsi** (*Sk.*). A name of the chief of the Kumâras Sanat-Sujâta, signifying the "waters". This epithet will become more comprehensible when we remember that the later type of Sanat-Sujâta was Michael, the Archangel, who is called in the Talmud "the Prince of *Waters*", and in the Roman Catholic Church is regarded as the patron of gulfs and promontories. Sanat-Sujâta is the immaculate son of the immaculate mother (Ambâ or Aditi, chaos and space) or the "waters" of limitless space. (See *S. D.*, Vol. I., p. 460.)

**Amdo** (*Tib.*). A sacred locality, the birthplace of Tson-kha-pa, the great Tibetan reformer and the founder of the Gelukpa (yellow caps), who is regarded as an Avatar of Amita-buddha.

**Amên**. In Hebrew is formed of the letters A M N = 1,40,50 =91,and is thus a simile of "Jehovah Adonai"=10, 5, 6, 5 and 1,4, 50, 10 =91 together; it is one form of the Hebrew word for "truth". In common parlance Amen is said to mean "so be it". [w.w.w.]

But, in *esoteric* parlance *Amen* means "the concealed". Manetho Sebennites says the word signifies *that which is hidden* and we know through Hecatæus and others that the Egyptians used the word to call upon their great God of Mystery, Ammon (or "Ammas, the hidden god ") to make himself conspicuous and manifest to them. Bonomi, the famous hieroglyphist, calls his worshippers very pertinently the "Amenoph", and Mr. Bonwick quotes a writer who says: "Ammon, the hidden god, will remain for ever hidden till anthropomorphically revealed; gods who are afar off are useless". Amen is styled "Lord of the new-moon festival". Jehovah-Adonai is a new form of the ram-headed god Amoun or Ammon (*q.v.*) who was invoked by the Egyptian priests under the name of Amen.

**Amenti** (*Eg.*). Esoterically and literally, the dwelling of the God Amen, or Amoun, or the "hidden", secret god. Exoterically the kingdom of Osiris divided into fourteen parts, each of which was set aside for some purpose connected with the after state of the defunct. Among other things, in one of these was the Hall of Judgment. It was the "Land of the West", the "Secret Dwelling", the *dark* land, and the "doorless house". But it was also *Ker-noter*, the "abode of the gods", and the "land of ghosts" like the "Hades" of the Greeks (*q.v.*). It was also the "Good Father's House" (in which there are "many mansions"). The fourteen divisions comprised, among many others, *Aanroo* (*q.v.*), the hall of the Two Truths, the Land of Bliss, *Neter-xev* "the funeral (or burial) place" *Otamer-xev*, the "Silence-loving Fields", and also many other mystical halls and dwellings, one like the Sheol of the Hebrews, another like the Devachan of the Occultists, etc., etc. Out of the fifteen gates of the abode of Osiris, there were two chief ones, the "gate of entrance" or *Rustu*, and the "gate of exit" (reincarnation) *Amh*. But there was no room in Amenti to represent the orthodox Christian Hell. The worst of all was the Hall of the eternal Sleep and Darkness. As Lepsius has it, the defunct "sleep (therein) in *incorruptible* forms, they wake not to see their brethren, they recognize no longer father and mother, their hearts feel nought toward their wife and children. This is the dwelling of the god All-Dead. . . . Each trembles to pray to him, for he hears not. Nobody can praise him, for he regards not those who adore him. Neither does he notice any offering brought to him." This god is *Karmic* Decree; the land of Silence—the abode of those who die absolute disbelievers, those dead from accident before their allotted time, and finally the dead on the threshold of *Avitchi*, which is never in Amenti or any other subjective state, save in one case, but on this land of forced re-birth. These tarried not very long even in their state of heavy sleep, of oblivion and darkness, but, were carried more or less speedily toward *Amh* the "exit gate".

**Amesha Spentas** (*Zend*). Amshaspends. The six angels or divine Forces personified as gods who attend upon Ahura Mazda, of which he is the synthesis and the seventh. They are one of the prototypes of the Roman Catholic "Seven Spirits" or Angels with Michael as chief, or the "Celestial Host"; the "Seven Angels of the Presence". They are the Builders, Cosmocratores, of the Gnostics and identical with the Seven Prajâpatis, the Sephiroth, etc. (*q.v.*).

**Amitâbha**. The Chinese perversion of the Sanskrit *Amrita Buddha*, or the "Immortal Enlightened", a name of Gautama Buddha. The name has such variations as Amita, Abida, Amitâya, etc., and. is explained as meaning both "Boundless Age" and "Boundless Light". The original conception of the ideal of an impersonal divine light has been anthrdpomorphized with time.

**Ammon** (*Eg.*). One of the great gods of Egypt. Ammon or Amoun is far older than Amoun-Ra, and is identified with Baal. Hammon, the Lord of Heaven. Amoun-Ra was Ra the Spiritual Sun, the "Sun of Righteousness", etc., for—"the Lord God is a Sun". He is the God of Mystery and the hieroglyphics of his name are often reversed. He is Pan, All-Nature esoterically, and therefore the universe, and the "Lord of Eternity". Ra, as declared by an old inscription, was "begotten by Neith but not engendered". He is called the "self-begotten" Ra,, and created goodness from a glance of his fiery eye, as Set-Typhon created evil from his. As Ammon (also Amoun and Amen), Ra, he is "Lord of the worlds enthroned on the Sun's disk and appears in the abyss of heaven". A very ancient hymn spells the name "*Amen-ra*", and hails the "Lord of the thrones of the earth...Lord of Truth, father of the gods, maker of man, creator of the beasts, Lord of Existence, Enlightener of the Earth, sailing in heaven in tranquillity. . . All hearts are softened at beholding thee, sovereign of life, health and strength We worship *thy spirit who alone made us*", etc., etc. (See Bonwick's *Egyptian Belief*.) Ammon Ra is called "his mother's husband" and her son. (See "Chnourmis" and "Chnouphis" and also *S. D.* I, pp. 91 and 393.) It was to the "ram-headed" god that the Jews sacrificed lambs, and the *lamb* of Christian theology is a disguised reminiscence of the ram.

**Ammonius Saccas**. A great and good philosopher who lived in Alexandria between the second and third centuries of our era, and who was the founder of the Neo-Platonic School of Philaletheians or "lovers of truth". He was of poor birth and born of Christian parents, but endowed with such prominent, almost divine, goodness as to he called *Theodidaktos,* the "god-taught". He honoured that which was good in Christianity, but broke with it and the churches very early, being unable to find in it any superiority over the older religions.

**Amrita** (*Sk.*). The ambrosial drink or food of the gods; the food giving immortality. The elixir of life churned out of the ocean of milk in the Purânic allegory. An old Vedic term applied to the sacred Soma juice in the Temple Mysteries.

**Amûlam Mûlam** (*Sk.*). Lit., the "rootless root"; Mulâprakriti of the Vedantins the spiritual "root of nature".

**Amun** (*Copt.*). The Egyptian god of wisdom, who had only Initiates or Hierophants to serve him as priests.

**Anâ** (*Chald.*). The "invisible heaven"or Astral Light; the heavenly mother of the terrestrial sea, *Mar,* whence probably the origin of *Anna,* the mother of *Mary.*

**Anacalypsis** (*Gr.*)., or an "Attempt to withdraw the veil of the Saitic Isis", by Godfrey Higgins. This is a very valuable work, now only obtainable at extravagant prices; it treats of the origin of all myths, religions and mysteries, and displays an immense fund of classical erudition. [w.w.w.]

**Anâgâmin** (*Sk.*). *Anagam.* One who is no longer to be reborn into the world of desire. One stage before becoming Arhat and ready for Nirvâna. The *third* of the four grades of holiness on the way to final Initiation.

**Anâhata Chakram** (*Sk.*). The seat or "wheel" of life; the heart, according to some commentators.

**Anâhata Shabda** (*Sk.*). The mystic voices and sounds heard by the Yogi at the incipient stage of his meditation, The third of the four states of sound, otherwise called Madhyamâ—the fourth state being when it is perceptible by the physical sense of hearing. The sound in its previous stages is not heard except by those who have developed their internal, highest spiritual senses. The four stages are called respectively, Parâ, Pashyantî, Madhyamâ and Vaikharî.

**Anaitia** (*Chald.*). A derivation from Anâ (*q.v.*), a goddess identical with the Hindu *Annapurna,* one of the names of Kâlî—the female aspect of Siva—at her best.

**Analogeticists**. The disciples of Ammonius Saccas (*q.v.*), so called because of their practice of interpreting all sacred legends, myths and mysteries by a principle of analogy and correspondence, which is now found in the Kabbalistic system, and pre-eminently so in the Schools of Esoteric Philosophy, in the East. (See "The Twelve Signs of the Zodiac," by T. Subba Row in *Five Years of Theosophy*.)

**Ânanda** (*Sk.*). Bliss, joy, felicity, happiness. A name of the favourite disciple of Gautama, the Lord Buddha.

**Ânanda-Lahari** (*Sk.*). "The wave of joy"; a beautiful poem written by Sankarâchârya, a hymn to Pârvati, very mystical and occult.

**Ânandamaya-Kosha** (*Sk.*). "The illusive Sheath of Bliss", i.e., the mâyâvic or illusory form, the appearance of that which is formless. "Bliss", or the higher soul. The Vedantic name for one of the five Koshas or "principles" in man; identical with our Âtmâ-Buddhi or the Spiritual Soul.

**Ananga** (*Sk.*). The "Bodiless". An epithet of Kâma, god of love.

**Ananta-Sesha** (*Sk.*). The Serpent of Eternity—the couch of Vishnu during Pralaya (lit., endless remain).

**Anastasis** (*Gr.*). The continued existence of the soul.

**Anatu** (*Chald.*). The female aspect of Anu (*q.v.*). She represents the Earth and Depth, while her consort represents the Heaven and Height. She is the mother of the god Hea, and produces heaven and earth. Astronomically she is Ishtar, Venus, the Ashtoreth of the Jews.

**Anaxagoras** (*Gr.*) A famous Ionian philosopher who lived 500 B.C., studied philosophy under Anaximenes of Miletus, and settled in the days of Pericles at Athens. Socrates, Euripides, Archelaus and other distinguished men and philosophers were among his disciples and pupils. He was a most learned astronomer and was one of the first to explain openly that which was taught by Pythagoras secretly, namely, the movements of the planets, the eclipses of the sun and moon, etc. It was he who taught the theory of Chaos, on the principle that "nothing comes from nothing"; and of atoms, as the underlying essence and substance of all bodies, "of the same nature as the bodies which they formed".

These atoms, he taught, were primarily put in motion by Nous (Universal Intelligence, the Mahat of the Hindus), which Nous is an immaterial, eternal, spiritual entity; by this combination the world was formed, the material gross bodies sinking down, and the ethereal atoms (or fiery ether) rising and spreading in the upper celestial regions. Antedating modern science by over 2000 years, he taught that the stars were of the same material as our earth, and the sun a glowing mass; that the moon was a dark, uninhabitable body, receiving its light from the sun; the comets, wandering stars or bodies; and over and above the said science, he confessed himself thoroughly convinced that the real existence of things, perceived by our senses, could not be demonstrably proved. He died in exile at Lampsacus at the age of seventy-two.

**Ancients**, The. A name given by Occultists to the seven creative Rays, born of Chaos, or the "Deep".

**Anda-Katâha** (*Sk.*). The outer covering, or the "shell" of Brahmâ's egg; the area within which our manifested universe is encompassed.

**Androgyne Goat** (of Mendes). See "Baphomet".

**Androgyne Ray** (*Esot.*). The first differentiated ray; the Second Logos; Adam Kadmon in the *Kabalah;* the "male and female created he them", of the first chapter of *Genesis.*

**Audumla** (*Scand.*). The symbol of nature in the Norse mythology; the cow who licks the salt rock, whence the divine Buri is born, before man's creation.

**Angâraka** (*Sk.*). Fire Star; the planet Mars; in Tibetan, *Mig-mar.*

**Angirasas** (*Sk.*). The generic name of several Purânic individuals and things; a class of *Pitris,* the ancestors of man; a river in *Plaksha,* one of the *Sapta dwîpas* (q.v).

**Angra Mainyus** (*Zend.*). The Zoroastrian name for Ahriman; the evil spirit of destruction and opposition who (in the *Vendidâd,* Fargard I.) is said by Ahura Mazda to "counter-create by his witchcraft" every beautiful land the God creates; for "Angra Mainyu is all death".

**AnimaMundi** (*Lat.*). The"Soul of the World", the same as the *Alaya* of the Northern Buddhists; the divine essence which permeates, animates and informs all, from the smallest atom of matter to man and god. It is in a sense the "seven-skinned mother" of the stanzas in the *Secret Doctrine,* the essence of seven planes of sentience, consciousness and differentiation, moral and physical. In its highest aspect it is *Nirvâna,* in its lowest Astral Light. It was feminine with the Gnostics, the early Christians and the Nazarenes; bisexual with other sects, who considered it only in its four lower planes. Of igneous, ethereal nature in the objective world of form (and then ether), and divine and spiritual in its three higher planes. When it is said that every human soul was born by detaching itself from the *Anima Mundi,* it means, esoterically, that our higher Egos are of an essence identical with It, which is a radiation of the ever unknown Universal ABSOLUTE.

**Anjala** (*Sk.*). One of the personified powers which spring from Brahmâ's body—the Prajâpatis.

**Anjana** (*Sk.*). A serpent, a son of Kasyapa Rishi.

**Annamaya Kosha** (*Sk.*). A Vedantic term. The same as *Sthûla Sharîra* or the physical body. It is the first "sheath" of the *five* sheaths accepted by the Vedantins, a sheath being the same as that which is called "principle" in Theosophy.

**Annapura** (*Sk.*). See "Anâ".

**Annedotus** (*Gr.*). The generic name for the Dragons or Men-Fishes, of which there were five. The historian Berosus narrates that there rose out of the Erythræan Sea on several occasions a semi-dæmon named Oannes or Annedotus, who although part animal yet taught the Chaldeans useful arts and everything that could humanise them. (See Lenormant *Chaldean Magic*, p. 203, and also "Oannes".) [w.w.w.]

**Anoia** (*Gr.*). "Want of understanding", "folly". *Anoia* is the name given by Plato and others to the lower Manas when too closely allied with Kâma, which is irrational (*agnoia*). The Greek word *agnoia* is evidently a derivation from and cognate to the Sanskrit word *ajnâna* (phonetically, *agnyana*) or ignorance, irrationality, absence of knowledge. (See "Agnoia" and "Agnostic".)

**Anouki** (*Eg.*). A form of Isis; the goddess of life, from which name the Hebrew *Ank*, life. (See "Anuki.")

**Ansumat** (*Sk.*). A Purânic personage, the "nephew of 60,000 uncles" King Sagara's sons, who were reduced to ashes by a single glance from Kapila Rishi's "Eye".

**Antahkarana** (*Sk.*)., or Antaskarana. The term has various meanings, which differ with every school of philosophy and sect. Thus Sankârachârya renders the word as "understanding"; others, as "the internal instrument, the Soul, formed by the thinking principle and egoism"; whereas the Occultists explain it as the *path* or bridge between the Higher and the Lower Manas, the divine *Ego*, and the *personal* Soul of man. It serves as a medium of communication between the two, and conveys from the Lower to the Higher Ego all those personal impressions and thoughts of men which can, by their nature, be assimilated and stored by the undying Entity, and be thus made immortal with it, these being the only elements of the evanescent *Personality* that survive death and time. It thus stands to reason that only that which is noble, spiritual and divine in man can testify in Eternity to his having lived.

**Anthesteria** (*Gr.*). The feast of Flowers (*Floralia*): during this festival the rite of Baptism or purification was performed in the Eleusinian Mysteries in the temple lakes, the Limnae, when the Mystæ were made to pass through the "narrow gate" of Dionysus, to emerge therefrom as full Initiates.

**Anthropology**. The Science of man; it embraces among other things:— *Physiology*, or that branch of natural science which discloses the mysteries of the organs and their functions in men, animals and plants; and also, and especially,—*Psychology* or the great, and in our days, too much neglected science of the soul, both as an entity distinct from the spirit, and in its relation to the spirit and body. In modern science, psychology deals only or principally with conditions of the nervous system, and almost absolutely ignores the psychical essence and nature. Physicians denominate the science of insanity psychology, and name the lunacy chair in medical colleges by that designation. (*Isis Unveiled*.)

**Anthropomorphism** (*Gr.*). From "anthropos" meaning man. The act of endowing god or gods with a human form and human attributes or qualities.

**Anu** (*Sk.*). An "atom", a title of Brahmâ, who is said to be an atom just as is the infinite universe. A hint at the pantheistic nature of the god.

**Anu** (*Chald.*). One of the highest of Babylonian deities, "King of Angels and Spirits, Lord of the city of Erech". He is the Ruler and God of Heaven and Earth. His symbol is a star and a kind of Maltese cross—emblems of divinity and sovereignty. He is an abstract divinity supposed to inform the whole expense of ethereal space or heaven, while his "wife" informs the more material planes. Both are the types of the Ouranos and Gaia of Hesiod. They sprang from the original Chaos. All his titles and attributes are grapfiic and indicate health, purity physical and moral, antiquity and holiness. Anu was the earliest god of the city of Erech. One of his sons was *Bil* or*Vil-Kan*, the god of fire, of various metals, and of weapons. George Smith very pertinently sees in this deity a close connection with a kind of cross breed between "the biblical Tubal Cain and the classical Vulcan" who is considered to be moreover "the most potent deity in relation to witchcraft and spells generally".

**Anubis** (*Gr.*) The dog -headed god, identical, in a certain aspect, with

Horus. He is pre-eminently the god who deals with the disembodied, or the resurrected in *post mortem* life. *Anepou* is his Egyptian name. He is a psychopompic deity, "the Lord of the Silent Land of the West, the land of the Dead, the preparer of the way to the other world ", to whom the dead were entrusted, to be led by him to Osiris, the Judge. In short, he is the "embalmer" and the "guardian of the dead". One of the oldest deities in Egypt, Mariette Bey having found the image of this deity in tombs of the Third Dynasty.

**Anugîtâ** (*Sk.*). One of the *Upanishads*. A very occult treatise. (*See The sacred Books of the East.*)

**Anugraha** (*Sk.*). The eighth creation in the *Vishnu Purâna.*

**Anuki** (*Eg.*). "See Anouki" *supra.* "The word *Ank* in Hebrew, means 'my life', my being, which is the personal pronoun Anocki, from the name of the Egyptian goddess *Anouki* ", says the author of the *Hebrew Mystery*, or the *Source of Measures.*

**Anumati** (*Sk.*). The moon at the full; when from a god—Soma—she becomes a goddess.

**Anumitis** (*Sk.*). Inference, deduction in philosophy.

**Anunnaki** (*Chald.*). Angels or Spirits of the Earth; terrestrial Elementals also.

**Anunit** (*Chald.*) The goddess of Akkad; Lucifer, the morning star. Venus as the evening star as Ishtar of Erech.

**Anupâdaka** (*Sk.*). Anupapâdaka, also Aupapâduka; means parentless", "self-existing", born without any parents or progenitors. A term applied to certain self-created gods, and the Dhyâni Buddhas.

**Anuttara** (*Sk.*). Unrivalled, peerless. Thus *Anuttara Bodhi* means unexcelled or unrivalled intelligence", *Anuttara Dharma*, unrivalled law or religion, &c.

**Anyâmsam Aniyasâm** (*Sk.*). A *no-raniyânsam* (in *Bhagavad gîtâ*). Lit., "the most atomic of the atomic; smallest of the small ". Applied to the universal deity, whose essence is everywhere.

**Aour** (*Chald.*). The synthesis of the two aspects of *astro-etheric* light; and the *od*—the life-giving, and the *ob*—the death-giving light.

**Apâm Napât** (*Zend*). A mysterious being, corresponding to the Fohat of the Occultists. It is both a Vedic and an Avestian name. Literally, the name means the "Son of the Waters" (of space, i.e., Ether), for in the *Avesta* Apâm Napât stands between the *fire-yazatas* and the *water-yazatas* .(See *S. D.*, Vol.

II., p. 400, note).

**Apâna** (*Sk.*). "Inspirational breath"; a practice in Yoga. *Prana* and *apâna* are the "expirational" and the "inspirational" breaths. It is called "vital wind" in *Anugîta.*

**Apap** (*Eg.*), in Greek *Apophis*. The symbolical Serpent of Evil. The Solar Boat and the Sun are the great Slayers of Apap in the *Book of the Dead.* It is Typhon, who having killed Osiris, incarnates in Apap, seeking to kill Horus. Like Taoer (or *Ta-ap-oer*) the female aspect of Typhon, Apap is called "the devourer of the Souls", and truly, since Apap symbolizes the animal body, as matter left soulless and to itself. Osiris, being, like all the other Solar gods, a type of the Higher Ego (Christos), Horus (his son) is the lower Manas or the *personal* Ego. On many a monument one can see Horus, helped by a number of dog-headed gods armed with crosses and spears, killing Apap. Says an Orientalist: "The God Horus standing as conqueror upon the Serpent of Evil, may be considered as the earliest form of our well-known group of St. George (who is Michael) and the Dragon, or holiness trampling down sin." Draconianism did not die with the ancient religions, but has passed bodily into the latest Christian form of the worship.

**Aparinâmin** (*Sk.*). The Immutable and the Unchangeable, the reverse of Parinâmin, that which is subject to modification, differentiation or decay.

**Aparoksha** (*Sk.*) *Direct perception.*

**Âpava** (*Sk.*) Lit. "He who sports in the Water". Another aspect of Nârâyana or Vishnu and of Brahmâ combined, for Âpava, like the latter, divides himself into two parts, male and female, and creates Vishnu, who creates Virâj, who creates Manu. The name is explained and interpreted in various ways in Brahmanical literature.

**Apavarga** (*Sk.*). Emancipation from repeated births.

**Apis** (*Eg.*), or *Hapi-ankh*. The "living deceased one" or Osiris incarnate in the sacred white Bull. Apis was the bull-god that, on reaching the age of twenty-eight, the age when Osiris was killed by Typhon—was put to death with great ceremony. It was not the Bull that was worshipped but the Osiridian symbol; just as Christians kneel now before the Lamb, the symbol of Jesus Christ, in their churches.

**Apocrypha** (*Gr.*). Very erroneously explained and adopted as doubtful, or spurious. The word means simply *secret, esoteric, hidden.*

**Apollo Belvidere.** Of all the ancient statues of Apollo, the son of Jupiter and Latona, called Phœbus, Helios, the radiant and the Sun, the best and most perfect is the one known by this name, which is in the Belvidere gallery of the Vatican at Rome. It is called the *Pythian Apollo*, as the god is represented in the moment of his victory over the serpent Python. The statue was found in the ruins of Antium, in 1503.

**Apollonius of Tyana** (*Gr.*). A wonderful philosopher born in Cappadocia about the beginning of the first century; an ardent Pythagorean, who studied the Phœnician sciences under Euthydemus; and Pythagorean philosophy and other studies under Euxenus of Heraclea. According to the tenets of this school he remained a vegetarian the whole of his long life, fed only on fruit and herbs, drank no wine, wore vestments made only of plant-fibres, walked barefooted, and let his hair grow to its full length, as all the Initiates before and after him. He was initiated by the priests of the temple of Æsculapius (Asciepios) at Ægae, and learnt many of the "miracles" for healing the sick wrought by the god of medicine. Having prepared himself for a higher initiation by a silence of five years, and by travel, visiting Antioch, Ephesus, Pamphylia and other parts, he journeyed via Babylon to India, all his intimate disciples having abandoned him, as they feared to go to the "land of enchantments". A casual disciple, Damis, however, whom he met on his way, accompanied him in his travels. At Babylon he was initiated by the Chaldees and Magi, according to Damis, whose narrative was copied by one named Philostratus a hundred years later. After his return from India, he showed himself a true Initiate, in that the pestilences and earthquakes, deaths of kings and other events, which he prophesied duly happened. At Lesbos, the priests of Orpheus, being jealous of him, refused to initiate him into their peculiar mysteries, though they did so several years later. He preached to the people of Athens and other cities the purest and noblest ethics, and the phenomena he produced were as wonderful as they were numerous and well attested. "How is it", enquires Justin Martyr in dismay—" how is it that the talismans (*telesmata*) of Apollonius have power, for they prevent, as we see, the fury of the waves and the violence of the winds, and the attacks of the wild beasts; and *whilst our Lord's miracles are preserved by tradition alone,* those of Apollonius *are most numerous and actually manifested in present facts?*" (*Quaest*, XXIV.). But an answer is easily found to this in the fact that after crossing the Hindu Kush, Apollonius had been directed by a king to the *abode of the Sages,* whose abode it may be to this day, by whom he was taught unsurpassed knowledge. His dialogues with the Corinthian Menippus indeed give us the esoteric catechism and disclose (when understood) many an important mystery of nature. Apollonius was the friend, correspondent and guest of kings and queens, and no marvellous or "magic" powers are better attested than his. At the end of his long and wonderful life he opened an esoteric school at Ephesus, and died aged almost one hundred years.

**Aporrheta** (*Gr.*). Secret instructions upon esoteric subjects given during the Egyptian and Grecian Mysteries.

**Apsaras** (*Sk.*). An Undine or Water-Nymph, from the Paradise or Heaven of Indra. The Apsarases are in popular belief the "wives of the gods" and called *Surânganâs*, and by a less honourable term, *Sumad-âtmajâs* or the "daughters of pleasure", for it is fabled of them that when they appeared at the churning of the Ocean neither Gods (Suras) nor Demons (Asuras) would take them for legitimate wives. Urvasi and several others of them are mentioned in the *Vedas*. In Occultism they are certain "sleep-producing" aquatic plants, and inferior forces of nature.

**Ar-Abu Nasr-al-Farabi**, called in Latin Alpharabius, a Persian, and the greatest Aristotelian philosopher of the age. He was born in 950 A.D., and is reported to have been murdered in 1047. He was an Hermetic philosopher and possessed the power of hypnotizing through music, making those who heard him play the lute laugh, weep, dance and do what he liked. Some of his works on Hermetic philosophy may be found in the Library of Leyden.

**Arahat** (*Sk.*). Also pronounced and written Arhat, Arhan, Rahat, &c., "the worthy one", lit., "deserving divine honours". This was the name first given to the Jain and subsequently to the Buddhist holy men initiated into the esoteric mysteries. The Arhat is one who has entered the best and highest path, and is thus emancipated from rebirth.

**Arani** (*Sk.*). The "female Arani" is a name of the Vedic Aditi (esoterically, the womb of the world). *Arani* is a *Swastika*, a disc-like wooden vehicle, in which the Brahmins generated fire by friction with *pramantha*, a stick, the symbol of the male generator. A mystic ceremony with a world of secret meaning in it and very sacred, perverted into phallic significance by the materialism of the age.

**Âranyaka** (*Sk.*). Holy hermits, sages who dwelt in ancient India in forests. Also a portion of the Vedas containing Upanishads, etc.

**Araritha** (*Heb.*). A very famous seven-lettered Kabbalistic wonder-word; its numeration is 813; its letters are collected by Notaricon from the sentence "one principle of his unity, one beginning of his individuality, his change is unity". [w.w.w.].

**Arasa Maram** (*Sk.*). The Hindu sacred tree of knowledge. In occult philosophy a mystic word.

**Arba-il** (*Chald.*). The Four Great Gods. *Arba* is Aramaic for four, and *il* is the same as Al or El. Three male deities, and a female who is virginal yet reproductive, form a very common ideal of Godhead. [w.w.w.]

**Archangel** (*Gr.*). Highest supreme angel. From the Greek *arch*, "chief" or "primordial", and *angelos*, "messenger ".

**Archæus** (*Gr.*). "The Ancient." Used of the oldest manifested deity; a term employed in the *Kabalah;* "archaic ", old, ancient.

**Archobiosis** (*Gr.*). Primeval beginning of life.

**Archetypal Universe** (*Kab.*). The ideal universe upon which the objective world was built. [w.w.w.]

**Archons** (*Gr.*). In profane and biblical language "rulers" and princes; in Occultism, primordial planetary spirits.

**Archontes** (*Gr.*). The archangels after becoming *Ferouers* (*q.v.*) or their own shadows, having mission on earth; a mystic ubiquity; implying a double life; a kind of hypostatic action, one of purity in a higher region, the other of terrestrial activity exercised on our plane.

(See Iamblichus, *De Mysteriis* II., Chap. 3.)

**Ardath** (*Heb.*). This word occurs in the Second Book of Esdras, ix., 26. The name has been given to one of the recent "occult novels" where much interest is excited by the visit of the hero to a field in the Holy Land so named; magical properties are attributed to it. In the Book of Esdras the prophet is sent to this field called Ardath "where no house is builded" and bidden "eat there only the flowers of the field, taste no flesh, drink no wine, and pray unto the highest continually, and then will I come and talk with thee". [w.w.w.]

**Ardha-Nârî** (*Sk.*). Lit., "half-woman". Siva represented as Androgynous, as half male and half female, a type of male and female energies combined. (See occult diagram in *Isis Unveiled,* Vol. II.)

**Ardhanârîswara** (*Sk.*). Lit., "the bi-sexual lord". Esoterically, the unpolarized states of cosmic energy symbolised by the Kabalistic Sephira, Adam Kadmon, &c.

**Ares.** The Greek name for Mars, god of war; also a term used by Paracelsus, the differentiated Force in Cosmos.

**Argha** (*Chald.*). The ark, the womb of Nature; the crescent moon, and a life-saving ship; also a cup for offerings, a vessel used for religious ceremonies.

**Arghyanâth** (*Sk.*). Lit., "lord of libations".

**Arian**. A follower of Arius, a presbyter of the Church in Alexandria in the fourth century. One who holds that Christ is a created and human being, inferior to God the Father, though a grand and noble man, a true adept versed in all the divine mysteries.

**Aristobulus** (*Gr*) An Alexandrian writer, and an obscure philosopher. A Jew who tried to prove that Aristotle explained the esoteric thoughts of Moses.

**Arithmomancy** (*Gr.*). The science of correspondences between gods, men, and numbers, as taught by Pythagoras. [w.w.w.]

**Arjuna** (*Sk.*) Lit., the "white". The third of the five Brothers Pandu or the reputed Sons of Indra (esoterically the same as Orpheus). A disciple of Krishna, who visited him and married Su-bhadrâ, his sister, besides many other wives, according to the allegory. During the fratricidal war between the *Kauravas* and the *Pândavas,* Krishna instructed him in the highest philosophy, while serving as his charioteer. (*See Bhaguvad Gîtâ.*)

**Ark of Isis**. At the great Egyptian annual ceremony, which took place in the month of Athyr, the boat of Isis was borne in procession by the priests, and *Collyrian* cakes or buns, marked with the sign of the cross (Tat), were eaten. This was in commemoration of the weeping of Isis for the loss of Osiris, the Athyr festival being very impressive. "Plato refers to the melodies on the occasion as being very ancient," writes Mr. Bonwick (*Eg. Belief and Mod. Thought*). "The *Miserere* in Rome has been said to be similar to its melancholy cadence, and to be derived from it Weeping, veiled virgins followed the ark. The *Nornes,* or veiled virgins, wept also for the loss of our Saxon forefathers' god, the ill-fated but good Baldur."

**Ark of the Covenant**. Every ark-shrine, whether with the Egyptians, Hindus, Chaldeans or Mexicans, was a phallic shrine, the symbol of the *yoni* or womb of nature. The *seket* of the Egyptians, the ark, or sacred chest, stood on the *ara*—its pedestal. The ark of Osiris, with the sacred relics of the god, was "of the same size as the Jewish ark", says S. Sharpe, the Egyptologist, carried by priests with staves passed through its rings in sacred procession, as the ark round which danced David, the King of Israel. Mexican gods also had their arks. Diana, Ceres, and other goddesses as well as gods had theirs. The ark was a boat—a vehicle in every case. "Thebes had a sacred ark 300 cubits long," and "the word *Thebes* is said to mean ark in Hebrew," which is but a natural recognition of the place to which the chosen people are indebted for their ark. Moreover, as Bauer writes, "the Cherub was not first used by Moses." The winged Isis was the cherub or *Arieh* in Egypt, centuries before the arrival there of even Abram or Sarai. "The external likeness of some of the Egyptian arks, surmounted by their two winged human figures, to the ark of the covenant, has often been noticed." (*Bible Educator*.) And not only the "external" but the *internal* "likeness" and sameness are now known to all. The arks, whether of the covenant, or of honest, straightforward, Pagan symbolism, had originally and now have one and the same meaning. The chosen people appropriated the idea and forgot to acknowledge its source. It is the same as in the case of the "Urim" and "Thummin" (*q.v.*). In Egypt, as shown by many Egyptologists, the two objects were the emblems of the *Two Truths*. "Two figures of Re and Thmei were worn on the breast-plate of the Egyptian High Priest. *Thmé*, plural *thmin*, meant truth in Hebrew. Wilkinson says the figure of Truth had closed eyes. Rosellini speaks of the *Thmei* being worn as a necklace. Diodorus gives such a necklace of gold and stones to the High Priest when delivering judgment. The Septuagint translates Thummin as *Truth*". (Bonwick's *Egyp. Belief*.)

**Arka** (*Sk.*). The Sun.

**Arkites**. The ancient priests who were attached to the Ark, whether of Isis, or the Hindu *Argua,* and who were seven in number, like the priests of the Egyptian *Tat* or any other cruciform symbol of the three and the *four*, the combination of which gives a male-female number. The *Avgha* (or ark) was the four-fold female principle, and the flame burning over it the triple *lingham*.

**Aroueris** (*Gr.*). The god Harsiesi, who was the elder Horus. He had a temple at Ambos. if we bear in mind the definition of the chief Egyptian gods by Plutarch, these myths will become more comprehensible; as he well says: "Osiris represents the beginning and principle; Isis, that which receives; and Horus, the compound of both. Horus engendered between them, is not eternal nor incorruptible, but, being always in generation, he endeavours by vicissitudes of imitations, and by periodical passion (yearly re-awakening to life) to continue always young, as if he should never die." Thus, since Horus is the personified physical world, Aroueris, or the "elder Horus", is the ideal Universe; and this accounts for the saying that "he was begotten by Osiris and Isis when these were still in the bosom of their mother"—Space. There is indeed, a good deal of mystery about this god, but the meaning of the symbol becomes clear once one has the key to it.

**Artephius.**—A great Hermetic philosopher, whose true name was never known and whose works are without dates, though it is known that he wrote his *Secret Book* in the XIIth century. Legend has it that he was one thousand years old at that time. There is a book on dreams by him in the possession of an Alchemist, now in Bagdad, in which he gives out the secret of seeing the past, the present, and the future, in sleep, and of remembering the things seen. There are but two copies of this manuscript extant. The book on *Dreams* by the Jew Solomon Almulus, published in Hebrew at Amsterdam in 1642, has a few reminiscences from the former work of Artephius.

**Artes** (*Eg.*). The Earth; the Egyptian god Mars.

**Artufas**. A generic name in South America and the islands for temples of *nagalism* or serpent worship.

**Arundhatî** (*Sk.*). The "Morning Star"; Lucifer-Venus.

**Arûpa** (*Sk.*). "Bodiless", formless, as opposed to *rûpa*, "body", or form.

**Arvâksrotas** (*Sk.*). The *seventh* creation, that of man, in the *Vishnu Purâna*.

**Arwaker** (*Scand.*). Lit., "early waker". The horse of the chariot of the Sun driven by the maiden Sol, in the *Eddas*.

**Ârya** (*Sk.*) Lit., "the holy"; originally the title of Rishis, those who had mastered the "Âryasatyâni" (*q.v.*) and entered the Âryanimârga path to Nirvâna or Moksha, the great "four-fold" path. But now the name has become the epithet of a race, and our Orientalists, depriving the Hindu Brahmans of their birth-right, have made Aryans of all Europeans. In esotericism, as the four paths, or stages, can be entered only owing to great spiritual development and "growth in holiness ", they are called the "four fruits". The degrees of Arhatship, called respectively Srotâpatti, Sakridâgamin, Anâgâmin, and Arhat, or the four classes of Âryas, correspond to these four paths and truths.

**Ârya-Bhata** (*Sk.*) The earliest Hindu algerbraist and astronomer, with the exception of Asura Maya (*q.v.*); the author of a work called *Ârya Siddhânta*, a system of Astronomy.

**Ârya-Dâsa** (*Sk.*) Lit., "Holy Teacher". A great sage and Arhat of the Mahâsamghika school.

**Aryahata** (*Sk.*) The "Path of Arhatship", or of holiness.

**Âryasangha** (*Sk.*) The Founder of the *first* Yogâchârya School. This Arhat, a direct disciple of Gautama, the Buddha, is most unaccountably mixed up and confounded with a personage of the same name, who is said to have lived in Ayôdhya (Oude) about the fifth or sixth century of our era, and taught Tântrika worship in addition to the Yogâchârya system. Those who sought to make it popular, claimed that he was the same Âryasangha, that had been a follower of Sâkyamuni, and that he was 1,000 years old. Internal evidence alone is sufficient to show that the works written by him and translated about the year 600 of our era, works full of Tantra worship, ritualism, and tenets followed now considerably by the "red-cap" sects in Sikhim, Bhutan, and Little Tibet, cannot be the same as the lofty system of the early Yogâcharya school of pure Buddhism, which is neither northern nor southern, but absolutely esoteric. Though none of the genunine Yogâchârya books (the *Narjol chodpa*) have ever been made public or marketable, yet one finds in the *Yogâchârya Bhûmi Shâstra* of the *pseudo-*Âryasangha a great deal from the older system, into the tenets of which he may have been initiated. It is, however, so mixed up with Sivaism and Tantrika magic and superstitions, that the work defeats its own end, notwithstanding its remarkable dialectical subtilty. How unreliable are the conclusions at which our Orientalists arrive, and how contradictory the dates assigned by them, may be seen in the case in hand. While Csoma de Körös (who, by-the-bye, never became acquainted with the Gelukpa (yellow-caps), but got all his information from "red-cap" lamas of the Borderland), places the *pseudo-*Âryasangha in the seventh century of our era; Wassiljew, who passed most of his life in China, proves him to have lived much earlier; and Wilson (see *Roy. As. Soc.*, Vol. VI., p. 240), speaking of the period when Âryasangha's works, which are still extant in Sanskrit, were written, believes it now "established, that they have been written *at the latest, from a century and a half before, to as much after*, the era of Christianity". At all events since it is beyond dispute that the Mahâyana religious works were all written far before Âryasangha's time—whether he lived in the "*second* century B.C.", or the "*seventh* .A.D."—and that these contain all and far more of the fundamental tenets of the Yogâchârya system, so disfigured by the Ayôdhyan imitator—the inference is that there must exist somewhere a genuine rendering free from popular Sivaism and left-hand magic.

**Aryasatyâni** (*Sk.*). The four truths or the four dogmas, which are (1) *Dukha,* or that misery and pain are the unavoidable concomitants of sentient (esoterically, physical) existence; (2) *Samudaya,* the truism that suffering is intensified by human passions; (3) *Nirôdha,* that the crushing out and extinction of all such feelings are possible for a man "on the path"; (4)

*Mârga*, the narrow way, or that path which leads to such a blessed result.

**Aryavarta** (*Sk.*). The "land of the Aryas", or India. The ancient name for Northern India. The Brahmanical invaders (" from the Oxus" say the Orientalists) first settled. It is erroneous to give this name to the whole,of India, since Manu gives the name of "the land of the Aryas" only to "the tract between the Himalaya and the Vindhya ranges, from the eastern to the western sea".

**Asakrit Samâdhi** (*Sk.*). A certain degree of ecstatic contemplation. A stage in *Samâdhi.*

**Âsana** (*Sk.*). The third stage of *Hatha Yoga*, one of the prescribed postures of meditation.

**Asat** (*Sk.*). A philosophical term meaning "non-being", or rather *non-be-ness.* The "incomprehensible nothingness". *Sat*, the immutable, eternal, ever-present, and the one real "Be-ness" (not Being) is spoken of as being "Born of Asat, and Asat begotten by Sat". The unreal, or Prakriti, objective nature regarded as an illusion. Nature, or the illusive shadow of its one true essence.

**Asathor** (*Scand*.). The same as Thor. The god of storms and thunder, a hero who receives Miölnir, the "storm-hammer", from its fabricators, the dwarfs. With it he conquer Alwin in a "battle of words" breaks the head of the giant Hrungir, chastises Loki for his magic; destroys the whole race of giants in Thrymheim; and, as a good and benevolent god, sets up therewith land-marks, sanctifies marriage bonds, blesses law and order, and produces every good and terrific feat with its help. A god in the *Eddas*, who is almost as great as Odin. (See "Miölnir" and "Thor's Hammer".)

**Asava Samkhaya** (*Pali*). The "finality of the stream", one of the six "Abhijnâs" (*q.v.*). A phenomenal knowledge of the finality of the stream of life and the series of re-births.

**Asburj**. One of the legendary peaks in the Teneriffe range. A great mountain in the traditions of Iran which corresponds in its allegorical meaning to the World-mountain, Meru. Asburj is that mount "at the foot of which the sun sets".

**Asch Metzareph** (*Heb.*). The Cleansing Fire, a Kabbalistic treatise, treating of Alchemy and the relation between the metals and the planets. [w.w.w.]

**Ases** (*Scand.*). The creators of the Dwarfs and Elves, the Elementals below men, in the Norse lays. They are the progeny of Odin; the same as the *Æsir*.

**Asgard** *(Scand.)*. The kingdom and the habitat of the Norse gods, the Scandinavian Olympus; situated "higher than the Home of the Light-Elves", but on the same plane as Jotunheim, the home of the Jotuns, the wicked giants versed in magic, with whom the gods are at eternal war. It is evident that the gods of Asgard are the same as the Indian *Suras* (gods) and the Jotuns as the *Asuras*, both representing the conflicting powers of nature—beneficent and maleficent. They are the prototypes also of the Greek gods and the Titans.

**Ash** *(Heb.)*. Fire, whether physical or symbolical fire; also found written in English as *As, Aish* and *Esch*.

**Ashen and Langhan** *(Kolarian)*. Certain ceremonies for casting out evil spirits, akin to those of exorcism with the Christians, in use with the Kolarian tribes in India.

**Asherah** *(Heb.)*. A word, which occurs in the Old Testament, and is commonly translated "groves" referring to idolatrous worship, but it is probable that it really referred to ceremonies of sexual depravity; it is a feminine noun. [w.w.w.]

**Ashmog** *(Zend)*. The Dragon or Serpent, a monster with a camel's neck in the *Avesta*; a kind of allegorical Satan, who after the Fall, "lost its nature and its name". Called in the old Hebrew (Kabbalistic) texts the "flying camel"; evidently a reminiscence or tradition in both cases of the prehistoric or antediluvian monsters, half bird, half reptile,

**Ashtadisa** *(Sk.)*. The eight-faced space. An imaginary division of space represented as an *octagon* and at other times as a *dodecahedron*.

**Ashta Siddhis** *(Sk.)*. The eight consummations in the practice of Hatha Yoga.

**Ashtar Vidyâ** *(Sk.)*. The most ancient of the Hindu works on Magic. Though there is a claim that the entire work is in the hands of some Occultists, yet the Orientalists deem it lost. A very few fragments of it are now extant, and even these are very much disfigured.

**Ash Yggdrasil** *(Scand.)*. The "Mundane Tree", the Symbol of the World with the old Norsemen, the "tree of the universe, of time and of life". It is ever green, for the Norns of Fate sprinkle It daily with the water of life from the fountain of Urd, which flows in Midgard. The dragon Nidhogg gnaws its roots incessantly, the dragon of Evil and Sin; but the Ash Yggdrasil cannot wither, until the Last Battle (the Seventh Race in the Seventh Round) is fought, when life, time, and the world will all vanish and disappear.

**Asiras** (*Sk.*). Elementals without heads; lit., "headless"; used also of the first two human races.

**Asita** (*Sk.*). A proper name; a son of Bharata; a Rishi and a Sage.

**Ask** (*Scand.*) or Ash tree. The "tree of Knowledge". Together with the *Embla* (alder) the Ask was the tree from which the gods of Asgard created the first man.

**Aski-kataski-haix-tetrax-damnameneus-aision.** These mystic words, which Athanasius Kircher tells us meant "Darkness, Light, Earth, Sun, and Truth", were, says Hesychius, engraved upon the zone or belt of the Diana of Ephesus. Plutarch says that the priests used to recite these words over persons who were possessed by devils. [w.w.w.]

**Asmodeus**. The Persian *Aêshma-dev,* the *Esham-dev* of the Parsis, "the evil Spirit of Concupiscence", according to Bréal, whom the Jews appropriated under the name of *Ashmedai,* "the Destroyer ", the *Talmud* identifying the creature with Beelzebub and Azrael (Angel of Death), and calling him the "King of the Devils ".

**Asmoneans**. Priest-kings of Israel whose dynasty reigned over the Jews for 126 years. They promulgated the Canon of the Mosaic Testament in contradistinction to the "Apocrypha" (*q.v.*) or Secret Books of the Alexandrian Jews, the Kabbalists, and maintained the dead-letter meaning of the former. Till the time of John Hyrcanus, they were Ascedeans (*Chasidim*) and Pharisees; but later they became Sadducees or Zadokites, asserters of Sacerdotal rule as contradistinguished from Rabbinical.

**Asoka** (*Sk.*). A celebrated Indian king of the Môrya dynasty which reigned at Magadha. There were two Asokas in reality, according to the chronicles of Northern Buddhism, though the first Asoka—the grand father of the second, named by Prof. Max Muller the "Constantine of India", was better known by his name of Chandragupta. It is the former who was called, *Piadasi* (Pali) "the beautiful", and *Devânam-piya* "the beloved of the gods", and also *Kâlâsoka;* while the name of his grandson was *Dharmâsôká*—the Asoka of the good law-—on account of his devotion to Buddhism. Moreover, according to the same source, the second Asoka had never followed the Brahmanical faith, but was a Buddhist born. It was his grandsire who had been first converted to the new faith, after which he had a number of edicts inscribed on pillars and rocks, a custom followed also by his grandson. But it was the second Asoka who was the most zealous supporter of Buddhism; he, who maintained in his palace from 60 to 70,000 monks and priests, who erected 84,000 *totes* and *stupas* throughout India, reigned 36 years, and sent missions to Ceylon, and throughout the world. The inscriptions of various edicts published by him display most noble ethical sentiments, especially the edict at Allahahad, on the so-called "Asoka's column ", in the Fort. The sentiments are lofty and poetical, breathing tenderness for animals as well as men, and a lofty view of a king's mission with regard to his people, that might be followed with great success in the present age of cruel wars and barbarous vivisection.

**Asomatous** (*Gr.*). Lit., without a material body, incorporeal; used of celestial Beings and Angels.

**Asrama** (*Sk.*). A sacred building, a monastery or hermitage for ascetic purposes. Every sect in India has its *Ashrams*.

**Assassins.** A masonic and mystic order founded by Hassan Sabah in Persia, in the eleventh century. The word is a European perversion of "Hassan", which forms the chief part of the name. They were simply *Sufis* and addicted, according to the tradition, to *hascheesl-eating,* in order to bring about celestial visions. As shown by our late brother, Kenneth Mackenzie, "they were teachers of the secret doctrines of Islamism; they encouraged mathematics and philosophy, and produced many valuable works. The chief of the Order was called Sheik-el-Jebel, translated the '*Old Man of the Mountains'*, and, as their Grand Master, he possessed power of life and death.'

**Assorus** (*Chald.*). The third group of progeny (Kissan and Assorus) from the Babylonian Duad, Tauthe and Apason, according to the Theogonies of Damascius. From this last emanated three others, of which series the last, Aus, begat Belus—"the fabricator of the World, the Demiurgus".

**Assur** (*Chald.*). A city in Assyria; the ancient seat of a library from which George Smith excavated the earliest known tablets, to which he assigns a date about 1500 B.C., called *Assur Kileh Shergat.*

**Assurbanipal** (*Chald.*). The Sardanapalus of the Greeks, "the greatest of the Assyrian Sovereigns, far more memorable on account of his magnificent patronage of learning than of the greatness of his empire", writes the late G. Smith, and adds: "Assurbanipal added more to the Assyrian royal library than *all the kings who had gone before him*". As the distinguished Assyriologist tells us in another place of his "Babylonian and Assyrian Literature" (*Chald. Account of Genesis*) that "the majority of the texts preserved belong to the earlier period previous to B.C. 1600", and yet asserts that "it is to tablets written in his (Assurbanipal's) reign (B.C. 673) that we owe almost all our knowledge of the Babylonian early history", one is well justified in asking, "How do you know?"

**Assyrian** *Holy Scriptures*. Orientalists show seven such books: the Books of Mamit, of Worship, of Interpretations, of Going to Hades; two Prayer Books *(Kanmagarri and Kanmikri:* Talbot) and the Kantolite, the lost Assyrian Psalter.

**Assyrian** *Tree of Life*. "*Asherah*" *(q.v.)*. It is translated in the Bible by "grove "and occurs 30 times. It is called an "idol"; and Maachah, the grandmother of Asa, King of Jerusalem, is accused of having made for herself such an idol, which was a *lingham*. For centuries this was a religious rite in Judæa. But the original Asherah was a pillar with seven branches on each side surmounted by a globular flower with three projecting rays, and no *phallic* stone, as the Jews made of it, but a metaphysical symbol. "Merciful One, who dead to life raises! was the prayer uttered before the Asherah, on the banks of the Euphrates. The "Merciful One", was neither the personal god of the Jews who brought the "grove" from their captivity, nor any extra-cosmic god, but the higher triad in man symbolized by the globular flower with its three rays.

**Asta-dasha** *(Sk.)*. Perfect, Supreme Wisdom; a title of Deity.

**Aster't** *(Heb.)*. Astarte, the Syrian goddess the consort of Adon, or Adonai.

**Astræa** *(Gr.)*. The ancient goddess of justice, whom the wickedness of men drove away from earth to heaven, wherein she now dwells as the constellation *Virgo*.

**Astral Body**, or Astral "Double". The ethereal counterpart or shadow of man or animal. The **Linga Sharira,** the "Doppelgäinger". The reader must not confuse it with the ASTRAL SOUL, another name for the lower Manas, or Kama-Manas so-called, the reflection of the HIGHER EGO.

**Astral Light** *(Occult)* The invisible region that surrounds our globe, as it does every other, and corresponding as the second Principle of Kosmos (the third being Life, of which it is the vehicle) to the *Linga Sharira* or the Astral Double in man. A subtle Essence visible only to a clairvoyant eye, and the lowest but one *(viz.,* the earth), of the Seven Akâsic or Kosmic Principles. Eliphas Levi calls it the great Serpent and the Dragon from which radiates on Humanity every evil influence. This is so; but why not add that the Astral Light gives out nothing but what it has received; that it is the great terrestrial crucible, in which the vile emanations of the earth (moral and physical) upon which the Astral Light is fed, are all converted into their subtlest essence, and radiated back intensified, thus becoming epidemics—moral, psychic and physical. Finally, the Astral Light is the same as the *Sidereal Light* of Paracelsus and other Hermetic philosophers. "Physically, it is the ether of modern science. Metaphysically, and in its spiritual, or occult sense, ether is a great deal more than is often imagined. In occult physics, and alchemy, it is well demonstrated to enclose within its shoreless waves not only Mr. Tyndall's *'promise* and potency of every quality of life', but also the *realization* of the potency of every quality of spirit. Alchemists and Hermetists believe that their *astral*, or sidereal ether, besides the above properties of sulphur, and white and red magnesia, or *magnes*, is the *anima mundi*, the workshop of Nature and of all the Kosmos, spiritually, as well as physically. The 'grand magisterium' asserts itself in the phenomenon of mesmerism, in the 'levitation' of human and inert objects; and may be called the ether from its spiritual aspect. The designation *astral* is ancient, and was used by some of the Neo-platonists, although it is claimed by some that the word was coined by the Martinists. Porphyry describes the celestial body which is always joined with the soul as 'immortal, luminous, and star-like'. The root of this word may be found, perhaps, in the Scythic *Aist-aer*—which means star, or the Assyrian *Istar,* which, according to Burnouf has the same sense." *(Isis Unveiled.)*

**Astrolatry** *(Gr.).* Worship of the Stars.

**Astrology** *(Gr.)* The Science which defines the action of celestial bodies upon mundane affairs, and claims to foretell future events from the position of the stars. Its antiquity is such as to place it among the very earliest records of human learning. It remained for long ages a secret science in the East, and its final expression remains so to this day, its exoteric application having been brought to any degree of perfection in the West only during the period of time since Varaha Muhira wrote his book on Astrology some 1400 years ago. Claudius Ptolemy, the famous geographer and mathematician, wrote his treatise *Tetrabiblos* about 135 A.D., which is still the basis of modern astrology. The science of Horoscopy is studied now chiefly under four heads: *viz.,* (1) *Mundane,* in its application to meteorology, seismology, husbandry, etc. (2) *State or civic,* in regard to the fate of nations, kings and rulers. (3) *Horary,* in reference to the solving of doubts arising in the mind upon any subject. (4) *Genethliacal,* in its application to the fate of individuals from the moment of their birth to their death. The Egyptians and the Chaldees were among the most ancient votaries of Astrology, though their modes of reading the stars and the modern practices differ considerably. The former claimed that Belus, the Bel or Elu of the Chaldees, a scion of the *divine* Dynasty, or the Dynasty of the king-gods, had belonged to the land of Chemi, and had left it, to found a colony from Egypt on the banks of the Euphrates, where a temple ministered by priests in the service of the "lords of the stars" was built, the said priests adopting the name of *Chaldees*. Two things are known: (a) that Thebes (in Egypt) claimed the honour of the invention of Astrology; and (b) that it was the Chaldees who taught that science to the other nations. Now Thebes antedated considerably not only "Ur of the Chaldees", but also Nipur, where Bel was first worshipped—Sin, his son (the moon), being the presiding deity of Ur, the land of the nativity of Terah, the Sabean and Astrolatrer, and of Abram, his son, the great Astrologer of biblical tradition. All tends, therefore, to corroborate the Egyptian claim. If later on the name of Astrologer fell into disrepute in Rome and elsewhere, it was owing to the fraud of those who wanted to make money by means of that which was part and parcel of the sacred Science of the Mysteries, and, ignorant of the latter, evolved a system based entirely upon mathematics, instead of on transcendental metaphysics and having the physical celestial bodies as its *upadhi* or material basis. Yet, all persecutions notwithstanding, the number of the adherents of Astrology among the most intellectual and scientific minds was always very great. If Cardan and Kepler were among its ardent supporters, then its later votaries have nothing to blush for, even in its now imperfect and distorted form. As said in *Isis Unveiled* (1. 259): "Astrology is to exact astronomy what psychology is to exact physiology. In astrology and psychology one has to step beyond the visible world of matter, and enter into the domain of transcendent spirit."

(See "*Astronomos.*")

**Astronomos** (*Gr.*). The title given to the Initiate in the Seventh Degree of the reception of the Mysteries. In days of old, Astronomy was synonymous with Astrology; and the great Astrological Initiation took place in Egypt at Thebes, where the priests perfected, if they did not wholly invent the science. Having passed through the degrees of *Pastophoros, Neocoros, Melanophoros, Kistophoros,* and *Balahala* (the degree of Chemistry of the Stars), the neophyte was taught the mystic signs of the Zodiac, in a circle dance representing the course of the planets (the dance of Krishna and the Gopis, celebrated to this day in Rajputana); after which he received a cross, the Tau (or Tat), becoming an *Astronomos* and a Healer. (*See Isis Unveiled*. Vol. II. 365). Astronomy and Chemistry were inseparable in these studies. "Hippocrates had so lively a faith in the influence of the stars on animated beings, and on their diseases, that he expressly recommends not to trust to physicians who are ignorant of astronomy." (Arago.) Unfortunately the key to the final door of Astrology or Astronomy is lost by the modern Astrologer; and without it, how can he ever be able to answer the pertinent remark made by the author of *Mazzaroth*, who writes: "people are said to be born under one sign, while in reality they are born under another, because *the sun is now seen among different stars at the equinox*"? Nevertheless, even the few truths he does know brought to his science such eminent and scientific believers as Sir Isaac Newton, Bishops Jeremy and Hall, Archbishop Usher, Dryden, Flamstead, Ashmole, John Milton, Steele, and a host of noted Rosicrucians.

**Asura Mazda** (*Sk.*). In the Zend, *Ahura Mazda*. The same as Ormuzd or Mazdeô; the god of Zoroaster and the Parsis.

**Asuramaya** (*Sk.*) Known also as *Mayâsura*. An Atlantean astronomer, considered as a great magician and sorcerer, well-known in Sanskrit works.

**Asuras** (*Sk.*). Exoterically, elementals and evil, gods—considered maleficent; demons, and *no* gods. But esoterically—the reverse. For in the most ancient portions of the *Rig Veda*, the term is used for the Supreme Spirit, and therefore the Asuras are spiritual and divine It is only in the last book of the *Rig Veda*, its latest part, and in the *Atharva Veda*, and the *Brâhmanas*, that the epithet, which had been given to Agni, the greatest Vedic Deity, to Indra and Varuna, has come to signify the reverse of gods. *Asu* means breath, and it is with his breath that Prajâpati (Brahmâ) creates the Asuras. When ritualism and dogma got the better of the Wisdom religion, the initial letter **a** was adopted as a negative prefix, and the term ended by signifying "not a god", and Sura only a deity. But in the Vedas the Suras have ever been connected with *Surya*, the sun, and regarded as *inferior* deities, devas.

**Aswamedha** (*Sk.*) The Horse-sacrifice; an ancient Brahmanical ceremony.

**Aswattha** (*Sk.*) The **Bo-tree**, the tree of knowledge, *ficus religiosa*.

**Aswins** (*Sk.*), or *Aswinau*, dual; or again, *Aswinî-Kumârau*, are the most mysterious and occult deities of all; who have "puzzled the oldest commentators". Literally, they are the "Horsemen", the "divine charioteers", as they ride in a *golden car* drawn by horses or birds or animals, and *"are possessed of many forms"*. They are two Vedic deities, the twin sons of the sun and the sky, which becomes the nymph Aswini. In mythological symbolism they are "the bright harbingers of Ushas, the dawn", who are "ever young and handsome, bright, agile, swift as falcons", who "prepare the way for the brilliant dawn to those who have patiently awaited through the night". They are also called time "physicians of Swarga" (or Devachan), inasmuch as they heal every pain and suffering, and cure all diseases. Astronomically, they are asterisms. They were enthusiastically worshipped, as their epithets show. They are the "Ocean-born" (i.e., *space* born) or *Abdhijau*, "crowned with lotuses" or **Pushhara-srajam,** etc., etc. Yâska, the commentator in the *Nirukta*, thinks that "the Aswins represent the transition from darkness to light "—cosmically, and we may add, metaphysically, also. But Muir and Goldstücker are inclined to see in them ancient "horsemen of great renown", because, forsooth, of the legend "that the gods refused the Aswins admittance to a sacrifice on the ground that *they had been on too familiar terms with men*". Just so, because as explained by the same Yâska "they are identified with heaven and earth", only for quite a different reason. Truly they are like the *Ribhus*, "originally renowned mortals (but also non-renowned occasionally) who in the course of time are translated into the companionship of gods"; and they show a negative character, "the result of the-alliance of light with darkness", simply because these *twins* are, in the esoteric philosophy, the **Kumâra-Egos,** the reincarnating "Principles" in this Manvantara.

**Atala** (*Sk*). One of the regions in the Hindu lokas, and one of the seven mountains; but esoterically Atala is on an astral plane, and was, once on a time, a real island upon this earth.

**Atalanta Fugiens** (*Lat*.). A famous treatise by the eminent Rosicrucian Michael Maier; it has many beautiful engravings of Alchemic symbolism: here is to be found the original of the picture of a man and woman within a circle, a triangle around it, then a square: the inscription is, "From the first *ens* proceed two contraries, thence come the three principles, and from them the four elementary states; if you separate the pure from the impure you will have the stone of the Philosophers". [w.w.w.]

**Atarpi** (*Chald*.), or *Atarpi-nisi*, the "man". A personage who was "pious to the gods"; and who prayed the god Hea to remove the evil of drought and other things before the Deluge is sent. The story is found on one of the most ancient Babylonian tablets, and relates to the sin of the world. In the words of G. Smith "the god Elu or Bel calls together an assembly of the gods, his sons, and relates to them that he is angry at the sin of the world"; and in the fragmentary phrases of the tablet: ". . . . I made them . . . . Their wickedness I am angry at, their punishment shall not be small . . . . let food be exhausted, above let Vul drink up his rain", etc., etc. In answer to Atarpi's prayer the god Hea announces his resolve to destroy the people he created, which he does finally by a deluge.

**Atash Behram** (*Zend*). The sacred fire of the Parsis, preserved perpetually in their fire-temples.

**Atef** (*Eg.*), or Crown of Horus. It consisted of a tall white cap with ram's horns, and the *urœus* in front. Its two feathers represent the two truths— *life and death.*

**Athamaz** (*Heb.*). The same as Adonis with the Greeks, the Jews having borrowed all their gods.

**Athanor** (*Occult.*) The "*astral*" fluid of the Alchemists, their Archimedean lever; exoterically, the furnace of the Alchemist.

**Atharva Veda** (*Sk.*) The fourth Veda; *lit.*, magic incantation containing aphorisms, incantations and magic formula One of the most ancient and revered Books of the Brahmans.

**Athenagoras** (*Gr.*) A Platonic philosopher of Athens, who wrote a Greek Apology for the Christians in A.D. 177, addressed to the Emperor Marcus Aurelius, to prove that the accusations brought against them, namely that they were incestuous and ate murdered children, were untrue.

**Athor** (*Eg.*) "Mother Night." Primeval Chaos, in the Egyptian cosmogony. The goddess of night.

**Atîvahikâs** (*Sk.*) With the Visishtadwaitees, these are the Pitris, or *Devas*, who help the disembodied soul or *Jiva* in its transit from its dead body to *Paramapadha.*

**Atlantidæ** (Gr.) The ancestors of the Pharaohs and the forefathers of the Egyptians, according to some, and as the Esoteric Science teaches. (See *S.D., Vol. II.*, and *Esoteric Buddhism.*) Plato heard of this highly civilized people, the last remnant of which was submerged 9,000 years before his day, from Solon, who had it from the High Priests of Egypt. Voltaire, the eternal scoffer, was right in stating that "the Atlantidæ (our *fourth* Root Race) made their appearance in Egypt It was in Syria and in Phrygia, as well as Egypt, that they established the worship of the Sun." Occult philosophy teaches that the Egyptians were a remnant of the last *Aryan* Atlantidæ.

**Atlantis** (*Gr.*) The continent that was submerged in the Atlantic and the Pacific Oceans according to the secret teachings and Plato.

**Atmâ** (or **Atman**) (*Sk.*). The Universal Spirit, the divine Monad, the 7th Principle, so-called, in the septenary constitution of man. The Supreme Soul.

**Atma-bhu** (*Sk.*). Soul-existence, or existing as soul. (See "*Alaya*".)

**Atmabodha** (*Sk.*). Lit., "Self-knowledge"; the title of a Vedantic treatise by Sankârachârya.

**Atma-jnâni** (*Sk.*) The Knower of the World-Soul, or Soul in general.

**Atma-matrasu** (*Sk.*) To enter into the elements of the "One-Self". (See *S. D. I.,334 Atmamâtra* is the spiritual atom, as contrasted with, and opposed to, the elementary differentiated atom or molecule.

**Atma Vidyâ** (*Sk.*). The highest form of spiritual knowledge; lit., "Soul-knowledge".

**Atri**, Sons of (*Sk.*). A class of Pitris, the "ancestors of man", or the so-called Prâjapâti, "progenitors"; one of the seven Rishis who form the constellation of the Great Bear.

**Attavada** (*Pali*). The sin of personality.

**Atyantika** (*Sk.*) One of the four kinds of *pralaya* or dissolution. The "absolute" pralaya.

**Atziluth** (*Heb.*) The highest of the Four Worlds of the Kabbalah referred only to the pure Spirit of God. [w. w. w.] See "Aziluth" for another interpretation.

**Audlang** (*Scand.*). The second heaven made by Deity above the field of Ida, in the Norse legends.

**Audumla** (*Scand.*) The Cow of Creation, the "nourisher", from which flowed four streams of milk which fed the giant Ymir or Örgelmir (matter in ebullition) and his sons, the Hrimthurses (Frost giants), before the appearance of gods or men. Having nothing to graze upon she licked the salt of the ice-rocks and thus produced Buri, "the Producer" in his turn, who had a son Bör (the born) who married a daughter of the Frost Giants, and had three sons, *Odin* (Spirit), *Wili* (Will), and We (Holy). The meaning of the allegory is evident. It is the precosmic union of the elements, of Spirit, or the creative Force, with Matter, cooled and still seething, which it forms in accordance with universal Will. Then the Ases, "the pillars and supports of the World" (***Cosmocratores***), step in and *create* as All-father wills them.

**Augiras**. One of the Prajâpatis. A son of Daksha; a lawyer, etc., etc.

**Augoeides** (*Gr.*). Bulwer Lytton calls it the "Luminous Self ", or our Higher Ego. But Occultism makes of it something distinct from this. It is a mystery. The *Augocides* is the luminous divine radiation of the EGO which, when incarnated, is but its shadow—pure as it is yet. This is explained in the *Amshaspends* and their *Ferouers*.

**Aum** (*Sk.*). The sacred syllable; the triple-lettered unit; hence the trinity in One.

**Aura** *(Gr. and Lat.)*. A subtle invisible essence or fluid that emanates from human and animal bodies and even things. It is a psychic effluvium, partaking of both the mind and the body, as it is the electro-vital, and at the same time an electro-mental aura; called in Theosophy the âkâsic or magnetic aura.

**Aurnavâbha** (*Sk.*) An ancient Sanskrit commentator.

**Aurva** (*Sk.*). The Sage who is credited with the invention of the "fiery weapon" called *Agneyâstra*.

**Ava-bodha** (*Sk.*). "Mother of Knowledge." A title of Aditi.

**Avâivartika** (*Sk.*) An epithet of every Buddha: lit., one who turns no more back; who goes straight to Nirvâna.

**Avalokiteswara** (*Sk.*) "The on-looking Lord" In the exoteric interpretation, he is Padmapâni (the lotus bearer and the lotus-born) in Tibet, the first divine ancestor of the Tibetans, the complete incarnation or Avatar of Avalokiteswara; but in esoteric philosophy Avaloki, the "on-looker", is the Higher Self, while Padmapâni is the Higher Ego or Manas. The mystic formula "Om mani padme hum" is specially used to invoke their joint help. While popular fancy claims for Avalokiteswara many incarnations on earth, and sees in him, not very wrongly, the spiritual guide of every believer, the esoteric interpretation sees in him the Logos, both celestial and human. Therefore, when the Yogâchârya School has declared Avalokiteswara as Padmâpani "to be the Dhyâni Bodhisattva of Amitâbha Buddha", it is indeed, because the former is *the spiritual reflex in the world of forms* of the latter, both being one—one in heaven, the other on earth.

**Avarasâila Sanghârama** (*Sk.*). Lit., the School of the Dwellers on the western mountain. A celebrated Vihâra (monastery) in Dhana-kstchâka, according to Eitel, "built 600 B.C., and deserted A.D. 600".

**Avastan** (*Sk.*) An ancient name for Arabia.

**Avasthas** (*Sk.*) States, conditions, positions.

**Avatâra** (*Sk.*) Divine incarnation. The descent of a god or some exalted Being, who has progressed beyond the necessity of Rebirths, into the body of a simple mortal. Krishna was an avatar of Vishnu. The Dalai Lama is regarded as an avatar of Avalokiteswara, and the Teschu Lama as one of Tson-kha-pa, or Amitâbha. There are two kinds of avatars: those born from woman, and the parentless, the *anupapâdaka*.

**Avebury** or **Abury**. In Wiltshire are the remains of an ancient megalithic Serpent temple: according to the eminent antiquarian Stukeley, 1740, there are traces of two circles of stones and two avenues; the whole has formed the representation of a serpent. [w.w.w.]

**Avesta** (*Zend*). Lit., "the Law". From the old Persian *Âbastâ*, "the law". The sacred Scriptures of the Zoroastrians. *Zend* means in the "Zend-Avesta"—a "commentary" or "interpretation". It is an error to regard "Zend" as a language, as "it was applied only to explanatory texts, to the translations of the Avesta"(Darmsteter).

**Avicenna**. The latinized name of Abu-Ali al Hoséen ben Abdallah Ibn Sina; a Persian philosopher, born 980 AD)., though generally referred to as an Arabian doctor. On account of his surprising learning he was called "the Famous", and was the author of the best and the first alchemical works known in Europe. All the Spirits of the Elements were subject to him, so says the legend, and it further tells us that owing to his knowledge of the Elixir of Life, he still lives, as an adept who will disclose himself to the profane at the end of a certain cycle.

**Avidyâ** (*Sk.*). Opposed to *Vidyâ*, Knowledge. Ignorance which proceeds from, and is produced by the illusion of the Senses or *Viparyaya.*

**Avikâra** (*Sk.*). Free from degeneration; changeless—used of Deity.

**Avitchi** (*Sk.*) A state: not necessarily after death only or between two births, for it can take place on earth as well. Lit., "uninterrupted hell". The last of the eight hells, we are told, "where the culprits *die and are reborn without interruption*—yet not without hope of final redemption. This is because Avitchi is another name for Myalba (our earth) and also a state to which some soulless men are condemned on this physical plane.

**Avyakta** (*Sk.*). The unrevealed cause; indiscrete or undifferentiated; the opposite of *Vyakta,* the differentiated. The former is used of the unmanifested, and the latter of the manifested Deity, or of Brahma and Brahmâ.

**Axieros** (*Gr.*). One of the Kabiri.

**Axiocersa** (*Gr.*). "         "

**Axiocersus** (*Gr.*).         "         "

**Ayana** (*Sk.*) A period of time; two Ayanas complete a year, one being the period of the Sun's progress northward, and the other south ward in the ecliptic.

**Ayin** (*Heb.*). Lit., "Nothing", whence the name of Ain-Soph. (See"Ain".)

**Aymar,** Jacques. A famous Frenchman who had great success in the use of the Divining Rod about the end of the 17th century; he was often employed in detecting criminals; two M.D's of the University of Paris, Chauvin and Garnier reported on the reality of his powers. See Colquhoun on *Magic.* [w.w.w.]

**Ayur Veda** (*Sk.*). Lit., "the Veda of Life".

**Ayuta** (*Sk.*). 100 Kôti, or a sum equal to 1,000,000,000.

**Azareksh** (*Zend*) A place celebrated for a fire-temple of the Zoroastrians and Magi during the time of Alexander the Great.

**Azazel** (*Heb.*) "God of Victory"; the scape-goat for the sins of Israel. He who comprehends the mystery of *Azazel,* says Aben-Ezra, "will learn the mystery of God's name", and truly. See "Typhon" and the scape-goat made sacred to him in ancient Egypt.

**Azhi-Dahaka** (*Zend*) One of the Serpents or Dragons in the legends of Iran and the Avesta Scriptures, the allegorical destroying Serpent or Satan.

**Aziluth** (*Heb.*) The name for the world of the Sephiroth, called the world of Emanations *Olam Aziluth.* It is the great and the highest prototype of the other worlds. "*Atzeelooth* is the Great Sacred Seal by means of which all the worlds are copied which have impressed on themselves the image on the Seal; and as this Great Seal comprehends three stages, which are three *zures* (prototypes) of *Nephesh* (the Vital Spirit or Soul), *Ruach* (the moral and reasoning Spirit), and the *Neshamah* (the Highest Soul of man), so the Sealed have also received three *zures,* namely *Breeah, Yetzeerah,* and *Aseeyah,* and these three zures are only one in the Seal" (*Myer's Qabbalah).* The globes A, Z, of our terrestial chain are in Aziluth. (See *Secret Doctrine.)*

**Azoth** (*Alch.*). The creative principle in Nature, the grosser portion of which is stored in the Astral Light. It is symbolized by a figure which is a cross (See "Eliphas Lévi"), the four limbs of which bear each one letter of the word *Taro,* which can be read also Rota, Ator, and in many other combinations, each of which has an occult meaning.

**A. and Ω.** Alpha and Omega, the First and the Last, the beginning and ending of all active existence; the Logos, hence (with the Christians) Christ. See *Rev.* xxi, 6., where John adopts "Alpha and Omega" as the symbol of a Divine Comforter who "will give unto him that is athirst of the fountain of the water of life freely". The word *Azot* or *Azoth* is a mediæval glyph of this idea, for the word consists of the first and last letters of the Greek alphabet, A and Ω of the Latin alphabet, A and Z, and of the Hebrew alphabet, A and T, or *aleph* and *tau.* (See also "Azoth".) [w.w.w.]

# B

**B.**—The second letter in almost all the alphabets, also the second in the Hebrew. Its symbol is a *house*, the form of *Beth*, the letter itself indicating a dwelling, a shed or a shelter. "As a compound of a root, it is constantly used for the purpose of showing that it had to do with stone; when stones at Beth-el are set up, for instance. The Hebrew value as a numeral is two. Joined with its predecessor, it forms the word Ab, the root of 'father', Master, one in authority, and it has the Kabalistical distinction of being the first letter in the Sacred Volume of the Law. The divine name connected with this letter is "*Bakhour.*" (*Royal Masonic Cyclopædia*)

**Baal** (*Chald. Heb.*). Baal or Adon (Adonai) was a phallic god. "Who shall ascend unto the hill (the high place) of the Lord; who shall stand in the place of his *Kadushu* (*q.v.*) ? "(*Psalms* XX1V. 3.) The "circle dance" performed by King David round the ark, was the dance prescribed by the Amazons in the Mysteries, the dance of the daughters of Shiloh (*Judges* xxi., *et seq.*) and the same as the leaping of the prophets of Baal (I. *Kings* xviii). He was named *Baal-Tzephon*, or god of the crypt (Exodus) and *Seth*, or the *pillar* (*phallus*), because he was the same as Ammon (or Baal-Hammon) of Egypt, called "the hidden god". Typhon, called Set, who was a great god in Egypt during the early dynasties, is an *aspect* of Baal and Ammon as also of Siva, Jehovah and other gods. Baal is the all devouring Sun, in one sense, the fiery Moloch.

**Babil Mound** (*Chald. Heb.*). The site of the Temple of Bel at Babylon.

**Bacchus** (*Gr.*). Exoterically and superficially the god of wine and the vintage, and of licentiousness and joy; but the esoteric meaning of this personification is more abstruse and philosophical. He is the Osiris of Egypt, and his life and significance belong to the same group as the other solar deities, all "sin-bearing," killed and resurrected; e.g., as Dionysos or Atys of Phrygia (Adonis, or the Syrian Tammuz), as Ausonius, Baldur (*q.v.*), &c., &c. All these were put to death, mourned for, and restored to life. The rejoicings for Atys took place at the *Hilaria* on the "pagan" Easter, March 15. Ausonius, a form of Bacchus, was slain "at the vernal equinox, March 21st, and rose in three days". Tammuz, the double of Adonis and Atys, was mourned by the women at the "grove" of his name "over Bethlehem, where the infant Jesus cried", says St. Jerome. Bacchus is murdered and his mother collects the fragments of his lacerated body as Isis does those of Osiris, and so on. Dionysos Iacchus, torn to shreds by the Titans, Osiris, Krishna, all descended into Hades and returned again.

Astronomically, they all represent the Sun; psychically they are all emblems of the ever-resurrecting "Soul" (the Ego in its re-incarnation); spiritually, all the innocent scape-goats, atoning for the sins of mortals, their own earthly envelopes, and in truth, the poeticized image of DIVINE MAN, the form of clay informed by its God.

**Bacon,** Roger. A Franciscan monk, famous as an adept in Alchemy and Magic Arts. Lived in the thirteenth century in England. He believed in the philosopher's stone in the way all the adepts of Occultism believe in it; and also in philosophical astrology. He is accused of having made a head of bronze which having an acoustic apparatus hidden in it, seemed to utter oracles which were words spoken by Bacon himself in another room. He was a wonderful physicist and chemist, and credited with having invented gunpowder, though he said he had the secret from "Asian (Chinese) wise men."

**Baddha** (*Sk.*). Bound, conditioned; as is every mortal who has not made himself free through Nirvâna.

**Bagavadam** (*Sk.*). A Tamil Scripture on Astronomy and other matters.

**Bagh-bog** (*Slavon.*). "God"; a Slavonian name for the Greek Bacchus, whose name became the prototype of the name God or *Bagh* and *bog* or *bogh*; the Russian for God.

**Bahak-Zivo** (*Gn.*). The "father of the Genii" in the Codex Nazarœus. The Nazarenes were an early semi-Christian sect.

**Bal** (*Heb.*). Commonly translated "Lord", but also Bel, the Chaldean god, and Baal, an "idol".

**Bala** (*Sk.*), or *Panchabalâni.* The "five powers" to be acquired in Yoga practice; full trust or faith; energy; memory; meditation; wisdom.

**Baldur** (*Scand.*). The "Giver of all Good". The bright God who is "the best and all mankind are loud in his praise; so fair and dazzling is he in form and features, that rays of light seem to issue from him *(Edda)*. Such was the birth-song chanted to Baldur who resurrects as Wali, the spring Sun. Baldur is called the "well-beloved", the "Holy one", "who alone is without sin". He is the "God of Goodness", who "shall be born again, when a new and purer world will have arisen from the ashes of the old, sin-laden world (Asgard)". He is killed by the crafty Loki, because Frigga, the mother of the gods, "while entreating all creatures and all lifeless things to swear that they will not injure the well-beloved", forgets to mention "the weak mistletoe bough", just as the mother of Achilles forgot her son's heel. A dart is made of it by Loki and he places it in the hands of blind Hödur who kills with it the sunny-hearted god of light. The Christmas misletoe is probably a reminiscence of the mistletoe that killed the Northern God of Goodness.

**Bal-ilu** (*Chal.*). One of the many titles of the Sun.

**Bamboo Books**. Most ancient and certainly pre-historic works in Chinese containing the antediluvian records of the *Annals of China*. They were found in the tomb of King Seang of Wai, who died 295 B.C., and claim to go back many centuries.

**Bandha** (*Sk.*). Bondage; life on this earth; from the same root as Baddha.

**Baphomet** (*Gr.*). The androgyne goat of Mendes. (See *S. D.*, I. 253). According to the Western, and especially the French Kabalists, the Templars were accused of worshipping Baphomet, and Jacques de Molay, the Grand Master of the Templars, with all his brother-Masons, suffered death in consequence. But esoterically, and philologically, the word never meant "goat", nor even anything so objective as an idol. The term means according to Von Hammer, "baptism" or *initiation into Wisdom,* from the Greek words βαφη and μητις and from the relation of Baphometus to Pan. Von Hammer must be right. It was a Hermetico Kabalistic symbol, but the whole story as invented by the Clergy was false. (See "Pan ".)

**Baptism** (*Gr.*). The rite of purification performed during the ceremony of initiation in the sacred tanks of India, and also the later identical rite established by John "the Baptist" and practised by his disciples and followers, who were not Christians. This rite was hoary with age when it was adopted by the *Chrestians* of the earliest centuries. Baptism belonged to the earliest Chaldeo-Akkadian theurgy; was religiously practised in the nocturnal ceremonies in the Pyramids where we see to this day the font in the shape of the sarcophagus; was known to take place during the Eleusinian mysteries in the sacred temple lakes, and is practised even now by the descendants of the ancient Sabians. The Mendæans (the *El Mogtasila* of the Arabs) are, notwithstanding their deceptive name of "St. John Christians", less Christians than are the Orthodox Mussulman Arabs around them. They are pure Sabians; and this is very naturally explained when one remembers that the great Semitic scholar Renan has shown in his *Vie de Jésus* that the Aramean verb *seba*, the origin of the name *Sabian*, is a synonym of the Greek βαπτιζω. The modern Sabians, the Mendæans whose vigils and religious rites, face to face with the silent stars, have been described by several travellers, have still preserved the theurgic, baptismal rites of their distant and nigh-for gotten forefathers, the Chaldean Initiates.

Their religion is one of multiplied baptisms, of seven purifications in the name of the seven planetary rulers, the "seven Angels of the Presence" of the Roman Catholic Church. The Protestant Baptists are but the pale imitators of the *El Mogtasila* or *Nazareans* who practise their Gnostic rites in the deserts of Asia Minor. (See "Boodhasp".)

**Bardesanes** or *Bardaisan*. A Syrian Gnostic, erroneously regarded as a Christian theologian, born at Edessa (*Edessene Chronicle*) in 155 of our era (Assemani *Bibl.. Orient.* i. 389). He was a great astrologer following the Eastern Occult System. According to Porphyry (who calls him the Babylonian, probably on account of his *Chaldeeism* or astrology), "Bardesanes . . . . held intercourse with the Indians that had been sent to the Cæsar with Damadamis at their head" (*De Abst.* iv. 17), and had his information from the Indian gymnosophists. The fact is that most of his teachings, however much they may have been altered by his numerous Gnostic followers, can be traced to Indian philosophy, and still more to the Occult teachings of the Secret System. Thus in his Hymns he speaks of the creative Deity as "Father-Mother", and elsewhere of "Astral Destiny" (Karma) of "Minds of Fire" (the *Agni-Devas*) &c. He connected the Soul (the personal Manas) with the Seven Stars, *deriving its origin* from the Higher Beings (the divine Ego); and therefore "admitted spiritual resurrection but denied the resurrection of the body", as charged with by the Church Fathers. Ephraim shows him preaching the signs of the Zodiac, the importance of the birth-hours and "proclaiming the seven". Calling the Sun the "Father of Life" and the Moon the "Mother of Life", he shows the latter "laying aside her garment of light (principles) for the renewal of the Earth". Photius cannot understand how, while accepting "the Soul free from the power of genesis (destiny of birth)" and possessing free will, he still placed the body under the rule of birth (genesis). For "they (the Bardesanists) say, that wealth and poverty and sickness and health and death and all things not within our control are works of destiny" (*Bibl. Cod.* 223, p.221—f). This is Karma, most evidently, which does not preclude at all free-will. Hippolytus makes him a representative of the Eastern School. Speaking of Baptism, Bardesanes is made to say (*loc. cit.* pp. 985-ff), "It is not however the Bath alone which makes us free, but the Knowledge of who we are, what we are become, where we were before, whither we are hastening, whence we are redeemed; what is generation (birth), what is re-generation (re.birth)". This points plainly to the doctrine of re-incarnation. His conversation (*Dialogue*) with Awida and Barjamina on Destiny and Free Will shows it. "What is called Destiny, is an order of outflow given to the Rulers (Gods) and the Elements, according to which order the Intelligences (Spirit-Egos) are changed by their descent into the Soul, and the Soul by its descent into the body". (See Treatise, found in its Syriac original, and published with English translation in 1855 by Dr. Cureton, *Spicileg. Syriac.* in British Museum.)

**Bardesanian** (*System*). The "Codex of the Nazarenes", a system worked out by one Bardesanes. It is called by some a Kabala within the Kabala; a religion or sect the esotericism of which is given out in names and allegories entirely *sui-generis*. A very old Gnostic system. This codex has been translated into Latin. Whether it is right to call the *Sabeanism* of the Mendaïtes (miscalled St. John's Christians), contained in the Nazarene Codex, "the Bardesanian system", as some do, is doubtful; for the doctrines of the Codex and the names of the Good and Evil Powers therein, are older than Bardaisan. Yet the names are identical in the two systems.

**Baresma** (*Zend*). A plant used by Mobeds (*Parsi priests*) in the fire-temples, wherein consecrated bundles of it are kept.

**Barhishad** (*Sk.*). A class of the "lunar" Pitris or "Ancestors", Fathers, who are believed in popular superstition to have kept up in their past incarnations the household sacred flame and made fire-offerings. Esoterically the Pitris who evolved their shadows or *chhayas* to make there-with the first man. (See *S. D.,* Vol. II.)

**Basileus** (*Gr.*). The Archon or Chief who had the outer super-vision during the Eleusinian Mysteries. While the latter was an initiated layman, and magistrate at Athens, the *Basileus* of the *inner* Temple was of the staff of the great Hierophant, and as such was one of the chief *Mystæ* and belonged to the inner mysteries.

**Basilidean** (*System*). Named after Basilides; the Founder of one of the most philosophical gnostic sects. Clement the Alexandrian speaks of Basilides, the Gnostic, as "a philosopher devoted to the contemplation of divine things". While he claimed that he had all his doctrines from the Apostle Matthew and from Peter through Glaucus, Irenaeus reviled him, Tertullian stormed at him, and the Church Fathers had not sufficient words of obloquy against the "heretic". And yet on the authority of St. Jerome himself, who describes with indignation what he had found *in the only genuine Hebrew copy* of the Gospel of Matthew (See *Isis Unv.*, ii., 181) which he got from the Nazarenes, the statement of Basilides becomes more than credible, and if accepted would solve a great and perplexing problem. His 24 vols. *of Interpretation of the Gospels*, were, as Eusebius tells us, burnt. Useless to say that these gospels were not our *present* Gospels. Thus, truth was ever crushed.

**Bassantin**, James. A Scotch astrologer. He lived in the 16th century and is said to have predicted to Sir Robert Melville, in 1562, the death and all the events connected therewith of Mary, the unfortunate Queen of Scots.

**Bath** (*Heb.*). Daughter.

**Bath Kol** (*Heb.*). Daughter of the Voice: the Divine afflatus, or inspiration, by which the prophets of Israel were inspired as by a voice from Heaven and the Mercy-Seat. In Latin *Filia Vocis*. An analogous ideal is found in Hindu exoteric theology named Vâch, the voice, the female essence, an aspect of Aditi, the mother of the gods and primæval Light; a mystery. [w.w.w.]

**Batoo** (*Eg.*). The first man in Egyptian folk-lore. *Noum*, the heavenly artist, creates a beautiful girl—the original of the Grecian Pandora—and sends her to Batoo, after which the happiness of the first man is destroyed.

**Batria** (*Eg.*). According to tradition, the wife of the Pharaoh and the teacher of Moses.

**Beel-Zebub** (*Heb.*). The disfigured *Baal* of the Temples. and more correctly Beel-Zebul. Beel-Zebub means literally "god of flies"; the derisory epithet used by the Jews, and the incorrect and confused rendering of the "god of the sacred scarabæi", the divinities watching the mummies, and symbols of transformation, regeneration and immortality. Beel-Zeboul means properly the "God of the Dwelling" and is spoken of in this sense in *Matthew* x. 25. As Apollo, originally not a Greek but a Phenician god, was the healing god, Paiàn, or physician, as well as the god of oracles, he became gradually transformed as such into the "Lord of Dwelling", a household deity, and thus was called Beel-Zeboul. He was also, in a sense, a psychopompic god, taking care of the souls as did Anubis. Beelzebub was always the oracle god, and was only confused and identified with Apollo latter on.

**Bel** (*Chald.*). The oldest and mightiest god of Babylonia, one of the earliest trinities,—Anu (*q.v.*); Bel, "Lord of the World", father of the gods, Creator, and "Lord of the City of Nipur'; and Hea, maker of fate, Lord of the Deep, God of Wisdom and esoteric Knowledge, and "Lord of the city of Eridu". The wife of Bel, or his female aspect (*Sakti*), was Belat, or Beltis, "the mother of the great gods", and the "Lady of the city of Nipur". The original Bel was also called Enu, Elu and Kaptu (see *Chaldean account of Genesis*, by G. Smith). His eldest son was the Moon God Sin (whose names were also

Ur, Agu and Itu), who was the presiding deity of the city of Ur, called in his honour by one of his names. Now Ur was the place of nativity of Abram (see "Astrology"). In the early Babylonian religion the Moon was, like *Soma* in India, a male, and the Sun a female deity. And this led almost every nation to great fratricidal wars between the lunar and the solar worshippers—e.g., the contests between the Lunar and the Solar Dynasties, the Chandra and Suryavansa in ancient Aryavarta. Thus we find the same on a smaller scale between the Semitic tribes. Abram and his father Terah are shown migrating from Ur and carrying their lunar god (or its scion) with them; for Jehovah Elohim or I—another form of *Elu*—has ever been connected with the moon. It is the Jewish lunar chronology which has led the European "civilized" nations into the greatest blunders and mistakes. Merodach, the son of Hea, became the later Bel and was worshipped at Babylon. His other title, Belas, has a number of symbolical meanings.

**Bela-Shemesh** (*Chald. Heb.*). "The Lord of the Sun", the name of the Moon during that period when the Jews became in turn solar and lunar worshippers, and when the Moon was a male, and the Sun a female deity. This period embraced the time between the allegorical expulsion of Adam and Eve from Eden down to the no less allegorical Noachian flood. (See *S. D.*, I. 397.)

**Bembo**, Tablet of; or *Mensa Isiaca*. A brazen tablet inlaid with designs in Mosaic (now in the Museum at Turin) which once belonged to the famous Cardinal Bembo. Its origin and date are unknown. It is covered with Egyptian figures and hieroglyphics, and is supposed to have been an ornament in an ancient Temple of Isis. The learned Jesuit Kircher wrote a description of it, and Montfaucon has a chapter devoted to it. [w.w.w.]

The only English work on the Isiac Tablet is by Dr. W. Wynn Westcott, who gives a photogravure in addition to its history, description, and occult significance.

**Ben** (*Heb.*). A son; a common prefix in proper names to denote the son of so-and-so, e.g., Ben Solomon, Ben Ishmael, etc.

**Be-ness.** A term coined by Theosophists to render more accurately the essential meaning of the untranslatable word Sat. The latter word does not mean "Being" for it presupposes a sentient feeling or some consciousness of existence. But, as the term Sat is applied solely to the absolute Principle, the universal, unknown, and ever unknowable Presence, which philosophical Pantheism postulates in Kosmos, calling it the basic root of

Kosmos. and Kosmos itself—"Being" was no fit word to express it. Indeed, the latter is not even, as translated by some Orientalists, "the incomprehensible Entity"; for it is no more an Entity than a non-Entity, but both. It is, as said, absolute *Be-ness*, not *Being*, the one secondless, undivided, and indivisible All—the root of all Nature visible and invisible, objective and subjective, to be sensed by the highest spiritual intuition, but never to be fully comprehended.

**Ben Shamesh** (*Heb.*). The children or the "Sons of the Sun". The term belongs to the period when the Jews were divided into sun and moon worshippers—Elites and Belites. (See "Bela-Shemesh".)

**Benoo** (*Eg.*). A word applied to two symbols, both taken to mean "Phœnix". One was the *Shen-shen* (the heron), and the other a nondescript bird, called the *Rech* (the red one), and both were sacred to Osiris. It was the latter that was the regular Phœnix of the great Mysteries, the typical symbol of self-creation and resurrection through death—a type of the Solar Osiris and of the divine Ego in man. Yet both the Heron and the Rech were symbols of cycles; the former, of the Solar year of 365 days; the latter of the tropical year or a period covering almost 26,000 years. In both cases the cycles were the types of the return of light from darkness, the yearly and great cyclic return of the sun-god to his birth-place, or—his Resurrection. The Rech-Benoo is described by Macrobius as living 660 years and then dying; while others stretched its life as long as 1,460 years. Pliny, the Naturalist, describes the Rech as a large bird with gold and purple wings, and a long blue tail. As every reader is aware, the Phœnix on feeling its end approaching, according to tradition, builds for itself a funeral pile on the top of the sacrificial altar, and then proceeds to consume himself thereon as a burnt-offering. Then a worm appears in the ashes, which grows and developes rapidly into a new Phœnix, resurrected from the ashes of its predecessor.

**Berasit** (*Heb.*). The first word of the book of *Genesis*. The English established version translates this as "In the beginning," but this rendering is disputed by many scholars. Tertullian approved of "In power"; Grotius "When first"; but the authors of the *Targum of Jerusalem*, who ought to have known Hebrew if anyone did, translated it "In Wisdom". Godfrey Higgins, in his Anacalypsis, insists on Berasit being the sign of the ablative case, meaning "in" and *ras, rasit,* an ancient word for *Chokmah,* "wisdom". Berasit or Berasheth is a mystic word among the Kabbalists of Asia Minor. [w.w.w.]

**Bergelmir** (*Scand.*). The one giant who escaped in a boat the general slaughter of his brothers, the giant Ymir's children, drowned in the blood of their raging Father. He is the Scandinavian Noah, as he, too, becomes the father of giants after the Deluge. The lays of the Norsemen show the grandsons of the divine Bun—Odin, Wili, and We—conquering and killing the terrible giant Ymir, and creating the world out of his body.

**Berosus** *(Chald.)*. A priest of the Temple of Belus who wrote for Alexander the Great the history of the Cosmogony, as taught in the Temples, from the astronomical and chronological records preserved in that temple. The fragments we have in the *soi-disant* translations of Eusebius are certainly as untrustworthy as the biographer of the Emperor Constantine—of whom he made a saint (!!)—could make them. The only guide to this Cosmogony may now be found in the fragments of the Assyrian tablets, evidently copied almost bodily from the earlier Babylonian records; which, say what the Orientalists may, are undeniably the originals of the Mosaic Genesis, of the Flood, the tower of Babel, of baby Moses set afloat on the waters, and of other events. For, if the fragments from the Cosmogony of Berosus, so carefully re-edited and probably mutilated and added to by Eusebius, are no great proof of the antiquity of these records in Babylonia—seeing that this priest of Belus lived three hundred years after the Jews were carried captive to Babylon, and they may have been borrowed by the Assyrians from them—later discoveries have made such a consoling hypothesis impossible. It is now fully ascertained by Oriental scholars that not only "Assyria borrowed its civilization and written characters from Babylonia," but the Assyrians copied their literature from Babylonian sources. Moreover, in his first Hibbert lecture, Professor Sayce shows the culture both of Babylonia itself and of the city of Eridu to have been of *foreign importation*; and, according to this scholar, the city of Eridu stood already "6,000 years ago on the shores of the Persian gulf," i.e., about the very time when Genesis shows the Elohim creating the world, sun, and stars out of nothing.

**Bes** *(Eg.)*. A phallic god, the god of concupiscence and pleasure. He is represented standing on a lotus ready to devour his own progeny (Abydos). A rather modern deity of foreign origin.

**Bestla** *(Scand.)*. The daughter of the "Frost giants", the sons of Ymir; married to Bun, and the mother of Odin and his brothers *(Edda)*.

**Beth** *(Heb.)*. House, dwelling.

**Beth Elohim** *(Heb.)*. A Kabbalistic treatise treating of the angels, souls of men, and demons. The name means "House of the Gods".

**Betyles** (*Phœn.*). Magical stones. The ancient writers call them the "animated stones"; oracular stones, believed in and used both by Gentiles and Christians. (See *S.D.* II. p. 342).

**Bhadra Vihara** (*Sk.*). Lit., "the Monastery of the Sages or Bodhisattvas". A certain *Vihara* or *Matham* in Kanyâkubdja.

**Bhadrakalpa** (*Sk.*). Lit., "The Kalpa of the Sages". Our present period is a Bhadra Kalpa, and the exoteric teaching makes it last 236 million years. It is "so called because 1,000 Buddhas or sages appear in the course of it". (*Sanshrit Chinese Dict.*) "Four Buddhas have already appeared" it adds; but as out of the 236 millions, over 151 million years have already elapsed, it does seem a rather uneven distribution of Buddhas. This is the way exoteric or popular religions confuse everything. Esoteric philosophy teaches us that every Root-race has its chief Buddha or Reformer, who appears also in the seven sub-races as a Bodhisattva (*q.v.*). Gautama Sakyamuni was the fourth, and also the fifth Buddha: the fifth, because we are the fifth root-race; the fourth, as the chief Buddha in this *fourth* Round. The Bhadra Kalpa, or the "period of stability", is the name of our present Round, esoterically—its duration applying, of course, only to our globe (D), the "1,000" Buddhas being thus in reality limited to but forty-nine in all.

**Bhadrasena** (*Sk.*). A Buddhist king of Magadha.

**Bhagats** (*Sk.*). Also called *Sokha* and *Sivnath* by the Hindus; one who exorcises evil spirits.

**Bhagavad-gita** (*Sk.*). Lit., "the Lord's Song". A portion of the Mahabharata, the great epic poem of India. It contains a dialogue wherein Krishna—the "Charioteer"—and Arjuna, his Chela, have a discussion upon the highest spiritual philosophy. The work is pre-eminently occult or esoteric.

**Bhagavat** (*Sk.*). A title of the Buddha and of Krishna. "The Lord" literally.

**Bhao** (*Sk.*). A ceremony of divination among the Kolarian tribes of Central India.

**Bhârata Varsha** (*Sk.*). The land of Bharata, an ancient name of India.

**Bhargavas** (*Sk.*). An ancient race in India; from the name of Bhrigu, the Rishi.

**Bhâshya** (*Sk*) A commentary.

**Bhâskara** (*Sk*). One of the titles of Surya, the Sun; meaning "life-giver" and "light-maker".

**Bhava** (*Sk.*). Being, or state of being; the world, a birth, and also a name of Siva.

**Bhikshu** (*Sk.*). In Pâli *Bihkhu*. The name given to the first followers of Sâkyamuni Buddha. Lit., "mendicant scholar". The *Sanskrit Chinese Dictionary* explains the term correctly by dividing Bhikshus into two classes of *Sramanas* (Buddhist monks and priests), viz., "esoteric mendicants who control their nature by the (religious) law, and exoteric mendicants who control their nature by *diet*;" and it adds, less correctly: "every true Bhikshu is supposed to work miracles".

**Bhons** (*Tib.*). The followers of the old religion of the Aborigines of Tibet; of pre-buddhistic temples and ritualism; the same as Dugpas, "red caps", though the latter appellation usually applies only to sorcerers.

**Bhrantidarsanatah** (*Sk.*). Lit., "false comprehension or apprehension"; something conceived of on false appearances as a *mayavic,* illusionary form.

**Bhrigu** (*Sk.*). One of the great Vedic Rishis. He is called "Son" by Manu, who confides to him his *Institutes*. He is one of the Seven *Prajâpatis* or progenitors of mankind, which is equivalent to identifying him with one of the creative gods, placed by the Purânas in Krita Yug, or the first age, that of purity. Dr. Wynn Westcott reminds us of the fact that the late and very erudite Dr. Kenealy (who spelt the name *Brighoo*), made of this Muni (Saint) the fourth, out of his twelve, "divine messengers" to the World, adding that he appeared in Tibet, A.N. 4800 and that his religion spread to Britain, where his followers raised the megalithic temple of Stonehenge. This, of course, is a hypothesis, based merely on Dr. Kenealy's personal speculations.

**Bhûmi** (*Sk.*). The earth, called also *Prithivî*.

**Bhur-Bhuva** (*Sk*). A mystic incantation, as *Om, Bhur, Bhuva, Swar*, meaning "Om, earth, sky, heaven, This is the exoteric explanation.

**Bhuranyu** (*Sk.*). "The rapid" or the swift. Used of a missile—an equivalent also of the Greek *Phoroneus.*

**Bhur-loka** (*Sk*). One of the 14 lokas or worlds in Hindu Pantheism; our Earth.

**Bhutadi** (*Sk.*). Elementary substances, the origin and the germinal essence of the elements.

**Bhutan.** A country of heretical Buddhists and Lamaists beyond Sikkhim, where rules the Dharma Raja, a nominal vassal of the Dalaï Lama.

**Bhûhta-vidyâ** (*Sk.*). The art of exorcising, of treating and curing demoniac possession. Literally, "Demon" or "Ghost-knowledge".

**Bhûta-sarga** *(Sk.)*. Elemental or incipient Creation, i.e., when matter was several degrees less material than it is now.

**Bhûtesa** *(Sk.)* Or *Bhûteswara;* lit., "Lord of beings or of existent lives". A name applied to Vishnu, to Brahmâ and Krishna.

**Bhûts** *(Sk.)*. *Bhûta.*: Ghosts, phantoms. To call them "demons", as do the Orientalists, is incorrect. For, if on the one hand, a Bhûta is "a malignant spirit which haunts cemeteries, lurks in trees, animates dead bodies, and deludes and devours human beings", in popular fancy, in India in Tibet and China, by Bhûtas are also meant "heretics" who besmear their bodies with ashes, or Shaiva ascetics (Siva being held in India for the King of Bhûtas).

**Bhuya-loka** *(Sk.)*. One of the 14 worlds.

**Bhuvana** *(Sk)*. A name of Rudra or Siva, one of the Indian *Trimurti* (Trinity).

**Bifröst** *(Scand.)*. A bridge built by the gods to protect Asgard. On it "the third Sword-god, known as Heimdal or Riger", stands night and day girded with his sword, for he is the watchman selected to protect Asgard, the abode of gods. Heimdal is the Scandinavian Cherubim with the flaming sword, "which turned every way to keep the way of the tree of life".

**Bihar Gyalpo** *(Tib.)*. A king deified by the Dugpas. A patron over all their religious buildings.

**Binah** *(Heb.)*. Understanding. The third of the 10 Sephiroth, the third of the Supernal Triad; a female potency, corresponding to the letter *hé* of the Tetragrammaton IHVH. Binah is called AIMA, the Supernal Mother, and "the great Sea". [w.w.w.]

**Birs Nimrud** *(Chald.)*. Believed by the Orientalists to be the site of the Tower of Babel. The great pile of Birs Nimrud is near Babylon. Sir H. Rawlinson and several Assyriologists examined the excavated ruins and found that the tower consisted of seven stages of brick-work, each stage of a different colour, which shows that the temple was devoted to the seven planets. Even with its three higher stages or floors in ruins, it still rises now 154 feet above the level of the plain. (See "Borsippa".)

**Black Dwarfs.** The name of the Elves of Darkness, who creep about in the dark caverns of the earth and fabricate weapons and utensils for their divine fathers, the Æsir or Ases. Called also "Black Elves".

**Black Fire** *(Zohar.)* A Kabbalistic term for Absolute Light and Wisdom;

"black" because it is incomprehensible to our finite intellects.

**Black Magic** (*Occult.*). Sorcery; necromancy, or the raising of the dead, and other selfish abuses of abnormal powers. This abuse may be unintentional; yet it is still "*black* magic" whenever anything is produced phenomenally simply for one's own gratification.

**B'ne Alhim** or *Beni Elohim* (*Heb.*). "Sons of God ", literally or more correctly "Sons of the gods", as Elohim is the plural of Eloah. A group of angelic powers referable by analogy to the Sephira Hôd.

[w. w. w.]

**Boat of the Sun.** This sacred solar boat was called *Sekti,* and it was steered by the dead. With the Egyptians the highest exaltation of the Sun was in *Aries* and the depression in *Libya.* (See "Pharaoh", the "Son of the Sun".) A blue light—which is the "Sun's Son"—is seen streaming from the bark. The ancient Egyptians taught that the real colour of the Sun was blue, and Macrobius also states that his colour is of a pure blue before he reaches the horizon and after he disappears below. It is curious to note in this relation the fact that it is only since 1881 that physicists and astronomers discovered that "our Sun is really blue". Professor Langley devoted many years to ascertaining the fact. Helped in this by the magnificent scientific apparatus of physical science, he has succeeded finally in proving that the apparent yellow-orange colour of the Sun is due only to the effect of absorption exerted by its atmosphere of vapours, chiefly metallic; but that in sober truth and reality, it is not "a white Sun but a blue one", i.e., something which the Egyptian priests had discovered without any known scientific instruments, many thousands of years ago!

**Boaz** (*Heb.*). The great-grandfather of David. The word is from B, meaning "in", and *oz* "strength", a symbolic name of one of the pillars at the porch of King Solomon's temple. [w. w. w.]

**Bodha-Bodhi** (*Sk.*). Wisdom-knowledge.

**Bodhi** or *Sambodhi* (*Sk.*). Receptive intelligence, in contradistinction to *Buddhi,* which is the potentiality of intelligence.

**Bodhi Druma** (*Sk.*). The Bo or Bodhi tree; the tree of "knowledge the *Pippala* or *ficus religiosa* in botany. It is the tree under which Sâkymuni meditated for seven years and then reached Buddhaship. It was originally 400 feet high, it is claimed; but when Hiouen-Tsang saw it, about the year 640 of our era, it was only 50 feet high. Its cuttings have been carried all over the Buddhist world and are planted in front of almost every Vihâra or temple of fame in China, Siam, Ceylon, and Tibet.

**Bodhidharma** *(Sk.)*. Wisdom-religion; or the wisdom contained in *Dharma* (ethics). Also the name of a great Arhat *Kshatriya* (one of the warrior-caste), the son of a king. It was Panyatara, his guru, who "gave him the name Bodhidharma to mark his understanding (bodhi) of the Law (dharma) of Buddha". (*Chin. San. Diet.*). Bodhidharma, who flourished in the sixth century, travelled to China, whereto he brought a precious relic, namely, the almsbowl of the Lord Buddha.

**Bodhisattva** *(Sk)*. Lit., "he, whose essence *(sattva)* has become intelligence *(bodhi)*"; those who need but one more incarnation to become perfect Buddhas, i.e., to be entitled to Nirvâna. This, as applied to *Manushi* (terrestrial) Buddhas. In the metaphysical sense, *Bodhisattva* is a title given to the sons of the celestial *Dhyâni* Buddhas.

**Bodhyanga** *(Sk.)*. Lit., the seven branches of knowledge or understanding. One of the 37 categories of the *Bodhi pakchika dharma,* comprehending seven degrees of intelligence (esoterically, seven states of consciousness), and these are (1) *Smriti* "memory"; (2) *Dharma pravitchaya,* "correct understanding" or discrimination of the Law; (3) *Virya,* "energy"; (4) *Priti,* "spiritual joy"; (5) *Prasrabdhi,* "tranquillity" or quietude; (6) *Samâdhi,* "ecstatic contemplation"; and (7) *Upeksha* "absolute indifference".

**Boehme** *(Jacob)*. A great mystic philosopher, one of the most prominent Theosophists of the mediæval ages. He was born about 1575 at Old Seidenburg, some two miles from Görlitz (Silesia), and died in 1624, at nearly fifty years of age. In his boyhood he was a common shepherd, and, after learning to read and write in a village school, became an apprentice to a poor shoemaker at Görlitz. He was a natural clairvoyant of most wonderful powers. With no education or acquaintance with science he wrote works which are now proved to be full of scientific truths; but then, as he says himself, what he wrote upon, he "saw it as in a great Deep in the Eternal". He had "a thorough view of the universe, as in a chaos", which yet "opened itself in him, from time to time, as in a young plant". He was a thorough born Mystic, and evidently of a constitution which is most rare one of those fine natures whose material envelope impedes in no way the direct, even if only occasional, intercommunion between the intellectual and the spiritual Ego. It is this Ego which Jacob Boehme, like so many other untrained mystics, mistook for God; "Man must acknowledge," he writes, "that his knowledge is not his own, but from God, who manifests the Ideas of Wisdom to the Soul of Man, in what measure he pleases." Had this great Theosophist mastered Eastern Occultism he might have expressed it otherwise. He would have known then that the "god" who spoke through his poor uncultured and untrained brain, was his own divine Ego, the omniscient Deity within himself, and that what that Deity gave out was not in "what measure pleased," but in the measure of the capacities of the mortal and temporary dwelling IT informed.

**Bonati,** Guido. A Franciscan monk, born at Florence in the XIIIth century and died in 1306. He became an astrologer and alchemist, but failed as a Rosicrucian adept. He returned after this to his monastery.

**Bona-Oma,** or *Bona Dea*. A Roman goddess, the patroness of female Initiates and Occultists. Called also Fauna after her father Faunus. She was worshipped as a prophetic and chaste divinity, and her cult was confined solely to women, men not being allowed to even pronounce her name. She revealed her oracles only to women, and the ceremonies of her Sanctuary (a grotto in the Aventine) were conducted by the Vestals, every 1st of May. Her aversion to men was so great that no male person was permitted to approach the house of the consuls where her festival was sometimes held, and even the portraits and the busts of men were carried out for the time from the building. Clodius, who once profaned such a sacred festival by entering the house of Caesar where it was held, in a female disguise, brought grief upon himself. Flowers and foliage decorated her temple and women made libations from a vessel (mellarium) full of milk. It is not true that the mellarium contained wine, as asserted by some writers, who being men thus tried to revenge themselves.

**Bono,** Peter. A Lombardian; a great adept in the Hermetic Science, who travelled to Persia to study Alchemy. Returning from his voyage he settled in Istria in 1330, and became famous as a Rosicrucian. A Calabrian monk named Lacinius is credited with having published in 1702 a condensed version of Bono's works on the transmutation of metals. There is, however, more of Lacinius than of Bono in the work. Bono was a genuine adept and an Initiate; and such do not leave their secrets behind them in MSS.

**Boodhasp** (*Chald.*) .An alleged Chaldean; but in esoteric teaching a Buddhist (a Bodhisattva), from the East, who was the founder of the esoteric school of Neo-Sabeism, and whose secret rite of baptism passed bodily into the Christian rite of the same name. For almost three centuries before our era, Buddhist monks overran the whole country of Syria, made their way into the Mesopotamian valley and visited even Ireland. The name *Ferho* and *Faho* of the Codex Nazaraeus is but a corruption of Fho, Fo and Pho, the name which the Chinese, Tibetans and even Nepaulese often give to Buddha.

**Book of the Dead.** An ancient Egyptian ritualistic and occult work attributed to Thot-Hermes. Found in the coffins of ancient mummies,

**Book of the Keys.** An ancient Kabbalistic work.

**Borj** (*Pers.*). The Mundane Mountain, a volcano or fire-mountain; the same as the Indian Meru.

**Borri,** Joseph Francis. A great Hermetic philosopher, born at Milan in the 17th century. He was an adept, an alchemist and a devoted occultist. He knew too much and was, therefore, condemned to death for heresy, in January, 1661, after the death of Pope Innocent X. He escaped and lived many years after, when finally he was recognised by a monk in a Turkish village, denounced, claimed by the Papal Nuncio, taken back to Rome and imprisoned, August 10th, 1675. But facts show that he escaped from his prison in a way no one could account for.

**Borsippa** (*Chald.*). The planet-tower, wherein Bel was worshipped in the days when *astrolaters* were the greatest astronomers. It was dedicated to Nebo, god of Wisdom. (See "Birs Nimrud ".)

**Both-al** (*Irish*). The Both-al of the Irish is the descendant and copy of the Greek Batylos and the Beth-el of Canaan, the "house of God" (*q.v.*).

**Bragadini,** Marco Antonio. A Venetian Rosicrucian of great achievements, an Occultist and Kabbalist who was decapitated in 1595 in Bavaria, for making gold.

**Bragi** (*Scand.*). The god of New Life, of the re-incarnation of nature and man. He is called "the divine singer" without spot or blemish. He is represented as gliding in the ship of the Dwarfs of Death during the death of nature (pralaya), lying asleep on the deck with his golden stringed harp near him and dreaming the dream of life. When the vessel crosses the threshold of Nain, the Dwarf of Death, Bragi awakes and sweeping the strings of his harp, sings a song that echoes over all the worlds, a song describing the rapture of existence, and awakens dumb, sleeping nature out of her long death-like sleep.

**Brahma** (*Sk.*). The student must distinguish between Brahma the neuter, and Brahmâ, the male creator of the Indian Pantheon. The former, Brahma or Brahman, is the impersonal, supreme and uncognizable Principle of the Universe from the essence of which all emanates, and into which all returns, which is incorporeal, immaterial, unborn, eternal, beginningless and endless. It is all-pervading, animating the highest god as well as the smallest mineral atom. Brahmâ on the other hand, the male and the alleged Creator, exists periodically in his manifestation only, and then again goes into pralaya, i.e., disappears and is annihilated.

**Brahmâ's Day.** A period of 2,160,000,000 years during which Brahmâ having emerged out of his golden egg *(Hiranyagarbha)*, creates and fashions the material world (being simply the fertilizing and creative force in Nature). After this period, the worlds being destroyed in turn, by fire and water, he vanishes with objective nature, and then comes Brahmâ's Night.

**Brahmâ's Night.** A period of equal duration, during which Brahmâ. is said to be asleep. Upon awakening he recommences the process, and this goes on for an AGE of Brahmâ composed of alternate "Days", and "Nights", and lasting 100 years (of 2,160,000,000 years each). It requires fifteen figures to express the duration of such an age; after the expiration of which the *Mahapralaya* or the Great Dissolution sets in, and lasts in its turn for the same space of fifteen figures.

**Brahmâ Prajâpati** *(Sk.).* "Brahmâ the Progenitor", literally the "Lord of Creatures". In this aspect Brahmâ is the synthesis of the Prajâpati or creative Forces.

**Brahmâ Vâch** *(Sk.)* Male and female Brahmâ. Vâch is also some-times called the female logos; for Vâch means Speech, literally. (See *Manu* Book I., and *Vishnu Purâna.*)

**Brahma Vidyâ** *(Sk.)* The knowledge, the esoteric science, about the two Brahmas and their true nature.

**Brahmâ Virâj.** *(Sk.)* The same: Brahmâ separating his body into two halves, male and female, creates in them Vâch and Virâj. In plainer terms and *esotericlly* Brahmâ the Universe, differentiating, produced thereby material nature, Virâj, and spiritual intelligent Nature, Vâch—which is the *Logos* of Deity or the manifested expression of the eternal divine Ideation.

**Brahmâcharî** *(Sk.)* A Brahman ascetic; one vowed to celibacy, a monk, virtually, or a religious student.

**Brahmajnâni** *(Sk.)* One possessed of complete Knowledge; an *Illuminatus* in esoteric parlance.

**Brâhman** *(Sk.)* The highest of the four castes in India, one supposed or rather fancying himself, as high among men, as Brahman, the ABSOLUTE of the Vedantins, is high among, or above the gods.

**Brâhmana period** *(Sk.)* One of the four periods into which Vedic literature has been divided by Orientalists.

**Brâhmanas** *(Sk.)* Hindu Sacred Books. Works composed by, and for

Brahmans. Commentaries on those portions of the Vedas which were intended for the ritualistic use and guidance of the "twice-born (Dwija) or Brahmans.

**Brahmanaspati** (*Sk.*). The planet Jupiter; a deity in the *Rig -Veda*, known in the exoteric works as Brihaspati, whose wife Târâ was carried away by Soma (the Moon). This led to a war between the gods and the Asuras.

**Brahmâpuri** (*Sk.*) Lit., "the City of Brahmâ.

**Brahmâputrâs** (*Sk.*) The Sons of Brahmâ.

**Brahmarandhra** (*Sk.*) A spot on the crown of the head connected by *Sushumna*, a cord in the spinal column, with the heart. A mystic term having its significance only in mysticism.

**Brahmârshîs** (*Sk.*). The Brahminical Rishis.

**Bread** and **Wine**. Baptism and the Eucharist have their direct origin in pagan Egypt. There the "waters of purification" were used (the Mithraic font for baptism being borrowed by the Persians from the Egyptians) and so were bread and wine. "Wine in the Dionysiak cult, as in the Christian religion, represents that blood which in different senses is the life of the world" (Brown, in the *Dionysiak Myth*). Justin Martyr says, "In imitation of which the devil did the like in the Mysteries of Mithras, for you either know or may *know that they also take bread and a cup of water* in the sacrifices of those that are initiated and *pronounce certain words over it*". (See "Holy Water".)

**Briareus** (*Gr.*) A famous giant in the Theogony of Hesiod. The son of Cœlus and Terra, a monster with 50 heads and 100 arms. He is conspicuous in the wars and battles between the gods.

**Briatic World** or *Briah* (*Heb.*) This world is the second of the Four worlds of the Kabbalists and referred to the highest created "Archangels", or to Pure Spirits. [w.w.w.]

**Bride**. The tenth Sephira, Malkuth, is called by the Kabbalists the Bride of Microprosopus; she is the final Hé of the Tetragrammaton; in a similar manner the Christian Church is called the Bride of Christ. [w.w.w.]

**Brihadâranyaka** (*Sk.*) The name of a *Upanishad*. One of the sacred and *secret* books of the Brahmins; an *Aranyaka* is a treatise appended to the Vedas, and considered a subject of special study by those who have retired to the jungle (forest) for purposes of religious meditation.

**Brihaspati** (*Sk.*) The name of a Deity, also of a *Rishi*. It is like wise the name of the planet Jupiter. He is the personified Guru and priest of the gods in India; also the symbol of exoteric ritualism as opposed to esoteric mysticism. Hence the opponent of King Soma—the moon, but also the sacred juice drunk at initiation—the parent of Budha, Secret Wisdom.

**Briseus** (*Gr.*) A name given to the god Bacchus from his nurse, Briso. He had also a temple at Brisa, a promontory of the isle of Lesbos.

**Brothers of the Shadow**. A name given by the Occultists to Sorcerers, and especially to the Tibetan *Dugpas,* of whom there are many in the Bhon sect of the *Red Caps (Dugpa)*. The word is applied to all practitioners of black or *left hand* magic.

**Bubasté** (*Eg.*) A city in Egypt which was sacred to the cats, and where was their principal shrine. Many hundreds of thousands of cats were embalmed and buried in the grottoes of Beni-Hassan-el Amar. The cat being a symbol of the moon was sacred to Isis, her goddess. It sees in the dark and its eyes have a phosphorescent lustre which frightens the night-birds of evil omen. The cat was also sacred to Bast, and thence called "the destroyer of the Sun's (Osiris') enemies".

**Buddha** (*Sk.*). Lit., "The Enlightened". The highest degree of knowledge. To become a Buddha one has to break through the bondage of sense and personality; to acquire a complete perception of the REAL SELF and learn not to separate it from all otherselves; to learn by experience the utter unreality of all phenomena of the visible Kosmos foremost of all; to reach a complete detachment from all that is evanescent and finite, and live while yet on Earth in the immortal and the everlasting alone, in a supreme state of holiness.

**Buddha Siddhârta** (*Sk.*) The name given to Gautama, the Prince of Kapilavastu, at his birth. It is an abbreviation of *sarvârtthasiddha* and means, the "realization of all desires". Gautama, which means, on earth (*gâu*) the most victorious (*tama*) "was the sacerdotal name of the Sâkya family, the kingly patronymic of the dynasty to which the father of Gautama, the King Suddhodhana of Kapilavastu, belonged. Kapilavastu was an ancient city, the birth-place of the Great Reformer and was destroyed during his life time. In the title *Sâkyamuni,* the last component, *muni,* is rendered as meaning one mighty in charity, isolation and silence", and the former Sâkya is the family name. Every Orientalist or Pundit knows by heart the story of Gautama, the Buddha, the most perfect of mortal men that the world has ever seen, but none of them seem to suspect the esoteric meaning underlying his prenatal biography, i.e., the significance of the popular story. The *Lalitavistûra* tells the tale, but abstains from hinting at the truth. The 5,000 *jâtakas,* or the events of former births (re-incarnations) are taken literally instead of esoterically. Gautama, the Buddha, would not have been a mortal man, had he not passed through hundreds and thousands of births previous to his last. Yet the detailed account of these, and the statement that during them he worked his way up through every stage of transmigration from the lowest animate and inanimate atom and insect, up to the highest—or *man,* contains simply the well-known occult aphorism: "a stone becomes a plant, a plant an animal, and an animal a man". Every human being who has ever existed, has passed through the same evolution. But the hidden symbolism in the sequence of these re-births *(jâtaka)* contains a perfect history of the evolution on this earth, *pre* and *post* human, and is a scientific exposition of natural facts. One truth not veiled but bare and open is found in their nomenclature, *viz.,* that as soon as Gautama had reached the human form he began exhibiting in every personality the utmost unselfishness, self-sacrifice and charity. Buddha Gautama, the fourth of the Sapta (Seven) Buddhas and Sapta Tathâgatas was born according to Chinese Chronology in 1024 B.C; but according to the Singhalese chronicles, on the 8th day of the second (or fourth) moon in the year 621 before our era. He fled from his father's palace to become an ascetic on the night of the 8th day of the second moon, 597 BC., and having passed six years in ascetic meditation at Gaya, and perceiving that physical self-torture was useless to bring enlightenment, be decided upon striking out a new path, until he reached the state of Bodhi. He became a full Buddha on the night of the 8th day of the twelfth moon, in the year 592, and finally entered Nirvâna in the year 543 according to Southern Buddhism. The Orientalists, however, have decided upon several other dates. All the rest is allegorical. He attained the state of Bodhisattva on earth when in the personality called Prabhâpala. Tushita stands for a place on this globe, not for a paradise in the invisible regions. The selection of the Sâkya family and his mother Mâyâ, as "the purest on earth," is in accordance with the model of the nativity of every Saviour, God or deified Reformer. The tale about his entering his mother's bosom in the shape of a white elephant is an allusion to his innate wisdom, the elephant of that colour being a symbol of every Bodhisattva. The statements that at Gautama's birth, the newly born babe walked *seven steps* in four directions, that an *Udumbara* flower bloomed in all its rare beauty and that the Nâga kings forthwith proceeded "*to baptise him*", are all so many allegories in the phraseology of the Initiates and well-understood by every Eastern Occultist. The whole events of his noble life are given in occult numbers, and every so-called *miraculous* event—so deplored by Orientalists as confusing the narrative and making it impossible to extricate truth from fiction—is simply the allegorical veiling of the truth, it is as comprehensible to an Occultist learned in symbolism, as it is difficult to understand for a European scholar ignorant of Occultism. Every detail of the narrative after his death and before cremation is a chapter of *facts* written in a language which must be studied before it is understood, otherwise its dead letter will lead one into absurd contradictions. For instance, having reminded his disciples of the immortality of Dharmakâya Buddha is said to have passed into Samâdhi, and lost himself in *Nirvâna—from which none can return.*, and yet, notwithstanding this, the Buddha is shown bursting open the lid of the coffin, and stepping out of it; saluting with folded hands his mother Mâyâ who had suddenly appeared in the air, though she had died seven (days after his birth, &c., &c. As Buddha. was a Chakravartti (he who turns the wheel of the Law), his body at its *cremation* could not be consumed by common fire. What happens Suddenly a jet of flame *burst out of the Swastica on his breast,* and reduced his body to ashes. Space prevents giving more instances. As to his being one of the true and undeniable Saviours of the World, suffice it to say that the most rabid orthodox missionary, unless he is hopelessly insane, or has not the least regard even for historical truth, cannot find one smallest accusation against the life and personal character of Gautama, the "Buddha". Without any claim to divinity, allowing his followers to fall into atheism, rather than into the degrading superstition of deva or idol-worship, his walk in life is from the beginning to the end, holy and divine. During the years of his mission it is blameless and pure as that of a god—or as the latter should be. He is a perfect example of a divine, godly man. He reached Buddhaship—i.e., complete enlightenment—entirely by his own merit and owing to his own individual exertions, no god being supposed to have any personal merit in the exercise of goodness and holiness. Esoteric teachings claim that he renounced Nirvâna and gave up the Dharmakâya vesture to remain a "Buddha of compassion" within the reach of the miseries of this world. And the religious philosophy he left to it has produced for over 2,000 years generations of good and unselfish men. His is the only *absolutely bloodless* religion among all the existing religions tolerant and liberal, teaching universal compassion and charity, love and self-sacrifice, poverty and contentment with one's lot, whatever it may he. No persecutions, and enforcement of faith by fire and sword, have ever disgraced it. No thunder-and-lightning-vomiting god has interfered with its chaste commandments; and if the simple, humane and philosophical code of daily life left to us by the greatest Man-Reformer ever known, should ever come to he adopted by mankind at large, then indeed an era of bliss and peace would dawn on Humanity.

**Buddhachhâyâ** (*Sk.*). Lit., "the shadow of Buddha". It is said to become visible at certain great events, and during some imposing ceremonies performed at Temples in commemoration of glorious acts of Buddhas life. Hiouen-tseng, the Chinese traveller, names a certain cave where it occasionally appears on the wall, but adds that only he whose mind is perfectly pure", can see it.

**Buddhaphala** (*Sk*) Lit., "the fruit of Buddha", the fruition of *Arahattvaphalla*, or Arhatship.

**Buddhi** (*Sk.*). Universal Soul or Mind. *Mahâbuddhi* is a name of Mahat (see "Alaya"); also the spiritual Soul in man (the sixth principle), the vehicle of Atmâ exoterically the seventh.

**Buddhism.** Buddhism is now split into two distinct Churches: the Southern and the Northern Church. The former is said to be the purer form, as having preserved more religiously the original teachings of the Lord Buddha. It is the religion of Ceylon, Siam, Burmah and other places, while Northern Buddhism is confined to Tibet, China and Nepaul. Such a distinction, however, is incorrect. If the Southern Church is nearer, in that it has not departed, except perhaps in some trifling dogmas due to the many councils held after the death of the Master, from the public or *exoteric* teachings of Sâkyamuni—the Northern Church is the outcome of Siddhârta Buddha's esoteric teachings which he confined to his elect Bhikshus and Arhats. In fact, Buddhism in the present age, cannot he justly judged either by one or the other of its exoteric popular forms. Real Buddhism can be appreciated only by blending the philosophy of the Southern Church and the metaphysics of the Northern Schools. If one seems too iconoclastic and stero:, and the other too metaphysical and transcendental, even to being overgrown with the weeds of Indian exotericism—many of the gods of its Pantheon having been transplanted under new names to Tibetan soil—it is entirely due to the popular expression of Buddhism in both Churches. Correspondentially they stand in their relation to each other as Protestantism to Roman Catholicism. Both err by an excess of zeal and erroneous interpretations, though neither the Southern nor the Northern Buddhist clergy have ever departed from truth consciously, still less have they acted under the dictates of *priestocracy,* ambition, or with an eye to personal gain and power, as the two Christian Churches have.

**Buddhochinga** (*Sk*) The name of a great Indian Arhat who went to China in the 4th century to propagate Buddhism and converted masses of people by means of miracles and most wonderful magic feats.

**Budha** (*Sk*. "The Wise and Intelligent", the Son of Soma, the Moon, and of Rokini or Taraka, wife of Brihaspati carried away by King Soma, thus leading to the great war between the Asuras, who sided with the Moon, and the Gods who took the defence of Brihaspati (Jupiter) who, was their *Purohita* (family priest). This war is known as the *Tarakamaya*. It is the original of the war in Olympus between the Gods and the Titans and also of the war (in *Revelation* between Michael (Indra) and the Dragon (personifying the Asuras).

**Bull-Worship** (See "Apis" ). The worship of the Bull and the Ram was addressed to one and the same power, that of generative creation, under two aspects—the celestial or cosmic, and the terrestrial or human. The ram-headed gods all belong to the latter aspect, the bull—to the former. Osiris to whom the Bull was sacred, was never regarded as a phallic deity; neither was Siva with his Bull Nandi, in spite of the *lingham*. As Nandi is of a pure milk-white colour, so was Apis. Both were the emblems of the generative, or of evolutionary power in the Universal Kosmos. Those who regard the solar gods and the bulls as of a phallic character, or connect the Sun with it, are mistaken, it is only the lunar gods and the rams, and lambs, which are priapic, and it little becomes a religion which, however unconsciously, has still adopted for its worship a god pre-eminently *lunar*, and accentuated its choice by the selection of the lamb, whose sire is the ram, a glyph as pre-eminently phallic, for its most sacred symbol—to vilify the older religions for using the same symbolism. The worship of the bull, Apis, Hapi Ankh, or the living Osiris, ceased over 3,000 years ago the worship of the ram and lamb continues to this day. Mariette Bey discovered the Serapeum, the Necropolis of the Apis-bulls, near Memphis, an imposing subterranean crypt 2,000 feet long and twenty feet wide, containing the mummies of thirty sacred bulls. If 1,000 years hence, a Roman Catholic Cathedral with the Easter lamb in it, were discovered under the ashes of Vesuvius or Etna, would future generations be justified in inferring therefrom that Christians were "lamb" and "dove" worshippers ? Yet the two symbols would give them as much right in the one case as in the other. Moreover, not all of the sacred "Bulls" were phallic, i.e., males; there were hermaphrodite and sexless "bulls". The black bull *Mnevis*, the son of Ptah, was sacred to the God Ra at Heliopolis; the Pacis of Hermonthis—to Amoun Horus, &c., &c., and Apis himself was a hermaphodite and not a male animal, which shows his cosmic character. As well call the *Taurus* of the Zodiac and all Nature *phallic.*

**Bumapa** (*Tib.*). A school of men, usually a college of mystic students.

**Bunda-hish.** An old Eastern work in which among other things anthropology is treated in an allegorical fashion.

**Burham-i-Kati.** A Hermetic Eastern work.

**Burî** (*Scand*) "The producer", the Son of Bestla, in Norse legends.

**Buru Bonga.** The "Spirit of the Hills". This Dryadic deity is worshipped by the Kolarian tribes of Central India with great ceremonies and magical display. There are mysteries connected with it, but the people are very jealous and will admit no stranger to their rites.

**Busardier.** A Hermetic philosopher born in Bohemia who is credited with having made a genuine powder of projection. He left the bulk of his *red* powder to a friend named Richthausen, an adept and alchemist of Vienna. Some years after Busardier's death, in 1637, Richthausen introduced himself to the Emperor Ferdinand III, who is known to have been ardently devoted to alchemy, and together they are said to have converted three pounds of mercury into the finest gold with one single grain of Busardier's powder. In 1658 the Elector of Mayence also was permitted to test the powder, and the gold produced with it was declared by the Master of the Mint to be such, that he had never seen finer. Such are the claims vouchsafed by the city records and chronicles.

**Butler.** An English name assumed by an adept, a disciple of some Eastern Sages, of whom many fanciful stories are current. It is said for instance, that Butler was captured during his travels in 1629, and sold into captivity. He became the slave of an Arabian philosopher, a great alchemist, and finally escaped, robbing his Master of a large quantity of red powder. According to more trustworthy records, only the last portion of this story is true. Adepts who can be robbed without knowing it would be unworthy of the name. Butler or rather the person who assumed this name, *robbed* his "Master" (whose free disciple he was) *of the secret of transmutation,* and abused of his knowledge—i.e., sought to turn it to his personal profit, but was speedily punished for it. After performing many wonderful cures by means of his "stone (i.e., the occult knowledge of an initiated adept), and producing extraordinary phenomena, to some of which Val Helmont, the famous Occultist and Rosicrucian, was witness, not for the benefit of men but his own vain glory, Butler was imprisoned in the Castle of Viloord, in Flanders, and passed almost the whole of his life in confinement. He lost his powers and died miserable and unknown. Such is the fate of every Occultist who abuses his power or desecrates the sacred science.

**Bythos** (*Gr.*). A Gnostic term meaning "Depth" or the "great Deep", Chaos. It is equivalent to space, before anything had formed itself in it from the primordial atoms that exist eternally in its spatial depths, according to the teachings of Occultism.

# C

**C.**—The third letter of the English alphabet, which has no equivalent in Hebrew except Caph, which see under K.

**Cabar Zio** (*Gnost.*). "The mighty Lord of Splendour" (*Codex Nazaraeus*), they who procreate *seven beneficent lives,* "who shine in their own form and light" to counteract the influence of the seven "badly-disposed" stellars or principles. These are the progeny of Karabtanos, the personification of concupiscence and matter. The latter are the seven physical planets, the former, their genii or Rulers.

**Cabeiri** or *Kabiri* (*Phœn.*) Deities, held in the highest veneration at Thebes, in Lemnos, Phrygia, Macedonia, and especially at Samothrace. They were mystery gods, no profane having the right to name or speak of them. Herodotus makes of them Fire-gods and points to Vulcan as their father. The Kabiri presided over the Mysteries, and their real number has never been revealed, their occult meaning being very sacred.

**Cabletow** (*Mas.*). A Masonic term for a certain object used in the Lodges. Its origin lies in the thread of the Brahman ascetics, a thread which is also used for magical purposes in Tibet.

**Cadmus** (*Gr.*). The supposed inventor of the letters of the alphabet. He may have been their originator and teacher in Europe and Asia Minor; but in India the letters were known and used by the Initiates ages before him.

**Caduceus** (*Gr.*). The Greek poets and mythologists took the idea of the Caduceus of Mercury from the Egyptians. The Caduceus is found as two serpents twisted round a rod, on Egyptian monuments built before Osiris. The Greeks altered this. We find it again in the hands of Æsculapius assuming a different form to the wand of Mercurius or Hermes. It is a cosmic, sidereal or astronomical, as well as a spiritual and even physiological symbol, its significance changing with its application.

Metaphysically, the Caduceus represents the fall of primeval and primordial matter into gross terrestrial matter, the one Reality becoming Illusion. (See *S. D.*, I. 550.) Astronomically, the head and tail represent the points of the ecliptic where the planets and even the sun and moon meet in close embrace. Physiologically, it is the symbol of the restoration of the equilibrium lost between Life, as a unit, and the currents of life performing various functions in the human body.

**Cæsar.** A far-famed astrologer and "professor of magic," i.e., an Occultist, during the reign of Henry IV of France. "He was reputed to have been strangled by the devil in 1611," as Brother Kenneth Mackenzie tells us.

**Cagliostro.** A famous Adept, whose real name is claimed (by his enemies) to have been Joseph Balsamo. He was a native of Palermo, and studied under some mysterious foreigner of whom little has been ascertained. His accepted history is too well known to need repetition, and his real history has never been told. His fate was that of every human being who proves that he knows more than do his fellow-creatures; he was "stoned to death" by persecutions, lies, and infamous accusations, and yet he was the friend and adviser of the highest and mightiest of every land he visited. He was finally tried and sentenced in Rome as a heretic, and was said to have died during his confinement in a State prison. (See "Mesmer".) Yet his end was not utterly undeserved, as he had been untrue to his vows in some respects, had fallen from his state of chastity and yielded to ambition and selfishness.

**Cain** or Kayn *(Heb.)* In Esoteric symbology he is said to be identical with Jehovah or the "Lord God" of the fourth chapter of *Genesis*. It is held, moreover, that Abel is not his brother, but his female aspect. (See *S. D., sub voce*.)

**Calvary Cross.** This form of cross does not date from Christianity. It was known and used for mystical purposes, thousands of years before our era. It formed part and parcel of the various Rituals, in Egypt and Greece, in Babylon and India, as well as in China, Mexico, and Peru. It is a cosmic, as well as a physiological (or *phallic*) symbol. That it existed among all the "heathen" nations is testified to by Tertullian. "How doth the Athenian Minerva differ from the body of a cross?" he queries. "The origin of your gods is derived from figures moulded on a cross. All those rows of images on your standards are the appendages of crosses; those hangings on your banners are the robes of crosses." And the fiery champion was right. The *tau* or T is the most ancient of all forms, and the cross or the *tat (q.v.)* as ancient. The *crux ansata*, the cross with a handle, is in the hands of almost every god, including Baal and the Phœnician Astarte. The *croix cramponnée* is the Indian *Swastica*. It has been exhumed from the lowest foundations of the ancient site of Troy, and it appears on Etruscan and Chaldean relics of antiquity. As Mrs. Jamieson shows: "The *ankh* of Egypt was the crutch of St. Anthony and the cross of St. Philip. The *Labarum* of Constantine . . . was an emblem long before, in Etruria. Osiris had the *Labarum* for his sign; Horus appears sometimes with the long Latin cross. The Greek pectoral cross is Egyptian. It was called by the Fathers the devil's invention before Christ . The *crux ansata* is upon the old coins of Tarsus, as the Maltese upon the breast of an Assyrian king ...The cross of Calvary, so common in Europe, occurs on the breasts of mummies. . . it was suspended round the necks of sacred Serpents in Egypt. . . . Strange Asiatic tribes bringing tribute in Egypt are noticed with garments studded with crosses, and Sir Gardner Wilkinson dates this picture B.C. 1500." Finally, "Typhon, the Evil One, is chained by a cross". *(Eg. Belief and Mod. Thought).*

**Campanella,** Tomaso. A Calabrese, born in 1568, who, from his childhood exhibited strange powers, and gave himself up during his whole life to the Occult Arts. The story which shows him initiated in his boyhood into the secrets of alchemy and thoroughly instructed in the secret science by a Rabbi-Kabbalist in a *fortnight* by means of *notavicon,* is a cock and bull invention. Occult knowledge, even when a heirloom from the preceding birth, does not come back into a new personality within fifteen days. He became an opponent of the Aristotelian materialistic philosophy when at Naples and was obliged to fly for his life. Later, the Inquisition sought to try and condemn him for the practice of magic arts, but its efforts were defeated. During his lifetime he wrote an enormous quantity of magical, astrological and alchemical works, most of which are no longer extant. He is reported to have died in the convent of the Jacobins at Paris on May the 21st, 1639.

**Canarese**. The language of the Karnatic, originally called Kanara, one of the divisions of South India.

**Capricornus** (*Lat.*) The 10th sign of the Zodiac (*Makâra* in Sanskrit), considered, on account of its hidden meaning, the most important among the constellations of the mysterious Zodiac. it is fully described in the *Secret Doctrine*, and therefore needs but a few words more. Whether, agreeably with exoteric statements, Capricornus was related in any way to the wet-nurse Amalthæa who fed Jupiter with her milk, or whether it was the god Pan who changed himself into a goat and left his impress upon the sidereal records, matters little. Each of the fables has its significance.

Everything in Nature is intimately correlated to the rest, and therefore the students of ancient lore will not be too much surprised when told that even the seven steps taken in the direction of every one of the four points of the compass, or −28 steps−taken by the new-born infant Buddha, are closely related to the 28 stars of the constellation of Capricornus.

**Cardan,** Jérome. An astrologer, alchemist, kabbalist and mystic, well known in literature. He was born at Pavia in 1501, and died at Rome in 1576.

**Carnac.** A very ancient site in Brittany (France) of a temple of cyclopean structure, sacred to the Sun and the Dragon; and of the same kind as Karnac, in ancient Egypt, and Stonehenge in England. (See the "Origin of the Satanic Myth" in *Archaic Symbolism.*) It was built by the prehistoric hierophant-priests of the Solar Dragon, or symbolized Wisdom (the Solar *Kumâras* who incarnated being the highest). Each of the stones was personally placed there by the successive priest-adepts in power, and commemorated in symbolic language the degree of power, status, and knowledge of each. (See further *S. D.* II. 381, *et seq.*, and also "Karnac".)

**Caste.** Originally the system of the four hereditary classes into which the Indian population was divided: Brahman, Kshatriya, Vaisya, and Sudra (or descendants of Brahmâ, Warriors, Merchants, and the lowest or Agriculturalists). Besides these original four, hundreds have now grown up in India.

**Causal Body.** This "body", which is no body either objective or subjective, but *Buddhi,* the Spiritual Soul, is so called because it is the direct cause of the Sushupti condition, leading to the *Turya* state, the highest state of *Samadhi.* It is called *Karanopadhi,* "the basis of the Cause", by the Târaka Raja Yogis; and in the Vedânta system it corresponds to both the *Vignânamaya* and *Anandamaya Kosha,* the latter coming next to Atma, and therefore being the vehicle of the universal Spirit. Buddhi alone could not be called a "Causal Body ", but becomes so in conjunction with Manas, the incarnating Entity or EGO.

**Cazotte,** *Jacques.* The wonderful Seer, who predicted the beheading of several royal personages and his own decapitation, at a gay supper some time before the first Revolution in France. He was born at Dijon in 1720, and studied mystic philosophy in the school of Martinez Pasqualis at Lyons. On the 11th of September 1791, he was arrested and condemned to death by the president of the revolutionary government, a man who, shameful to state, had been his fellow-student and a member of the Mystic

Lodge of Pasqualis at Lyons. Cazotte was executed on the 25th of September on the Place du Carrousel.

**Cecco d'Ascolî.** Surnamed "Francesco Stabili." He lived in the thirteenth century, and was considered the most famous astrologer in his day. A work of his published at Basle in 1485, and called *Commentarii in Sphaeram Joannis de Sacrabosco*, is still extant. He was burnt alive by the Inquisition in 1327.

**Cerberus** (*Gr., Lat.*). Cerberus, the three-headed canine monster, which was supposed to watch at the threshold of Hades, came to the Greeks and Romans from Egypt. It was the monster, half-dog and half-hippopotamus, that guarded the gates of Amenti. The mother of Cerberus was Echidna—a being, half-woman, half-serpent, much honoured in Etruria. Both the Egyptian and the Greek Cerberus are symbols of Kâmaloka and its uncouth monsters, the cast-off shells of mortals.

**Ceres** (*Lat.*) In Greek *Demeter*. As the female aspect of Pater Æther, Jupiter, she is esoterically the productive principle in the all-pervading Spirit that quickens every germ in the material universe.

**Chabrat Zereh Aur Bokher** (*Heb.*) An Order of the Rosicrucian stock, whose members study the Kabbalah and Hermetic sciences; it admits both sexes, and has many grades of instruction. The members meet in private, and the very existence of the Order is generally unknown. [w.w.w.]

**Chadâyatana** (*Sk.*). Lit., the six dwellings or *gates* in man for the reception of sensations; thus, on the physical plane, the eyes, nose, ear, tongue, body (or touch) and mind, as a product of the physical brain and on the mental plane (esoterically), *spiritual* sight, smell, hearing, taste, touch and perception, the whole synthesized by the *Buddhi-atmic* element. Chadâyatana is one of the 12 Nidânas, which form the chain of incessant causation and effect.

**Chaitanya** (*Sk*) The founder of a mystical sect in India. A rather modern sage, believed to be an *avatar* of Krishna.

**Chaitya**, or *Tchaitya* (*Sk.*). Any locality made sacred through some event in the life of Buddha; a term signifying the same in relation to gods, and any kind of place or object of worship.

**Chakchur**, or *Tchakchur* (*Sk.*). The first *Vidjnâna* (*q.v.*). Lit., "the eye", meaning the faculty of sight, or rather, an occult perception of spiritual and subjective realities (*Chakshur*).

**Chakna-padma-karpo** (*Tib.*) "He who holds the lotus", used of *Chenresi*, the Bodhisattva. It is not a genuine Tibetan word, but half Sanskrit.

**Chakra**, or *Tchakra* (*Sk.*). A spell. The disk of Vishnu, which served as a weapon; the wheel of the Zodiac, also the wheel of time, etc. With Vishnu, it was a symbol of divine authority. One of the sixty-five figures of the *Sripâda*, or the mystic foot-print of Buddha which contains that number of symbolical figures. The Tchakra is used in mesmeric phenomena and other abnormal practices.

**Chakshub** (*Sk.*) The "eye ". *Loka-chakshub* or "the eye of the world" is a title of the Sun.

**Chaldean Book of Numbers**. A work which contains all that is found in the *Zohar* of Simeon Ben-Jochai, and much more. It must be the older by many centuries, and in one sense its original, as it contains all the fundamental principles taught in the Jewish Kabbalistic works, but none of their blinds. It is very rare indeed, there being perhaps only two or three copies extant, and these in private hands.

**Chaldeans**, or *Kasdim*. At first a tribe, then a caste of learned Kabbalists. They were the *savants*, the magians of Babylonia, astrologers and diviners. The famous Hillel, the precursor of Jesus in philosophy and in ethics, was a Chaldean. Franck in his *Kabbala* points to the close resemblance of the "secret doctrine" found in the *Avesta* and the religious metaphysics of the Chaldees.

**Chandâlas**, or *Tchhandâlas* (*Sk.*). Outcasts, or people without caste, a name now given to all the lower classes of the Hindus; but in antiquity it was applied to a certain class of men, who, having forfeited their right to any of the four castes-—Brâhmans, Kshatriyas, Vaisyas and Sûdras—were expelled from cities and sought refuge in the forests. Then they became "bricklayers", until finally expelled they left the country, some 4,000 years before our era. Some see in them the ancestors of the earlier Jews, whose tribes began with A-brahm or "No Brahm". To this day it is the class most despised by the Brahmins in India.

**Chandra** (*Sk.*) The Moon; also a deity. The terms *Chandra* and Soma are synonyms.

**Chandragupta**, or *Tchandragupta* (*Sk.*). The first Buddhist King in India, the grand-sire of Asoka; the *Sandracottus* of the all-bungling Greek writers who went to India in Alexander's time. (See "Asoka".) Also, the son of Nanda, the first Buddhist King of the Morya Dynasty, the grandfather of King Asoka, "the beloved of the gods" (*Piyadasi*).

**Chandra-kanta** (*Sk.*) "The moon-stone", a gem that is claimed to be formed and developed under the moon-beams, which give it occult and magical properties. It has a very cooling influence in fever if applied to both temples.

**Chandramanam** *(Sk.)* The method of calculating time by the Moon.

**Chandrayana** *(Sk.)* The lunar year chronology.

**Chandra-vansa** *(Sk.)* The "Lunar Race", in contradistinction to *Suryavansa*, the "Solar Race". Some Orientalists think it an inconsistency that Krishna, a *Chandravansa* (of the Yadu branch) should have been declared an Avatar of Vishnu, who is a *manifestation of the solar energy* in Rig -Veda, a work of unsurpassed authority with the Brahmans. This shows, however, the deep occult meaning of the Avatar; a meaning which only esoteric philosophy can explain. A glossary is no fit place for such explanations; but it may be useful to remind those who know, and teach those who do not, that in Occultism, man is called a *solar-lunar* being, solar in his higher triad, and lunar in his quaternary. Moreover, it is the Sun who imparts his light to the Moon, in the same way as the human *triad* sheds its divine light on the mortal shell of sinful man. Life celestial quickens life terrestrial. Krishna stands metaphysically for the *Ego* made one with Atma-Buddhi, and performs mystically the same function as the *Christos* of the Gnostics, both being "the inner god in the temple"—man. Lucifer is "the bright morning star", a well known symbol in *Revelations,* and, as a planet, corresponds to the EGO. Now Lucifer (or the planet Venus) is the *Sukra-Usanas* of the Hindus; and Usanas is the Daitya-guru, i.e., the spiritual guide and instructor of the Danavas and the Daityas. The latter are the giant-demons in the *Purânas,* and in the esoteric interpretations, the antetypal symbol of the man of flesh, physical mankind. The Daityas can raise themselves, it is said, through knowledge "austerities and devotion" to "the rank of the gods and of the ABSOLUTE". All this is very suggestive in the legend of Krishna; and what is more suggestive still is that just as Krishna, the Avatar of a great God in India, is of time race of Yadu, so is another incarnation, "God incarnate himself"—or the "God-man Christ", also of the race *Iadoo*—the name for the Jews all over Asia. Moreover, as his mother, who is represented as Queen of Heaven standing on the crescent, is identified in Gnostic philosophy, and also in the esoteric system, with the Moon herself, like all the other lunar goddesses such as Isis, Diana, Astarte and others—mothers of the Logoi, so Christ is called repeatedly in the Roman Catholic Church, the Sun-Christ, the *Christ-Soleil* and so on. If the later is a metaphor so also is the earlier.

**Chantong** *(Tib.)* "He of the 1,000 Eyes", a name of Padmapani or Chenresi

(Avalokitesvara).

**Chaos** (*Gr.*) The Abyss, the "Great Deep". It was personified in Egypt by the Goddess Neïth, anterior to all gods. As Deveria says, "the only God, without form and sex, who gave birth to itself, and without fecundation, is adored under the form of a Virgin Mother". She is the vulture-headed Goddess found in the oldest period of Abydos, who belongs, accordingly to Mariette Bey, to the first Dynasty, which would make her, even on the confession of the time-dwarfing Orientalists, about 7,000 years old. As Mr. Bonwick tells us in his excellent work on Egyptian belief—"Neïth, Nut, Nepte, Nuk (her names as variously read !) is a philosophical conception worthy of the nineteenth century after the Christian era, rather than the thirty-ninth before it or earlier than that". And he adds: "Neith or Nout is neither more nor less than the *Great Mother*, a yet the *Immaculate Virgin*, or female God from whom all things proceeded". Neïth is the "Father-mother" of the *Stanzas* of the *Secret Doctrine*, the Swabhavat of the Northern Buddhists, the *immaculate* Mother indeed, the prototype of the latest "Virgin" of all; for, as Sharpe says, "the Feast of Candlemas—in honour of the goddess Neïth—is yet marked in our Almanacs as Candlemas day, or the Purification of the Virgin Mary"; and Beauregard tells us of "the Immaculate Conception of the Virgin, who can henceforth, as well as the Egyptian Minerva, the mysterious Neïth, boast of having come from herself, and of having given birth to God". He who would deny the working of cycles and the recurrence of events, let him read what Neïth was years ago, in the conception of the Egyptian Initiates, trying to popularize a philosophy too abstract for the masses; and then remember the subjects of dispute at the Council of Ephesus in 431, when Mary was declared Mother of God; and her Immaculate Conception forced on the World as by command of God, by Pope and Council in 1858. Neïth is *Swabhdvat* and also the Vedic *Aditi* and the Purânic *Akâsa*, for "she is not only the celestial vault, or ether, but is made to appear in a tree, from which she gives the fruit of the Tree of Life (like another Eve) or pours upon her worshippers some of the divine water of life". Hence she gained the favourite appellation of "Lady of the Sycamore", an epithet applied to another Virgin (Bonwick). The resemblance becomes still more marked when Neïth is found on old pictures represented as a Mother embracing the ram-headed god, the "Lamb". An ancient stele declares her to be "Neut, the luminous, who has engendered the gods"—the Sun included, for Aditi is the mother of the Marttanda, the Sun—an Aditya. She is *Naus,* the celestial ship; hence we find her on the prow of the Egyptian vessels, like

Dido on the prow of the ships of the Phœnician mariners, and forth with we have the Virgin Mary, from *Mar*, the "Sea", called the "Virgin of the Sea", and the "Lady Patroness" of all Roman Catholic seamen. The Rev. Sayce is quoted by Bonwick, explaining her as a principle in the Babylonian *Bahu* (Chaos, or confusion) i.e., "merely the Chaos of Genesis... and perhaps also Môt, the primitive substance that was the mother of all the gods". Nebuchadnezzar seems to have been in the mind of the learned professor, since he left the following witness in cuneiform language, "I built a temple to the Great Goddess, my Mother". We may close with the words of Mr. Bonwick with which we thoroughly agree "She (Neïth) is the *Zerouâna* of the Avesta, 'time without limits'. She is the Nerfe of the Etruscans, half a woman and half a fish" (whence the connection of the Virgin Mary with the fish and *pisces*); of whom it is said: "From holy good Nerfe the navigation is happy. She is the *Bythos* of the Gnostics, the *One* of the Neoplatonists, the All of German metaphysicians, the *Anaita* of Assyria."

**Charaka** (*Sk.*). A writer on Medicine who lived in Vedic times. He is believed to have been an incarnation (*Avatara*) of the Serpent *Sesha*, i.e., an embodiment of divine Wisdom, since Sesha-Naga, the King of the "Serpent" race, is synonymous with Ananta, the seven-headed Serpent, on which Vishnu sleeps during the *pralayas*. *Ananta* is the "endless" and the symbol of eternity, and as such, one with Space, while Sesha is only periodical in his manifestations. Hence while Vishnu is identified with *Ananta,* Charaka is only the Avatar of Sesha. (See "Ananta" and "Sesha".)

**Charnook**, Thomas. A great alchemist of the sixteenth century; a surgeon who lived and practiced near Salisbury, studying the art in some neighbouring cloisters with a priest. It is said that he was initiated into the final secret of transmutation by the famous mystic William Bird, who "had been a prior of Bath and defrayed the expense of repairing the Abbey Church from the gold which he made by the red and white elixirs" (*Royal Mas. Cyc.*). Charnock wrote his *Breviary of Philosophy* in the year 1557 and the *Enigma of Alchemy*, in 1574.

**Charon** (*Gr.*) The Egyptian *Khu-en-ua,* the hawk-headed Steersman of the boat conveying the Souls across the black waters that separate life from death. Charon, the Sun of Erebus and Nox, is a variant of Khu en-ua. The dead were obliged to pay an *obolus*, a small piece of money, o this grim ferryman of the Styx and Acheron; therefore the ancients always placed a coin under the tongue of the deceased. This custom has been preserved in our own times, for most of the lower classes in Russia place coppers in the coffin under the head of the dead for *post mortem* expenses.

**Châryâka** (*Sk.*) There were two famous beings of this name. One a *Rakshasa* (demon) who disguised himself as a Brâhman and entered Hastinâ-pura; whereupon the Brahmans discovered the imposture and reduced Châryâka to ashes with the fire of their eyes,—i.e., magnetically by means of what is called in Occultism the "black glance" or evil eye. The second was a terrible materialist and denier of all but matter, who if he could come back to life, would put to shame all the "Free thinkers" and "Agnostics" of the day. He lived before the Râmâyanic period, but his teachings and school have survived to this day, and he has even now followers, who are mostly to be found in Bengal.

**Chastanier**, *Benedict*. A French mason who established in London in 1767 a Lodge called "The Illuminated Theosophists".

**Chatur Mahârâja,** *or Tchatur Mahârâja* (*Sk.*). The "four kings", Devas, who guard the four quarters of the universe, and are connected with Karma.

**Chatur mukha** (*Sk*) The "four-faced one", a title of Brahmâ.

**Chatur varna** (*Sk.*) The four castes (*lit.*, colours).

**Châturdasa Bhuvanam** (*Sk.*) The fourteen lokas or planes of existence. Esoterically, the dual seven states.

**Chaturyonî** (*Sk.*) Written also *tchatur-yoni*. The same as *Karmaya* or "the four modes of birth"—four ways of entering on the path of Birth as decided by Karma: (a) birth from the womb, as men and mammalia (b) birth from an egg, as birds and reptiles; (c) from moisture and air-germs, as insects; and (d) by sudden *self-transformation*, as Bodhisattvas and Gods (*Anupadaka*).

**Chava** (*Heb.*) The same as Eve: "the Mother of all that lives" "Life"

**Chavigny,** *Jean Aimé de*. A disciple of the world-famous Nostradamus, an astrologer and an alchemist of the sixteenth century. He died in the year 1604. His life was a very quiet one and he was almost unknown to his contemporaries; but he left a precious manuscript on the pre-natal and post-natal influence of the stars on certain marked individuals, a secret revealed to him by Nostradamus. This treatise was last in the possession of the Emperor Alexander of Russia.

**Chelâ** (*Sk.*) A disciple, the pupil of a Guru or Sage, the follower of some adept of a school of philosophy (*lit.*, child).

**Chemi** (*Eg.*). The ancient name of Egypt.

**Chenresi** (*Tib.*) The Tibetan Avalokitesvara. The Bodhisattva Padmâpani, a divine Buddha.

**Cheru** (*Scand*) Or Heru. A magic sword, a weapon of the "sword god" Heru. In the *Edda*, the Saga describes it as destroying its possessor, should he be unworthy of wielding it. It brings victory and fame only in the hand of a virtuous hero.

**Cherubim** (*Heb.*) According to the Kabbalists, a group of angels, which they specially associated with the Sephira Jesod. in Christian teaching, an order of angels who are "watchers". *Genesis* places Cherubim to guard the lost Eden, and the O.T. frequently refers to them as guardians of the divine glory. Two winged representations in gold were placed over the Ark of the Covenant; colossal figures of the same were also placed in the Sanctum Sanctorum of the Temple of Solomon. Ezekiel describes them in poetic language. Each Cherub appears to have been a compound figure with four faces—of a man, eagle, lion, and ox, and was certainly winged. Parkhurst, *in voc. Cherub,* suggests that the derivation of the word is from K, a particle of similitude, and RB or RUB, greatness, master, majesty, and so an image of godhead. Many other nations have displayed similar figures as symbols of deity; e.g., the Egyptians in their figures of Serapis. as Macrohius describes in his *Saturnalia*; the Greeks had their triple-headed Hecate, and the Latins had three-faced images of Diana, as Ovid tells us, *ecce procul ternis Hecate variata figuris*. Virgil also describes her in the fourth Book of the Æneid. Porphyry and Eusebius write the same of Proserpine. The Vandals had a many-headed deity they called Triglaf. The ancient German races had an idol Rodigast with human body and heads of the ox, eagle, and man. The Persians have some figures of Mithras with a man's body, lion's head, and four wings. Add to these the Chimæra Sphinx of Egypt, Moloch, Astarte of the Syrians, and some figures of Isis with Bull's horns and feathers of a bird on the head. [w.w.w.]

**Chesed** (*Heb.*) "Mercy ", also named *Gedulah*, the fourth of the ten Sephiroth; a masculine or active potency. [w.w. w.]

**Chhanda Riddhi Pâda,** or *Tchhanda Riddhi Pâda* (*Sk.*). "The step of desire", a term used in Râja Yoga. It is the final renunciation of all desire as a *sine quânon* condition of phenomenal powers, and entrance on the direct path of Nirvâna.

**Chhâyâ** (*Sk.*) "Shade" or "Shadow". The name of a creature produced by Sanjnâ, the wife of Surya, from herself (astral body). Unable to endure the ardour of her husband, Sanjnâ left Chhâyâ in her place as a wife, going herself away to perform austerities. Chhâyâ is the astral image of a person in esoteric philosophy.

**Chhandoga** (*Sk*) A *Samhitâ* collection of Sama Veda; also a priest, a chanter of the Sama Veda.

**Chhanmûka** (Sk) A great Bodhisattva with the Northern Buddhists, famous for his ardent love of Humanity; regarded in the esoteric schools as a *Nirmanakâya*.

**Chhannagarikah** (*Tib*.). Lit., the school of six cities. A famous philosophical school where Chelas are prepared before entering on the Path.

**Chhassidi** or *Chasdim*. In the Septuagint *Assidai*, and in English *Assideans*. They are also mentioned in *Maccabees* I., vii., 13, as being put to death with many others. They were the followers of Mattathias, the father of the Maccabeans, and were all initiated mystics, or Jewish adepts. The word means "skilled learned in all wisdom, human and divine". Mackenzie (*Royal Masonic Cyclopedia, RMC*) regards them as the guardians of the Temple for the preservation of its purity; but as Solomon and his Temple are both allegorical and had no real existence, the Temple means in this case the "body of Israel "and its morality." Scaliger connects this Society of the *Assideans* with that of the Essenes, deeming it the predecessor of the latter."

**Chhaya loka** (*Sk*.) The world of Shades; like Hades, the world of the *Eidola* and *Umbræ*. We call it *Kâmaloka*.

**Chiah** (*Heb*.) Life; Vita, *Revivificatio*. In the Kabbala, the second highest essence of the human soul, corresponding to Chokmah (Wisdom).

**Chichhakti** (*Sk*.) *Chih-Sakti*; the power which generates thought.

**Chidagnikundum** (*Sk*.). Lit., "the fire-hearth in the heart"; the seat of the force which extinguishes all individual desires.

**Chidâkâsam** (Sk); The field, or basis of consciousness.

**Chiffilet,** *Jean*. A Canon-Kabbalist of the XVIIth century, reputed to have learned a key to the Gnostic works from Coptic Initiates; he wrote a work on Abraxas in two portions, the esoteric portion of which was burnt by the Church.

**Chiim** (*Heb*.) A plural noun—"lives"; found in compound names Elohim Chum, the gods of lives, Parkhurst translates "the living God" and Ruach Chiim, Spirit of lives or of life. [w.w. w.]

**Chikitsa Vidyâ Shâstra** , or *Tchikitsa Vidyâ Shâstra*(*Sk*.). A treatise on occult medicine, which contains a number of "magic" prescriptions. It is one of the *Pancha Vidyâ Shâstra*s or Scriptures.

**China**, The Kabbalah of. One of the oldest known Chinese books is the *Yih King, or Book of Changes*. It is reported to have been written 2850 B.C., in the dialect of the Accadian black races of Mesopotamia. It is a most abstruse system of Mental and Moral Philosophy, with a scheme of universal relation and divination. Abstract ideas are represented by lines, half lines, circle, and points. Thus a circle represents YIH, the Great Supreme; a line is referred to YIN, the Masculine Active Potency; two half lines are YANG, the Feminine Passive Potency. KWEI is the animal soul, SHAN intellect, KHIEN heaven or Father, KHWAN earth or Mother, KAN or QHIN is Son; male numbers are odd, represented by light circles, female numbers are even, by black circles. There are two most mysterious diagrams, one called "HO or the River Map", and also associated with a Horse; and the other called "The Writing of LO"; these are formed of groups of white and black circles, arranged in a Kabbalistic manner. The text is by a King named Wan, and the commentary by Kan, his son; the text is allowed to be older than the time of Confucius. [w.w.w.]

**Chit** (*Sk.*) Abstract Consciousness.

**Chitanuth our** (*Heb.*). *Chitons*, a priestly garb; the coats of skin given by *Java Aleim* to Adam and Eve after their fall,

**Chitkala** (*Sk.*). In Esoteric philosophy, identical with the Kumâras those who first incarnated into the men of the Third Root-Race. (See *S. D.*, Vol. 1. p. 288 n.)

**Chitra Gupta** (*Sk.*) The deva (or god) who is the recorder of Yâma (the god of death), and who is supposed to read the account of every Soul's life from a register called *Agra Sandhâni*, when the said soul appears before the seat of judgment. (See "*Agra Sandhâni* ".)

**Chitra Sikkandinas** (*Sk*). The constellation of the great Bear; the habitat of the seven Rishis (*Sapta Riksha*). Lit., "bright-crested".

**Chitta Riddhi Pâda**, or *Tchitta Riddhi Pâda*(*Sk*) "The step of memory." The third condition of the mystic series which leads to the acquirement of adept-ship; i.e., the renunciation of physical memory, and of all thoughts connected with worldly or personal events in one's life—benefits, personal pleasures or associations. physical memory has to be sacrificed, and recalled by will power only when absolutely needed. The *Riddhi Pâda*, lit., the four "Steps to Riddhi", are the four modes of controlling and finally of annihilating desire, memory, and finally meditation itself—so far as these are connected with any effort of the physical brain—meditation then becomes absolutely spiritual.

**Chitta Smriti Upasthâna,** *Tchitta Smriti Upasthâna(Sk.).* One of the four aims of *Smriti Upasthâna,* i.e., the keeping ever in mind the transitory character of man's life, and the incessant revolution of the wheel of existence.

**Chnoumis** (*Gr*) The same as Chnouphis and Kneph. A symbol of creative force; Chnoumis or Kneph is "the unmade and eternal deity" according to Plutarch. He is represented as blue (ether), and with his ram's head with an asp between the horns, he might be taken for Ammon or Chnouphis (*q.v.* ). The fact is that all these gods are solar, and represent under various aspects the phases of generation and impregna tion. Their ram's heads denote this meaning, a ram ever symbolizing generative energy in the abstract, while the bull was the symbol of strength and the creative function. All were one god, whose attributes were individualised and personified. According to Sir G. Wilkinsen, Kneph or Chnoumis was "the idea of the Spirit of God"; and Bonwick explains that, as *Av,* "matter" or "flesh", he was criocephalic (ram-headed), wearing a solar disk on the head, standing on the Serpent Mehen, with a viper in his left and a cross in his right hand, and bent upon the function of creation in the underworld (the earth, esoterically). The Kabbalists identify him with "Binah, the third Sephira of the Sephirothal Tree, or Binah, represented by the Divine name of Jehovah". If as Chnoumis-Kneph, he represents the Indian Narayâna, the Spirit of ( moving on the waters of space, as *Eichton* or Ether he holds in his mouth an Egg, the symbol of evolution; and as *Av* he is Siva, the Destroyer and the Regenerator; for, as Deveria explains:"His Journey to the lower hemispheres appears to symbolize the evolutions of substances, which are born to die and to be reborn." Esoterically, however, and as taught by the Initiates of the inner temple, Chnoumis-Kneph was pre-eminently *the god of reincarnation.* Says an inscription: "I am Chnoumis, Son of the Universe, 700", a mystery having a direct reference to the reincarnating EGO.

**Chnouphis** (*Gr.*). *Nouf* in Egyptian. Another aspect of Ammon, and the personification of his generative power *in actu,* as Kneph is of the same in *potentia.* He is also ram-headed. If in his aspect as Kneph he is the Holy Spirit with the creative ideation brooding in him, as Chnouphis, he is the angel who "comes in" into the Virgin soil and flesh. A prayer on a papyrus, translated by the French Egyptologist Chabas, says; "O Sepui, Cause of being, who hast formed thine own body! O only Lord, proceeding from Noum ! O divine substance, created from itself! O God, who hast made the substance which is in him! O God, who has made his own father and impregnated his own mother." This shows the origin of the Christian doctrines of the Trinity and immaculate conception. He is seen on a monument seated near a potter's wheel, and forming men out of clay. The fig-leaf is sacred to him, which is alone sufficient to prove him a phallic god—an idea which is carried out by the inscription: "he who made that which is, the creator of beings, the first existing, he who made to exist all that exists." Some see in him the incarnation of Ammon-Ra, but he is the latter himself in his phallic aspect, for, like Ammon, he is "his mother's husband", i.e., the male or impregnating side of Nature. His names vary, as Cnouphis, Noum, Khem, and Khnum or Chnoumis. As he represents the Demiurgos (or Logos) from the material, lower aspect of the Soul of the World, he is the Agathodæmon, symbolized sometimes by a Serpent; and his wife Athor or Maut (Môt mother), or Sate, "the daughter of the Sun", carrying an arrow on a sunbeam (the ray of conception), stretches "mistress over the lower portions of the atmosphere". below the constellations, as Neïth expands over the starry heavens. (See "Chaos".)

**Chohan** (*Tib.*) "Lord" or "Master"; a chief; thus *Dhyan-Chohan* would answer to "Chief of the Dhyanis", or celestial Lights—which in English would he translated Archangels.

**Chokmah** (Heb) Wisdom; the second of the ten Sephiroth, and the second of the supernal Triad. A masculine potency corresponding to the Yod (ʼ) of the Tetragrammaton IHVH, and to *Ab*, the Father. [w.w.w.]

**Chréstos** (*Gr.*) The early Gnostic form of Christ. It was used in the fifth century B.C. by Æschylus, Herodotus, and others. The *Manteumata pythochresta,* or the "oracles delivered by a Pythian god" "through a pythoness, are mentioned by the former (*Choeph.* 901). *Chréstian* is not only "the seat of an oracle", but an offering to, or for, the oracle.

*Chréstés* is one who explains oracles, "a prophet and soothsayer", and Chrésterios one who serves an oracle or a god. The earliest Christian writer, Justin Martyr, in his first *Apology* calls his co-religionists Chréstians. It is only through ignorance that men call themselves Christians instead of Chréstians," says Lactantius (lib. iv., cap. vii.). The terms Christ and Christians, spelt originally Chrést and Chréstians, were borrowed from the Temple vocabulary of the Pagans. Chréstos meant in that vocabulary a disciple on probation, a candidate for hierophantship. When he had attained to this through initiation, long trials, and suffering, and had been "*anointed*" (i.e., "rubbed with oil", as were Initiates and even idols of the gods, as the last touch of ritualistic observance), his name was changed into Christos, the "purified", in esoteric or mystery language. In mystic symbology, indeed, *Christés*, or *Christos*, meant that the "Way", the Path, was already trodden and the goal reached; when the fruits of the arduous labour, uniting the personality of evanescent clay with the indestructible INDIVIDUALITY, transformed it thereby into the immortal EGO. "At the end of the Way stands the *Chréstes*", the *Purifier*, and the union once accomplished, the *Chrestos*, the "man of sorrow", became *Christos* himself. Paul, the Initiate, knew this, and meant this precisely, when he is made to say, in bad translation: "I travail in birth again until Christ be formed in you" (Gal. iv.19), the true rendering of which is . . . "until ye form the Christos within yourselves" But the profane who knew only that Chréstés was in some way connected with priest and prophet, and knew nothing about the hidden meaning of Christos, insisted, as did Lactantius and Justin Martyr, on being called *Chréstians* instead of Christians. Every good individual, therefore, may find Christ in his "inner man" as Paul expresses it (Ephes. iii. 16,17), whether he be Jew, Mussulman, Hindu, or Christian. Kenneth Mackenzie seemed to think that the word *Chréstos* was a synonym of Soter, "an appellation assigned to deities, great kings and heroes," indicating "Saviour,"—and he was right. For, as he adds: "It has been applied redundantly to Jesus Christ, whose name Jesus or Joshua bears the same interpretation. The name Jesus, in fact, is rather a title of honour than a name—the true name of the Soter of Christianity being Emmanuel, or God with us (*Matt*.i, 23.).Great divinities among all nations, who are represented as expiatory or self-sacrificing, have been designated by the same title." (*R.M. Cyclopædia*) The Asklepios (or Æsculapius) of the Greeks had the title of *Soter*.

**Christian Scientist**. A newly-coined term for denoting the practitioners of an art of healing by will. The name is a misnomer, since Buddhist or Jew, Hindu or Materialist, can practise this new form of Western Yoga, with like success, if he can only guide and control his will with sufficient firmness. The "Mental Scientists" are another rival school. These work by a universal denial of every disease and evil imaginable, and claim syllogistically that since Universal Spirit cannot be subject to the failings of flesh, and since every atom is Spirit and in Spirit, and since finally, they— the healers and the healed—are all absorbed in this Spirit or Deity, there is not, nor can there he, such a thing as disease. This prevents in no wise both Christian and Mental Scientists from succumbing to disease, and nursing chronic diseases in their own bodies just like ordinary mortals.

**Chthonia** (*Gr.*) Chaotic earth in the Hellenic cosmogony.

**Chuang**. A great Chinese philosopher.

**Chubilgan** (*Mongol.*) Or *Khubilkhan.* The same as *Chutuktu.*

**Chutuktu** (*Tib.*) An incarnation of Buddha or of some Bodhisattva, as believed in Tibet, where there are generally five manifesting and two *secret* Chutuktus among the high Lamas.

**Chyuta** (*Sk.*) Means, "the fallen" into generation, as a Kabbalist would say; the opposite of *achyuta*, something which is not subject to change or differentiation; said of deity.

**Circle**. There are several "Circles" with mystic adjectives attached to them. Thus we have: (1) the "Decussated or Perfect Circle" of Plato, who shows it decussated in the form of the letter X; (2) the "Circle-dance" of the Amazons, around a Priapic image, the same as the dance of the *Gopis* around the Sun (Krishna), the shepherdesses representing the signs of the Zodiac; (3) the "Circle of Necessity" of 3,000 years of the Egyptians and of the Occultists, the duration of the cycle between rebirths or reincarnations being from 1,000 to 3,000 years on the average. This will be treated under the term "Rebirth" or "Reincarnation".

**Clairaudience**. The faculty, whether innate or acquired by occult training, of hearing all that is said at whatever distance.

**Clairvoyance**. The faculty of seeing with the inner eye or spiritual sight. As now used it is a loose and flippant term, embracing under its meaning a happy guess due to natural shrewdness or intuition, and also that faculty which was so remarkably exercised by Jacob Boehme and Swedenborg. Real clairvoyance means the faculty of seeing through the densest matter (the latter disappearing at the will and before the spiritual eye of the Seer), and irrespective of time (past, present and future) or distance.

**Clemens Alexandrinus**. A Church Father and a voluminous writer, who had been a Neo-Platonist and a disciple of Ammonius Saccas. He lived between the second and the third centuries of our era, at Alexandria.

**Cock**. A very occult bird, much appreciated in ancient augury and symbolism. According to the *Zohar*, the cock crows three times before the death of a person; and in Russia and all Slavonian countries whenever a person is ill on the premises where a cock is kept, its crowing is held to be a sign of inevitable death, unless the bird crows at the hour of midnight, or immediately afterwards, when its crowing is considered natural. As the cock was sacred to Æsculapius, and a the latter was called the *Soter* (Saviour) who raised the dead to life, the Socratic exclamation "We owe a cock to Æculapius", just before the Sage's death, is very suggestive. As the cock was always connected in symbology with the Sun (or solar gods),

Death and Resurrection, it has found its appropriate place in the four Gospels in the prophecy about Peter repudiating his Master before the cock crowed thrice. The cock is the most magnetic and sensitive of all birds, hence its Greek name *alectruon*.

**Codex Nazaraeus** (Lat.) The "Book of Adam"—the latter name meaning *anthropos*, Man or Humanity. The Nazarene faith is called sometimes the Bardesanian system, though Bardesanes (B.C. 155 to 228) does not seem to have had any connection with it. True, he was born at Edessa in Syria, and was a famous astrologer and Sabian before his alleged conversion. But he was a well-educated man of noble family, and would not have used the almost incomprehensible Chaldeo dialect mixed with the mystery language of the Gnostics, in which the Codex is written. The sect of the Nazarenes was pre-Christian. Pliny and Josephus speak of the Nazarites as settled on the banks of the Jordan 150 years B.C. (*Ant.Jud.* xiii. p. 9); and Munk says that the "Naziareate was an institution established before the laws of Musah" or Moses. (Munk p. 169.) Their modern name is in Arabic—*El Mogtasila*; in European languages—the Mendæans or "Christians of St. John". (See "Baptism".) But if the term Baptists may well be applied to them, it is not with the Christian meaning: for while they were, and still are Sabians, or pure astrolaters, the Mendæans of Syria, called the Galileans, are pure polytheists, as every traveller in Syria and on the Euphrates can ascertain, once he acquaints himself with their mysterious rites and ceremonies. (*See Isis Unv. ii. 290, et seq.*) So secretly did they preserve their beliefs from the very beginning, that Epiphanius who wrote against the Heresies in the14th century confesses himself unable to say what they believed in (i. 122); he simply states that they never mention the name of Jesus, nor do they call themselves Christians (*loc. cit.* 190. Yet it is undeniable that some of the alleged philosophical views and doctrines of Bardesanes are found in the codex of the Nazarenes. (See Norberg's *Codex Nazaræous* or the "Book of Adam", and also "Mendæans ".)

**Coeur**, *Jacques*. A famous Treasurer of France, born in 1408, who obtained the office by black magic. He was reputed as a great alchemist and his wealth became fabulous; but he was soon banished from the country, and retiring to the Island of Cyprus, died there in 1460, leaving behind enormous wealth, endless legends and a bad reputation.

**Coffin-Rite**, or *Pastos*. This was the final rite of Initiation in the Mysteries in Egypt, Greece and elsewhere. The last and supreme secrets of Occultism could not be revealed to the Disciple until he had passed through this allegorical ceremony of Death and Resurrection into new light. "The Greek verb *teleutaó*," says Vronsky, "signifies in the active voice 'I die', and in the middle voice 'I am initiated' ". Stobæus quotes an ancient author, who says, "The mind is affected in death, just as it is in the initiation into the Mysteries; and word answers to word, as well as thing to thing; for *teleutan* is 'to die', and *teleisthai* 'to be initiated'". And thus, as Mackenzie corroborates, when the Aspirant was placed in the *Pastos*, Bed, or Coffin (in India on the *lathe*, as explained in the *Secret Doctrine*), "he was symbolically said to die."

**Collanges, *Gabriel de*.** Born in 1524. The best astrologer in the XVlth century and a still better Kabbalist. He spent a fortune in the unravelling of its mysteries. It was rumoured that he died through poison administered to him by a Jewish Rabbin-Kabbalist.

**College of Rabbis.** A college at Babylon; most famous during the early centuries of Christianity. Its glory, however, was greatly darkened by the appearance in Alexandria of Hellenic teachers, such as Philo Judæus, Josephus, Aristobulus and others. The former avenged themselves on their successful rivals by speaking of the Alexandrians as theurgists and unclean prophets. But the Alexandrian believers in thaumaturgy were not regarded as sinners or impostors when orthodox Jews were at the head of such schools of "*hazim*". These were colleges for teaching prophecy and occult sciences. Samuel was the chief of such a college at Ramah; Elisha at Jericho. Hillel had a regular academy for prophets and seers; and it is Hillel, a pupil of the Babylonian College, who was the founder of the Sect of the Pharisees and the great orthodox Rabbis.

**Collemann, *Jean*.** An Alsatian, born at Orleans, according to K. Mackenzie; other accounts say he was a Jew, who found favour owing to his astrological studies, with both Charles VII. and Louis XI., and that he had a bad influence on the latter.

**Collyridians.** A sect of Gnostics who, in the early centuries of Christianity, transferred their worship and reverence from Astoreth to Mary, as Queen of Heaven and Virgin. Regarding the two as identical, they offered to the latter as they had done to the former, buns and cakes on certain days, with sexual symbols represented on them.

**Continents.** In the Buddhist cosmogony, according to Gautama Buddha's exoteric doctrine, there are numberless systems of worlds (or *Sakwala*) all of which are born, mature, decay, and are destroyed periodically. Orientalists translate the teaching about "the four great continents which do not communicate with each other", as meaning that "upon the earth there are four great continents" (see Hardy's *Eastern Monachism*, p. 4), while the doctrine means simply that around or *above* the earth there are on either side four worlds, i.e., the earth appearing as the fourth on each side of the arc.

**Corybantes,** *Mysteries of the.* These were held in Phrygia in honour of Atys, the youth beloved by Cybele. The rites were very elaborate within the temple and very noisy and tragic in public. They began by a public bewailing of the death of Atys and ended in tremendous rejoicing at his resurrection. The statue or image of the victim of Jupiter's jealousy was placed during the ceremony in a pastos (coffin), and the priests sang his sufferings. Atys, as Visvakarma in India, was a representative of Initiation and Adeptship. He is shown as being born impotent, because chastity is a requisite of the life of an aspirant. Atys is said to have established the rites and worship of Cybele, in Lydia. (See *Pausan.*, vii., c. 17.)

**Cosmic Gods.** Inferior gods, those connected with the formation of matter.

**Cosmic ideation** (*Occult.*) Eternal thought, impressed on substance or spirit-matter, in the eternity; thought which becomes active at the beginning of every new life-cycle.

**Cosmocratores** (*Gr.*). "Builders of the Universe", the "world architects", or the Creative Forces personified.

**Cow-worship.** The idea of any such "worship" is as erroneous as it is unjust. No Egyptian worshipped the cow, nor does any Hindu worship this animal now, though it is true that the cow and bull were sacred then as they are to-day, but only as the natural physical symbol of a metaphysical ideal; even as a church made of bricks and mortar is sacred to the civilized Christian because of its associations and not by reason of its walls. The cow was sacred to Isis, the Universal Mother, Nature, and to the Hathor, the female principle in Nature, the two goddesses being allied to both sun and moon, as the disk and the cow's horns (*crescent*) prove. (See "Hathor ' and "Isis".) In the *Vedas,* the Dawn of Creation is represented by a cow. This dawn is Hathor, and the day which follows, or Nature already formed, is Isis, for both are one except in the matter of time. Hathor the elder is "the mistress of the seven mystical cows "and Isis, "the Divine Mother is the "cow-horned" *the cow of plenty* (or Nature, Earth), and, as the mother of Horus (the physical world)—the "mother of all that lives The *outa* was the symbolic eye of Horus, the right being the sun, and the left the moon. The right "eye" of Horus was called "the cow of Hathor", and served as a powerful amulet, as the dove in a nest of rays or glory, with or without the cross, is a talisman with Christians, Latins and Greeks. The *Bull* and the *Lion* which we often find in company with Luke and Mark in the frontispiece of their respective Gospels in the Greek and Latin texts, are explained as symbols—-which is indeed the fact. Why not admit the same in the case of the Egyptian sacred Bulls, Cows, Rams, and Birds?

**Cremer**, *John.* An eminent scholar who for over thirty years studied Hermetic philosophy in pursuance of its practical secrets, while he was at the same time Abbot of Westminster While on a voyage to Italy, he met the famous Raymond Lully whom he induced to return with him to England. Lully divulged to Cremer the secrets of the stone, for which service the monastery offered daily prayers for him. Cremer, says the *Royal Masonic Cyclopedia*, "having obtained a profound knowledge of the secrets of Alchemy, became a most celebrated and learned adept in occult philosophy . . . lived to a good old age, and died in the reign of King Edward III."

**Crescent.** *Sin* was the Assyrian name for the moon, and *Sin-ai* the Mount, the birth-place of Osiris, of Dionysos, Bacchus and several other gods. According to Rawlinson, the moon was held in higher esteem than the sun at Babylon, *because darkness preceded light.* The crescent was, therefore, a sacred symbol with almost every nation, before it became the 'standard of the Turks. Says the author of *Egyptian Belief,* "The crescent is not essentially a Mahometan ensign. On the contrary, it was a Christian one, derived through Asia from the Babylonian Astarte, Queen of Heaven, or from the Egyptian Isis . . . . whose emblem was the crescent. The Greek Christian Empire of Constantinople held it as their palladium. Upon the conquest of the Turks, the Mahometan Sultan adopted it for the symbol of his power. Since that time the *crescent* has been made to oppose the idea of the cross."

**Criocephale** (*Gr.*). Ram-headed, applied to several deities and emblematic figures, notably those of ancient Egypt, which were designed about the period when the Sun passed, at the Vernal Equinox, from the sign Taurus to the sign Aries. Previously to this period, bull-headed and horned deities prevailed. Apis was the type of the Bull deity, Ammon that of the ram-headed type: Isis, too, had a Cow's head allotted to her. Porphyry writes that the Greeks united the Ram to Jupiter and the Bull to Bacchus. [w.w.w.]

**Crocodile**. "The great reptile of Typhon." The seat of its "worship" was Crocodilopolis and it was sacred to Set and Sebak—its alleged creators. The primitive Rishis in India, the *Manus*, and Sons of Brahmâ, are each the progenitors of some animal species, of which he is the alleged "father"; in Egypt, each god was credited with the formation or creation of certain animals which were sacred to him. Crocodiles must have been numerous in Egypt during the early dynasties, if one has to judge by the almost incalculable number of their mummies. Thousands upon thousands have been excavated from the grottoes of Moabdeh, and many a vast *necropolis* of that Typhonic animal is still left untouched. But the Crocodile was only worshipped where his god and "father" received honours. Typhon (*q.v.*) had once received such honours and, as Bunsen shows, had been considered a great god. His words are, "Down to the time of Ramses B.C. 1300, Typhon was one of the most venerated and powerful gods, a god who pours blessings and life on the rulers of Egypt." As explained elsewhere, Typhon is the material aspect of Osiris. When Typhon, the Quaternary, *kills* Osiris, the triad or divine Light, and cuts it metaphorically into 14 pieces, and separates himself from the "god", he incurs the execration of the masses; he becomes the evil god, the storm and hurricane god, the burning sand of the Desert, the constant enemy of the Nile, and the "slayer of the evening beneficent dew", because Osiris is the ideal Universe, Siva the great Regenerative Force, and Typhon the material portion of it, the evil side of the god, or the Destroying Siva. This is why the crocodile is also partly venerated and partly execrated. The appearance of the crocodile in the Desert, far from the water, prognosticated the happy event of the coming inundation—hence its adoration at Thebes and Ombos. But he destroyed thousands of human and animal beings yearly—hence also the hatred and persecution of the Crocodile at Elephantine and Tentyra.

**Cross.** Mariette Bey has shown its antiquity in Egypt by proving that in all the primitive sepulchres "the plan of the chamber has the form of a cross". It is the symbol of the Brotherhood of races and men; and was laid on the breast of the corpses in Egypt, as it is now placed on the corpses of deceased Christians, and, in its *Swastica* form (*croix*, cramponnée) on the hearts of the Buddhist adepts and Buddhas. (See "Calvary Cross".)

**Crux Ansata** (*Lat.*). The handled cross, T; whereas the tau is T, in this form,

and the oldest Egyptian cross or the *tat* is thus ✚. The *crux ansata* was the symbol of immortality, but the *tat*-cross was that of spirit-matter and had the significance of a sexual emblem. The *crux ansata* was the foremost symbol in the Egyptian Masonry instituted by Count Cagliostro; and Masons must have indeed forgotten the primitive significance of their highest symbols, if some of their authorities still insist that the *crux ansata* is only a combination of the *cteis* (or yoni) and *phallus* (or *lingham*). Far from this. The handle or *ansa* had a double significance, but never a phallic one; as an attribute of Isis it was the mundane circle; as symbol of law on the breast of a mummy it was that of immortality, of an endless and beginningless eternity, that which descends upon and grows out of the plane of material nature, the horizontal feminine line, surmounting the vertical male line—the fructifying male principle in nature or spirit. Without the handle the *crux ansata* became the *tau* T, which, left by itself, is an androgyne symbol, and becomes purely phallic or sexual only when it takes the shape +.

**Crypt** (*Gr.*) A secret subterranean vault, some for the purpose of initiation, others for burial purposes. There were crypts under every temple in antiquity. There was one on the Mount of Olives, lined with red stucco, and built before the advent of the Jews.

**Curetes**. The Priest-Initiates of ancient Crete, in the service of Cybele. Initiation in their temples was very severe; it lasted twenty-seven days, during which time the aspirant was left by himself in a crypt, undergoing terrible trials. Pythagoras was initiated into these rites and came out victorious.

**Cutha**. An ancient city in Babylonia after which a tablet giving an account of "creation" is named. The "Cutha tablet" speaks of a temple of Sittam", in the sanctuary of Nergal, the "giant king of war, lord of the city of Cutha", and is purely esoteric, it has to be read symbolically, if at all.

**Cycle.** From the Greek *Kuklos*. The ancients divided time into end less cycles, wheels within wheels, all such periods being of various durations, and each marking the beginning or the end of some event either cosmic, mundane, physical or metaphysical. There were cycles of only a few years, and cycles of immense duration, the great Orphic cycle, referring to the ethnological change of races, lasting 120,000 years, and the cycle of Cassandrus of 136,000, which brought about a complete change in planetary influences and their correlations between men and gods—a fact entirely lost sight of by modern astrologers.

**Cynocephalus** (*Gr.*) The Egyptian *Hapi*. There was a notable difference between the ape-headed gods and the "Cynocephalus" (*Simia hamadryas*), a dog-headed baboon from upper Egypt. The latter, whose sacred city was Hermopolis, was sacred to the lunar deities and Thoth Hermes, hence an emblem of secret wisdom—as was Hanuman, the monkey-god of India, and later, the elephant-headed Ganesha. The mission of the Cynocephalus was to show the way for the Dead to the Seat of Judgment and Osiris, whereas the ape-gods were all phallic. They are almost invariably found in a crouching posture, holding on one hand the *outa* (the eye of Horus), and in the other the sexual cross. Isis is seen sometimes riding on an ape, to designate the fall of divine nature into generation.

# D

**D.**—Both in the English and Hebrew alphabets the fourth letter, whose numerical value is four. The symbolical signification in the *Kabbala* of the *Daleth* is "door". It is the Greek *delta* Δ, through which the world (whose symbol is the *tetrad* or number four,) issued, producing the divine seven. The name of the Tetrad was Harmony with the Pythagoreans, "because it is a diatessaron in sesquitertia". With the Kabbalists, the divine name associated with Daleth was Daghoul.

**Daath** (*Heb.*) Knowledge; "the conjunction of Chokmah and Binah, Wisdom and Understanding": sometimes, in error, called a Sephira. [w.w.w.]

**Dabar** (*Heb.*) D (*a*) B (*a*) R (*im*), meaning the "Word", and the "Words" in the Chaldean Kabbala, *Dabar* and *Logoi*. (See *S. D.*, I. p. 350, and "Logos", or "Word".)

**Dabistan** (*Pers.*) The land of Iran; ancient Persia.

**Dache-Dachus** (*Chald.*) The dual emanation of Moymis, the progeny of the dual or androgynous World-Principle, the male Apason and female Tauthe. Like all theocratic nations possessing Temple mysteries, the Babylonians never mentioned the "One" Principle of the Universe, nor did they give it a name. This made Damascious (*Theogonies*) remark that like the rest of "barbarians" the Babylonians passed it over in silence. Tauthe was the mother of the gods, while Apason was her self-generating male power, Moymis, the ideal universe, being her only-begotten son, and *emanating* in his turn Dache-Dachus, and at last Belus, the Demiurge of the objective Universe.

**Dactyli** (*Gr.*) From *daktulos*, "a finger". The name given to the Phrygian Hierophants of Kybele, who were regarded as the greatest magicians and exorcists. They were five or ten in number because of the five fingers on one hand that blessed, and the ten on both hands which evoke the gods. They also healed by manipulation or mesmerism.

**Dadouchos** (*Gr.*) The torch-bearer, one of the four celebrants in the Eleusinian mysteries. There were several attached to the temples but they appeared in public only at the Panathenaic Games at Athens, to preside over the so-called "torch-race". (See Mackenzie's *R.M. Cyclopædia.*)

**Dæmon** (*Gr.*) In the original Hermetic works and ancient classics it has a meaning identical with that of "god", "angel" or "genius". The Dæmon of Socrates is the incorruptible part of the man, or rather the real inner man which we call Nous or the rational divine Ego. At all events the Dæmon (or Daimon of the great Sage was surely not the demon of the Christian Hell or of Christian orthodox theology. The name was given by ancient peoples, and especially the philosophers of the Alexandrian school, to all kinds of spirits, whether good or bad, human or otherwise. The appellation is often synonymous with that of gods or angels. But some philosophers tried, with good reason, to make a just distinction between the many classes.

**Dænam** (*Pahlavi*) Lit., "Knowledge", the principle of understanding in man, rational Soul, or *Manas*, according to the *Avesta*.

**Dag, Dagon** (*Heb.*). "Fish" and also "Messiah". Dagon was the Chaldean man-fish Oannes, the mysterious being who arose daily out of the depths of the sea to teach people every useful science. He was also called *Annedotus*.

**Dâgoba** (*Sk.*), or *Stûpa*. Lit: a sacred mound or tower for Buddhist holy relics. These are pyramidal-looking mounds scattered all over India and Buddhist countries, such as Ceylon, Burmah, Central Asia, etc. They are of various sizes, and generally contain some small relics of Saints or those claimed to have belonged to Gautama, the Buddha. As the human body is supposed to consist of 84,000 *dhâtus* (organic cells with definite vital functions in them), Asoka is said for this reason to have built 84,000 *dhâtu-gopas* or Dâgobas in honour of every cell of the Buddha's body, each of which has now become a *dhârmadhâtu* or holy relic. There is in Ceylon a Dhâtu-gopa at Anurâdhapura said to date from160 years B.C. They are now built pyramid-like, but the primitive Dâgobas were all shaped like towers with a cupola and several tchhatra (umbrellas) over them. Eitel states that the Chinese Dâgobas have all from 7 to 14 *tchhatras* over them, a number which is symbolical of the human body.

**Daitya Guru** (*Sk.*) The instructor of the giants, called *Daityas* (*q.v.*) Allegorically, it is the title given to the planet Venus-Lucifer, or rather to its indwelling Ruler, *Sukra*, a male deity (See *S. D.*. II. p. 30).

**Daityas** *(Sk.)* Giants, Titans, and exoterically demons, but in truth identical with certain Asuras, the intellectual gods, the opponents of the useless gods of ritualism and the enemies of *puja* sacrifices.

**Daivi-prakriti** *(Sk.)* Primordial, homogeneous light, called by some Indian Occultists "the Light of the Logos" (see *Notes on the Bhagavat Gita*, by T. Subba Row, B.A., L.L.B.); when differentiated this light becomes FOHAT.

**Dâkinî** *(Sk.)* Female demons, vampires and blood-drinkers *(asra-pas)*. In the *Purânas* they attend upon the goddess Kâli and feed on human flesh. A species of evil "Elementals" *(q.v.)*.

**Daksha** *(Sk.)* A form of Brahmâ and his son in the Purânas But the *Rig Veda* states that "Daksha sprang from Aditi, and Aditi from Daksha", which proves him to be a personified correlating Creative Force acting on *all the planes*. The Orientalists seem very much perplexed what to make of him; but Roth is nearer the truth than any, when saying that Daksha is the spiritual power, and at the same time the male energy that generates the gods in eternity, which is represented by Aditi. The Purânas as a matter of course, anthropomorphize the idea, and show Daksha instituting "sexual intercourse on this earth", after trying every other means of procreation. The generative Force, spiritual at the commencement, becomes of course at the most material end of its evolution a procreative Force on the physical plane; and so far the Purânic allegory is correct, as the Secret Science teaches that our present mode of procreation began towards the end of the third Root-Race.

**Daladâ** *(Sk.)*A very precious relic of Gautama the Buddha; viz., his supposed left canine tooth preserved at the great temple at Kandy, Ceylon. Unfortunately, the relic shown is not genuine. The latter has been securely secreted for several hundred years, ever since the shameful and bigoted attempt by the Portuguese (the then ruling power in Ceylon) to steal and make away with the real relic. That which is shown in the place of the real thing is the monstrous tooth of some animal.

**Dama** *(Sk.)*. Restraint of the senses.

**Dambulla** *(Sk.)* The name of a huge rock in Ceylon. It is about 400 feet above the level of the sea. Its upper portion is excavated, and several large cave-temples, or Vihâras, are cut out of the solid rock, all of these being of pre-Christian date. They are considered as the best-preserved antiquities in the island. The North side of the rock is vertical and quite inaccessible, but on the South side, about 150 feet from its summit, its huge overhanging granite mass has been fashioned into a platform with a row of large cave-temples excavated in the surrounding walls—evidently at an enormous sacrifice of labour and money. Two Vihâras may he mentioned out of the many: the *Maha Râja Vihâra*, 172 ft. in length and 75 in breadth, in which there are upwards of fifty figures of Buddha, most of them larger than life and all formed from the solid rock. A well has been dug out at the foot of the central *Dâgoba* and from a fissure in the rock there constantly drips into it beautiful clear water which is kept for sacred purposes. In the other, the *Maha Dewiyo Vihâra*, there is to be seen a gigantic figure of the dead Gautama Buddha, 7 feet long, reclining on a couch and pillow cut out of solid rock like the rest. "This long, narrow and dark temple, the position and placid aspect of Buddha, together with the stillness of the place, tend to impress the beholder with the idea that he is in the chamber of death. The priest asserts . . . . that such was Buddha, and such were those (at his feet stands an attendant) who witnessed the last moments of his mortality" (Hardy's *East. Monachism*). The view from Dambulla is magnificent. On the large rock platform which seems to he now more visited by very intelligent tame white monkeys than by monks, there stands a huge Bo-Tree, one of the numerous scions from the original Bo-Tree under which the Lord Siddhârtha reached Nirvâna. "About 50 ft. from the summit there is a pond which, as the priests assert, is never without water." (The *Ceylon Almanac*, 1834.)

**Dammâpadan** (*Pali.*) A Buddhist work containing moral precepts.

**Dâna** (*Sk.*). Almsgiving to mendicants, lit., "charity", the first of the six Paramitas in Buddhism.

**Dânavas** (*Sk.*). Almost the same as *Daityas*; giants and demons, the opponents of the ritualistic gods.

**Dangma** (*Sk.*) In Esotericism a purified Soul. A Seer and an Initiate; one who has attained full wisdom.

**Daos** (*Chald.*) The seventh King (Shepherd) of the divine Dynasty, who reigned over the Babylonians for the space of *ten sari,* or 36,000 years, a saros being of 3,600 years' duration. In his time four Annedoti, or Men-fishes (Dagons) made their appearance.

**Darâsta** (*Sk*) Ceremonial magic practised by the central Indian tribes, especially among the Kolarians.

**Dardanus** (*Gr.*) The Son of Jupiter and Electra, who received the Kabeiri gods as a dowry, and took them to Samothrace, where they were worshipped long before the hero laid the foundations of Troy, and before Tyre and Sidon were ever heard of, though Tyre was built 2,760 years B.C.

(See for fuller details "*Kabiri*".)

**Darha** (*Sk.*) The ancestral spirits of the Kolarians.

**Darsanas** (*Sk.*) The Schools of Indian philosophy, of which there are six; *Shad-darsanas* or six demonstrations.

**Dasa-sil** (*Pali.*) The ten obligations or commandments taken by and binding upon the priests of Buddha; the five obligations or *Pansil* are taken by laymen.

**Dava** (*Tib.*) The moon, in Tibetan astrology.

**Davkina** (*Chald.*) The wife of Hea, "the goddess of the lower regions, the consort of the Deep", the mother of Merodach, the Bel of later times, and mother to many river-gods, Hea being the god of the lower regions, the "lord of the Sea or abyss", and also the lord of Wisdom.

**Dayanisi** (*Aram.*). The god worshipped by the Jews along with other Semites, as the "Ruler of men"; Dionysos—the Sun; whence Jehovah Nissi, or Iao-Nisi, the same as Dio-nysos or Jove of Nyssa. (See *Isis Unveil.* II. 526.)

**Day of Brahmâ**. See "Brahmâ's Day" etc.

**Dayus** or *Dyaus* (*Sk*). A Vedic term. The unrevealed Deity, or that which reveals Itself only as light and the bright day—metaphorically.

**Death**, *Kiss of.* According to the Kabbalah, the earnest follower does not die by the power of the Evil Spirit, Yetzer ha Rah, but by a kiss from the mouth of Jehovah Tetragrammaton, meeting him in the Haikal Ahabah or Palace of Love. [w.w.w.]

**Dei termini** (*Lat.*). The name for pillars with human heads representing Hermes, placed at cross-roads by the ancient Greeks and Romans. Also the general name for deities presiding over boundaries and frontiers.

**Deist.** One who admits the existence of a god or gods, but claims to know nothing of either and denies revelation. A Freethinker of olden times.

**Demerit.** In Occult and Buddhistic parlance, a constituent of Karma. It is through *avidya* or ignorance of *vidya*, divine illumination, that merit and demerit are produced. Once an Arhat obtains full illumination and perfect control over his personality and lower nature, he ceases to create merit and demerit

**Demeter** The Hellenic name for the Latin Ceres, the goddess of corn and tillage. The astronomical sign, Virgo. The Eleusinian Mysteries were celebrated in her honour.

**Demiurgic Mind**.The same as "Universal Mind". Mahat, the first "product" of Brahmâ, or himself.

**Demiurgos** (*Gr*) The Demiurge or Artificer; the Supernal Power which built the universe. Freemasons derive from this word their phrase of "Supreme Architect ". With the Occultists it is the third manifested Logos, or Plato's "second god", the second logos being represented by him as the "Father", the only Deity that he dared mention as an Initiate into the Mysteries.

**Demon est Deus inversus** (*Lat*) A Kabbalistic axiom; lit., "the devil is god reversed"; which means that there is neither evil nor good, but that the forces which create the one create the other, according to the nature of the materials they find to work upon.

**Demonologia** *(Gr.)*. Treatises or Discourses upon Demons, or Gods in their dark aspects.

**Demons.** According to the Kabbalah, the demons dwell in the world of Assiah, the world of matter and of the "shells"' of the dead. They are the Klippoth. There are Seven Hells, whose demon dwellers represent the vices personified. Their prince is Samael, his female companion is Isheth Zenunim—the woman of prostitution: united in aspect, they are named "The Beast", Chiva. [w.w.w.]

**Demrusch** (*Pers.*). A Giant in the mythology of ancient Iran.

**Denis,** *Angoras.* "A physician of Paris, astrologer and alchemist in the XIVth century" (*R.M. Cyclopædia*).

**Deona Mati**. In the Kolarian dialect, one who exorcises evil spirits.

**Dervish.** A Mussulman—Turkish or Persian—ascetic. A nomadic and wandering monk. Dervishes, however, sometimes live in communities. They are often called the "whirling charmers". Apart from his austerities of life, prayer and contemplation, the Turkish, Egyptian, or Arabic devotee presents but little similarity with the Hindu fakir, who is also a Mussulman. The latter may become a saint and holy mendicant the former will never reach beyond his second class of occult manifestations. The dervish may also be a strong mesmerizer, but he will never voluntarily submit to the abominable and almost incredible self-punishment which the fakir invents for himself with an ever-increasing avidity, until nature succumbs and he dies in slow and excruciating tortures. The most dreadful operations, such as flaying the limbs alive; cutting off the toes, feet, and legs; tearing out the eyes and causing one's self to be buried alive up to the chin in the earth, and passing whole months in this posture, seem child's play to them. The Dervish must not be confused with the Hindu *sanyâsi or yogi*. (See "Fakir").

**Desatir**. A very ancient Persian work called the *Book of Shet*. It speaks of the *thirteen* Zoroasters, and is very mystical.

**Deva** (*Sk.*). A god, a "resplendent" deity. Deva-Deus, from the root *div* "to shine". A Deva is a celestial being—whether good, bad, or indifferent. Devas inhabit "the three worlds", which are the *three planes* above us. There are 33 groups or 330 millions of them.

**Deva Sarga** (*Sk.*). Creation: the origin of the principles, said to be Intelligence born of the qualities or the attributes of nature.

**Devachan** (*Sk.*). The "dwelling of the gods". A state intermediate between two earth-lives, into which the EGO (Atmâ-Buddhi-Manas, or the Trinity made One) enters, after its separation from Kâma Rupa, and the disintegration of the lower principles on earth.

**Devajnânas** (*Sk.*). or *Daivajna*. The higher classes of celestial beings, those who possess divine knowledge.

**Devaki** (*Sk.*). The mother of Krishna. She was shut up in a dungeon by her brother, King Kansa, for fear of the fulfilment of a prophecy which stated that a son of his sister should dethrone and kill him. Notwithstanding the strict watch kept, Devaki was overshadowed by Vishnu, the holy Spirit, and thus gave birth to that god's *avatara*, Krishna. (See "Kansa".)

**Deva-laya** (*Sk.*). "The shrine of a Deva". The name given to all Brahmanical temples.

**Deva-lôkas** (*Sk.*). The abodes of the Gods or Devas in superior spheres. The seven celestial worlds above Meru.

**Devamâtri** (*Sk.*). Lit., "the mother of the gods". A title of Aditi, Mystic Space.

**Dêvanâgarî** (*Sk.*). Lit., "the language or letters of the dêvas" or gods. The characters of the Sanskrit language. The alphabet and the art of writing were kept secret for ages, as the *Dwijas* (Twice-born) and the *Dikshitas* (Initiates) alone were permitted to use this art. It was a crime for a. Sudra to recite a verse of the *Vedas*, and for any of the two lower castes (Vaisya and Sudra) to know the letters was an offence punishable by death. Therefore is the word *lipi*, "writing", absent from the oldest MSS., a fact which gave the Orientalists the erroneous and rather incongruous idea that writing was not only unknown before the day of Pânini, but even to that sage himself That the greatest grammarian the world has ever produced should be ignorant of writing would indeed be the greatest and most incomprehensible phenomenon of all.

**Devapi** (*Sk.*). A Sanskrit Sage of the race of Kuru, who, together with another Sage (Moru), is supposed to live throughout the four ages and until the coming of *Maitreya Buddha*, or *Kalki* (the last Avatar of Vishnu); who, like all the Saviours of the World in their last appearance, like Sosiosh of the Zoroastrians and the *Rider* of St. Johns *Revelation*, will appear seated on a *White Horse*. The two, Devapi and Moru, are supposed to live in a Himalayan retreat called *Kalapa* or *Katapa*. This is a Purânic allegory.

**Devarshis,** or *Deva-rishi* (*Sk*). Lit., "gods rishis"; the divine or god like saints, those sages who attain a fully divine nature on earth.

**Devasarman** (*Sk.*). A very ancient author who died about a century after Gautama Buddha. He wrote two famous works, in which he denied the existence of both Ego and non-Ego, the one as successfully as the other.

**Dhârana** (*Sk*). That state in Yoga practice when the mind has to be fixed unflinchingly on some object of meditation.

**Dhâranî**(*Sk.*). In Buddhism—both Southern and Northern—and also in Hinduism, it means simply a *mantra* or *mantras*—sacred verses from the *Rig Veda*. In days of old these mantras or Dhâranî were all considered mystical and practically efficacious in their use. At present, however, it is the Yogâchârya school alone which proves the claim in practice. When chanted according to given instructions a **Dhâranî** produces wonderful effects. Its occult power, however, does not reside in the *words* but in the inflexion or accent given and the resulting sound originated thereby. (See "Mantra" and "Akasa").

**Dharma** (*Sk.*). The sacred Law; the Buddhist Canon.

**Dharmachakra** (*Sk.*). Lit., The turning of the "wheel of the Law". The emblem of Buddhism as a system of cycles and rebirths or reincarnations.

**Dharmakâya** (*Sk*). Lit., "the glorified spiritual body" called the "Vesture of Bliss". The third, or highest of the *Trikâya* (Three Bodies), the attribute developed by every "Buddha", i.e., every initiate who has crossed or reached the end of what is called the "fourth Path" (in esotericism the sixth "portal" prior to his entry on the seventh). The highest of the *Trikâya*, it is the *fourth* of the *Buddhakchêtra*, or Buddhic planes of consciousness, represented figuratively in Buddhist asceticism as a robe or vesture of luminous Spirituality. In popular Northern Buddhism these vestures or robes are: (1) Nirmanakâya (2) Sambhogakâya (3) and Dharmakâya the last being the highest and most sublimated of all, as it places the ascetic on the threshold of Nirvâna. (See, however, the *Voice of the Silence,* page 96, *Glossary,* for the true *esoteric* meaning.)

**Dharmaprabhasa** (*Sk*). The name of the Buddha who will appear during the seventh Root-race. (See "Ratnâvabhâsa Kalpa", when sexes will exist no longer).

**Dharmasmriti Upasthâna** (*Sk*). A very long compound word containing a very mystical warning. "Remember, the constituents (of human nature) originate *according to the Nidânas, and are-not* originally the Self", which means—that, which the Esoteric Schools teach, and not the ecclesiastical interpretation.

**Dharmâsôka** (*Sk.*). The name given to the first Asoka after his conversion to Buddhism,—King Chandragupta, who served all his long life "Dharma", or the law of Buddha. King Asoka (the second) was not *converted,* but was born a Buddhist.

**Dhâtu** (*Pali*). Relics of Buddha's body collected after his cremation.

**Dhruva** (*Sk*). An Aryan Sage, now the Pole Star. A *Kshatriya* (one of the warrior caste) who became through religious austerities a *Rishi,* and was, for this reason, raised by Vishnu to this eminence in the skies. Also called *Grah-Âdhâr* or "the pivot of the planets".

**Dhyan Chohans** (*Sk*). Lit., "The Lords of Light". The highest gods, answering to the Roman Catholic Archangels. The divine Intelligences charged with the supervision of Kosmos.

**Dhyâna** (*Sk.*). In Buddhism one of the six Paramitas of perfection, a state of abstraction which carries the ascetic practising it far above this plane of sensuous perception and out of the world of matter. Lit., "contemplation". The six stages of Dhyan differ only in the degrees of abstraction of the personal Ego from sensuous life.

**Dhyani Bodhisattyas** (*Sk.*). In Buddhism, the five sons of the Dhyani-Buddhas. They have a mystic meaning in Esoteric Philosophy.

**Dhyani Buddhas** (*Sk.*). They "of the Merciful Heart"; worshipped especially in Nepaul. These have again a secret meaning.

**Dhyani Pasa** (*Sk.*). "The rope of the Dhyanis" or Spirits; the Ring "Pass not" (See *S. D.,* Stanza V., Vol. I., p. 129).

**Diakka.** Called by Occultists and Theosophists "spooks" and "shells", i.e., phantoms from *Kâma Loka.* A word invented by the great American Seer, Andrew Jackson Davis, to denote what he considers untrustworthy

"Spirits". In his own words: "A *Diakka* (from the Summerland) is one who takes insane delight in *playing parts,* in juggling tricks, in *personating* opposite characters; to whom prayer and profane utterances are of equivalue; surcharged with a passion for lyrical narrations; . . . morally deficient, he is without the active feelings of justice, philanthropy, or tender affection. He knows nothing of what men call the sentiment of gratitude; the ends of hate and love are the same to him; his motto is often fearful and terrible to others—SELF is the whole of private living, and exalted annihilation *the end of all private life.* Only yesterday, one said to a lady medium, signing himself *Swedenborg,* this: 'Whatsoever is, has been, will be, or may be, that I AM.; and private life is but the aggregative phantasms of thinking throb-lets, rushing in their rising onward to the central heart of eternal death' (*The Diakka and their Victims*; "an explanation of the False and Repulsive in Spiritualism.") These "Diakka" are then simply the communicating and materializing so-called "Spirits" of Mediums and Spiritualists.

**Dianoia** (*Gr.*). The same as the Logos. The eternal source of thought, "divine ideation", which is the root of all thought. (See "Ennoia.")

**Dido,** or *Elissa.* Astarte; the Virgin of the Sea—who crushes the Dragon under her foot; The patroness of the Phœnician mariners. A Queen of Carthage who fell in love with Æneas according to Virgil.

**Digambara** (*Sk.*). A naked mendicant. Lit., "clothed with Space". A name of Siva in his character of Rudra, the Yogi.

**Dii Minores** (*Lat.*). The inferior or "reflected group of the twelve gods "or *Dii Majores,* described by Cicero in his *De Natura Deorum*, I. 13.

**Dîk** (*Sk*). Space, Vacuity.

**Diktamnon** (*Gr.*), or *Dictemnus (Dittany).* A curious plant possessing very occult and mystical properties and well-known from ancient times. It was sacred to the Moon-Goddesses. Luna, Astarte, Diana. The Cretan name of Diana was *Diktynna,* and as such the goddess wore a wreath made of this magic plant. The *Dihtamnon* is an evergreen shrub whose contact, as claimed in Occultism, develops and at the same time cures somnambulism. Mixed with Verbena it will produce clairvoyance and ecstasy. Pharmacy attributes to the *Dihtamnon* strongly sedative and quieting properties. It grows in abundance on Mount Dicte, in Crete, and enters into many *magical* performances resorted to by the *Cretans* even to this day.

**Diksha** (*Sk*). Initiation. *Dikshit,* an Initiate.

**Dingir** and *Mul-lil* (*Akkad.*). The Creative Gods.

**Dinur** (*Heb.*). The River of Fire whose flame burns the Souls of the guilty in the Kabbalistic allegory.

**Dionysos** (*Sk.*). The Demiurgos, who, like Osiris, was killed by the Titans and dismembered into fourteen parts. He was the personified Sun, or as the author of the *Great Dionysiak Myth* says "He is Phanes, the spirit of material visibility, Kyklops giant of the Universe, with one bright solar eye, the growth-power of the world, the all-pervading animism of things, son of Semele Dionysos was born at Nysa or Nissi, the name given by the Hebrews to Mount Sinai (Exodus xvii. 15), the birthplace of Osiris, which identifies both suspiciously with "Jehovah Nissi". (See *Isis Unv.* II. 165, 526.)

**Dioscuri** (*Gr.*). The name of Castor and Pollux, the sons of Jupiter and Leda. Their festival, the *Dioscuria*, was celebrated with much rejoicing by the Lacedæmonians.

**Dîpamkara** (*Sk.*). Lit., "the Buddha of fixed light"; a predecessor of Gautama, the Buddha.

**Diploteratology** (*Gr.*). Production of mixed Monsters; in abbreviation *teratology*.

**Dis** (*Gr.*). In the Theogony of Damascius, the same as *Protogonos*, the "first born light", called by that author "the disposer of all things.

**Dises** (*Scand.*). The later name for the divine women called Walky-rics, Norns, &c., in the *Edda*.

**Disk**-worship. This was very common in Egypt but not till later times, as it began with Amenoph III., a Dravidian, who brought it from Southern India and Ceylon. It was Sun-worship under another form, the *Aten-Nephru*, Aten-Ra being identical with the Adonai of the Jews, the "Lord of Heaven" or the Sun. The winged disk was the emblem of the Soul. The Sun was at one time the symbol of Universal Deity shining *on the whole world and all creatures;* the Sabæans regarded the Sun as the Demiurge and a Universal Deity, as did also the Hindus, and as do the Zoroastrians to this day. The Sun is undeniably the one creator of physical nature. Lenormant was obliged, notwithstanding his orthodox Christianity, to denounce the resemblance between disk and Jewish worship. "Aten represents the Adonai or Lord, the Assyrian Tammuz, and the Syrian Adonis"(*The Gr. Dionys. Myth.*)

**Divyachakchus** (*Sk.*). Lit., "celestial Eye" or divine seeing, perception. It is the first of the six "Abhijnas" (*q.v.*); the faculty developed by Yoga practice to perceive any object in the Universe, at whatever distance.

**Divyasrôtra** *(Sk)*. Lit., "celestial Ear" Or divine hearing. The second "Abhijna", or the faculty of understanding the language or sound produced by any living being on Earth.

**Djâti** *(Sk.)*. One of the twelve "Nidanas" (*q.v.*); the cause and the effect in the mode of birth taking place according to the "Chatur Yoni"(*q.v.*), when in each case a being, whether man or animal, is placed in one of the six (esoteric seven) Gâti or paths of sentient existence, which esoterically, counting downward, are: (1) the highest Dhyani (*Anupadaka*); (2) Devas; (3) Men; (4) Elementals or Nature Spirits; (5) Animals; (6) lower Elementals; (7) organic Germs. These are in the popular or exoteric nomenclature, Devas, Men, Asûras, Beings in Hells, Prêtas (hungry demons), and Animals.

**Djin** *(Arab.)*. Elementals; Nature Sprites; Genii. The *Djins* or *Jins* are much dreaded in Egypt, Persia and elsewhere.

**Djnâna** *(Sk)*, or *Jnâna.* Lit., Knowledge; esoterically, "supernal or divine knowledge acquired by Yoga". Written also *Gnyana.*

**Docetæ** *(Gr.)*. Lit.,"The Illusionists". The name given by orthodox Christians to those Gnostics who held that Christ did not, nor could he, suffer death actually, but that, if such a thing had happened, it was merely an illusion which they explained in various ways.

**Dodecahedron** *(Gr.)*. According to Plato, the Universe is built by "the first begotten" on the geometrical figure of the Dodecahedron. (See *Timaeus*).

**Dodona** *(Gr.)*. An ancient city in Thessaly, famous for its Temple of Jupiter and its oracles. According to ancient legends, the town was founded by a *dove.*

**Donar** *(Scand.)*, or *Thunar, Thor.* In the North the God of Thunder. He was the Jupiter Tonans of Scandinavia. Like as the oak was devoted to Jupiter so was it sacred to Thor, and his altars were over shadowed with oak trees. Thor, or Donar, was the offspring of Odin, "the omnipotent God of Heaven", and of Mother Earth.

**Dondam-pai-den-pa** *(Tib.)*. The same as the Sanskrit term *Paramarthasatya* or "absolute truth", the highest spiritual self-consciousness and perception, divine self-consciousness, a very mystical term.

**Doppelgänger** *(Germ.)*. A synonym of the "Double" and of the "Astral body" in occult parlance.

**Dorjesempa** *(Tib.)*. The "Diamond Soul", a name of the celestial Buddha.

**Dorjeshang** *(Tib.)*. A title of Buddha in his highest aspect; a name of the supreme Buddha; also *Dorje*.

**Double.** The same as the "Astral body" or "Doppelgänger".

**Double Image.** The name among the Jewish Kabbalists for the *Dual Ego*, called respectively: the Higher, *Metatron*, and the Lower, *Samael*. They are figured allegorically as the two inseparable companions of man through life, the one his Guardian Angel, the other his Evil Demon.

**Dracontia** *(Gr.)*. Temples dedicated to the Dragon, the emblem of the Sun, the symbol of Deity, of Life and Wisdom. The Egyptian Karnac, the Carnac in Britanny, and Stonehenge are Dracontia well known to all.

**Drakôn** *(Gr.)* or Dragon. Now considered a "mythical" monster, perpetuated in the West only on seals,. &c., as a heraldic griffin, and the Devil slain by St. George, &c. In fact an extinct antediluvian monster In Babylonian antiquities it is referred to as the "scaly one" and connected on many gems with Tiamat the sea. "The Dragon of the Sea" is repeatedly mentioned. In Egypt, it is the star of the Dragon (then the North Pole Star), the origin of the connection of almost all the gods with the Dragon. Bel and the Dragon, Apollo and Python, Osiris and Typhon, Sigur and Fafnir, and finally St. George and the Dragon, are the same. They were all solar gods, and wherever we find the Sun there also is the Dragon, the symbol of Wisdom—Thoth-Hermes. The Hierophants of Egypt and of Babylon styled themselves "Sons of the Serpent-God" and "Sons of the Dragon". "I am a Serpent, I am a Druid", said the Druid of the Celto-Britannic regions, for the Serpent and the Dragon were both types of Wisdom, Immortality and Rebirth. As the serpent casts its old skin only to reappear in a new one, so does the immortal Ego cast off one personality but to assume another.

**Draupnir** *(Scand.)*. The golden armlet of Wodan or Odin, the companion of the spear Gungnir which he holds in his right hand; both are endowed with wonderful magic properties.

**Dravidians.** A group of tribes inhabiting Southern India; the aborigines.

**Dravya** *(Sk.)*. Substance (metaphysically).

**Drishti** *(Sk.)*. Scepticism; unbelief.

**Druids.** A sacerdotal caste which flourished in Britain and Gaul. They were Initiates who admitted females into their sacred order, and initiated them into the mysteries of their religion. They never entrusted their sacred verses and scriptures to writing, but, like the Brahmans of old, committed them to memory; a feat which, according to the statement of Cæsar took twenty years to accomplish. Like the Parsis they had no images or statues of their gods. The Celtic religion considered it blasphemy to represent any god, even of a minor character, under a human figure. It would have been well if the Greek and Roman Christians had learnt this lesson from the "pagan" Druids. The three chief commandments of their religion were:— "Obedience to divine laws; concern for the welfare of mankind; suffering with fortitude all the evils of life".

**Druzes.** A large sect, numbering about 100,000 adherents, living on Mount Lebanon in Syria. Their rites are very mysterious, and no traveller, who has written anything about them, knows for a certainty the whole truth. They are the *Sufis* of Syria. They resent being called Druzes as an insult, but call themselves the "disciples of Hamsa ", their Messiah, who came to them in the ninth century from the "Land of the Word of God", which land and word they kept religiously secret. The Messiah to come will be the same Hamsa, but called *Hakem*—the "All-Healer ". (See *Isis Unveiled,* II 308, *et seq.*)

**Dudaim** (*Heb.*). Mandrakes. The *Atropa Mandragova* plant is mentioned in *Genesis,* xxx., 14, and in *Canticles*: the name is related in Hebrew to words meaning "breasts" and "love", the plant was notorious as a love charm, and has been used in many forms of black magic. [w.w.w.]

Dudaim in Kabbalistic parlance is the Soul and Spirit; any two things united in love and friendship *(dodim)*. "Happy is he who preserves his *dudai*m (higher and lower Manas) inseparable."

**Dugpas** (*Tib.*). Lit., "Red Caps," a sect in Tibet. Before the advent of *Tsong-ka-pa* in the fourteenth century, the Tibetans, whose Buddhism had deteriorated and been dreadfully adulterated with the tenets of the old *Bhon* religion,—were all Dugpas. From that century, however, and after the rigid laws imposed upon the *Gelukpas* (yellow caps) and the general reform and purification of Buddhism (or Lamaism), the Dugpas have given themselves over more than ever to sorcery, immorality, and drunkenness. Since then the word Dugpas has become a synonym of "sorcerer", "adept of black magic" and everything vile. There are few, if any, Dugpas in Eastern Tibet, but they congregate in Bhutan, Sikkim, and the borderlands generally. Europeans not being permitted to penetrate further than those borders, the Orientalists never having studied Buddho-Lamaism in Tibet proper, but judging of it on hearsay and from what Cosmo di Köros, Schlagintweit, and a few others have learnt of it from

Dugpas, confuse both religions and bring them under one head. They thus give out to the public pure Dugpaism instead of Buddho-Lamaism. In short Northern Buddhism in its purified, metaphysical form is almost entirely unknown.

**Dukkha** (*Sk.*). Sorrow, pain.

**Dumah** (*Heb.*). The Angel of Silence (Death) in the Kabbala.

**Durga** (*Sk*). Lit., "inaccessible". The female potency of a god; the name of Kali, the wife of Siva, the *Mahesvara*, or "the great god".

**Dustcharitra** (*Sk.*). The "ten evil acts"; namely, three acts of the body viz., taking life, theft and adultery; four evil acts of the mouth, viz., lying, exaggeration in accusations, slander, and foolish talk; and three evil acts of mind (Lower Manas), viz., envy, malice or revenge, and unbelief.

**Dwapara Yuga** (*Sk.*). The third of the "Four Ages" in Hindu Philosophy; or the second age counted from below.

**Dwarf of Death**. In the *Edda* of the Norsemen, Iwaldi, the Dwarf of Death, hides Life in the depths of the great ocean, and then sends her up into the world at the right time. This Life is Iduna, the beauti-ful maiden, the daughter of the "Dwarf". She is the Eve of the Scandinavian Lays, for she gives of the apples of ever-renewed youth to the gods of Asgard to eat; but these, instead of being cursed for so doing and doomed to die, give thereby renewed youth yearly to the earth and to men, after every short and sweet sleep in the arms of the Dwarf. Iduna is raised from the Ocean when Bragi (*q.v.*), the Dreamer of Life, without spot or blemish, crosses asleep the silent waste of waters. Bragi is the divine ideation of Life, and Iduna living Nature—Prakriti, Eve.

**Dwellers** (on the Threshold). A term invented by Bulwer Lytton in *Zanoni*; but in Occultism the word "Dweller" is an occult term used by students for long ages past, and refers to certain maleficent astral Doubles of defunct persons.

**Dwesa** (*Sk.*). Anger. One of the three principal states of mind (of which 63 are enumerated), which are *Râga*—pride or evil desire; *Dwesa*—anger, of which hatred is a part; and *Moha*—the ignorance of truth. These three are to be steadily avoided.

**Dwijâ** (*Sk.*). "Twice-born". In days of old this term was used only of the Initiated Brahmans; but now it is applied to every man belonging to the first of the four castes, who has undergone a certain ceremony.

**Dwija Brahman** (*Sk.*). The investure with the sacred thread that now constitutes the "second birth". Even a Sudra who chooses to pay for the honour becomes, after the ceremony of passing through a silver or golden cow—a *dwijâ*.

**Dwipa** *(Sk.)*. An island or a continent. The Hindus have seven *(Sapta dwipa)*; the Buddhists only four. This is owing to a misunderstood reference of the Lord Buddha who, using the term metaphorically, applied the word *dwipa* to the races of men. The four Root-races which preceded our fifth, were compared by Siddhârtha to four continents or isles which studded the ocean of birth and death—*Samsâra*.

**Dynasties.** In India there are two, the Lunar and the Solar, or the *Somavansa* and the *Suryavansa*. In Chaldea and Egypt there were also two distinct kinds of dynasties, the *divine* and the *human*. In both countries people were ruled in the beginning of time by Dynasties of Gods. In Chaldea they reigned one hundred and twenty Sari, or in all 432,000 years; which amounts to the same figures as a Hindu Mahayuga 4,320,000 years. The chronology prefacing the *Book of Genesis* (English translation) is given "Before Christ, 4004". But the figures are a rendering by solar years. In the original Hebrew, which preserved a lunar calculation, the figures are 4,320 years. This "coincidence" is well explained in Occultism.

**Dyookna** *(Kab.)*. The shadow of eternal Light. The "Angels of the Presence" or archangels. The same as the *Ferouer* in the *Vendidad* and other Zoroastrian works.

**Dzyn** or Dzyan *(Tib.)*. Written also *Dzen*. A corruption of the Sanskrit Dhyan and *jnâna* (or *gnyâna* phonetically)—Wisdom, divine knowledge. In Tibetan, learning is called *dzin*.

# E

**E.**—The fifth letter of the English alphabet. The *he* (soft) of the Hebrew alphabet becomes in the Ehevi system of reading that language an E. Its numerical value is five, and its symbolism is a *window*; the womb, in the Kabbala. In the order of the divine names it stands for the fifth, which is *Hadoor* or the "majestic" and the "splendid."

**Ea** *(Chald.)* also *Hea*. The second god of the original Babylonian trinity composed of Anu, Hea and Bel. Hea was the "Maker of Fate", "Lord of the Deep", "God of Wisdom and Knowledge", and "Lord of the City of Eridu".

**Eagle.** This symbol is one of the most ancient. With the Greeks and Persians it was sacred to the Sun; with the Egyptians, under the name of

*Ah*, to Horus, and the Kopts worshipped the eagle under the name of *Ahom*. It was regarded as the sacred emblem of Zeus by the Greeks, and as that of the highest god by the Druids. The symbol has passed down to our day, when following the example of the pagan Marius, who, in the second century B.C. used the double-headed eagle as the ensign of Rome, the Christian crowned heads of Europe made the double-headed sovereign of the air sacred to themselves and their scions. Jupiter was satisfied with a one-headed eagle and so was the Sun. The imperial houses of Russia, Poland, Austria, Germany, and the late Empire of the Napoleons, have adopted a two-headed eagle as their device.

**Easter.** The word evidently comes from Ostara, the Scandinavian goddess of spring. She was the symbol of the resurrection of all nature and was worshipped in early spring. It was a custom with the pagan Norsemen at that time to exchange coloured eggs called the eggs of Ostara. These have now become Easter-Eggs. As expressed in *Asgard and the Gods:* "Christianity put another meaning on the old custom, by connecting it with the feast of the Resurrection of the Saviour, who, like the hidden life in the egg, slept in the grave for three days before he awakened to new life". This was the more natural since Christ was identified with that same Spring Sun which awakens in all his glory, after the dreary and long death of winter. (See "Eggs".)

**Ebionites** (*Heb.*). Lit., "the poor"; the earliest sect of Jewish Christians, the other being the Nazarenes. They existed when the term "Christian" was not yet heard of. Many of the relations of *Iassou* (Jesus), the adept ascetic around whom the legend of Christ was formed, were among the Ebionites. As the existence of these mendicant ascetics can be traced at least a century earlier than chronological Christianity, it is an additional proof that *Iassou* or *Jeshu* lived during the reign of Alexander Jannæus at Lyd (or Lud), where he was put to death as stated in the *Sepher Toldos Jeshu.*

**Ecbatana**. A famous city in Media worthy of a place among the seven wonders of the world. It is thus described by Draper in his *Conflict between Religion and Science*, chap. i, . . "The cool summer retreat of the Persian Kings, was defended by seven encircling walls of hewn and polished blocks, the interior ones in succession of increasing height, and of different colours, in astrological accordance with the seven planets. The palace was roofed with silver tiles; its beams were plated with gold. At midnight in its halls, the sun was rivalled by many a row of naphta cressets. A paradise, that luxury of the monarchs of the East, was planted in the midst of the city. The Persian Empire was truly the garden of the world."

**Echath** (*Heb.*). The same as the following—the "One", but feminine.

**Echod** (*Heb.*) or *Echad*. "One", masculine, applied to Jehovah.

**Eclectic Philosophy**. One of the names given to the Neo-Platonic school of Alexandria.

**Ecstasis** (*Gr.*). A psycho-spiritual state; a physical trance which induces clairvoyance and a beatific state bringing on visions.

**Edda** (*Iceland.*). Lit., "great-grandmother"of the Scandinavian Lays. It was Bishop Brynjüld Sveinsson, who collected them and brought them to light in 1643. There are two collections of Sagas, translated by the Northern Skalds, and there are two *Eddas*. The earliest is of unknown authorship and date and its antiquity is very great. These Sagas were collected in the XIth century by an Icelandic priest; the second is a collection of the history (or myths) of the gods spoken of in the first, which became the Germanic deities, giants, dwarfs and heroes.

**Eden** (*Heb.*). "Delight", pleasure. In *Genesis* the "Garden of Delight" built by God; in the Kabbala the "Garden of Delight", a place of Initiation into the mysteries. Orientalists identify it with a place which was situated in Babylonia in the district of Karduniyas, called also Gan-dunu, which is almost like the Gan-eden of the Jews. (See the works of Sir H. Rawlinson, and G. Smith.) That district has four rivers, Euphrates, Tigris, Surappi, Ukni. The two first have been adopted without any change by the Jews; the other two they have probably transformed into "Gihon and Pison", so as to have something original. The following are some of the reasons for the identification of Eden, given by Assyriologists. The cities of Babylon, Larancha and Sippara, were founded before the flood, according to the chronology of the Jews. "Surippak was the city of the ark, the mountain east of the Tigris was the resting place of the ark, Babylon was the site of the tower, and Ur of the Chaldees the birthplace of Abraham." And, as Abraham, "the first leader of the Hebrew race, migrated from Ur to Harran in Syria and from thence to Palestine", the best Assyriologists think that it is "so much evidence in favour of the hypothesis that Chaldea was the original home of these stories (in the Bible) and that the Jews received them originally from the Babylonians".

**Edom** (*Heb.*). Edomite Kings. A deeply concealed mystery is to he found in the allegory of the seven Kings of Edorn, who "reigned in the land of Edom before there reigned any King over the children of Israel". (*Gen. xxxvi*. 31.) The Kabbala teaches that this Kingdom was one of "unbalanced forces' and necessarily of unstable character. The world of Israel is a type of the condition of the worlds which came into existence subsequently to the later period when the equilibrium had become established. [w.w. w.]

On the other hand the Eastern Esoteric philosophy teaches that the seven Kings of Edom are not the type of perished worlds or unbalanced forces, but the symbol of the seven human Root-races, four of which have passed away, the fifth is passing, and two are still to come. Though in the language of esoteric *blinds*, the hint in St. John's *Revelation* is clear enough when it states in chapter xvii , 10: "And there are seven Kings; five are fallen, and one (the fifth, still) is, and the other (the sixth Root-race) is not yet come Had all the seven Kings of Edom perished as worlds of "unbalanced forces", how could the fifth still be, and the other or others "not yet come"? In The *Kabbalah Unveiled*, we read on page 48, "The seven Kings had died and their possessions had been broken up", and a footnote emphasizes the statement by saying, "these seven Kings are the Edomite Kings".

**Edris** (*Arab.*), or *Idris*. Meaning "the learned One", an epithet applied by the Arabs to Enoch.

**Eggs** (Easter). Eggs were symbolical from an early time. There was the "Mundane Egg", in which Brahmâ gestated, with the Hindus the *Hiranya-Gharba*, and the Mundane Egg of the Egyptians, which proceeds from the mouth of the "unmade and eternal deity", Kneph, and which is the emblem of generative power. Then the Egg of Babylon, which hatched Ishtar, and was said to have fallen from heaven into the Euphrates. Therefore coloured eggs were used yearly during spring in almost every country, and in Egypt were exchanged as sacred symbols in the spring-time, which was, is, and ever will be, the emblem of birth or rebirth, cosmic and human, celestial and terrestrial. They were hung up in Egyptian temples and are so suspended to this day in Mahometan mosques.

**Egkosmioi** (*Gk*). "The intercosmic gods, each of which presides over a great number of daemons to whom they impart their power and change it from one to another at will", says Proclus, and he adds, that which is taught in the esoteric doctrine. In his system he shows the uppermost regions from the zenith of the Universe to the moon belonging to the gods, or planetary Spirits, according to their hierarchies and classes. The highest among them were the twelve *Huper-ouranioi*, the super-celestial gods. Next to the latter, in rank and power, came the *Egkosmioi*.

**Ego** (*Lat.*). "Self"; the consciousness in man "I am I"—or the feeling of "I-am-ship". Esoteric philosophy teaches the existence of two Egos in man, the mortal or personal, and the Higher, the Divine and the Impersonal, calling the former "personality" and the latter "Individuality Egoity. From the word "Ego". Egoity means "individuality", never "personality", and is the opposite of egoism or "selfishness", the characteristic par excellence of the latter.

**Egregores.** Eliphas Lévi calls them "the chiefs of the souls who are the spirits of energy and action"; whatever that may or may not mean. The Oriental Occultists describe the *Egregores* as Beings whose bodies and essence is a tissue of the so-called *astral light.* They are the shadows of the higher Planetary Spirits whose bodies are of the essence of the higher divine light.

**Eheyeh** (*Heb.*). "I am", according to Ibn Gebirol, but not in the sense of "I am that I am".

**Eidolon** (*Gr.*). The same as that which we term the human phantom, the astral form.

**Eka** (*Sk.*). "One"; also a synonym of *Mahat,* the *Universal Mind,* as the principle of Intelligence.

**Ekana-rupa** (*Sk.*). The One (and the Many) bodies or forms; a term applied by the Purânas to Deity.

**Ekasloka Shastra** (*Sk.*). A work on the *Shastras* (Scriptures) by Nagarjuna; a mystic work translated into Chinese.

**El-Elion** (*Heb.*). A name of the Deity *borrowed* by the Jews from the *Phœnician Elon*, a name of the Sun.

**Elementals.** Spirits of the Elements. The creatures evolved in the four Kingdoms or Elements—earth, air, fire, and water. They are called by the Kabbalists, Gnomes (of the earth), Sylphs (of the air), Salamanders (of the fire), and Undines (of the water). Except a few of the higher kinds, and their rulers, they are rather forces of nature than ethereal men and women. These forces, as the servile agents of the Occultists, may produce various effects; but if employed by" Elementaries" (*q.v.*) in which case they enslave the mediums—they will deceive the credulous. All the lower invisible beings generated on the 5th 6th, and 7th planes of our terrestrial atmosphere, are called Elementals Peris, Devs, Djins, Sylvans, Satyrs, Fauns, Elves, Dwarfs, Trolls, Kobolds, Brownies, Nixies, Goblins, Pinkies, Banshees, Moss People, White Ladies, Spooks, Fairies, etc., etc., etc.

**Elementaries**. Properly, the disembodied souls of the depraved; these souls having at some time prior to death separated from themselves their divine spirits, and so lost their chance for immortality; but at the present stage of learning it has been thought best to apply the term to the spooks or phantoms of disembodied persons, in general, to those whose temporary habitation is the Kâma Loka. Eliphas Lévi and some other Kabbalists make little distinction between elementary spirits who have been men, and those beings which people the elements, and are the blind forces of nature. Once divorced from their higher triads and their bodies, these souls remain in their *Kâma-rupic* envelopes, and are irresistibly drawn to the earth amid elements congenial to their gross natures. Their stay in the Kâma Loka varies as to its duration; but ends invariably in disintegration, dissolving like a column of mist, atom by atom, in the surrounding elements.

**Elephanta.** An island near Bombay, India, on which are the well-preserved ruins of the cave-temple, of that name. It is one of the most ancient in the country and is certainly a Cyclopeian work, though the late J. Fergusson has refused it a great antiquity.

**Eleusinia** (*Gr.*). The Eleusinian Mysteries were the most famous and the most ancient of all the Greek Mysteries (save the Samothracian), and were celebrated near the hamlet of Eleusis, not far from Athens. Epiphanius traces them to the days of Inachos (1800 B.C.), founded, as another version has it, by Eumolpus, a King of Thrace and a Hierophant. They were celebrated in honour of Demeter, the Greek Ceres and the Egyptian Isis; and the last act of the performance referred to a sacrificial victim of atonement and a resurrection, when the Initiate was admitted to the highest degree of "Epopt" (*q.v.*). The festival of the Mysteries began in the month of Boëdromion (September), the time of grape-gathering, and lasted from the 15th to the 22nd, seven days. The Hebrew feast of Tabernacles, the feast of *Ingatherings,* in the month of Ethanim (the seventh), also began on the 15th and ended on the 22nd of that month, The name of the month (Ethanim) is derived, according to some, from Adonim, Adonia, Attenim, Ethanim, and was in honour of Adonai or Adonis (Thammuz), whose death was lamented by the Hebrews in the groves of Bethlehem. The sacrifice of both "Bread and Wine" was performed before the Mysteries of initiation, and during the ceremony the mysteries were divulged to the candidates from the *petroma,* a kind of book made of two stone tablets (*petrai*), joined at one side and made to open like a volume. (See *Isis Unveiled* II., pp. 44 and 91, *et seq.,* for further explanations.)

**Elivagar** *(Scand.)*. The waters of Chaos, called in the cosmogony of the Norsemen "the stream of Elivagar".

**Elohîm** *(Heb.)*. Also *Alhim*, the word being variously spelled. Godfrey Higgins, who has written much upon its meaning, always spells it *Aleim*. The Hebrew letters are *aleph, lamed, hé, yod, mem*, and are numerically 1, 30, 5, 10, 40 = 86. It seems to be the plural of the feminine noun *Eloah*, ALH, formed by adding the common plural form IM, a masculine ending; and hence the whole seems to imply the emitted active and passive essences. As a title it is referred to "Binah" the Supernal Mother, as is also the fuller title IHVH ALHIM, Jehovah Elohim. As Binah leads on to seven succeedent Emanations, so "Elohim" has been said to represent a sevenfold power of godhead. [w.w. w.]

**Eloï** *(Gn.)*. The genius or ruler of Jupiter; its Planetary Spirit. (See Origen, *Contra Celsum*.)

**Elu** *(Sing.)*. An ancient dialect used in Ceylon.

**Emanation** *the Doctrine of*. In its metaphysical meaning, it is opposed to Evolution, yet one with it. Science teaches that evolution is physiologically a mode of generation in which the germ that develops the foetus pre-exists already in the parent, the development and final form and characteristics of that germ being accomplished in nature; and that in cosmology the process takes place blindly through the correlation of the elements, and their various compounds. Occultism answers that this is only the *apparent* mode, the real process being Emanation, guided by intelligent Forces under an immutable LAW. Therefore, while the Occultists and Theosophists believe thoroughly in the doctrine of Evolution as given out by Kapila and Manu, they are *Emanationists* rather than *Evolutionists*. The doctrine of Emanation was at one time universal. It was taught by the Alexandrian as well as by the Indian philosophers, by the Egyptian, the Chaldean and Hellenic Hierophants, and also by the Hebrews (in their Kabbala, and even in *Genesis)*. For it is only owing to deliberate mistranslation that the Hebrew word asdt has been translated "angels" from the Septuagint, when it means *Emanations, Æons*, precisely as with the Gnostics. Indeed, in Deuteronomy (xxxiii., 2) the word *asdt* or *ashdt* is translated as" fiery law", whilst the correct rendering of the passage should be "from his right hand went [not a fiery law, but a fire according to law"; viz., that the fire of one flame is imparted to, and caught up by another like as in a trail of inflammable substance. This is precisely emanation. As shown in Isis Unveiled: "In Evolution, as it is now beginning to he understood, there is supposed to be in all matter an impulse to take on a higher form—a supposition clearly expressed by Manu and other Hindu philosophers of the highest antiquity. The philosopher's tree illustrates it in the case of the zinc solution. The controversy between the followers of this school and the Emanationists may he briefly stated thus The Evolutionist stops all inquiry at the borders of ' the Unknowable "; the Emanationist believes that nothing can be evolved—or, as the word means, unwombed or born—except it has first been involved, thus indicating that life is from a spiritual potency above the whole."

**Empusa** (*Gr.*). A ghoul, a vampire, an evil demon taking various forms.

**En** (or **Ain**) **Soph** (*Heb.*). The endless, limitless and boundless. The absolute deific Principle, impersonal and unknowable. It means literally "no-thing" i.e., nothing that could be classed with anything else. The word and ideas are equivalent to the Vedantic conceptions of Parabrahmn. [w.w.w.]

Some Western Kabbalists, however, contrive to make of IT, a personal "He", a male deity instead of an impersonal deity.

**En** (*Chald.*). A negative particle, like a in Greek and Sanskrit. The first syllable of "En-Soph" (*q.v.*), or nothing that begins or ends, the "Endless".

**Enoichion** (*Gr.*). Lit., the *inner* Eye"; the "Seer", a reference to the third *inner*, or Spiritual Eye, the true name for Enoch disfigured from *Chanoch*.

**Ens** (*Gr.*). The same as the Greek To On "Being", or the real Presence in Nature.

**Ephesus** (*Gr.*). Famous for its great metaphysical College where Occultism (Gnosis) and Platonic philosophy were taught in the days of the Apostle Paul. A city regarded as the focus of secret sciences, and that Gnôsis. or Wisdom, which is the antagonist of the perversion of Christo-Esotericism to this day. It was at Ephesus where was the great College of the Essenes and all the lore the Tanaim had brought from the *Chaldees,*

**Epimetheus** (*Gr.*). Lit., "He who takes counsel *after*" the event. A brother of Prometheus in Greek Mythology.

**Epinoia** (*Gr.*). Thought, invention, design. A name adopted by the Gnostics for the first passive Æon.

**Episcopal Crook.** One of the insignia of Bishops, derived from the sacerdotal sceptre of the Etruscan Augurs. it is also found in the hand of several gods.

**Epoptes** (*Gr.*). An Initiate. One who has passed his last degree of initiation.

**Eridanus** (*Lat.*). *Ardan,* the Greek name for the river Jordan.

**Eros** (*Gr.*). Hesiod makes of the god Eros the third personage of the Hellenic primordial Trinity composed of Ouranos, Gæa and Eros. It is the personified procreative Force in nature in its abstract sense, the propeller to "creation" and procreation. Exoterically, mythology makes of Eros the god of lustful, animal desire, whence the term *erotic* esoterically, it is different. (See "Kâma".)

**Eshmim** (*Heb.*). The Heavens, the Firmament in which are the Sun, Planets and Stars; from the root **Sm**, meaning to place, dispose; hence, the planets, as disposers. [w.w.w.]

**Esoteric** (*Gr.*). Hidden, secret. From the Greek *esotericos*, "inner" concealed.

**Esoteric Bodhism.** Secret wisdom or intelligence from the Greek *esotericos* "inner", and the Sanskrit *Bodhi,* "knowledge", intelligence—in contradistinction to *Buddhi,* "the *faculty* of knowledge or intelligence" and *Buddhism,* the philosophy or Law of Buddha (the Enlightened). Also written "Budhism", from *Budha* (Intelligence and Wisdom) the Son of Soma.

**Essasua.** The African and Asiatic sorcerers and serpent charmers.

**Essenes**. A hellenized word, from the Hebrew *Asa,* a "healer". A mysterious sect of Jews said by Pliny to have lived near the Dead Sea *per millia sæculorum*—for thousands of ages. "Some have supposed them to be extreme Pharisees, and others—which may be the true theory—the descendants of the *Benim-nabim* of the *Bible,* and think that they were 'Kenites and *Nazarites*. They had many Buddhistic ideas and practices; and it is noteworthy that the priests of the *Great Mother* at Ephesus, Diana-Bhavani with many breasts, were also so denominated. Eusebius, and after him De Quincey, declared them to be the same as the early Christians, which is more than probable. The title ' brother', used in the early Church, was Essenean; they were a fraternity, or a koinobion or community like the early converts." (*Isis Unveiled.*)

**Ether**. Students are but too apt to confuse this with Akâsa and with Astral Light. It is neither, in the sense in which ether is described by physical Science. Ether is a material agent, though hitherto undetected by any physical apparatus; whereas Akâsa is a distinctly spiritual agent, identical, in one sense, with the Anima Mundi, while the Astral Light is only the seventh and highest principle of the terrestrial atmosphere, as undetectable as Akâsa and real Ether, because it is something quite on another plane. The seventh principle of the earth's atmosphere, as said, the

Astral Light, is only the second on the Cosmic scale. The scale of Cosmic Forces, Principles and Planes, of Emanations—on the metaphysical—and Evolutions—on the physical plane—is the Cosmic Serpent biting its own tail, the Serpent reflecting the Higher, and reflected in its turn by the lower Serpent. The Caduceus explains the mystery, and the four-fold Dodecahedron on the model of which the universe is said by Plato to have been built by the manifested Logos—synthesized by the unmanifested First-Born—yields geometrically the key to Cosmogony and its microcosmic reflection—our Earth.

**Eurasians.** An abbreviation of "European-Asians". The mixed coloured races: the children of the white fathers and the dark mothers of India, or *vice versa*.

**Evapto**. Initiation; the same as *Epopteia*.

**Evolution**. The development of higher orders of animals from lower. As said in *Isis Unveiled:* "Modern Science holds but to a one-sided physical evolution, prudently avoiding and ignoring the higher or spiritual evolution, which would force our contemporaries to confess the superiority of the ancient philosophers and psychologists over themselves. The ancient sages, ascending to the UNKNOWABLE, made their starting-point from the first manifestation of the unseen, the unavoidable, and, from a strictly logical reasoning, the absolutely necessary creative Being, the Demiurgos of the universe. Evolution began with them from pure spirit, which descending lower and lower down, assumed at last a visible and comprehensible form, and became matter. Arrived at this point, they speculated in the Darwinian method, but on a far more large and comprehensive basis." (See "Emanation".)

**Exoteric**. Outward, public; the opposite of esoteric or hidden.

**Extra-Cosmic**. Outside of Kosmos or Nature; a nonsensical word invented to assert the existence of a *personal* god, independent of, or out side, Nature *per se*, in opposition to the Pantheistic idea that the whole Kosmos is animated or informed with the Spirit of Deity, Nature being but the garment, and matter the illusive shadow, of the real unseen Presence.

**Eye of Horus**. A very sacred symbol in ancient Egypt. It was called the *outa* the right eye represented the sun, the left, the moon. Says Macrobius: "The *outo* (or *uta*) is it not the emblem of the sun, king of the world, who from his elevated throne sees all the Universe below him"?

**Eyes** (*divine*). The "eyes" the Lord Buddha developed in him at the twentieth hour of his vigil when sitting under the BO-tree, when he was attaining Buddhaship. They are the eyes of the glorified Spirit, to which matter is no longer a physical impediment, and which have the power of seeing all things within the space of the limitless Universe. 0n the following morning of that night, at the close of the third watch, the "Merciful One" attained the Supreme Knowledge.

**Ezra** (*Heb.*). The Jewish priest and scribe, who, circa 450 B.C., compiled the Pentateuch if indeed he was not the author of it) and the rest of the Old Testament, except Nehemiah and Malachi. [w.w.w.]

**Ezra** (*Heb.*). The same as Azareel and Azriel, a great Hebrew Kabbalist. His full name is Rabbi Azariel ben Manahem. He flourished at Valladolid, Spain, in the twelfth century, and was famous as a philosopher and Kabbalist. He is the author of a work on the Ten Sephiroth.

# F

**F.**—The sixth letter of the English alphabet, for which there is no equivalent in Hebrew. It is the double F F of the Æolians which became the *Digamma* for some mysterious reasons. It corresponds to the Greek *phi*. As a Latin numeral it denotes 40, with a dash over the letter (F) 400,000.

**Faces** (*Kabbalistic*), or, as in Hebrew, *Partzupheem.* The word usually refers to *Areekh Anpeen* or Long Face, and *Zeir-Anpeen*, or Short Face, and *Resha Hivrah* the "White Head" or Face. The Kabbala states that from the moment of their appearance (the hour of differentiation of matter) all the material for future forms was contained in the three Heads which are one, and called *Atteekah Kadosha* (Holy Ancients and the Faces). It is when the Faces look toward each other, that the Holy Ancients" in three Heads, or *Atteekah Kadosha,* are called *Areek Appayem*, i.e., "Long Faces". (See *Zohar* iii., 292a.) This refers to the three Higher Principles, cosmic and human.

**Fafnir** (*Scand.*). The Dragon of Wisdom.

**Fahian** (*Chin.*). A Chinese traveller and writer in the early centuries of Christianity, who wrote on Buddhism.

**Fa-Hwa-King** (*Chin.*). A Chinese work on Cosmogony.

**Faizi** (*Arab.*). Literally the "heart". A writer on occult and mystic subjects.

**Fakir** (Arab.). A Mussulman ascetic in India, a Mahometan "Yogi". The name is often applied, though erroneously. to Hindu ascetics; for strictly speaking only Mussulman ascetics are entitled to it. This loose way of calling things by general names was adopted in *Isis Unveiled* but is now altered.

**Falk**, *Caïn Chenul*. A Kabbalistic Jew, reputed to have worked "miracles". Kenneth Mackenzie quotes in regard to him from the German annalist Archenoiz' work on England (1788):—" There exists in London an extraordinary man who for thirty years has been celebrated in Kabbalistic records. He is named Caïn Chenul Falk. A certain Count de Rautzow, lately dead in the service of France, with the rank of Field-Marshal, certifies that he has seen this Falk in Brunswick, and that evocations of spirits took place in the presence of credible witnesses." These "spirits" were Elementals, whom Falk brought into view by the conjurations used by every Kabbalist. His son, Johann Friedrich Falk, likewise a Jew, was also a Kabbalist of repute, and was once the head of a Kabbalistic college in London. His occupation was that of a jeweller and appraiser of diamonds, and he was a wealthy man. To this day the mystic writings and rare Kabbalistic works bequeathed by him to a trustee may be perused in a certain half-public library in London, by every genuine student of Occultism. Falk's own writings are all still in MS., and some in cypher.

**Farbauti** (*Scand.*). A giant in the *Edda*; lit., "the oarsman"; the father of Loki, whose mother was the giantess Laufey (leafy isle); a genealogy which makes W. S. W. Anson remark in *Asgard and the Gods* that probably the oarsman or Farbauti "was the giant who saved himself from the flood in a boat, and the latter (Laufey) the island to which he rowed"—which is an additional variation of the Deluge.

**Fargard** (*Zend.*). A section or chapter of verses in the *Vendidad* of the Parsis.

**Farvarshi** (*Mazd.*). The same as *Ferouer*, or the opposite (as contrasted) double. The spiritual counterpart of the still more spiritual original. Thus, Ahriman is the *Ferouer* or the *Farvarshi* of Ormuzd—"*demon est deus inversus*"—Satan of God. Michael the Archangel, "he like god", is a *Ferouer* of that god. A *Farvarshi* is the shadowy or dark side of a Deity—or its darker lining.

**Ferho** (*Gnost.*). The highest and greatest creative power with the Nazarene Gnostics. (*Codex Nazaræus.*)

**Fetahil** (*Gr.*). The lower creator, in the same *Codex*.

**First Point**. Metaphysically the first point of manifestation, the germ of primeval differentiation, or the point in the infinite Circle "whose centre is everywhere, and circumference nowhere". The Point is the Logos.

**Fire** (*Living*). A figure of speech to denote deity, the "One" life. A theurgic term, used later by the Rosicrucians. The symbol of the *living fire* is the sun, *certain of whose rays develope the fire of life in a diseased body, impart the* *knowledge of the future* to the sluggish mind, and stimulate to active function a certain psychic and generally dormant faculty in man. The meaning is very occult.

**Fire-Philosophers**. The name given to the Hermetists and Alchemists of the Middle Ages, and also to the Rosicrucians. The latter, the successors of the Theurgists, regarded fire as the symbol of Deity. It was the source, not only of material atoms, but the container of the spiritual and psychic Forces energizing them. Broadly analyzed, fire is a triple principle; esoterically, a septenary, as are all the rest of the Elements. As man is composed of Spirit, Soul and Body, plus a four fold aspect: so is Fire. As in the works of Robert Fludd (de Fluctibus) one of the famous Rosicrucians, Fire contains (1) a visible flame (Body); (2) an invisible, astral fire (Soul); and (3) Spirit. The four aspects are heat (life), light (mind), electricity (Kâmic, or molecular powers) and the Synthetic Essence, *beyond* Spirit, or the radical cause of its existence and manifestation. For the Hermetist or Rosicrucian, when a flame is extinct on the objective plane it has only passed from the seen world unto the unseen, from the knowable into the unknowable.

**Fifty Gates of Wisdom** (*Kab.*). The number is a *blind*, and there are really 49 gates, for Moses, than whom the Jewish world has no higher adept, reached, according to the Kabbalas, and passed only the 49th. These "gates" typify the different planes of Being or *Ens*. They are thus the "gates" of Life and the "gates" of understanding or degrees of occult knowledge. These 49 (or 50) gates correspond to the seven gates in the seven caves of Initiation into the Mysteries of Mithra (see Celsus and Kircher). The division of the 50 gates into five chief gates, each including *ten*—is again a blind. It is in the fourth gate of these five, from which begins, ending at the tenth, the world of Planets, thus making seven, corresponding to the seven lower Sephiroth—that the key to their meaning lies hidden. They are also called the "gates of Binah" or understanding.

**Flagæ** (*Herm.*). A name given by Paracelsus to a particular kind of guardian angels or genii.

**Flame** (*Holy*). The "Holy Flame" is the name given by the Eastern Asiatic Kabbalists (Semites) to the *Anima Mundi* the "world-soul" The Initiates were called the "Sons of the Holy Flame.

**Fludd** (*Robert*), generally known as Robertus de Fluctibus, the chief of the "Philosophers by Fire". A celebrated English Hermetist of the sixteenth century, and a voluminous writer. He wrote on the essence of gold and other mystic and occult subjects.

**Fluvii Transitus** (*Lat.*). Or crossing of the River (Chebar). Cornelius Agrippa gives this alphabet. In the *Ars Quatuor Coronatorum,* Vol. III., part 2, 1890, which work is the Report of the proceedings of the Quatuor Coronati Lodge of Freemasons, No. 2076, will be found copies of this alphabet, and also the curious old letters called Melachim, and the Celestial alphabet, supplied by W. Wynn Westcott, P.M. This Lodge seems to be the only one in England which really does study "the hidden mysteries of Nature and Science" in earnest.

**Fohat** (*Tib.*). A term used to represent the active (male) potency of the Sakti (female reproductive power) in nature. The essence of cosmic electricity. An occult Tibetan term for *Daiviprakriti* primordial light: and in the universe of manifestation the ever-present electrical energy and ceaseless destructive and formative power. Esoterically, it is the same, Fohat being the universal propelling Vital Force, at once the propeller and the resultant.

**Foh-tchou** (*Chin.*). Lit., "Buddha's Lord", meaning, however, simply the teacher of the doctrines of Buddha. Foh means a Guru who lives generally in a temple of Sakyamuni Buddha — the Foh-Maeyu.

**Fons Yitæ** (*Lat.*). A work of Ibn Gehirol, the Arabian Jewish philosopher of the XIth century, who called it *Me-gôr Hayyûn* or the "Fountain of Life" (*De Materia Universali and Fons Vitæ*). The Western Kabbalists have proclaimed it a really Kabbalistic work. Several MSS.,Latin and Hebrew, of this wonderful production have been discovered by scholars in public libraries; among others one by Munk, in 1802. The Latin name of Ibn Gebirol was Avicebron, a name well-known to all Oriental scholars.

**FourAnimals.** The symbolical animals of the vision of Ezekiel (the *Mercabah*). "With the first Christians the celebration of the Mysteries of the Faith was accompanied by the burning of seven lights, with incense, the Trishagion, and the reading of the book of the gospels, upon which was wrought, both on covers and pages, the winged man, lion, bull, and eagle" (*Qabbalah,* by Isaac Myer, LL.B.). To this day these animals are represented along with the four Evangelists and prefixing their respective gospels in the editions of the Greek Church. Each represents one of the four lower classes of worlds or planes, into the similitude of which each *personality* is cast. Thus the Eagle (associated with St. John) represents cosmic Spirit or Ether, the all-piercing Eye of the Seer; the Bull of St. Luke, the waters of

Life, the all-generating element and cosmic strength; the Lion of St. Mark, fierce energy, undaunted courage and cosmic fire; while the human Head or the Angel, which stands near St. Matthew is the synthesis of all three combined in the higher Intellect of man, and in cosmic Spirituality. All these symbols are Egyptian, Chaldean, and Indian. The Eagle, Bull and Lion-headed gods are plentiful, and all represented the same idea, whether in the Egyptian, Chaldean, Indian or Jewish religions, but beginning with the Astral body they went no higher than the cosmic Spirit or the Higher Manas—Atma-Buddhi, or Absolute Spirit and Spiritual Soul its vehicle, being incapable of being symbolised by concrete images.

**Fravasham** (*Zend*). Absolute spirit.

**Freya** or *Frigga* (*Scand.*). In the *Edda*, Frigga is the mother of the gods like Aditi in the *Vedas*. She is identical with the Northern Frea of the Germans, and in her lowest aspect was worshipped as the all-nourishing Mother Earth. She was seated on her golden throne, formed of webs of golden light, with three divine virgins as her handmaidens and messengers, and was occupied with spinning golden threads with which to reward good men. She is Isis and Diana at the same time, for she is also Holda, the mighty huntress, and she is Ceres-Demeter, who protects agriculture—the moon and nature.

**Frost Giants** or *Hrimthurses* (*Scand.*). They are the great builders, the Cyclopes and Titans of the Norsemen, and play a prominent part in the *Edda*. It is they who build the strong wall round Asgard (the Scandinavian Olympus) to protect it from the Jotuns, the wicked giants.

**Fylfot** (*Scand.*). A weapon of Thor, like the Swastika, or the Jaina, the four-footed cross; generally called "Thor's Hammer".

# G

**G.**—The seventh letter in the English alphabet. "In Greek, Chaldean, Syriac, Hebrew, Assyrian, Samaritan, Etrurian, Coptic, in the modern Romaic and Gothic, it occupies the third place in the alphabet, while in Cyrillic, Glagolitic, Croat, Russian, Servian and Wallachian, it stands fourth." As the name of "god" begins with this letter (in Syriac, *gad*; Swedish, *gud:* German, *gott*; English, *god*; Persian, *gada,* etc., etc.), there is an occult reason for this which only the students of esoteric philosophy and of the *Secret Doctrine*, explained esoterically, will understand thoroughly; it refers to the three logoi—the last, the Elohim, and the emanation of the latter, the androgynous Adam Kadmon. All these peoples have derived the name of "god" from their respective traditions, the more or less clear echoes of the esoteric tradition. Spoken and "Silent Speech" (writing) are a "gift of the gods", say all the national traditions, from the old Aryan Sanskrit-speaking people who claim that their alphabet, the *Devanâgari* (*lit.*, the language of the *devas* or gods) was given to them from heaven, down to the Jews, who speak of an alphabet, the parent of the one which has survived, as having been a celestial and mystical symbolism given by the angels to the patriarchs. Hence, every letter had its manifold meaning. A symbol itself of a celestial being and objects, it was in its turn represented on earth by like corresponding objects whose form symbolised the shape of the letter. The present letter, called in Hebrew *gimel* and symbolised by a long camel's neck, or rather a serpent erect, is associated with the third sacred divine name, *Ghadol* or *Magnus* (great). Its numeral is four, the Tetragrammaton and the sacred Tetraktys; hence its sacredness. With other people it stood for 400 and with a dash over it, for 400,000.

**Gabriel.** According to the Gnostics, the "Spirit" or Christos, the "messenger of life", and Gabriel are one. The former "is called some-times the Angel Gabriel Hebrew 'the mighty one of God'," and took with the Gnostics the place of the Logos, while the Holy Spirit was considered one with the Æon Life, (see *Irenæus* I., xii.). Therefore we find Theodoret saying (in *Hævet. Fab.*, II vii.): "The heretics agree with us (Christians) respecting the beginning of all things. But they say there is not one Christ (God), *but one above* and *the other below.* And this last *formerly dwelt in many;* but the Jesus, they at one time say is *from* God, at another they call him a Spirit;" The key to this is given in the esoteric philosophy. The "spirit" with the Gnostics was a female potency exoterically, it was the ray proceeding from the Higher Manas, the Ego, and that which the Esotericists refer to as the *Kâma Manas* or the lower personal Ego, which is radiated in every human entity by the Higher Ego or Christos, the god within us. Therefore, they were right in saying: "there is not one Christ, but one above and the other below". Every student of Occultism will understand this, and also that Gabriel — or "the mighty one of God" — is one with the Higher Ego. (See *Isis Unveiled.*)

**Gæa** (*Gr.*). Primordial Matter, in the Cosmogony of Hesiod; Earth, as some think; the wife of Ouranos, the sky or heavens. The female personage of the primeval Trinity, composed of Ouranos, Gæa and Eros.

**Gaffarillus.** An Alchemist and philosopher who lived in the middle of the seventeenth century. He is the first philosopher known to maintain that every natural object (e.g., plants, living creatures, etc.), when burned, retained its form in its ashes and that it could be raised again from them. This claim was justified by the eminent chemist Du Chesne, and after him Kircher, Digby and Vallemont have assured themselves of the fact, by demonstrating that the astral forms of burned plants could be raised from their ashes. A receipt for raising such astral phantoms of flowers is given in a work of Oetinger, *Thoughts on the Birth and Generation of Things.*

**Gaganeswara** (*Sk.*). "Lord of the Sky", a name of Garuda.

**Gal-hinnom** (*Heb.*) The name of Hell in the Talmud.

**Gambatrin** (*Scand.*). The name of Hermodur's "magic staff" in the *Edda.*

**Ganadevas** (*Sk.*)A certain class of celestial Beings who are said to inhabit *Maharloka.* They are the rulers of our Kalpa (Cycle) and therefore termed Kalpâdhikârins, or Lord of the Kalpas. They last only "One Day" of Brahmâ.

**Gandapada** (*Sk.*) A celebrated Brahman teacher, the author of the Commentaries on the *Sankhya Karika, Mandukya Upanishad*, and other works.

**Gândhâra** (*Sk.*) A musical note of great occult power in the Hindu gamut—the third of the diatonic scale.

**Gandharva** (*Sk.*) The celestial choristers and musicians of India. in the *Vedas* these deities reveal the secrets of heaven and earth and esoteric science to mortals. They had charge of the sacred Soma plant and its juice, the ambrosia drunk in the temple which gives "omniscience".

**Gan-Eden** (*Heb.*) Also *Ganduniyas.* (See "Eden".)

**Ganesa** (*Sk.*) The elephant-headed God of Wisdom, the *son* of Siva. He is the same as the Egyptian Thoth-Hermes, and Anubis or Hermanubis (*q.v.*). The legend shows him as having lost his human head, which was replaced by that of an elephant.

**Gangâ** (*Sk.*) The Ganges, the principal sacred river in India. There are two versions of its myth: one relates that Gangâ (the goddess) having transformed herself into a river, flows from the big toe of Vishnu; the other, that the Gangâ drop from the ear of Siva into the Anavatapta lake, thence passes out, through the mouth of the silver cow (*gômukhi*), crosses all Eastern India and falls into the Southern Ocean. "An 'heretical superstition' ", remarks Mr. Eitel in his *Sanskrit, Chinese Dictionary* "ascribes to the waters of the Ganges *sin-cleansing power.*" No more a "superstition" one would say, than the belief that the waters of Baptism and the Jordan have "sin-cleansing power".

**Gangâdwâra** (*Sk.*) "The gate or door of the Ganges", literally; the name of a town now called Hardwar, at the foot of the Himalayas.

**Gangi** (*Sk.*) A renowned Sorcerer in the time of Kâsyapa Buddha (a predecessor of Gautama). Gangi was regarded as an incarnation of Apalâla, the Nâga (Serpent), the guardian Spirit of the Sources of Subhavastu, a river in Udyâna. Apalâla is said to have been converted by Gautama Buddha, to the good Law, and become an Arhat. The allegory of the name is comprehensible: all the Adepts and Initiates were called *nâgas,* "Serpents of Wisdom".

**Ganinnânse.** A Singhalese priest who has not yet been ordained—from *gana*, an assemblage or brotherhood. The higher ordained priests "are called *terunnânse* from the Pali *théro*, an elder"(Hardy).

**Garm** (*Scand.*). The Cerberus of the *Edda*. This monstrous dog lived in the Gnypa cavern in front of the dwelling of Hel, the goddess of the netherworld.

**Garuda** (*Sk.*) A gigantic bird in the *Ramâyana*, the steed of Vishnu. Esoterically—the symbol of the great Cycle.

**Gâthâ** (*Sk.*) Metrical chants or hymns, consisting of moral aphorisms. A gâthâ of thirty-two words is called Âryâgiti.

**Gâti** (*Sk.*) The six (esoterically *seven*) conditions of sentient existence. These are divided into two groups: the three higher and the three lower *paths.* To the former belong the devas, the asuras and (immortal) men; to the latter (in exoteric teachings) creatures in hell, *prêtas* or hungry demons, and animals. Explained *esoterically*, however, the last three are the *personalities* in Kâmaloka, elementals and animals. The seventh mode of existence is that of the Nirmanakâya (*q.v.*).

**Gâtra** (*Sk.*) Lit., the *limbs* (of Brahmâ) from which the "mind-born" sons, the seven Kumâras, were born.

**Gautama** (*Sk.*) The Prince of Kapilavastu, son of Sudhôdana, the Sâkya king of a small realm on the borders of Nepaul, born in the seventh century B.C., now called the "Saviour of the World". Gautama or Gôtama was the sacerdotal name of the Sâkya family, and Sidhârtha was Buddha's name before he became a Buddha. Sâkya Muni, means the Saint of the Sâkya family. Born a simple mortal he rose to Buddhaship through his own personal and unaided merit. A man—verily greater than any god!

**Gayâ** (*Sk.*) Ancient city of Magadha, a little north-west of the modern Gayah. It is at the former that Sakyamuni reached his Buddha-ship, under the famous Bodhi-tree, *Bodhidruma*.

**Gayâtri** (*Sk.*) also *Sâvitri*. A most sacred verse, addressed to the Sun, in the Rig -Veda, which the Brahmans have to repeat mentally every morn and eve during their devotions.

**Geber** (*Heb.*) or *Gibborim*. "Mighty men"; the same as the *Kabirim*. In heaven, they are regarded as powerful angels, on earth as the giants mentioned in chapter vi. of *Genesis*.

**Gebirol,** *Solomon Ben Jehudah*. Called in literature Avicebron. An Israelite by birth, a philosopher, poet and Kabbalist, a voluminous writer and a mystic. He was born in the eleventh Century at Malaga (1021), educated at Saragossa, and died at Valencia in 1070, murdered by a Mahommedan. His fellow-religionists called him Salomon the Sephardi, or the Spaniard, and the Arabs, Abu Ayyub Suleiman ben ya'hya Ibn Dgebirol; whilst the scholastics named him Avicebron. (See Myer's *Qabbalah.*) Ibn Gebirol was certainly one of the greatest philosophers and scholars of his age. He wrote much in Arabic and most of his MSS. have been preserved. His greatest work appears to be the *Megôr Hayyîm*, i.e., the *Fountain of Life*, "one of the earliest exposures of the secrets of the Speculative Kabbalah", as his biographer informs us. (See "*Fons Vitæ*".)

**Geburah** (*Heb.*) A Kabbalistic term; the fifth Sephira, a female and passive potency, meaning severity and power; from it is named the Pillar of Severity. [w. w w.]

**Gedulah** (*Heb.*) Another name for the Sephira *Chesed*.

**Gehenna,** in Hebrew *Hinnom*. No hell at all, but a valley near Jerusalem, where Israelites immolated their children to Moloch. In that valley a place named *Tophet* was situated, where a fire was perpetually preserved for sanitary purposes. The prophet Jeremiah informs us that his countrymen, the Jews, used to sacrifice their children on that spot.

**Gehs** (*Zend*) Parsi prayers.

**Gelukpa** (*Tib.*) "Yellow Caps" literally; the highest and most orthodox Buddhist sect in Tibet, the antithesis of the Dugpa ("Red Caps"), the old "devil worshippers".

**Gemara** (*Heb.*) The latter portion of the Jewish Talmud, begun by Rabbi Ashi and completed by Rabbi Mar and Meremar, about 300 A.D. Lit., to finish. It is a commentary on the Mishna. [w.w.w.]

**Gematria** (*Heb.*) A division of the practical Kabbalah. It shows the numerical value of Hebrew words by summing up the values of the letters composing them and further, it shows by this means, analogies between words and phrases. [w.w.w.]

One of the methods (arithmetical) for extracting the hidden meaning from letters, words and sentences.

**Gems,** *Three precious.* In Southern Buddhism these are the sacred books, the Buddhas and the priesthood. In Northern Buddhism and its secret schools, the Buddha, his sacred teachings, and the Narjols (Buddhas of Compassion).

**Genesis.** The whole of the Book of Genesis down to the death of Joseph, is found to he a hardly altered version of the Cosmogony of the Chaldeans, as is now repeatedly proven from the Assyrian tiles. The first three chapters are transcribed from the allegorical narratives of the beginnings common to all nations. Chapters four and five are a new allegorical adaptation of the same narration in the secret *Book of Numbers*; chapter six is an astronomical narrative of the Solar year and the seven *cosmocratores* from the Egyptian original of the Pymander and the symbolical visions of a series of *Enoichioi* (Seers)—from whom came also the Book of Enoch. The beginning of Exodus, and the story of Moses is that of the Babylonian Sargon, who having flourished (as even that unwilling authority Dr. Sayce tells us) 3750 B.C. preceded the Jewish lawgiver by almost 2300 years. (See *S. D.,* Vol. II., pp. 691 et seq.) Nevertheless, *Genesis* is an undeniably esoteric work. It has not borrowed, nor has it disfigured the universal symbols and teachings on the lines of which it was written, but simply adapted the eternal truths to its own national spirit and clothed them in cunning allegories comprehensible only to its Kabbalists and Initiates. The Gnostics have done the same, each sect in its own way, as thousands of years before, India, Egypt, Chaldea and Greece, had also dressed the same incommunicable truths each in its own national garb. The key and solution to all such narratives can be found *only in the esoteric teachings.*

**Genii** (*Lat.*) A name for Æons, or angels, with the Gnostics. The names of their hierarchies and classes are simply legion.

**Geonic Period.** The era of the Geonim may be found mentioned in works treating of the Kabbalah; the ninth century AD. is implied. [w.w.w.]

**Gharma** (*Sk.*) A title of Karttikeya, the Indian god of war and the Kumâra born of Siva's drop of sweat that fell into the Ganges.

**Ghôcha** (*Sk.*) Lit., "the miraculous Voice". The name of a great Arhat, the author of Abhidharmamrita Shastra, who restored sight to a blind man by anointing his eyes with the tears of the audience moved by his (Ghôcha's) supernatural eloquence.

**Gilgoolem** (*Heb.*) The cycle of rebirths with the Hebrew Kabbalists; with the orthodox Kabbalists, the "whirling of the soul" after death, which finds-no rest until it reaches Palestine, the "promised land", and its body is buried there.

**Gimil** (*Scand.*). "The Cave of Gimil" or Wingolf. A kind of Heaven or Paradise, or perhaps a New Jerusalem, built by the "Strong and Mighty God" who remains nameless in the *Edda*, above the Field of Ida, and after the new earth rose out of the waters.

**Ginnungagap** (*Scand.*). The "cup of illusion" literally; the abyss of the great deep, or the shoreless, beginningless, and endless, yawning gulf; which in esoteric parlance we call the "World's Matrix", the primordial living space. The cup that contains the universe, hence the "cup of illusion".

**Giöl** (*Scand.*) The, Styx, the river Giöl which had to be crossed before the nether-world was reached, or the cold Kingdom of Hel. It was spanned by a gold-covered bridge, which led to the gigantic iron fence that encircles the palace of the Goddess of the Under-World or Hel.

**Gna** (*Scand.*) One of the three handmaidens of the goddess Freya. She is a female Mercury who bears her mistress' messages into all parts of the world.

**Gnâna** (*Sk.*) Knowledge as applied to the esoteric sciences.

**Gnân Devas** (*Sk.*) Lit., "the gods of knowledge". The higher classes of gods or devas; the "mind-born" sons of Brahmâ, and others including the Manasa-putras (the Sons of Intellect). Esoterically, our reincarnating Egos.

**Gnânasakti** (*Sk.*) The power of true knowledge, one of the seven great forces in Nature (*six*, exoterically).

**Gnatha** (*Sk.*) The Kosmic *Ego*; the conscious, intelligent Soul of Kosmos.

**Gnomes** (*Alch.*) The Rosicrucian name for the mineral and earth elementals,

**Gnôsis** (*Gr.*) Lit., "knowledge". The technical term used by the schools of religious philosophy, both before and during the first centuries of so-called Christianity, to denote the object of their enquiry. This Spiritual and Sacred Knowledge, the *Gupta Vidya* of the Hindus, could only be obtained by Initiation into Spiritual Mysteries of which the ceremonial "Mysteries" were a type.

**Gnostics** (*Gr.*) The philosophers who formulated and taught the Gnôsis or Knowledge (*q.v.*). They flourished in the first three centuries of the Christian era: the following were eminent, Valentinus, Basilides, Marcion, Simon Magus, etc. [w.w.w.]

**Gnypa** (*Scand.*) The cavern watched by the dog Garm (*q.v.*).

**Gogard** (*Zend.*) The Tree of Life in the *Avesta.*

**Golden Age.** The ancients divided the life cycle into the Golden, Silver, Bronze and Iron Ages. The Golden was an age of primeval purity, simplicity and general happiness.

**Gonpa** (*Tib.*) A temple or monastery; a *Lamasery.*

**Gonpîs** (*Sk.*). Shepherdesses — the playmates and companions of Krishna, among whom was his wife Raddha.

**Gossain** (*Sk.*). The name of a certain class of ascetics in India.

**Great Age.** There were several "great ages" mentioned by the ancients. In India it embraced the whole Maha-manvantara, the "age of Brahmâ", each "Day" of which represents the life cycle of a chain—i.e. it embraces a period of seven Rounds. (See *Esoteric Buddhism*, by A. P. Sinnett.) Thus while a "Day" and a "Night" represent, as Manvantara and Pralaya, 8,640,000,000 years, an "age" lasts through a period of 311,040,000,000,000 years; after which the Pralaya, or dissolution of the universe, becomes universal. With the Egyptians and Greeks the "great age" referred only to the tropical or sidereal year, the duration of which is 25,868 solar years. Of the complete age—that of the gods—they say nothing, as it was a matter to he discussed and divulged only in the Mysteries, during the initiating ceremonies. The "great age" of the Chaldees was the same in figures as that of the Hindus.

**Grihastha** (*Sk.*) Lit., "a householder", "one who lives in a house with his family". A Brahman "family priest" in popular rendering, and the sarcerdotal hierarchy of the Hindus.

**Guardian Wall.** A suggestive name given to the host of translated adepts (Narjols) or the Saints collectively, who are supposed to watch over, help and protect Humanity. This is the so-called "Nirmanâkâya" doctrine in Northern mystic Buddhism. (See *Voice of the Silence*, Part III.)

**Guff** (*Heb.*) Body; physical form; also written Gof.

**Guhya** (*Sk.*) Concealed, secret.

**Guhya Vidyâ**(*Sk.*) The secret knowledge of mystic Mantras.

**Gullweig** (*Scand.*) The personification of the "golden" ore. It is said in the

*Edda* that during the Golden Age, when lust for gold and wealth was yet unknown to man, "when the gods played with golden disks, and no passion disturbed the rapture of mere existence", the whole earth was happy. But, no sooner does "Gullweig (Gold ore) the bewitching enchantress come, who, thrice cast into the fire, arises each time more beautiful than before, and fills the souls of gods and men with unappeasable longing ", than all became changed. It is then that the Norns, the Past, Present and Future, entered into being, the blessed peace of childhood's dreams passed away and Sin came into existence with all its evil consequences. *(Asgard and the Gods.)*

**Gunas** (*Sk*) Qualities, attributes (See" Triguna"); a thread, also a cord.

**Gunavat** (*Sk.*) That which is endowed with qualities.

**Gupta Vidyâ** (*Sk.*) The same as Guhya Vidyâ; Esoteric or Secret Science; knowledge.

**Guru** (*Sk.*) Spiritual Teacher; a master in metaphysical and ethical doctrines; used also for a teacher of any science.

**Guru Deva** (*Sk.*) Lit., "divine Master".

**Gyan-Ben-Giân** (*Pers.*) The King of the Peris, the Sylphs, in the old mythology of Iran.

**Gyges** (*Gr.*) "The ring of Gyges" has become a familiar metaphor in European literature. Gyges was a Lydian who, after murdering the King Candaules, married his widow. Plato tells us that Gyges descended once into a chasm of the earth and discovered a brazen horse, within whose open side was the skeleton of a man who had a brazen ring on his finger. This ring when placed on his own finger made him invisible.

**Gymnosophists** (*Gr.*) The name given by Hellenic writers to a class of naked or "air-clad" mendicants; ascetics in India, extremely learned and endowed with great mystic powers. It is easy to recognise in these gymnosophists the Hindu *Aranyaka* of old, the learned yogis and ascetic-philosophers who retired to the jungle and forest, there to reach, through great austerities, superhuman knowledge and experience.

**Gyn** (*Tib.*) Knowledge acquired under the tuition of an adept teacher or guru.

# H

H.—The eighth letter and aspirate of the English alphabet, and also the eighth in the Hebrew. As a Latin numeral it signifies 200, and with the addition of a dash 200,000; in the Hebrew alphabet Châth is equivalent to *h*, corresponds to eight, and is symbolised by a Fence and *Venus* according to Seyffarth, being in affinity and connected with *Hê*, and therefore with the opening or womb. It is pre-eminently a *Yonic* letter.

**Ha** (*Sk.*) A magic syllable used in sacred formulæ it represents the power of *Akâsa Sakti*. Its efficacy lies in the expirational accent and the sound produced.

**Habal de Garmin** (*Heb.*) According to the Kabbalah this is the Resurrection Body: a *tzelem* image or *demooth* similitude to the deceased man; an inner fundamental spiritual type remaining after death. It is the "Spirit of the Bones "mentioned in Daniel and Isaiah and the Psalms, and is referred to in the Vision of Ezekiel about the clothing of the dry bones with life: consult C, de Leiningen on the Kabbalah, T.P.S. Pamphlet, Vol. II., No. 18. [w.w.w.]

**Hachoser** (*Heb.*) Lit., "reflected Lights"; a name for the minor or inferior powers, in the Kabbalah.

**Hades** (*Gr.*), or *Aïdes*. The "invisible", i.e., the land of the shadows, one of whose regions was Tartarus, a place of complete darkness, like the region of profound dreamless sleep in the Egyptian Amenti. Judging by the allegorical description of the various punishments inflicted therein, the place was purely Karmic. Neither Hades nor Amenti were the hell still preached by some retrograde priests and clergymen; but whether represented by the Elysian Fields or by Tartarus, Hades was a place of retributive justice and no more. This could only be reached by crossing the river to the "other shore", i.e. by crossing the river Death, and being once more reborn, for weal or for woe. As well expressed in Egyptian Belief: "The story of Charon, the ferryman (of the, Styx) is to be found not only in Homer, but in the poetry of many lands. The River must be crossed before gaining the Isles of the Blest. The Ritual of Egypt described a Charon and his boat long ages before Homer. He is Khu-en-ua, the hawk-headed steersman." (See "Amenti", "Hel" and "Happy Fields".)

**Hagadah** (*Heb.*) A name given to parts of the Talmud which are legendary. [w.w.w.]

**Hahnir** (*Scand.*), or *Hönir*. One of the three mighty gods (Odin, Hahnir and Lodur) who, while wandering on earth, found lying on the sea-shore two human forms, motionless, speechless, and senseless. Odin gave them souls; Hahnir, motion and senses; and Lodur, blooming complexions.

Thus were men created.

**Haima** (*Heb.*) The same as the Sanskrit *hiranya* (golden), as "the golden Egg" *Hiranyagarbha.*

**Hair.** Occult philosophy considers the hair (whether human or animal) as the natural receptacle and retainer of the vital essence which often escapes with other emanations from the body. It is closely connected with many of the brain functions—for instance memory. With the ancient Israelites the cutting of the hair and beard was a sign of defilement, and "the Lord said unto Moses. . . They shall not make baldness upon their head", etc. (Lev. XX1., 1-5.) "Baldness", whether natural or artificial, was a sign of calamity, punishment, or grief, as when Isaiah (iii., 24) enumerates, "instead of well-set hair baldness", among the evils that are ready to befall the chosen people. And again, "On all their heads baldness and every beard cut" (*Ibid.* xv., 2). The Nazarite was ordered to let his hair and beard grow, and never to permit a razor to touch them. With the Egyptians and Buddhists it was only the initiated priest or ascetic to whom life is a burden, who shaved. The Egyptian priest was supposed to have become master of his body, and hence shaved his head for cleanliness; yet the Hierophants wore their hair long. The Buddhist still shaves his head to this day—as sign of scorn for life and health. Yet Buddha, after shaving his hair when he first became a mendicant, let it grow again and is always represented with the top-knot of a Yogi. The Hindu priests and Brahmins, and almost all the castes, shave the rest of the head but leave a long lock to grow from the centre of the crown. The ascetics of India wear their hair long, and so do the war-like Sikhs, and almost all the Mongolian peoples. At Byzantium and Rhodes the shaving of the beard was prohibited by law, and in Sparta the cutting of the beard was a mark of slavery and servitude. Among the Scandinavians, we are told, it was considered a disgrace, "a mark of infamy", to cut off the hair. The whole population of the island of Ceylon (the Buddhist Singhalese) wear their hair long. So do the Russian, Greek and Armenian clergy, and monks. Jesus and the Apostles are always represented with their hair long, but fashion in Christendom proved stronger than Christianity, the old ecclesiastical rules (*Constit. Apost. lib.* I. C. 3) enjoining the clergy "to wear their hair and beards long" (See Riddle's *Ecclesiastical Antiquities.*) The Templars were commanded to wear their beards long. Samson wore his hair long, and the biblical allegory shows that health and strength and the very life are connected with the length of the hair. If a cat is shaved it will die in nine cases out of ten. A dog whose coat is not interfered with lives longer and is more intelligent than one whose coat is shaven. Many old people as they lose their hair lose much of their memory and become weaker. While the life of the Yogis is proverbially long, the Buddhist priests (of Ceylon and elsewhere) are not generally long-lived. Mussulmen shave their heads but wear their beards; and as their head is always covered, the danger is less.

**Hajaschar** (*Heb.*) The Light Forces in the Kabbalah; the "Powers of Light", which are the creative but inferior forces.

**Hakem.** Lit., "the Wise One", the Messiah to come, of the Druzes or the "Disciples of Hamsa".

**Hakim** (*Arab.*) A doctor, in all the Eastern countries, from Asia Minor to India.

**Halachah** (*Heb.*) A name given to parts of the Talmud, which are arguments on points of doctrine; the word means "rule". [w.w.w.]

**Hallucination.** A state produced sometimes by physiological disorders, sometimes by mediumship, and at others by drunkenness. But the cause that produces the visions has to be sought deeper than physiology. All such visions, especially when produced through mediumship, are preceded by a relaxation of the nervous system, in variably generating an abnormal magnetic condition which attracts to the sufferer waves of astral light. It is the latter that furnishes the various hallucinations. These, however, are not always what physicians would make them, empty, and unreal dreams. No one can see that which does not exist—i.e., which is not impressed—in or on the astral waves. A Seer may, however, perceive objects and scenes (whether past, present, or future) which have no relation whatever to himself, and also perceive several things entirely disconnected with each other at one and the same time, thus producing the most grotesque and absurd combinations. Both drunkard and Seer, medium and Adept, see their respective visions in the Astral Light; but while the drunkard, the madman, and the untrained medium, or one suffering from brain-fever, see, because they cannot help it, and evoke the jumbled visions unconsciously to themselves, the Adept and the trained Seer have the choice and the control of such visions. They know where to fix their gaze, how to steady the scenes they want to observe, and how to see beyond the upper outward layers of the Astral Light. With the former such glimpses into the waves are hallucinations: with the latter they become the faithful reproduction of what actually has been, is, or will be, taking place. The glimpses at random caught by the medium, and his flickering visions in the deceptive light, are transformed under the guiding will of the Adept and Seer into steady pictures, the truthful representations of that which he wills to come within the focus of his perception.

**Hamsa** or Hansa (*Sk.*) "Swan or goose", according to the Orientalists; a mystical bird in Occultism analogous to the Rosicrucian Pelican. The sacred mystic name which, when preceded by that of KALA (infinite time), i.e. *Kalahansa*, is name of Parabrahm; meaning the "Bird out of space and time". Hence Brahmâ (male)is called *Hansa Vahana* "the Vehicle of Hansa" (the Bird). We find the same idea in the *Zohar,* where *Ain Suph* (the endless and infinite) is said to descend into the universe, for purposes of manifestation, using Adam Kadmon (Humanity) as a chariot or vehicle.

**Hamsa** (*Arab.*). The founder of the mystic sect of the Druzes of Mount Lebanon. (See "Druzes" .)

**Hangsa** (*Sk*) A mystic syllable standing for evolution, and meaning in its literal sense "I am he", or *Ahamsa*.

**Hansa** (*Sk.*) The name, according to the *Bhâgavata Purâna*, of the "One Caste" when there were as yet no varieties of caste, but verily "one Veda, one Deity and one Caste".

**Hanuman** (*Sk.*) The monkey god of the *Ramayana*; the *generalissimo* of Rama's army; the son of Vayu, the god of the wind, and of a virtuous she-demon. Hanuman was the faithful ally of Rama and by his unparalleled audacity and wit, helped the Avatar of Vishnu to finally conquer the demon-king of Lanka, Ravana, who had carried off the beautiful Sita, Rama's wife, an outrage which led to the celebrated war described in the Hindu epic poem.

**Happy Fields.** The name given by the Assyrio-Chaldeans to their Elysian Fields, which were intermingled with their Hades. As Mr. Boscawen tells his readers—"The Kingdom of the underworld was the realm of the god Hea, and the Hades of the Assyrian legends was placed in the underworld, and was ruled over by a goddess, Nin-Kigal, or 'the Lady of the Great Land'. She is also called Allât." A translated inscription states:— "After the gifts of these present days, in the feasts of the land of the silver sky, the resplendent courts, the abode of blessedness, and in the light of the Happy Fields, may he dwell in life eternal, holy, in the presence of the gods who inhabit Assyria". This is worthy of a Christian tumulary inscription. Ishtar, the beautiful goddess, descended into Hades after her beloved Tammuz, and found that this dark place of the shades had seven spheres and seven gates, at each of which she had to leave something belonging to her.

**Hara** (*Sk.*) A title of the god Siva.

**Hare-Worship.** The hare was sacred in many lands and especially among the Egyptians and Jews. Though the latter consider it an unclean, *hoofed* animal, unfit to eat, yet it was held sacred by some tribes. The reason for this was that in a certain species of hare the male suckled the little ones. It was thus considered to be androgynous or hermaphrodite, and so typified an attribute of the Demiurge, or creative Logos. The hare was a symbol of the moon, wherein the face of the prophet Moses is to be seen to this day, say the Jews. Moreover the moon is connected with the worship of Jehovah, a deity pre-eminently the god of generation, perhaps also for the same reason that Eros, the god of sexual love, is represented as carrying a hare. The hare was also sacred to Osiris. Lenormand writes that the hare "has to be considered as the symbol of the Logos . . . the Logos ought to be hermaphrodite and we know that the hare is an androgynous type".

**Hari** (*Sk.*) A title of Vishnu, but used also for other gods.

**Harikesa** (*Sk.*). The name of one of the seven rays of the Sun.

**Harivansa** (*Sk.*) A portion of the *Mahâbhârata*, a poem on the genealogy of Vishnu, or Hari.

**Harmachus** (*Gr.*) The Egyptian Sphinx, called *Har-em-chu* or "Horus (the Sun) in the Horizon", a form of Ra the sun-god; esoterically the risen god. An inscription on a tablet reads "O blessed Ra Harmachus Thou careerest by him in triumph. O shine, Amoun-Ra Harmachus self-generated". The temple of the Sphinx was discovered by Mariette Bey close to the Sphinx, near the great Pyramid of Gizeh All the Egyptologists agree in pronouncing the Sphinx and her temple the "oldest religious monument of the world "—at any rate of Egypt.

"The principal chamber", writes the late Mr. Fergusson "*in the form of a cross*, is supported by piers, simple prisms of Syenite granite without base or capital . . . no sculptures or inscriptions of any sort are found on the walls of this temple, no ornament or symbol nor any image in the sanctuary". This proves the enormous antiquity of both the Sphinx and the temple. "The great bearded Sphinx of the Pyramids of Gizeh is the symbol of Harmachus, the same as each Egyptian Pharaoh who bore, in the inscriptions, the name of 'living form of the Solar Sphinx upon the Earth '," writes Brugsh Bey. And Renan recalls that "at one time the Egyptians were said to have temples without sculptured images" (Bonwick). Not only the Egyptians but every nation of the earth began with temples devoid of idols and even of symbols. It is only when the remembrance of the great abstract truths and of the primordial Wisdom taught to humanity by the dynasties of the divine kings died out that men had to resort to mementos and symbology. In the story of Horus in some tablets of Edfou, Rouge found an inscription showing that the god had once assumed "the shape of a human-headed lion to gain advantage over his enemy Typhon. Certainly Horus was so adored in Leontopolis. He is the real Sphinx. That accounts, too, for the lion figure being sometimes seen on each side of Isis. . . It was her child." (Bonwick.) And yet the story of Harmachus, or Har em-chu, is still left untold to the world, nor is it likely to he divulged to this generation. (See "Sphinx".)

**Harpocrates** (*Gr.*). The child Horus or *Ehoou* represented with a finger on his mouth, the solar disk upon his head and golden hair. He is the "god of Silence" and of Mystery. (See "Horus"). Harpocrates was also worshipped by both Greeks and Romans in Europe as a son of *Isis*.

**Harshana** (*Sk.*) A deity presiding over offerings to the dead, or *Srâddha*.

**Harvîri** (*Eg.*) Horns, the elder: the ancient name of a solar god: the rising sun represented as a god reclining on a full-blown lotus, the symbol of the Universe.

**Haryaswas** (*Sk.*) The five and ten thousand sons of Daksha, who instead of peopling the world as desired by their father, all became yogis, 'as advised by the mysterious sage Narada, and remained celibates. "They dispersed through the regions and have not returned." This means, according to the secret science, that they had all incarnated in mortals. The name is given to natural born mystics and celibates, who are said to be incarnations of the "Haryaswas".

**Hatchet**. In the Egyptian Hieroglyphics a symbol of power, and also of death. The hatchet is called the "Severer of the Knot "i.e., of marriage or any other tie.

**Hatha Yoga** (*Sk.*) The lower form of Yoga practice; one which uses physical means for purposes of spiritual self-development The opposite of *Râja Yoga*.

**Hathor** (*Eg.*) The lower or infernal aspect of Isis, corresponding to the Hecate of Greek mythology.

**Hawk**. The hieroglyphic and type of the Soul. The sense varies with the postures of the bird. Thus when lying as dead it represents the transition, larva state, or the passage from the state of one life to another. When its wings are opened it means that the defunct is resurrected in Amenti and once more in conscious possession of his soul. The chrysalis has become a butterfly.

**Hayo Bischat** (*Heb.*) The Beast, in the *Zohar:* the Devil and Tempter. Esoterically our lower animal passions.

**Hay-yah** (*Heb.*) One of the metaphysical human "Principles". Eastern Occultists divide men into seven such Principles; Western Kabbalists, we are told, into three only—namely, *Nephesh Ruach* and *Neshamah*. But in truth, this division is as loose and as mere an abbreviation as our "Body, Soul, Spirit ". For, in the *Qabbalah* of Myer (*Zohar* ii.,141 b., *Cremona Ed.* ii., fol. 63 b., col. 251) it is stated that *Neshamah* or Spirit has three divisions, "the highest being *Ye'hee-dah* (Atmâ) the middle, *Hay-yah* (Buddhi), and the last and third, the *Neshamah,* properly speaking (Manas)". Then comes *Mahshabah,* Thought (the lower Manas, or conscious Personality), in which the higher then manifest themselves, thus making *four;* this is followed by *Tzelem,* Phantom of the Image (*Kama-rupa* in life the Kamic element); *D'yooq-nah,* Shadow of the image (*Linga Sharira,* the Double); and *Zurath,* Prototype, which is Life—seven in all, even without the *D'mooth,* Likeness or Similitude, which is called a lower manifestation, and is in reality the *Guf,* or Body. Theosophists of the E. S. who know the transposition made of Atmâ and the part taken by the *auric* prototype, will easily find which are the *real seven,* and assure themselves that between the division of Principles of the Eastern Occultists and that of the real Eastern Kabbalists there is no difference. Do not let us forget that neither the one nor the other are prepared to give out the real and *final* classification in their public writings.

**Hay-yoth ha Qadosh** (*Heb.*) The holy living creatures of Ezekiel's vision of the *Merkabah,* or vehicle, or chariot. These are the four symbolical beasts, the cherubim of Ezekiel, and in the Zodiac Taurus, Leo, Scorpio (or the Eagle), and Aquarius, the man.

**Hea** (*Chald.*) The god of the Deep and the Underworld; some see in him Ea or Oannes, the fish-man, or Dagon.

**Heabani** (*Chald.*) A famous astrologer at the Court of Izdubar, frequently mentioned in the fragments of the Assyrian tablets in reference to a dream of Izdubar, the great Babylonian King, or Nimrod, the "mighty hunter before the Lord ". After his death, his soul being unable to rest underground, the ghost of Heabani was raised by .Merodach, the god, his body restored to life and then transferred alive, like Elijah, to the regions of the Blessed.

**Head of all Heads** (*Kab*). Used of the "Ancient of the Ancients" *Atteehah D'atteekeen,* who is the "Hidden of the Hidden, the Concealed of the Concealed". In this cranium of the "White Head", *Resha Hivrah,* "dwell daily 13,000 myriads of worlds, which rest upon It, lean upon It" *(Zohar iii. Idrah Rabbah)* . . . "In that *Atteehah* nothing is revealed except the Head alone, because it is the Head of all Heads. . . The Wisdom above, which is the Head, is hidden in it, the Brain which is tranquil and quiet, and none knows it but Itself. . . . And this Hidden Wisdom . . . the Concealed of the Concealed, the Head of all Heads, a Head which is not a Head, nor does any one know, nor is it ever known, what is in that Head which Wisdom and Reason cannot comprehend" (*Zohar* iii., fol. 288 a). This is said of the Deity of which the Head (i.e., Wisdom perceived by all) is alone manifested. Of that Principle which is still higher nothing is even predicated, except that its universal presence and actuality are a philosophical necessity.

**Heavenly Adam.** The synthesis of the Sephirothal Tree, or of all the Forces in Nature and their informing deific essence. In the diagrams, the Seventh of the lower Sephiroth, Sephira *Malkhooth*—the Kingdom of Harmony—represents the feet of the ideal Macrocosm, whose head reaches to the first manifested Head. This Heavenly Adam is the *natura naturans,* the abstract world, while the Adam of Earth (Humanity) is the *natura naturata* or the material universe. The former is the presence of Deity in its universal essence; the latter the manifestation of the intelligence of that essence. In the *real Zohar* not the fantastic and anthropomorphic caricature which we often find in the writings of Western Kabbalists—there is not a particle of the personal deity which we find so prominent in the dark cloaking of the Secret Wisdom known as the Mosaic Pentateuch.

**Hebdomad** (*Gr.*) The Septenary.

**Hebron** or *Kirjath-Arba.* The city of the Four Kabeiri, for *Kirjath Arba* signifies "the City of the Four". It is in that city, according to the legend, that an Isarim or an Initiate found the famous Smaragdine tablet on the dead body of Hermes.

**Hel** or Hela (*Scand.*). The Goddess-Queen of the Land of the Dead; the inscrutable and direful Being who reigns over the depths of Helheim and Nifelheim. In the earlier mythology, Hel was the earth-goddess, the good and beneficent mother, nourisher of the weary and the hungry. But in the later Skalds she became the female Pluto, the dark Queen of the Kingdom of Shades, she who brought death into this world, and sorrow afterwards.

**Helheim** (*Scand.*), The Kingdom of the Dead in the Norse mythology. In the *Edda,* Helheim surrounds the Northern Mistworld, called Nifelheim.

**Heliolatry** (*Gr.*). Sun-Worship.

**Hell.** A term with the Anglo-Saxons, evidently derived from the name of the goddess *Hela* (*q.v.*), and by the Sclavonians from the Greek Hades: hell being in Russian and other Sclavonian tongues—*ad,* the only difference between the Scandinavian cold hell and the hot hell of the Christians, being found in their respective temperatures. But even the idea of those overheated regions is not original with the Europeans, many peoples having entertained the conception of an underworld climate; as well may we if we localise our Hell in the centre of the earth. All exoteric religions—the creeds of the Brahmans, Buddhists, Zoroastrians, Mahommedans, Jews, and the rest, make their hells hot and dark, though many are more attractive than frightful. The idea of a hot hell is an afterthought, the distortion of an astronomical allegory. With the Egyptians, Hell became a place of punishment by fire not earlier than the seventeenth or eighteenth dynasty, when Typhon was transformed from a god into a devil. But at whatever time this dread superstition was implanted in the minds of the poor ignorant masses, the scheme of a burning hell and souls tormented therein is purely Egyptian. Ra (the Sun) became the Lord of the Furnace in Karr, the hell of the Pharaohs, and the sinner was threatened with misery "in the heat of infernal fires". "A lion was there" says Dr. Birch "and was called the roaring monster". Another describes the place as "the bottomless pit and lake of fire, into which the victims are thrown" (compare *Revelation*). The Hebrew word *gaï-hinnom* (Gehenna) never really had the significance given to it in Christian orthodoxy.

**Hemadri** (*Sk.*) The golden Mountain; Meru.

**Hemera** (*Gr.*) "The light of the inferior or terrestrial regions" as Ether is the light of the superior heavenly spheres. Both are born of *Erebos* (darkness) and *Nux* (night).

**Heptakis** (*Gr.*) "The Seven-rayed One "of the Chaldean astrolaters: the same as IAO.

**Herakies** (*Gr.*). The same as Hercules.

**Heranasikha** (*Sing.*) From *Herana* "novice" and *Sikha* "rule" or precept: manual of Precepts. A work written in *Elu* or the ancient Singhalese, for the use of young priests.

**Hermanubis** (*Gr.*). Or Hermes Anubis" the revealer of the mysteries of the lower world "—not of Hell or Hades as interpreted, but of our Earth (*the* *lowest world of the septenary chain of worlds*)—and also of the sexual mysteries. Creuzer must have guessed at the truth of the right interpretation, as he calls Anubis-Thoth-Hermes "*a symbol of science and of the intellectual world*". He was always represented with a cross in his hand, one of the earliest symbols of the mystery of generation, or procreation on this earth. In the Chaldean Kabbala (*Book of Numbers*) the Tat symbol, or +, is referred to as Adam and Eve, the latter being the transverse or horizontal bar drawn out of the side (or rib) of *Hadam*, the perpendicular bar. The fact is that, esoterically, Adam and Eve while representing the early *third* Root Race—those who, being still mindless, imitated the animals and degraded themselves with the latter—stand also as the dual symbol of the sexes. Hence Anubis, the Egyptian god of generation, is represented with the head of an animal, a dog or a jackal, and is also said to be the "Lord of the underworld" or "Hades "into which he introduces the souls of the dead (the reincarnating entities), for Hades is in one sense the womb, as some of the writings of the Church Fathers fully show.

**Hermaphrodite** (*Gr.*). Dual-sexed; a male and female Being, whether man or animal.

**Hermas** (Gr.). An ancient Greek writer of whose works only a few fragments are now extant.

**Hermes-fire.** The same as "Elmes-fire". (See *Isis Unveiled* Vol. I.,p. 125.)

**Hermes Sarameyas** (*Greco-Sanskrit*) The God Hermes, or Mercury, "he who watches over the flock of stars" in the Greek mythology.

**Hermes Trismegistus** (*Gr.*). The "thrice great Hermes", the Egyptian. The mythical personage after whom the Hermetic philosophy was named. In Egypt the God Thoth or Thot. A generic name of many ancient Greek writers on philosophy and Alchemy. Hermes Trismegistus is the name of Hermes or Thoth in his human aspect, as a god he is far more than this. As *Hermes-Thoth-Aah*, he is Thoth, the moon, i.e., his symbol is the bright side of the moon, supposed to contain the essence of creative Wisdom, "the elixir of Hermes ". As such he is associated with the Cynocephalus, the dog-headed monkey, for the same reason as was Anubis, one of the aspects of Thoth. (See "Hermanubis".) The same idea underlies the form of the Hindu God of Wisdom, the elephant-headed Ganesa, or Ganpat, the son of Parvati and Siva. (See "Ganesa".) When he has the head of an *ibis,* he is the sacred scribe of the gods; but even then he wears the crown *atef* and the lunar di*Sk.* He is the most mysterious of gods. As a serpent, Hermes Thoth is the divine creative 'Wisdom. The Church Fathers speak at length of Thoth-Hermes. (See "Hermetic".)

**Hermetic.** Any doctrine or writing connected with the esoteric teachings of Hermes, who, whether as the Egyptian Thoth or the Greek Hermes, was the God of Wisdom with the Ancients, and, according to Plato, "discovered numbers, geometry, astronomy and letters". Though mostly considered as spurious, nevertheless the Hermetic writings were highly prized by St. Augustine, Lactantius, Cyril and others. In the words of Mr. J. Bonwick, "They are more or less touched up by the Platonic philosophers among the early Christians (such as Origen and Clemens Alexandrinus) who sought to substantiate their Christian arguments by appeals to these heathen and revered writings, though they could not resist the temptation of making them say a little too much. Though represented by some clever and interested writers as teaching pure monotheism, the Hermetic or Trismegistic books are, nevertheless, purely pantheistic. The Deity referred to in them is defined by Paul as that in *which* "we live, and move and have our being"—notwithstanding the "in Him" of the translators.

**Hetu** (*Sk.*). A natural or physical cause.

**Heva** (*Heb.*). Eve, "the mother of all that lives".

**Hiarchas** (*Gr.*). The King of the "Wise Men", in the Journey of Apollonius of Tyana to India.

**Hierogrammatists.** The title given to those Egyptian priests who were entrusted with the writing and reading of the sacred and secret records. The "scribes of the secret records" literally. They were the instructors of the neophytes preparing for initiation.

**Hierophant**. From the Greek "Hierophantes"; literally, "One who explains sacred things ". The discloser of sacred learning and the Chief of the Initiates. A title belonging to the highest Adepts in the temples of antiquity, who were the teachers and expounders of the Mysteries and the Initiators into the final great Mysteries. The Hierophant represented the Demiurge, and explained to the postulants for Initiation the various phenomena of Creation that were produced for their tuition. "He was the sole expounder of the esoteric secrets and doctrines. It was forbidden even to pronounce his name before an uninitiated person. He sat in the East, and wore as a symbol of authority a golden globe suspended from the neck. He was also called *Mystagogus*" (Kenneth R. H. Mackenzie, ix., F.T.S., in *The Royal Masonic Cyclopædia*). In Hebrew and Chaldaic the term was *Peter*, the opener, discloser; hence the Pope as the successor of the hierophant of the ancient Mysteries, sits in the Pagan chair of St. Peter.

**Higher Self.** The Supreme Divine Spirit overshadowing man. The crown of the upper spiritual Triad in man—Atmân.

**Hillel.** A great Babylonian Rabbi of the century preceding the Christian era. He was the founder of the sect of the Pharisees, a learned and a sainted man.

**Himachala Himadri** (*Sk.*). The Himalayan Mountains.

**Himavat** *(Sk)*. The personified Himalayas; the father of the river Ganga, or Ganges.

**Hinayana** (*Sk.*). The "Smaller Vehicle"; a Scripture and a School of the Northern Buddhists, opposed to the *Mahayana,* "the Greater Vehicle", in Tibet. Both schools are mystical. (See "Mahayana".) Also in exoteric superstition the lowest form of transmigration.

**Hiouen Thsang.** A great Chinese writer and philosopher who travelled in India in the sixth century, in order to learn more about Buddhism, to which he was devoted.

**Hippocrates** (*Gr.*). A famous physician of Cos, one of the Cyclades, who flourished at Athens during the invasion of Artaxerxes, and delivered that town from a dreadful pestilence. He was called "the father of Medicine ". Having studied his art from the votive tablets offered by the cured patients at the temples of Æsculapius, he became an Initiate and the most proficient healer of his day, so much so that he was almost deified. His learning and knowledge were enormous. Galen says of his writings that they are truly the voice of an oracle. He died in his 100th year, 361 B.C.

**Hippopotamus** (*Gr.*) In Egyptian symbolism Typhon was called "the hippopotamus who slew his father and violated his mother," Rhea (mother of the gods). His father was Chronos. As applied therefore to Time and Nature (Chronos and Rhea), the accusation becomes comprehensible. The type of Cosmic Disharmony, Typhon, who is also Python, the monster formed of the slime of the Deluge of Deucalion, "violates" his mother, Primordial Harmony, whose beneficence was so great that she was called "The Mother of the Golden Age". It was Typhon, who put an end to the latter, i.e., produced the first war of elements.

**Hiquet** *(Eg.)*. The frog-goddess; one of the symbols of immortality and of the "water" principle. The early Christians had their church lamps made in the form of a frog, to denote that baptism in water led to immortality.

**Hiram Abiff**. A biblical personage; a skilful builder and a "Widow's Son", whom King Solomon procured from Tyre, for the purpose of superintending the works of the Temple, and who became later a masonic character, the hero on whom hangs all the drama, or rather play, of the Masonic Third Initiation. The Kabbala makes a great deal of Hiram Abiff.

**Hiranya** (*Sk.*). Radiant, golden, used of the "Egg of Brahmâ".

**Hiranya Garbha** (*Sk.*). The radiant or golden egg or womb. Esoterically the luminous "fire mist" or ethereal stuff from which the Universe was formed.

**Hiranyakasipu** (*Sk.*). A King of the Daityas, whom Vishnu—in his *avatar* of the "man lion"—puts to death.

**Hiranyaksha** (*Sk.*). "The golden-eyed," the king and ruler of the 5th region of *Pâtala*, the nether-world; a snake-god in the Hindu Pantheon. It has various other meanings.

**Hiranyapura** (*Sk.*). The Golden City.

**Hisi** (*Fin.*). The "Principle of Evil" in the *Kalevala*, the epic poem of Finland.

**Hitopadesa** (*Sk.*). "Good Advice." A work composed of a collection of ethical precepts, allegories and other tales from an old Scripture, the *Panchatantra.*

**Hivim** or *Chivim* (*Heb.*). Whence the Hivites who, according to some Roman Catholic commentators, descend from Heth, son of Canaan, son of Ham, "the accursed". Brasseur de Bourbourg, the missionary translator of the Scripture of the Guatemalians, the *Popol Vuh,* indulges in the theory that the *Hivim* of the *Quetzo Cohuatl*, the Mexican Serpent Deity, and the "descendants of Serpents" as they call themselves, are identical with the descendants of Ham (! !) "whose ancestor is Cain". Such is the conclusion, at any rate, drawn from Bourhourg's writings by Des Mousseaux, the demonologist. Bourbourg hints that the chiefs of the name of Votan, the Quetzo Cohuati, are the descendants of Ham and Canaan. "I am Hivim", they say. "Being a Hivim, I am of the great Race of the Dragons. I am a snake, myself, for I am a Hivim' (*Cortes* 51). But Cain is allegorically shown as the ancestor of the Hivites, the Serpents, because Cain is held to have been *the first initiate in the mystery of procreation.* The "race of the Dragons" or Serpents means the Wise Adepts. The names *Hivi* or Hivite, and Levi—signify a Serpent "; and the Hivites or Serpent-tribe of Palestine, were, like all Levites and Ophites of Israel, *initiated* Ministers to the temples, i.e., Occultists, as are the priests of Quetzo Cohuatl. The Gibeonites whom Joshua assigned *to the service of the sanctuary* were Hivites. (See *Isis Unveiled*, Vol. II. 481.)

**Hler** (*Scand.*). The god of the One of the three mighty sons of the Frost-giant, Ymir. These sons were Kari, god of the air and the storms; Hler of the Sea; and Logi of the fire. They are the Cosmic trinity of the Norsemen.

**Hoa** (*Heb.*). That, from which proceeds *Ab*, the "Father"; therefore the Concealed *Logos*.

**Hoang Ty** (*Chin.*). "The Great Spirit." His Sons are said to have acquired new wisdom, and imparted what they knew before to mortals, by falling—like the rebellious angels—into the "Valley of Pain", which is allegorically our Earth. In other words they are identical with the "Fallen Angels" of exoteric religions, and with the reincarnating Egos, esoterically.

**Hochmah** (*Heb.*). See "Chochmah".

**Hod** (*Heb.*). Splendour, the eighth of the ten Sephiroth, a female passive potency. [w.w.w.]

**Holy of Holies.** The Assyriologists, Egyptologists, and Orientalists, in general, show that such a place existed in every temple of antiquity. The great temple of Bel-Merodach whose sides faced the four cardinal points, had in its extreme end a "Holy of Holies" hidden from the profane by a veil: here, "at the beginning of the year 'the divine king of heaven and earth, the lord of the heavens, seats himself'." According to Herodotus, here was the golden image of the god with a golden table in front like the Hebrew table for the shew bread, and upon this, food appears to have been placed. in some temples there also was "a little coffer or ark with two engraved stone tablets on it". (Myer's *Qabbalah.*) In short, it is now pretty well proven, that the "chosen people" had nothing original of their own, but that every detail of their ritualism and religion was borrowed from older nations. The *Hibbert Lectures* by Prof. Sayce and others show this abundantly. The story of the birth of Moses is that of Sargon, the Babylonian, who preceded Moses by a couple of thousand years; and no wonder, as Dr. Sayce tells us that the name of Moses, *Mosheh,* has a connection with the name of the Babylonian sun-god as the "hero" or "leader". (*Hib. Lect.*, p. 46 *et seq.*) Says Mr. J. Myer, "The orders of the priests were divided into high priests, those attached or bound to certain deities, like the Hebrew Levites; anointers or cleaners; the *Kali*, 'illustrious' or 'elders'; the soothsayers, and the *Makhkhu* or 'great one', in which Prof. Delitzsch sees the *Rab-mag* of the Old Testament. . . The Akkadians and Chaldeans kept a Sabbath day of rest every seven days, they also had thanksgiving days, and days for humiliation and prayer. There were sacrifices of vegetables and animals, of meats and wine. . . . The number seven was especially sacred. . . . The great temple of Babylon existed long before 2,250 B.C. Its 'Holy of Holies' was with in the shrine of Nebo, the prophet god of wisdom." It is from the Akkadians that the god Mardak passed to the Assyrians, and he had been before Merodach, "the merciful", of the Babylonians, the only son and interpreter of the will of Ea or *Hea*, the great Deity of Wisdom. The Assyriologists have, in short, unveiled the whole scheme of the "*chosen* people".

**Holy Water.** This is one of the oldest rites practised in Egypt, and thence in Pagan Rome. It accompanied the rite of bread and wine. "Holy water was sprinkled by the Egyptian priest alike upon his gods' images and the faithful. It was both poured and sprinkled. A brush has been found, supposed to have been used for that purpose, as at this day." (Bonwick's *Egyptian Belief.*) As to the bread, "the cakes of Isis were placed upon the altar. Gliddon writes that they were 'identical in shape with the consecrated cake of the Roman and Eastern Churches'. Melville assures us 'the Egyptians marked this holy bread with St. Andrew's cross'. The Presence bread was broken before being distributed by the priests to the people, and was supposed to become the flesh and blood of the Deity. The miracle was wrought by the hand of the officiating priest, who blessed the food. . . . Rouge tells us 'the bread offerings bear the imprint of the fingers, the mark of consecration '." (*Ibid*, page 458.) (See also "Bread and Wine".)

**Homogeneity.** From the Greek words *homos* "the same" and *genos* "kind". That which is of the same nature throughout, undifferentiated, non-compound, as gold is *supposed* to be.

**Honir** (*Scand.*). A creative god who furnished the first man with intellect and understanding after man had been created by him jointly with Odin and Lodur from an ash tree.

**Honover** (*Zend*). The Persian *Logos*, the manifested Word.

**Hor Ammon** (*Eg.*). "The Self-engendered", a word in theogony which answers to the Sanskrit *Anupadaka*, parentless. Hor-Ammon is a combination of the ram-headed god of Thebes and of Horus.

**Horchia** (*Chald.*). According to Berosus, the same as Vesta, goddess of the Hearth.

**Horus** (*Eg.*). The last in the line of divine Sovereigns in Egypt, said to he the son of Osiris and Isis. He is the great god "loved of Heaven", the "beloved of the Sun, the offspring of the gods, the subjugator of the world". At the time of the Winter Solstice (our Christmas), his image, in the form of a small newly-born infant, was brought out from the sanctuary for the adoration of the worshipping crowds. As he is the type of the vault of heaven, he is said to have come from the *Maem Misi,* the sacred birthplace (the womb of the World), and is, therefore, the "mystic Child of the Ark" or the *argha*, the symbol of the matrix. Cosmically, he is the Winter Sun. A tablet describes him as the "substance of his father", Osiris, of whom he is an incarnation and also identical with him. Horus is a chaste deity, and "like Apollo has no amours. His part in the lower world is associated with the judgment. He introduces souls to his father, the judge" (Bonwick). An ancient hymn says of him, "By him the world is judged in that which it contains. Heaven and earth are under his immediate presence. He rules all human beings. The sun goes round according to his purpose. He brings forth abundance and dispenses it to all the earth. Everyone adores his beauty. Sweet is his love in us."

**Hotri** (*Sk.*). A priest who recites the hymns from the *Rig Veda*, and makes oblations to the fire.

**Hotris** (*Sk*). A symbolical name for the *seven* senses called, in the *Anugita* "the Seven Priests". "The senses supply the fire of mind (i.e., desire) with the oblations of external pleasures." An occult term used metaphysically.

**Hrimthurses** (*Scand.*). The Frost-giants; Cyclopean builders in the *Edda*.

**Humanity.** Occultly and Kabbalistically, the whole of mankind is symbolised, by Manu in India; by Vajrasattva or Dorjesempa, the head of the Seven Dhyani, in Northern Buddhism; and by Adam Kadmon in the Kabbala. All these represent the totality of mankind whose beginning is in this androgynic protoplast, and whose end is in the Absolute, beyond all these symbols and myths of human origin. Humanity is a great Brotherhood by virtue of the sameness of the material from which it is formed physically and morally. Unless, however, it becomes a Brotherhood also intellectually, it is no better than a superior genus of animals.

**Hun-desa** (*Sk.*). The country around lake Mansaravara in Tibet.

**Hvanuatha** (*Mazd.*). The name of the earth on which we live. One of the seven *Karshvare* (Earths), spoken of in *Orma Ahr*. (See Introduction to the *Vendidad* by Prof. Darmsteter.)

**Hwergelmir** (*Scand.*). A roaring cauldron wherein the souls of the evil doers perish.

**Hwun** (*Chin.*). Spirit. The same as Atmân.

**Hydranos** (*Gr.*). Lit., the "Baptist". A name of the ancient Hierophant of the

Mysteries who made the candidate pass through the "trial by water", wherein he was plunged thrice. This was his baptism by the Holy Spirit which moves on the waters of Space. Paul refers to St. John as *Hydranos*, the Baptist. The Christian Church took this rite from the ritualism of the Eleusinian and other Mysteries.

**Hyksos** (*Eg.*). The mysterious nomads, the Shepherds, who invaded Egypt at a period unknown and far anteceding the days of Moses. They are called the "Shepherd Kings".

**Hyle** (*Gr.*). Primordial stuff or matter; esoterically the homogeneous sediment of Chaos or the Great Deep. The first principle out of which the objective Universe was formed.

**Hypatia** (*Gr.*). The girl-philosopher, who lived at Alexandria during the fifth century, and taught many a famous man—among others Bishop Synesius. She was the daughter of the mathematician Theon, and became famous for her learning. Falling a martyr to the fiendish conspiracy of Theophilos, Bishop of Alexandria, and his nephew Cyril, she was foully murdered by their order. With her death fell the Neo Platonic School.

**Hyperborean** (*Gr.*). The regions around the North Pole in the Arctic Circle.

**Hypnotism** (*Gr.*). A name given by Dr. Braid to various processes by which one person of strong will-power plunges another of weaker mind into a kind of trance; once in such a state the latter will do anything *suggested* to him by the hypnotiser. Unless produced for beneficial purposes, Occultists would call it *black magic* or Sorcery. It is the most dangerous of practices, morally and physically, as it interferes with the nerve fluid and the nerves controlling the circulation in the capillary blood-vessels.

**Hypocephalus** (*Gr.*). A kind of a pillow for the head of the mummy. They are of various kinds, *e.g.*, of stone, wood, etc., and very often of circular disks of linen covered with cement, and inscribed with magic figures and letters. They are called "rest for the dead" in the *Ritual*, and every mummy-coffin has one.

# I

I .—The ninth letter in the English, the tenth in the Hebrew alphabet. As a numeral it signifies in both languages *one*, and also *ten* in the Hebrew (see J), in which it corresponds to the Divine name *Jah*, the male side, or aspect, of the hermaphrodite being, or the male-female Adam, of which *hovah* Jah-hovah) is the female aspect. It is symbolized by a hand with bent fore-finger, to show its phallic signification.

**Iacchos** (*Gr.*). A synonym of Bacchus. Mythology mentions three persons so named: they were Greek ideals adopted later by the Romans. The word Iacchos is stated to be of Phœnician origin, and to mean "an infant at the breast ". Many ancient monuments represent Ceres or Demeter with Bacchus in her arms. One Iacchos was called Theban and Conqueror, son of Jupiter and Semele; his mother died before his birth and he was preserved for some time in the thigh of his father; he was killed by the Titans. Another was son of Jupiter, as a Dragon, and Persephone; this one was named Zagræmus. A third was Iacchos of Eleusis, son of Ceres: he is of importance because he appeared on the sixth day of the Eleusinian Mysteries. Some see an analogy between Bacchus and Noah, both cultivators of the Vine, and patrons of alcoholic excess. [w.w.w.]

**Iachus** (*Gr.*). An Egyptian physician, whose memory, according to Ælian, was venerated for long centuries on account of his wonderful occult knowledge. Iachus is credited with having stopped epidemics simply by *certain fumigations*, and cured diseases by making his patients inhale herbs.

**Iaho**. Though this name is more fully treated under the word"Yaho" and "Iao", a few words of explanation will not be found amiss. Diodorus mentions that the God of Moses was Iao; but as the latter name denotes a "mystery god", it cannot therefore be confused with Iaho or Yaho (*q.v.*). The Samaritans pronounced it Iabe, Yahva, and the Jews Yaho, and then Jehovah, by change of Masoretic vowels, an elastic scheme by which any change may be indulged in. But "Jehovah" is a later invention and invocation, as originally the name was Jah, or Iacchos (Bacchus). Aristotle shows the ancient Arabs representing Iach (Iacchos) by a horse, *i.e.*, *the horse of the Sun* (Dionysus), which followed the chariot on which Ahura Mazda, the god of the Heavens, daily rode.

**Iamblichus** (*Gr.*). A great Theurgist, mystic, and writer of the third and fourth centuries, a Neo-Platonist and philosopher, born at Chalcis in Cœle-Syria. Correct biographies of him have never existed because of the hatred of the Christians; but that which has been gathered of his life in isolated fragments from works by impartial pagan and independent writers shows how excellent and holy was his moral character, and how great his learning. He may be called the founder of theurgic magic among the Neo-Platonists and the reviver of the practical mysteries outside of temple or fane. His school was at first distinct from that of Plotinus and Porphyry, who were strongly against ceremonial magic and practical theurgy as dangerous, though later he convinced Porphyry of its. advisability on some occasions, and both master and pupil firmly believed in theurgy and magic, of which the former is principally the highest and most efficient mode of communication with one's Higher Ego, through the medium of one's astral body. Theurgic is benevolent magic, and it becomes goetic, or dark and evil, only when it is used for necromancy or selfish purposes; but such dark magic has never been practised by any theurgist or philosopher, whose name has descended to us unspotted by any evil deed. So much was Porphyry (who became the teacher of Iamblichus in Neo-Platonic philosophy) convinced of this, that though he himself never practised theurgy, yet he gave instructions for the acquirement of this sacred science. Thus he says in one of his writings, "Whosoever is acquainted with the nature of *divinely luminous appearances fasmata* knows also on what account it is requisite to abstain from all birds (and animal food) and especially for him who hastens to be liberated from terrestrial concerns and to be established with the celestial gods". (*See Select Works* by T. Taylor, p. 159.) Moreover, the same Porphyry mentions in his Life of Plotinus a priest of Egypt, who, "at the request of a certain friend of Plotinus, exhibited to him, in the temple of Isis at Rome, the familiar *daimon* of that philosopher ". In other words, he produced the theurgic invocation (see "Theurgist") by which Egyptian Hierophant or Indian Mahâtma, of old, could clothe their own or any other person's astral *double* with the appearance of its Higher EGO, or what Bulwer Lytton terms the "Luminous Self", the *Augoeides,* and confabulate with It. This it is which Iamblichus and many others, including the mediæval Rosicrucans, meant by *union with Deity.* Iamblichus wrote many books but only a few of his works are extant, such as his "Egyptian Mysteries" and a treatise "On Dæmons", in which he speaks very severely against any intercourse with them. He was a biographer of Pythagoras and deeply versed in the system of the latter, and was also learned in the Chaldean Mysteries. He taught that the One, or universal MONAD, was the principle of all unity as well as diversity, or of Homogeneity and Heterogeneity; that the Duad, or two ("Principles"), was the intellect, or that which we call Buddhi-Manas; three, was the Soul (the lower Manas), etc. etc. There is much of the theosophical in his teachings, and his works on the various kinds of dæmons (Elementals) are a well of esoteric knowledge for the student. His austerities, purity of life and earnestness were great. Iamblichus is credited with having been once levitated ten cubits high from the ground, as are some of the modern Yogis, and even great mediums.

**Iao** (*Gr.*). See Iaho. The highest god of the Phœnicians the light conceivable only by intellect", the physical and spiritual Principle of all things, "the male Essence of Wisdom ". It is the ideal Sun light.

**Iao Hebdomai** (*Gr.*). The collective "Seven Heavens" (also angels) according to Irenæus. The mystery-god of the Gnostics. The same as the Seven *Manasa-putras* (*q.v.*) of the Occultists. (See also "Yah" and "Yaho".)

**Ibis Worship.** The Ibis, in Egyptian *Hab*, was sacred to Thoth at Hermopolis. It was called the messenger of Osiris, for it is the symbol of Wisdom, Discrimination, and Purity, as it loathes water if it is the least impure. Its usefulness in devouring the eggs of the crocodiles and serpents was great, and its credentials for divine honours as a symbol were: (a) its black wings, which related it to primeval darkness—chaos; and (b) the triangular shape of them—the triangle being the first geometrical figure and a symbol of the trinitarian mystery. To this day the Ibis is a sacred bird with some tribes of Kopts who live along the Nile.

**Ibn Gebirol**. *Solomon Ben Yehudah*: a great philosopher and scholar, a Jew by birth, who lived in the eleventh century in Spain. The same as Avicenna (*q.v.*).

**Ichchha** (*Sk.*). Will, or will-power.

**Ichchha Sakti** (*Sk.*). Will-power; force of desire; one of the occult Forces of nature. That power of the will which, exercised in occult practices, generates the nerve-currents necessary to set certain muscles in motion and to paralyze certain others.

**Ichthus** (*Gr.*). A Fish: the symbol of the Fish has been frequently referred to Jesus, the Christ of the New Testament, partly because the five letters forming the word are the initials of the Greek phrase, *Iesous* Christos *Theou Uios Soter,* Jesus Christ the Saviour, Son of God. Hence his followers in the early Christian centuries were often called *fishes,* and drawings of fish are found in the Catacombs. Compare also the narrative that some of his early disciples were fishermen, and the assertion of Jesus— "I will make you fishers of men". Note also the Vesica Piscis, a conventional shape for fish in general, is frequently found enclosing a picture of a Christ, holy virgin, or saint; it is a long oval with pointed ends, the space marked out by the intersection of two equal circles, when less than half the area of one. Compare the Christian female recluse, a Nun—this word is the Chaldee name for fish, and fish is connected with the worship of Venus, a goddess, and the Roman Catholics still eat fish on the Dies Veneris or Friday. [w.w.w.]

**Ida** (*Scand.*). The plains of Ida, on which the gods assemble to hold counsel in the *Edda*. The field of peace and rest.

**Ideos.** In Paracelsus the same as Chaos, or *Mysterium Magnum* as that philosopher calls it.

**Idises** (*Scand.*). The same as the Dises, the Fairies and Walkyries, the divine women in the Norse legends; they were reverenced by the Teutons before the day of Tacitus, as the latter shows.

**Idæic Finger.** An iron finger strongly magnetized and used in the temples for healing purposes. It produced wonders in that direction, and therefore was said to possess magical powers.

**Idol.** A statue or a picture of a heathen god; or a statue or picture of a Romish Saint, or a fetish of uncivilized tribes.

**Idospati** (*Sk.*). The same as Narayana or Vishnu; resembling Poseidon in some respects.

**Idra Rabba** (*Heb.*). "The Greater Holy Assembly ' a division of the *Zohar*.

**Idra Suta** (*Heb.*). "The Lesser Holy Assembly", another division of the *Zohar*.

**Iduna** (*Scand.*). The goddess of immortal youth. The daughter of Iwaldi, the Dwarf. She is said in the *Edda* to have hidden "life" in the Deep of the Ocean, and when the right time came, to have restored it to Earth once more. She was the wife of Bragi, the god of poetry; a most charming myth. Like Heimdal, "born of nine mothers", Bragi at his birth rises upon the crest of the wave from the bottom of the sea (see "Bragi"). He married Iduna, the immortal goddess, who accompanies him to Asgard where every morning she feeds the gods with the apples of eternal youth and health. (*See Asgard and the Gods*.)

**Idwatsara** (*Sk.*). One of the five periods that form the Yuga. This cycle is pre-eminently the Vedic cycle, which is taken as the basis of calculation for larger cycles.

**Ieu.** The "first man"; a Gnostic term used in *Pistis-Sophia*.

**Iezedians** or *Iezidi* (*Pers.*). This sect came to Syria from Basrah. They use baptism, believe in the archangels, but reverence Satan at the same time. Their prophet Iezad, who preceded Mahomet by long centuries, taught that a messenger from heaven would bring them a book written from the eternity.

**Ifing** (*Scand.*). The broad river that divides Asgard, the home of the gods, from that of the Jotuns, the great and strong magicians. Below Asgard was

Midgard, where in the sunny æther was built the home of the Light Elves. In their disposition and order of locality, all these Homes answer to the Deva and other Lokas of the Hindus, inhabited by the various classes of gods and Asuras.

**Igaga** (Chald.) Celestial angels, the same as Archangels.

**I.H.S.** This triad of initials stands for the *in hoc signo* of the alleged vision of Constantine, of which, save Eusebius, its author, no one ever knew. I.H.S. is interpreted *Jesus Hominum Salvator*, and *In hoc signo*. It is, however, well known that the Greek IHS was one of the most ancient names of Bacchus. As Jesus was never identical with Jehovah, but with his own "Father" (as all of us are), and had come rather to destroy the worship of Jehovah than to enforce it, as the Rosicrucians well maintained, the scheme of Eusebius is very transparent. *In hoc signo Victor ens,* or *the Labarum* T (the *tau* and the *resh*) is a very old *signum*, placed on the foreheads of those who were just initiated. Kenealy translates it as meaning "he who is initiated into the Naronic Secret, or the 600, shall be Victor" but it is simply "through this sign hast thou conquered"; i.e., through the *light* of Initiation—Lux. (See "Neophyte and "Naros".)

**Ikhir Bonga.** A "Spirit of the Deep" of the Kolarian tribes.

**Ikshwaku** (*Sk.*). The progenitor of the Solar tribe (the Suryavansas) in India, and the Son of Vaivaswata Manu, the progenitor of the present human Race.

**Ila** (*Sk.*). Daughter of Vaivaswata Manu; wife of Buddha, the son of Soma; one month a woman and the other a man by the decree of Saraswati; an allusion to the androgynous second race. Ila is also Vâch in another aspect.

**Ilavriti** (*Sk.*). A region in the centre of which is placed Mount Meru, the habitat of the gods.

**Ilda Baoth.** *Lit.,* "the child from the Egg", a Gnostic term. He is the creator of our physical globe (the earth) according to the Gnostic teaching in the *Codex Nazaræus* (the Evangel of the Nazarenes and the Ebionites). The latter identifies him with Jehovah the God of the Jews. Ildabaoth is "the Son of Darkness" in a bad sense and the father of the six terrestrial "Stellar", dark spirits, the antithesis of the bright Stellar spirits. Their respective abodes are the seven spheres, the upper of which begins in the "middle space", the region of their mother Sophia Achamôth, and the lower ending on this earth—the seventh region (See *Isis Unveiled,* Vol. II., 183.) Ilda-Baoth is the genius of Saturn, the planet; or rather the evil spirit of its ruler.

**Iliados.** In Paracelsus the same as "Ideos" (*q.v.*). Primordial matter in the subjective state.

**Illa-ah**, *Adam (Heb.).* Adam Illa-ah is the celestial, superior Adam, in the *Zohar.*

**Illinus.** One of the gods in the Chaldean Theogony of Damascius.

**Ilmatar** *(Finn.).* The Virgin who falls from heaven into the sea before creation. She is the "daughter of the air" and the mother of seven Sons (the seven forces in nature). (See Kalevala, the epic poem of Finland.)

**Illusion.** In Occultism everything finite (like the universe and all in it) is called illusion or *maya.*

**Illuminati** *(Lat.).* The "Enlightened", the initiated adepts.

**Ilus** *(Gr.).* Primordial mud or slime; called also Hyle.

**Image.** Occultism permits no other image than that of the living image of divine man (the symbol of Humanity) on earth. The *Kabbala* teaches that this divine Image, the copy of the *sublime and holy upper Image* (the Elohim) has now changed into *another similitude,* owing to the development of men's sinful nature. It is only the *upper divine Image* (the Ego) which is the same; the lower (personality) has changed, and man, now fearing the wild beasts, has grown to bear on his face the similitude of many of them. (*Zohar* I. fol. 71a.) In the early period of Egypt there were no images; but later, as Lenormand says, "In the sanctuaries of Egypt they divided the properties of nature and consequently of Divinity (the Elohim, or the Egos), into seven abstract qualities, characterised each by an emblem, which are matter, cohesion, fluxion, coagulation, accumulation, station and division ". These were all attributes symbolized in various images.

**Imagination.** In Occultism this is not to be confused with fancy, as it is one of the plastic powers of the higher Soul, and is the memory of the preceding incarnations, which, however disfigured by the lower Manas, yet rests always on a ground of truth.

**Imhot-pou** or *Imhotep (Eg.).* The god of learning (the Greek Imouthes). He was the son of Ptah, and in one aspect Hermes, as he is represented as imparting wisdom with a book before him. He is a solar god; lit., "the god of the handsome face ".

**Immah** *(Heb.).* Mother, in contradistinction to *Abba,* father.

**Immah Illa-ah** *(Heb.).* The upper mother; a name given to Shekinah.

**In** *(Chin.).* The female principle of matter, impregnated by Yo, the male ethereal principle, and precipitated thereafter down into the universe.

**Incarnations** *(Divine)* or *Avatars*. The Immaculate Conception is as pre-eminently Egyptian as it is Indian. As the author of *Egyptian Belief* has it: "It is not the vulgar, coarse and sensual story as in Greek mythology, but refined, moral and spiritual "; and again the incarnation idea was found revealed on the wall of a Theban temple by Samuel Sharpe, who thus analyzes it: "First the god Thoth . . . as the messenger of the gods, like the Mercury of the Greeks (or the Gabriel of the first Gospel), tells the *maiden* queen Mautmes, that she is to give birth to a son, who is to be king Amunotaph III. Secondly, the god Kneph, the Spirit . . . . and the goddess Hathor (Nature) both take hold of the queen by the hands and put into her mouth the character for life, a cross, which is to be the life of the coming child", etc., etc. Truly divine incarnation, or the *avatar* doctrine, constituted the grandest mystery of every old religious system!

**Incas** *(Peruvian)*. The name given to the creative gods in the Peruvian theogony, and later to the rulers of the country. "The Incas, *seven* in number have repeopled the earth after the Deluge ', Coste makes them say (I. iv., p. 19). They belonged at the beginning of the *fifth* Root-race to a dynasty of divine kings, such as those of Egypt, India and Chaldea.

**Incubus** *(Lat.)*. Something more real and dangerous than the ordinary meaning given to the word, viz., that of "nightmare ". An *Incubus* is the male Elemental, and *Succuba* the female, and these are undeniably the spooks of mediæval demonology, called forth from the invisible regions by human passion and lust. They are now called "Spirit brides" and "Spirit husbands" among some benighted Spiritists and spiritual mediums. But these poetical names do not prevent them in the least being that which they are—Ghools, Vampires and soulless Elementals; formless centres of Life, devoid of sense; in short, *subjective protoplasms* when left alone, but called into a definite being and form by the creative and diseased imagination of certain mortals. They were known under every clime as in every age, and the Hindus can tell more than one terrible tale of the dramas enacted in the life of young students and mystics by the *Pisachas*, their name in India.

**Individuality.** One of the names given in Theosophy and Occultism to the Human Higher EGO. We make a distinction between the immortal and divine Ego, and the mortal human Ego which perishes. The latter, or "personality" (personal Ego) survives the dead body only for a time in the Kama Loka; the Individuality prevails forever.

**Indra** *(Sk.)*. The god of the Firmament, the King of the sidereal gods. A Vedic Deity.

**Indrâni** (*Sk.*). The female aspect of Indra.

**Indriya** or *Deha Sanyama (Sk.)*. The control of the senses in Yoga practice. These are the ten external agents; the five senses which are used for perception are called *Jnana-indriya,* and the five used for action—*Karma-indriya. Pancha-indryani* means literally and in its occult sense "the live roots producing life"(eternal). With the Buddhists, it is the five positive agents producing five supernal qualities.

**Induvansa** (*Sk.*). Also *Somavansa* or the lunar race (dynasty), from *Indu,* the Moon. ("See "Suryavansa".)

**Indwellers.** A name or the substitute for the right Sanskrit esoteric name, given to our "inner enemies", which are seven in the esoteric philosophy. The early Christian Church called them the "seven capital Sins ': the Nazarene Gnostics named them, the "seven badly disposed Stellars", and so on. Hindu exoteric teachings speak only of the "*six* enemies" and under the term *Arishadwarga* enumerate them as follows: (1) Personal desire, lust or any passion (*Kâma*); (2) Hatred or malice (*Krodha*); ( Avarice or cupidity (*Lobha*); ( Ignorance (*Moha*); ( Pride or arrogance (*Mada*); (6) Jealousy, envy (*Matcharya*); forgetting the seventh, which is the "unpardonable sin", and the worst of all in Occultism. (See *Theosophist,* May, 1890, p. 431.)

**Ineffable Name.** With the Jews, the substitute for the "*mystery* name" of their tribal deity *Eh-yeh,* "I am", or Jehovah. The third commandment prohibiting the using of the latter name "in vain", the Hebrews substituted for it that of *Adonai* or "the Lord". But the Protestant Christians who, translating indifferently Jehovah and Elohim—which is also a substitute *per se*, besides being an *inferior* deity name—by the words "Lord" and "God", have become in this instance more Catholic than the Pope, and include in the prohibition both the names. At the present moment, however, neither Jews nor Christians seem to remember, or so much as suspect, the occult reason why the qualification of Jehovah or YHVH had become reprehensible; most of the Western Kabbalists also seem to be unaware of the fact. The truth is, that the name they bring forward as "ineffable", is not in the least so. It is the "unpronounceable", or rather the name *not to be pronounced,* if any thing; and this for symbological reasons. To begin with, the "Ineffable Name" of the true Occultist, is *no name* at all, least of all is it that of Jehovah. The latter implies, even in its Kabbalistical, esoteric meaning, an androgynous nature, YHVH, or one of a male and female nature. It is simply Adam and Eve, or man and woman blended in one, and as now written and pronounced, is itself a substitute. But the Rabbins do not care to remember the Zoharic admission that YHVH means "not as I Am written, Am I read" (*Zohar*, fol. III., 23Oa). One has to know how to divide the Tetragrammaton *ad infinitum* before one arrives at the *sound* of the truly unpronounceable name of the Jewish mystery-god. That the Oriental Occultists have their own "Ineffable name" it is hardly necessary to repeat.

**Initiate**. From the Latin *Initiatus*. The designation of anyone who was received into and had revealed to him the mysteries and secrets of either Masonry or Occultism. In times of antiquity, those who had been initiated into the arcane knowledge taught by the Hierophants of the Mysteries; and in our modern days those who have been initiated by the adepts of mystic lore into the mysterious knowledge, which, notwithstanding the lapse of ages, has yet a few real votaries on earth.

**Initiation**. From the same root as the Latin *initia,* which means the basic or first principles of any Science. The practice of initiation or admission into the sacred Mysteries, taught by the Hierophants and learned priests of the Temples, is one of the most ancient customs. This was practised in every old national religion. In Europe it was abolished with the fall of the last pagan temple. There exists at present but one kind of initiation known to the public, namely that into the Masonic rites. Masonry, however, has no more secrets to give out or conceal. In the palmy days of old, the Mysteries, according to the greatest Greek and Roman philosophers, were the most sacred of all solemnities as well as the most beneficent, and greatly promoted virtue. The Mysteries represented the passage from mortal life into finite death, and the experiences of the disembodied Spirit and Soul in the world of subjectivity. In our own day, as the secret is lost, the candidate passes through sundry meaningless ceremonies and is initiated into the solar allegory of Hiram Abiff, the "Widow's Son".

**Inner Man.** An occult term, used to designate the true and immortal Entity in us, not the outward and mortal form of clay that we call our body. The term applies, strictly speaking, only to the Higher Ego, the "astral man" being the appellation of the Double and of Kâma Rupa (*q.v.*) or the surviving *eidolon*.

**Innocents**. A nick-name given to the Initiates and Kabbalists before the Christian era. The "Innocents" of Bethlehem and of Lud (or Lydda) who were put to death by Alexander Janneus, to the number of several thousands (B.C. 100, or so), gave rise to the legend of the 40,000 innocent babes murdered by Herod while searching for the infant Jesus. The first is a little known historical fact, the second a fable, as sufficiently shown by Renan in his *Vie de Jésus*.

**Intercosmic gods.** The Planetary Spirits, Dhyan-Chohans, Devas of various degrees of spirituality, and "Archangels" in general.

**Iranian Morals.** The little work called *Ancient Iranian and Zoroastrian Morals*, compiled by Mr. Dhunjibhoy Jamsetjee Medhora, a Parsi Theosophist of Bombay, is an excellent treatise replete with the highest moral teachings, in English and Gujerati, and will acquaint the student better than many volumes with the ethics of the ancient Iranians.

**Irdhi** (*Sk.*). The synthesis of the ten "supernatural" occult powers in Buddhism and Brahmanism.

**Irkalla** (*Chald.*). The god of Hades, called by the Babylonians "the country unseen".

**Isarim** (*Heb.*). The Essenian Initiates.

**Ishim** (*Chald.*). The B'ne-Aleim, the "beautiful sons of god", the originals and prototypes of the later "Fallen Angels".

**Ishmonia** (*Arab.*). The city near which is buried the so-called "petrified city" in the Desert. Legend speaks of immense subterranean halls and chambers, passages, and libraries secreted in them. Arabs dread its neighbourhood after sunset.

**Ishtar** (*Chald.*). The Babylonian Venus, called "the eldest of heaven and earth", and daughter of Anu, the god of heaven. She is the goddess of love and beauty. The planet Venus, as the evening star, is identified with Ishtar, and as the morning star with Anunit, the goddess of the Akkads. There exists a most remarkable story of her descent into Hades, on the sixth and seventh Assyrian tiles or tablets deciphered by the late G. Smith. Any Occultist who reads of her love for Tammuz, his assassination by Izdubar, the despair of the goddess and her descent in search of her beloved through the seven gates of Hades, and finally her liberation from the dark realm, will recognise the beautiful allegory of the soul in search of the Spirit.

**Isiac table.** A true monument of Egyptian art. It represents the goddess Isis under many of her aspects. The Jesuit Kircher describes it as a table of copper overlaid with black enamel and silver incrustations. It was in the possession of Cardinal Bembo, and therefore called "*Tabula Bembina sive Mensa Isiaca* ". Under this title it is described by W. Wynn Westcott, M.B., who gives its "History and Occult Significance" in an extremely interesting and learned volume (with photographs and illustrations). The tablet was believed to have been a votive offering to Isis in one of her numerous temples. At the sack of Rome in 1525, it came into the possession of a soldier who sold it to Cardinal Bembo. Then it passed to the Duke of Mantua in 1630, when it was lost.

**Isis.** In Egyptian *Issa*, the goddess Virgin-Mother; personified nature. In Egyptian or Koptic *Uasari,* the female reflection of *Uasar* or Osiris. She is the "woman clothed with the sun" of the land of Chemi. Isis Latona is the Roman Isis.

**Isitwa** (*Sk.*). The divine Power.

**Israel** (*Heb.*). The Eastern Kabbalists derive the name from *Isaral* or *Asar*, the Sun-God. "Isra-el" signifies "striving with god": the "sun rising upon Jacob-Israel" means the Sun-god Isaral (or Isar-el) striving with, and to fecundate matter, which has power with "God and with man" and often prevails over both. Esau, Æsaou, Asu, is also the Sun. Esau and Jacob, the allegorical twins, are the emblems of the ever struggling dual principle in nature—good and evil, darkness and sunlight, and the "Lord" (Jehovah) is their antetype. Jacob-Israel is the feminine principle of Esau, as Abel is that of Cain, both Cain and Esau being the male principle. Hence, like Malach-Iho, the "Lord" Esau fights with Jacob and prevails not. In *Genesis* xxxii. the God-Sun first strives with Jacob, breaks his *thigh* (a phallic symbol) and yet is defeated by his terrestrial type—matter; and the Sun-God rises on Jacob and his *thigh* in covenant. All these biblical personages, their "Lord God" included, are types represented in an allegorical sequence. They are types of Life and Death, Good and Evil, Light and Darkness, of Matter and Spirit in their synthesis, all these being under their contrasted aspects.

**Iswara** (*Sk.*). The "Lord" or the personal god—*divine Spirit in man. Lit.*, sovereign (independent) existence. A title given to Siva and other gods in India. Siva is also called Iswaradeva, or sovereign deva.

**Ithyphallic** (*Gr.*). Qualification of the gods as males and hermaphrodites, such as the bearded Venus, Apollo in woman's clothes, Ammon the generator, the embryonic Ptah, and so on. Yet the phallus, so conspicuous and, according to *our* prim notions, so indecent, in the Indian and Egyptian religions, was associated in the earliest symbology far more with another and much purer idea than that of sexual creation. As shown by many an Orientalist, it expressed *resurrection, the rising in life from death.* Even the other meaning had nought indecent in it: "These images only symbolise in a very expressive manner the creative force of nature, without obscene intention," writes Mariette Bey, and adds, "It is but another way to express *celestial generation*, which should cause the deceased to enter into a new life". Christians and Europeans are very hard on the phallic symbols of the ancients. The nude gods and goddesses and their generative emblems and statuary have secret departments assigned to them in our museums; why then adopt and preserve the same symbols for Clergy and Laity? The love-feasts in the early Church—its *agapæ* as pure (or as impure) as the Phallic festivals of the Pagans; the long priestly robes of the Roman and Greek Churches, and the long hair of the latter, the holy water sprinklers and the rest, are there to show that Christian ritualism has preserved in more or less modified forms all the symbolism of old Egypt. As to the symbolism of a purely *feminine* nature, we are bound to confess that in the sight of every impartial archæologist the half nude toilets of our cultured ladies of Society are far more suggestive of female-sex worship than are the rows of yoni-shaped lamps, lit along the highways to temples in India.

**Iurbo Adunaï.** A Gnostic term, or the compound name for Iao Jehovah, whom the Ophites regarded as an emanation of their Ilda-Baoth, the Son of Sophia Achamoth—the proud, ambitious and jealous god, and impure Spirit, whom many of the Gnostic sects regarded as the god of Moses. "Iurbo is called by the Abortions (the Jews) Adunai" says the *Codex Nazaræus* (vol. iii., p.13 The "Abortions" and *Abortives* was the nickname given to the Jews by their opponents the Gnostics.

**Iu-Kabar Zivo** (*Gn.*). Known also as Nebat-Iavar-bar-Iufin-Ifafin, "Lord of the Æons" in the Nazarene System. He is the procreator (Emanator) of the *seven holy lives* (the seven primal Dhyan Chohans, or Archangels, each representing one of the cardinal Virtues), and is himself called the third life (*third* Logos). In the Codex he is addressed as "the Helm and *Vine* of the food of life". Thus, he is identical with Christ (Christos) who says "I am the *true Vine* and my Father is the Husband-man "(John xv. i). It is well known that Christ is regarded in the Roman Catholic Church, as the "chief of the Æons", and also as Michael "who is like god". Such was also the belief of the Gnostics.

**Iwaldi** (*Scand.*). The dwarf whose sons fabricated for Odin the magic spear. One of the subterranean master-smiths who, together with other gnomes, contrived to make an enchanted sword for the great war-god Cheru. This two-edged-sword figures in the legend of the Emperor Vitellius, who got it from the god, "to his own hurt", according to the oracle of a "wise woman", neglected it and was finally killed with it at the foot of the capitol, by a German soldier who had purloined the weapon. The "sword of the war-god" has a long biography, since it also re-appears in the half-legendary biography of Attila. Having married against her will

Ildikd, the beautiful daughter of the King of Burgundy whom he had slain, his bride gets the magic sword from a mysterious old woman, and with it kills the King of the Huns.

**Izdubar**. A name of a hero in the fragments of Chaldean History and Theogony on the so-called Assyrian tiles, as read by the late George Smith and others. Smith seeks to identify Izdubar with Nimrod. Such may or may not be the case; but as the name of that Babylonian King itself only "appears" as Izduhar, his identification with the son of Cush may also turn out more apparent than real. Scholars are but too apt to check their archæological discoveries by the far later statements found in the Mosaic books, instead of acting *vice versa*. "The chosen people" have been fond at all periods of history of helping themselves to other people's property. From the appropriation of the early history of Sargon, King of Akkad, and its wholesale application to Moses born (if at all) some thousands of years later, down to their "spoiling" the Egyptians under the direction and divine advice of their Lord God, the whole Pentateuch seems to be made up of unacknowledged *mosaical* fragments from other people's Scriptures. This ought to have made Assyriologists more cautious; but as many of these belong to the clerical caste, such coincidences as that of Sargon affect them very little. One thing is certain Izdubar, or whatever may be his name, is shown in all the tablets as a mighty giant who towered in size above all other men as a cedar towers over brushwood—a hunter, according to cuneiform legends, who contended with, and destroyed the lion, tiger, wild bull, and buffalo, the most formidable animals.

# J

**J.**—The tenth letter in the English and Hebrew alphabet, in the latter of which it is equivalent to *y,* and *i,* and is numerically number 10, the perfect number (See *Jodh* and *Yodh*), or one. (See also "I".)

**Jâbalas** (*Sk.*). Students of the mystical portion of the White *Yajur Veda*.

**Jachin** (*Heb.*). "In Hebrew letters IKIN, from the root KUN "to establish", and the symbolical name of one of the Pillars at the porch of King Solomon's Temple" [w.w.w.]

The other pillar was called Boaz, and the two were respectively white and black. They correspond to several mystic ideas, one of which is that they represent the dual Manas or the higher and the lower Ego; another connected these two pillars in Slavonian mysticism with God and the

Devil,to the"WHITE" and the "BLACK GOD" or *Byeloy Bog* and *Tchernoy Bog.* (See "Yakin and Boaz" *infra*).

**Jacobites.** A Christian sect in Syria of the VIth cent. (550) which held that Christ had only one nature and that confession was not of divine origin. They had secret signs, passwords and a solemn initiation with mysteries.

**Jadoo** (*Hind.*). Sorcery, black magic, enchantment.

**Jadoogar** (*Hind.*). A Sorcerer, or Wizard.

**Jagaddhatri** (*Sk.*). Substance; the name of "the nurse of the world", the designation of the power which carried Krishna and his brother Balarama into Devaki, their mother's bosom. A title of Sarasvati and Durga.

**Jagad-Yoni** (*Sk*). The womb of the world; space.

**Jagat** (*Sk.*). The Universe.

**Jagan-Natha** (*Sk.*). Lit., "Lord of the World", a title of Vishnu. The great image of Jagan-natha on its car, commonly pronounced and spelt Jagernath. The idol is that of Vishnu Krishna. Puri, near the town of Cuttack in Orissa, is the great seat of its worship; and twice a year an immense number of pilgrims attend the festivals of the Snâna yâtra and Ratha-âtra During the first, the image is bathed, and during the second it is placed on a car, between the images of *Balarâma* the brother, and *Subhadrâ* the sister of Krishna and the huge vehicle is drawn by the devotees, who deem it felicity to be crushed to death under it.

**Jagrata** (*Sk.*). The waking state of consciousness. When mentioned in Yoga philosophy, *Jagrata-avastha* is the waking condition, one of the four states of Pranava in ascetic practices, as used by the Yogis.

**Jâhnavî** (*Sk.*). A name of *Ganga,* or the river Ganges.

**Jahva Alhim** (*Heb.*). The name that in *Genesis* replaces "Alhim", or Elohim, *the gods.* It is used in chapter I., while in chapter II. the "Lord God" or Jehovah steps in. In Esoteric philosophy and exoteric tradition, Jahva Alhim (*Java Aleim*) was the title of the chief of the Hierophants, who initiated into the good and the evil of this world in the college of priests known as the Aleim College in the land of Gandunya or Babylonia. Tradition and rumour assert, that the chief of the temple *Fo-maïyu,* called Foh-tchou (teacher of Buddhist law), a temple situated in the fastnesses of the great mount of Kouenlong-sang (between China and Tibet), teaches once every three years under a tree called *Sung-Mîn-Shû,* or the" Tree of Knowledge and (the tree) of life", which is the Bo (Bodhi) tree of Wisdom.

**Jaimini** (*Sk.*). A great sage, a disciple of Vyâsa the transmitter and teacher of the Sama Veda which as claimed he received from his Guru. He is also the famous founder and writer of the Pûrva Mimânsâ philosophy.

**Jaina Gross.** The same as the "Swastika" (*q.v.*), "Thor's hammer" also, or the Hermetic cross.

**Jainas** (*Sk.*). A large religious body in India closely resembling Buddhism, but who preceded it by long centuries. They claim that Gautama, the Buddha, was a disciple of one of their Tirtankaras, or Saints. They deny the authority of the Vedas and the existence of any *personal* supreme god, but believe in the eternity of matter, the periodicity of the universe and the immortality of men's minds (*Manas*) as also of that of the animals. An extremely mystic sect.

**Jalarupa** (*Sk.*). Lit., "water-body, or form". One of the names of Makâra (the sign *capricornus*). It is one of the most occult and mysterious of the Zodiacal signs; it figures on the banner of Kama, god of love, and is connected with our immortal Egos. (See *Secret Doctrine.*)

**Jambu-dwipa** (*Sk.*). One of the main divisions of the globe, in the Purânic system. It includes India. Some say that it was a continent,—others an island—or one of the seven islands (*Sapta dwipa*) It is "the dominion of Vishnu". In its astronomical and mystic sense it is the name of our globe, separated by the plane of objectivity from the six other globes of our planetary chain.

**Jamin** (*Heb.*). The right side of a man, esteemed the most worthy. Benjamin means "son of the right side", *i.e., testis.* [w.w.w.]

**Janaka** (*Sk.*). One of the Kings of Mithilâ of the Solar race. He was a great royal sage, and lived twenty generations before Janaka the father of Sita who was King of Videha.

**Jana-loka** (*Sk.* The world wherein the Munis (the Saints) are supposed to dwell after their corporeal death (See *Purânas*). Also a terrestrial locality.

**Janârddana** (*Sk.*). Lit., "the adored of mankind", a title of Krishna.

**Japa** (*Sk.*). A mystical practice of certain Yogis. It consists in the repetition of various magical formulæ and mantras.

**Jaras** (*Sk.*). "Old Age". The allegorical name of the hunter who killed Krishna by mistake, a name showing the great ingenuity of the Brahmans and the symbolical character of the World-Scriptures in general. As Dr. Crucefix, a high mason well says, "to preserve the occult mysticism of their order from all except their own class, the priests invented symbols and hieroglyphics to embody sublime truths ".

**Jatayu** (*Sk.*). The Son of Garuda. The latter is the great cycle, or *Mahakalpa* symbolized by the giant bird which served as a steed for Vishnu, and other gods, when related to space and time. Jatayu is called in the *Ramayana* "the King of the feathered tribe". For defending Sita carried away by Ravana, the giant king of Lanka, he was killed by him. Jatayu is also called "the king of the vultures".

**Javidan Khirad** (Pers) A work on moral precepts.

**Jayas** (*Sk.*), The twelve great gods in the *Purânas* who neglect to create men, and are therefore, cursed by Brahmâ to be *reborn* "in every (racial) Manvantara till the seventh". Another form or aspect of the reincarnating Egos.

**Jebal Djudi** (*Arab.*). The "Deluge Mountain" of the Arabic legends. The same as Ararat, and the Babylonian Mount of *Nizir* where Xisuthrus landed with his ark.

**Jehovah** (*Heb.*). The Jewish "Deity name J'hovah, is a compound of two words, *viz* of *Jah* (y, i, or j, *Yôdh*, the tenth letter of the alphabet) and *hovah* (Hâvah, or Eve)," says a Kabalistic authority, Mr. J. Ralston Skinner of Cincinnati, U.S.A. And again, "The word Jehovah, or *Jah-Eve*, has the primary meaning of existence or being as male female". It means Kabalistically the latter, indeed, and nothing more; and as repeatedly shown is entirely phallic. Thus, verse 26 in the IVth chapter of *Genesis*, reads in its disfigured translation . . . . "then began men to call upon the name of the Lord", whereas it ought to read correctly . . . . "then began men to call themselves by the name of *Jah-hovah*" or males and females, which they had become after the separation of sexes. In fact the latter is described in the same chapter, when Cain (the male or *Jah*) "rose up against Abel, his (*sister*, not) brother and slew him"(*spilt his blood*, in the original). Chapter IV of *Genesis* contains in truth, the allegorical narrative of that period of anthropological and physiological evolution which is described in the *Secret Doctrine* when treating of the third Root race of mankind. It is followed by Chapter V *as a blind*; but ought to be succeeded by Chapter VI, where the Sons of God took as their wives the daughters of men or of the giants. For this is an allegory hinting at the mystery of the Divine Egos incarnating in mankind, after which the hitherto senseless races "became mighty men, . . . men of renown" (v. 4), having acquired minds (*manas*) which they had not before.

**Jehovah Nissi** (*Heb.*). The androgyne of Nissi (See "Dionysos"). The Jews worshipped under this name Bacchus-Osiris, *Dio-Nysos*, and the multiform

Joves of Nyssa, the Sinai of Moses. Universal tradition shews Bacchus reared in a cave of Nyssa. Diodorus locates Nysa between Phœnicia and Egypt, and adds, "Osiris was brought up in Nysa he was son of Zeus and was named from his father (nominative Zeus, genitive Dios) and the place *Dio-nysos*"—the Zeus or Jove of Nyssa.

**Jerusalem,** *Jerosalem (Septuag.)* and *Hierosolyma (Vulgate).* In Hebrew it is written Yrshlim or "city of peace", but the ancient Greeks called it pertinently *Hierosalem* or "Secret Salem", since Jerusalem is a rebirth from Salem of which Melchizedek was the King-Hierophant, a declared Astrolator and worshipper of the Sun, "the Most High" by-the-bye. There also Adoni-Zedek reigned in his turn, and was the last of its Amorite Sovereigns. He allied himself with four others, and these five kings went to conquer back Gideon, but (according to *Joshua* X) came out of the affray second best. And no wonder, since these five kings were opposed, not only by Joshua but by the "Lord God", and by the Sun and the Moon also. On that day, we read, at the command of the successor of Moses, "the sun stood still and the moon stayed" (v. 13) for the whole day. No mortal man, king or yeoman, could withstand, of course, such a shower "of great stones from heaven" as was cast upon them by the Lord himself . . . . "from Beth-horon unto Azekah" "and they died" (v. ii). After having died they "fled and hid themselves in a cave at Makkedah" (v. i6). It appears, however, that such undignified behaviour in a God received its Karmic punishment afterwards. At different epochs of history, the Temple of the Jewish Lord was sacked, ruined and burnt (See "Mount Moriah")—holy ark of the covenant, cherubs, Shekinah and all, but that deity seemed as powerless to protect his property from desecration as though they were no more stones left in heaven. After Pompey had taken the Second Temple in 63 B.C., and the third one, built by Herod the Great, had been razed to the ground by the Romans, in 70 A.D., no new temple was allowed to be built in the capital of the "chosen people" of the Lord. In spite of the Crusades, since the XIIIth century Jerusalem has belonged to the Mahommedans, and almost every site holy and dear to the memory of the old Israelites, and also of the Christians, is now covered by minarets and mosques, Turkish barracks and other monuments of Islam.

**Jesod** *(Heb.).* Foundation; the ninth of the Ten Sephiroth, a masculine active potency, completing the six which form the Microprosopus. [w.w.w.]

**Jetzirah** *(Heb.).* See "Yetzirah".

**Jetzirah,** Sepher; or *Book of the Creation.* The most occult of all the

Kabalistic works now in the possession of modern mystics. Its alleged origin, of having been written by Abraham, is of course nonsense; but its intrinsic value is great. It is composed of six *Perakim* (chapters), subdivided into *thirty-three* short *Mishnas* or Sections; and treats of the evolution of the Universe on a system of correspondences and numbers. Deity is said therein to have formed ("created") the Universe by means of numbers "by thirty-two paths (or ways) of secret wisdom ", these ways being made to correspond with the twenty-two letters of the Hebrew alphabet and the ten fundamental numbers. These ten are the primordial numbers whence proceeded the whole Universe, and these are followed by the twenty-two letters divided into Three Mothers, the seven double consonants and the twelve simple consonants. He who would well understand the system is advised to read the excellent little treatise upon *Sepher Jetzirah,* by Dr. W. WynnWestcott. (See "Yetzirah".)

**Jhâna** *(Sk.)* or *Jnana.* Knowledge; Occult Wisdom.

**Jhâna Bhaskara** *(Sk.).* A work on Asuramâya, the Atlantean astronomer and magician, and other prehistoric legends.

**Jigten Gonpo** *(Tib.).* A name of Avalokitêswara, or *Chenres-Padma-pani,* the "Protector against Evil".

**Jishnu** *(Sk.).* "Leader of the Celestial Host", a title of Indra, who, in the War of the Gods with the Asuras, led the "host of devas". He is the "Michael, the leader of the Archangels" of India.

**Jiva** *(Sk.).* Life, as the Absolute; the Monad also or "Atma-Buddhi".

**Jivanmukta** *(Sk.).* An adept or yogi who has reached the ultimate state of holiness, and separated himself from matter; a Mahatma, or *Nirvânee,* a "dweller in bliss" and emancipation. Virtually one who has reached Nirvâna during life.

**Jivatma** *(Sk.).* The ONE universal life, generally; but also the divine Spirit in Man.

**Jnânam** *(Sk.).* The same as "Gnâna", etc., the same as "Jhâna" *(q.v.).*

**Jnânendriyas** *(Sk.).* The five channels of knowledge.

**Jnâna Sakti** *(Sk.).* The power of intellect.

**Jörd.** In Northern Germany the goddess of the Earth, the same as Nerthus and the Scandinavian Freya or Frigg.

**Jotunheim** *(Scand.).* The land of the Hrimthurses or Frost-giants.

**Jotuns** *(Scand.).* The Titans or giants. Mimir, who taught Odin magic, the "thrice wise", was a Jotun.

**Jul** (*Scand.*). The wheel of the Sun from whence *Yuletide,* which was sacred to Freyer, or Pro, the Sun-god, the ripener of the fields and fruits, admitted later to the circle of the Ases. As god of sunshine and fruitful harvests he lived in the Home of the Light Elves.

**Jupiter** *(Lat.).* From the same root as the Greek Zeus, the greatest god of the ancient Greeks and Romans, adopted also by other nations. His names are among others: (1) Jupiter-Aërios; (2) Jupiter-Ammon of Egypt; (3) Jupiter Bel-Moloch, the Chaldean; (4) Jupiter-Mundus, Deus Mundus, "God of the World"; (5) Jupiter-Fulgur, "the Fulgurant", etc.,etc.

**Jyotisha** *(Sk.).* Astronomy and Astrology; one of the Vedângas.

**Jyotisham Jyotch** *(Sk.).* The "light of lights", the Supreme Spirit, so called in the *Upanishads*.

**Jyotsna** *(Sk.).* Dawn; one of the bodies assumed by Brahmâ the morning twilight.

# K

**K.**—The eleventh letter in both the English and the Hebrew alphabets. As a numeral it stands in the latter for 20, and in the former for 250, and with a stroke over it (K) for 250,000. The Kabalists and the Masons appropriate the word Kodesh or Kadosh as the name of the Jewish god under this letter.

**Ka** *(Sk.).* According to Max Muller, the interrogative pronoun "who?"— raised to the dignity of a deity without cause or reason. Still it has its esoteric significance and is a name of Brahmâ in his phallic character as generator or Prajâpati (*q.v.*).

**Kabah** or *Kaaba* (*Arab*). The name of the famous Mahommedan temple at Mecca, a great place of pilgrimage. The edifice is not large but very original; of a cubical form 23 X 24 cubits in length and breadth and 27 cubits high, with only one aperture on the East side to admit light. In the north-east corner is the "black stone" of Kaaba, said to have been lowered down direct from heaven and to have been as white as snow, but subsequently it became black, owing to the sins of mankind The "white stone", the reputed tomb of Ismael, is in the north side and the place of Abraham is to the east. If, as the Mahommedans claim, this temple was, at the prayer of Adam after his exile, transferred by Allah or Jehovah direct from Eden down to earth, then the "heathen" may truly claim to have far exceeded the divine primordial architecture in the beauty of their edifices.

**Kabalist.** From Q B L H, KABALA, an unwritten or oral tradition. The kabalist is a student of "secret science", one who interprets the hidden meaning of the Scriptures with the help of the symbolical Kabala, and explains the real one by these means. The Tanaim were the first kabalists among the Jews; they appeared at Jerusalem about the beginning of the third century before the Christian era. The books of *Ezekiel, Daniel, Henoch,* and the *Revelation* of St. John, are purely kabalistical. This secret doctrine is identical with that of Chaldeans, and includes at the same time much of the Persian wisdom, or "magic". History catches glimpses of famous kabalists ever since the eleventh century. The Mediæval ages, and even our own times, have had an enormous number of the most learned and intellectual men who were students of the Kabala (or Qabbalah, as some spell it). The most famous among the former were Paracelsus, Henry Khunrath, Jacob Böhmen, Robert Fludd, the two Van Helmonts, the Abbot John Trithemius, Cornelius Agrippa, Cardinal Nicolao Cusani, Jerome Carden, Pope Sixtus IV., and such Christian scholars as Raymond Lully, Giovanni Pico de la Mirandola, Guillaume Postel, the great John Reuchlin, Dr. Henry More, Eugenius Philalethes (Thomas Vaughan), the erudite Jesuit Athanasius Kircher, Christian Knorr (Baron) von Rosenroth; then Sir Isaac Newton., Leibniz, Lord Bacon, Spinosa, etc., etc., the list being almost inexhaustible. As remarked by Mr. Isaac Myer, in his Qabbalah, the ideas of the Kabalists have largely influenced European literature. "Upon the practical Qabbalah, the Abbé ,de Villars (nephew of de Montfaucon) in 1670, published his celebrated satirical novel, 'The Count de Gabalis', upon which Pope based his 'Rape of the Lock'. Qabbalism ran through the Mediæval poems, the 'Romance of the Rose', and permeates the writings of Dante." No two of them, however, agreed upon the origin of the Kabala, the *Zohar, Sepher Yetzirah,* etc. Some show it as coming from the Biblical Patriarchs, Abraham, and even Seth; others from Egypt, others again from Chaldea. The system is certainly very old; but like all the rest of systems, whether religious or philosophical, the Kabala is derived directly from the primeval Secret Doctrine of the East; through the Vedas, the Upanishads, Orpheus and Thales, Pythagoras and the Egyptians. Whatever its source, its substratum is at any rate identical with that of all the other systems from the *Book of the Dead* down to the later Gnostics. The best exponents of the *Kabala* in the Theosophical Society were among the earliest, Dr. S. Pancoast, of Philadelphia, and Mr. G. Felt; and among the latest, Dr. W. Wynn Westcott, Mr. S. L. Mac Gregor Mathers (both of the Rosicrucian College) and a few others. (See "Qabbalah ".)

**Kabalistic Faces.** These are Nephesch, Ruach and Neschamah, or the animal (vital), the Spiritual and the Divine Souls in man—Body, Soul and Mind.

**Kabalah** (*Heb.*). The hidden wisdom of the Hebrew Rabbis of the middle ages derived from the older secret doctrines concerning divine things and cosmogony, which were combined into a theology after the time of the captivity of the Jews in Babylon. All the works that fall under the esoteric category are termed Kabalistic.

**Kabiri** (*Phœn.*) or the *Kabirim*. Deities and very mysterious gods with the ancient nations, including the Israelites, some of whom—as Terah, Abram's father—worshipped them under the name of *Teraphim*. With the Christians, however, they are now devils, although the modern Archangels are the direct transformation of these same Kabiri. In Hebrew the latter name means "the mighty ones", Gibborim. At one time all the deities connected with fire—whether they were divine, infernal or volcanic—were called Kabirian.

**Kadmon** (*Heb.*). Archetypal man. See."Adam Kadmon".

**Kadosh** (*Heb.*). Consecrated, holy; also written *Kodesh*. Something set apart for temple worship. But between the etymological meaning of the word, and its subsequent significance in application to the *Kadeshim* (the "priests" set apart for certain temple rites)—there is an abyss. The words *Kadosh* and *Kadeshim* are used in II. Kings as rather an opprobrious name, for the *Kadeshuth* of the Bible were identical in their office and duties with the Nautch girls of some Hindu temples. They were Galli, the mutilated priests of the lascivious rites of Venus Astarte, who lived "by the house of the Lord". Curiously enough the terms *Kadosh,* etc., were appropriated and used by several degrees of Masonic knighthood.

**Kailasa** (*Sk.*). In metaphysics "heaven", the abode of gods; geographically a mountain range in the Himalayas, north of the Mansaravâra lake, called also lake *Manasa.*

**Kailem** (*Heb.*). Lit., vessels or vehicles; the vases for the source of the Waters of Life; used of the Ten Sephiroth, considered as the primeval *nuclei* of all Kosmic Forces. Some Kabalists regard them as manifesting in the universe through twenty-two canals, which are represented by the twenty-two letters of the Hebrew alphabet, thus making with the Ten Sephiroth thirty-two paths of wisdom. [w. w. w.]

**Kaimarath** (*Pers.*). The last of the race of the *prehuman* kings. He is identical with Adam Kadmon. A fabulous Persian hero.

**Kakodæmon** (*Gr.*). The evil genius as opposed to *Agathodæmon* the good genius, or deity. A Gnostic term.

**Kala** (*Sk.*). A measure of time; four hours, a period of thirty Kashthas.

**Kala** (*Sk.*). Time, fate; a cycle and a proper name, or title given to Yama, King of the nether world and Judge of the Dead.

**Kalabhana** (*Sk.*). The same as Taraka (See *S. D.*, Vol. II., p. 382, foot-note).

**Kalagni** (*Sk.*). The flame of time. A divine Being created by Siva, a monster with 1,000 heads. A title of Siva meaning "the fire of fate".

**Kalahansa** or *Hamsa* (*Sk*). A mystic title given to Brahma (or Parabrahman); means "the swan *in* and *out* of time". Brahmâ (male) is called Hansa-Vahan, the vehicle of the "Swan".

**Kalavingka** (*Sk.*), also *Kuravikaya* and *Karanda*, etc. "The sweet-voiced bird of immortality". Eitel identifies it with *cuculus melanoleicus*, though the bird itself is allegorical and non-existent. Its voice is heard at a certain stage of Dhyana in Yoga practice. It is said to have awakened King Bimbisara and thus saved him from the sting of a cobra. In its esoteric meaning this sweet-voiced bird is our Higher Ego.

**Kalevala.** The Finnish Epic of Creation.

**Kali** (*Sk.*). The "black", now the name of Parvati, the consort of Siva, but originally that of one of the seven tongues of Agni, the god of fire—"the black, fiery tongue". Evil and wickedness.

**Kalidasa** (*Sk.*). The greatest poet and dramatist of India.

**Kaliya** (*Sk.*). The five-headed serpent killed by Krishna in his childhood. A mystical monster symbolizing the passions of man—the river or water being a symbol of matter.

**Kaliyuga** (*Sk.*). The fourth, the black or iron age, our present period, the duration of which us 432,000 years. The last of the ages into which the evolutionary period of man is divided by a series of such ages. It began 3,102 years B.C. at the moment of Krishna's death, and the first cycle of 5,000 years will end between the years 1897 and 1898.

**Kalki Avatar** (*Sk.*). The "White Horse Avatar", which will be the last manvantaric incarnation of Vishnu, according to the Brahmins; of Maitreya Buddha, agreeably to Northern Buddhists; of Sosiosh, the last hero and Saviour of the Zoroastrians, as claimed by Parsis; and of the "Faithful and True" on the white Horse (*Rev.* xix.,2 ). In his future epiphany or tenth *avatar*, the heavens will open and Vishnu will appear "seated on a milk-white steed, with a drawn sword blazing like a comet, for the final destruction of the wicked, the renovation of 'creation' and the 'restoration of purity'". (Compare *Revelation*.) This will take place at the end of the Kaliyuga 427,000 years hence. The latter end of every Yuga is called "the destruction of the world", as then the earth changes each time its outward form, submerging one set of continents and upheaving another set.

**Kalluka Bhatta** (*Sk.*). A commentator of the Hindu *Manu Smriti* Scriptures; a well-known writer and historian.

**Kalpa** (*Sk.*). The period of a mundane revolution, generally a cycle of time, but usually, it represents a "day" and "night" of Brahmâ, a period of 4,320,000,000 years.

**Kama** (*Sk.*) Evil desire, lust, volition; the cleaving to existence. Kama is generally identified with *Mara* the tempter.

**Kamadeva** (*Sk.*). In the popular notions the god of love, a Visva-deva, in the Hindu Pantheon. As the *Eros* of Hesiod, degraded into Cupid by exoteric law, and still more degraded by a later popular sense attributed to the term, so is Kama a most mysterious and metaphysical subject. The earlier Vedic description of Kama alone gives the key-note to what he emblematizes. Kama is the first conscious, *all embracing desire* for universal good, love, and for all that lives and feels, needs help and kindness, the first feeling of infinite tender compassion and mercy that arose in the consciousness of the creative ONE Force, as soon as it came into life and being as a ray from the ABSOLUTE. Says the *Rig Veda*, "Desire first arose in IT, which was the primal germ of mind, and which Sages, searching with their intellect, have discovered in their heart to be the bond which connects Entity with non-Entity", or *Manas* with pure *Atma-Buddhi*. There is no idea of sexual love in the conception. Kama is pre-eminently the divine desire of creating happiness and love; and it is only ages later, as mankind began to materialize by anthropomorphization its grandest ideals into cut and dried dogmas, that Kama became the power that gratifies desire on the animal plane. This is shown by what every *Veda* and some *Brahmanas* say. In the *Atharva Veda*, Kama is represented as the Supreme Deity and Creator. In the Taitarîya Brahmana, he is the child of Dharma, the god of Law and Justice, of Sraddha and faith. In another account he springs from the heart of Brahmâ. Others show him born from water, i.e., from primordial chaos, or the "Deep". Hence one of his many names, *Irâ-ja,* "the water-born"; and *Aja,* "unborn"; and *Atmabhu* or "Self-existent". Because of the sign of *Makara* (Capricornus) on his banner, he is also called "Makara Ketu". The allegory about Siva, the "Great Yogin ", reducing Kama to ashes by the fire from his *central* (or third) *Eye,* for inspiring the Mahadeva with thoughts of his wife, while he was at his devotions—is very suggestive, as it is said that he thereby reduced Kama to his primeval spiritual form.

**Kamadhâtu** (*Sk.*). Called also Kamâvatchara, a region including Kâmalôka. In exoteric ideas it is the first of the Trailâkya—or three regions (applied also to celestial beings) or seven planes or degrees, each broadly represented by one of the three chief characteristics; namely, *Kama, Rupa* and *Arupa,* or those of desire, form and formlessness. The first of the Trailokyas, *Kamadhâtu,* is thus composed of the earth and the six inferior Devalokas, the earth being followed by *Kamaloka* (*q.v.*). These taken together constitute the seven degrees of the material world of form and sensuous gratification. The second of the Trailôkya (or Trilôkya) is called Rupadhâtu or "material form" and is also composed of seven Lokas (or localities). The third is Arupadhâtu or "immaterial lokas". "Locality", however, is an incorrect word to use in translating the term dhâtu, which does not mean in some of its special applications a "place" at all. For instance, *Arupadhâtu* is a purely subjective world, a "state" rather than a place. But as the European tongues have no adequate metaphysical terms to express certain ideas, we can only point out the difficulty.

**Kamaloka** (*Sk.*). The *semi*-material plane, to us subjective and invisible, where the disembodied "personalities", the astral forms, called *Kamarupa* remain, until they fade out from it by the complete exhaustion of the effects of the mental impulses that created these eidolons of human and animal passions and desires; (See "Kamarupa".) It is the Hades of the ancient Greeks and the Amenti of the Egyptians, the land of Silent Shadows; a division of the first group of the *Trailôkya.* (See "Kamadhâtu".)

**Kamarupa** (*Sk.*). Metaphysically, and in our esoteric philosophy, it is the subjective form created through the mental and physical desires and thoughts in connection with things of matter, by all sentient beings, a form which survives the death of their bodies. After that death three of the seven "principles"—or let us say planes of senses and consciousness on which the human instincts and ideation act in turn—viz., the body, its astral prototype and physical vitality,—being of no further use, remain on earth; the three higher principles, grouped into one, merge into the state of Devachan (*q.v.*), in which state the Higher Ego will remain until the hour for a new reincarnation arrives; and the *eidolon* of the ex-Personality is left alone in its new abode. Here, the pale copy of the man that was, vegetates for a period of time, the duration of which is variable and according to the element of materiality which is left in it, and which is determined by the past life of the defunct. Bereft as it is of its higher mind, spirit and physical senses, if left alone to its own senseless devices, it will gradually fade out and disintegrate. But, if forcibly drawn back into the terrestrial sphere whether by the passionate desires and appeals of the surviving friends or by regular necromantic practices—one of the most pernicious of which is medium-ship—the "spook" may prevail for a period greatly exceeding the span of the natural life of its body. Once the Kamarupa has learnt the way back to living human bodies, it becomes a vampire, feeding on the vitality of those who are so anxious for its company. In India these *eidolons* are called *Pisâchas,* and are much dreaded, as already explained elsewhere.

**Kamea** (*Heb.*). An amulet, generally a magic square.

**Kandu** .(*Sk.*). A holy sage of the second root-race, a yogi, whom Pramlôcha, a "nymph" sent by Indra for that purpose, beguiled, and lived with for several centuries. Finally, the Sage returning to his senses, repudiated and chased her away. Whereupon she gave birth to a daughter, Mârishâ. The story is in an allegorical fable from the *Purânas.*

**Kanishka** (*Sk.*). A King of the Tochari, who flourished when the third Buddhist Synod met in Kashmir, i.e., about the middle of the last century B.C., a great patron of Buddhism, he built the finest *stûpas* or dagobas in Northern India and Kabulistan.

**Kanishthas** (*Sk.*). A class of gods which will manifest in the fourteenth or last manvantara of our world—according to the Hindus.

**Kanya** (*Sk.*). A virgin or maiden. *Kanya Kumârî* "the virgin-maiden" is a title of Durga-Kali, worshipped by the Thugs and Tantrikas.

**Kapila Rishi** (*Sk.*). A great sage, a great adept of antiquity; the author of the Sankhya philosophy.

**Kapilavastu** (*Sk.*). The birth-place of the Lord Buddha; called "the yellow dwelling": the capital of the monarch who was the father of Gautama Buddha.

**Karabtanos** (*Gr.*). The spirit of blind or animal desire; the symbol of Kama-rupa. The Spirit "without sense or judgment" in the Codex of the Nazarenes. He is the symbol of matter and stands for the father of the seven spirits of concupiscence begotten by him on his mother, the "Spiritus" or the Astral Light.

**Karam** (*Sk.*). A great festival in honour of the Sun-Spirit with the Kolarian tribes.

**Kârana** (*Sk.*). Cause (metaphysically).

**Kârana Sarîra** *(Sk.)*. The "Causal body". It is dual in its meaning. Exoterically, it is Avidya, ignorance, or that which is the cause of the evolution of a human ego and its reincarnation; hence the lower Manas esoterically—the causal body or Kâranopadhi stands in the Taraka Raja yoga as corresponding to Buddhi and the Higher "Manas," or Spiritual Soul.

**Karanda** *(Sk.)*. The "sweet-voiced bird," the same as *Kalavingka (q.v.)*

**Kâranopadhi** *(Sk.)*. The basis or *upadhi* of Karana, the "causal soul". In Taraka Rajayoga, it corresponds with both *Manas* and *Buddhi*. See Table in the *S. D.*, Vol. I, p. 157.

**Kardecists**. The followers of the spiritistic system of Allan Kardec, the Frenchman who founded the modern movement of the Spiritist School. The Spiritists of France differ from the American and English Spiritualists in that their "Spirits" teach reincarnation, while those of the United States and Great Britain denounce this belief as a heretical fallacy and abuse and slander those who accept it. "When Spirits disagree..."

**Karma** *(Sk.)*. Physically, action: metaphysically, the LAW OF RETRIBUTION, the Law of cause and effect or Ethical Causation. Nemesis, only in one sense, that of bad Karma. It is the eleventh *Nidana* in the concatenation of causes and effects in orthodox Buddhism; yet it is the power that controls all things, the resultant of moral action, the meta physical *Samskâra*, or the moral effect of an act committed for the attainment of something which gratifies a personal desire. There is the Karma of merit and the Karma of demerit. Karma neither punishes nor rewards, it is simply *the one* Universal LAW which guides unerringly, and, so to say, blindly, all other laws productive of certain effects along the grooves of their respective causations. When Buddhism teaches that "Karma is that moral kernel (of any being) which alone survives death and continues in transmigration ' or reincarnation, it simply means that there remains nought after each Personality but the causes produced by it; causes which are undying, i.e., which cannot be eliminated from the Universe until replaced by their legitimate effects, and wiped out by them, so to speak, and such causes—unless compensated during the life of the person who produced them with adequate effects, will follow the reincarnated Ego, and reach it in its subsequent reincarnation until a harmony between effects and causes is fully reestablished. No "personality"—a mere bundle of material atoms and of instinctual and mental characteristics—can of course continue, as such, in the world of pure Spirit. Only that which is immortal in its very nature and divine in its essence, namely, the Ego, can exist for ever. And as it is that Ego which chooses the personality it will inform, after each Devachan, and which receives through these personalities the effects of the Karmic causes produced, it is therefore the Ego, that *self* which is the "moral kernel" referred to and embodied karma, "which alone survives death."

**Karnak** (*Eg*.). The ruins of the ancient temples, and palaces which now stand on the emplacement of ancient Thebes. The most magnificent representatives of the art and skill of the earliest Egyptians. A few lines quoted from Champollion, Denon and an English traveller, show most eloquently what these ruins are. Of Karnak Champollion writes:—"The ground covered by the mass of remaining buildings is square; and each side measures 1,800 feet. One is astounded and *overcome by the grandeur* of the sublime remnants, the prodigality and magnificence of workmanship to be seen everywhere. No people of ancient or modern times has conceived the art of architecture upon a scale so sublime, so grandiose as it existed among the ancient Egyptians; and the imagination, which in Europe soars far above our porticos, arrests itself *and falls powerless* at the foot of the hundred and forty columns of the hypostyle of Karnak! In one of its halls, the Cathedral of Notre Dame might stand and not touch the ceiling, but be considered as a small ornament in the centre of the hall."

Another writer exclaims: "Courts, halls, gateways, pillars, obelisks, monolithic figures, sculptures, long rows of sphinxes, are found in such profusion at Karnak, that the sight is too much for modern comprehension." Says Denon, the French traveller: "It is hardly possible to believe, after seeing it, in the reality of the existence of so many buildings collected together on a single point, in their dimensions, in the resolute perseverance which their construction required, and in the incalculable expenses of so much magnificence! It is necessary that the reader should fancy what is before him to be a dream, as he who views the objects themselves occasionally yields to the doubt whether he be perfectly awake. . . . There are lakes and mountains within the *periphery of the sanctuary*. These two edifices are selected as examples from a list *next to inexhaustible*. The whole valley and delta of the Nile, from the cataracts to the sea, was covered with temples, palaces, tombs, pyramids, obelisks, and pillars. The execution of the sculptures is beyond praise. The mechanical perfection with which artists wrought in granite, serpentine, breccia, and basalt, is wonderful, according to all the experts animals and plants look as good as natural, and artificial objects are beautifully sculptured; battles by sea and land, and scenes of domestic life are to be found in all their *bas-*

*reliefs."*

**Karnaim** (*Heb.*). Horned, an attribute of Ashtoreth and Astarte; those horns typify the male element, and convert the deity into an androgyne. Isis also is at times horned. Compare also the idea of the Crescent Moon—symbol of Isis—as horned. [w.w.w.]

**Karneios** (*Gr.*). "Apollo *Karneïos*," is evidently an *avatar* of the Hindu "Krishna *Karna*". Both were Sun-gods; both "Karna" and Karneios meaning "radiant". (See the *S. D.*,Vol. II., p. 44, note.)

**Karshipta** (*Mazd.*). The holy bird of Heaven in the Mazdean Scriptures, of which Ahura Mazda says to Zaratushta that *"he recites the Avesta in the language of birds"* (*Bund.* xix. *et seq.*). The bird is the symbol of "Soul" of Angel and Deva in every old religion. It is easy to see, therefore, that this "holy bird" means the divine Ego of man, or the "Soul". The same as *Karanda* (*q.v.*).

**Karshvare** (*Zend*). The "seven earths" (our septenary chain) over which rule the *Amesha Spenta*, the Archangels or Dhyan Chohans of the Parsis. The seven earths, of which one only, namely Hvanirata—our earth—is known to mortals. The Earths (esoterically), or seven divisions (exoterically), are our own planetary chain as in *Esoteric Buddhism* and the *Secret Doctrine*. The doctrine is plainly stated in Fargard XIX., 39, of the *Vendidad*.

**Kartikeya** (*Sk*), or *Kartika*. The Indian God of War, son of Siva, born of his seed fallen into the Ganges. He is also the personification of the power of the Logos. The planet Mars. Kartika is a very occult personage, a nursling of the Pleiades, and a Kumâra. (See *Secret Doctrine*.)

**Karunâ-Bhâwanâ** (*Sk.*). The meditation of pity and compassion in Yoga.

**Kasbeck.** The mountain in the Caucasian range where Prometheus was bound.

**Kasi** (*Sk.*). Another and more ancient name of the holy city of Benares.

**Kasina** (*Sk.*). A mystic Yoga rite used to free the mind from all agitation and bring the *Kamic* element to a dead stand-still.

**KâsiKhanda** (*Sk.*). A long poem, which forms a part of the *Skanda Purâna* and contains another version of the legend of Daksha's head. Having lost it in an affray, the gods replaced it with the head of a ram *Mekha Shivas*, whereas the other versions describe it as the head of a goat, a substitution which changes the allegory considerably.

**Kasyapa** (*Sk.*). A Vedic Sage; in the words of *Atharva Veda*, "The self-born who sprang from Time". Besides being the father of the Adityas headed by Indra, Kasyapa is also the progenitor of serpents, reptiles, birds and other walking, flying and creeping beings.

**Katha** (*Sk.*) One of the Upanishads commented upon by Sankarâchârya.

**Kaumara** (*Sk.*). The "Kumara Creation", the virgin youths who sprang from the body of Brahmâ.

**Kauravya** (*Sk.*). The King of the Nagas (Serpents) in Pâtâla, exoterically a hall. But esoterically it means something very different. There is a tribe of the *Nâgas* in Upper India; Nagal is the name in Mexico of the chief medicine men to this day, and was that of the chief adepts in the twilight of history; and finally *Patal* means the Antipodes and is a name of America. Hence the story that Arjuna travelled to Pâtâla, and married *Ulupi*, the daughter of the King Kauravya, may he as historical as many others regarded first as fabled and then found out to be true.

**Kayanim** (*Heb.*). Also written Cunim; the name of certain mystic cakes offered to *Ishtar*, the Babylonian Venus. Jeremiah speaks of these Cunim offered to the "Queen of Heaven", vii. 18. Nowadays we do not offer the buns, but eat them at Easter. [w.w.w.]

**Kavyavahana** (*Sk.*). The fire of the Pitris.

**Kchana** (*Sk.*). A second incalculably short: the 90th part or fraction of a thought, the 4,500th part of a minute, during which from 90 to 100 births and as many deaths occur on this earth.

**Kebar-Zivo** (*Gnostic*). One of the chief creators in the *Codex Nasaræus*.

**Keherpas** (*Sk.*). Aerial form,

**Keshara** (*Sk.*). "Sky Walker", i.e., a Yogi who can travel in his astral form.

**Kether** (*Heb.*). The Crown, the highest of the ten Sephiroth; the first of the Supernal Triad. It corresponds to the Macroprosopus, vast countenance, or Arikh Anpin, which differentiates into Chokmah and Binah. [w.w.w.]

**Ketu** (*Sk.*). The descending node in astronomy; the tail of the celestial dragon who attacks the Sun during the eclipses; also a comet or meteor.

**Key.** A symbol of universal importance, the emblem of silence among the ancient nations. Represented on the threshold of the Adytum, a key had a double meaning: it reminded the candidates of the obligations of silence, and promised the unlocking of many a hitherto impenetrable mystery to the profane. In the "Œdipus Coloneus" of Sophocles, the chorus speaks of "the golden key which had come upon the tongue of the ministering Hierophant in the mysteries of Eleusis", (1051). "The priestess of Ceres, according to Callimachus, bore a key as her ensign of office, and the key was, in the Mysteries of Isis, symbolical of the opening or disclosing of the heart and conscience before the forty-two assessors of the dead". (*R. M. Cyclopædia*).

**Khado** (*Tib.*). Evil female demons in popular folk-lore. In the Esoteric Philosophy occult and evil Forces of nature. Elementals known in Sanskrit as *Dakini*.

**Khaldi.** The earliest inhabitants of Chaldea who were first the worshippers of the Moon god, Deus Lunus, a worship which was brought to them by the great stream of early Hindu emigration, and later a caste of regular Astrologers and Initiates.

**Kha** (*Sk.*). The same as "Akâsa".

**Khamism.** A name given by the Egyptologists to the ancient language of Egypt. *Khami*, also.

**Khanda Kâla** (*Sk.*). Finite or conditioned time in contradistinction to infinite time, or eternity—*Kala*.

**Khem** (*Eg.*). The same as Horus. "The God Khem will avenge his father Osiris"; says a text in a papyrus.

**Khepra** (*Eg.*). An Egyptian god presiding over rebirth and transmigration. He is represented with a scarabæus instead of a head.

**Khi** (*Chin.*). Lit., "breath"; meaning Buddhi.

**Khnoom** (*Eg.*). The great Deep, or Primordial Space.

**Khoda** (*Pers.*). The name for the Deity.

**Khons,** or *Chonso.* (*Eg.*) The Son of Maut and Ammon, the personification of morning. He is the Theban Harpocrates, according to some. Like Horus he crushes under his foot a crocodile, emblem of night and darkness or Seb (Sebek) who is Typhon. But in the inscriptions, he is addressed as "the Healer of diseases and banisher of all evil". He is also the "god of the hunt", and Sir Gardner Wilkinson would see in him the Egyptian Hercules, probably because the Romans had a god named Consus who presided over horse races and was therefore called "the concealer of secrets". But the latter is a later variant on the Egyptian Khons, who is more probably an aspect of Horus, as he wears a hawk's head, carries the whip and crook of Osiris the *tat* and the *crux ansata*.

**Khoom** (*Eg.*), or *Knooph*. The Soul of the world; a variant of *Khnoom*.

**Khubilkhan** (*Mong.*), or *Shabrong*. In Tibet the names given to the supposed incarnations of Buddha. Elect Saints.

**Khunrath**, *Henry*. A famous Kabalist, chemist and physician born in 1502, initiated into Theosophy (Rosicrucian) in 1544. He left some excellent Kabalistic works, the best of which is the "Amphitheatre of Eternal Wisdom" (1598).

**Kimapurushas** (*Sk.*). Monstrous Devas, half-men, half-horses.

**Kings of Edom.** Esoterically, the early, tentative, malformed races of men. Some Kabalists interpret them as "sparks", worlds in formation disappearing as soon as formed.

**Kinnaras** (*Sk.*). Lit., "What men?" Fabulous creatures of the same description as the *Kim-purushas*, One of the four classes of beings called "Maharajas".

**Kioo-tche** (*Chin.*). An astronomical work.

**Kirâtarjuniya** of *Bharavi (Sk.)*. A Sanskrit epic, celebrating the strife and prowess of Arjuna with the god Siva disguised as a forester.

**Kiver-Shans** (*Chin.*). The *astral* or "Thought Body".

**Kiyun** (*Heb.*). Or the god *Kivan* which was worshipped by the Israelites in the wilderness and was probably identical with Saturn and even with the god Siva. Indeed, as the Zendic H is S in India (their "hapta" is "sapta", etc.), and as the letters K, H, and S, are interchangeable, Siva may have easily become *Kiva* and *Kivan*.

**Klesha** (*Sk.*). Love of life, but literally "pain and misery". Cleaving to existence, and almost the same as *Kama*.

**Klikoosha** (*Russ.*). One possessed by the Evil one. Lit., a "crier out", a "screamer", as such unfortunates are periodically attacked with fits during which they crow like cocks, neigh, bray and prophesy.

**Klippoth** (*Heb.*). Shells: used in the Kabbalah in several senses; (1) evil spirits, demons; (2) the shells of dead human beings, not the physical body, but the remnant of the personality after the spirit has departed; (3) the Elementaries of some authors. [w.w.w.]

**Kneph** (*Eg.*). Also *Cneph* and *Nef*, endowed with the same attributes as Khem. One of the gods of creative Force, for he is connected with the Mundane Egg. He is called by Porphyry "the creator of the world"; by Plutarch the "unmade and eternal deity"; by Eusebius he is identified with the *Logos*; and Jamblichus goes so far as almost to identify him with Brahmâ since he says of him that "this god is intellect itself, intellectually perceiving itself, and consecrating intellections to itself; and *is to be worshipped in silence*". One form of him, adds Mr. Bonwick "was *Av* meaning *flesh*. He was criocephalus, with a solar disk on his head, and standing on the serpent Mehen. In his left hand was a viper, and a cross was in his right. He was actively engaged in the underworld upon a mission of creation." Deveria writes: "His journey to the lower hemisphere appears to symbolise the evolutions of substances which are born to die and to be reborn". Thousands of years before Kardec, Swedenborg, and Darwin appeared, the old Egyptians entertained their several philosophies. (*Eg. Belief and Mod. Thought.*)

**Koinobi** (*Gr.*). A sect which lived in Egypt in the early part of the first Christian century; usually confounded with the *Therapeutæ*. They passed for magicians.

**Kokab** (*Chald.*). The Kabalistic name associated with the planet Mercury; also the Stellar light. [w.w.w.]

**Kol** (*Heb.*). A voice, in Hebrew letters QUL. The Voice of the divine. (See "Bath Kol" and "Vâch".) [w.w.w.]

**Kols**. One of the tribes in central India, much addicted to magic. They are considered to he great sorcerers.

**Konx-Om-Pax** (*Gr.*). Mystic words used in the Eleusinian mysteries. It is believed that these words are the Greek imitation of ancient Egyptian words once used in the secret ceremonies of the Isiac cult. Several modern authors give fanciful translations, but they are all only guesses at the truth. [w.w.w.]

**Koorgan** (*Russ.*). An artificial mound, generally an old tomb. Traditions of a supernatural or magical character are often attached to such mounds.

**Koran** (*Arab.*), or *Quran*. The sacred Scripture of the Mussulmans, revealed to the Prophet Mohammed by Allah (god) himself. The revelation differs, however, from that given by Jehovah to Moses. The Christians abuse the Koran calling it a hallucination, and the work of an Arabian impostor. Whereas, Mohammed preaches in his Scripture the unity of Deity, and renders honour to the Christian prophet "*Issa Ben Yussuf*" (Jesus, son of Joseph). The Koran is a grand poem, replete with ethical teachings proclaiming loudly Faith, Hope and Charity.

**Kosmos** (*Gr.*). The Universe, as distinguished from the world, which may mean our globe or earth.

**Kounboum** (*Tib.*). The sacred Tree of Tibet, the "tree of the 10,000 images" as Huc gives it. It grows in an enclosure on the Monastery lands of the Lamasery of the same name, and is well cared for. Tradition has it that it grew out of the hair of Tson-ka-pa, who was buried on that spot. This "Lama" was the great Reformer of the Buddhism of Tibet, and is regarded as an incarnation of Amita Buddha. In the words of the Abbé Huc, who lived several months with another missionary named Gabet near this phenomenal tree: "Each of its leaves, in opening, bears either a letter or a religious sentence, written in sacred characters, and these letters are, of their kind, of such a perfection that the type-foundries of Didot contain nothing to excel them. Open the leaves, which vegetation is about to unroll, and you will there discover, on the point of appearing, the letters or the distinct words which are the marvel of this unique tree! Turn your attention from the leaves of the plant to the bark of its branches, and new characters will meet your eyes! Do not allow your interest to flag; raise the layers of this bark, and still OTHER CHARACTERS will show themselves below those whose beauty had surprised you. For, do not fancy that these super posed layers repeat the same printing. No, quite the contrary; for each lamina you lift presents to view its distinct type. How, then, can we suspect jugglery? I have done my best in that direction to discover the slightest trace of human trick, and my baffled mind could not retain the slightest suspicion." Yet promptly the kind French Abbé suspects the Devil.

**Kratudwishas** (*Sk.*). The enemies of the Sacrifices; the Daityas, Danavas, Kinnaras, etc., etc., all represented as great ascetics and Yogis. This shows who are really meant. They were the enemies of religious mummeries and ritualism.

**Kravyâd** (*Sk.*). A flesh-eater; a carnivorous man or animal.

**Krisâswas** Sons of (*Sk.*). The weapons called *Agneyastra.* The magical living weapons endowed with intelligence, spoken of in the *Ramayana* and elsewhere. An occult allegory.

**Krishna** (*Sk.*).. The most celebrated avatar of Vishnu, the "Saviour" of the Hindus and their most popular god. He is the-eighth Avatar, the son of Devaki, and the nephew of Kansa, the Indian King Herod, who while seeking for him among the shepherds and cow-herds who concealed him, slew thousands of their newly-born babes. The story of Krishna's conception, birth, and childhood are the exact prototype of the New Testament story. The missionaries, of course, try to show that the Hindus stole the story of the Nativity from the early Christians who came to India.

**Krita-Yuga** (*Sk.*). The first of the four Yugas or Ages of the Brahmans; also called *Satya-Yuga*, a period lasting 1,728,000 years.

**Krittika** (*Sk.*). The Pleiades. The seven nurses of Karttikiya, the god of War.

**Kriyasakti** (Gk.). The power of thought; one of the seven forces of Nature. Creative potency of the *Siddhis* (powers) of the full Yogis.

**Kronos** (*Gr.*). Saturn. The God of Boundless Time and of the Cycles.

**Krura-lochana** (*Sk.*). The "evil-eyed"; used of Sani, the Hindu Saturn, the planet.

**Kshanti** (*Sk.*). Patience, one of the *Paramîtas* of perfection.

**Kahatriya** (*Sk.*). The second of the four castes into which the Hindus were originally divided.

**Kshetrajna** or *Kshetrajneswara* (*Sk.*). Embodied spirit, the Conscious Ego in its highest manifestations; the reincarnating Principle; the "Lord" in us.

**Kshetram** (*Sk.*). The "Great Deep" of the Bible and *Kabala*. Chaos, Yoni; Prakriti, Space.

**Kshira Samudra** (*Sk.*). Ocean of milk, churned by the gods.

**Kuch-ha-guf** (*Heb.*). The astral body of a man. In Franz Lambert it is written "Coach-ha-guf". But the Hebrew word is Kuch, meaning *vis,* "force", motive origin of the earthy body. [w.w.w.]

**Kuklos Anagkês** (*Gr.*). Lit., "The Unavoidable Cycle" or the "Circle of Necessity"-. Of the numerous catacombs in Egypt and Chaldea the most renowned were the subterranean crypts of Thebes and Memphis. The former began on the Western side of the Nile extending toward the Libyan desert, and were known as the *serpents'* (Initiated Adepts) catacombs. It was there that the Sacred Mysteries of the *Kuklos Anagkês* were performed, and the candidates were acquainted with the inexorable laws traced for every disembodied soul from the beginning of time. These laws were that every reincarnating Entity, casting away its body should pass from this life on earth unto another life on a more subjective plane, a state of bliss, unless the sins of the personality brought on a complete separation of the higher from the lower "principles"; that the "circle of necessity" or the *unavoidable cycle* should last a given period (from one thousand to even three thousand years in a few cases), and that when closed the Entity *should return to its mummy,* i.e., to a new incarnation. The Egyptian and Chaldean teachings were those of the "Secret Doctrine" of the Theosophists. The Mexicans had the same. Their demi-god, Votan, is made to describe in *Popol Vu* (see de Bourbourg's work) the *ahugero de colubra* which is identical with the "Serpent's Catacombs", or passage, adding that it ran underground and "terminated at the root of heaven", into which *serpent's hole,* Votan was, admitted because he was himself "a son of the Serpents", or a *Dragon of Wisdom*, i.e., an Initiate. The world over, the priest-adepts called themselves "Sons of the Dragon" and "Sons of the Serpent-god".

**Kukkuta Padagiri** (*Sk.*), called also *Gurupadagiri*, the "teacher's mountain". It is situated about seven miles from Gaya, and is famous owing to a persistent report that Arhat Mahâkâsyapa even to this day dwells in its caves.

**Kumâra** (*Sk.*). A virgin boy, or young celibate. The first Kumâras are the seven sons of Brahmâ born out of the limbs of the god, in the so-called ninth creation. It is stated that the name was given to them owing to their formal refusal to "procreate their species", and so they "remained Yogis", as the legend says.

**Kumârabudhi** (*Sk.*). An epithet given to the human "Ego".

**Kumâra guha** (*Sk.*). Lit., "the mysterious, virgin youth". A title given to Karttikeya owing to his strange origin.

**Kumbhaka** (*Sk.*). Retention of breath, according to the regulations of the Hatha Yoga system.

**Kumbhakarna** (*Sk.*). The brother of King Ravana of Lanka, the ravisher of Rama's wife, Sita. As shown in the *Ramayana,* Kumbhakarna under a curse of Brahmâ slept for six months, and then remained awake one day to fall asleep again, and so on, for many hundreds of years. He was awakened to take part in the war between Rama and Ravana, captured Hanuman, but was finally killed himself.

**Kundalini Sakti** (*Sk.*). The power of life; one of the Forces of Nature; that power that generates a certain light in those who sit for spiritual and clairvoyant development. It is a power known only to those who practise concentration and Yoga.

**Kunti** (*Sk.*). The wife of Pandu and the mother of the Pandavas, the heroes and the foes of their cousins the Kauravas, in the *Bhagavad-gita*. It is an allegory of the Spirit-Soul or Buddhi. Some think that Draupadi, the wife in common of the five brothers, the Pandavas, is meant to represent Buddhi: but this is not so, for Draupadi stands for the *terrestrial life* of the Personality. As such, we see it made little of, allowed to be insulted and even taken into slavery by Yudhishthira, the *elder* of the Pandavas and her chief lord, who represents the Higher Ego with all its qualifications.

**Kurios** (*Gr.*). 'The Lord, the Master.

**Kurus** *(Sk.)* or *Kauravas*. The foes of the Pandavas in the *Bhagavad Gita*, on the plain of Kurukshetra. This plain is but a few miles from Delhi.

**Kusa** (*Sk.*). A sacred grass used by the ascetics of India, called the grass of lucky augury. It is very occult.

**Kusadwipa** (*Sk.*). One of the seven islands named *Saptadwipa* in the *Puranas*. (See *S. D., Vol. II.,* p. 404, Note.)

**Kusala** (*Sk.*). Merit, one of the two chief constituents of Karma.

**Kusînara** *(Sk.)*. The city near which Buddha died. It is near Delhi, though some Orientalists would locate it in Assam.

**Kuvera** (*Sk.*). God of the Hades, and of wealth like Pluto. The king of the evil demons in the Hindu Pantheon.

**Kwan-shai-yîn** (*Chin.*). The male logos of the Northern Buddhists and those of China; the "manifested god".

**Kwan-yin** (*Chin.*). The female logos, the "Mother of Mercy".

**Kwan-yin-tien** (*Chin.*). The heaven where Kwan-yin and the other logoi dwell.

# L

**L.**—The twelfth letter of the English Alphabet, and also of the Hebrew, where *Lamed* signifies an Ox-goad, the sign of a form of the god Mars, the *generative* deity. The letter is an equivalent of number 30. The Hebrew divine name corresponding to L, is Limmud, or *Doctus*.

**Labarum** (*Lat.*). The standard borne before the old Roman Emperors, having an eagle upon it as an emblem of sovereignty. It was a long lance with a cross staff at right angles. Constantine replaced the eagle by the christian monogram with the motto εν τουτω νικα which was later interpreted into *In hoc signo vinces*. As to the monogram, it was a combination of the letter X, *Chi*, and P, *Rho*, the initial syllable of Christos. But the *Labarum* had been an emblem of Etruria ages before Constantine and the Christian era. It was the sign also of Osiris and of Horus who is often represented with the long Latin cross, while the Greek pectoral cross is purely Egyptian. In his "Decline and Fall" Gibbon has exposed the Constantine imposture. The emperor, if he ever had a vision at all, must have seen the Olympian Jupiter, in whose faith he died.

**Labro.** A Roman saint, solemnly beatified a few years ago. His great holiness consisted in sitting at one of the gates of Rome night and day for forty years, and remaining unwashed through the whole of that time. He was eaten by vermin to his bones.

**Labyrinth** (*Gr.*). Egypt had the "celestial labyrinth" whereinto the souls of the departed plunged, and also its type on earth, the famous Labyrinth, a subterranean series of halls and passages with the most extraordinary windings. Herodotus describes it as consisting of 3,000 chambers, half below and half above ground. Even in his day strangers were not allowed into the subterranean portions of it as they contained the sepulchres of the kings who built it and other mysteries. The "Father of History" found the Labyrinth already almost in ruins, yet regarded it even in its state of dilapidation as far more marvellous than the pyramids.

**Lactantius.** A Church Father, who declared the heliocentric system a heretical doctrine, and that of the antipodes as a "fallacy invented by the devil".

**Ladakh.** The upper valley of the Indus, inhabited by Tibetans, but belonging to the Rajah of Cashmere.

**Ladder.** There are many "ladders" in the mystic philosophies and schemes, all of which were, and some still are, used in the respective mysteries of various nations. The *Brahmanical Ladder* symbolises the *Seven* Worlds or *Sapta Loka*; the *Kabalistical Ladder*, the seven lower Sephiroth; *Jacob's Ladder* is spoken of in the Bible; the *Mithraic Ladder* is also the "Mysterious Ladder". Then there are the Rosicrucian, the Scandinavian, the Borsippa Ladders, etc., etc., and finally the *Theological Ladder* which, according to Brother Kenneth Mackenzie, consists of the four cardinal and three theological virtues.

**Lady of the Sycamore**. A title of the Egyptian goddess Neïth, who is often represented as appearing in a tree and handing therefrom the fruit of the Tree of Life, as also the Water of Life, to her worshippers.

**Laena** (*Lat.*). A robe worn by the Roman Augurs with which they covered their heads while sitting in contemplation on the flight of birds.

**Lahgash** (*Kab.*). Secret speech; esoteric incantation; almost identical with the mystical meaning of Vâch.

**Lajja** (*Sk.*). "Modesty"; a demi-goddess, daughter of Daksha.

**Lakh** (*Sk.*). 100,000 of units, either in specie or anything else.

**Lakshana** (*Sk.*). The thirty-two bodily signs of a Buddha, marks by which he is recognised.

**Lakshmi** (*Sk.*) "Prosperity", fortune; the Indian Venus, born of the churning of the ocean by the gods; goddess of beauty and wife of Vishnu.

**Lalita Vistara** (*Sk.*). A celebrated biography of Sakya Muni, the Lord Buddha, by Dharmarakcha, A.D. 308.

**Lama** (*Tib.*). Written "Clama". The title, if correctly applied, belongs only to the priests of superior grades, those who can hold office as gurus in the monasteries. Unfortunately every common member of the *gedun* (clergy) calls himself or allows himself to be called "Lama". A real Lama is an ordained and *thrice* ordained Gelong. Since the reform produced by Tsong-ka-pa, many abuses have again crept into the *theocracy* of the land. There are "Lama-astrologers", the *Chakhan*, or common *Tsikhan* (from *tsigan*, "gypsy"), and Lama-soothsayers, even such as are allowed to marry and do not belong to the clergy at all. They are very scarce, however, in Eastern Tibet, belonging principally to Western Tibet and to sects which have nought to do with the *Gelukpas* (yellow caps). Unfortunately, Orientalists knowing next to nothing of the true state of affairs in Tibet, confuse the Choichong, of the Gurmakhayas Lamasery (Lhassa)—the Initiated Esotericists, with the Charlatans and *Dugpas* (sorcerers) of the Bhon sects. No wonder if—as Schagintweit says in his *Buddhism in Tibet*—"though the images of King Choichong (the "god of astrology") are met with in most monasteries of Western Tibet and the Himalayas, my brothers never saw a Lama Choichong". This is but natural. Neither the Choichong, nor the *Kubilkhan (q.v.)* overrun the country. As to the "God" or "King Choichong" he is no more a "god of astrology" than any other "Planetary" Dhyan Chohan.

**Lamrin** (*Tib.*). A sacred volume of precepts and rules, written by Tson-kha-pa, "for the advancement of knowledge".

**Land of the Eternal Sun.** Tradition places it beyond the Arctic regions at the North Pole. It is "the land of the gods where the sun never sets".

**Lang-Shu** (*Chin.*). The title of the translation of Nagarjuna's work, the *Ekasloka-Shastra.*

**Lanka** (*Sk.*). The ancient name of the island now called Ceylon. It is also the name of a mountain in the South East of Ceylon, where, as tradition says, was a town peopled with demons named Lankapuri. It is described in the epic of the *Ramayana* as of gigantic extent and magnificence, "with seven broad moats and seven stupendous walls of stone and metal". Its foundation is attributed to Visva-Karma, who built it for Kuvera, the king of the demons, from whom it was taken by Ravana, the ravisher of Sita.

The *Bhâgavat Purâna* shows Lanka or Ceylon as primarily the summit of Mount Meru, which was broken off by Vayu, god of the wind, and hurled into the ocean. It has since become the seat of the Southern Buddhist Church, the Siamese Sect (headed at present by the High Priest Sumangala), the representation of the purest exoteric Buddhism on this side of the Himalayas.

**Lanoo** (*Sk.*). A disciple, the same as "chela".

**Lao-tze** (*Chin.*). A great sage, saint and philosopher who preceded Confucius.

**Lapis philosophorum** (*Lat.*). The "Philosopher's stone"; a mystic term in alchemy, having quite a different meaning from that usually attributed to it.

**Lararium** (*Lat.*). An apartment in the house of ancient Romans where the *Lares* or household gods were preserved, with other family relics.

**Lares** (*Lat.*). These were of three kinds: *Lares familiares*, the guardians and invisible presidents of the family circle; *Lares parvi*, small idols used for divinations and augury: and *Lares præstites*, which were supposed to maintain order among the others. The Lares are the *manes* or ghosts of disembodied people. Apuleius says that the tumulary in scription, *To the gods manes who lived*, meant that the Soul had been transformed in a *Lemure;* and adds that though "the human Soul is a demon that our languages may name genius", and "is an *immortal god* though in *a certain sense she is born at the same time as the man in whom she is*, yet we may say *that she dies in the same way that she is born*". Which means in plainer language that *Lares* and *Lemures* are simply the shells cast off by the EGO, the high spiritual and immortal Soul, whose *shell,* and also its astral reflection, the *animal* Soul, die, whereas the higher Soul prevails throughout eternity.

**Larva** (*Lat.*). The animal Soul. *Larvæ* are the shadows of men that have lived and died.

**Law of Retribution**. (See "Karma".)

**Laya** or *Layam* (*Sk.*). From the root *Li* "to dissolve, to disintegrate" a point of equilibrium (*zero-point*) in physics and chemistry. In occultism, that point where substance becomes homogeneous and is unable to act or differentiate.

**Lebanon** (*Heb.*). A range of mountains in Syria, with a few remnants of the gigantic cedar trees, a forest of which once crowned its summit. Tradition says that it is here, that the timber for King Solomon's temple was obtained. (See "Druzes".)

**Lemuria.** A modern term first used by some naturalists, and now adopted by Theosophists, to indicate a continent that, according to the *Secret Doctrine* of the East, preceded Atlantis. Its Eastern name would not reveal much to European ears.

**Leon,** *Moses de.* The name of a Jewish Rabbi in the XIIIth century, accused of having composed the *Zohar* which he gave out as the true work of Simeon Ben Jachaï. His full name is given in Myer's *Qabbalah* as Rabbi Moses ben-Shem-Tob de Leon, of Spain, the same author proving very cleverly that de Leon was *not* the author of the *Zohar.* Few will say he was, but everyone must suspect Moses de Leon of perverting considerably the original *Book of Splendour* (Zohar). This sin, however, may be shared by him with the Mediæval "Christian Kabalists" and by Knorr von Rosenroth especially. Surely, neither Rabbi Simeon, condemned to death by Titus, nor his son, Rabbi Eliezer, nor his Secretary Rabbi Abba, can be charged with introducing into the *Zohar* purely Christian dogmas and doctrines invented by the Church Fathers several centuries after the death of the former Rabbis. This would be stretching alleged divine prophecy a little too far.

**Lévi, Éliphas.** The real name of this learned Kabalist was Abbé Alphonse Louis Constant. Eliphas Lévi Zahed was the author of several works on philosophical magic. Member of the *Fratres Lucis* (Brothers of Light), he was also once upon a time a priest, an *abbé* of the Roman Catholic Church, which promptly proceeded to unfrock him, when he acquired fame as a Kabalist. He died some twenty years ago, leaving five famous works — *Dogme et Rituel de la Haute Magie* (1856); *Histoire de la Magie* (1860); *La Clef des grands Mystères* (1861); *Legendes et Symboles* (1862); and *La Science des Esprits* (1865); besides some other works of minor importance. His style is extremely light and fascinating; but with a rather too strong characteristic of mockery and paradox in it to be the ideal of a serious Kabalist.

**Leviathan.** In biblical esotericism, Deity in its double manifestation of good and evil. The meaning may be found in the *Zohar* (II. 34*b*.) "Rabbi Shimeon said: The work of the beginning (of 'creation') the companions (candidates) study and understand it; but the *little ones* (the full or perfect Initiates) are those who understand the allusion to the work of the beginning *by the Mystery of the Serpent of the Great Sea* (to wit) *Thanneen, Leviathan.*" (See also *Qabbalah,* by I. Myer.)

**Levânah** (*Heb.*). The moon, as a planet and an astrological influence.

**Lha** (*Tib.*). Spirits of the highest spheres, whence the name of Lhassa, the residence of the Dalaï-Lama. The title of Lha is often given in Tibet to some *Narjols* (Saints and Yogi adepts) who have attained great occult powers.

**Lhagpa** (*Tib.*). Mercury, the planet.

**Lhakang** (*Tib.*). A temple; a crypt, especially a subterranean temple for mystic ceremonies.

**Lhamayin** (*Tib.*). Elemental sprites of the lower terrestrial plane. Popular fancy makes of them demons and devils.

**Lif** (*Scand.*). Lif and Lifthresir, the only two human beings who were allowed to be present at the "Renewal of the World". Being "pure and innocent and free from sinful desires, they are permitted to enter the world where peace now reigns". The *Edda* shows them hidden in Hoddmimir's forest dreaming the dreams of childhood while the last conflict was taking place. These two creatures, and the allegory in which they take part, are allusions to the few nations of the Fourth Root Race, who, surviving the great submersion of their continent and the majority of their Race, passed into the Fifth and continued their ethnical evolution in our present Human Race.

**Light,** *Brothers of.* This is what the great authority on secret societies, Brother Kenneth R. H. Mackenzie IX., says of this Brotherhood. "A mystic order, *Fratres Lucis,* established in Florence in 1498. Among the members of this order were Pasqualis, Cagliostro, Swedenborg, St. Martin, Eliphaz Lévi, and many other eminent mystics. Its members were very much persecuted by the Inquisition. It is a small but compact body, the members being spread all over the world."

**Lila** (*Sk*) Sport, literally; or pastime. In the orthodox Hindu Scriptures it is explained that "the acts of the divinity are *lila* ", or sport.

**Lilith** (*Heb.*). By Jewish tradition a demon who was the first wife of Adam, before Eve was created: she is supposed to have a fatal influence on mothers and newly-born infants. LIL is night, and LILITH is also the owl: and in mediæval works is a synonym of Lamia or female demon. [w.w.w.]

**Lil-in** (*Heb.*). The children of Lilith, and their descendants. "Lilith is the Mother of the *Shedim* and the *Muquishim* (the ensnarers)". Every class of the Lil-ins, therefore, are devils in the demonology of the Jews. (See *Zohar* ii. 268*a*.)

**Limbus Major** *(Lat.)*. A term used by Paracelsus to denote primordial (alchemical) matter; "Adam's earth".

**Linga** or *Lingam* *(Sk.)*. A sign or a symbol of abstract creation. Force becomes the organ of procreation only on this earth. In India there are 12 great Lingams of Siva, some of which are on mountains and rocks, and also in temples. Such is the *Kedâresa* in the Himalaya, a huge and shapeless mass of rock. In its origin the Lingam had never the gross meaning connected with the phallus, an idea which is altogether of a later date. The symbol in India has the same meaning which it had in Egypt, which is simply that the creative or procreative Force is divine. It also denotes who was the dual Creator—male and female, Siva and his Sakti. The gross and immodest idea connected with the phallus is not Indian but Greek and pre-eminently Jewish. The Biblical *Bethels* were real priapic stones, the "Beth-el" (phallus) wherein God dwells. The same symbol was concealed within the ark of the Covenant, the "Holy of Holies". Therefore the "Lingam" even as a phallus is not "a symbol of Siva" only, but that of every "Creator" or creative god in every nation, including the Israelites and their "God of Abraham and Jacob".

**Linga Purâna** *(Sk.)*. A scripture of the Saivas or worshippers of Siva. Therein *Maheswara*, "the great Lord", concealed in the Agni Linga explains the ethics of life—duty, virtue, self-sacrifice and finally liberation by and through ascetic life at the end of the *Agni Kalpa* (the Seventh Round). As Professor Wilson justly observed "the Spirit of the worship (phallic) is as little influenced by the character of the type as can well be imagined. *There is nothing like the phallic orgies of antiquity; it is all mystical and spiritual.*"

**Linga Sharîra** *(Sk.)*. The "body", i.e., the aerial symbol of the body. This term designates the *döppelganger* or the "astral body" of man or animal. It is the *eidolon* of the Greeks, the vital and *prototypal* body; the reflection of the men of flesh. It is born *before* and dies or fades out, with the disappearance of the last atom of the body.

**Lipi** *(Sk.)* To write. See "Lipikas"in Vol. I. of the *Secret Doctrine*.

**Lipikas** *(Sk.)*. The celestial recorders, the "Scribes", those who record every word and deed, said or done by man while on this earth. As Occultism teaches, they are the agents of KARMA—the retributive Law.

**Lobha** *(Sk.)*. Covetousness: cupidity, a son sprung from Brahmâ in an evil hour.

**Lodur** *(Scand.)*. The second personage in the trinity of gods in the *Eddas* of the Norsemen; and the father of the twelve great gods. It is Lodur who endows the first man—made of the ash-tree (*Ask*), with blood and colour.

**Logi** (*Scand.*). Lit., "flame". This giant with his sons and kindred, made themselves finally known as the authors of every cataclysm and conflagration in heaven or on earth, by letting mortals perceive them in the midst of flames. These giant-fiends were all enemies of man trying to destroy his work wherever they found it. A symbol of the cosmic elements.

**Logia** (*Gr.*). The secret discourses and teachings of Jesus contained in the Evangel of Matthew—in the original Hebrew, not the spurious Greek text we have—and preserved by the Ebionites and the Nazarenes in the library collected by Pamphilus, at Cæsarea. This "Evangel" called by many writers "the genuine Gospel of Matthew", was used according to (St.) Jerome, by the Nazarenes and Ebionites of Beroea, Syria, in his own day (4th century). Like the *Aporrheta* or secret discourses, of the Mysteries, these Logia could only be understood with a key. Sent by the Bishops Chromatius and Heliodorus, Jerome, after having obtained permission, translated them, but found it "a difficult task" (truly so!) to reconcile the text of the "genuine" with that of the spurious Greek gospel he was acquainted with. See *Isis Unveiled* II., 180 *et seq.*)

**Logos** (*Gr.*). The manifested deity with every nation and people; the outward expression, or the effect of the cause which is ever concealed. Thus, speech is the Logos of thought; hence it is aptly translated by the "Verbum" and "Word" in its metaphysical sense.

**Lohitanga** (*Sk.*). The planet, Mars.

**Loka** (*Sk.*). A region or circumscribed place. In metaphysics, a world or sphere or plane. The Purânas in India speak incessantly of seven and fourteen Lokas, above, and below our earth; of heavens and hells,

**Loka Chakshub** (*Sk.*). The "Eye of the World"; a title of the Sun, *Surya*.

**Loka Pâlas** (*Sk.*). The supporters, rulers and guardians of the world. The deities (planetary gods) which preside over the eight cardinal points, among which are the Tchatur (Four) Maharajahs.

**Loki** (*Scand.*). The Scandinavian Evil Spirit exoterically. In esoteric philosophy "an opposing power" only because differentiating from primordial harmony. In the *Edda*, he is the father of the terrible Fenris Wolf, and of the Midgard Snake. By blood he is the brother of Odin, the good and valiant god; but in nature he is his opposite. Loki Odin is simply two in one. As Odin is, in one sense, vital heat, so is Loki the symbol of the passions produced by the intensity of the former.

**Loreley.** The German copy of the Scandinavian "Lake Maiden". Undine is one of the names given to these maidens, who are known in exoteric Magic and Occultism as the Water-Elementals.

**Lost Word** *(Masonic).* It ought to stand as "lost words" and lost secrets, in general, for that which is termed the lost "Word" is no word at all, as in the case of the Ineffable Name *(q.v.)* The Royal Arch Degree in Masonry, has been "in search of it" since it was founded. But the "dead"—-especially those *murdered* — do not speak; and were even "the Widow's Son" to come back to life "materialized", he could hardly reveal that which never existed in the form in which it is *now* taught. The SHEMHAMPHORASH (the separated name, through the power of which according to his detractors, Jeshu Ben Pandira is said to have wrought his miracles, after stealing it from the Temple)—whether derived from the "self existent substance" of Tetragrammaton, or not, can never be a substitute, for the lost LOGOS of divine magic.

**Lotus** *(Gr.).* A most occult plant, sacred in Egypt, India and else where; called "the child of the Universe bearing the likeness of its mother in its bosom". There was a time "when the world was a golden lotus" *(padma)* says the allegory. A great variety of these plants, from the majestic Indian lotus, down to the marsh-lotus (bird's foot trefoil) and the Grecian "Dioscoridis", is eaten at Crete and other islands. It is a species of nymphala, first introduced from India to Egypt to which it was-not indigenous. See the text of *Archaic Symbolism* in the Appendix Viii. "The Lotus, as a Universal Symbol".

**Lotus,** *Lord of the.* A title applied to the various creative gods, as also to the Lords of the Universe of which this plant is the symbol. ("See Lotus".)

**Love Feasts,** *Agapae (Gr.).* These banquets of charity held by the earliest Christians were founded at Rome by Clemens, in the reign of Domitian. Professor A. Kestner's *The Agapæ or the Secret World Society (Wiltbund) of the Primitive Christians"* (published 1819 at Jena) speaks of these Love Feasts as "having a hierarchical constitution, and a groundwork of Masonic symbolism and Mysteries"; and shows a direct connection between the old Agapæ and the Table Lodges or Banquets of the Freemasons. Having, however, exiled from their suppers the "holy kiss" and women, the banquets of the latter are rather "drinking" than "love" feasts. The early Agapæ were certainly the same as the *Phallica,* which "were once as pure as the Love Feasts of early Christians" as Mr. Bonwick very justly remarks, "though like them rapidly degenerating into licentiousness". *(Eg. Bel. and Mod. Thought,* p. 260.)

**Lower Face** *or Lower Countenance* (*Kab.*). A term applied to Microprosopus, as that of "Higher Face" is to Macroprosopus. The two are identical with *Long Face* and *Short Face*.

**Lubara** (*Chald.*). The god of Pestilence and. Disease.

**Lucifer** (*Lat.*). The planet Venus, as the bright "Morning Star". Before Milton, Lucifer had never been a name of the Devil. Quite the reverse, since the Christian Saviour is made to say of himself in *Revelations* (xvi. 22.) "I am . . . the bright morning star" or Lucifer. One of the early Popes of Rome bore that name; and there was even a Christian sect in the fourth century which was called the *Luciferians.*

**Lully**, *Raymond*. An alchemist, adept and philosopher, born in the 13th century, on the island of Majorca. It is claimed for him that, in a moment of need, he made for King Edward III. of England several millions of gold "rose nobles", and thus helped him to carry on war victoriously. He founded several colleges for the study of Oriental languages, and Cardinal Ximenes was one of his patrons and held him in great esteem, as also Pope John XXI. He died in 1314, at a good old age. Literature has preserved many wild stories about Raymond Lully, which would form a most extraordinary romance. He was the elder son of the Seneshal of Majorca and inherited great wealth from his father.

**Lunar Gods.** Called in India the Fathers, "Pitris" or the lunar ancestors. They are subdivided, like the rest, into seven classes or Hierarchies, In Egypt although the moon received less worship than in Chaldea or India, still Isis stands as the representative of Luna-Lunus, "the celestial Hermaphrodite". Strange enough while the modern connect the moon only with lunacy and generation, the ancient nations, who knew better, have, individually and collectively, connected their "wisdom gods" with it. Thus in Egypt the lunar gods are Thoth-Hermes and Chons; in India it is Budha, the Son of *Soma,* the moon; in Chaldea Nebo is the lunar god of Secret Wisdom, etc., etc. The wife of Thoth, *Sifix,* the lunar goddess, holds a pole with five rays or the five-pointed star, symbol of man, the Microcosm, in distinction from the Septenary Macrocosm. As in all theogonies a goddess precedes a god, on the principle most likely that the chick can hardly precede its egg, in Chaldea the moon was held as older and more venerable than the Sun, because, as they said, darkness precedes light at every periodical rebirth (or "creation") of the universe. Osiris although connected with the Sun and a Solar god is, nevertheless, born on Mount *Sinai,* because *Sin* is the Chaldeo-Assyrian word for the moon; so was Dio-Nysos, god of Nyssi or *Nisi,* which latter appelation was that of

Sinai in Egypt, where it was called Mount Nissa. The *crescent* is not—as proven by many writers—an ensign of the Turks, but was adopted by Christians for their symbol before the Mahommedans. For ages the crescent was the emblem of the Chaldean Astarte, the Egyptian Isis, and the Greek Diana, all of them Queens of Heaven, and finally became the emblem of Mary the Virgin. "The Greek Christian Empire of Constantinople held it as their palladium. Upon the conquest by the Turks, the Sultan adopted it . . . and since that, the crescent has been made to oppose the idea of the *cross*". (*Eg. Belief.*)

**Lupercalia** (*Lat.*). Magnificent popular festivals celebrated in ancient Rome on February 15th in honour of the God Pan, during which the *Luperci*, the most ancient and respectable among the sacerdotal functionaries, sacrificed two goats and a dog, and two of the most illustrious youths were compelled to run about the city naked (except the loins) whipping all those whom they met. Pope Gelasius abolished the Lupercalia in 496, but substituted for them on the same day the procession of lighted candles.

**Luxor** (*Occ.*). A compound word from *lux* (light) and *aur* (fire), thus meaning the "Light of (divine) Fire."

**Luxor,** *Brotherhood of*. A certain Brotherhood of mystics. Its name had far better never have been divulged, as it led a great number of well-meaning people into being deceived, and relieved of their money by a certain bogus Mystic Society speculators, born in Europe, only to be exposed and fly to America. The name is derived from the ancient *Lookshur* in Beloochistan, lying between Bela and Kedjee. The order is very ancient and the most secret of all. It is useless to repeat that its members disclaim all connection with the "H.B. of L.", and the *tutti quanti* of commercial mystics, whether from Glasgow or Boston.

**Lycanthropy** (*Gr.*). Physiologically, a disease or mania, during which a person imagines he is a wolf, and acts as such. Occultly, it means the same as "were-wolf", the psychological faculty of certain sorcerers to *appear* as wolves. Voltaire states that in the district of Jura, in two years between 1598 and 1600, over 600 lycanthropes were put to death by a too-Christian judge. This does not mean that Shepherds accused of sorcery, and seen as wolves, had indeed the power of changing themselves physically into such; but simply that they had the hypnotizing power of making people (or those they regarded as enemies), believe they saw a wolf when there was none in fact. The exercise of such power is truly sorcery. "Demoniacal" possession is *true* at bottom, minus the devils of Christian theology. But this is no place for a long disquisition upon occult mysteries and magic powers.

# M

**M.**—The thirteenth letter of the Hebrew and of the English alphabets, and the twenty-fourth of the Arabic. As a Roman numeral, this letter stands for 1,000, and with a dash on it (M̄) signifies one million. In the Hebrew alphabet *Mem* symbolized water, and as a numeral is equivalent to 40. The Sanskrit *ma* is equivalent to number 5, and is also connected with water through the sign of the Zodiac, called Makâra (*q.v.*). Moreover, in the Hebrew and Latin numerals the *m,* stands "as the definite numeral for an indeterminate number"(Mackenzie's Mason. *Cyc.*), and "the Hebrew sacred name of God app]ied to this letter is *Meborach, Benedictus.*" With the Esotericists the *M* is the symbol of the Higher Ego—Manas, Mind.

**Mâ** (*Sk.*). Lit., "five". A name of Lakshmi.

**Ma**, *Mut* (*Eg.*). The goddess of the lower world, another form of Isis, as she is nature, the eternal mother. She was the sovereign and Ruler of the North wind, the precursor of the overflow of the Nile, and thus called "the opener of the nostrils of the living". She is represented offering the *ankh*, or cross, emblem of physical life to her worshippers, and is called the "Lady of Heaven".

**Machagistia.** Magic, as once taught in Persia and Chaldea, and raised in its occult practices into a religio-magianism. Plato, speaking of Machagistia, or Magianism, remarks that it is the purest form of the worship of *things divine.*

**Macrocosm** (*Gr.*). The "Great Universe" literally, or Kosmos.

**Macroprosopus** (*Gr.*). 'A Kabalistic term, made of a compound Greek word: meaning the Vast or Great Countenance (See "Kabalistic Faces"); a title of Kether, the Crown, the highest Sephira. It is the name of the Universe, called *Arikh-Anpin*, the totality of that of which Microprosopus or *Zauir-Anpin* "the lesser countenance", is the part and antithesis. In its high or abstract metaphysical sense, Microprosopus is Adam Kadmon, the *vehicle of Ain-Suph*, and the crown of the Sephirothal Tree, though since Sephira and Adam Kadmon are in fact one under two aspects, it comes to the same thing. Interpretations are many, and they differ.

**Madhasadana** or *Madhu-Sûdana* (*Sk.*). "Slayer of Madhu" (a demon), a title of Krishna from his killing the latter.

**Mâdhava** (*Sk*). (1) A name of Vishnu or Krishna; (2) The month of April; (3) A title of Lakshmi when written *Madhavi.*

**Madhya** (*Sk.*). Ten thousand billions.

**Madhyama** (*Sk.*). Used of something beginningless and endless. Thus Vâch (Sound, the female Logos, or the female counterpart of Brahmâ is said to exist in several states, one of which is that of *Mâdhyama*, which is equivalent to saying that Vâch is *eternal* in one sense "the Word (Vâch) was with God, and *in* God", for the two are one.

**Mâdhyamikas** (*Sk.*). A sect mentioned in the *Vishnu Purâna*. Agreeably to the Orientalists, a "Buddhist sect, which is an anachronism. It was probably at first a sect of Hindu atheists. A later school of that name, teaching a system of sophistic nihilism, that reduces every proposition into a thesis and its antithesis, and then denies both, has been started in Tibet and China. It adopts a few principles of Nâgârjuna, who was one of the founders of the esoteric Mahayâna systems, not their *exoteric* travesties. The allegory that regarded Nâgârjuna's "Paramartha" as a gift from the *Nâgas* (Serpents) shows that he received his teachings from the secret school of adepts, and that the real tenets are therefore kept secret.

**Maga** (*Sk.*). The priests of the Sun, mentioned in the *Vishnu Purâna*. They are the later Magi of Chaldea and Iran, the forefathers of the modern Parsis.

**Magadha** (*Sk.*). An ancient country in India, under Buddhist Kings.

**Mage,** or *Magian*. From *Mag* or *Maha*. The word is the root of the word magician. The Maha-âtma (the great Soul or Spirit) in India had its priests in the pre-Vedic times. The Magians were priests of the fire-god; we find them among the Assyrians and Babylonians, as well as among the Persian fire-worshippers. The three Magi, also denominated kings, that are said to have made gifts of gold, incense and myrrh to the infant Jesus, were fire-worshippers like the rest, and astrologers; for they saw his star. The high priest of the Parsis, at Surat, is called Mobed. Others derived the name from Megh; Meh-ab signifying some thing grand and noble. Zoroaster's disciples were called *Meghestom*, according to Kleuker.

**Magi** (*Lat.*). The name of the ancient hereditary priests and learned adepts in Persia and Media, a word derived from *Mâha* great, which became later *mog* or *mag,* a priest in Pehlevi. Porphyry describes them (*Abst.* iv. 16) as "The learned men who are engaged among the Persians in the service of the Deity are called Magi", and Suidas informs us that "among the Persians the lovers of wisdom (*philalethai*) are called Magi". The *Zendavesta* (ii. 171, 261) divides them into three degrees: (1) The *Herbeds* or "Noviciates"; (2) *Mobeds* or "Masters"; (3) *Destur Mobeds,* or "Perfect Masters". The Chaldees had similar colleges, as also the Egyptians, *Destur Mobeds* being identical with the Hierophants of the mysteries, as practised in Greece and Egypt.

**Magic.** The great "Science". According to Deveria and other Orientalists, "magic was considered as a sacred science inseparable from religion" by the oldest and most civilized and learned nations. The Egyptians, for instance, were one of the most sincerely religious nations, as were and still are the Hindus. "Magic consists of, and is acquired by the worship of the gods", said Plato. Could then a nation, which, owing to the irrefragable evidence of inscriptions and papyri, is proved to have firmly believed in magic for thousands of years, have been deceived for so long a time. And is it likely that generations upon generations of a learned and pious hierarchy, many among whom led lives of self-martyrdom, holiness and asceticism, would have gone on deceiving themselves and the people (or even only the latter) for the pleasure of perpetuating belief in "miracles" ? Fanatics, we are told, will do anything to enforce belief in their god or idols. To this we reply: in such case, Brahmans and Egyptian *Rekhget-amens* (*q.v.*) or Hierophants would not have popularized belief *in the power of man by magic practices to command the services of the gods: which gods,* are in truth, but the occult powers or potencies of Nature, personified by the learned priests themselves, in which they reverenced only the attributes of the one unknown and nameless Principle. As Proclus the Platonist ably puts it: "Ancient priests, when they considered that there is a certain alliance and sympathy in natural things to each other, and of things manifest to occult powers, and discovered that all things subsist in all, *fabricated a sacred science from this mutual sympathy and similarity......*and applied for occult purposes, both celestial and terrene natures, by means of which, through a certain similitude, they deduced divine virtues into this inferior abode". Magic is the science of communicating with and directing supernal, supramundane Potencies, as well as of commanding those of the lower spheres; a practical knowledge of the hidden mysteries of nature known to only the few, because they are so difficult to acquire, without falling into sins against nature. Ancient and mediæval mystics divided magic into three classes—*Theurgia, Goëtia* and natural *Magic.* "Theurgia has long since been appropriated as the peculiar sphere of the theosophists and metaphysicians", says Kenneth Mackenzie. Goëtia is *black* magic, and "natural (or white) magic has risen with healing in its wings to the proud position of an exact and progressive study". The comments added by our late learned Brother are remarkable. "The realistic desires of modern times have contributed to bring magic into disrepute and ridicule. . . . Faith (in one's own self) is an essential element in magic, and existed long before other ideas which presume its pre-existence. It is said that it takes a wise man to make a fool; and a man's ideas must be exalted almost to madness, i.e., his brain susceptibilities must be increased far beyond the low, miserable status of modern civilization, before he can become a true magician; (for) a pursuit of this science implies a certain amount of isolation and *an abnegation of Self*". A very great isolation, certainly, the achievement of which constitutes a wonderful phenomenon, a miracle in itself. Withal magic is not something *supernatural*. As explained by Jamblichus, "they through the sacerdotal theurgy announce that they are able to ascend *to more elevated and universal Essences, and to those that are established above fate, viz.,* to god and the demiurgus: neither employing matter, nor assuming any other things besides, except the observation of a sensible time". Already some are beginning to recognise the existence of subtle powers and influences in nature of which they have hitherto known nought. But as Dr. Carter Blake truly remarks, "the nineteenth century is not that which has observed the genesis of new, nor the completion of old, methods of thought"; to which Mr. Bonwick adds that "if the ancients knew but little of our mode of investigations into the secrets of nature, we know still less of their mode of research".

**Magic, White**, or "Beneficent Magic", so-called, is *divine* magic, devoid of selfishness, love of power, of ambition, or lucre, and bent only on doing good to the world in general, and one's neighbour in particular. The smallest attempt to use one's abnormal powers for the gratification of self, makes of these powers sorcery or black magic.

**Magic, Black.** (Vide *Supra*.)

**Magician**. This term, once a title of renown and distinction, has come to he wholly perverted from its true meaning. Once the synonym of all that was honourable and reverent, of a possessor of learning and wisdom, it has become degraded into an epithet to designate-one who is a pretender and a juggler; a charlatan, in short, or one who has "sold his soul to the Evil One", who misuses his knowledge, and employs it for low and dangerous uses, according to the teachings of the clergy, and a mass of superstitious fools who believe the magician a sorcerer and an "Enchanter". The word is derived from *Magh, Mah* in Sanskrit Mâha—great; a man well versed in esoteric knowledge. (*Isis Unveiled.*)

**Magna Mater** (*Lat.*). "Great Mother". A title given in days of old, to all the chief goddesses of the nations, such as Diana of Ephesus, Isis, Mauth, and many others.

**Magnes**. An expression used by Paracelsus and the mediæval Theosophists. It is the spirit of light, or *Akâsa*. A word much used by the mediæval Alchemists.

**Magnetic Masonry**. Also called "Iatric" masonry. It is described as a Brotherhood of Healers (from *iatrikê* a Greek word meaning "the art of healing"), and is greatly used by the "Brothers of Light "as Kenneth Mackenzie states in the *Royal Masonic Cyclopedia*. There appears to be a tradition in some secret Masonic works—so says Ragon at any rate, the great Masonic authority—to the effect that there was a Masonic degree called the Oracle of Cos, "instituted in the eighteenth century B.C., from the fact that Cos was the birthplace of Hippocrates". The *iatrikê* was a distinct characteristic of the priests who took charge of the patients in the ancient *Asclepia*, the temples where the god Asclepios (Æsculapius) was said to heal the sick and the lame.

**Magnetism**. A Force in nature and in man. When it is the former, it is an agent which gives rise to the various phenomena of attraction, of polarity, etc. When the latter, it becomes "animal" magnetism, in contradistinction to cosmic, and terrestrial magnetism.

**Magnetism,** *Animal*. While official science calls it a "supposed" agent, and utterly rejects its actuality, the teeming millions of antiquity and of the now living Asiatic nations, Occultists, Theosophists, Spiritualists, and Mystics of every kind and description proclaim it as a well established fact. Animal magnetism is a *fluid*, an emanation. Some people can emit it for curative purposes through their eyes and the tips of their fingers, while the rest of all creatures, mankind, animals and even every inanimate object, emanate it either as an *aura*, or a varying light, and that whether consciously or not. When acted upon by Contact: with a patient or by the will of a human operator it is called "Mesmerism" (*q.v.*).

**Magnum Opus** (*Lat.*). In Alchemy the final completion, the "Great Labour" or Grand *Œuvre*; the production of the "Philosopher's Stone" and "Elixir of Life" which, though not by far the myth some sceptics would have it, has yet to be accepted symbolically, and is full of mystic meaning.

**Magus** (*Lat.*). in the New Testament it means a Sage, a wise man of the Chaldeans; it is in English often used for a Magician, any wonder-worker; in the Rosicrucian Society it is the title of the highest members, the IXth grade; the Supreme Magus is the Head of the Order in the "Outer"; the Magi of the "Inner" are unknown except to those of the VIIIth grade. [w.w.w.]

**Mahâ Buddhi** (*Sk.*). *Mahat*. The Intelligent Soul of the World. The seven *Prakritis* or seven "natures" or planes, are counted from Mahâbuddhi downwards.

**Mahâ Chohan** (*Sk.*). The chief of a spiritual Hierarchy, or of a school of Occultism; the head of the trans-Himalayan mystics.

**Mahâ Deva** (*Sk.*). Lit., "great god"; a title of Siva.

**Mahâ Guru** (*Sk.*). Lit., "great teacher". The Initiator.

**Mahâjwala** (*Sk.*). A certain hell.

**Mahâ Kâla** (*Sk.*). "Great Time". A name of Siva as the "Destroyer", and of Vishnu as the "Preserver".

**Mahâ Kalpa** (*Sk.*). The "great age".

**Mahâ Manvantara** (*Sk.*). Lit., the great interludes between the "Manus". The period of universal activity. Manvantara implying here simply a period of activity, as opposed to Pralaya, or rest—without reference to the length of the cycle.

**Mahâ Mâyâ** (*Sk.*). The great illusion of manifestation. This universe, and all in it in their mutual relation, is called the great Illusion or *Mahâmâyâ* It is also the usual title given to Gautama the Buddha's Immaculate Mother—Mayâdêvi, or the "Great Mystery", as she is called by the Mystics.

**Mahâ Pralaya** (*Sk.*). The opposite of Mahâmanvantara, literally "the great Dissolution", the "Night" following the "Day of Brahmâ". It is the great rest and sleep of all nature after a period of active manifestation; orthodox Christians would refer to it as the "Destruction of the World".

**Mahâ Parinibbâna Sutta** (*Pali.*). One of the most authoritative of the Buddhist sacred writings.

**Mahâ Purusha** (*Sk.*). Supreme or Great Spirit. A title of Vishnu.

**Mahâ Râjikâs** (*Sk.*). A *gana* or class of gods 236 in number. Certain *Forces* in esoteric teachings.

**Mahâ Sûnyata** (*Sk.*). Space, or eternal law; the great void or chaos.

**Mahâ Vidyâ** (*Sk.*). The great esoteric science. The highest Initiates alone are in possession of this science, which embraces almost universal knowledge.

**Mahâ Yogin** (*Sk.*). The "great ascetic". A title of Siva.

**Mahâ Yuga** (*Sk.*). The aggregate of four *Yugas* or ages, of 4,320,000 solar years; a "Day of Brahmâ", in the Brahmanical system; lit., "the great age".

**Mahâbhârata** (*Sk.*). Lit., the "great war"; the celebrated epic poem of India (probably the longest poem in the world) which includes both the *Ramayana* and the *Bhagavad Gîtâ* "the Song Celestial". No two Orientalists agree as to its date. But it is undeniably extremely ancient.

**Mahâbhâratian period**. According to the best Hindu Commentators and Swami Dayanand Saraswati, 5,000 years B.C.

**Mahâbhashya** (*Sk.*). The great commentary on Pânini's grammar by Patanjali.

**Mahâbhautic** (*Sk.*). Belonging to the Macrocosmic principles.

**Mahâbhutas** (*Sk.*). Gross elementary principles of matter.

**Mahârâjahs,** *The Four* (*Sk.*). The four great Karmic deities with the Northern Buddhists placed at the four cardinal points to watch mankind.

**Mahar Loka** (*Sk.*). A region wherein dwell the *Munis* or "Saints" during Pralaya; according to the Purânic accounts. It is the usual abode of Bhrigâ, a Prajâpati (Progenitor) and a Rishi, one of the seven who are said to be co-existent with Brahmâ.

**Mahâsura** (*Sk.*). The great Asura; exoterically—Satan, esoterically—the great god.

**Mahat** (*Sk.*). Lit., "The great one". The first principle of Universal Intelligence and Consciousness. In the Purânic philosophy the first product of root-nature or *Pradhâna* (the same as Mulaprakriti); the producer of *Manas* the thinking principle, and of *Ahankâra*, egotism or the feeling of "I am I" (in the lower Manas).

**Mahâtma.** Lit., "great soul". An adept of the highest order. Exalted beings who, having attained to the mastery over their lower principles are thus living unimpeded by the "man of flesh", and are in possession of knowledge and power commensurate with the stage they have reached in their spiritual evolution. Called in Pali Rahats and Arhats.

**Mâhâtmya** (*Sk.*). "Magnanimity", a legend of a shrine, or any holy place.

**Mahatowarat** (*Sk.*). Used of Parabrahm; greater than the greatest spheres.

**Mahattattwa** (*Sk*). The first of the seven creations called respectively in the *Purânas*—Mahattattwa, Chûta, Indriya, Mukhya, Tiryaksrotas, Urdhwasrotas and Arvaksrotas.

**Mahoraga** (*Sk.*). *Mahâ uraga,* "great serpent"—Sesha or any others.

**Mahavanso** (*Pali.*). A Buddhist historical work written by Bhikshu Mohânâma, the uncle of King Dhatusma. An authority on the history of Buddhism and its spread in the island of Ceylon.

**Mahayâna** (*Pal.*). A school; lit., "the great vehicle". A mystical system founded by Nâgârjuna. Its books were written in the second century B.C.

**Maitreya Buddha** (*Sk.*). The same as the *Kalki Avatar* of Vishnu (the "White Horse" Avatar), and of Sosiosh and other Messiahs. The only difference lies in the dates of their appearances. Thus, while Vishnu is expected to appear on his white horse at the end of the present *Kali Yuga* age "for the final destruction of the wicked, the renovation of creation and the restoration of purity", Maitreya is expected earlier. Exoteric or popular teaching making slight variations on the esoteric doctrine states that Sakyamuni (Gautama Buddha) visited him in Tushita (a celestial abode) and commissioned him to issue thence on earth as his successor at the expiration of five thousand years after his (Buddha's) death. This would be in less than 3,000 years hence. Esoteric philosophy teaches that the next Buddha will appear during the seventh (sub) race of this Round. The fact is that Maitreya was a follower of Buddha, a well-known Arhat, though not his direct disciple, and that he was the founder of an esoteric philosophical school. As shown by Eitel (*Sanskrit-Chinese Dict.*), "statues were erected in his honour as early as B.C. 350".

**Makâra** (*Sk.*). "The Crocodile." In Europe the same as Capricorn; the tenth sign of the Zodiac. Esoterically, a mystic class of devas. With the Hindus, the vehicle of Varuna, the water-god.

**Makâra Ketu** (*Sk.*). A name of Kâma, the Hindu god of love and desire.

**Makâram** or *Panchakaram* (*Sk.*). In occult symbology a pentagon, the five-pointed star, the five limbs, or extremities, of man. Very mystical.

**Makâras** (*Sk.*). The five M's of the Tantrikas. (See "Tantra").

**Malachim** (*Heb.*). The messengers or angels.

**Malkuth** (*Heb.*). The Kingdom, the tenth Sephira, corresponding to the final H (*hé*) of the Tetragrammaton or IHVH. It is the Inferior Mother, the Bride of the Microprosopus (*q.v.*); also called the "Queen" It is, in one sense, the Shekinah. [w.w.w.]

**Mamitu** (*Chald.*). The goddess of Fate. A kind of Nemesis.

**Manas** (*Sk.*). Lit., "the mind", the mental faculty which makes of man an intelligent and moral being, and distinguishes him from the mere animal; a synonym of *Mahat*. *Esoterically*, however, it means, when unqualified, the Higher EGO, or the sentient reincarnating Principle in man. When qualified it is called by Theosophists *Buddhi-Manas* or the Spiritual Soul in contradistinction to its human reflection—*Kâma-Manas*.

**Manas, Kâma** (*Sk.*). Lit., "the mind of desire." With the Buddhists it is the *sixth* of the Chadâyatana (*q.v.*), or the six organs of knowledge, hence the highest of these, synthesized by the seventh called *Klichta*, the spiritual perception of that which defiles this (lower) Manas, or the "Human-animal Soul", as the Occultists term it. While the Higher Manas or the Ego is directly related to *Vijnâna* (the 10th of the 12 Nidânas)—which is the perfect knowledge of all forms of knowledge, whether relating to object or subject in the nidânic concatenation of causes and effects; the lower, the Kâma Manas is but one of the *Indriya* or organs (roots) of Sense. Very little can be said of the dual Manas here, as the doctrine that treats of it, is correctly stated only in esoteric works. Its mention can thus be only very superficial.

**Manas Sanyama** (*Sk.*). Perfect concentration of the mind, and control over it, during Yoga practices.

**Manas Taijasi** (*Sk.*). Lit., the "radiant" Manas; a state of the Higher Ego, which only high metaphysicians are able to realize and comprehend.

**Mânasa** or *Manaswin* (*Sk.*). "The efflux of the *divine* mind," and explained as meaning that this efflux signifies the *manasa* or divine sons of Brahmâ-Virâj. Nilakantha who is the authority for this statement, further explains the term "manasa" by *manomâtrasarira*. These Manasa are the *Arupa* or incorporeal sons of the Prajâpati Virâj, in another version. But as Arjuna Misra identifies Virâj with Brahmâ, and as Brahmâ is Mahat, the universal mind, the exoteric blind becomes plain. The Pitris are identical with the Kumâra, the Vairaja, the Manasa-Putra (mind sons), and are finally identified with the human "Egos".

**Mânasa Dhyânis** (*Sk.*). The highest Pitris in the *Purânas*; the Agnishwatthas, or Solar Ancestors of Man, those who made of Man a rational being, by incarnating in the senseless forms of semi-ethereal flesh of the men of the third race. (See Vol. II. of *Secret Doctrine*.)

**Mânasas** (*Sk.*). Those who endowed humanity with *manas* or intelligence, the immortal EGOS in men. (See "Manas".)

**Manasasarovara** (*Sk.*). Phonetically pronounced *Mansoravara*. A sacred lake in Tibet, in the Himalayas, also called *Anavatapta*. Manasasarovara is the name of the tutelary deity of that lake and, according to popular folk-lore, is said to be a *nâga*, a "serpent". This, translated esoterically, means a great adept, a sage. The lake is a great place of yearly pilgrimage for the Hindus, as the *Vedas* are claimed to have been written on its shores.

**Mânava** (*Sk.*). A land of ancient India; a Kalpa or Cycle. The name of a weapon used by Râma; meaning of "Manu" as,—

**Mânava Dharma Shâstra**—is the ancient code of law of, or by Manu.

**Mandala** (*Sk.*). A circle; also the ten divisions of the Vedas.

**Mandara** (*Sk.*). The mountain used by the gods as a stick to churn the ocean of milk in the *Purânas*.

**Mandâkinî** (*Sk.*). The heavenly *Ganga* or Ganges.

**Mandragora** (*Gr.*). A plant whose root has the human form. In Occultism it is used by *black* magicians for various illicit objects, and some of the "left-hand" Occultists make *homunculi* with it. It is commonly called *mandrake*, and is supposed to cry out when pulled out of the ground.

**Manes** or *Manus* (*Lat.*). Benevolent "gods", i.e., "spooks" of the lower world *(Kâmaloka)*; the deified shades of the dead—of the ancient profane, and the "materialized"*ghosts* of the modern Spiritualists, believed to be the souls of the departed, whereas, in truth, they are only their empty *shells*, or images.

**Manichæans** (*Lat.*). A sect of the third century which believed in *two* eternal principles of good and evil; the former furnishing mankind with souls, and the latter with bodies. This sect was founded by a certain half-Christian mystic named Mani, who gave himself out as the expected "Comforter", the Messiah and Christ. Many centuries later, after the sect was dead, a Brotherhood arose, calling itself the "Manichees", of a masonic character with several degrees of initiation. Their ideas were Kabalistic, but were misunderstood.

**Mano** (*Gnost.*). The Lord of Light. *Rex Lucis*, in the *Codex Nazaræus*. He is the Second "Life" of the second or manifested trinity "the heavenly life and light, and older than the architect of heaven and earth" (*Cod. Naz.*, Vol. I. p. 145). These trinities are as follows. The Supreme Lord of splendour and of light, luminous and refulgent, before which no other existed, is called Corona (the crown); Lord Ferho, the unrevealed life which existed in the former from eternity; and Lord Jordan—the spirit, the living water of grace (*Ibid.* II pp. 45-51). He is the one through whom alone we can be saved. These three constitute the trinity *in abscondito*. The second trinity is composed of the three lives. The first is the similitude of Lord Ferho, through whom he has proceeded forth; and the second Ferho is the King of Light—MANO. The second life is *Ish Amon* (Pleroma), the vase of election, containing the visible thought of the *Jordanus Maximus*—the *type* (or its intelligible reflection), the prototype of the living water, who is the "spiritual Jordan". (*Ibid.* II., p. 211.) The third life, which is produced by the other two, is ABATUR (*Ab*, the Parent or Father). This is the mysterious and decrepit "Aged of the Aged", the Ancient "*Senem sui obtegentem et grandævum mundi.*" This latter third Life is the Father of the Demiurge

Fetahil, the Creator of the world, whom the Ophites call Ilda-Baoth *(q.v.)*, though Fetahil is the *only-begotten one*, the reflection of the Father, Abatur, who begets him by looking into the "dark water". Sophia Achamoth also begets her Son Ilda-Baoth the *Demiurge*, by looking into the chaos of matter. But the Lord Mano, "the Lord of loftiness, the Lord of all genii", is higher than the Father, in this kabalistic *Codex* — one is purely spiritual, the other material. So, for instance, while Abatur's "only-begotten" one is the genius Fetahil, the Creator of the physical world, Lord Mano, the "Lord of Celsitude", who is the son of Him, who is "the Father of all who preach the Gospel", produces also an "only-begotten" one, the Lord Lehdaio, "a just Lord". He is the Christos, the anointed, who pours out the "grace" of the Invisible Jordan, the Spirit of the *Highest Crown.* (See for further information *Isis Unveiled.* Vol. II., pp. 227, *et. seq.*)

**Manodhâtu** *(Sk.).* Lit., the "World of the mind", meaning not only all our mental faculties, but also one of the divisions of the plane of mind. Each human being has his *Manodhatu* or plane of thought proportionate with the degree of his intellect and his mental faculties, beyond which he can go only by studying and developing his higher spiritual faculties in one of the higher spheres of thought.

**Manomaya Kosha** *(Sk.).* A Vedantic term, meaning the *Sheath* (*Kosha*) of the *Manomaya*, an equivalent for fourth and fifth "principles" in man. In esoteric philosophy this "Kosha" corresponds to the dual *Manas.*

**Manticism**, or *Mantic Frenzy.* During this state was developed the gift of prophecy. The two words are nearly synonymous. One was as honoured as the other. Pythagoras and Plato held it in high esteem, and Socrates advised his disciples to study Manticism. The Church Fathers, who condemned so severely the *mantic frenzy* in Pagan priests and Pythiæ, were not above applying it to their own uses. The Montanists, who took their name from Montanus, a bishop of Phrygia, who was considered divinely inspired, contended with the μάντεις (manteis) or prophets. "Tertullian, Augustine, and the martyrs of Carthage, were of the number", says the author of *Prophecy, Ancient and Modern.* "The Montanists seem to have resembled the *Bacchantes* in the wild enthusiasm that characterized their orgies," he adds. There is a diversity of opinion as to the origin of the word *Manticism.* There was the famous Mantis the Seer, in the days of Melampus and Prœtus King of Argos; and there was Manto, the daughter of the prophet of Thebes, herself a prophetess. Cicero describes prophecy and mantic frenzy, by saying, that "in the inner recesses of the mind is divine prophecy hidden and confined, a divine impulse, which when it burns more vividly is called furor", frenzy. (*Isis Unveiled*.)

**Mantra period** (*Sk.*). One of the four periods into which Vedic literature has been divided.

**Mantra Shâstra** (*Sk.*). Brahmanical writings on the occult science of incantations.

**Mantra Tantra Shâstras** (*Sk.*). Works on incantations, but specially on magic.

**Mantras** (*Sk.*). Verses from the Vedic works, used as incantations and charms. By Mantras are meant all those portions of the Vedas which are distinct from the *Brahmanas*, or their interpretation.

**Mantrika Sakti** (*Sk.*). The power, or the occult potency of mystic words, sounds, numbers or letters in these Mantras.

**Manjusri** (*Tib.*). The God of Wisdom. In Esoteric philosophy a certain Dhyan Chohan.

**Manu** (*Sk.*). The great Indian legislator. The name comes from the Sanskrit root *man* "to think"—mankind really, but stands for Swâyambhuva, the first of the Manus, who started from *Swâyambhu*, "the self-existent" hence the *Logos*, and the progenitor of mankind. Manu is the first Legislator, almost a Divine Being.

**Manu Swâyambhuva** (*Sk*). The heavenly man. Adam-Kadmon, the synthesis of the fourteen Manus.

**Manus** (*Sk.*). The fourteen Manus are the patrons or guardians of the race cycles in a Manvantara, or Day of Brahmâ. The primeval Manus are seven, they become fourteen in the *Purânas*.

**Manushi** or *Manushi Buddhas* (*Sk.*). Human Buddhas, Bodhisattvas, or incarnated Dhyan Chohans.

**Manvantara** (*Sk.*). A period of manifestation, as opposed to Pralaya (dissolution, or rest), applied to various cycles, especially to a Day of Brahmâ, 4,320,000,000 Solar years—and to the reign of one Manu—308,448,000. (See *S. D.*, Vol. II, p. 68 *et. seq.*) Lit., *Manuantara*—between Manus.

**Maquom** (*Chald.*) "A secret place" in the phraseology of the Zohar, a concealed spot, whether referring to a sacred shrine in a temple, to the "Womb of the World", or the human womb. A Kabalistic term.

**Mâra** (*Sk.*). The god of Temptation, the *Seducer* who tried to turn away Buddha from his PATH. He is called the "Destroyer" and "Death" (of the Soul). One of the names of Kâma, God of love.

**Marabut**. A Mahometan pilgrim who has been to Mekka, a saint. After his death his body is placed in an open sepulchre built above ground, like other buildings, but in the middle of the streets and public places of populated cities. Placed inside the small and only room of the tomb (and several such public sarcophagi of brick and mortar may be seen to this day in the streets and squares of Cairo), the devotion of the way farers keeps a lamp ever burning at his head. The tombs of some of these marabuts are very famous for the miracles they are alleged to perform.

**Marcionites**. An ancient Gnostic Sect founded by Marcion who was a devout Christian as long as no dogma of human creation came to mar the purely transcendental, and metaphysical concepts, and the *original* beliefs of the early Christians. Such primitive beliefs were those of Marcion. He denied the *historical* facts (as now found in the Gospels) of Christ's birth, incarnation and passion, and also the resurrection of the body of Jesus, maintaining that such statements were simply the *carnalization* of metaphysical allegories and symbolism, and a degradation of the true spiritual idea. Along with all the other Gnostics, Marcion accused the "Church Fathers", as Irenæus himself complains, of "framing their (Christian) doctrine according to the capacity of their hearers, fabling blind things for the blind, according to their blindness; for the dull, according to their dulness: for those in error, according to their errors."

**Mârga** (*Sk.*). "The "Path", The *Ashthânga mârga*, the "holy" or sacred path is the one that leads to Nirvâna. The eight-fold path has grown out of the seven-fold path, by the addition of the (now) first of the eight Marga; *i.e.*, "the possession of orthodox views"; with which a *real Yogâcharya* would have nothing to do.

**Mârîchi** (*Sk.*). One of the "mind-born" sons of Brahmâ in the *Purânas*. Brahmans make of him the personified light, the parent of Sûrya, the Sun and the direct ancestor of Mahâkâsyapa. The Northern Buddhists of the Yogachârya School, see in Mârîchi Deva, a Bodhisattva, while Chinese Buddhists (especially the Tauists), have made of this conception the Queen of Heaven, the goddess of light, ruler of the sun and moon. With the pious but illiterate Buddhists, her magic formula "Om Mârîchi svâha" is very powerful. Speaking of Mârîchi, Eitel mentions "Georgi, who explains the name as a 'Chinese transcription of the name of the holy Virgin Mary'" (!!). As Mârîchi is the chief of the Maruts and one of the seven primitive Rishis, the supposed derivation does seem a little far fetched.

**Mârishâ** (*Sk.*). The daughter of the Sage Kanda and Pramlochâ, the Apsara-demon from Indra's heaven. She was the mother of Daksha. An allegory referring to the Mystery of the Second and Third human Races.

**Martinists.** A Society in France, founded by a great mystic called the Marquis de St. Martin, a disciple of Martinez Pasqualis. It was first established at Lyons as a kind of occult Masonic Society, its members believing in the possibility of communicating with Planetary Spirits and minor Gods and genii of the ultramundane Spheres. Louis Claude de St. Martin, born in 1743, had commenced life as a brilliant officer in the army, but left it to devote himself to study and the *belles lettres*, ending his career by becoming an ardent Theosophist and a disciple of Jacob Boehmen. He tried to bring back Masonry to its primeval character of Occultism and Theurgy, but failed. He first made his "Rectified Rite" to consist of ten degrees, but these were brought down owing to the study of the original Masonic orders—to seven. Masons complain that he introduced certain ideas and adopted rites "at variance with the archæological history of Masonry"; but so did Cagliostro and St Germain before him, as all those who knew well the origin of Free masonry.

**Mârttanda,** (*Sk.*). The Vedic name of the Sun.

**Mârut Jivas** (*Sk.*). The monads of Adepts who have attained the final liberation, but prefer to re-incarnate on earth for the sake of Humanity. Not to be confused, however, with the *Nirmânakâyas,* who are far higher.

**Mâruts** (*Sk.*). With the Orientalists Storm-Gods, but in the *Veda* something very mystical. In the esoteric teachings as they incarnate in every round, they are simply identical with some of the Agnishwatta Pitris, the Human intelligent Egos. Hence the allegory of Siva transforming the *lumps of flesh into boys*, and calling them Maruts, to show senseless men transformed by becoming the Vehicles of the Pitris or Fire Maruts, and thus rational beings.

**Masben** ∴ (*Chald.*). A Masonic term meaning "the Sun in putrefaction". Has a direct reference—perhaps forgotten by the Masons—to their "Word at Low Breath".

**Mash-Mak.** By tradition an Atlantean word of the fourth Race, to denote a mysterious Cosmic fire, or rather Force, which was said to be able to pulverize in a second whole cities and disintegrate the world.

**Masorah** (*Heb.*). The name is especially applied to a collection of notes, explanatory, grammatical and critical, which are found on the margin of ancient Hebrew MSS., or scrolls of the Old Testament. The Masoretes were also called Melchites.

**Masoretic Points,** or *Vowels* (*Heb.*). Or, as the system is now called, *Masóra* from *Massoreh* or *Massoreth*, "tradition", and *Mâsar*, to "hand down". The Rabbins who busied themselves with the *Masorah*, hence called Masorites, were also the inventors of the Masoretic points, which are supposed to give the vowelless words of the Scriptures their true pronunciation, by the addition of points representing vowels to the consonants. This was the invention of the learned and cunning Rabbins of the School of Tiberias (in the ninth century of our era), who, by doing so, have put an entirely new construction on the chief words and names in the Books of Moses, and made thereby confusion still more confounded. The truth is, that this scheme has only added additional blinds to those already existing in the *Pentateuch* and other works.

**Mastaba** (*Eg.*). The upper portion of an Egyptian tomb, which, say the Egyptologists, consisted always of three parts: namely (1) the *Mastaba* or memorial chapel above ground, (2) a Pit from twenty to ninety feet in depth, which led by a passage, to (3) the *Burial Chamber*, where stood the *Sarcophagus*, containing the *mummy* sleeping its sleep of long ages. Once the latter interred, the pit was filled up and the entrance to it concealed. Thus say the Orientalists, who divide the last resting place of the mummy on almost the same principles as theologians do man—into body, soul, and spirit or mind. The fact is, that these tombs of the ancients were symbolical like the rest of their sacred edifices, and that this symbology points directly to the septenary division of man. But in death the order is reversed; and while the Mastaba with its scenes of daily life painted on the walls, its *table of offerings*, to the *Larva*, the *ghost*, or "Linga Sarira", was a memorial raised to the two Principles and Life which had quitted that which was a lower *trio* on earth; the Pit, the Passage, the Burial Chambers and the mummy in the Sarcophagus, were the objective symbols raised to the two perishable "principles", the *personal* mind and Kama, and the three imperishable, the higher Triad, now merged into one. This "One" was the Spirit of the Blessed now resting in the Happy Circle of Aanroo.

**Matari Svan** (*Sk.*). An ærial being shown in *Rig-Veda* bringing down *agni* or fire to the *Bhrigus*; who are called "The Consumers", and are described by the Orientalists as "a class of mythical beings who belonged to the middle or ærial class of gods". In Occultism the Bhrigus are simply the "Salamanders" of the Rosicrucians and Kabalists.

**Materializations.** In Spiritualism the word signifies the objective appearance of the so-called "Spirits" of the dead, who reclothe themselves occasionally in matter; *i.e.*, they form for themselves out of the materials at hand, which are found in the atmosphere and the emanations of those present, a temporary body hearing the human likeness of the defunct as he appeared, when alive. Theosophists accept the phenomenon of "materialization"; but they reject the theory that it is produced by "Spirits", *i.e.*, the immortal principles of the disembodied persons. Theosophists hold that when the phenomenon is genuine—and it is a fact of rarer occurrence than is generally believed—it is produced by the *larvæ*, the *eidola* or Kamalokic "ghosts" of dead personalities. (See "Kâmadhâtu", "Kâmaloka" and "Kâmarupa".) As Kâmaloka is on the earth plane and differs from its degree of materiality only in the degree of its plane of consciousness, for which reason it is concealed from our normal sight, the occasional apparition of such shells is as natural as that of electric balls and other atmospheric phenomena. Electricity as a fluid, or atomic matter (for Theosophists hold with Maxwell that it *is* atomic), though invisible, is ever present in the air, and manifests under various shapes, but only when certain conditions are there to "materialize" the fluid, when it passes from its own on to our plane and makes itself objective. Similarly with the *eidola* of the dead. They are present, around us, but being on another plane do not see us any more than we see them. But whenever the strong desires of living men and the conditions furnished by the abnormal constitutions of mediums are combined together, these *eidola* are drawn—nay, *pulled* down from their plane on to ours and made objective. This is *Necromancy;* it does no good to the dead, and great harm to the living, in addition to the fact that it interferes with a law of nature. The occasional materialization of the "astral bodies" or *doubles* of living persons is quite another matter. These "astrals" are often mistaken for the apparitions of the dead, since, chameleon-like, our own "Elementaries", along with those of the disembodied and cosmic Elementals, will often assume the appearance of those images which are strongest in our thoughts. In short, at the so-called "materialization" seances it is those present and the medium, who *create* the peculiar likeness of the *apparitions*. Independent "apparitions" belong to another kind of psychic phenomena. Materializations are also called "form-manifestations" and "portrait statues". To call them materialized spirits is inadmissible, for they are not spirits but animated portrait-statues, indeed.

**Mathadhipatis** (*Sk.*). Heads of various religious Brotherhoods in India, High Priests in Monasteries.

**Matrâ** (*Sk.*). The shortest period of time as applied to the duration of sounds, equal to the twinkling of the eye.

**Mâtrâ** (*Sk.*). The quantity of a Sanskrit Syllable.

**Mâtripadma** (*Sk.*). The mother-lotus; the womb of Nature.

**Mâtris** (*Sk.*). "Mothers," the divine mothers. Their number is seven. They are the female aspects and powers of the gods.

**Matronethah** (*Heb. Kab.*). Identical with *Malcuth*, the tenth Sephira. *Lit.*, Matrona is the "inferior mother".

**Matsya** (*Sk.*). "A fish." *Matsya avatar* was one of the earliest incarnations of Vishnu.

**Matsya Purâna** (*Sk.*). The Scripture or Purâna which treats of that incarnation.

**Mâyâ** (*Sk.*). Illusion; the cosmic power which renders phenomenal existence and the perceptions thereof possible. In Hindu philosophy that alone which is changeless and eternal is called *reality;* all that which is subject to change through decay and differentiation and which has therefore a begining and an end is regarded as *mâyâ—*illusion.

**Mâyâ Moha** (*Sk.*). An illusive form assumed by Vishnu in order to deceive ascetic Daityas who were becoming too holy through austerities and hence too dangerous in power, as says the *Vishnu Purâna.*

**Mâyâvi Rûpa** (*Sk.*). "Illusive form"; the "double" in esoteric philosophy; *döppelganger or perisprit* in German and French.

**Mayavic Upadhi** (*Sk.*). The covering of illusion, phenomenal appearance.

**Mazdeans.** From (Ahura) Mazda. (See Spiegel's *Yasna*, xl.) They were the ancient Persian nobles who worshipped Ormazd, and, rejecting images, inspired the Jews with the same horror for every concrete representation of the Deity. They seem in Herodotus' time to have been superseded by the Magian religionists. The Parsis and Gebers, (*geberim*, mighty men, of *Genesis* vi. and x. 8) appear to be Magian religionists.

**Mazdiasnian.** Zoroastrian; lit., "worshipping god".

**M'bul** (*Heb.*). The "waters of the flood". Esoterically, the periodical outpourings of astral impurities on to the earth; periods of psychic crimes and iniquities, or of regular moral cataclysms.

**Medinî**(*Sk.*). The earth; so-called from the marrow (*medas*) of two demons. These monsters springing from the ear of the sleeping Vishnu, were preparing to kill Brahmâ who was lying on the lotus which grows from Vishnu's navel, when the god of Preservation awoke and killed them. Their bodies being thrown into the sea produced such a quantity of fat and marrow that Nârâyana used it to form the earth with.

**Megacosm** (*Gr.*). The world of the Astral light, or as explained by a puzzled Mason "a great world, not identical with Macrocosm, the Universe, but something between it and Microcosm, the little world" or man.

**Mehen** (*Eg.*). In popular myths, the great serpent which represents the lower atmosphere. In Occultism, the world of the *Astral light,* called symbolically the Cosmic Dragon and the Serpent. (See the works of Eliphaz Lévi, who called this light *le Serpent du Mal,* and by other names, attributing to it all the evil influences on the earth.)

**Melekh** (*Heb.*). Lit., "a King". A title of the Sephira Tiphereth, the V, or *vau* in the tetragrammaton — the son or *Microprosopus* (the Lesser Face).

**Melhas** (*Sk.*). A class of fire-gods or Salamanders.

**Memrab** (*Heb.*). In the Kabala, "the voice of the will" i.e., the collective forces of nature in activity, called the "Word", or Logos, by the Jewish Kabalists.

**Mendæans** (*Gr.*). Also called *Sabians,* and St. John Christians. The latter is absurd, since, according to all accounts, and even their own, they have nothing at all to do with Christianity, *which they abominate.* The modern sect of the Mendæans is widely scattered over Asia Minor and elsewhere, and is rightly believed by several Orientalists to be a direct surviving relic of the Gnostics. For as explained in the *Dictionnaire des Apocryphes* by the Abbé Migrie (art. "Le Code Nazaréan" vulgaire-ment appele "*Livre d'Adam*"), the Mendæans (written in French *Mandaïtes,* which name they pronounce as *Mandai*) "properly signifies science, knowledge or Gnosis. Thus it is the equivalent of Gnostics" (*loc. cit.* note p. 3). As the above cited work shows, although many travellers have spoken of a sect whose followers are variously named Sabians, St. John's Christians and Mendæans, and who are scattered around *Schat-Etarab* at the junction of the Tigris and Euphrates (principally at Bassorah, Hoveïza, Korna, etc.), it was Norberg who was the first to point out a tribe belonging to the same sect established in Syria. And they are the most interesting of all. This tribe, some 14,000 or 15,000 in number, lives at a day's march east of Mount Lebanon, principally at Elmerkah, (Lata-Kieh). They call themselves indifferently Nazarenes and Galileans, as they originally come to Syria from Galilee. They claim that their religion is the same as that of St. John the Baptist, and that it has not changed one bit since his day. On festival days they clothe them selves in camel's skins, sleep on camel's skins, and eat locusts and honey as did their "Father, St. John the Baptist". Yet they call Jesus Christ an *impostor, a false Messiah,* and Nebso (or the planet Mercury in its evil side), and show him as a production of the Spirit of the "seven badly-disposed stellars" (or planets). See *Codex Nazaræus,* which is their Scripture.

**Mendes** (*Gr.*). The name of the *demon-goat,* alleged by the Church of Rome to have been *worshipped* by the Templars and other Masons. But this goat was a myth created by the evil fancy of the *odium theologicum.* There never was such a creature, nor was its worship known among Templars or their predecessors, the Gnostics. The god of Mendes, or the Greek Mendesius, a name given to Lower Egypt in pre-Christian days, was the ram-headed god Ammon, the living and holy spirit of *Ra,* the life-giving sun; and this led certain Greek authors into the error of affirming that the Egyptians called the "goat" (or the *ram*-headed god) himself, Mendes. Ammon was for ages the chief deity of Egypt, the supreme god; *Amoun-Ra* the "hidden god", or *Amen* (the concealed) the *Self-engendered* who is "his own father and his own son". Esoterically, he was *Pan*, the god of nature or nature personified, and probably the cloven foot of Pan the *goat-footed*, helped to produce the error of this god being a goat. As Ammon's shrine was at *Pa-bi-neb-tat,* "the dwelling of *Tat* or Spirit, Lord of Tat" (*Bindedi* in the Assyrian inscriptions), the Greeks first corrupted the name into *Bendes* and then into *Mendes* from "Mendesius". The "error" served ecclesiastical purposes too well to be made away with, even when recognized.

**Mensambulism** (*Lat.*). A word coined by some French Kabalists to denote the phenomenon of "table turning" from the Latin *mensa,* a table.

**Meracha phath** (*Heb.*). Used of the "breathing" of the divine Spirit when in the act of hovering over the waters of space before creation (See *Siphra Dzeniutha*).

**Mercavah** or *Mercabah* (*Heb.*). A chariot: the Kabalists say that the Supreme after he had established the Ten Sephiroth used them as a chariot or throne of glory on which to descend upon the souls of men.

**Merodach** (*Chald.*). God of Babylon, the Bel of later times. He is the son of Davkina, goddess of the lower regions, or the earth, and of Hea, God of the Seas and Hades with the Orientalists; but esoterically and with the Akkadians, the Great God of Wisdom, "he who resurrects the dead". Hea, Ea, Dagon or Oannes and Merodach are one.

**Meru** (*Sk.*). The name of an alleged mountain in the centre (or "navel") of the earth where Swarga, the Olympus of the indians, is placed. It contains the "cities" of the greatest gods and the abodes of various Devas. Geographically accepted, it is an unknown mountain north of the

Himalayas. In tradition, Meru was the "Land of Bliss" of the earliest Vedic times. It is also referred to as *Hemâdri* "the golden mountain", *Ratnasânu*, "jewel peak", *Karnikâchala*, "lotus-mountain", and *Amarâdri* and *Deva-parvata*, "the mountain of the gods" The Occult teachings place it in the very centre of the North Pole, pointing it out as the site of the first continent on our earth, after the solidification of the globe.

**Meshia** and *Meshiane (Zend)*. The Adam and Eve of the Zoroastrians, in the early Persian system; the first human couple.

**Mesmer**, *Friedrich Anton*. The famous physician who rediscovered and applied practically that magnetic fluid in man which was called animal magnetism and since then Mesmerism. He was born in Schwaben, in 1734 and died in 1815. He was an initiated member of the Brotherhoods of the *Fratres Lucis* and of Lukshoor (or Luxor), or the Egyptian Branch of' the latter. It was the Council of "Luxor" which selected him—according to the orders of the "Great Brotherhood"—to act in the XVIIIth century as their usual pioneer, sent in the last quarter of every century to enlighten a small portion of the Western nations in occult lore. It was St. Germain who supervised the development of events in this case; and later Cagliostro was commissioned to help, but having made a series of mistakes, more or less fatal, he was *recalled*. Of these three men who were at first regarded as quacks, Mesmer is already vindicated. The justification of the two others will follow in the next century. Mesmer founded the "Order of Universal Harmony" in 1783, in which presumably only animal magnetism was taught, but which in reality expounded the tenets of Hippocrates, the methods of the ancient *Asclepieia*, the Temples of Healing, and many other occult sciences.

**Metatron** *(Heb.)*. The Kabbalistic "Prince of Faces", the Intelligence of the First Sephira, and the reputed ruler of Moses. His numeration is 314, the same as the deity title "Shaddai", Almighty. He is also the Angel of the world of Briah, and he who conducted the Israelites through the Wilderness, hence, the same as "the Lord God" Jehovah. The name resembles the Greek words *metathronon* or "beside the Throne". [w.w.w.]

**Metempsychosis.** The progress of the soul from one stage of existence to another. Symbolized as and vulgarly believed to be rebirths in animal bodies. A term generally misunderstood by every class of European and American society, including many scientists. *Metempsychosis* should apply to animals alone. The kabalistic axiom, "A stone becomes a plant, a plant an animal, an animal a man, a man a spirit, and a spirit a god", receives an explanation in Manu's *Mânava-Dharma-Shâstra* and other Brahmanical books.

**Metis** (*Gr.*). Wisdom. The Greek theology associated Metis—Divine Wisdom, with Eros—Divine Love. The word is also *said* to form part of the Templars' deity or idol Baphomet, which some authorities derive from *Baphe*, baptism, and *Metis*, wisdom; while others say that the idol represented the two teachers whom the Templars equally denied, *viz.*, Papa or the Pope, and Mahomet. [w.w.w.]

**Midgard** (*Scand.*). The great snake in the *Eddas* which gnaws the roots of the *Yggdrasil*—the Tree of Life and the Universe in the legend of the Norsemen. Midgard is the Mundane Snake of Evil.

**Midrashim** (*Heb.*). "Ancient"—the same as *Purâna;* the ancient writings of the Jews as the *Purânas* are called the "Ancient" (Scriptures) of India.

**Migmar** (*Tib.*). The planet Mars.

**Mîmânsâ** (*Sk.*). A school of philosophy; one of the six in India. There are two Mîmânsâ the older and the younger. The first, the "Pârva-Mîmânsâ", was founded by Jamini, and the later or "Uttara Mîmânsâ", by a Vyasa—and is now called the Vedânta school. Sankarâchârya was the most prominent apostle of the latter. The Vedânta school is the oldest of all the six *Darshana* (lit., "demonstrations"), but even to the Pûrva-Mîmânsâ no higher antiquity is allowed than 500 B.C. Orientalists in favour of the absurd idea that all these schools are "due to Greek influence", in order to have them fit their theory would make them of still later date. The *Shaddarshana* (or Six Demonstrations) have all a starting point in common, and maintain that *ex nihilo nihil fit*.

**Mimir** (*Scand.*). A wise giant in the *Eddas*. One of the Jotuns or Titans. He had a well which he watched over (Mimir's well), which contained the waters of Primeval Wisdom, by drinking of which Odin acquired the knowledge of all past, present, and future events.

**Minas** (*Sk.*). The same as Meenam, the Zodiacal sign *Pisces* or Fishes.

**Minos** (*Gr.,*). The great Judge in Hades. An ancient King of Crete.

**Miölner** (Scand.) The storm-hammer of Thor (See "Svastica") made for him by the Dwarfs; with it the God conquered men and gods alike. The same kind of magic weapon as the Hindu *Agneyastra*, the fire-weapon.

**Mirror**. The Luminous Mirror, *Aspaqularia nera,* a Kabbalistic term, means the power of foresight and farsight, prophecy such as Moses had. Ordinary mortals have only the *Aspaqularia della nera* or Non Luminous Mirror, they see only in a glass darkly: a parallel symbolism is that of the conception of the Tree of Life, and that only of the Tree of Knowledge. [w.w.w.]

**Mishnah** (*Heb.*). The older portion of the Jewish Talmud, or oral law,, consisting of supplementary regulations for the guidance of the Jews with an ample commentary. The contents are arranged in six sections, treating of Seeds, Feasts, Women, Damages, Sacred Things and Purification. Rabbi Judah Haunasee codified the Mishnah about AM. 140. [w.w.w.]

**Mistletoe.** This curious plant, which grows only as a parasite upon other trees, such as the apple and the oak, was a mystic plant in several ancient religions, notably that of the Celtic Druids: their priests cut the Mistletoe with much ceremony at certain seasons, and then only with a specially consecrated golden knife. Hislop suggests as a religious explanation that the Mistletoe being a Branch growing out of a Mother tree was worshipped as a Divine Branch out of an Earthly Tree, the union of deity and humanity. The name in German means "all heal". Compare the Golden Branch in Virgil's Æneid, Vi. 126: and Pliny, Hist. Nat., xvii. 4 *"Sacerdos candida veste cultus arborem scandit, falce aurea demetit."* [w.w.w.]

**Mitra** or *Mithra*. (*Pers.*) An ancient Iranian deity, a sun-god, as evidenced by his being lion-headed. The name exists also in India and means a form of the sun. The Persian Mithra, he who drove out of heaven Ahriman, is a kind of Messiah who is expected to return as the judge of men, and is a sin-bearing god who atones for the iniquities of mankind. As such, however, he is directly connected with the highest Occultism, the tenets of which were expounded during the Mithraic Mysteries which thus bore his name.

**Mitre.** The head-dress of a religious dignitary, as of a Roman Catholic Bishop: a capending upwards in two lips, like a fish's head with open mouth—*os tincæ* associated with Dagon, the Babylonian deity, the word *dag* meaning fish. Curiously enough the *os uteri* has been so called in the human female and the fish is related to the *goddess* Aphrodite who sprang from the sea. It is curious also that the ancient Chaldee legends speak of a religious teacher coming to them springing out of the sea, named Oannes and Annedotus, half fish, half man. [w.w.w.]

**Mizraim** (*Eg.*). The name of Egypt in very ancient times, This name is now connected with Freemasonry. See the rite of Mizraim and the rite of Memphis in Masonic Cyclopædias.

**Mlechchhas** (*Sk.*). Outcasts. The name given to all foreigners, and those who are non-Aryas.

**Mnevis** (*Eg.*). The bull Mnevis, the Son of Ptah, and the symbol of the Sun-god Ra, as Apis was supposed to be Osiris in the sacred bull-form. His abode was at Heliopolis, the City of the Sun. He was black and carried on his horns the sacred uræus and di*Sk.*

**Mobeds** (*Zend*). Parsi, or Zoroastrian priests.

**Moira** (*Gr.*). The same as the Latin *Fatum*—fate, destiny, the power which rules over the actions, sufferings, the life and struggles of men. But this is not *Karma*; it is only one of its agent-forces.

**Moksha** (*Sk.*). "Liberation." The same as Nirvâna; a post mortem state of rest and bliss of the "Soul-Pilgrim".

**Monad** (*Gr.*). The Unity, the *one;* but in Occultism it often means the unified triad, Atma-Buddhi-Manas, or the duad, Atma-Buddhi, that immortal part of man which reincarnates in the lower kingdoms, and gradually progresses through them to Man and then to the final goal—Nirvâna.

**Monas** (*Gr.*). The same as the term *Monad*; "Alone", a unit. In the Pythagorean system the duad emanates from the higher and solitary Monas, which is thus the "First Cause".

**Monogenes** (*Gr.*). Lit., "the only-begotten"; a name of Proserpine and other gods and goddesses.

**Moon**. The earth's satellite has figured very largely as an emblem in the religions of antiquity; and most commonly has been represented as Female, but this is not universal, for in the myths of the Teutons and Arabs, as well as in the conception of the Rajpoots of India (see Tod, *Hist.*), and in Tartary the moon was male. Latin authors speak of Luna. and also of Lunus, but with extreme rarity. The Greek name is Selene, the Hebrew Lebanah and also Yarcah. In Egypt the moon was associated with Isis, in Phenicia with Astarte and in Babylon with Ishtar. From certain points of view the ancients regarded the moon also as Androgyne. The astrologers allot an Influence to the moon over the several parts of a man, according to the several Zodiacal signs she traverses; as well as a special influence produced by the house she occupies in a figure.

The division of the Zodiac into the 28 mansions of the moon appears to be older than that into 12 signs: the Copts, Egyptians, Arabs, Persians and Hindoos used the division into 28 parts centuries ago, and the Chinese use it still.

The Hermetists said the moon gave man an astral form, while Theosophy teaches that the Lunar Pitris were the creators of our human bodies and lower principles. (See *S. D., Vol.* 1, p. 386.) [w.w.w.]

**Moriah, Mount**. The site of King Solomon's first temple at Jerusalem according to tradition. It is to that mount that Abraham journeyed to offer Isaac in sacrifice.

**Morya** (*Sk.*). One of the royal Buddhist houses of Magadha; to which belonged Chandragupta and Asoka his grandson; also the name of a Rajpoot tribe.

**Môt** (*Phœn.*). The same as *ilus,* mud, primordial chaos; a word used in the Tyrrhenian Cosmogony (See "*Suidas*").

**Mout** or *Mooth* (*Eg.*). The mother goddess; the primordial goddess, for "all the gods are born from Mooth", it is said. Astronomically, the moon.

**Mu** (*Senzar*). The mystic word (or rather a portion of it) in Northern Buddhism. It means the "destruction of temptation" during the course of Yoga practice.

**Mudra** (*Sk.*). Called the mystic seal. A system of occult signs made with the fingers. These signs imitate ancient Sanskrit characters of magic efficacy. First used in the Northern Buddhist Yogâcharya School, they were adopted later by the Hindu Tantrikas, but often misused by them for black magic purposes.

**Mukta** and **Mukti** (*Sk.*). Liberation from sentient life; one beatified or liberated; a candidate for *Moksha,* freedom from flesh and matter, or life on this earth.

**Mûlaprakriti** (*Sk.*). The Parabrahmic root, the abstract deific feminine principle—undifferentiated substance. Akâsa. Literally, "the root of Nature" (*Prakriti*) or Matter.

**Mulil** (*Chald.*). A name of the Chaldean Bel.

**Muluk-Taoos** (*Arab.*). From *Maluk,* "Ruler", a later form of Moloch, Melek, Malayak and *Malachim,* "messengers", angels. It is the Deity worshipped by the *Yezidis,* a sect in Persia, kindly called by Christian theology "devil worshippers", under the form of a peacock. The Lord "Peacock" is not Satan, nor is it the devil; for it is simply the symbol of the *hundred eyed* Wisdom; the bird of Saraswati, goddess of Wisdom; of *Karttikeya* the *Kumâra,* the Virgin celibate of the Mysteries of Juno, and all the gods and goddesses connected with the secret learning.

**Mummy**. The name for human bodies embalmed and preserved according to the ancient Egyptian method. The process of mummification is a rite of extreme antiquity in the land of the Pharaohs, and was considered as one of the most sacred ceremonies. It was, moreover, a process showing considerable learning in chemistry and surgery. Mummies 5,000 years old and more, reappear among us a preserved and fresh as when they first came from the hands of the *Parashistes*.

**Mumukshatwa** *(Sk.)*. Desire for liberation (from reincarnation and thraldom of matter).

**Mundakya Upanishad** *(Sk.)*. Lit., the "Mundaka esoteric doctrine", a work of high antiquity. It has been translated by Raja Rammohun Roy.

**Mundane** *Egg* or *Tree,* or any other such symbolical object in the world Mythologies. *Meru* is a "Mundane Mountain"; the Bodhi Tree, or *Ficus religiosa,* is the Mundane Tree of the Buddhists; just as the Yggdrasil is the "*Mundane* Tree" of the Scandinavians or Norsemen.

**Munis** *(Sk.)*. Saints, or Sages.

**Murâri** *(Sk.)*. An epithet of Krishna or Vishnu; lit., the enemy of *Mura*—an Asura.

**Mûrti***(Sk.)*. A form, or a sign, or again a face, e.g., "Trimûrti", the "three Faces" or Images.

**Murttimat** *(Sk.)*. Something inherent or incarnate in something else and inseparable from it; like *wetness* in water, which is coexistent and coeval with it. Used of some attributes of Brahmâ and other gods.

**Muspel** *(Scand.)*. A giant in the *Edda*, the Fire-god, and the father of the Flames. It was these evil sons of the good Muspel Who after threatening evil in Glowheim (Muspelheim) finally gathered into a formidable army, and fought the "Last Battle" on the field of Wigred. Muspel is rendered as "World (or Mundane) Fire". The conception Dark Surtur (black smoke) out of which flash tongues of flame, connects Muspel with the Hindu Agni.

**Mutham** or *Mattam.* *(Sk.)*. Temples in India with cloisters and monasteries for regular ascetics and scholars.

**Myalba** *(Tib.)*. In the Esoteric philosophy of Northern Buddhism, the name of our Earth, called **Hell** for those who reincarnate in it for punishment. Exoterically, Myalba is translated a Hell.

**Mystagogy** *(Gr.)*. The doctrines or interpretations of the sacred mysteries.

**Mysterium Magnum** *(Lat.)*. "The great Mystery", a term used in Alchemy in connection with the fabrication of the "Philosopher's Stone" and the "Elixir of Life".

**Mysteries**. Greek *teletai*, or finishings, celebrations of initiation or the

Mysteries. They were observances, generally kept secret from the profane and uninitiated, in which were taught by dramatic representation and other methods, the origin of things, the nature of the human spirit, its relation to the body, and the method of its purification and restoration to higher life. Physical science, medicine, the laws of music, divination, were all taught in the same manner. The Hippocratic oath was but a mystic obligation. Hippocrates was a priest of Asklepios, some of whose writings chanced to become public. But the Asklepiades were initiates of the Æsculapian serpent-worship, as the Bacchantes were of the Dionysia; and both rites were eventually incorporated with the Eleusinia. The Sacred Mysteries were enacted in the ancient Temples by the initiated Hierophants for the benefit and instruction of the candidates. The most solemn and occult Mysteries were certainly those which were performed in Egypt by "the band of secret-keepers", as Mr. Bonwick calls the Hierophants. Maurice describes their nature very graphically in a few lines. Speaking of the Mysteries performed in Philæ (the Nile-island), he says that "it was in these gloomy caverns that the grand and mystic arcana of the goddess (Isis) were unfolded to the adoring aspirant, while the solemn hymn of initiation resounded through the long extent of these stony recesses". The word "mysteries" is derived from the Greek *muô*, "to close the mouth", and every symbol connected with them had, a hidden meaning. As Plato and many other sages of antiquity affirm, the Mysteries were highly religious, moral and beneficent as a school of ethics. The Grecian mysteries, those of Ceres and Bacchus, were only imitations of the Egyptian; and the author of *Egyptian Belief and Modern Thought*, informs us that our own "word *chapel* or *capella* is said to be the *Caph-El* or college of *El*, the Solar divinity". The well-known *Kabiri* are associated with the Mysteries. In short, the Mysteries were in every country a series of dramatic performances, in which the mysteries of cosmogony and nature, in general, were personified by the priests and neophytes, who enacted the part of various gods and goddesses, repeating supposed scenes (allegories) from their respective lives. These were explained in their hidden meaning to the candidates for initiation, and incorporated into philosophical doctrines.

**Mystery Language.** The sacerdotal secret jargon employed by the initiated priests, and used only when discussing sacred things. Every nation had its own "mystery" tongue, unknown save to those admitted to the Mysteries.

**Mystes** (*Gr.*). In antiquity, the name of the new Initiates; now that of Roman Cardinals, who having borrowed all their other rites and dogmas from Aryan, Egyptian and Hellenic "heathen", have helped themselves also to the **musiz** of the neophytes. They have *to keep their eyes and mouth shut on their* consecration and are, therefore, called *Mystæ*

**Mystica Vannus Iacchi**. Commonly translated the mystic Fan: but in an ancient terra-cotta in the British Museum the fan is a Basket such as the Ancients' Mysteries displayed with mystic contents: Inman says with emblematic *testes*. [w.w.w.]

# N

**N.**—The 14th letter in both the English and the Hebrew alphabets. In the latter tongue the N is called Nun, and signifies a fish. It is the symbol of the female principle or the womb. Its numerical value is 50 in the Kabalistic system, but the Peripatetics made it equivalent to 900, and with a stroke over it (900) 9,000. With the Hebrews, however, the *final Nun* was 700.

**Naaseni**. The Christian Gnostic sect, called Naasenians, or serpent worshippers, who considered the constellation of the Dragon as the symbol of their Logos or Christ.

**Nabatheans**. A sect almost identical in their beliefs with the Nazarenes and Sabeans, who had more reverence for John the Baptist than for Jesus. Maimonides identifies them with the astrolaters. "Respecting the beliefs of the Sabeans", he says, "the most famous is the book, *The agriculture of the Nabatheans*". And we know that the Ebionites, the first of whom were the friends and relatives of Jesus, according to tradition, in other words, the earliest and first Christians, "were the direct followers and disciples of the Nazarene sect", according to Epiphanius and Theodoret (See the *Contra Ebionites* of Epiphanius, and also "Galileans" and "Nazarenes").

**Nabhi** (*Sk.*). The father of Bhârata, who gave his name to *Bhârata Varsha* (land) or India.

**Nabia** (*Heb.*). Seership, soothsaying. This oldest and most respected of mystic phenomena is the name given to prophecy in the *Bible*, and is correctly included among the spiritual powers, such as divination, clairvoyant visions, trance-conditions, and oracles. But while enchanters, diviners, and even astrologers are strictly condemned in the Mosaic books, prophecy, seership, and *nabia* appear as the special gifts of heaven. In early ages they were all termed *Epoptai* (Seers), the Greek word for Initiates; they were also designated *Nebim*, "the plural of Nebo, the Babylonian god of wisdom." The Kabalist distinguishes between the *seer* and the *magician*; one is passive, the other active; *Nebirah*, is one who looks into futurity and a clairvoyant; *Nebi-poel*, he who possesses *magic powers*. We notice that Elijah and Apollonius resorted to the same means to isolate themselves from the disturbing influences of the outer world, viz., wrapping their heads entirely in a woollen mantle, from its being an electric non-conductor we must suppose.

**Nabu** *(Chald.)*. Nebu or Nebo, generally; the Chaldean god of Secret Wisdom, from which name the Biblical, Hebrew term **Nabiim** (prophets) was derived. This son of Anu and Ishtar was worshipped chiefly at Borsippa; but he had also his temple at Babylon, above that of Bel, devoted to the seven planets. (See "Nazarenes" and "Nebo".)

**Nâga** *(Sk.)*. Literally "Serpent". The name in the Indian Pantheon of the Serpent or Dragon Spirits, and of the inhabitants of Pâtâla, hell. But as Pâtâla means the *antipodes*, and was the name given to America by the ancients, who knew and visited that continent before Europe had ever heard of it, the term is probably akin to the Mexican Nagals the (now) sorcerers and medicine men. The Nagas are the Burmese *Nats*, serpent-gods, or "dragon demons". In Esotericism, however, and as already stated, this is a nick-name for the "wise men" or adepts in China and Tibet, the "Dragons." are regarded as the titulary deities of the world, and of various spots on the earth, and the word is explained as meaning adepts, yogis, and narjols. The term has simply reference to their great knowledge and wisdom. This is also proven in the ancient Sûtras and Buddha's biographies. The Nâga is ever a wise man, endowed with extraordinary magic powers, in South and Central America as in India, in Chaldea as also in ancient Egypt. In China the "worship" of the Nâgas was widespread, and it has become still more pronounced since Nâgarjuna (the "great Nâga", the "great adept" literally), the fourteenth Buddhist patriarch, visited China. The "Nâgas" are regarded by the Celestials as "the tutelary Spirits or gods of the five regions or the four points of the compass and the centre, as the guardians of the five lakes and four oceans" (Eitel). This, traced to its origin and translated esoterically, means that the five continents and their five root-races had always been under the guardianship of "terrestrial deities", i.e., Wise Adepts. The tradition that Nâgas washed Gautama Buddha at his birth, protected him and guarded the relics of his body when dead, points again to the Nâgas being only wise men, Arhats, and no monsters or Dragons. This is also corroborated by the innumerable stories of the conversion of Nâgas to Buddhism. The

Nâga of a lake in a forest near Râjagriha and many other "Dragons" were thus converted by Buddha to the good Law.

**Nâgadwîpa** (*Sk.*). Lit., "the island of the Dragons"; one of the *Seven Divisions* of Bhâratavarsha, or modern India, according to the Purânas. No proofs remain as to who were the Nâgas (a historical people however), the favourite theory being that they were a Scythic race. But there is no proof of this. When the Brahmans invaded India they "found a race of *wise* men, half-gods, half-demons", says the legend, men who were the teachers of other races and became likewise the instructors of the Hindus and the Brahmans themselves. Nagpur is justly believed to be the surviving relic of Nâgadwîpa. Now Nagpur is virtually in Râjputana near Oodeypore, Ajmere, etc. And is it not well known that there was a time when Brahmans went to learn Secret Wisdom from the Râjputs? Moreover a tradition states that Apollonius of Tyana was instructed in magic by the Nâgas of Kashmere.

**Nagal.** The title of the chief Sorcerer or "medicine man" of some tribes of Mexican Indians. These keep always a *daimon* or god, in the shape of a serpent—and sometimes some other sacred animal—who is said to inspire them.

**Nâgarâjas** (*Sk.*). The usual name given to all the supposed "guardian Spirits" of lakes and rivers, meaning literally "Dragon Kings". All of these are shown in the Buddhist chronicles as having been converted to the Buddhist monastic life: *i.e* , as becoming Arhats from the Yogis that they were before.

**Nâgârjuna** (*Sk.*). An Arhat, a hermit (a native of Western India) converted to Buddhism by Kapimala and the fourteenth Patriarch, and now regarded as a Bodhisattva-Nirmanakaya. He was famous for his dialectical subtlety in metaphysical arguments; and was the first teacher of the Amitâbha doctrine and a representative of the Mahayâna School. Viewed as the greatest philosopher of the Buddhists, he was referred to as "one of the four suns which illumine the world". He was born 223 B.C, and going to China after his conversion converted in his turn the whole country to Buddhism.

**Nagkon Wat** (*Siam.*). Imposing ruins in the province of Siamrap (Eastern Siam), if ruins they may be called. An abandoned edifice of most gigantic dimensions, which, together with the great temple of Angkorthâm, are the best preserved relics of the past in all Asia. After the Pyramids this is the most occult edifice in the whole world. Of an oblong form, it is 796 feet in length and 588 in width, entirely built of stone, the roof included, but *without cement* like the pyramids of Ghizeh, the stones fitting so closely that the joints are even now hardly discernible. It has a central pagoda 250 feet in height from the first floor, and four smaller pagodas at the four corners, about 175 feet each. In the words of a traveller, (*The Land of the White Elephant*, Frank Vincent, p. 209) "in style and beauty of architecture, solidity of construction, and magnificent and elaborate carving and sculpture, the great Nagkon Wat has no superior, certainly no rival, standing at the present day." (See *Isis Unv.*, Vol. I. pp. 561-566.)

**Nahash** (*Heb.*). "The Deprived"; the Evil one or the Serpent, according to the Western Kabalists.

**Nahbkoon** (*Eg*). The god who unites the "doubles", a mystical term referring to the human disembodied "principles".

**Naimittika** (*Sk.*). Occasional, or incidental; used of one of the four kinds of Pralayas (See "Pralaya").

**Naïn** (*Scand.*). The "Dwarf of Death".

**Najo** (*Hind.*). Witch; a sorceress.

**Nakshatra** (*Sk.*). Lunar asterisms.

**Namah** (*Sk.*). In Pali *Namo*. The first word of a daily invocation among Buddhists, meaning "I humbly trust, or adore, or acknowledge" the Lord; as: "Namo tasso Bhagavato Arahato" etc., addressed to Lord Buddha. The priests are called "Masters of Namah"—both Buddhist and Taoist, because this word is used in liturgy and prayers, in the invocation of the *Triratna* (*q.v.*), and with a slight change in the occult incantations to the *Bodhisvattvas* and *Nirmânakâyas*.

**Nanda** (*Sk.*). One of the Kings of Magadha (whose dynasty was overthrown by Chandragupta *q.v.*).

**Nandi** (*Sk.*). The sacred white bull of Siva and his *Vâhan* (Vehicle).

**Nanna** (*Scand.*). The beautiful bride of Baldur, who fought with the blind Hodur ("he who rules over darkness") and received his death from the latter by magic art. Baldur is the personification of Day, Hodur of Night, and the lovely Nanna of Dawn.

**Nannak** (*Chald.*), also *Nanar* and *Sin*. A name of the moon; said to be the son of *Mulil*, the older Bel and the Sun, in the later mythology. In the earliest, the Moon is far older than the Sun.

**Nara** (*Sk.*). "Man", the original, eternal man.

**Nârâ.** (*Sk.*). The waters of Space, or the Great Deep, whence the name of

Nârâyana or Vishnu.

**Nara Sinha** *(Sk.)*. Lit., "Man-lion"; an Avatar of Vishnu.

**Nârada** *(Sk.)*. One of the Seven great Rishis, a Son of Brahmâ This "Progenitor" is one of the most mysterious personages in the Brahmanical sacred symbology. Esoterically Nârada is the Ruler of events during various Karmic cycles, and the personification, in a certain sense, of the great human cycle; a Dhyan Chohan. He plays a great part in Brahmanism, which ascribes to him some of the most occult hymns in the *Rig Veda*, in which sacred work he is described as "of the Kanwa family". He is called Deva-Brahmâ, but as such has a distinct character from the one he assumes on earth—or Pâtâla. Daksha cursed him for his interference with his 5,000 and 10,000 sons, whom he persuaded to remain Yogins and *celibates*, to be reborn time after time on this earth (*Mahâbhârata*). But this is an allegory. He was the inventor of the Vina, a kind of lute, and a great "lawgiver". The story is too long to be given here.

**Nâraka** *(Sk.)*. In the popular conception, a hell, a "prison under earth". The hot and cold hells, each eight in number, are simply emblems of the globes of our septenary chain, with the addition of the "eighth sphere" supposed to be located in the moon. This is a transparent *blind*, as these "hells" are called *vivifying hells* because, as explained, any being dying in one is immediately born in the second, then in the third, and so on; life lasting in each 500 years (a blind on the number of cycles and reincarnations). As these hells constitute one of the six *gâti* (conditions of sentient existence), and as people are said to be reborn in one or the other according to their Karmic merits or demerits, the blind becomes self-evident. Moreover, these Nârakas are rather purgatories than hells, since release from each is possible through *the prayers and intercessions of priests for a consideration*, just as in the Roman Catholic Church, which seems to have copied the Chinese-ritualism in this pretty closely. As said before, esoteric philosophy traces every hell to life on earth, in one or another form of sentient existence.

**Nârâyana** *(Sk.)*. The "mover on the Waters" of space: a title of Vishnu, in his aspect of the Holy Spirit, moving on the Waters of Creation. (See *Mânu*, Book II.) In esoteric symbology it stands for the primeval manifestation of the *life-principle,* spreading in infinite Space.

**Nargal** *(Chald.)*. The Chaldean and Assyrian chiefs of the Magi (Rab Mag).

**Narjol** *(Tib.)*. A Saint; a glorified Adept.

**Naros** or *Neros* *(Heb.)*. A cycle, which the Orientalists describe as consisting of 600 years. But what years? There were three kinds of Neros:

the greater, the middle and the less. It is the latter cycle only which was of 600 years. (See "Neros".)

**Nâstika** (*Sk.*). Atheist, or rather he who does not worship or recognize the gods and idols.

**Nâth** (*Sk.*). A Lord: used of gods and men; a title added to the first name of men and things as *Badrinath* (lord of mountains), a famous place of pilgrimage; *Gopinath* (lord of the shepherdesses), used of Krishna.

**Nava Nidhi** (*Sk.*). Lit., "the nine Jewels"; a consummation of spiritual development, in mysticism.

**Nazar** (*Heb.*). One "set apart"; a temporary monastic class of celibates spoken of in the *Old Testament*, who married not, nor did they use wine during the time of their vow, and who wore their hair long, cutting it only at their initiation. Paul must have belonged to this class of Initiates, for he himself tells the *Galatians* (i. x5) that he was *separated* or "set apart" from the moment of his birth; and that he had his hair cut at Cenchrea, because "he had a vow" (*Acts* xviii.18), i.e., had been initiated as a Nazar; after which he became a "master-builder" (i *Corinth.* iii.10). Joseph is styled a Nazar (*Gen.* xlix. 26). Samson and Samuel were also Nazars, and many more.

**Nazarenes** (*Heb.*). The same as the St. John Christians; called the Mend or Sabeans. Those Nazarenes who left Galilee several hundred years ago and settled in Syria, east of Mount Lebanon, call themselves also Galileans; though they designate Christ "a false Messiah" and recognise only St. John the Baptist, whom they call the "Great Nazar". The Nabatheans with very little difference adhered to the same belief as the Nazarenes or the Sabeans. More than this—the Ebionites, whom Renan shows as numbering among their sect all the surviving relatives of Jesus, seem to have been followers of the same sect if we have to believe St. Jerome, who writes: "I received permission from the Nazaræans who at Beræa of Syria used this (Gospel of Matthew written in Hebrew) to translate it.... The Evangel which the Nazarenes and Ebionites use which recently I translated from Hebrew into Greek.' (Hieronymus' *Comment.* to *Matthew*, Book II., chapter xii., and Hieronymus' *De Viris Illust. cap* 3.) Now this supposed Evangel of Matthew, by whomsoever written, "exhibited matter", as Jerome complains (bc. cit.), "not for edification but for destruction"(of Christianity). But the fact that the Ebionites, the *genuine primitive Christians*, "rejecting the rest of the apostolic writings, made use only of this (Matthew's Hebrew) Gospel" (Adv. Hær., i. 26) is very suggestive. For, as Epiphanius declares, the Ebionites firmly believed, with the Nazarenes, that Jesus was but a man "of the seed of a man" (Epiph. *Contra Ebionites*). Moreover we know from the Codex of the Nazarenes, of which the "Evangel according to Matthew" formed a portion, that these Gnostics, whether Galilean, Nazarene or Gentile, call Jesus, in their hatred of astrolatry, in their Codex *Naboo-Meschiha* or "Mercury". (See "Mendæans"). This does not shew much orthodox Christianity either in the Nazarenes or the Ebionites; but seems to prove on the contrary that the Christianity of the early centuries and modern Christian theology are two entirely opposite things.

**Nebban** or **Neibban** (*Chin.*). The same as Nirvâna, *Nippang* in Tibet.

**Nebo** (*Chald.*). The same as the Hindu Budha, son of Soma the Moon, and Mercury the planet. (See "Nabu".)

**Necromancy** (*Gr.*). The raising of the images of the dead, considered in antiquity and by modern Occultists as a practice of black magic. Iamblichus, Porphyry and other Theurgists have deprecated the practice, no less than did Moses, who condemned the "witches" of his day to death, the said witches being only Necromancers—as in the case of the Witch of Endor and Samuel.

**Nehaschim** (*Kab.*). "The serpent's works." It is a name given to the Astral Light, "the great deceiving serpent" (Mâyâ), during certain practical works of magic. (See *S. D.*, Vol. II, p. 409.)

**Neilos** (*Gr.*). The river Nile; also a god.

**Neith** (*Eg.*). *Neithes*. The Queen of Heaven; the moon-goddess in Egypt. She is variously called *Nout, Nepte, Nur*. (For symbolism, see "Nout".)

**Neocoros** (*Gr.*). With the Greeks the guardian of a Temple.

**Neophyte** (*Gr.*). A novice; a postulant or candidate for the Mysteries. The methods of initiation varied. Neophytes had to pass in their trials through all the four elements, emerging in the fifth as glorified Initiates. Thus having passed through Fire (Deity), Water (Divine Spirit), Air (the Breath of God), and the Earth (Matter), they received a sacred mark, a *tat* and a *tau*, or a + and a T. The latter was the monogram of the Cycle called the Naros, or Neros. As shown by Dr. E. V. Kenealy, in his Apocalypse, the cross in symbolical language (one of the seven meanings) "+ exhibits at the same time three primitive letters, of which the word LVX or Light is compounded. . . . The Initiates were marked with this sign, when they were admitted into the perfect mysteries. We constantly see the Tau and the Resh united thus ♀. Those two letters in the old Samaritan, as found on coins, stand, the first for 400, the second for 200 = 600. This is the staff of Osiris." Just so, but this does not prove that the Naros was a cycle of 600 years; but simply that one more pagan symbol had been appropriated by the Church. (See "Naros" and "Neros" and also "I. H. S.")

**Neo-platonism.** Lit.,"The *new* Platonism" or Platonic School. An eclectic pantheistic school of philosophy founded in Alexandria by Ammonius Saccas, of which his disciple Plotinus was the head (A.D. 189-270). It sought to reconcile Platonic teachings and the Aristotelean system with oriental Theosophy. Its chief occupation was pure spiritual philosophy, metaphysics and mysticism. Theurgy was introduced towards its later years. It was the ultimate effort of high intelligences to check the ever-increasing ignorant superstition and *blind* faith of the times; the last product of Greek philosophy, which was finally crushed and put to death by brute force.

**Nephesh Chia** (*Kab.*). Animal or living Soul.

**Nephesh** (*Heb.*). Breath of life. *Anima, Mens, Vita,* Appetites. This term is used very loosely in the Bible. It generally means *prana* "life"; in the Kabbalah it is the animal passions and the animal Soul. [w.w.w.] Therefore, as maintained in theosophical teachings, *Nephesh* is the synonym of the Prâna-Kâmic Principle, or the vital animal Soul in man. [H. P. B.]

**Nephilim** (*Heb.*). Giants, Titans, the Fallen Ones.

**Nephtys** (*Eg.*). The sister of Isis, philosophically only one of her aspects. As Osiris and Typhon are one under two aspects, so Isis and Nephtys are one and the same symbol of nature under its dual aspect. Thus, while Isis is the wife of Osiris, Nephtys is the wife of Typhon, the foe of Osiris and his slayer, although she weeps for him. She is often represented at the bier of the great Sun-god, having on her head a disk between the two horns of a crescent. She is the genius of the lower world, and Anubis, the Egyptian Pluto, is called her son. Plutarch has given a fair esoteric explanation of the two sisters. Thus he writes:

Nephtys designs that which is under the earth, and which one sees not (i.e., its disintegrating and reproducing power), and Isis that which is above earth, and which is visible (or physical nature). . . . The circle of the horizon which divides these two hemispheres and which is common to both, is Anubis." The identity of the two goddesses is shown in that Isis is also called the mother of Anubis. Thus the two are the Alpha and Omega of Nature.

**Nergal** (*Chald.*). On the Assyrian tablets he is described as the "giant king of war, lord of the city of Cutha". It is also the Hebrew name for the planet Mars, associated invariably with ill-luck and danger. Nergal-Mars is the "shedder of blood". In occult astrology it is less malefic than Saturn, but is more active in its associations with men and its influence on them.

**Neros** (*Heb.*). As shown by the late E. V. Kenealy this "Naronic Cycle" was a *mystery*, a true "secret of god", to disclose which during the prevalence of the religious mysteries and the authority of the priests, meant death. The learned author seemed to take it for granted that the Neros was of 600 years duration, but he was mistaken. (See "Natos".) Nor were the establishment of the Mysteries and the rites of Initiation due merely the necessity of perpetuating the knowledge of the true meaning of the Naros and keeping this cycle secret from the profane; for the Mysteries are as old as the present human race, and there were far more important secrets to veil than the figures of any cycle. (See "Neophyte" and "I. H. S.", also "Naros".) The mystery of 666, "the number of the great heart" so called, is far better represented by the *Tau* and the *Resh* than 600.

**Nerthus** (*Old Sax.*). The goddess of the earth, of love and beauty with the old Germans; the same as the Scandinavian Freya or Frigga. Tacitus mentions the great honours paid to Nerthus when her idol was carried on a car in triumph through several districts.

**Neshamah** (*Heb.*). Soul, *anima, afflatus.* In the Kabbalah, as taught in the Rosicrucian order, one of the three highest essences of the Human Soul, corresponding to the *Sephira Binah*. [w.w.w.]

**Nesku** or *Nusku* (*Chald.*). Is described in the Assyrian tablets as the "holder of the golden sceptre, the lofty god".

**Netzach** (*Heb.*). "Victory". The seventh of the Ten Sephiroth, a masculine active potency. [w.w.w.]

**Nidâna** (*Sk.*). The 12 causes of existence, or a chain of causation, "a concatenation of cause and effect in the whole range of existence through 12 links". This is the fundamental dogma of Buddhist thought, "the understanding of which solves the riddle of life, revealing the insanity of existence and preparing the mind for Nirvâna". (Eitel's *Sans. Chin. Dict.*) The 12 links stand thus in their enumeration. (1) *Jâti*, or birth, according to one of the four modes of entering the stream of life and reincarnation—or *Chatur Yoni* (*q.v.*), each mode placing the being born in one of the six *Gâti* (*q.v.*). (2) *Jarârnarana*, or decrepitude and death, following the maturity of the *Skandhas* (*q.v.*). (3) *Bhava,* the Karmic agent which leads every new sentient being to be born in this or another mode of existence in the

*Trailokya* and Gâti. (4) *Upâdâna,* the creative cause of *Bhava* which thus becomes the cause of *Jati* which is the effect; and this creative cause is the *clinging to life.* ( 5) *Trishnâ,* love, whether pure or impure. (6) *Vêdâna,* or sensation; perception by the senses, it is the 5th Skandha. (7) *Sparsa,* the sense of touch. (8) *Chadâyatana,* the organs of sensation. (9) *Nâmarûpa,* personality, i.e., a form with a name to it, the symbol of the unreality of material phenomenal appearances. (10) *Vijnâna,* the perfect knowledge of every perceptible thing and of all objects in their concatenation and unity. (11) *Samskâra,* action on the plane of illusion. (12) *Avidyâ,* lack of true perception, or ignorance. The Nidânas belonging to the most subtle and abstruse doctrines of the Eastern metaphysical system, it is impossible to go into the subject at any greater length.

**Nidhi** *(Sk)* A treasure. Nine treasures belonging to the god Kuvera—the Vedic Satan—each treasure being under the guardianship of a demon; these are personified, and are the objects of worship of the Tantrikas.

**Nidhogg** *(Scand.).* The "Mundane" Serpent.

**Nidra** *(Sk.).* Sleep. Also the female form of Brahmâ.

**Nifiheim** *(Scand.).* The cold Hell, in the *Edda.* A place of eternal non-consciousness and inactivity. (See *S. D.,* Vol. II., p. 245).

**Night of Brahmâ.** The period between the dissolution and the active life of the Universe which is called in contrast the "Day of Brahmâ".

**Nilakantha** *(Sk.).* A name of Siva meaning "blue throated". This is said to have been the result of some poison administered to the god.

**Nile-God** *(Eg.).* Represented by a wooden image of the river god receiving honours in gratitude for the bounties its waters afford the country. There was a "celestial" Nile, called in the Ritual *Nen-naou* or "primordial waters"; and a terrestrial Nile, worshipped at *Nilopolis* and Hapimoo. The latter was represented as an androgynous being with a beard and breasts, and a fat blue face; green limbs and reddish body. At the approach of the yearly inundation, the image was carried from one place to another in solemn procession.

**Nimbus** *(Lat.).* The aureole around the heads of the Christ and Saints in Greek and Romish Churches is of Eastern origin. As every Orientalist knows, Buddha is described as having his head surrounded with shining glory six cubits in width; and, as shown by Hardy *(Eastern Monachism),* "his principal disciples are represented by the native painters as having a similar mark of eminence". In China, Tibet and Japan, the heads of the saints are always surrounded with a nimbus.

**Nimitta** (*Sk.*). 1. An interior illumination developed by the practice of meditation. 2. The efficient spiritual cause, as contrasted with Upadana, the material cause, in Vedânta philosophy. See also *Pradhâna* in Sankhya philosophy.

**Nine.** The "Kabbalah of the Nine Chambers" is a form of secret writing in cipher, which originated with the Hebrew Rabbis, and has been used by several societies for purposes of concealment notably some grades of the Freemasons have adopted it. A figure is drawn of two horizontal parallel lines and two vertical parallel lines across them, this process forms nine chambers, the centre one a simple square, the others being either two or three sided figures, these are allotted to the several letters in any order that is agreed upon. There is also a Kabbalstic attribution of the ten Sephiroth to these nine chambers, but this is not published. [w.w.w.]

**Nirguna** (*Sk.*). Negative attribute; unbound, or without *Gunas* (attributes), i.e., that which is devoid of all qualities, the opposite of Saguna, that which has attributes (*S. D.*, Vol. II, p. 95), e.g., Parabrahmam is Nirguna; Brahmâ, Saguna. Nirguna is a term which shows the impersonality of the thing spoken of.

**Nirmânakâya** (*Sk.*). Something entirely different in esoteric philosophy from the popular meaning attached to it, and from the fancies of the Orientalists. Some call the *Nirmânakâya* body "Nirvana with remains" (Schlagintweit, etc.) on the supposition, probably, that it is a kind of Nirvânic condition during which consciousness and form are retained. Others say that it is one of the *Trikâya* (three bodies), with the "power of assuming any form of appearance in order to propagate Buddhism" (Eitel's idea); again, that "it is the incarnate avatâra of a deity" (*ibid.*), and so on. Occultism, on the other hand, says:that Nirmânakâya, although meaning literally a transformed "body", is a state. The form is that of the adept or yogi who enters, or chooses, that *post mortem* condition in preference to the Dharmakâya or *absolute* Nirvânic state. He does this because the latter *kâya* separates him for ever from the world of form, conferring upon him a state of *selfish* bliss, in which no other living being can participate, the adept being thus precluded from the possibility of helping humanity, or even *devas*. As a Nirmânakâya, however, the man leaves behind him only his physical body, and retains every other "principle" save the Kamic—for he has crushed this out for ever from his nature, during life, and it can never resurrect in his post mortem state. Thus, instead of going into selfish bliss, he chooses a life of self-sacrifice, an existence which ends only with the life-cycle, in order to be enabled to help mankind in an invisible yet most effective manner. (See *The Voice of the Silence*, third treatise, "The Seven Portals".) Thus a Nirmânakâya is not, as popularly believed, the body "in which a Buddha or a Bodhisattva appears on earth", but verily one, who whether a *Chutuktu* or a *Khubilkhan*, an adept or a yogi during life, has since become a member of that invisible Host which ever protects and watches over Humanity within Karmic limits. Mistaken often for a "Spirit", a Deva, God himself, &c., a Nirmânakâya is ever a protecting, compassionate, verily a *guardian* angel, to him who becomes worthy of his help. Whatever objection may be brought forward against this doctrine; however much it is denied, because, forsooth, it has never been hitherto made public in Europe and therefore since it is unknown to Orientalists, it must needs be "a myth of modern invention"—no one will be bold enough to say that this idea of helping suffering mankind at the price of one's own almost interminable self-sacrifice, is not one of the grandest and noblest that was ever evolved from human brain.

**Nirmathya** (*Sk.*). The sacred fire produced by the friction of two pieces of wood—the "fire" called *Pavamâna* in the *Purânas*. The allegory contained therein is an occult teaching.

**Nirriti** (*Sk.*). A goddess of Death and Decay.

**Nirukta** (*Sk.*). An *anga* or limb, a division of the *Vedas*; a glossarial comment.

**Nirupadhi** (*Sk.*). Attributeless; the negation of attributes.

**Nirvâna** (*Sk.*). According to the Orientalists, the entire "blowing out", like the flame of a candle, the utter extinction of existence. But in the esoteric explanations it is the state of absolute existence and absolute consciousness, into which the Ego of a man who has reached the highest degree of perfection and holiness during life goes, after the body dies, and occasionally, as in the case of Gautama Buddha and others, during life. (See "Nirvânî".)

**Nirvânî** (*Sk.*). One who has attained Nirvana—an emancipated soul. That Nirvâna means nothing of the kind asserted by Orientalists every scholar who has visited China, India and Japan is well aware. It is "*escape* from misery" but only from that of matter, freedom from *Klêsha*, or *Kâma*, and the complete extinction of animal desires. If we are told that *Abidharma* defines Nirvâna "as a state of absolute annihilation", we concur, adding to the last word the qualification "of everything connected with matter or the physical world", and this simply because the latter (as also all in it) is illusion, *mâyâ*. Sâkya-mûni Buddha said in the last moments of his life that "the spiritual body is immortal" (See *Sans. Chin. Dict.*). As Mr. Eitel, the scholarly Sinologist, explains it: "The popular exoteric systems agree in defining Nirvâna *negatively* as a state of absolute exemption from the circle of transmigration; as a state of entire freedom from all forms of existence; to begin with, freedom from all passion and exertion; a state of indifference to all sensibility" and he might have added "death of all compassion for the world of suffering". And this is why the Bodhisattvas who prefer the Nirmânakâya to the Dharmakâya vesture, stand higher in the popular estimation than the Nirvânîs. But the same scholar adds that: "Positively (and esoterically) they define Nirvâna as the highest state of spiritual bliss, as absolute immortality through absorption of the soul (spirit rather) into itself, but *preserving individuality* so that, e.g., Buddhas, after entering Nirvâna, may reappear on earth"—i.e., in the future Manvantara.

**Nîshada** (*Sk.*). (1) One of the seven qualities of sound—the one and sole attribute of Akâsa; (2) the *seventh* note of the Hindu musical scale; (3) an outcast offspring of a Brahman and a Sudra mother; (4) a range of mountains south of Meru—north of the Himalayas.

**Nissi** (*Chald.*) One of the seven Chaldean gods.

**Nîti** (*Sk.*). Lit., Prudence, ethics.

**Nitya Parivrita**. (*Sk.*). Lit., continuous extinction.

**Nitya Pralaya** (*Sk.*). Lit., "perpetual" Pralaya or dissolution. It is the constant and imperceptible changes undergone by the atoms which last as long as a Mahâmanvantara, a whole age of Brahmâ, which takes fifteen figures to sum up. A stage of chronic change and dissolution, the stages of growth and decay. It is the duration of "Seven Eternities". (See *S. D.*, Vol. I, p. 371; Vol. II, pp. 69, 310.) There are four kinds of Pralayas, or states of changelessness. The Naimittika, when Brahmâ slumbers; the Prakritika, a partial Pralaya of anything during Manvantara; Atyantika, when man has identified himself with the One Absolute synonym of Nirvâna; and Nitya, for physical things especially, as a state of profound and dreamless sleep.

**Nitya Sarga** (*Sk.*). The state of constant creation or evolution, as opposed to *Nitya Pralaya*—the state of perpetual incessant dissolution (or change of atoms) disintegration of molecules, hence change of forms.

**Nizir** (*Chald.*). The "Deluge Mountain"; the Ararat of the Babylonians with "Xisuthrus" as Noah.

**Nixies**. The water-sprites; Undines.

**Niyashes** (*Mazd.*). Parsi prayers.

**Nofir-hotpoo** (*Eg.*). The same as the god *Khonsoo*, the lunar god of Thebes. Lit., "he who is in absolute rest". Nofir-hotpoo is one of the three persons of the Egyptian trinity, composed of Ammon, Mooth, and their son Khonsoo or Nofir-hotpoo.

**Nogah** (*Chald.*). Venus, the planet; glittering splendour.

**Noo** (*Eg.*). Primordial waters of space called "Father-Mother"; the "face of the deep" of the Bible; for above Noo hovers the Breath of Kneph, who is represented with the Mundane Egg in his mouth.

**Noom** (*Eg.*). A celestial sculptor, in the Egyptian legends, who creates a beautiful girl whom he sends like another Pandora to *Batoo* (or "man"), whose happiness is thereafter destroyed. The "sculptor" or artist is the same as Jehovah, the architect of the world, and the girl is "Eve".

**Noon** (*Eg.*). The celestial river which flows in *Noot*, the cosmic abyss or Noo. As all the gods have been generated in the *river* (the Gnostic *Pleroma*), it is called "the Father-Mother of the gods".

**Noor Ilahee** (*Arab.*). "The light of the Elohim", literally. This light is believed by some Mussulmen to be transmitted to mortals "through a hundred prophet-leaders". Divine knowledge; the Light of the Secret Wisdom.

**Noot** (*Eg.*). The heavenly abyss in the *Ritual* or the Book of the Dead. It is infinite space personified in the *Vedas* by Aditi, the goddess who, like Noon (*q.v.*) is the "mother of all the gods".

**Norns** (*Scand.*). The three sister goddesses in the *Edda*, who make known to men the decrees of *Orlog* or Fate. They are shown as coming out of the unknown distances *enveloped in a dark veil* to the Ash Yggdrasil (*q.v.*), and "sprinkle it daily with water from the Fountain of Urd, that it may not wither but remain green and fresh and strong" (*Asgard and the Gods*). Their names are "Urd", the Past; "Werdandi", the Present; and "Skuld", the Future, "which is either rich in hope or dark with tears". Thus they reveal the decrees of Fate "for out of the past and present the events and actions of the future are born" (*loc. cit.*).

**Notaricon** (*Kab.*). A division of the practical Kabbalah; treats of the formation of words from the initials or finals of the words in every sentence; or conversely it forms a sentence of words whose initials or finals are those of some word. [w.w.w.]

**Noumenon** (*Gr.*). The true essential nature of being as distinguished from the illusive objects of sense.

**Nous** (*Gr.*). A Platonic term for the Higher Mind or Soul. It means Spirit as distinct from animal Soul—*psyche*; divine consciousness or mind in man: *Nous* was the designation given to the Supreme deity (third *logos*) by Anaxagoras. Taken from Egypt where it was called *Nout*, it was adopted by the Gnostics for their first conscious Æon which, with the Occultists, is the third *logos*, cosmically, and the third "principle" (from above) or *manas,* in man. (See "Nout".)

**Nout** (*Gr.*). In the Pantheon of the Egyptians it meant the "One-only-One", because they did not proceed in their popular or exoteric religion higher than the third manifestation which radiates from the *Unknown* and the *Unknowable*, the first unmanifested and the second *logoi* in the esoteric philosophy of every nation. The Nous of Anaxagoras was the *Mahat* of the Hindu Brahmâ, *the first manifested* Deity—"the Mind or Spirit self-potent"; this creative Principle being of course the *primum mobile* of everything in the Universe—its Soul and Ideation. (See "Seven Principles" in man.)

**Number Nip**. An Elf, the mighty King of the Riesengebirge, the most powerful of the genii in Scandinavian and German folk-lore.

**Nuns.** There were nuns in ancient Egypt as well as in Peru and old Pagan Rome. They were the "virgin brides" of their respective (Solar) gods. Says Herodotus, "The brides of Ammon are excluded from all intercourse with men", they are "the brides of Heaven"; and virtually they became dead to the world, just as they are now. In Peru they were "Pure Virgins of the Sun", and the *Pallakists* of Ammon-Ra are referred to in some inscriptions as the "divine spouses". "The sister of Oun-nefer, the chief prophet of Osiris, during the reign of Rameses II.," is described as "Taia, Lady Abbess of Nuns" (Mariett e Bey).

**Nuntis** (*Lat.*). The "Sun-Wolf", a name of the planet Mercury. He is the Sun's attendant, *Solaris luminis particeps*. (See *S. D.*, Vol. II, p. 28.)

**Nyâya** (*Sk.*). One of the six *Darshanas* or schools of Philosophy in India; a system of Hindu logic founded by the Rishi Gautama.

**Nyima** (*Tib.*). The Sun—astrologically.

**Nyingpo** (*Tib.*). The same as Alaya, "the World Soul"; also called *Tsang*.

# O

**O.**—The fifteenth letter and fourth vowel in the English alphabet. It has no equivalent in Hebrew, whose alphabet with one exception is vowelless. As a numeral, it signified with the ancients 11; and with a dash on it 11,000. With other ancient people also, it was a very sacred letter. In the Dêvanâgari, or the characters of the gods, its significance is varied, but there is no space to give instances.

**Oak**, *sacred*. With the Druids the oak was a most holy tree, and so also with the ancient Greeks, if we can believe Pherecydes and his cosmogony, who tells us of the sacred oak "in whose luxuriant branches a serpent (i.e., wisdom) dwelleth, and cannot be dislodged". Every nation had its own sacred trees, pre-eminently the Hindus.

**Oannes.** (*Gr.*). Musarus Oannes, the Annedotus, known in the Chaldean "legends", transmitted through Berosus and other ancient writers, as Dag or Dagon, the "man-fish". Oannes came to the early Babylonians as a reformer and an instructor. Appearing from the Erythræan Sea, he brought to them civilisation, letters and sciences, law, astronomy and religion, teaching them agriculture, geometry and the arts in general. There were Annedoti who came after him, five in number (our race being *the fifth* )—"all like Oannes inform and teaching the same"; but Musarus Oannes was the first to appear, and this he did during the reign of Ammenon, the third of the ten antediluvian Kings whose dynasty ended with Xisuthrus, the Chaldean Noah (See "Xisuthrus"). Oannes was "an *animal* endowed with reason whose body was that of a fish, but *who had a human head under the fish's with feet also below, similar to those of a man,* subjoined to the fish's tail, and *whose voice and language too were articulate and human"* (Polyhistor and Apollodorus). This gives the key to the allegory. It points out Oannes, as a *man* and a "priest", an *Initiate.* Layard showed long ago (See *Nineveh*) that the "fish's head" was simply a head gear, the *mitre* worn by priests and gods, made in the form of a fish's head, and which in a very little modified form is what we see even now on the heads of high Lamas and Romish Bishops. Osiris had such a mitre. The fish's tail is simply the train of a long stiff mantle as depicted on some Assyrian tablets, the form being seen reproduced in the sacerdotal gold cloth garment worn during service by the modern Greek priests. This allegory of Oannes, the Annedotus, reminds us of the "Dragon" and "Snake-Kings "; the *Nâgas* who in Buddhist legends instruct people in wisdom on lakes and rivers, and end by becoming converts to the good

Law and *Arhats*. The meaning is evident. The "fish" is an old and very suggestive symbol in the Mystery-language, as is also "water". Ea or Hea was the god of the sea and Wisdom, and the sea serpent was one of his emblems, his priests being "serpents "or Initiates. Thus one sees why Occultism places Oannes and the other Annedoti in the group of those ancient "adepts" who were called "marine" or "water dragons"—Nâgas. Water typified their human origin (as it is a symbol of earth and matter and also of purification), in distinction to the "fire Nâgas" or the immaterial, Spiritual Beings, whether celestial Bodhisattvas or Planetary Dhyânis, also regarded as the instructors of mankind. The hidden meaning becomes clear to the Occultist, once he is told that "this being (Oannes) was accustomed to pass the day among men, teaching; and when the Sun had set, he retired again into the sea, passing the night in the deep, "*for he was amphibious*", i.e., he belonged to two planes: the spiritual and the physical. For the Greek word *amphibios* means simply "life on two planes", from *amphi,* "on both sides", and *bios,* "life". The word was often applied in antiquity to those men who, though still wearing a human form, had made themselves almost divine through knowledge, and lived as much in the spiritual supersensuous regions as on earth. Oannes is dimly reflected in Jonah, and even in John, the Precursor, both connected with Fish and Water.

**Ob** (*Heb.*). The astral light-—or rather, its pernicious evil currents—was personified by the Jews as a Spirit, the Spirit of *Ob*. With them, any one who dealt with spirits and necromancy was said to be possessed by the Spirit of *Ob*.

**Obeah**. Sorcerers and sorceresses of Africa and the West Indies. A sect of black magicians, snake-charmers, enchanters, &c.

**Occult Sciences.** The science of the secrets of nature—physical and psychic, mental and spiritual; called Hermetic and Esoteric Sciences. In the West, the Kabbalah may be named; in the East, mysticism, magic, and Yoga philosophy, which latter is often referred to by the Chelas in India as the *seventh* "Darshana" (school of philosophy), there being only *six* Darshanas in India known to the world of the profane. These sciences are, and have been for ages, hidden from the vulgar for the very good reason that they would never be appreciated by the selfish educated classes, nor understood by the uneducated; whilst the former might misuse them for their own profit, and thus turn the divine science into *black magic*. It is often brought forward as an accusation against the Esoteric philosophy and the Kabbalah that their literature is full of "a barbarous and meaningless jargon" unintelligible to the ordinary mind. But do not exact Sciences—medicine, physiology, chemistry, and the rest—do the same? Do not official Scientists equally veil their facts and discoveries with a newly coined and most barbarous Græco-Latin terminology? As justly remarked by our late brother, Kenneth Mackenzie—"To juggle thus with words, when the facts are so simple, is the art of the Scientists of the present time, in striking contrast to those of the XVIIth century, who called spades spades, and not 'agricultural implements '."Moreover, whilst their facts would be as simple and as comprehensible if rendered in ordinary language, the facts of Occult Science are of so abstruse a nature, that in most cases no words exist in European languages to express them; in addition to which our "jargon" is a *double* necessity—(a) for the purpose of describing clearly these *facts* to him who is versed in the Occult terminology; and (b) to conceal them from the profane.

**Occultist.** One who studies the various branches of occult science. The term is used by the French Kabbalists (See Eliphas Lévi's works). Occultism embraces the whole range of psychological, physiological, cosmical, physical, and spiritual phenomena. From the word occultus hidden or secret. It therefore applies to the study of the **Kabbalah**, astrology, alchemy, and all arcane sciences.

**Od** (*Gr.*). From *odos*, "passage", or passing of that force which is developed by various minor forces or agencies such as magnets, chemical or vital action, heat, light, &c. It is also called "odic" and "odylic force", and was regarded by Reichenbach and his followers as an independent entitative force—which it certainly is—stored in man as it is in Nature.

**Odacon.** The fifth Annedotus, or *Dagon* (See "Oannes") who appeared during the reign of Euedoreschus from Pentebiblon, also "from the Erythræan Sea like the former, having the same *complicated form between a fish and a man*" (*Apollodorus*, Cory p. 30).

**Odem** or *Adm (Heb.*). A stone (the cornelian) on the breast-plate of the Jewish High Priest. It is of red colour and possesses a great medicinal power.

**Odin** (*Scand.*). The god of battles, the old German *Sabbaoth*, the same as the Scandinavian *Wodan*. He is the great hero in the *Edda* and one of the creators of man. Roman antiquity regarded him as one with Hermes or Mercury (Budha), and modern Orientalism (Sir W. Jones) accordingly confused him with Buddha. In the Pantheon of the Norse men, he is the "father of the gods" and divine wisdom, and as such he is of course

Hermes or the creative wisdom. Odin or Wodan in creating the first man from trees—the Ask (ash) and Embla (the alder)_ endowed them with life and soul, Honir with intellect, and Lodur with form and colour.

**Odur** (*Scand.*). The human husband of the goddess Freya, a scion of divine ancestry in the Northern mythology.

**Oeaihu,** or *Oeaihwu*. The manner of pronunciation depends on the accent. This is an esoteric term for the six in one or the mystic seven. The occult name for the "seven vowelled" ever-present manifestation of the Universal Principle.

**Ogdoad** (*Gr.*). The tetrad or "quaternary" reflecting itself produced the ogdoad, the "eight", according to the Marcosian Gnostics. The eight great gods were called the "sacred Ogdoad".

**Ogham** (Celtic). A mystery language belonging to the early Celtic races, and used by the Druids. One form of this language consisted in the association of the leaves of certain trees with the letters, this was called *Beth-luis-nion Ogham*, and to form words and sentences the leaves were strung on a cord in the proper order. Godfrey Higgins suggests that to complete the mystification certain other leaves which meant nothing were interspersed. [w.w.w.]

**Ogir** or *Hler* (*Scand*). A chief of the giants in the *Edda* and the ally of the gods. The highest of the Water-gods, and the same as the Greek Okeanos.

**Ogmius.** The god of wisdom and eloquence of the Druids, hence Hermes in a sense.

**Ogygia** (*Gr.*). An ancient submerged island known as the isle of Calypso, and identified by some with Atlantis. This is in a certain sense correct. But then what portion of Atlantis, since the latter was a continent rather than an "enormous" island!

**Oitzoe** (*Pers.*). The invisible goddess whose voice spoke through the rocks, and whom, according to Pliny, the *Magi* had to consult for the election of their kings.

**Okhal** (*Arab.*). The "High"priest of the Druzes, an Initiator into their mysteries.

**Okhema** (*Gr.*). A Platonic term meaning "vehicle" or body.

**Okuthor** (*Scand.*). The same as Thor, the "thunder god".

**Olympus** (*Gr.*). A mount in Greece, the abode of the gods according to Homer and Hesiod.

**Om** or Aum (*Sk.*). A mystic syllable, the most solemn of all words in India.

It is "an invocation, a benediction, an affirmation and a promise and it is so sacred, as to be indeed *the word at low breath* of occult, *primitive* masonry. No one must be near when the syllable is pronounced for a purpose. This word is usually placed at the beginning of sacred Scriptures, and is prefixed to prayers. It is a compound of three letters a,u,m, which, in the popular belief, are typical of the three Vedas, also of three gods—A (Agni) V (Varuna) and M (Maruts) or Fire, Water and Air. In esoteric philosophy these are the three sacred fires, or the "triple fire"in the Universe and Man, besides many other things. Occultly, this "triple fire" represents the highest *Tetraktys* also, as it is typified by the Agni named Abhimânin and his transformation into his three sons, Pâvana, Pavamâna and Suchi, "who drinks up water", i.e., destroys material desires. This monosyllable is called Udgîtta, and is sacred with both Brahmins and Buddhists.

**Omito-Fo** (*Chin.*). The name of Amita-Buddha, in China.

**Omkâra** (*Sk.*). The same as Aum or Om. It is also the name of one of the twelve *lingams,* that was represented by a secret and most sacred shrine at Ujjain—no longer existing, since the time of Buddhism.

**Omoroka** (*Chald.*). The "sea" and the woman who personifies it according to Berosus, or rather of Apollodorus. As the *divine* water, however, Omoroka is the reflection of Wisdom from on high.

**Onech** (*Heb.*). The Phœnix so named after Enoch or Phenoch. For Enoch (also Khenoch) means literally the *initiator* and *instructor,* hence the Hierophant who reveals the *last mystery.* The bird Phœnix is always associated with a tree, the mystical *Ababel* of the Koran, the *Tree of Initiation* or of knowledge.

**Onnofre** or *Oun-nofre* (*Eg.*). The King of the land of the Dead, the Underworld, and in this capacity the same as Osiris, "who resides in Amenti at Oun-nefer, king of eternity, great god manifested in the celestial abyss". (A hymn of the XIXth dynasty.) (See also "Osiris".)

**Ophanim** (*Heb.*). More correctly written Auphanim. The "wheels" seen by Ezekiel and by John in the Revelation—world.spheres (*S. D.*, Vol. I, p. 92.) The symbol of the Cherubs or Karoubs (the Assyrian Sphinxes). As these beings are represented in the Zodiac by Taurus, Leo, Scorpio and Aquarius, or the Bull, the Lion, the Eagle and Man, the occult meaning of these creatures being placed in company of the four Evangelists becomes evident. In the *Kabbalah* they are a group of beings allotted to the Sephira Chokmah, Wisdom.

**Ophis** (*Gr.*). The same as Chnuphis or *Kneph,* the *Logos*; the good serpent or Agathodæmon.

**Ophiomorphos** (*Gr.*). The same, but in its material aspect, as the Ophis-Christos. With the Gnostics the Serpent represented "Wisdom in Eternity".

**Ophis-Christos** (*Gr.*). The serpent Christ of the Gnostics.

**Ophiozenes** (*Gr.*). The name of the Cypriote charmers of venomous serpents and other reptiles and animals.

**Ophites** (*Gr.*). A Gnostic Fraternity in Egypt, and one of the earliest sects of Gnosticism, or *Gnosis* (Wisdom, Knowledge), known as the "Brotherhood of the Serpent". It flourished early in the second century, and while holding some of the principles of Valentinus had its own occult rites and symbology. A living serpent, representing the Christos-principle (i.e., the divine reincarnating Monad, not Jesus the man), was displayed in their mysteries and reverenced as a symbol of wisdom, Sophia, the type of the all-good and all-wise. The Gnostics were not a Christian sect, in the common acceptation of this term, as the *Christos* of pre-Christian thought and the Gnosis was *not* the "god-man" Christ, but the divine EGO, made one with Buddhi. Their Christos was the "Eternal Initiate", the Pilgrim, typified by hundreds of Ophidian symbols for several thousands of years before the "Christian" era, so-called. One can see it on the "Belzoni tomb" from Egypt, *as a winged serpent with three heads* (Atma-Buddhi-Manas), and *four* human legs, typifying its androgynous character; on the walls of the descent to the sepulchral chambers of Rameses V., it is found as a snake with vulture's wings—the vulture and hawk being solar symbols. "The heavens are scribbled over with interminable snakes ' writes Herschel of the Egyptian chart of stars. "The *Meissi* (Messiah?) meaning the *Sacred Word*, was a good serpent", writes Bonwick in his *Egyptian Belief*. "This serpent of goodness, with its head crowned, was mounted upon a cross and formed a sacred standard of Egypt." The Jews *borrowed* it in their "brazen serpent of Moses". It is to this "Healer" and "Saviour", therefore, that the Ophites referred, and not to Jesus or his words, "As Moses lifted up the serpent in the desert, so it behoves the Son of Man to be lifted up"— when explaining the meaning of their *ophis*. Tertullian, whether wittingly or unwittingly, mixed up the two. The four-winged serpent is the god Chnuphis. The good serpent bore the cross of life around its neck, or suspended from its mouth. The winged serpents become the Seraphim (Seraph, *Saraph)* of the Jews. In the 87th chapter of the *Ritual* (the Book of the Dead) the human soul transformed into *Bata*, the omniscient serpents says:—" I am the serpent Ba-ta, of long years, Soul of the Soul, laid out and born daily; I am the Soul that descends on the earth", i.e., the Ego.

**Orai** (*Gr.*). The name of the angel-ruler of Venus, according to the Egyptian Gnostics.

**Orcus** (*Gr.*). The bottomless pit in the Codex of the Nazarenes.

**Örgelmir** (*Scand.*). Lit., "seething clay". The same as Ymir, the giant, the unruly, turbulent, erratic being, the type of primordial matter, out of whose body, after killing him, the sons of Bör created a new earth. He is also the cause of the Deluge in the Scandinavian Lays, for he flung his body into Ginnungagap, the yawning abyss; the latter being filled with it, the blood flowed over and produced a great flood in which all the Hrimthurses, the frost giants, were drowned; one of them only the cunning Bergelmir saves himself and wife in a boat and became the father of a new race of giants. "And there were giants on the earth in those days."

**Orion** (*Gr.*). The same as Atlas, who supports the world on his shoulders.

**Orlog** (*Scand.*). Fate, destiny, whose agents were the three Norns, the Norse *Parcæ*.

**Ormazd** or *Ahura Mazda* (*Zend*). The god of the Zoroastrians or the modern Parsis. He is symbolized by the sun, as being the Light of Lights. Esoterically, he is the synthesis of his six *Amshaspends* or Elohim, and the creative Logos. In the Mazdean exoteric system, Ahura Mazda is the supreme god, and one with the supreme god of the Vedic age—Varuna, if we read the *Vedas* literally.

**Orpheus** (*Gr.*). Lit., the "tawny one". Mythology makes him the son of Æager and the muse Calliope. Esoteric tradition identifies him with Arjuna, the son of Indra and the disciple of Krishna. He went round the world teaching the nations wisdom and sciences, and establishing mysteries. The very story of his losing his Eurydice and finding her in the underworld or Hades, is another point of resemblance with the story of Arjuna, who goes to Pâtàla (*Hades* or hell, but in reality the Antipodes or America) and finds there and marries Ulupi, the daughter of the Nâga king. This is as suggestive as the fact that he was considered *dark* in complexion even by the Greeks, who were never very fair-skinned themselves.

**Orphic Mysteries** or *Orphica* (*Gr.*). These followed, but differed greatly from, the mysteries of Bacchus. The system of Orpheus is one of the purest morality and of severe asceticism. The theology taught by him is again purely Indian. With him the divine Essence is inseparable from whatever is in the infinite universe, all forms being concealed from all eternity in It. At determined periods these forms are manifested from the divine Essence or manifest themselves. Thus through this law of emanation (or evolution) all things participate in this Essence, and are parts and members instinct with divine nature, which is omnipresent. All things having proceeded from, must necessarily return into it; and therefore, innumerable transmigrations or reincarnations and purifications are needed before this final consummation can take place. This is pure Vedânta philosophy. Again, the Orphic Brotherhood ate no animal food and wore white linen garments, and had many ceremonies like those of the Brahmans.

**Oshadi Prastha** (*Sk.*). Lit., "the place of medicinal herbs". A mysterious city in the Himalayas mentioned even from the Vedic period. Tradition shows it as once inhabited by sages, great adepts in the healing art, who used only herbs and plants, as did the ancient Chaldees. The city is mentioned in the *Kumâra Sambhava* of Kalidasa.

**Osiris.** (*Eg.*). The greatest God of Egypt, the Son of Seb (Saturn), celestial fire, and of Neith, primordial matter and infinite space. This shows him as the self-existent and self-created god, the first manifesting deity (our third Logos), identical with Ahura Mazda and other "First Causes". For as Ahura Mazda is one with, or the synthesis of, the Amshaspends, so Osiris, the collective unit, when differentiated and personified, becomes Typhon, his brother, Isis and Nephtys his sisters, Horus his son and his other aspects. He was born at Mount Sinai, the Nyssa of the O. T. (See-*Exodus* xvii. 15), and buried at Abydos, after being killed by Typhon at the early age of twenty-eight, according to the allegory. According to Euripides he is the same as Zeus and Dionysos or *Dio-Nysos* "the god of Nysa", for Osiris is said by him to have been brought up in Nysa, in Arabia "the Happy". Query: how much did the latter tradition influence, or have anything in common with, the statement in the Bible, that "Moses built an altar and called the name Jehovah Nissi", or Kabbalistically—"Dio-Iao-Nyssi"? (See *Isis Unveiled* Vol. II. p. 165.) The four chief aspects of Osiris were—Osiris-Phtah (Light), the spiritual aspect; Osiris-Horus (Mind), the intellectual *manasic* aspect; Osiris-Lunus, the "Lunar" or psychic, astral aspect; Osiris-Typhon, Daïmonic, or physical, material, therefore passional turbulent aspect. In these four aspects he symbolizes the dual Ego—the divine and the human, the cosmico-spiritual and the terrestrial.

Of the many supreme gods, this Egyptian conception is the most suggestive and the grandest, as it embraces the whole range of physical and metaphysical thought. As a solar deity he had twelve minor gods under him—the twelve signs of the Zodiac. Though his name is the "Ineffable", his forty-two attributes bore each one of his names, and his seven dual aspects completed the forty-nine, or 7 X 7; the former symbolized by the fourteen members of his body, or twice seven. Thus the god is blended in man, and the man is deified into a god. He was addressed as Osiris-Eloh. Mr. Dunbar T. Heath speaks of a Phœnician inscription which, when read, yielded the following tumular inscription in honour of the mummy: "Blessed be Ta-Bai, daughter of Ta-Hapi, priest of Osiris-Eloh. She did nothing against anyone in anger. She spoke no falsehood against any one. Justified before Osiris, blessed be thou from before Osiris! Peace be to thee." And then he adds the following remarks: "The author of this inscription ought, I suppose, to be called a heathen, as justification before Osiris is the object of his religious aspirations. We find, however, that he gives to Osiris the appellation *Eloh*. Eloh is the name used by the Ten Tribes of Israel for the Elohim of Two Tribes. Jehovah-Eloh (*Gen*. iii. 21.) in the version used by Ephraim corresponds to Jehovah Elohim in that used by Judah and ourselves. This being so, the question is sure to be asked, and ought to be humbly answered—What was the meaning meant to be conveyed by the two phrases respectively, *Osiris-Eloh* and *Jehovah-Eloh*? For my part I can imagine but one answer, viz., that Osiris was the national God of Egypt, Jehovah that of Israel, and that Eloh is equivalent to *Deus, Gott* or *Dieu*". As to his human development, he is, as the author of the *Egyptian Belief* has it . . . "One of the Saviours or Deliverers of Humanity . . . . As such he is born in the world. He came as a benefactor, to relieve man of trouble . . . . In his efforts to do good he encounters evil . . . and he is temporarily overcome. He is killed . . Osiris is buried. His tomb was the object of pilgrimage for thousands of years. But he did not rest in his grave. At the end of three days, or forty, he rose again and ascended to Heaven. This is the story of his Humanity" (*Egypt. Belief*). And Mariette Bey, speaking of the Sixth Dynasty, tells us that "the name of Osiris . . commences to be more used. The formula of *Justified* is met with": and adds that "it proves that this name (of *the Justified* or *Makheru* was not given to the dead only". But it also proves that the legend of Christ was found ready in almost all its details thousands of years before the Christian era, and that the Church fathers had no greater difficulty than to simply apply it to a new personage.

**Ossa.** (*Gr.*) A mount, the tomb of the giants (allegorical).

**Otz-Chiim.** (*Heb.*). The Tree of Life, or rather of Lives, a name given to the Ten Sephiroth when arranged in a diagram of three columns. [w.w.w.]

**Oulam,** or *Oulom* (*Heb.*). This word does not mean "eternity" or *infinite* duration, as translated in the texts, but simply an extended time, neither the beginning nor the end of which can be known.

**Ouranos** (*Gr.*). The whole expanse of Heaven called the "Waters of Space", the Celestial Ocean, etc. The name very likely comes from the Vedic Varuna, personified as the water god and regarded as the chief Aditya among the seven planetary deities. In Hesiod's Theogony, Ouranos (or Uranus) is the same as Cœlus (Heaven) the oldest of all the gods and the father of the divine Titans.

# P

**P.**—The 16th letter in both the Greek and the English alphabets, and the 17th in the Hebrew, where it is called *pé* or *pay*, and is symbolized by the mouth, corresponding also, as in the Greek alphabet, to number 80. The Pythagoreans also made it equivalent to 100, and with a dash thus ($\overline{P}$) it stood for 400,000. The Kabbalists associated with it the sacred name of *Phodeh* (Redeemer), though no valid reason is given for it.

**P and Cross**, called generally the Labarum of Constantine. It was, however, one of the oldest emblems in Etruria before the Roman Empire. It was also the sign of Osiris. Both the long Latin and the Greek pectoral crosses are Egyptian, the former being very often seen in the hand of Horus. "The cross and Calvary so common in Europe, occurs on the breasts of mummies" (Bonwick).

**Pachacamac** (*Peruv.*). The name given by the Peruvians to the Creator of the Universe, represented as *a host of creators*. On his altar only the first-fruits and flowers were laid by the pious.

**Pacis Bull**. The divine Bull of Hermonthes, sacred to Amoun-Horus, the Bull Netos of Heliopolis being sacred to Amoun-Ra.

**Padârthas** (*Sk.*). Predicates of existing things; so-called in the *Vaiseshika* or "atomic" system of philosophy founded by Kanâda. This school is one of the six *Darshanas*.

**Padmâ** (*Sk.*). The Lotus; a name of Lakshmi, the Hindu Venus, who is the *wife* or the female aspect, of Vishnu.

**Padma Âsana** (*Sk.*). A posture prescribed to and practised by some Yogis for developing concentration.

**Padma Kalpa** (*Sk.*). The name of the last Kalpa or the preceding Manvantara, which was a year of Brahmâ.

**Padma Yoni** (Sk). A title of Brahmâ (also called *Abjayoni*), or the "lotus-born".

**Pæan** (*Gr.*). A hymn of rejoicing and praise in honour of the sun-god Apollo or Helios.

**Pagan** (*Lat.*). Meaning at first no worse than a dweller in the country or the woods; one far removed from the city-temples, and therefore unacquainted with the state religion and ceremonies. The word "heathen" has a similar significance, meaning one who lives on the heaths and in the country. Now, however, both come to mean *idolaters.*

**Pagan Gods**. The term is erroneously understood to mean idols. The philosophical idea attached to them was never that of something objective or anthropomorphic, but in each case an abstract potency, a virtue, or quality in nature. There are gods who are divine planetary spirits (Dhyan Chohans) or Devas, among which are also our Egos. With this exception, and especially whenever represented by an idol or in anthropomorphic form, the gods represent symbolically in the Hindu, Egyptian, or Chaldean Pantheons—formless spiritual Potencies of the "Unseen Kosmos".

**Pahans** (*Prakrit*). Village priests.

**Paksham** (*Sk.*). An astronomical calculation; one half of the lunar month or 14 days; two *paksham* (or *paccham*) making a month of mortals, but only a day of the *Pitar devata* or the "father-gods".

**Palæolithic** A newly-coined term meaning in geology "ancient stone" age, as a contrast to the term *neolithic,* the "newer" or later stone age.

**Palâsa** *Tree* (*Sk.*) Called also Kanaka (*butea frondosa*) a tree with red flowers of very occult properties.

**Pâli**. The ancient language of Magadha, one that preceded the more refined Sanskrit. The Buddhist Scriptures are all written in this language.

**Palingenesis** (*Gr.*). Transformation; or new birth.

**Pan** (*Gr.*). The nature-god, whence Pantheism; the god of shepherds, huntsmen, peasants, and dwellers on the land. Homer makes him the son of Hermes and Dryope. His name means ALL. He was the inventor of the Pandæan pipes; and no nymph who heard their sound could resist the fascination of the great Pan, his grotesque figure not withstanding. Pan is related to the Mendesian goat, only so far as the latter represents, as a talisman of great occult potency, nature's creative force. The whole of the Hermetic philosophy is based on nature's hidden secrets, and as Baphomet was undeniably a Kabbalistic talisman, so was the name of Pan of great magic efficiency in what Eliphas Lévi would call the "Conjuration of the

Elementals". There is a well-known pious legend which has been current in the Christian world ever since the day of Tiberias, to the effect that the "great Pan is dead". But people are greatly mistaken in this; neither nature nor any of her Forces can ever die. A few of these may be left unused, and being forgotten lie dormant for long centuries. But no sooner are the proper conditions furnished than they awake, to act again with tenfold power.

**Panænus**(*Gr.*). A Platonic philosopher in the Alexandrian school of Philaletheans.

**Pancha Kosha** (*Sk.*). The five "sheaths". According to Vedantin philosophy, Vijnânamaya Kosha, the fourth sheath, is composed of Buddhi, or is Buddhi. The five sheaths are said to belong to the two higher principles — *Jivâtma* and *Sâkshi*, which represent the *Upathita* and *An-upahita*, divine spirit respectively. The division in the esoteric teaching differs from this, as it divides man's physical-metaphysical aspect into seven principles.

**Pancha Krishtaya** (*Sk.*). The five races.

**Panchakâma** (*Sk.*). Five methods of sensuousness and sensuality.

**Panchakritam** (*Sk.*). An element combined with small portions of the other four elements.

**Panchama** (*Sk.*). One of the *five* qualities of musical sound, the fifth, Nishâda and Daivata completing the seven; G of the diatonic scale.

**Panchânana** (*Sk.*). "Five-faced", a title of Siva; an allusion to the five races (since the beginning of the first) which he represents, as the ever reincarnating Kumâra throughout the Manvantara. In the sixth root-race he will be called the "six-faced".

**Panchâsikha** (*Sk.*). One of the seven Kumâras who went to pay worship to Vishnu on the island of Swetadwipa in the allegory.

**Panchen Rimboche** (*Tib.*). Lit., "the great Ocean, or Teacher of Wisdom". The title of the Teshu Lama at Tchigadze; an incarnation of Amitabha the celestial "father" of Chenresi, which means to say that he is an *Avatar* of Tson-kha-pa (See "Sonkhapa"). *De jure* the Teshu Lama is second after the Dalaï Lama; *de facto*, he is higher, since it is Dharma Richen, the successor of Tson-kha-pa at the golden monastery founded by the latter Reformer and established by the Gelukpa sect (yellow caps) who created the Dalaï Lamas at Llhassa, and was the first of the dynasty of the "Panchen Rimboche". While the former (Dalaï Lama are addressed as "Jewel of Majesty", the latter enjoy a far higher title, namely "Jewel of Wisdom", as they are high Initiates.

**Pândavârani** (*Sk.*). Lit., the "Pandava Queen"; Kunti, the mother of the Pandavas. (All these are highly important personified symbols in esoteric philosophy.)

**Pandavas** (*Sk.*). The descendants of Pandu.

**Pandora** (*Gr.*). A beautiful woman created by the gods under the orders of Zeus to be sent to Epimetheus, brother of Prometheus; she had charge of a casket in which all the evils, passions and plagues which torment humanity were locked up. This casket Pandora, led by curiosity, opened, and thus set free all the ills which prey on mankind.

**Pandu** (*Sk.*). "The Pale", literally; the father of the Pandavas Princes, the foes of the *Kurava* in the *Mahâbhârata*.

**Pânini** (*Sk.*). A celebrated grammarian, author of the famous work called Pâninîyama; a Rishi, supposed to have received his work from the god Siva. Ignorant of the epoch at which he lived, the Orientalists place his date between 600 B.C. and 300 A.D.

**Pantacle** (*Gr.*). The same as Pentalpha; the triple triangle of Pythagoras or the five-pointed star. It was given the name because it reproduces the letter **A** (alpha) on the five sides of it or in five different positions—its number, moreover, being composed of the first odd ( and the first even (2) numbers. It is very occult. In Occultism and the Kabala it stands for man or the Microcosm, the "Heavenly Man", and as such it was a powerful talisman for keeping at bay evil spirits or the Elementals. In Christian theology it refers to the five wounds of Christ; its interpreters failing, however, to add that these "five wounds" were themselves symbolical of the Microcosm, or the "Little Universe", or again, Humanity, this symbol pointing out the fall of pure Spirit (Christos) into matter (Iassous, "life", or man). In esoteric philosophy the Pentalpha, or five-pointed star, is the symbol of the EGO or the Higher Manas. Masons use it, referring to it as the five-pointed star, and connecting it with their own fanciful interpretation. (See the word "Pentacle" for its difference in meaning from "Pantacle".)

**Pantheist.** One who identifies God with Nature and vice versa. Pantheism is often objected to by people and regarded as reprehensible. But how can a philosopher regard Deity as infinite, omnipresent and eternal unless Nature is an aspect of IT, and IT informs every atom in Nature?

**Panther** (*Heb.*). According to the *Sepher Toldosh Jeshu*, one of the so-called Apocryphal Jewish Gospels, Jesus was the son of Joseph Panther and

Mary, hence Ben Panther. Tradition makes of Panther a Roman soldier. [w.w.w.]

**Pâpa-purusha** (*Sk.*). Lit., "Man of Sin": the personification in a human form of every wickedness and sin. Esoterically, one who is reborn, or reincarnated from the state of *Avitchi*—hence, "Soulless".

**Para** (*Sk.*). "Infinite" and "supreme" in philosophy—the final limit. **Param** is the end and goal of existence; **Parâpara** is the boundary of boundaries.

**Parabrahm** (*Sk.*). "Beyond Brahmâ", literally. The Supreme Infinite Brahma, "Absolute"—the attributeless, the secondless reality. The impersonal and nameless universal Principle.

**Paracelsus.** The symbolical name adopted by the greatest Occultist of the middle ages—Philip Bombastes Aureolus Theophrastus von Hohenheim—born in the canton of Zurich in 1493. He was the cleverest physician of his age, and the most renowned for curing almost any illness by the power of talismans prepared by himself. He never had a friend, but was surrounded by enemies, the most bitter of whom were the Churchmen and their party. That he was accused of being in league with the devil stands to reason, nor is it to be wondered at that finally he was murdered by some unknown foe, at the early age of forty-eight. He died at Salzburg, leaving a number of works behind him, which are to this day greatly valued by the Kabbalists and Occultists. Many of his utterances have proved prophetic. He was a clairvoyant of great powers, one of the most learned and erudite philosophers and mystics, and a distinguished Alchemist. Physics is indebted to him for the discovery of nitrogen gas, or Azote.

**Paradha** (*Sk.*). The period of one-half the Age of Brahmâ.

**Parama** (*Sk.*). The "one Supreme".

**Paramapadâtmava** (*Sk.*). Beyond the condition of Spirit, "supremer" than Spirit, bordering on the Absolute.

**Paramapadha** (*Sk.*). The place where—according to Visishtadwaita Vedantins—bliss is enjoyed by those who reach *Moksha* (Bliss). This "place" is not material but made, says the Catechism of that sect, "of *Suddhasatwa*, the essence of which the body of Iswara", the lord, "is made".

**Paramapaha** (*Sk*) A state which is already a conditioned existence.

**Paramartha** (*Sk*) Absolute existence.

**Pâramârthika** (*Sk.*). The one true state of existence according to Vedânta.

**Paramarshis** (*Sk.*). Composed of two words: parama, "supreme", and

Rishis, or supreme Rishis—Saints.

**Paramâtman** (*Sk.*). The Supreme Soul of the Universe.

**Paranellatons.** In ancient Astronomy the name was applied to certain stars and constellations which are extra Zodiacal, lying above and below the constellations of the Zodiac; they were 36 in number: allotted to the Decans, or one-third parts of each sign. The paranellatons ascend or descend with the Decans alternately, thus when Scorpio rises, Orion in its paranellaton sets, also Auriga; this gave rise to the fable that the horses of Phaeton, the Sun, were frightened by a Scorpion, and the Charioteer fell into the River Po; that is the constellation of the River Eridanus which lies below Auriga the star. [w.w.w.]

**Paranirvâna** (*Sk.*). Absolute *Non-Being*, which is equivalent to absolute *Being* or "Be-ness", the state reached by the human Monad at the end of the great cycle (See *S. D.*, Vol. I, p. 135). The same as *Paraniskpanna*.

**Parasakti** (*Sk.*). "The great Force"—one of the six Forces of Nature; that of light and heat.

**Parâsara** (*Sk.*). A Vedic Rishi, the narrator of *Vishnu Purâna*.

**Paratantra** (*Sk.*). That which has no existence of, or by itself, but only through a dependent or causal connection.

**Paroksha** (*Sk.*). Intellectual apprehension of a truth.

**Parsees.** Written also Parsis. The followers of Zoroaster. This is the name given to the remnant of the once-powerful Iranian nation, which remained true to the religion 'of its forefathers—the fire-worship. This remnant now dwells in India, some 50,000 strong, mostly in Bombay and Guzerat.

**Pâsa** (*Sk.*). The crucifixion noose of Siva, the noose held in his right hand in some of his representations.

**Paschalis**, *Martinez*. A very learned man, a mystic and occultist. Born about 1700, in Portugal. He travelled extensively, acquiring knowledge wherever he could in the East, in Turkey, Palestine, Arabia, and Central Asia. He was a great Kabbalist. He was the teacher of the Initiator of the Marquis de St. Martin, who founded the mystical Martinistic School and Lodges. Paschalis is reported to have died in St. Domingo about 1779, leaving several excellent works behind him.

**Pasht** (*Eg.*). The cat-headed goddess, the Moon, called also Sekhet. Her statues and representations are seen in great numbers at the British Museum. She is the wife or female aspect of Ptah (the son of Kneph), the creative principle, or the Egyptian Demiurgus. She is also called *Beset* or

*Bubastis,* being then both the re-uniting and the separating principle. Her motto is: "punish the guilty and remove defilement", and one of her emblems is the cat. According to Viscount Rouge, her worship is extremely ancient (B.C. 3000), and she is the mother of the Asiatic race, the race that settled in Northern Egypt. As such she is called Ouato.

**Pashut** (*Heb.*). "Literal interpretation." One of the four modes of interpreting the Bible used by the Jews.

**Pashyantî** (*Sk.*). The second of the four degrees (Parâ, Pashyantî, Madhyamâ and Vaikharî), in which sound is divided according to its differentiation.

**Pass not**, *The Ring*. The circle within which are confined all those who still labour under the delusion of separateness.

**Passing of the River** (*Kab.*). This phrase may be met with in works referring to mediæval magic: it is the name given to a cypher alphabet used by Kabbalistic Rabbis at an early date; the river alluded to is the Chebar—the name will also be found in Latin authors as Literæ Transitus. [w.w.w.]

**Pastophori** (*Gr.*). A certain class of candidates for initiation, those who bore in public processions (and also in the temples) the sacred coffin or funeral couch of the Sun-gods—killed and resurrected, of Osiris, Tammuz (or Adonis), of Atys and others. The Christians adopted their coffin from the pagans of antiquity.

**Pâtâla** (*Sk*). The nether world, the antipodes; hence in popular superstition the infernal regions, and philosophically the two Americas, which are antipodal to India. Also, the South Pole as standing opposite to Meru, the North Pole.

**Pâtaliputra** (*Sk.*). The ancient capital of Magadha, a kingdom of Eastern India, now identified with Patna.

**Pâtanjala** (*Sk.*). The Yoga philosophy; one of the six *Darshanas* or Schools of India.

**Patanjali** (*Sk.*). The founder of the Yoga philosophy. The date assigned to him by the Orientalists is 200 B.C.; and by the Occultists nearer to 700 than 600 B.C. At any rate he was a contemporary of Pânini.

**Pâvaka** (*Sk.*). One of the three personified *fires* eldest sons of Abhimânim or Agni, who had forty-five sons; these with the original son of Brahmâ, their father Agni, and his three descendants, constitute the mystic 49 fires. Pâvaka is the electric fire.

**Pavamâna** (*Sk.*). Another of the three fires (*vide supra*)—the fire produced by friction.

**Pavana** (*Sk*) God of the wind; the alleged father of the monkey-god Hanuman (See "Râmâyana").

**Peling** (*Tib.*). The name given to all foreigners in Tibet, to Europeans especially.

**Pentacle** (*Gr.*). Any geometrical figure, especially that known as the double equilateral triangle, the six-pointed star (like the theosophical pentacle); called also Solomon's seal, and still earlier "the sign of Vishnu"; used by all the mystics, astrologers, etc.

**Pentagon** (*Gr.*), from *pente* "five", and *gonia* "angle"; in geometry a plane figure with five angles.

**Per-M-Rhu** (*Eg.*). This name is the recognised pronunciation of the ancient title of the collection of mystical lectures, called in English *The Book of the Dead*. Several almost complete papyri have been found, and there are numberless extant copies of portions of the work. [w.w.w.]

**Personality.** In Occultism—which divides man into seven principles, considering him under the three aspects of the *divine*, the *thinking* or the *rational*, and the *animal* man—the lower *quaternary* or the purely astrophysical being; while by *Individuality* is meant the Higher Triad, considered as a Unity. Thus the *Personality* embraces all the characteristics and memories of one physical life, while the *Individuality* is the imperishable *Ego* which re-incarnates and clothes itself in one personality after another.

**Pesh-Hun** (*Tib.*). From the Sanskrit *pesuna* "spy"; an epithet given to Nârada, the meddlesome and troublesome Rishi.

**Phala** (*Sk.*). Retribution; the fruit or result of causes.

**Phâlguna** (*Sk.*). A name of Arjuna; also of a month.

**Phallic** (*Gr.*). Anything belonging to sexual worship; or of a sexual character externally, such as the Hindu *lingham* and *yoni*—the emblems of the male and female generative power—which have none of the unclean significance attributed to it by the Western mind.

**Phanes** (Gr.). One of the Orphic triad—*Phanes, Chaos* and *Chronos*. It was also the trinity of the Western people in the pre-Christian period.

**Phenomenon** (*Gr.*). In reality "an appearance", something previously unseen, and puzzling when the cause of it is unknown. Leaving aside various kinds of phenomena, such as cosmic, electrical, chemical, etc., and holding merely to the phenomena of spiritism, let it be remembered that theosophically and esoterically every "miracle"—from the biblical to the theumaturgic—is simply a phenomenon, but that no phenomenon is ever a miracle, *i.e.*, something supernatural or outside of the laws of nature, as all such are impossibilities in nature.

**Philaletheans** (*Gr.*). Lit., "the lovers of truth"; the name is given to the Alexandrian Neo-Platonists, also called Analogeticists and Theosophists. (See *Key to Theosophy,* p. 1, *et seq.*) The school was founded by Ammonius Saccas early in the third century, and lasted until the fifth. The greatest philosophers and sages of the day belonged to it.

**Philalethes**, *Eugenius*. The Rosicrucian name assumed by one Thomas Vaughan, a mediæval English Occultist and Fire Philosopher. He was a great Alchemist. [w.w.w.]

**Philæ** (*Gr.*). An island in Upper Egypt where a famous temple of that name was situated, the ruins of which may be seen to this day by travellers.

**Philo Judæus.** A Hellenized Jew of Alexandria, and a very famous historian and writer; born about 30 B.C, died about 45 A.D. He ought thus to have been well acquainted with the greatest event of the 1st century of our era, and the facts about Jesus, his life, and the drama of the Crucifixion. And yet he is absolutely silent upon the subject, both in his careful enumeration of the then existing Sects and Brotherhoods in Palestine and in his accounts of the Jerusalem of his day. He was a great mystic and his works abound with metaphysics and noble ideas, while in esoteric knowledge he had no rival for several ages among the best writers. [under "Philo Judæus" in the Glossary of the *Key to Theosophy.*]

**Philo-Judaeus.** A Hellenized Jew of Alexandria, a famous historian and philosopher of the first century, born about the year 30 B. C., and died between the years 45 and 50 A. D. Philo's symbolism of the Bible is very remarkable. The animals, birds, reptiles, trees, and places mentioned in it are all, it is said, "allegories of conditions of the soul, of faculties, dispositions, or passions; the useful plants were allegories of virtues, the noxious of the affections of the unwise and so on through the mineral kingdom; through heaven, earth and stars; through fountains and rivers, fields and dwellings; through metals, substances, arms, clothes, ornaments, furniture, the body and its parts, the sexes, and our outward condition." (*Dict. Christ. Biog.*) All of which would strongly corroborate the idea that Philo was acquainted with the ancient Kabbala.

**Philosopher's Stone.** Called also the "Powder of Projection". It is the

*Magnum Opus* of the Alchemists, an object to be attained by them at all costs, a substance possessing the power of transmuting the baser metals into pure gold. Mystically, however, the Philosopher's Stone symbolises the transmutation of the lower animal nature of man into the highest and divine.

**Philostratus** (*Gr.*). A biographer of Apollonius of Tyana, who described the life, travels and adventures of this sage and philosopher.

**Phla** (*Gr.*). A small island in the lake Tritonia, in the days of Herodotus.

**Phlegiæ** (*Gr.*). A submerged ancient island in prehistoric days and identified by some writers with Atlantis; also a people in Thessaly.

**Pho** (*Chin.*). The animal Soul.

**Phœbe** (*Gr.*). A name given to Diana, or the moon.

**Phœbus-Apollo** (*Gr.*). Apollo as the Sun, "the light of life and of the world".

**Phoreg** (*Gr.*). The name of the seventh Titan not mentioned in the cosmogony of Hesiod. The "mystery" Titan.

**Phorminx** (*Gr.*). The seven-stringed lyre of Orpheus.

**Phoronede** (*Gr.*). A poem of which Phoroneus is the hero; this work is no longer extant.

**Phoroneus** (*Gr.*). A Titan; an ancestor and generator of mankind. According to a legend of Argolis, like Prometheus he was credited with bringing fire to this earth (Pausanias). The god of a river in Peloponnesus.

**Phren** (*Gr.*). A Pythagorean term denoting what we call the Kâma-Manas still overshadowed by the Buddhi-Manas.

**Phtah** (*Eg.*). The God of death; similar to Siva, the destroyer. In later Egyptian mythology a sun-god. It is the seat or locality of the Sun and its occult Genius or Regent in esoteric philosophy.

**Phta-Ra** (*Eg.*). One of the 49 mystic (occult) Fires.

**Picus,** *John, Count of Mirandola.* A celebrated Kabbalist and Alchemist, author of a treatise "on gold" and other Kabbalistic works. He defied Rome and Europe in his attempt to prove divine *Christian* truth in the *Zohar*. Born in 1463, died 1494.

**Pillaloo Codi** (*Tamil*). A nickname in popular astronomy given to the Pleiades, meaning "hen and chickens". The French also, curiously enough, call this constellation, "Poussinière".

**Pillars,** *The Two.* Jachin and Boaz were placed at the entrance to the

Temple of Solomon, the first on the right, the second on the left. Their symbolism is developed in the rituals of the Freemasons.

**Pillars**, *The Three*. When the ten Sephiroth are arranged in the Tree of Life, two vertical lines separate them into 3 Pillars, namely the Pillar of Severity, the Pillar of Mercy, and the central Pillar of Mildness. Binah, Geburah, and Hod form the first, that of Severity; Kether, Tiphereth, Jesod and Malkuth the central pillar; Chokmah, Chesed and Netzach the Pillar of Mercy. [w.w.w.]

**Pillars of Hermes**. Like the "pillars of Seth" (with which they are identified) they served for commemorating occult events, and various esoteric secrets symbolically engraved on them. It was a universal practice. Enoch is also said to have constructed pillars.

**Pingala** *(Sk.)*. The great Vedic authority on the Prosody and *chhandas* of the Vedas. Lived several centuries B.C.

**Pippala** *(Sk.)*. The tree of knowledge: the mystic fruit of that tree "upon which came Spirits who love Science". This is allegorical and occult.

**Pippalâda** *(Sk.)*. A magic school wherein *Atharva Veda* is explained founded by an Adept of that name.

**Pisâchas** *(Sk.)*. In the *Purânas*, goblins or demons created by Brahmâ. In the southern Indian folk-lore, ghosts, demons, larvæ and vampires—generally female—who haunt men. Fading remnants of human beings in *Kâmaloka*, as shells and Elementaries.

**Pistis Sophia** *(Sk.)*. "Knowledge-Wisdom." A sacred book of the early Gnostics or the primitive Christians.

**Pitar Devata** *(Sk.)*. The "Father-Gods", the lunar ancestors of mankind.

**Pitaras** *(Sk.)*. Fathers, Ancestors. The fathers of the human races.

**Pitris** *(Sk.)*. The ancestors, or creators of mankind. They are of seven classes, three of which are incorporeal, *arupa,* and four corporeal. In popular theology they are said to be created from Brahmâ's side. They are variously genealogized, but in esoteric philosophy they are as given in the *Secret Doctrine*. In *Isis Unveiled* it is said of them "It is generally believed that the Hindu term means the spirits of our ancestors, of disembodied people, hence the argument of some Spiritualists that fakirs (and yogis) and other Eastern wonder-workers, are *mediums*. This is in more than one sense erroneous. The Pitris are not the ancestors of the present living men, but those of the human kind, or Adamic races; the spirits of human races, which on the great scale of descending evolution *preceded our races* of men, and they *were physically, as well as spiritually, far superior* to our modern pigmies. In *Mânava Dharma Shâstra* they are called the *Lunar Ancestors*." The *Secret Doctrine* has now explained that which was cautiously put forward in the earlier Theosophical volumes.

**Pîyadasi** (*Pali*). "The beautiful", a title of King Chandragupta (the "Sandracottus" of the Greeks) and of Asoka the Buddhist king, his grandson. They both reigned in Central India between the fourth and third centuries B.C., called also Devânâmpiya, "the beloved of the gods".

**Plaksha** (*Sk.*). One of the seven *Dwipas* (continents or islands) in the Indian Pantheon and the *Purânas*.

**Plane.** From the Latin *planus* (level, flat) an extension of space or of something in it, whether physical or metaphysical, *e.g.*, a "plane of consciousness". As used in Occultism, the term denotes the range or extent of some state of consciousness, or of the perceptive power of a particular set of senses, or the action of a particular force, or the state of matter corresponding to any of the above.

**Planetary Spirits.** Primarily the rulers or governors of the planets. As our earth has its hierarchy of terrestrial planetary spirits, from the highest to the lowest plane, so has every other heavenly body. In Occultism, however, the term "Planetary Spirit" is generally applied only to the seven highest hierarchies corresponding to the Christian archangels. These have all passed through a stage of evolution corresponding to the humanity of earth on other worlds, in long past cycles. Our earth, being as yet only in its fourth round, is far too young to have produced high planetary spirits. The highest planetary spirit ruling over any globe is in reality the "Personal God" of that planet and far more truly its "over-ruling providence" than the self-contradictory Infinite Personal Deity of modern Churchianity.

**Plastic Soul.** Used in Occultism in reference to the *linga sharira* or the astral body of the lower Quaternary. It is called "plastic" and also "Protean" Soul from its power of assuming any shape or form and moulding or modelling itself into or upon any image impressed in the astral light around it, or in the minds of the medium or of those present at séances for materialization. The *linga sharira* must not be confused with the *mayavi rupa* or "thought body"—the image created by the thought and will of an adept or sorcerer; for while the "astral form" or *linga sharira* is a real entity, the "thought body" is a temporary illusion created by the mind.

**Plato**. An Initiate into the Mysteries and the greatest Greek philosopher, whose writings are known the world over. He was the pupil of Socrates and the teacher of Aristotle. He flourished over 400 years before our era.

**Platonic School**, or the "Old Akadéme", in contrast with the later or *Neo-Platonic* School of Alexandria (See "Philalethean").

**Pleroma** (*Gr.*). "Fulness", a Gnostic term adopted to signify the divine world or Universal Soul. Space, developed and divided into a series of æons. The abode of the invisible gods. It has three degrees.

**Plotinus**. The noblest, highest and grandest of all the Neo-Platonists after the founder of the school, Ammonius Saccas. He was the most enthusiastic of the *Philaletheans* or "lovers of truth", whose aim was to found a religion on a system of intellectual abstraction, which is true Theosophy, or the whole substance of Neo-Platonism. If we are to believe Porphyry, Plotinus has never disclosed either his birth-place or connexions, his native land or his race. Till the age of twenty-eight he had never found teacher or teaching which would suit him or answer his aspirations. Then he happened to hear Ammonius Saccas, from which day he continued to attend his school. At thirty-nine he accompanied the Emperor Gordian to Persia and India with the object of learning their philosophy. He died at the age of sixty-six after writing fifty-four books on philosophy. So modest was he that it is said he "blushed to think he had a body". He reached *Samâdhi* (highest ecstasy or "re-union with God" the divine *Ego*) several times during his life. As said by a biographer, "so far did his contempt for his bodily organs go, that he refused to use a remedy, regarding it as unworthy of a man to use means of this kind". Again we read, "as he died, a dragon (or serpent) that had been under his bed, glided through a hole in the wall and disappeared"—a fact suggestive for the student of symbolism. He taught a doctrine identical with that of the Vedantins, namely, that the Spirit-Soul emanating from the One deific principle was, after its pilgrimage, re-united to It.

**Point within a Circle**. In its esoteric meaning the first unmanifested *logos* appearing on the infinite and shoreless expanse of Space, represented by the Circle. It is the plane of Infinity and Absoluteness. This is only one of the numberless and hidden meanings of this symbol, which is the most important of all the geometrical figures used in metaphysical emblematology. As to the Masons, they have made of the point "an individual brother" whose duty to God and man is bounded by the circle, and have added John the Baptist and John the Evangelist to keep company with the "brother", representing them under two perpendicular parallel lines.

**Popes-Magicians.** There are several such in history; *e.g.*, Pope Sylvester II., the artist who made an "oracular head", like the one fabricated by Albertus Magnus, the learned Bishop of Ratisbon. Pope Sylvester was considered a great "enchanter and sorcerer" by Cardinal Benno, and the "head" was smashed to pieces by Thomas Aquinas, because it talked too much. Then there were Popes Benedict IX., John XX., and the VIth and VIIth Gregory, all regarded by their contemporaries as magicians. The latter Gregory was the famous Hildebrand. As to Bishops and lesser Priests who studied Occultism and became expert in magic arts, they are numberless.

**Popol Vuh.** The Sacred Books of the Guatemalians. Quiché MSS., discovered by Brasseur de Bourbourg.

**Porphyry,** or *Porphyrius*. A Neo-Platonist and a most distinguished writer, only second to Plotinus as a teacher and philosopher. He was born before the middle of the third century A.D., at Tyre, since he called himself a Tyrian and is supposed to have belonged to a Jewish family. Though himself thoroughly Hellenized and a Pagan, his name *Melek* (a king) does seem to indicate that he had Semitic blood in his veins. Modern critics very justly consider him the most practically philosophical, and the soberest, of all the Neo-Platonists. A distinguished writer, he was specially famous for his controversy with Iamblichus regarding the evils attendant upon the practice of Theurgy. He was, however, finally converted to the views of his opponent. A natural-born mystic, he followed, as did his master Plotinus, the pure Indian Râj-Yoga training, which leads to the union of the Soul with the Over-Soul or Higher Self (Buddhi-Manas). He complains, however, that, all his efforts notwithstanding, he did not reach this state of ecstacy before he was sixty, while Plotinus was a proficient in it. This was so, probably because while his teacher held physical life and body in the greatest contempt, limiting philosophical research to those regions where life and thought become eternal and divine, Porphyry devoted his whole time to considerations of the hearing of philosophy on practical life. "The end of philosophy is with him morality", says a biographer, "we might almost say, holiness—the healing of man's infirmities, the imparting to him a purer and more vigorous life. Mere knowledge, however true, is not of itself sufficient; knowledge has for its object *life* in accordance with *Nous*"—"reason", translates the biographer. As we interpret *Nous*, however, not as Reason, but mind (Manas) or the divine eternal *Ego* in man, we would translate the idea esoterically, and make it read "the occult or secret *knowledge* has for its object terrestrial *life* in accordance with *Nous*, or our everlasting reincarnating *Ego*", which would be more consonant with Porphyry's idea, as it is with esoteric philosophy. (*See* Porphyry's *De Abstinentia* ., 29.) Of all the Neo-Platonists, Porphyry approached the nearest to real Theosophy as now taught by the Eastern secret school. This is shown by all our modern critics and writers on the Alexandrian school, for "he held that the Soul should be as far as possible freed from the bonds of matter, . . . be ready . . . to cut off the whole body". (*Ad Marcellam*, 34.) He recommends the practice of abstinence, saying that "we should be like the gods if we could abstain from vegetable as well as animal food". He accepts with reluctance theurgy and mystic incantation as those are "powerless to purify the *noëtic* (manasic) principle of the soul": theurgy can "but cleanse the lower or psychic portion, and make it capable of perceiving lower beings, such as spirits, angels and gods" (Aug. *De Civ. Dei.* X., 9), just as Theosophy teaches. "Do not defile the divinity", he adds, with the vain imaginings of men you will not injure that which is for ever blessed (Buddhi-Manas) but you will blind yourself to the perception of the greatest and most vital truths". (*Ad Marcellam*,18.) "If we would he free from the assaults of evil spirits, we must keep ourselves clear of those things over which evil spirits have power, for they attack not the pure soul which has no affinity with them". *(De Abstin.* ii., 43.) This is again our teaching. The Church Fathers held Porphyry as the bitterest enemy, the most irreconcilable to Christianity. Finally, and once more as in modern Theosophy, Porphyry— as all the Neo-Platonists, according to St. Augustine—"praised Christ while they disparaged Christianity"; Jesus, they contended, as we contend, "said nothing himself against the pagan deities, but wrought wonders by their help". "They could not call him as his disciples did, God, but they honoured him as one of the best and wisest of men". (*De Civ. Dei.*, X1X., 23.) Yet, "even in the storm of controversy, scarcely a word seems to have been uttered against the private life of Porphyry. His system prescribed purity and . . . he practised it". (See *A Dict. of Christian Biography*, Vol. IV., "Porphyry".)

**Poseidonis** *(Gr.).* The last remnant of the great Atlantean Continent. Plato's island Atlantis is referred to as an equivalent term in Esoteric Philosophy.

**Postel**, *Guillaume*. A French adept, born in Normandy in 1510. His learning brought him to the notice of Francis I., who sent him to the Levant in search of occult MSS., where he was received into and initiated by an Eastern Fraternity. On his return to France he became famous. He was persecuted by the clergy and finally imprisoned by the Inquisition, but was released by his Eastern brothers from his dungeon. His *Clavis Absconditorum*, a key to things hidden and forgotten, is very celebrated.

**Pot-Amun.** Said to be a Coptic term. The name of an Egyptian priest and hierophant who lived under the earlier Ptolemies. Diogenes Laertius tells us that it signifies one consecrated to the "Amun", the god of wisdom and secret learning, such as were Hermes, Thoth, and Nebo of the Chaldees. This must be so, since in Chaldea the priests consecrated to Nebo also bore his name, being called the Neboïm, or in some old Hebrew Kabbalistic works, "Abba Nebu". The priests generally took the names of their gods. Pot-Amun is credited with having been the first to teach Theosophy, or the outlines of the Secret Wisdom-Religion, to the uninitiated.

**Prabhavâpyaya** (*Sk.*). That whence all originates and into which all things resolve at the end of the life-cycle.

**Prachetâs** (*Sk.*). A name of Varuna, the god of water, or esoterically—its principle.

**Prâchetasas** (*Sk.*). See *S. D.*, Vol. II., p. 176 *et seq.* Daksha is the son of the Prâchetasas, the ten sons of Prachinavahis. Men endowed with magic powers in the *Purânas* who, while practising religious austerities, remained immersed at the bottom of the sea for 10,000 years. The name also of Daksha, called *Prâchetasa*.

**Pradhâna** (*Sk.*). Undifferentiated substance, called elsewhere and in other schools—Akâsa; and Mulaprakriti or Root of Matter by the Vedantins. In short, Primeval Matter.

**Pragna** (*Sk.*) or *Prajna*. A synonym of *Mahat* the Universal Mind. The capacity for perception. (*S. D.*, I. 139) Consciousness.

**Prahlâda** (*Sk.*). The son of Hiranyakashipu, the King of the Asuras. As Prahlâda was devoted to Vishnu, of whom his father was the greatest enemy, he became subjected in consequence to a variety of tortures and punishments. In order to save his devotee from these, Vishnu assumed the form of *Nri-Sinha* (man-lion, his fourth *avatar*) and killed the father.

**Prajâpatis** (*Sk.*). Progenitors; the givers of life to all on this Earth. They are seven and then ten—corresponding to the seven and ten Kabbalistic Sephiroth; to the Mazdean Amesha-Spentas, &c. Brahmâ the creator, is called Prajâpati as the synthesis of the Lords of Being.

**Prâkrita** (*Sk.*). One of the provincial dialects of Sanskrit—"the language of the gods", and therefore, its materialisation.

**Prâkritika Pralaya** (*Sk.*). The Pralaya succeeding to the Age of Brahmâ, when everything that exists is resolved into its primordial essence (or Prakriti).

**Prakriti** (*Sk.*). Nature in general, nature as opposed to Purusha—spiritual nature and Spirit, which together are the "two primeval aspects of the One Unknown Deity". (*S. D., Vol.* I, p. 51.)

**Pralaya** (*Sk.*). A period of obscuration or repose—planetary, cosmic or universal—the opposite of Manvantara (*S. D.,* I. 370.).

**Pramantha** (*Sk.*). An accessory to producing the sacred fire by friction. The sticks used by Brahmins to kindle fire by friction.

**Prameyas** (*Sk.*). Things to be proved; objects of *Pramâna* or proof.

**Pram-Gimas** (*Lithuanian*). Lit., "Master of all", a deity-title.

**Pramlochâ** (*Sk.*). A female *Apsaras*—a water-nymph who beguiled Kandu. (See "Kandu".)

**Prâna** (*Sk.*). Life-Principle; the breath of Life.

**Prânamâya Kosha** (*Sk.*). The vehicle of *Prâna*, life, or the *Linga Sarîra* a Vedantic term.

**Pranâtman** (*Sk.*). The same as *Sutrâtmâ*, the eternal germ-thread on which are strung, like beads, the personal lives of the EGO.

**Pranava** (*Sk.*). A sacred word, equivalent to *Aum*.

**Prânâyâma** (*Sk.*). The suppression and regulation of the breath in Yoga practice.

**Pranidhâna** (*Sk.*). The fifth observance of the Yogis; ceaseless devotion. (See *Yoga Shâstras*, ii. 32.)

**Prâpti** (*Sk.*). From *Prâp*, to reach. One of the eight *Siddhis* (powers) of Râj-Yoga. The power of transporting oneself from one place to another, instantaneously, by the mere force of will; the faculty of divination, of healing and of prophesying, also a Yoga power.

**Prasanga Madhyamika** (*Sk.*). A Buddhist school of philosophy in Tibet. it follows, like the Yogâchârya system, the *Mahâyâna* or "Great Vehicle" of precepts; but, having been founded far later than the Yogâchârya, it is not half so rigid and severe. It is a semi-exoteric and very popular system among the *literati* and laymen.

**Prashraya**, or *Vinaya* (*Sk.*). "The progenetrix of affection." A title bestowed upon the Vedic Aditi, the "Mother of the Gods".

**Pratibhâsika** (*Sk.*). The apparent or illusory life.

**Pratisamvid** (*Sk.*). The four "unlimited forms of wisdom" attained by an

Arhat; the last of which is the absolute knowledge of and power over the twelve Nidânas. See "Nidâna".)

**Pratyâbhâva** (*Sk.*). The state of the Ego under the necessity of repeated births.

**Pratyagâtmâ** (*Sk.*). The same as Jivâtmâ, or the one living Universal Soul — Alaya.

**Pratyâhâra** (*Sk.*). The same as "Mahâpralaya".

**Pratyâharana** (*Sk.*). The preliminary training in practical Râj -Yoga.

**Pratyaksha** (*Sk*). Spiritual perception by means of senses.

**Pratyasarga** (*Sk.*). In Sankhya philosophy the "intellectual evolution of the Universe"; in the *Purânas* the 8th creation.

**Pratyêka Buddha** (*Sk*). The same as "*Pasi*-Buddha". The Pratyêka Buddha is a degree which belongs exclusively to the Yogâchârya school, yet it is only one of high intellectual development with no true spirituality. It is the *dead-letter* of the Yoga laws, in which intellect and comprehension play the greatest part, added to the strict carrying out of the rules of the inner development. It is one of the three paths to Nirvâna, and the lowest, in which a Yogi — "without teacher and without saving others" — by the mere force of will and technical observances, attains to a kind of nominal Buddhaship individually; doing no good to anyone, but working selfishly for his own salvation and himself alone. The Pratyêkas are respected outwardly but are despised inwardly by those of keen or spiritual appreciation. A Pratyêka is generally compared to a "Khadga" or solitary rhinoceros and called *Ekashringa Rishi*, a selfish solitary Rishi (or saint). "As crossing Sansâra ('the ocean of birth and death' or the series of incarnations), suppressing errors, and yet not attaining to absolute perfection, the Pratyêka Buddha is compared with a horse which crosses a river swimming, without touching the ground." (*Sanskrit-Chinese Dict.*) He is far below a true "Buddha of Compassion". He strives only for the reaching of Nirvâna.

**Pre-existence.** The term used to denote that we have lived before. The same as reincarnation in the past. The idea is derided by some, rejected by others, called absurd and inconsistent by the third yet it is the oldest and the most universally accepted belief from an immemorial antiquity. And if this belief was universally accepted by the most subtle philosophical minds of the pre-Christian world, surely it is not amiss that some of our modern intellectual men should also believe in it, or at least give the doctrine the benefit of the doubt. Even the Bible hints at it more than once,

St. John the Baptist being regarded as the reincarnation of Elijah, and the Disciples asking whether the blind man *was born blind because of his sins,* which is equal to saying that he had *lived and sinned before being born blind.* As Mr. Bonwick well says: it was "the work of spiritual progression and soul discipline. The pampered sensualist returned a beggar; the proud oppressor, a slave; the selfish woman of fashion, a seamstress. A turn of the wheel gave a chance for the development of neglected or abused intelligence and feeling, hence the popularity of reincarnation in all climes and times. . . . thus the expurgation of evil was . . . gradually but certainly accomplished." Verily "an evil act follows a man, passing through one hundred thousand transmigrations" (*Panchatantra*). "All souls have a subtle vehicle, image of the body, which carries the passive soul from one material dwelling to another" says Kapila; while Basnage explains of the Jews: "By this second death is not considered hell, but that which happens when a soul has a second time animated a body". Herodotus tells his readers, that the Egyptians "are the earliest who have spoken of this doctrine, according to which the soul of man is immortal, and after the destruction of the body, *enters into a newly born being.* When, say they, it has passed through all the animals of the earth and sea, and all the birds, it will re-enter the body of a new born man." This is *Pre-existence.* Deveria showed that the funeral books of the Egyptians say plainly "that *resurrection* was, in reality, but a renovation, leading to a new infancy, and a new youth. (See "Reincarnation".)

**Prêtas** (*Sk.*). "Hungry demons in popular folk-lore. "Shells", of the avaricious and selfish man after death; "Elementaries" reborn as Prêtas, in Kâma-loka, according to the esoteric teachings;

**Priestesses**. Every ancient religion had its priestesses in the temples. In Egypt they were called the **Sâ** and served the altar of Isis and in the temples of other goddesses. *Canephorœ* was the name given by the Greeks to those consecrated priestesses who bore the baskets of the gods during the public festivals of the Eleusinian Mysteries. There were female prophets in Israel as in Egypt, diviners of dreams and oracles; and Herodotus mentions the *Hierodules*, the virgins or nuns dedicated to the Theban Jove, who were generally the Pharaohs' daughters and other Princesses of the Royal House. Orientalists speak of the wife of Cephrenes, the builder of the so-called second Pyramid, who was a priestess of Thoth. (See "Nuns".)

**Primordial Light**. In Occultism, the light which is born in, and through the preternatural darkness of chaos, which contains "the all in all", the seven rays that become later the seven Principles in Nature.

**Principles**. The Elements or original essences, the basic differentiations upon and of which all things are built up. We use the term to denote the seven individual and fundamental aspects of the One Universal Reality in Kosmos and in man. Hence also the seven aspects in the anifestation in the human being—divine, spiritual, psychic, astral, physiological and simply physical.

**Priyavrata** (*Sk.*). The name of the son of Swâyambhûva Manu in exoteric Hinduism. The occult designation of one of the primeval races in Occultism.

**Proclus** (*Gr.*). A Greek writer and mystic philosopher, known as a Commentator of Plato, and surnamed the Diadochus. He lived in the fifth century, and died, aged 75, at Athens A.D. 485. His last ardent disciple and follower and the translator of his works was Thomas Taylor of Norwich, who, says Brother Kenneth Mackenzie, "was a modern mystic who adopted the pagan faith as being the only veritable faith, and actually sacrificed doves to Venus, a goat to Bacchus and designed to immolate a bull to Jupiter" but was prevented by his landlady.

**Prometheus** (*Gr.*). The Greek *logos*; he, who by bringing on earth divine fire (intelligence and consciousness) endowed men with reason and mind. Prometheus is the Hellenic type of our Kumâras or *Egos,* those who, by incarnating in men, made of them latent gods instead of animals. The gods (or Elohim) were averse to men becoming "as one of us (*Genesis* iii., 22), and knowing "good and evil". Hence we see these gods in every religious legend punishing man for his desire to know. As the Greek myth has it, for stealing the fire he brought to men from Heaven, Prometheus was chained by the order of Zeus to a crag of the Caucasian Mountains.

**Propator** (*Gr*) Gnostic term. The "Depth" of Bythos, or En-Aiôr, the unfathomable light. The latter is alone the Self-Existent and the Eternal—Propator is only periodical.

**Protogonos** (*Gr.*). The "first-born"; used of all the manifested gods and of the Sun in our system.

**Proto-îlos** (*Gr.*). The first primordial matter.

**Protologoi** (*Gr.*). The primordial seven creative Forces when anthropomorphized into Archangels or Logoi.

**Protyle** (*Gr.*). A newly-coined word in chemistry to designate the first homogeneous, primordial substance.

**Pschent** (*Eg.*). A symbol in the form of a double crown, meaning the presence of Deity in death as in life, on earth as in heaven. This *Pschent* is only worn by certain gods.

**Psyche** (*Gr.*). The animal, terrestrial Soul; the lower *Manas*.

**Psychism,** from the Greek *psyche*. A term now used to denote very loosely every kind of mental phenomena, e.g., mediumship, and the higher sensitiveness, hypnotic receptivity, and inspired prophecy, simple clairvoyance in the astral light, and real divine seership; in short, the word covers every phase and manifestation of the powers and potencies of the *human* and the *divine* Souls.

**Psychography**. A word first used by theosophists; it means writing under the dictation or the influence of one's "soul-power", though Spiritualists have now adopted the term to denote writing produced by their mediums under the guidance of returning "Spirits".

**Psychology.** The Science of Soul, in days of old: a Science which served as the unavoidable basis for physiology. Whereas in our modern day, it is psychology that is being based (by our *great* scientists) upon physiology.

**Psychometry.** Lit., "Soul-measuring"; reading or seeing, not with the physical eyes, but with the soul or inner Sight.

**Psychophobia.** Lit., "Soul-fear," applied to materialists and certain atheists, who become struck with madness at the very mention of Soul or Spirit.

**Psylli** (*Gr.*). Serpent-charmers of Africa and Egypt.

**Ptah,** or *Pthah* (*Eg.*). The son of Kneph in the Egyptian Pantheon. He is the Principle of Light and Life through which "creation" or rather evolution took place. The Egyptian logos and creator, the Demiurgos. A very old deity, as, according to Herodotus, he had a temple erected to him by Menes, the first king of Egypt. He is "giver of life" and the self-born, and the father of Apis, the sacred bull, conceived through a ray from the Sun. Ptah is thus the prototype of Osiris, a later deity. Herodotus makes him the father of the Kabiri, the mystery-gods; and the *Targum of Jerusalem* says: "Egyptians called the wisdom of the First Intellect Ptah"; hence he is *Mahat* the "divine wisdom"; though from another aspect he is *Swabhâvat*, the self-created substance, as a prayer addressed to him in the *Ritual of the Dead* says, after calling Ptah "father of fathers and of all gods, generator of all men produced from his substance": "Thou art without father, being. engendered by thy own will; thou art without mother, *being born by the renewal of thine own substance from whom proceeds substance*".

**Pâjâ** (*Sk.*). An offering; worship and divine honours offered to an idol or something sacred.

**Pulastya** (*Sk.*). One of the seven "mind-born sons" of Brahmâ; the reputed father of the *Nâgas* (serpents, also *Initiates*) and other symbolical creatures.

**Pums** *(Sk.)*. Spirit, supreme Purusha, Man.

**Punarjanma** (*Sk.*). The power of evolving objective manifestations; motion of forms; also, re-birth.

**Pundarîk-aksha** (*Sk.*). Lit., "lotus-eyed", a title of Vishnu. "Supreme and imperishable glory", as translated by some Orientalists.

**Pûraka** (*Sk.*). Inbreathing process; a way of breathing as regulated according to the prescribed rules of Hatha 'yoga.

**Purânas** (*Sk.*). Lit., "ancient". A collection of symbolical and allegorical writings—eighteen in number now—supposed to have been composed by Vyâsa, the author of *Mahâbhârata*.

**Purohitas** (*Sk.*). Family priests; Brahmans.

**Pururavas** (*Sk.*). The son of Budha the son of Soma (the moon), and of Ila famous for being the first to produce fire by the friction of two pieces of wood, and make it (the fire) *triple*. An occult character.

**Purusha** (*Sk.*). "Man", *heavenly man*. Spirit, the same as Nârâyana in another aspect. "The Spiritual Self."

**Purusha Nârâyana** (*Sk.*). Primordial male—Brahmâ.

**Purushottama** (*Sk.*). Lit., "best of men"; metaphysically, however, it is spirit, the Supreme Soul of the universe; a title of Vishnu.

**Pûrvaja** (*Sk.*). "Pregenetic", the same as the Orphic *Protologos*; a title of Vishnu.

**Purvashadha** (*Sk.*). An asterism.

**Pûshan** (*Sk.*). A Vedic deity, the real meaning of which remains unknown to Orientalists. It is qualified as the "Nourisher", the feeder of all (helpless) beings. Esoteric philosophy explains the meaning. Speaking of it the *Taittirîya Brâhmana* says that, "When Prajâpati formed living beings, Pûshan nourished them". This then is the same mysterious force that nourishes the fœtus and unborn babe, by *Osmosis*, and which is called the"atmospheric (or *akâsic*) nurse", and the "father nourisher". When the lunar Pitris had evolved men, these remained senseless and helpless, and it is "Pûshan who fed primeval man". Also a name of the Sun.

**Pushkala** (*Sk*) or *Puskola*. A palm leaf prepared for writing on, used in Ceylon. All the native books are written on such palm leaves, and last for centuries.

**Pushkara** (*Sk.*). A blue lotus; the seventh Dwîpa or zone of Bhâratavarsha (India). A famous lake near Ajmere; also the proper name of several persons.

**Pûto** (*Sk.*). An island in China where Kwan-Shai-Yin and Kwan-Yin have a number of temples and monasteries.

**Putra** (*Sk.*). A son.

**Pu-tsi K'iun-ling** (*Chin.*). Lit., "the Universal Saviour of all beings". A title of Avalokiteswara, and also of Buddha.

**Pygmalion** (*Gr.*). A celebrated sculptor and statuary in the island of Cyprus, who became enamoured of a statue he had made. So the Goddess of beauty, taking pity on him, changed it into a living woman (*Ovid, Met.*). The above is an allegory of the soul.

**Pymander** (Gr.). The "Thought divine". The Egyptian Prometheus and the personified Nous or divine light, which appears to and instructs Hermes Trismegistus, in a hermetic work called "Pymander".

**Pyrrha** (*Gr.*). A daughter of Epimatheos and Pandora, who was married to Deucalion. After a deluge when mankind was almost annihilated, Pyrrha and Deucalion made men and women out of stones which they threw behind them.

**Pyrrhonism** (*Gr.*). The doctrine of Scepticism as first taught by Pyrrho, though his system was far more philosophical than the blank denial of our modern Pyrrhonists.

**Pythagoras** (*Gr.*). The most famous of mystic philosophers, born at Samos, about 586 B.C. He seems to have travelled all over the world, and to have culled his philosophy from the various systems to which he had access. Thus, he studied the esoteric sciences with the *Brachmanes* of India, and astronomy and astrology in Chaldea and Egypt. He is known to this day in the former country under the name of Yavanâchârya ("Ionian teacher"). After returning he settled in Crotona, in Magna Grecia, where he established a college to which very soon resorted all the best intellects of the civilised centres. His father was one Mnesarchus of Samos, and was a man of noble birth and learning. It was Pythagoras. who was the first to teach the heliocentric system, and who was the greatest proficient in geometry of his century. It was he also who created the word "philosopher", composed of two words meaning a "lover of wisdom"— *philo-sophos*. As the greatest mathematician, geometer and astronomer of historical antiquity, and also the highest of the metaphysicians and scholars, Pythagoras has won imperishable fame. He taught reincarnation as it is professed in India and much else of the Secret Wisdom.

**Pythagorean Pentacle** (*Gr.*). A Kabbalistic six-pointed star with an eagle at the apex and a bull and a lion under the face of a man; a mystic symbol adopted by the Eastern and Roman Christians, who place these animals beside the four Evangelists.

**Pythia** or *Pythoness* (*Gr.*). Modern dictionaries inform us that the term means one who delivered the oracles at the temple of Delphi, and "any female supposed to have the spirit of divination in her—*a witch*" (Webster). This is neither true, just nor correct. On the authority of Iamblichus, Plutarch and others, a Pythia was a priestess chosen among the *sensitives* of the poorer classes, and placed in a temple where oracular powers were exercised. There she had a room secluded from all but the chief Hierophant and Seer, and once admitted, was, like a nun, lost to the world. Sitting on a tripod of brass placed over a fissure in the ground, through which arose intoxicating vapours, these subterranean exhalations, penetrating her whole system, produced the prophetic *mania*, in which abnormal state she delivered oracles. Aristophanes in Væstas "I., reg. 28, calls the Pythia *ventriloqua vates* or the "ventriloquial prophetess", on account of her *stomach*-voice. The ancients placed the soul of man (the lower *Manas*) or his personal self-consciousness, in the pit of his stomach. We find in the fourth verse of the second *Nâbhânedishta* hymn of the Brahmans: "Hear, O sons of the gods, one who speaks through his name (*nâbhâ*), for he hails you in your dwellings!" This is a modern somnambulic phenomenon. The navel was regarded in antiquity as "the circle of the sun", the seat of divine internal light. Therefore was the oracle of Apollo at *Delphi*, the city of *Delphus*, the womb or abdomen—while the seat of the temple was called the *omphalos*, navel. As well-known, a number of mesmerized subjects can read letters, hear, smell and see through that part of their body. In India there exists to this day a belief (also among the Parsis) that adepts have flames in their navels, which enlighten for them all darkness and unveil the spiritual world. It is called with the Zoroastrians *the lamp of Deshtur* or the "High Priest"; and the light or radiance of the *Dikshita* (the initiate) with the Hindus.

**Pytho** (*Gr.*). The same as *Ob*—a fiendish, devilish influence; the *ob* through which the sorcerers are said to work.

# Q

Q.—The seventeenth letter of the English Alphabet. It is the obsolete

Æolian *Qoppa* and the Hebrew *Koph*. As a numeral it is 100, and its symbol is the back of the head from the ears to the neck. With the Æolian Occultists it stood for the symbol of differentiation.

**Qabbalah** (*Heb.*). The ancient Chaldean Secret Doctrine, abbreviated into Kabala. An occult system handed clown by oral transmission; but which, though accepting tradition, is not in itself composed of merely traditional teachings, as it was once a fundamental science, now disfigured by the additions of centuries, and by interpolation by the Western Occultists, especially by *Christian* Mystics. It treats of hitherto esoteric interpretations of the Jewish Scriptures, and teaches several methods of interpreting Biblical allegories. Originally the doctrines were transmitted "from mouth to ear" only, says Dr. W. Wynn Westcott, "in an oral manner from teacher to pupil who received them; hence the name Kabbalah, Qabalah, or Cabbala from the Hebrew root QBL, to receive. Besides this Theoretic Kabbalah, there was created a Practical branch, which is concerned with the Hebrew letters, as types a like of Sounds, Numbers, and Ideas." (See "Gematria", "Notaricon", "Temura".) For the original book of the *Qabbalah*—the *Zohar*—see further on. But the *Zohar* we have now is not the *Zohar* left by Simeon Ben Jochai to his son and secretary as an heirloom. The author of the present *approximation* was one Moses de Leon, a Jew of the XIIIth century. (See "Kabalah" and "Zohar".)

**Qadmon, Adam**, or *Adam Kadmon (Heb.*). The Heavenly or Celestial Man, the Microcosm (*q.v.*), He is the manifested Logos; the *third* Logos according to Occultism, or the Paradigm of Humanity.

**Qai-yin** (*Heb.*). The same as Cain.

**Qaniratha** (*Mazd.*). Our earth, in the Zoroastrian Scriptures, which is placed, as taught in the *Secret Doctrine*, in the midst of the other six *Karshwars*, or globes of the terrestrial chain. (See *S. D.*, Vol. II, p. 759.)

**Q'lippoth** (*Heb.*), or *Klippoth*. The world of Demons or Shells; the same as the Aseeyatic World, called also *Olam Klippoth*. It is the residence of *Samâel*, the Prince of Darkness in the Kabbalistic allegories. But note what we read in the *Zohar* (ii.43*a*) "For the service of the Angelic World, the Holy. . . . made Samâel and his legions, *i.e.*, the world of action, who are as it were the clouds to be used (by the higher or upper Spirits, our *Egos*) to ride upon in their descent to the earth, and serve, as it were, for their horses". This, in conjunction with the fact that Q'lippoth contains the matter of which stars, planets, and even men are made, shows that Samâel with his legions is simply chaotic, turbulent matter, which is used in its finer state by spirits to robe themselves in. For speaking of the "vesture" or form *(rupa)* of the incarnating *Egos*, it is said in the Occult Catechism that they, the Mânasaputras or Sons of Wisdom, use for the consolidation of their forms, in order to descend into lower spheres, the *dregs of Swabhavat*, or that plastic matter which is throughout Space, in other words, primordial *ilus*. And these dregs are what the Egyptians have called Typhon and modern Europeans Satan, Samâel, etc., etc. *Deus est Demon inversus*—the Demon is the *lining* of God.

**Quadrivium** *(Lat.)*. A term used by the Scholastics during the Middle Ages to designate the last four paths of learning—of which there were originally seven. Thus grammar, rhetoric and logic were called the *trivium*, and arithmetic, geometry, music and astronomy (the Pythagorean obligatory sciences) went under the name of *quadrivium*.

**Quetzo-Cohuatl** *(Mex.)*. The serpent-god in the Mexican Scriptures and legends. His wand and other "land-marks" show him to be some great Initiate of antiquity, who received the name of "Serpent" on account of his wisdom, long life and powers. To this day the aboriginal tribes of Mexico call themselves by the names of various reptiles, animals and birds.

**Quiche Cosmogony**. Called *Popol Vuh*; discovered by the Abbé Brasseur de Bourbourg. (See "Popol Vuh".)

**Quietists**. A religious sect founded by a Spanish monk named Molinos. Their chief doctrine was that contemplation (an internal state of complete rest and passivity) was the only religious practice possible, and constituted the whole of religious observances. They were the Western *Hatha Yogis* and passed their time in trying to separate their minds from the objects of sense. The practice became a fashion in France and also in Russia during the early portion of this century.

**Quinanes**. A very ancient race of giants, of whom there are many traditions, not only in the folk-lore but in the history of Central America. Occult science teaches that the race which preceded our own human race was one of giants, which gradually decreased, after the Atlantean deluge had almost swept them off the face of the earth, to the present size of man.

**Quindecemvir** *(Lat.)*. The Roman priest who had charge of the Sibylline books.

**Qû-tamy** *(Chald.)*. The name of the mystic who receives the revelations of the moon-goddess in the ancient Chaldean work, translated into Arabic, and retranslated by Chwolsohn into German, under the name of *Nabathean Agriculture*.

# R

R.—The eighteenth letter of the alphabet; "the canine", as its sound reminds one of a snarl. In the Hebrew alphabet it is the twentieth, and its numeral is 200. It is equivalent as *Resh* to the divine name *Rahim* (clemency); and its symbols are, a sphere, a head, or a circle.

**Ra** (*Eg.*). The divine Universal Soul in its manifested aspect—the ever-burning light; also the personified Sun.

**Rabbis** (*Heb.*). Originally teachers of the Secret Mysteries, the *Qabbalah;* later, every Levite of the priestly caste became a teacher and a Rabbin. (See the series of Kabbalistic Rabbis by w.w.w.)

1 **Rabbi Abulafia** of Saragossa born in 1240, formed a school of Kabbalah named after him; his chief works were *The Seven Paths of the Law* and *The Epistle to Rabbi Solomon.*

2 **Rabbi Akiba.** Author of a famous Kabbalistic work, the "Alphabet of R.A.", which treats every letter as a symbol of an idea and an emblem of some sentiment; the *Book of Enoch* was originally a portion of this work, which appeared at the close of the eighth century. It was not purely a Kabbalistic treatise.

3 **Rabbi Azariel ben Menachem** (A.D. 1160). The author of the *Commentary on the Ten Sephiroth,* which is the oldest purely Kabbalistic work extant, setting aside the *Sepher Yetzirah,* which although older, is not concerned with the Kabbalistic Sephiroth. He was the pupil of Isaac the Blind, who is the reputed father of the European Kabbalah, and he was the teacher of the equally famous R. Moses Nachmanides.

4 **Rabbi Moses Botarel** (1480). Author of a famous commentary on the *Sepher Yetzirah*; he taught that by ascetic life and the use of invocations, a man's dreams might be made prophetic.

5 **Rabbi Chajim Vital** (1600) ( The great exponent of the Kabbalah as taught R. Isaac Loria: author of one of the most famous works, *Otz Chiim,* or *Tree of Life*; from this Knorr von Rosenroth has taken the *Book on the Rashith ha Gilgalim,* revolutions of souls, or scheme of reincarnations.

6 **Rabbi Ibn Gebirol**. A famous Hebrew Rabbi, author of the hymn *Kether Malchuth,* or Royal Diadem, which appeared about 1050; it is a beautiful poem, embodying the cosmic doctrines of Aristotle, and it even now forms part of the Jewish special service for the evening preceding the great annual Day of Atonement (See Ginsburg and Sachs on the

*Religious Poetry of the Spanish Jews*). This author is also known as Avicebron.

**7 Rabbi Gikatilla.** A distinguished Kabbalist who flourished about 1300: he wrote the famous books, *The Garden of Nuts, The Gate to the Vowel Points, The mystery of the shining Metal,* and *The Gates of Righteousness.* He laid especial stress on the use of Gematria, Notaricon and Temura.

**8 Rabbi Isaac the Blind** of Posquiero. The first who publicly taught in Europe, about A.D. 1200, the Theosophic doctrines of the *Kabbalah.*

**9 Rabbi Loria** (also written *Luria,* and also named *Ari* from his initials). Founded a school of the *Kabbalah* circa 1560. He did not write any works, but his disciples treasured up his teachings, and R. Chajim Vital published them.

**10 Rabbi Moses Cordovero** (A.D. 1550). The author of several Kabbalistic works of a wide reputation, *viz., A Sweet Light, The Book of Retirement,* and *The Garden of Pomegranates*; this latter can be read in Latin in Knorr von Rosenroth's *Kabbalah Denudata,* entitled *Tractatus de Animo, ex libro Pardes Rimmonim.* Cordovero is notable for an adherence to the strictly metaphysical part, ignoring the wonder-working branch which Rabbi Sabbatai Zevi practised, and almost perished in the pursuit of.

**11 Rabbi Moses de Leon** (circa A.D. 1290). The editor and first publisher of the *Zohar,* or "Splendour", the most famous of all the Kabbalistic volumes, and almost the only one of which any large part has been translated into English. This *Zohar* is asserted to be in the main the production of the still more famous Rabbi Simon ben Jochai, who lived in the reign of the Emperor Titus.

**12 Rabbi Moses Maimonides** (died 1304). A famous Hebrew Rabbi and author, who condemned the use of charms and amulets, and objected to the Kabbalistic use of the divine names.

**13 Rabbi Sabbatai Zevi** (born 1641). A very famous Kabbalist, who passing beyond the dogma became of great reputation as a thaumaturgist, working wonders by the divine names. Later in life he claimed Messiahship and fell into the hands of the Sultan Mohammed IV. of Turkey, and would have been murdered, but saved his life by adopting the Mohammedan religion. (See Jost on *Judaism and its Sects.*)

**14 Rabbi Simon ben Jochai** (circa A.D. 70-80). It is round this name that cluster the mystery and poetry of the origin of the *Kabbalah* as a gift of the deity to mankind. Tradition has it that the *Kabbalah* was a divine theosophy first taught by God to a company of angels, and that some glimpses of its perfection were conferred upon Adam; that the wisdom passed from him unto Noah; thence to Abraham, from whom the Egyptians of his era learned a portion of the doctrine. Moses derived a partial initiation from the land of his birth, and this was perfected by direct communications with the deity. From Moses it passed to the seventy elders of the Jewish nation, and from them the theosophic scheme was handed from generation to generation; David and Solomon especially became masters of this concealed doctrine. No attempt, the legends tell us, was made to commit the sacred knowledge to writing until the time of the destruction of the second Temple by Titus, when Rabbi Simon ben Jochai, escaping from the besieged Jerusalem, concealed himself in a cave, where he remained for twelve years. Here he, a Kabbalist already, was further instructed by the prophet Elias. Here Simon taught his disciples, and his chief pupils, Rabbi Eliezer and Rabbi Abba, committed to writing those teachings which in later ages became known as the *Zohar*, and were certainly published afresh in Spain by Rabbi Moses de Leon, about 1280. A fierce contest has raged for centuries between the learned Rabbis of Europe around the origin of the legend, and it seems quite hopeless to expect ever to arrive at an accurate decision as to what portion of the Zohar, if any, is as old as Simon ben Jochai. (See "Zohar".) [w.w.w.]

**Râdhâ** (*Sk.*). The shepherdess among the *Gopis* (shepherdesses) of Krishna, who was the wife of the god.

**Râga** (Sk). One of the five *Kleshas* (afflictions) in Patânjali's Yoga philosophy. In *Sânkhya Kârikâ*, it is the "obstruction" called love and desire in the physical or terrestrial sense. The five *Kleshas* are: *Avidyâ*, or ignorance; *Asmitâ*, selfishness, or "I-am-ness"; *Râga*, love; *Dwesha*, hatred; and *Abhinivesa,* dread of suffering.

**Ragnarök** (*Scand.*). A kind of metaphysical entity called the "Destroyer" and the "Twilight of the Gods", the two-thirds of whom are destroyed at the "Last Battle" in the *Edda*. Ragnarök lies in chains on the ledge of a rock so long as there are some good men in the world; but when all laws are broken and all virtue and good vanish from it, then Ragnarok will he unbound and allowed to bring every imaginable evil and disaster on the doomed world.

**Ragon**, *J. M.* A French Mason, a distinguished writer and great symbologist, who tried to bring Masonry back to its pristine purity. He was born at Bruges in 1789, was received when quite a boy into the Lodge and Chapter of the "Vrais Amis", and upon removing to Paris founded the Society of the Trinosophes. it is rumoured that he was the possessor of a number of papers given to him by the famous Count de St. Germain, from which he had all his remarkable knowledge upon early Masonry. He died at Paris in 1866, leaving a quantity of books written by himself and masses of MSS., which were bequeathed by him to the "Grand Orient". Of the mass of his published works very few are obtainable, while others have entirely disappeared. This is due to mysterious persons (Jesuits, it is believed) who hastened to buy up every edition they could find after his death. In short, his works are now extremely rare.

**Rahasya** (*Sk.*). A name of the Upanishads. *Lit.*, secret essence of knowledge.

**Rahat.** The same as "Arhat"; the adept who becomes entirely free from any desires on this plane, by acquiring divine knowledge and powers.

**Ra'hmin Seth** (*Heb.*). According to the *Kabala* (or *Qabbalah*), the "soul-sparks", contained in Adam (Kadmon), went into three sources, the heads of which were his three sons. Thus, while the "soul spark" (or *Ego*) called Chesed went into Habel, and Geboor-ah into Qai-yin (Cain)—Ra'hmin went into Seth, and these three sons were divided into seventy human species, called "the principal roots of the human race".

**Râhu** (*Sk.*). A *Daitya* (demon) whose lower parts were like a dragon's tail. He made himself immortal by robbing the gods of some *Amrita*—the elixir of divine life—for which they were churning the ocean of milk. Unable to deprive him of his immortality, Vishnu exiled him from the earth and made of him the constellation Draco, his head being called Râhu and his tail Ketu—astronomically, the ascending and descending nodes. With the latter appendage he has ever since waged a destructive war on the denouncers of his robbery, the sun and the moon, and (during the eclipses) is said to swallow them. Of course the fable has a mystic and occult meaning.

**Rahula** (*Sk.*). The name of Gautama Buddha's son.

**Raibhyas** (*Sk.*). A class of gods in the 5th Manvantara.

**Raivata Manvantara** (*Sk.*). The life-cycle presided over by Raivata Manu. As he is the fifth of the fourteen Manus (in Esotercism, *Dhyan Chohans*), there being seven *root*-Manus and seven *seed*-Manus for the seven Rounds of our terrestrial chain of globes (See *Esot. Buddhism* by A. P. Sinnett, and the *Secret Doctrine*, Vol.1., "Brahminical Chronology"), Raivata presided over the third Round and was its *root*-Manu.

**Râjâ** (*Sk.*). A Prince or King in India.

**Râjagriha** *(Sk.)*. A city in Magadha famous for its conversion to Buddhism in the days of the Buddhist kings. It was their residence from Bimbisara to Asoka, and was the seat of the first Synod, or Buddhist Council, held 510 B.C.

**Râjârshis** (*Sk.*). The King-Rishis or King-Adepts, one of the three classes of Rishis in India; the same as the King-Hierophants of ancient Egypt.

**Râjas** (*Sk.*). The "quality of foulness" (*i.e.*, differentiation), and activity in the *Purânas*. One of the three *Gunas* or divisions in the correlations of matter and nature, representing form and change.

**Rajasâs** (*Sk.*). The elder *Agnishwattas* —the Fire-Pitris, "fire" standing as a symbol of enlightenment and intellect.

**Râja-Yoga** (*Sk.*). The true system of developing psychic and spiritual powers and union with one's *Higher Self*—or the Supreme Spirit, as the profane express it. The exercise, regulation and concentration of thought. Râja-Yoga is opposed to Hatha-Yoga, the physical or psycho physiological training in asceticism.

**Râkâ** (*Sk.*). The day of the full moon: a day for occult practices.

**Râkshâ** (*Sk.*). An amulet prepared during the full or new moon.

**Râkshasas** (*Sk.*). *Lit.*, "raw eaters", and in the popular superstition evil spirits, demons. Esoterically, however, they are the *Gibborim* (giants) of the Bible, the Fourth Race or the Atlanteans. (See *S. D.*, Vol. II, p. 165.)

**Râkshasi-Bhâshâ** (*Sk.*). *Lit.*, the language of the Râkshasas. In reality, the speech of the Atlanteans, our gigantic forefathers of the fourth Root-race.

**Ram Mohum Roy** (*Sk.*). The well-known Indian reformer who came to England in 1833 and died there.

**Râma** (*Sk.*). The seventh *avatar* or incarnation of Vishnu; the eldest son of King Dasaratha, of the Solar Race. His full name is Râma-Chandra, and he is the hero of the *Râmâyana*. He married Sîta, who was the female *avatar* of Lakshmi, Vishnu's wife, and was carried away by Râvana the Demon-King of Lanka, which act led to the famous war.

**Râmâyana** (*Sk.*). The famous epic poem collated with the *Mahâbhârata*. It looks as if this poem was either the original of the *Iliad* or *vice versa*, except that in *Râmâyana* the allies of Râma are monkeys, led by Hanuman, and monster birds and other animals, all of whom fight against the *Râkshasas*, or demons and giants of Lankâ.

**Râsa** (*Sk.*). The mystery-dance performed by Krishna and his *Gopis*, the shepherdesses, represented in a yearly festival to this day, especially in Râjastan. Astronomically it is Krishna—the *Sun*—around whom circle the planets and the signs of the Zodiac symbolised by the *Gopis*. The same as the "circle-dance" of the Amazons around the priapic image, and the dance of the daughters of Shiloh (*Judges* xxi.), and that of King David around the ark. (See *Isis Unveiled*, II., pp. 45, 331 and 332.)

**Râshi** (*Sk.*). An astrological division, the sixth, relating to Kanya (*Virgo*) the sixth sign in the Zodiac.

**Rashi-Chakra** (*Sk.*), The Zodiac.

**Rasit** (*Heb.*). Wisdom.

**Rasollâsâ** (*Sk.*). The first of the eight physical perfections, or *Siddhis* (phenomena), of the Hatha Yogis. Rasollâsâ is the prompt evolution *at will* of the juices of the body independently of any nutriment from without.

**Rasshoo** (*Eg.*). The solar fires formed in and out of the primordial "waters", or substance, of Space.

**Ratnâvabhâsa Kalpa** (*Sk.*). The age in which all sexual difference will have ceased to exist, and birth will take place in the *Anupâdaka* mode, as in the second and third Root-races. Esoteric philosophy teaches that it will take place at the end of the sixth and during the seventh and last Root-race in this Round.

**Râtri** (*Sk.*). Night; the body Brahmâ assumed for purposes of creating the Râkshasas or alleged giant-demons.

**Raumasa** (*Sk.*). A class of devas (gods) said to have originated from the pores of Verabhadra's skin. An allusion to the *pre-Adamic* race called the "sweat-born". (*S. D.*, Vol. II.)

**Ravail.** The true name of the Founder of modern Spiritism in France, who is better known under the pseudonym of *Allan Kardec*.

**Râvana** (*Sk.*). The King-Demon (the Râkshasas), the Sovereign of Lankâ (Ceylon), who carried away Sîta, Râma's wife, which led to the great war described in the *Râmâyana*.

**Ravi** (*Sk.*). A name of the Sun.

**Rechaka** (*Sk.*). A practice in Hatha Yoga, during the performance of Prânâyâma or the regulation of breath: namely, that of opening one nostril and emitting breath therefrom, and keeping the other closed; one of the three operations respectively called Pûraka, Kumbhaka and Rechaka—operations very pernicious to health.

**Red Colour.** This has always been associated with male characteristics, especially by the Etruscans and Hindoos. In Hebrew it is Adam, the same as the word for "earth" and "the first man". It seems that nearly all myths represent the first perfect man as white. The same word without the initial A is Dam or Dem, which means Blood, also of red colour. [w.w.w.]

The colour of the fourth Principle in man—*Kâma*, the seat of desires is represented red.

**Reincarnation.** The doctrine of rebirth, believed in by Jesus and the Apostles, as by all men in those days, but denied now by the Christians. All the Egyptian converts to Christianity, Church Fathers and others, believed in this doctrine, as shown by the writings of several. In the still existing symbols, the human-headed bird flying towards a mummy, a body, or "the soul uniting itself with its *sahou* (glorified body of the Ego, and also the *kâmalokic shell*) proves this belief. "The song of the Resurrection" chanted by Isis to recall her dead husband to life, might be translated "Song of Rebirth", as Osiris is collective Humanity. "Oh! Osiris [here follows the name of the Osirified mummy, or the departed], rise again in holy earth (matter), august mummy in the coffin, under thy corporeal substances", was the funeral prayer of the priest over the deceased. "Resurrection" with the Egyptians never meant the resurrection of the mutilated mummy, but of the *Soul* that informed it, the Ego in a new body. The putting on of flesh periodically by the Soul or the Ego, was a universal belief; nor can anything be more consonant with justice and Karmic law. (See "Pre-existence".)

**Rekh-get-Amen** *(Eg.)*. The name of the priests, hierophants, and teachers of Magic, who, according to Lenormant, Maspero, the Champollions, etc., etc., "could levitate, walk the air, live under water, sustain great pressure, harmlessly suffer mutilation, read the past, foretell the future, make themselves invisible, and cure diseases" (Bonwick, *Religion of Magic)*. And the same author adds: "Admission to the mysteries did not confer magical powers. These depended upon two things: the possession of innate capacities, and the knowledge of certain formulæ employed under suitable circumstances". Just the same as it is now.

**Rephaim** *(Heb.)*. Spectres, phantoms. *(S. D.,* Vol. II, p. 279.)

**Resha-havurah** *(Heb., Kab.)*. Lit., the "White Head", from which flows the fiery fluid of life and intelligence in three hundred and seventy streams, in all the directions of the Universe. The "White Head" is the first Sephira, the Crown, or first active light.

**Reuchlin**, *John*. Nicknamed the "Father of the Reformation"; the friend of

Pico di Mirandola, the teacher and instructor of Erasmus, of Luther and Melancthon. He was a great Kabbalist and Occultist.

**Rig Veda** (*Sk.*). The first and most important of the four *Vedas*. Fabled to have been "created" from the Eastern mouth of Brahmâ; recorded in Occultism as having been delivered by great sages on Lake Man(a)saravara beyond the Himalayas, dozens of thousands of years ago.

**Rik** (*Sk.*). A verse of *Rig-Veda*.

**Riksha** (*Sk.*). Each of the twenty-seven constellations forming the Zodiac. Any fixed star, or constellation of stars.

**Rimmon** (*Heb.*). A Pomegranate, the type of abundant fertility; occurs in the Old Testament; it figures in Syrian temples and was deified there, as an emblem of the celestial prolific mother of all; also a type of the full womb. [w.w.w.]

**Rings, Magic**. These existed as talismans in every folk-lore. In Scandinavia such rings are always connected with the elves and dwarfs who were alleged to be the possessors of talismans and who gave them occasionally to human beings whom they wished to protect. In the words of the chronicler: "These magic rings brought good luck to the owner so long as they were carefully preserved; but their loss was attended with terrible misfortunes and unspeakable misery".

**Rings and Rounds**. Terms employed by Theosophists in explanation of Eastern cosmogony. They are used to denote the various evolutionary cycles in the Elemental, Mineral, &c., Kingdoms, through which the Monad passes on any one globe, the term Round being used only to denote the cyclic passage of the Monad round the complete chain of seven globes. Generally speaking, Theosophists use the term ring as a synonym of cycles, whether cosmic, geological, metaphysical or any other.

**Riphæus** (*Gr.*). In mythology a mountain chain upon which slept the frozen-hearted god of snows and hurricanes. In Esoteric philosophy a real prehistoric continent which from a tropical ever sunlit land has now become a desolate region beyond the Arctic Circle.

**Rishabha** (*Sk.*). A sage supposed to have been the first teacher of the Jain doctrines in India.

**Rishabham** (*Sk*). The Zodiacal sign Taurus.

**Rishi-Prajâpati** (*Sk.*). *Lit.*, "revealers", holy sages in the religious history of Âryavarta. Esoterically the highest of them are the Hierarchies of "Builders" and Architects of the Universe and of living things on earth;

they are generally called Dhyan Chohans, Devas and gods.

**Rishis** (*Sk.*). Adepts; the inspired ones. In Vedic literature the term is employed to denote those persons through whom the various Mantras were revealed.

**Ri-thlen.** *Lit.*, "snake-keeping". It is a terrible kind of sorcery practised at Cherrapoonjee in the Khasi-Hills. The former is the ancient capital of the latter. As the legend tells us: ages ago a *thlen* (serpent-dragon) which inhabited a cavern and devoured men and cattle was put to death by a local St. George, and cut to pieces, every piece being sent out to a different district to be burnt. But the piece received by the Khasis was preserved by them and became a kind of household god, and their descendants developed into *Ri-thlens* or "snake keepers", for the piece they preserved grew into a dragon *(thlen)* and ever since has obsessed certain Brahmin families of that district. To acquire the good grace of their *thlen* and save their own lives, these "keepers" have often to commit murders of women and children, from whose bodies they cut out the toe and finger nails, which they bring to their *thlen,* and thus indulge in a number of black magic practices connected with sorcery and necromancy.

**Roger Bacon.** A very famous Franciscan monk who lived in England in the thirteenth century. He was an Alchemist who firmly believed in the existence of the Philosopher's Stone, and was a great mechanician, chemist, physicist and astrologer. In his treatise on the *Admirable Force of Art and Nature,* he gives hints about gunpowder and predicts the use of steam as a propelling power, describing besides the hydraulic press, the diving-bell and the kaleidoscope. He also made a famous brazen head fitted with an acoustic apparatus which gave out oracles.

**Ro** *and* **Ru** *(Eg.).* The gate or outlet, the spot in the heavens whence proceeded or was born primeval light; synonymous with "cosmic womb".

**Rohinilâ** (*Sk.*). The ancient name of a monastery visited by Buddha Sâkyamuni, now called Roynallah, near Balgada, in Eastern Behar.

**Rohit** (*Sk.*). A female deer, a hind; the form assumed by Vâch (the female Logos and female aspect of Brahmâ who created her out of one half of his body) to escape the amorous pursuits of her "father", who transformed himself for that purpose into a buck or *red* deer (the colour of Brahmâ being red).

**Rohitaka Stupa** (*Sk.*). The "red stupa", or dagoba, built by King Asoka, and on which Maitribala-râjâ fed starving Yakshas with his blood. The Yakshas are inoffensive demons (Elementaries) called *pynya-janas* or "good people".

**Rosicrucians** (*Mys.*). The name was first given to the disciples of a learned Adept named Christian Rosenkreuz, who flourished in Germany, circa 1460. He founded an Order of mystical students whose early history is to be found in the German work, *Fama Fraternitatis* (1614), which has been published in several languages. The members of the Order maintained their secrecy, but traces of them have been found in various places every half century since these dates. The *Societas Rosicruciana in Anglia* is a Masonic Order, which has adopted membership in the "outer"; the Chabrath Zereh Aur Bokher, or Order of the G. D., which has a very complete scheme of initiation into the Kabbalah and the Higher Magic of the Western or Hermetic type, and admits both sexes, is a direct descendant from mediæval sodalities of Rosicrucians, themselves descended from the Egyptian Mysteries. [w.w.w.]

**Rostan.** Book of the Mysteries of Rostan; an occult work in manuscript.

**Rowhanee** (*Eg.*) or *Er-Roohanee*. is the Magic of modern Egypt, supposed to proceed from Angels and Spirits, that is Genii, and by the use of the mystery names of Allah; they distinguish two forms—Ilwee, that is the Higher or White Magic; and Suflee and Sheytanee, the Lower or Black Demoniac Magic. There is also Es-Seemuja, which is deception or conjuring. Opinions differ as to the importance of a branch of Magic called Darb el Mendel, or as Barker calls it in English, the Mendal: by this is meant a form of artificial clairvoyance, exhibited by a young boy before puberty, or a virgin, who, as the result of self-fascination by gazing on a pool of ink in the hand, with coincident use of incense and incantation, sees certain scenes of real life passing over its surface. Many Eastern travellers have narrated instances, as E. W. Lane in his *Modern Egyptians* and his *Thousand and One Nights*, and E. B. Barker; the incidents have been introduced also into many works of fiction, such as Marryat's *Phantom Ship*, and a similar idea is interwoven with the story of Rose Mary and the Beryl stone, a poem by Rossetti. For a superficial attempt at explanation, see the *Quarterly Review*, No.117. [w.w.w.]

**Ruach** (*Heb.*). Air, also Spirit; the Spirit, one of the "human principles" (Buddhi-Manas).

**Ruach Elohim** (*Heb.*). The Spirit of the gods; corresponds to the Holy Ghost of the Christians. Also the wind, breath and rushing water. [w.w.w.]

**Rudra** (*Sk.*). A title of Siva, the Destroyer.

**Rudras** (*Sk.*). The mighty ones; the lords of the three upper worlds. One of the classes of the "fallen" or incarnating spirits; they are all born of Brahmâ.

**Runes** (*Scand.*). The Runic language and characters are the mystery or sacerdotal tongue and alphabet of the ancient Scandinavians. *Runes* are derived from the word *rûna* (secret). Therefore both language and character could neither be understood nor interpreted without having the key to it. Hence while the written *runes* consisting of sixteen letters are known, the ancient ones composed of marks and signs are indecipherable. They are called the magic characters. "It is clear", says E. W. Anson, an authority on the folk-lore of the Norsemen, "that the runes were from various causes regarded even in Germany proper as full of mystery and endowed with supernatural power". They are said to have been invented by Odin.

**Rûpa** (*Sk.*). Body; any form, applied even to the forms of the gods, which are subjective to us.

**Ruta** (*Sk.*). The name of one of the last islands of Atlantis, which perished ages before *Poseidonis*, the "Atlantis" of Plato.

**Rutas** (*Sk.*). An ancient people that inhabited the above island or continent in the Pacific Ocean.

# S

**S.**—The nineteenth letter; numerically, *sixty*. In Hebrew it is the fifteenth letter, Samech, held as holy because "the sacred name of god is *Samech*". Its symbol is a prop, or a pillar, and a phallic egg. In occult geometry it is represented as a circle quadrated by a cross, ⊕. In the *Kabbalah* the "divisions of Gan-Eden or paradise" are similarly divided.

**Sa** or **Hea** (*Chald.*). The synthesis of the seven Gods in Babylonian mythology.

**Sabalâswâs** (*Sk.*). Sons of Daksha (*S. D.*, Vol. II, p. 275).

**Sabao** (*Gr.*). The Gnostic name of the genius of Mars.

**Sabaoth** (*Heb.*). An army or host, from Sâbô go to war; hence the name of the fighting god—the" Lord of Sabaoth ".

**Sabda** (*Sk.*). The Word, or Logos.

**Sabda Brahmam** (*Sk.*). "The Unmanifested Logos." The *Vedas*; "Ethereal Vibrations diffused throughout Space ".

**Sabhâ** (*Sk.*). An assembly; a place for meetings, social or political. Also

*Mahâsabhâ* , "the bundle of wonderful (mayavic or illusionary) things" the gift of Mayâsur to the Pândavas (*Mahâbhârata.*)

**Sabianism.** The religion of the ancient Chaldees. The latter believing in one impersonal, universal, deific Principle, never mentioned It, but offered worship to the solar, lunar, and planetary gods and rulers, regarding the stars and other celestial bodies as their respective symbols.

**Sabians.** *Astrolaters,* so called; those who worshipped the stars, or rather their "regents ".(See "Sabianism ".)

**Sacha Kiriya** (*Sk.*). A power with the Buddhists akin to a magic mantram with the Brahmans. It is a miraculous energy which can be exercised by any adept, whether priest or layman, and "most efficient when accompanied by *bhâwanâ* "(meditation). It consists in a recitation of one's "acts of merit done either in this or some former birth"—as the Rev. Mr. Hardy thinks and puts it, but in reality it depends on the intensity of one's will, added to an absolute faith in one's own powers, whether of yoga— willing—or of prayer, as in the case of Mussulmans and Christians. Sacha means "true", and *Kiriyang,* "action". It is the *power of merit,* or of a saintly life.

**Sacrarium** *(Lat.).* The name of the room in the houses of the ancient Romans, which contained the particular deity worshipped by the family; also the adytum of a temple.

**Sacred Heart.** In Egypt, of Horus; in Babylon, of the god Bel; and the lacerated heart of Bacchusin Greece and elsewhere. Its symbol was the *persea.* The pear-like shape of its fruit, and of its kernel especially, resembles the heart in form. It is sometimes seen on the head of Isis, the mother of Horus, the fruit being cut open and the heart-like kernel exposed to full view. The Roman Catholics have since adopted the worship of the "sacred heart" of Jesus and of the Virgin Mary.

**Sacred Science.** The name given to the *inner* esoteric philosophy, the secrets taught in days of old to the initiated candidates, and divulged during the last and supreme Initiation by the Hierophants.

**Sadaikarûpa** (*Sk.*). The essence of the immutable nature.

**Sadducees.** A sect, the followers of one Zadok, a disciple of Anti-gonus Saccho. They are accused of having denied the immortality of the (personal) soul and that of the resurrection of the (physical and personal) body. Even so do the Theosophists; though they deny neither the immortality of the Ego nor the resurrection of all its numerous and successive lives, which survive *in the memory of the Ego.* But together with the Sadducees—a sect of learned philosophers who were to all the other Jews that which the polished and learned Gnostics were to the rest of the Greeks during the early centuries of our era—we certainly deny the immortality of the *animal* soul and the resurrection of the physical body. The Sadducees were the scientists and the learned men of Jerusalem, and held the highest offices, such as of high priests and judges, while the Pharisees were almost from first to last the Pecksniffs of Judæa.

**Sâdhyas** (*Sk.*). One of the names of the "twelve great gods" created by Brahmâ. Kosmic gods; lit., "divine sacrificers". The Sâdhyas are important in Occultism.

**Sadik.** The same as the Biblical Melchizedec, identified by the mystic Bible-worshippers with Jehovah, and Jesus Christ. But Father Sadik's identity with Noah being proven, he can be further identified with Kronos-Saturn.

**Safekh** (*Eg.*). Written also *Sebek* and *Sebakh*, god of darkness and night, with the crocodile for his emblem. In the Typhonic legend and transformation he is the same as Typhon. He is connected with both Osiris and Horus, and is their great enemy on earth. We find him often called the "triple crocodile ". In astronomy he is the same as Mâkâra or Capricorn, the most mystical of the signs of the Zodiac.

**Saga** (*Scand.*). The goddess "who sings of the deeds of gods and heroes ", and to whom the black ravens of Odin reveal the history of the Past and of the Future in the Norsemen's *Edda*.

**Sâgara** (*Sk.*). Lit., "the Ocean"; a king, the father of 60,000 Sons, who, for disrespect shown to the sage Kapila, were reduced to ashes by a single glance of his eye.

**Sagardagan.** One of the four paths to Nirvana.

**Saha** (*Sk.*). "The world of suffering"; any inhabited world in the chilio-cosmos.

**Sahampati** (*Sk.*). Maha or Parabrahm.

**Saharaksha** (*Sk.*). The fire of the Asuras; the name of a son of Pavamâna, one of the three chief occult fires.

**Saint Martin**, *Louis Claude de*. Born in France (Amboise), in 1743. A great mystic and writer, who pursued his philosophical and theosophical studies at Paris, during the Revolution. He was an ardent disciple of Jacob Boehme, and studied under Martinez Paschalis, finally founding a mystical semi-Masonic Lodge, "the Rectified Rite of St. Martin ", with seven degrees. He was a true Theosophist. At the present moment some ambitious charlatans in Paris are caricaturing him and passing themselves off as initiated Martinists, and thus dishonouring the name of the late Adept.

**Sais** (*Eg.*). The place where the celebrated temple of Isis-Neith was found, wherein was the ever-veiled statue of Neith (Neith and Isis being interchangeable), with the famous inscription, "I am all that has been, and is, and shall be, and my peplum no mortal has withdrawn ". (See "Sirius".)

**Saka** (*Sk.*). Lit., "the One", or the Ekas; used of the "Dragon of Wisdom" or the manifesting deities, taken collectively.

**Saka** (*Sk.*). According to the Orientalists the same as the classical *Sacæ*. It is during the reign of their King Yudishtira that the *Kali Yuga* began.

**Sâka Dwîpa** (*Sk.*). One of the seven islands or continents mentioned in the *Purânas* (ancient works).

**Sakkayaditthi.** Delusion of personality; the erroneous idea that "I am I ", a man or a woman with a special name, instead of being an inseparable part of the whole.

**Sakradagamin** (*Sk.*). Lit., "he who will receive birth (only) once more" before Nirvâna is reached by him; he who has entered the second of the four paths which lead to Nirvana and has almost reached perfection.

**Sakshi** (*Sk.*). The name of the hare, who in the legend of the "moon and the hare" threw himself into the fire to save some starving pilgrims who would not kill him. For this sacrifice Indra is said to have transferred him to the centre of the moon.

**Sakti** (*Sk.*). The active female energy of the gods; in popular Hinduism, their wives and goddesses; in Occultism, the crown of the astral light. Force and the six forces of nature synthesized. Universal Energy.

**Sakti-Dhara** (*Sk.*). Lit., the "Spear-holder", a title given to Kartikeya for killing Târaka, a Daitya or giant-demon. The latter, demon though he was, seems to have been such a great Yogin, owing to his religious austerities and holiness, that he made all the gods tremble before him. This makes of Kartikeya, the war god, a kind of St. Michael.

**Sakwala.** This is a *bana* or "word" uttered by Gautama Buddha in his oral instructions. Sakwala is a mundane, or rather a solar system, of which there is an infinite number in the universe, and which denotes that space to which the light of every sun extends. Each Sakwala contains earths, hells and heavens (meaning good and bad spheres, our earth being considered as hell, in Occultism); attains its prime, then falls into decay and is finally destroyed at regularly recurring periods, in virtue of one immutable law. Upon the earth, the Master taught that there have been already four great "continents" (the Land of the Gods, Lemuria, Atlantis, and the present "continent" divided into five parts of the *Secret Doctrine*), and that three more have to appear. The former did *not communicate* with each other", a sentence showing that Buddha was not speaking of the actual continents known in his day (for *Pâtâla* or America was perfectly familiar to the ancient Hindus), but of the four geological formations of the earth, with their four distinct *root*-races which had already disappeared.

**Sâkya** *(Sk.)*. A patronymic of Gautama Buddha.

**Sâkyamuni Buddha** *(Sk.)*. A name of the founder of Buddhism, the great Sage, the Lord Gautama.

**Salamanders.** The Rosicrucian name for the Elementals of Fire. The animal, as well as its name, is of most occult significance, and is widely used in poetry. The name is almost identical in all languages. Thus, in Greek, Latin, French, Spanish, Italian, etc., it is Salamandra, in Persian Samandel, and in Sanskrit Salamandala.

**Salmalî** *(Sk.)*. One of the seven zones; also a kind of tree.

**Sama** *(Sk.)*. One of the *bhâva pushpas,* or "flowers of sanctity Sama is the fifth, or "resignation". There are eight such flowers, namely: clemency or charity, self-restraint, affection (or love for others), patience, resignation, devotion, meditation and veracity. Sama is also the repression of any mental perturbation,

**Sâma Veda** *(Sk.)*. Lit., "the Scripture, or *Shâstra*, of peace". One of the four Vedas.

**Samâdhâna** *(Sk.)*. That state in which a Yogi can no longer diverge from the path of spiritual progress; when everything terrestrial, except the visible body, has ceased to exist for him.

**Samâdhi** *(Sk.)*. A state of ecstatic and complete trance. The term comes from the words *Sam-âdha*, "self-possession ". He who possesses this power is able to exercise an absolute control over all his faculties, physical or mental; it is the highest state of Yoga.

**Samâdhindriya** *(Sk.)*. Lit., "the root of concentration"; the fourth of the five roots called Pancha Indriyâni, which are said in esoteric philosophy to be the agents in producing a highly moral life, leading to sanctity and liberation; when these are reached, the two *spiritual roots* lying latent in the body (Atmâ and Buddhi) will send out shoots and blossom. *Samâdhindriya* is the organ of ecstatic meditation in Râj-yoga practices.

**Samael** (*Heb.*). The Kabbalistic title of the Prince of those evil spirits who represent incarnations of human vices; the angel of Death. From this the idea of Satan has been evolved. [w.w.w.]

**Samajna** (*Sk.*). Lit., "an enlightened (or *luminous*) Sage". Translated verbally, *Samgharana Samajna*, the famous Vihâra near Kustana (China), means "the monastery of the luminous Sage".

**Samâna** (*Sk.*). One of the five breaths (Prânas) which carry on the chemical action in the animal body.

**Sâmanêra**. A novice; a postulant for the Buddhist priesthood.

**Samanta Bhadra** (*Sk.*). Lit., "Universal Sage". The name of one of the four Bodhisattvas of the Yogâchârya School, of the Mâhâyana (the Great Vehicle) of Wisdom of that system. There are four terrestrial and three celestial Bodhisattvas: the first four only act in the present races, but in the middle of the fifth Root-race appeared the fifth Bodhisattva, who, according to an esoteric legend, was Gautama Buddha, but who, having appeared too early, had to disappear bodily from the world for a while.

**Sâmanta Prabhâsa** (*Sk.*). Lit., "universal brightness" or dazzling light. The name under which each of the 500 perfected Arhats reappears on earth as Buddha.

**Sâmânya** (*Sk.*). Community, or commingling of qualities, an abstract notion of genus, such as humanity.

**Samâpatti** (*Sk.*). Absolute concentration in Râja-Yoga; the process of development by which perfect indifference (*Sams*) is reached (*apatti*). This state is the last stage of development before the possibility of entering into Samâdhi is reached.

**Samaya** (*Sk.*). A religious precept.

**S'ambhala** (*Sk*). A very mysterious locality on account of its future associations. A town or village mentioned in the *Purânas*, whence, it is prophesied, the Kalki Avatar will appear. The "Kalki"is Vishnu, *the Messiah on the White Horse* of the Brahmins; Maitreya Buddha of the Buddhists, Sosiosh of the Parsis, and Jesus of the Christians (See *Revelations*). All these "messengers" are to appear "before the destruction of the world", says the one; before the end of Kali Yuga say the others. It is in S'ambhala that the future Messiah will be born. Some Orientalists make modern Murâdâbâd in Rohilkhand (N.W.P.) identical with S'ambhala, while Occultism places it in the Himalayas. It is pronounced *Shambhala*.

**Sambhogakâya** (*Sk.*). One of the three "Vestures" of glory, or bodies, obtained by ascetics on the "Path". Some sects hold it as the second, while others as the third of the *Buddhahshêtras*; or forms of Buddha. Lit., the "Body of Compensation" (See *Voice of the Silence*, Glossary iii). Of such *Buddhakshêtras* there are seven, those of Nirmanakâya, Sambhogakáya and Dharmakâya, belonging to the *Trikâya*, or three-fold quality.

**Samgha** (*Sk.*). The corporate assembly, or a quorum of priests; called also Bhikshu Samgha; the word "church" used in translation does not at all express the real meaning.

**Samkhara** (*Pali*). One of the five Shandhas or attributes in Buddhism.

**Samkhara** (*Pali*). "Tendencies of mind" (See "Skandhas").

**Samma Sambuddha** (*Pali*). The recollection of all of one's past incarnations; a yoga phenomenon.

**Samma Sambudha** (*Pali*). A title of the Lord Buddha, the "Lord of meekness and resignation"; it means "perfect illumination".

**Samothrace** (*Gr.*). An island famous for its Mysteries, perhaps the oldest ever established in our present race. The Samothracian Mysteries were renowned all over the world.

**Samothraces** (*Gr.*). A designation of the Five gods worshipped at the island of that name during the Mysteries. They are considered as identical with the Cabeiri, Dioscuri and Corybantes. Their names were mystical, denoting Pluto, Ceres or Proserpine, Bacchus and Æsculapius, or Hermes.

**Sampajnâna** (*Sk.*). A power of internal illumination.

**Samskâra** (*Sk.*). Lit., from *Sam* and *Krî*, to improve, refine, impress. In Hindu philosophy the term is used to denote the impressions left upon the mind by individual actions or external circumstances, and capable of being developed on any future favourable occasion—even in a future birth. The *Samskâra* denotes, therefore, the germs of propensities and impulses from previous births to be developed in this, or the coming *janmâs* or reincarnations. In Tibet, Samskâra is called Doodyed, and in China is defined as, or at least connected with, action or Karma. It is, strictly speaking, a metaphysical term, which in exoteric philosophies is variously defined; *e.g.*, in Nepaul as illusion, in Tibet as notion, and in Ceylon as discrimination. The true meaning is as given above, and as such is connected with Karma and its working.

**Samtan** (*Tib.*). The same as Dhyâna or meditation.

**Samvara** *(Sk.)*. A deity worshipped by the Tantrikas.

**Samvarta** *(Sk.)*. A minor Kalpa. A period in creation after which a partial annihilation of the world occurs.

**Samvartta Kalpa** *(Sk.)*. The Kalpa or period of destruction, the same as *Pralaya*. Every root-race and sub-race is subject to such Kalpas of destruction; the fifth root-race having sixty-four such Cataclysms periodically; namely: fifty-six by fire, seven by water, and one small Kalpa by winds or cyclones.

**Samvat** *(Sk.)*. The name of an Indian chronological era, supposed to have commenced fifty-seven years B.C.

**Samvriti** *(Sk.)*. False conception—the origin of illusion.

**Samvritisatya** *(Sk.)*. Truth mixed with false conceptions (Samvriti); the reverse of absolute truth—or *Paramârthasatya,* self-consciousness in absolute truth or reality.

**Samyagâjiva** *(Sk.)*. Mendicancy for religious purposes: the correct profession. It is the fourth Mârga (path), the vow of poverty, obligatory on every Arhat and monk.

**Samyagdrishti** *(Sk.)*. The ability to discuss truth. The first of the eight Mârga (paths) of the ascetic.

**Samyakkarmânta** *(Sk.)*. The last of the eight Mârgas. Strict purity and observance of honesty, disinterestedness and unselfishness, the characteristic of every Arhat.

**Samyaksamâdhi** *(Sk.)*. Absolute mental coma. The sixth of the eight Mârgas; the full attainment of Samâdhi.

**Samyaksambuddha** *(Sk.)* or *Sammâsambuddha* as pronounced in Ceylon. Lit., the Buddha of correct and harmonious knowledge, and the third of the ten titles of Sâkyamuni.

**Samyattaka Nikaya** *(Pali)*. A Buddhist work composed mostly of dialogues between Buddha and his disciples.

**Sana** *(Sk.)*. One of the three *esoteric* Kumâras, whose names are Sana, Kapila and Sanatsujâta, the mysterious triad which contains the mystery of generation and reincarnation.

**Sana** or *Sanaischara* *(Sk.)*. The same as Sani or Saturn the planet. In the Hindu Pantheon he is the son of Surya, the Sun, and of Sanjna, Spiritual Consciousness, who is the daughter of Visva-Karman, or rather of Chhâyâ the shadow left behind by Sanjna. Sanaischara, the "slow-moving ".

**Sanaka** (*Sk.*). A sacred plant, the fibres of which are woven into yellow robes for Buddhist priests.

**Sanat Kumâra** (*Sk.*). The most prominent of the seven Kumâras, the Vaidhâtra the first of which are called Sanaka, Sananda, Sanâtana and Sanat Kumâra; which names are all significant qualifications of the degrees of human intellect.

**Sanat Sujâtîya** (*Sk.*). A work treating of Krishna's teachings, such as in *Bhagavad Gitâ* and *Anugîta*.

**Sancha-Dwîpa** (*Sk.*). One of the seven great islands *Sapta-Dwîpa*.

**Sanchoniathon** (*Gr.*). A pre-christian writer on Phœnician Cosmogony, whose works are no longer extant. Philo Byblus gives only the so-called fragments of Sanchoniathon.

**Sandalphon** (*Heb.*). The Kabbalistic Prince of Angels, emblematically represented by one of the *Cherubim* of the Ark.

**Sandhyâ** (*Sk.*). A period between two Yugas, morning-evening; anything coming between and joining two others. Lit., "twilight"; the period between a full Manvantara, or a "Day ", and a full Pralaya or a "Night of Brahmâ".

**Sandhyâmsa** (*Sk.*). A period following a Yuga.

**Sanghai Dag-po** (*Tib.*). The "concealed Lord"; a title of those who have merged into, and identified themselves with, the Absolute. Used of the "Nirvânees" and the "Jîvanmuktas".

**Sangye Khado** (*Sk.*). The Queen of the *Khado* or female genii; the *Dâkini* of the Hindus and the *Lilith* of the Hebrews.

**Sanjnâ** (*Sk.*). Spiritual Consciousness. The wife of Surya, the Sun.

**Sankara** (*Sk.*). The name of Siva. Also a great Vedantic philosopher.

**Sânkhya** (*Sk.*). The system of philosophy founded by Kapila Rishi, a system of analytical metaphysics, and one of the six *Darshanas* or schools of philosophy. It discourses on numerical categories and the meaning of the twenty-five *tatwas* (the forces of nature in various degrees). This "atomistic school", as some call it, explains nature by the interaction of twenty-four elements with *purusha* (spirit) modified by the three gunas (qualities), teaching the eternity of *pradhâna* (primordial, homogeneous matter), or the self-transformation of nature and the eternity of the human Egos.

**Sânkhya Kârikâ** (*Sk.*). A work by Kapila, containing his aphorisms.

**Sânkhya Yoga** (*Sk.*). The system of Yoga as set forth by the above school.

**Sanna** (*Pali*). One of the five Skandhas, namely the attribute of abstract ideas.

**Sannyâsi** (*Sk.*). A Hindu ascetic who has reached the highest mystic knowledge; whose mind is fixed only upon the supreme truth, and who has entirely renounced everything terrestrial and worldly.

**Sansâra** (*Sk.*). Lit., "rotation"; the ocean of births and deaths. Human rebirths represented as a continuous circle, a wheel ever in motion.

**Sanskrit** (*Sk.*). The classical language of the Brahmans, never known *nor spoken in its true systematized form* (given later *approximately* by Pânini), except by the initiated Brahmans, as it was pre-eminently "a mystery language". It has now degenerated into the so-called Prâkrita.

**Santa** (*Sk.*). Lit., "placidity". The primeval quality of the latent, undifferentiated state of elementary matter.

**Santatih** (*Sk.*). The "offspring."

**Saphar** (*Heb.*). Sepharim; one of those called in the *Kabbalah—Sepher, Saphar and Sipur*, or "Number, Numbers and Numbered", by whose agency the world was formed.

**Sapta** (*Sk.*). Seven.

**Sapta Buddhaka** (*Sk.*). An account in *Mahânidâna Sûtra* of *Sapta Buddha*, the seven Buddhas of our Round, of which Gautama Sâkyamuni is esoterically the fifth, and exoterically, as a blind, the seventh.

**Sapta Samudra** (*Sk.*). The "seven oceans". These have an occult significance on a higher plane.

**Sapta Sindhava** (*Sk.*). The "seven sacred rivers". A Vedic term. In Zend works they are called *Hapta Heando*. These rivers are closely united with the esoteric teachings of the Eastern schools, having a very occult significance.

**Sapta Tathâgata** (*Sk.*). The chief seven *Nirmânakâyas* among the numberless ancient world-guardians. Their names are inscribed on a heptagonal pillar kept in a secret chamber in almost all Buddhist temples in China and Tibet. The Orientalists are wrong in thinking that these are "the seven Buddhist substitutes for the Rishis of the Brahmans." (See "Tathâgata-gupta").

**Saptadwîpa** (*Sk.*). The seven sacred islands or "continents" in the *Purânas*.

**Saptaloka** (*Sk.*). The seven higher regions, beginning from the earth upwards.

**Saptaparna** (*Sk.*). The "sevenfold". A plant which gave its name to a famous cave, a *Vihâra*, in Râjâgriha, now near Buddhagaya, where the Lord Buddha used to meditate and teach his Arhats, and where after his death the first Synod was held. This cave had seven chambers, whence the name. In Esotericism *Saptaparna* is the symbol of the "seven fold Man-Plant".

**Saptarshi** (*Sk.*). The seven Rishis. As stars they are the constellation of 'the Great Bear, and called as such the *Riksha* and *Chitrasikhandinas,* bright-crested.

**Sar** or Saros (*Chald.*). A Chaldean god from whose name, represented by a circular horizon, the Greeks borrowed their word *Saros*, the cycle.

**Saramâ** (*Sk.*). In the *Vedas*, the dog of Indra and mother of the two dogs called *Sârameyas. Saramâ* is the "divine watchman" of the god and the same as he who watched "over the golden flock of stars and solar rays"; the same as Mercury, the planet, and the Greek Hermes, called *Sârameyas*.

**Saraph** (*Heb.*). A flying serpent.

**Sarasvati** (*Sk.*). The same as Vâch, wife and daughter of Brahmâ produced from one of the two halves of his body. She is the goddess of speech and of sacred or esoteric knowledge and wisdom. Also called *Sri*.

**Sarcophagus** (*Gr.*). A stone tomb, a receptacle for the dead; *sarc* = flesh, and *phagein* = to eat. *Lapis assius,* the stone of which the sarcophagi were made, is found in Lycia, and has the property of consuming the bodies in a very few weeks. In Egypt sarcophagi were made of various other stones, of black basalt, red granite, alabaster and other materials, as they served only as outward receptacles for the wooden coffins containing the mummies. The epitaphs on some of them are as remarkable as they are highly ethical, and no Christian could wish for anything better. One epitaph, dating thousands of years before the year one of our modern era, reads:—" I have given water to him who was thirsty, and clothing to him who was naked. I have done harm to no man." Another: "I have done actions desired by men and those which are commanded by the gods". The beauty of some of these tombs may be judged by the alabaster sarcophagus of Oimenephthah I., at Sir John Soane's Museum, Lincoln's Inn. "It was cut out of a single block of fine alabaster stone, and is 9 ft. 4 in.. long, by 22 to 24 in. in width, and 27 to 32 in. in height. . . . Engraved dots, etc., outside were once filled with blue copper to represent the heavens. To attempt a description of the wonderful figures inside and out is beyond the scope of this work. Much of our knowledge of the mythology of the people is derived from this precious monument, with its hundreds of figures to illustrate the last judgment, and the life beyond the grave. Gods, men, serpents, symbolical animals and plants are there most beautifully carved." (*Funeral Rites of the Egyptians.*)

**Sargon** (*Chald.*). A Babylonian king. The story is now found to have been the original of Moses and the ark of bulrushes in the Nile.

**Sarîra** (*Sk.*). Envelope or body.

**Sarisripa** (*Sk.*). Serpents, crawling insects, reptiles, "the infinitesimally small".

**Sarku** (*Chald.*). Lit., the light race; that of the gods in contradistinction to the dark race called *zahmat gagnadi*, or the race that fell, i.e., mortal men.

**Sarpas** (*Sk.*). Serpents, whose king was Sesha, the serpent, or rather an aspect of Vishnu, who reigned in Pâtâla.

**Sârpa-rajnî** (*Sk.*). The queen of the serpents in the *Brâhmanas*.

**Sarva Mandala** (*Sk.*) A name for the "Egg of Brahmâ".

**Sarvada** (*Sk.*). Lit., "all-sacrificing" A title of Buddha, who in a former Jataha (birth) sacrificed his kingdom, liberty, and even life, to save others.

**Sarvaga** (*Sk.*). The supreme "World-Substance".

**Sarvâtmâ** (*Sk.*). The supreme Soul; the all-pervading Spirit.

**Sarvêsha** (*Sk.*). Supreme Being. Controller of every action and force in the universe.

**Sat** (*Sk.*). The one ever-present Reality in the infinite world; the divine essence which is, but cannot be said to exist, as it is Absoluteness, Be-ness itself.

**Sata rûpa** (*Sk.*). The "hundred-formed one"; applied to Vâch, who to be the female Brahmâ assumes a hundred forms, i.e., Nature.

**Sati** (*Eg.*). The triadic goddess, with Anouki of the Egyptian god Khnoum.

**Sattâ** (*Sk.*). The "one and sole Existence"—Brahma (neut.).

**Satti** or *Suttee*, (*Sk.*). The burning of living widows together with their dead husbands—a custom now happily abolished in India; lit., "a chaste and devoted wife".

**Sattva** (*Sk.*). Understanding; quiescence in divine knowledge. It follows 'generally the word *Bodhi* when used as a compound word, e.g., "Bodhisattva".

**Sattva** or *Satwa*, (*Sk.*). Goodness; the same as Sattva, or purity, one of the trigunas or three divisions of nature.

**Satya** (*Sk.*). Supreme truth.

**Satya Loka** (*Sk.*). The world of infinite purity and wisdom, the celestial abode of Brahmâ and the gods.

**Satya Yuga** (*Sk.*). The golden age, or the age of truth and purity; the first of the four Yugas, also called Krita Yuga.

**Satyas** (*Sk.*). One of the names of the twelve great gods.

**Scarabæus**, In Egypt, the symbol of resurrection, and also of rebirth; of resurrection for the mummy or rather of the highest aspects of the *personality* which animated it, and of rebirth for the Ego, the "spiritual body" of the lower, human Soul. Egyptologists give us but half of the truth, when in speculating upon the meaning of certain inscriptions, they say, "the justified soul, once arrived at a certain period of its peregrinations (simply at the death of the physical body) should be united to its body (*i.e.*, the Ego) never more *to be separated from it* ". (Rougé.) What is this so-called body? Can it be the mummy? Certainly not, for the emptied mummified corpse can never resurrect. It can only be the eternal, spiritual vestment, the EGO that never dies but gives immortality to whatsoever becomes united with it. "The delivered Intelligence (which) retakes its luminous envelope and (re)becomes Daïmon", as Prof. Maspero says, is the *spiritual* Ego; the *personal* Ego or *Kâma Manas*, its direct ray, or the lower soul, is that which aspires to become *Osirified*, i.e., to unite itself with its "god"; and that portion of it which will succeed in so doing, will never more be separated from it (the god), not even when the latter incarnates again and again, descending periodically on earth in its pilgrimage, in search of further experiences and following the decrees of Karma. Khem, "the sower of seed", is shown on a stele in a picture of Resurrection after physical death, as the creator and the sower of the grain of corn, which, after corruption, springs up afresh each time into a new ear, on which a scarab beetle is seen poised; and Deveria shows very justly that "Ptah is the inert, material form of Osiris, who will become Sokari (the eternal Ego) to be reborn, and afterwards be Harmachus", or Horus in his transformation, the *risen* god. The prayer so often found in the tumular inscriptions, "the wish for the resurrection in one's *living* soul" or the Higher Ego, has ever a scarabæus at the end, standing for the personal soul. The scarabæus is the most honoured, as the most frequent and familiar, of all Egyptian symbols. No mummy is without several of them; the favourite ornament on engravings, house hold furniture and utensils is this sacred beetle, and Pierret pertinently shows in his *Livre des Morts* that the secret meaning of this hieroglyph is sufficiently explained in that the Egyptian name for the scarabæus *Kheper* signifies to *be*, to *become*, to *build again*.

**Scheo** (*Eg.*). The god who, conjointly with Tefnant and Seb, inhabits Aanroo, the region called "the land of the rebirth of the gods".

**Schesoo-Hor** (*Eg.*). Lit., the servants of Horus; the early people who settled in Egypt and who were Aryans.

**Schools of the Prophets.** Schools established by Samuel for the training of the *Nabiim* (prophets). Their method was pursued on the same lines as that of a Chela or candidate for initiation into the occult sciences, i.e., the development of abnormal faculties or clairvoyance leading to Seership. Of such schools there were many in days of old in Palestine and Asia Minor. That the Hebrews worshipped Nebo, the Chaldean god of secret learning, is quite certain, since they adopted his name as an equivalent of Wisdom.

**Séance.** A word which has come to mean with Theosophists and Spiritualists a sitting with a medium for phenomena, the materialisation of "spirits" and other manifestations.

**Seb** (*Eg.*). The Egyptian Saturn; the father of Osiris and Isis. Esoterically, the sole principle before creation, nearer in meaning to Parabrahm than Brahmâ. From as early as the second Dynasty, there were records of him, and statues of Seb are to be seen in the museums represented with the goose or black swan that laid the egg of the world on his head. Nout or Neith, the "Great Mother" and yet the "Immaculate Virgin", is Seb's wife; she is the oldest goddess on record, and is to be found on monuments of the first dynasty, to which Mariette Bey assigns the date of almost 7000 years B.C.

**Secret Doctrine.** The general name given to the esoteric teachings of antiquity.

**Sedecla** (*Heb.*). The Obeah woman of Endor.

**Seer.** One who is a clairvoyant; who can see things visible, and invisible— for others—at any distance and time with his spiritual or inner sight or perceptions.

**Seir Anpin,** or *Zauir Anpin (Heb.*). In the *Kabbalah,* "the Son of the concealed Father", he who unites in himself all the Sephiroth. Adam Kadmon, or the first manifested "Heavenly Man", the Logos.

**Sekhem** (*Eg.*). The same as Sekten.

**Sekhet** (*Eg.*). See "Pasht".

**Sekten** (Eg.). Dêvâchân; the place of post mortem reward, a state of bliss, not a locality.

**Senâ** (*Sk.*). The female aspect or Sakti of Kârttikeya; also called Kaumâra.

**Senses**. The ten organs of man. In the exoteric Pantheon and the allegories of the. East, these are the emanations of ten minor gods, the terrestrial Prajâpati or "progenitors". They are called in contradistinction to the five physical and the seven superphysical, the "elementary senses". In Occultism they are closely allied with various forces of nature, and with our *inner* organisms, called cells in physiology.

**Senzar**. The mystic name for the secret sacerdotal language or the "Mystery-speech" of the initiated Adepts, all over the world.

**Sepher Sephiroth** (*Heb.*). A Kabbalistic treatise concerning the gradual evolution of Deity from negative repose to active emanation and creation. [w.w.w.]

**Sepher Yetzirah** (*Heb.*). "The Book of Formation". A very ancient Kabbalistic work ascribed to the patriarch Abraham. It illustrates the creation of the universe by analogy with the twenty-two letters of the Hebrew alphabet, distributed into a triad,, a heptad, and a dodecad, corresponding with the-three mother letters, A, M, S, the seven planets, and the twelve signs of the Zodiac. It is written in the Neo-Hebraic of the *Mishnah.* [w.w.w.]

**Sephira** (*Heb.*) An emanation of Deity; the parent and synthesis of the ten Sephiroth when she stands at the head of the Sephirothal Tree; in the Kabbalah, Sephira,or the "Sacred Aged", is the divine Intelligence (the same as Sophia or Metis), the first emanation from the "Endless" or Ain-Suph.

**Sephiroth** (*Heb.*). The ten emanations of Deity; the highest is formed by the concentration of the Ain Soph Aur, or the Limitless Light, and each: Sephira produces by emanation another Sephira. The names of the Ten Sephiroth are—1. Kether—The Crown; 2. Chokmah—Wisdom; 3. Binah—Understanding; 4. Chesed-—Mercy; 5. Geburah—Power; 6. Tiphereth—Beauty; 7. Netzach—Victory; 8. Hod—Splendour; 9. Jesod_Foundation; and 10. Malkuth—The Kingdom.

The conception of Deity embodied in the Ten Sephiroth is a very sublime one, and each Sephira is a picture to the Kabbalist of a group of exalted ideas, titles and attributes, which the name but faintly represents. Each Sephira is called either active or passive, though this attribution may lead to error; passive does not mean a return to negative existence; and the two words only express the relation between individual Sephiroth, and not any absolute quality. [w.w.w.]

**Septerium** (*Lat.*) A great religious festival held in days of old every ninth year at Delphi, in honour of Helios, the Sun, or Apollo, to commemorate his triumph over darkness, or Python; Apollo-Python being the same as Osiris-Typhon in Egypt.

**Seraphim** (*Heb.*). Celestial beings described by Isaiah (vi., 2,) as of human form with the addition of three pair of wings. The Hebrew word is ShRPIM, and apart from the above instance, is translated serpents, and is related to the verbal root ShRP, *to burn up* . The word is used for serpents in *Numbers* and *Deuteronomy*. Moses is said to have raised in the wilderness a ShRP or Seraph of Brass as a type. This bright serpent is also used as an emblem of Light. Compare the myth of Æsculapius, the healing deity, who is said to have been brought to Rome from Epidaurus as a serpent, and whose statues show him holding a wand on which a snake is twisted. (See Ovid, *Metam.*, lib. xv.). The Seraphim of the *Old Testament* seem to be related to the Cherubim (*q.v.*). In the *Kabbalah* the Seraphim are a group of angelic powers allotted to the Sephira Geburah—Severity. [w.w.w.]

**Serapis** (*Eg.*). A great solar god who replaced Osiris in the popular worship, and in whose honour the seven vowels were sung. He was often made to appear in his representations as a serpent, a "Dragon of Wisdom ". The greatest god of Egypt during the first centuries of Christianity.

**Sesha** (*Sk.*) *Ananta*, the great Serpent of Eternity, the couch of Vishnu; the symbol of infinite Time in Space. In the exoteric beliefs Sesha is represented as a *thousand*-headed and *seven*-headed cobra; the former the king of the nether world, called Pâtâla, the latter the carrier or support of Vishnu on the Ocean of Space.

**Set** or *Seth* (*Eg.*). The same as the Son of Noah and Typhon—who is the dark side of Osiris. The same as Thoth and Satan, the adversary, not the devil represented by Christians.

**Sevekh** (*Eg.*). The god of time; Chronos; the same as *Sefekh*. Some Orientalists translate it as the "Seventh".

**Shaberon** (*Tib.*). The Mongolian Shaberon or Khubilgan (or Khubilkhans) are the reincarnations of Buddha, according to the Lamaists; great Saints and *Avatars*, so to say.

**Shaddai**, *El* (*Heb.*). A name of the Hebrew Deity, usually translated God Almighty, found in *Genesis, Exodus, Numbers, Ruth* and *Job*. Its Greek equivalent is Kurios Pantokrator; but by Hebrew derivation it means rather "the pourer forth", *shad* meaning a breast, and indeed *shdi* is also used for "a nursing mother". [w.w.w.]

**Shamans**. An order of Tartar or Mongolian priest-magicians, or as some say, priest-sorcerers. They are not Buddhists, but a sect of the old Bhon religion of Tibet. They live mostly in Siberia and its borderlands. Both men and women may be Shamans. They are all magicians, or rather sensitives or mediums artificially developed. At present those who act as priests among the Tartars are generally very ignorant, and far below the fakirs in knowledge and education.

**Shânâh** (*Heb*). The Lunar Year.

**Shangna** (*Sk*.). A mysterious epithet given to a robe or "vesture in a metaphorical sense". To put on the "Shangna robe" means the acquirement of Secret Wisdom, and Initiation. (See *Voice of the Silence,* pp. 84 and 85, Glossary.)

**Shâstra** or *S'âstra* (*Sk*.). A treatise or book; any work of divine or accepted authority, including law books. A Shâstri means to this day, in India, a man learned in divine and human law.

**Shedim** (*Heb*.). See "Siddim ".

**Shekinah** (*Heb*.). A title applied to Malkuth, the tenth Sephira, by the Kabbalists; but by the Jews to the cloud of glory which rested on the Mercy-seat in the Holy of Holies. As taught, however, by all the Rabbins of Asia Minor, its nature is of a more exalted kind, Shekinah being the veil of Ain-Soph, the Endless and the Absolute; hence a kind of Kabbalistic Mûlaprakriti. [w.w.w.]

**Shells.** A Kabbalistic name for the phantoms of the dead, the "spirits" of the Spiritualists, figuring in physical phenomena; so named on account of their being simply illusive forms, empty of their higher principles.

**Shemal** (*Chald*.). Samâel, the spirit of the earth, its presiding ruler and genius.

**Shemhamphorash** (*Heb*.). The separated name. The mirific name derived from the substance of deity and showing its self-existent essence. Jesus was accused by the Jews of having stolen this name from the Temple by magic arts, and of using it in the production of his miracles.

**Sheol** (*Heb*.). The hell of the Hebrew Pantheon; a region of stillness and inactivity as distinguished from Gehenna, (*q.v.*).

**Shien-Sien** (Chin.). A state of bliss and soul-freedom, during which a man can travel in spirit where he likes.

**Shiites** (*Pers.*). A sect of Mussulmen who place the prophet **Ali** higher than Mohammed, rejecting Sunnah or tradition.

**Shîla** (*Pali*). The second virtue of the ten Pâramitâs of perfection. Perfect harmony in words and acts.

**Shinto** (*Jap.*). The ancient religion of Japan before Buddhism, based upon the worship of spirits and ancestors.

**Shoel-ob** (*Heb.*). A consulter with familiar "spirits"; a necromancer, a raiser of the dead, or of their phantoms.

**Shoo** (*Eg.*). A personification of the god Ra; represented as the "great cat of the Basin of Persea in Anu".

**Shûdâla Mâdan** (*Tam.*) The vampire, the ghoul, or graveyard spook.

**Shûle Mâdan** (*Tam.*). The elemental which is said to help the "jugglers" to grow mango trees and do other wonders.

**Shutukt** (*Tib.*). A collegiate monastery in Tibet of great fame, containing over 30,000 monks and students.

**Sibac** (*Quiché*). The reed from the pith of which the third race of men was created, according to the scripture of the Guatemalians, called the *Popol Vuh.*

**Sibikâ** (*Sk.*). The weapon of Kuvera, god of wealth (a Vedic deity living in Hades, hence a kind of Pluto), made out of the parts of the divine splendour of Vishnu, residing in the Sun, and filed off by Visvarkarman, the god Initiate.

**Siddhânta** (*Sk.*). Any learned work on astronomy or mathematics, in India.

**Siddhârtha** (*Sk.*). A name given to Gautama Buddha.

**Siddhas** (*Sk.*). Saints and sages who have become almost divine also a hierarchy of Dhyan Chohans.

**Siddhâsana** (*Sk.*). A posture in Hatha-yoga practices.

**Siddha-Sena** (*Sk.*). Lit., "the leader of Siddhas"; a title of Kârttikeya, the "mysterious youth" (*kumâra guha*).

**Siddhis** (*Sk.*). Lit., "attributes of perfection"; phenomenal powers acquired through holiness by Yogis.

**Siddim** (*Heb.*). The Canaanites, we are told, worshipped these evil powers as deities, the name meaning the "pourers forth"; a valley was named after them. There seems to be a connection between these, as types of Fertile Nature, and the many-bosomed Isis and Diana of Ephesus. In Psalm cvi.,

37, the word is translated "devils ", and we are told that the Canaanites shed the blood of their sons and daughters to them. Their title seems to come from the same root ShD, from which the god name El Shaddai is derived. [w.w.w.]

The Arabic Shedim means "Nature Spirits ", Elementals; they are the *afrits* of modern Egypt and *djins* of Persia,.India, etc.

**Sidereal.** Anything relating to the stars, but also, in Occultism, to various influences emanating from such regions, such as "sidereal force ", as taught by Paracelsus, and sidereal (luminous), ethereal body, etc.

**Si-dzang** (*Chin.*). The Chinese name for Tibet; mentioned in the Imperial Library of the capital of Fo Kien, as the "great seat of Occult learning", 2,207 years B.C. (*S. D.*, Vol. I, p. 271.)

**Sige** (*Gr.*). "Silence"; a name adopted by the Gnostics to signify the root whence proceed the Æons of the second series.

**Sighra** or *Sighraga* (*Sk.*). The father of *Moru*, "who is still living through the power of Yoga, and will manifest himself in the beginning of the *Krita* age in order to re-establish the *Kshattriyas* in the nineteenth Yuga" say the Purânic prophecies. "Moru" stands here for "Morya ", the dynasty of the Buddhist sovereigns of Pataliputra which began with the great King Chandragupta, the grandsire of King Asoka. It is the first Buddhist Dynasty. (*S. D.*, Vol. I, p. 378.)

**Sigurd** (*Scand.*). The hero who slew Fafnir, the "Dragon", roasted his heart and ate it, after which he became the wisest of men. An allegory referring to Occult study and initiation.

**Simeon-ben-Jochai.** An Adept-Rabbin, who was the author of the *Zohar,* (*q.v.*).

**Simon Magus.** A very great Samaritan Gnostic and Thaumaturgist, called "the great Power of God".

**Simorgh** (*Pers.*). The same as the winged Siorgh, a kind of gigantic griffin, half phœnix, half lion, endowed in the Iranian legends with oracular powers. Simorgh was the guardian of the ancient Persian Mysteries. It is expected to reappear at the end of the cycle as a gigantic bird-lion. Esoterically, it stands as the symbol of the Manvantaric cycle. Its Arabic name is *Rahshi*.

**Sinaï** (*Heb.*). Mount Sinaï, the Nissi of *Exodus* (xvii., ii), the birth place of almost all the solar gods of antiquity, such as Dionysus, born at Nissa or Nysa, Zeus of Nysa, Bacchus and Osiris, (*q.v.*). Some ancient people believed the Sun to be the progeny of the Moon, who was herself a Sun once upon a time. *Sin-aï* is the "Moon Mountain ", hence the connexion.

**Sing Bonga**. The Sun-spirit with the Kollarian tribes.

**Singha** (*Sk.*). The constellation of Leo; *Singh* meaning "lion".

**Sinika** (*Sk.*). Also Sinita and Sanika, etc., as variants. The Vishnu *Purâna* gives it as the name of a future sage who will be taught by him who will become Maitreya, at the end of Kali Yuga, and adds that this is a great mystery.

**Sinîvâlî** (*Sk.*). The first day of the new moon, which is greatly connected with Occult practices in India.

**Siphra Dtzeniouta** (*Chald.*). The Book of Concealed Mystery; one division of the *Zohar*. (See Mathers' *Kabbalah Unveiled.*)

**Sirius** (*Gr.*). In Egyptian, *Sothis*. The dog-star: the star worshipped in Egypt and reverenced by the Occultists; by the former because its heliacal rising with the Sun was a sign of the beneficent inundation of the Nile, and by the latter because it is mysteriously associated with Thoth-Hermes, god of wisdom, and Mercury, in another form. Thus Sothis-Sirius had, and still has, a mystic and direct influence over the whole *living* heaven, and is connected with almost every god and goddess. It was "Isis in the heaven "and called *Isis-Sothis*, for Isis was "in the constellation of the dog ", as is declared on her monuments. "The soul of Osiris was believed to reside in a personage who walks with great steps in front of *Sothis,* sceptre in hand and a whip upon his shoulder." Sirius is also Anuhis, and is directly connected with the ring "Pass me not"; it is, moreover, identical with Mithra, the Persian Mystery god, and with Horus and even Hathor, called sometimes the goddess Sothis. Being connected with the Pyramid, Sirius was, therefore, connected with the initiations which took place in it. A temple to Sirius-Sothis once existed within the great temple of Denderah. To sum up, all religions are not, as Dufeu, the French Egyptologist, sought to prove, derived from Sirius, the dog-star, but Sirius-Sothis is certainly found in connection with every religion of antiquity.

**Sishta** (*Sk.*). The great elect or Sages, left after every minor *Pralaya* (that which is called "obscuration" in Mr. Sinnett's *Esoteric Buddhism*), when the globe goes into its night or rest, to become, on its re-awakening, the seed of the next humanity. Lit. "remnant."

**Sisthrus** (*Chald.*). According to Berosus, the last of the ten kings of the dynasty of the divine kings, and the "Noah" of Chaldea. Thus, as Vishnu foretells the coming deluge to Vaivasvata-Manu, and, fore warning, commands him to build an ark, wherein he and seven Rishis are saved; so the god Hea foretells the same to Sisithrus (or Xisuthrus) commanding him to prepare a vessel and save himself with a few elect. Following suit, almost 800,000 years later, the Lord God of Israel repeats the warning to Noah. Which is prior, therefore? The story of Xisuthrus, now deciphered from the Assyrian tablets, corroborates that which was said of the Chaldean deluge by Berosus, Apollodorus, Abydenus, etc., etc. (See eleventh tablet in G. Smith's *Chaldean Account of Genesis,* page 263, *et seq.*). This tablet xi. covers every point treated of in chapters six and seven of Genesis—the gods, the sins of men, the command to build an ark, the Flood, the destruction of men, the dove and the raven sent out of the ark, and finally the Mount of Salvation in Armenia (Nizi r-Ararat); all is there. The words "the god Hea heard, and his liver was angry, because his men had corrupted his purity", and the story of his destroying all his seed, were engraved on stone tablets many thousand years before the Assyrians reproduced them on their baked tiles, and even these most assuredly antedate the Pentateuch, "written from memory" by Ezra, hardly four centuries B.C.

**Sistrum** (*Gr.*). Egyptian *ssesh* or *kemken*. An instrument, usually made of bronze but sometimes of gold or silver, of an open circular form, with a handle, and four wires passed through holes, to the end of which jingling pieces of metal were attached; its top was ornamented with a figure of Isis, or of Hathor. It was a sacred instrument, used in temples for the purpose of producing, by means of its combination of *metals, magnetic currents, and sounds.* To this day it has survived in Christian Abyssinia, under the name of *sanasel,* and the good priests use it to "drive devils from the premises", an act quite comprehensible to the Occultist, even though it does provoke laughter in the sceptical Orientalist. The priestess usually held it in her right hand during the ceremony of *purification of the air,* or the "conjuration of the elements", as E. Lévi would call it, while the priests held the Sistrurn in their left hand, using the right to manipulate the "key of life"—the handled cross or Tau.

**Sisumara** (*Sk.*). An imaginary rotating belt, upon which all the celestial bodies move. This host of stars and constellations is represented under the figure of *Sisumara,* a tortoise (some say a *porpoise* !), dragon, crocodile, and what not. But as it is a symbol of the Yoga-meditation of holy Vasudeva or Krishna, it must be a crocodile, or rather, a dolphin, since it is identical with the zodiacal Makâra. Dhruva, the ancient pole-star, is placed at the tip of the tail of this sidereal monster, whose head points southward and whose body bends in a ring. Higher along the tail are the Prajâpati Agni, etc., and at its root are placed Indra, Dharma, and the seven Rishis (the Great Bear), etc., etc. The meaning is of course mystical.

**Siva** (*Sk.*). The third person of the Hindu Trinity (the Trimûrti). He is a god of the first order, and in his character of Destroyer higher than Vishnu, the Preserver, as he destroys only to regenerate on a higher plane. He is born as Rudra, the Kumâra, and is the patron of all the Yogis, being called, as such, Mahâdeva the great ascetic, His titles are significant *Trilochana*, "the three-eyed", *Mahâdeva*, "the great god ", *Sankara*, etc., etc., etc.

**Siva-Rudra** (*Sk.*). Rudra is the Vedic name of Siva, the latter being absent from the Veda.

**Skandha** or *Skhanda* (*Sk.*). Lit., "bundles", or groups of attributes; everything finite, inapplicable to the eternal and the absolute. There are five—esoterically, *seven*—attributes in every human living being, which are known as the *Pancha Shandhas*. These are (1) form, *rûpa*; (2) perception, *vidâna*; (3) consciousness, *sanjnâ*; (4) action, *sanskâra*; (5) knowledge, *vidyâna*. These unite at the birth of man and constitute his personality. After the maturity of these Skandhas, they begin to separate and weaken, and this is followed by *jarâmarana*, or decrepitude and death.

**Skrymir** (*Scand.*). One of the famous giants in the *Eddas*.

**Sloka**, (*Sk.*). The Sanskrit epic metre formed of thirty-two syllables: verses in four half-lines of eight, or in two lines of sixteen syllables each.

**Smaragdine Tablet of Hermes**. As expressed by Eliphas Lévi,"this Tablet of Emerald is the whole of magic in a single page"; but India has a single word which, when understood, contains "the whole of magic". This is a tablet, however, alleged to have been found by Sarai, Abraham's wife (!) *on the dead body of Hermes*. So say the Masons and Christian Kabbalists. But in Theosophy we call it an allegory. May it not mean that *Sarai-swati*, the wife of Brahmâ, or the goddess of secret wisdom and learning, finding still much of the ancient wisdom latent in the dead body of Humanity, revivified that wisdom? This led to the rebirth of the Occult Sciences, so long forgotten and neglected, the world over. The tablet itself, however, although containing the "whole of magic", is too long to be reproduced here.

**Smârtava** (*Sk.*). The Smârta Brahmans; a sect founded by Sankarâchârya.

**Smriti** (*Sk.*). Traditional accounts imparted orally, from the word *Smriti*, "Memory" a daughter of Daksha. They are now the legal and ceremonial writings of the Hindus; the opposite of, and therefore less sacred, than the

*Vedas*, which are *Sruti,* or "revelation".

**Sod** (*Heb.*). An "Arcanum", or religious mystery. The Mysteries of Baal, Adonis and Bacchus, all sun-gods having serpents as symbols, or, as in the case of Mithra, a "solar serpent". The ancient Jews had their Sod also, symbols not excluded, since they had the "brazen serpent" lifted in the Wilderness, which particular serpent was the Persian Mithra, the symbol of Moses as an Initiate, but was certainly never meant to represent the *historical Christ*. "The secret (Sod) of the Lord is with them that fear him ", says David, in *Psalm* xxv., 14. But this reads in the original Hebrew, "Sod Ihoh (or the Mysteries) of Jehovah are for those who fear him". So terribly is the Old Testament mistranslated, that verse 7 in *Psalm* lxxxix., which stands in the original "Al (El) is terrible in the great *Sod* of the *Kedeshim*" (the *Galli,* the priests of the inner Jewish mysteries), reads now in the mutilated translation "God is greatly to be feared in the assembly of the saints". Simeon and Levi held their *Sod*, and it is repeatedly mentioned in the Bible. "Oh my soul", exclaims the dying Jacob, "come not thou into their secret (Sod, in the orig.), unto their assembly", *i.e..* into the *Sodalily* of Simeon and Levi (*Gen.* xlix., 6). (See Dunlap, *Sôd, the Mysteries of Adoni.*)

**Sodales** (*Lat.*). The members of the Priest-colleges. (See Freund's *Latin Lexicon*, iv., 448.) Cicero tells us also (*De Senectute,* 13) that "*Sodalities* were constituted in the Idæn Mysteries of the MIGHTY MOTHER". Those initiated into the Sod were termed the "Companions".

**Sodalian Oath**. The most sacred of all oaths. The penalty of death followed the breaking of the Sodalian oath or pledge. The oath and the Sod (the secret learning) are earlier than the *Kabbalah* or Tradition, and the ancient *Midrashim* treated fully of the Mysteries or Sod before they passed into the *Zohar.* Now they are referred to as the *Secret Mysteries* of the Thorah, or Law, to break which is fatal.

**Soham** (*Sk.*). A mystic syllable representing *involution*: lit., "THAT I AM".

**Sokaris** (*Eg.*). A fire-god; a solar deity of many forms. He is Ptah Sokaris, when the symbol is purely cosmic, and "Ptah-Sokaris-Osiris" when it is phallic. This deity is hermaphrodite, the sacred bull Apis being its son, conceived in it by a solar ray. According to Smith's *History of the East*, Ptah is a "second Demiurgus, an emanation from the first creative Principle" (the *first* Logos). The upright Ptah, with cross and staff, is the "creator of the eggs of the sun and moon". Pierret thinks that he represents the primordial Force that preceded the gods and "created the stars, and the eggs of the sun and moon". Mariette Bey sees in him "Divine Wisdom scattering the stars in immensity", and he is corroborated by the Targum of Jerusalem, which states that the "Egyptians called the Wisdom of the First Intellect Ptah".

**Sokhit** (*Eg.*). A deity to whom the cat was sacred.

**Solomon's Seal**. The symbolical double triangle, adopted by the T.S. and by many Theosophists. Why it should be called "Solomon's Seal" is a mystery, unless it came to Europe from Iran, where many stories are told about that mythical personage and the magic seal used by him to catch the *djins* and imprison them in old bottles. But this seal or double triangle is also called in India the "Sign of Vishnu ", and may be seen on the houses in every village as a talisman against evil. The triangle was sacred and used as a religious sign in the far East ages before Pythagoras proclaimed it to be the first of the geometrical figures, as well as the most mysterious. it is found on pyramid and obelisk, and is pregnant with occult meaning, as are, in fact, all triangles. Thus the pentagram is the triple triangle—the six-pointed being the *hexalp ha*. (See "Pentacle" and "Pentagram".) The way a triangle points determines its meaning. If upwards, it means the male element and *divine fire;* downwards, the female and the *waters* of matter; upright, but with a bar across the top, *air* and astral light; downwards, with a bar—the earth or gross matter, etc., etc. When a Greek Christian priest in blessing holds his two fingers and thumb together, he simply makes the magic sign—by the power of the *triangle* or "trinity".

**Soma** (*Sk.*). The moon, and also the juice of the plant of that name used in the temples for trance purposes; a sacred beverage. Soma, the moon, is the symbol of the Secret Wisdom. In the *Upanishads* the word is used to denote gross matter (with an association of moisture) capable of producing life under the action of heat. (See "Soma-drink".)

**Soma-drink**. Made from a rare mountain plant by initiated Brahmans. This Hindu sacred beverage answers to the Greek ambrosia or nectar, quaffed by the gods of Olympus. A cup of Kykeôn was also quaffed by the Mystes at the Eleusinian initiation. He who drinks it easily reaches *Bradhna*, or the place of splendour (Heaven). The Soma-drink known to Europeans is not the *genuine* beverage, but its substitute; for the initiated priests alone can taste of the real Soma; and even kings and Rajas, when sacrificing, receive the substitute. Haug, by his own confession, shows in his *Aitareya Brâhmana*, that it was not the Soma that he tasted and found nasty, but the juice from the roots of the Nyagradha, a plant or bush which grows on the hills of Poona. We were positively informed that the majority of the sacrificial priests of the Dekkan have lost the secret of the true Soma.

It can be found neither in the ritual books nor through oral information. The true followers of the primitive Vedic religion are very few; these are the alleged descendants of the Rishis, the real Agnihôtris, the initiates of the great Mysteries. The Soma drink is also commemorated in the Hindu Pantheon, for it is called King-Soma. He who drinks thereof is made to participate in the heavenly king; he becomes filled with his essence, as the Christian apostles and their converts were. filled with the Holy Ghost, and purified of their sins. The Soma makes a new man of the initiate; he is reborn and transformed, and his spiritual nature overcomes the physical; it bestows the divine power of inspiration, and develops the clairvoyant faculty to the utmost. According to the exoteric explanation the soma is a plant, but at the same time it is an angel. It forcibly connects the inner, highest "spirit" of man, which spirit is an angel like the mystical Soma, with his "irrational soul ", or astral body, and thus united by the power of the magic drink, they soar together above physical nature and participate during life in the beatitude and ineffable glories of Heaven, Thus the Hindu Soma is mystically and in all respects the same that the Eucharist supper is to the Christian. The idea is similar. By means of the sacrificial prayers—the mantras—this liquor is supposed to be immediately transformed into the real Soma, or the angel, and even into Brahmâ himself. Some missionaries have expressed themselves with much indignation about this ceremony, the more so, seeing that the Brahmans generally use *a kind of spirituous liquor* as a substitute. But do the Christians believe less fervently in the transubstantiation of the communion wine into the blood of Christ, because this wine happens to be more or less spirituous? Is not the idea of the symbol attached to it the same? But the missionaries say that this hour of soma-drinking is the golden hour of Satan, who lurks at the bottom of the Hindu sacrificial cup. (*Isis Unveiled.*)

**Soma-loka** (*Sk.*). A kind of lunar abode where the god Soma, the regent of the moon, resides. The abode of the Lunar Pitris—or *Pitriloka*.

**Somapa** (*Sk.*). A class of Lunar Pitris. (See "Trisuparna.")

**Somnambulism** Lit., "sleep-walking", or moving, acting, writing, reading and performing every function of waking consciousness in one's sleep, with utter oblivion of the fact on awakening. This is one of the great psycho-physiological phenomena, the least understood as it is the most puzzling, to which Occultism alone holds the key.

**Son-kha-pa** (*Tib.*). Written also *Tsong-kha-pa.* A famous Tibetan reformer of the fourteenth century, who introduced a purified Buddhism into his country. He was a great Adept, who being unable to witness any longer the desecration of Buddhist philosophy by the false priests who made of it a marketable commodity, put a forcible stop thereto by a timely revolution and the exile of 40,000 sham monks and Lamas from the country. He is regarded as an Avatar of Buddha, and is the founder of the *Gelukpa* ("yellow-cap") Sect, and of the mystic Brotherhood connected with its chiefs. The "tree of the 10,000 images" *(khoom boom)* has, it is said, sprung from the long hair of this ascetic, who leaving it behind him disappeared for ever from the view of the profane.

**Sooniam.** A magical ceremony for the purpose of removing a sickness from one person to another. Black magic, sorcery.

**Sophia** *(Gr.)*. Wisdom. The female *Logos* of the Gnostics; the Universal Mind; and the female Holy Ghost with others.

**Sophia Achamoth** *(Gr.)*. The daughter of Sophia. The personified Astral Light, or the lower plane of Ether.

**Sortes Sanctorum** *(Lat.)*. The "holy casting of lots for purposes of divination", practised by the early and mediæval Christian clergy. St. Augustine, who does not "disapprove of this method of learning futurity, provided it be not used for worldly purposes, practised it himself "(*Life of St. Gregory of Tours*). If, however, "it is practised by laymen, heretics, or heathen" of any sort, *sortes sanctorum* become—if we believe the good and pious fathers—*sortes diabolorum or sortilegium*—sorcery.

**Sosiosh** *(Zend)*. The Mazdean Saviour who, like Vishnu, Maitreya Buddha and others, is expected to appear on a white horse at the end of the cycle to save mankind. (See "S'ambhala".)

**Soul.** The yuch, or *nephesh* of the *Bible*; the vital principle, or the breath of life, which every animal, down to the infusoria, shares with man. In the translated Bible it stands indifferently for *life*, blood and soul. "Let us not kill his *nephesh*", says the original text: "let us not kill *him*", translate the Christians (*Genesis* xxxvii. 21), and so on.

**Sowan** *(Pali)*. The first of the "four paths" which lead to Nirvâna, in Yoga practice.

**Sowanee** *(Pali)*. He who entered upon that "path".

**Sparsa** *(Sk)*. The sense of touch.

**Spenta Armaita** *(Zend)*. The female genius of the earth; the "fair daughter of Ahura Mazda". With the Mazdeans, *Spenta Armaita* is the personified Earth.

**Spirit.** The lack of any mutual agreement between writers in the use of this word has resulted in dire confusion. It is commonly made synonymous with *soul*; and the lexicographers countenance the usage. In Theosophical teachings. the term "Spirit" is applied solely to that which *belongs directly to Universal Consciousness*, and which is its homogeneous and unadulterated emanation. Thus, the higher Mind in Man or his Ego (Manas) is, when linked indissolubly with Buddhi, a spirit; while the term "Soul", human or even animal (the lower Manas acting in animals as instinct), is applied only to Kâma-Manas, and qualified as the living soul. This is *nephesh*, in Hebrew, the "breath of life". Spirit is formless and *immaterial*, being, when individualised, of the highest spiritual substance— *Suddasatwa*, the divine essence, of which the body of the manifesting *highest* Dhyanis are formed. Therefore, the Theosophists reject the appellation "Spirits" for those phantoms which appear in the phenomenal manifestations of the Spiritualists, and call them "shells", and various other names. (See "Sukshma Sarîra".) Spirit, in short, is no entity in the sense of having form; for, as Buddhist philosophy has it, where there is a form, there is a cause for pain and suffering. But each *individual* spirit—this individuality lasting only throughout the manvantaric life-cycle—may be described as a *centre of consciousness*, a self-sentient and self-conscious centre; a state, not a conditioned individual. This is why there is such a wealth of words in Sanskrit to express the different States of Being, Beings and Entities, each appellation showing the philosophical difference, the plane to which such *unit* belongs, and the degree of its spirituality or materiality. Unfortunately these terms are almost untranslatable into our Western tongues.

**Spiritualism**. In philosophy, the state or condition of mind opposed to materialism or a material conception of things. Theosophy, a doctrine which teaches that all which exists is animated or informed by the Universal Soul or Spirit, and that not an atom in our universe can be outside of this omnipresent Principle—is pure Spiritualism. As to the belief that goes under that name, namely, belief in the constant communication of the living with the dead, whether through the mediumistic powers of oneself or a so-called medium—it is no better than the materialisation of spirit, and the degradation of the human and the divine, souls. Believers in such communications are simply dishonouring the dead and performing constant sacrilege. It was well called "Necromancy" in days of old. But our modern Spiritualists take offence at being told this simple truth.

**Spook.** A ghost, a hobgoblin. Used of the various apparitions in the seance-rooms of the Spiritualists.

**Sraddha** (*Sk*). Lit., faith, respect, reverence.

**Srâddha** (*Sk*.). Devotion to the memory and care for the welfare of the *manes* of dead relatives. A *post-mortem* rite for newly kindred. There are also monthly rites of *Srâddha*.

**Srâddhadeva** (*Sk*.). An epithet of Yama, the god of death and king of the nether world, or Hades.

**Srâmana** (*Sk*.). Buddhist priests, ascetics and postulants for Nirvâna, "they who have to place a restraint on their thoughts". The word Saman, now "Shaman" is a corruption of this primitive word.

**Srastara** (*Sk*.). A couch consisting of a mat or a tiger's skin, strewn with *darbha, kusa* and other grasses, used by ascetics—gurus and chelas—and spread on the floor.

**Sravah** (*Mazd*.). The Amshaspends, in their highest aspect.

**Srâvaka** (*Sk*.). Lit., "he who causes to hear"; a preacher. But in Buddhism it denotes a disciple or chela.

**Sri Sankarâchârya** (*Sk*.). The great religious reformer of India, and teacher of the Vedânta philosophy—the greatest of all such teachers, regarded by the *Adwaitas* (Non-dualists) as an incarnation of Siva and a worker of miracles. He established many *mathams* (monasteries), and founded the most learned sect among Brahmans, called the Smârtava. The legends about him are as numerous as his philosophical writings. At the age of thirty-two he went to Kashmir, and reaching Kedarânâth in the Himalayas, entered a cave alone, whence he never returned. His followers claim that he did not die, but only retired from the world.

**Sringa Giri** (*Sk*.). A large and wealthy monastery on the ridge of the Western Ghauts in Mysore (Southern India); the chief *matham* of the Adwaita and Smârta Brahmans, founded by Sankarâchârya. There resides the religious head (the latter being called Sankarâchârya) of all the Vedantic Adwaitas, credited by many with great abnormal powers.

**Sri-pâda** (*Sk*.). The impression of Buddha's foot. *Lit*., "the step or foot of the Master or exalted Lord".

**Srivatsa** (*Sk*.). A mystical mark worn by Krishna, and also adopted by the Jains.

**Sriyantra** (*Sk*.). The double triangle or the seal of Vishnu, called also "Solomon's seal ", and adopted by the Theosophical Society.

**Srotâpatti** (*Sk*) Lit., "he who has entered the stream ", *i.e.*, the stream or path that leads to Nirvâna, or figuratively, to the Nirvânic Ocean. The same as *Sowanee.*

**Srotriya** (*Sk*) The appellation of a Brahman who practises the Vedic rites he studies, as distinguished from the *Vedavit*, the Brahman who studies them only theoretically.

**Sruti** (*Sk.*). Sacred tradition received by revelation; the *Vedas* are such a tradition as distinguished from "Smriti "(*q.v.*).

**St. Germain**, *the Count of.* Referred to as an enigmatical personage by modern writers. Frederic II., King of Prussia, used to say of him that he was a man whom no one had ever been able make out. Many are his "biographies", and each is wilder than the other. By some he was regarded as an incarnate god, by others as a clever Alsatian Jew. One thing is certain, Count de St. Germain—whatever his real patronymic may have been—had a right to his name and title, for he had bought a property called San Germano, in the Italian Tyrol, and paid the Pope for the title. He was uncommonly handsome, and his enormous erudition and linguistic capacities are undeniable, for he spoke English, Italian, French, Spanish, Portuguese, German, Russian, Swedish, Danish, and many Slavonian and Oriental languages, with equal facility with a native. He was extremely wealthy, never received a *sou* from anyone—in fact never accepted a glass of water or broke bread with anyone—made most extravagant presents of superb jewellery to all his friends, even to the royal families of Europe. His proficiency in music was marvellous; he played on every instrument, the violin being his favourite. "St. Germain rivalled Paganini himself", was said of him by an octogenarian Belgian in 1835, after hearing the "*Genoese maestro*". "It is St. Germain resurrected who plays the violin in the body of an Italian skeleton", exclaimed a Lithuanian baron who had heard both.

He never laid claim to spiritual powers, but proved to have a right to such claim. He used to pass into a dead trance from thirty-seven to forty-nine hours without awakening, and then knew all he had to know, and demonstrated the fact by prophesying futurity and never making a mistake. It is he who prophesied before the Kings Louis XV. and XVI., and the unfortunate Marie Antoinette. Many were the still living witnesses in the first quarter of this century who testified to his marvellous memory; he could read a paper in the morning and, though hardly glancing at it, could repeat its contents without missing one word days afterwards; he could write with two hands at once, the right hand writing a piece of poetry, the left a diplomatic paper of the greatest importance. He read sealed letters without touching them, while still in the hand of those who brought them

to him. He was the greatest adept in transmuting metals, making gold and the most marvellous diamonds, an art, he said, he had learned from certain Brahmans in India, who taught him the artificial crystallisation ("quickening") of pure carbon. As our Brother Kenneth Mackenzie has it:—
"In 1780, when on a visit to the French Ambassador to the Hague, he broke to pieces with a hammer a superb diamond of his own manufacture, the counterpart of which, also manufactured by himself, he had just before sold to a jeweller for 5500 louis d'or". He was the friend and confidant of Count Orloff in 1772 at Vienna, whom he had helped and saved in St. Petersburg in 1762, when concerned in the famous political conspiracies of that time; he also became intimate with Frederick the Great of Prussia. As a matter of course, he had numerous enemies, and therefore it is not to be wondered at if all the gossip invented about him is now attributed to his own confessions: e.g., that he was over five hundred years old; also, that he claimed personal intimacy "with the Saviour and his twelve Apostles, and that he had reproved Peter for his bad temper "—the latter clashing somewhat in point of time with the former, if he had really claimed to be only five hundred years old. if he said that "he had been born in Chaldea and professed to possess the secrets of the Egyptian magicians and sages ", he may have spoken truth without making any miraculous claim. There are Initiates, and not the highest either, who are placed in a condition to remember more than one of their past lives. But we have good reason to know that St. Germain could never have claimed "personal intimacy" with the Saviour. How ever that may be, Count St. Germain was certainly the greatest Oriental Adept Europe has seen during the last centuries. But Europe knew him not. Perchance some may recognise him at the next *Terreur* which will affect all Europe when it comes, and not one country alone.

**Sthâla Mâyâ** (*Sk.*). Gross, concrete and—because differentiated—an illusion.

**Sthâna** (*Sk.*). Also *Ayâna*; the place or abode of a god.

**Sthâvara** (*Sk*). From *sthâ* to stay or remain motionless. The term for all conscious, sentient objects deprived of the power of locomotion—fixed and rooted like the trees or plants; while all those sentient things, which add motion to a certain degree of consciousness, are called *Jangama*, from *gam*, to move, to go.

**Sthâvirâh,** or *Sthâviranikaya* (*Sk.*). One of the earliest philosophical contemplative schools, founded 300 B.C. In the year 247 before the Christian era, it split into three divisions: the *Mahâvihâra Vâsinâh* (School of the great monasteries), *Jêtavaniyâh,* and *Abhayagiri Vâsinâh.* It is one of the four branches of the *Vaibhâchika* School founded by Kâtyâyana, one of the great disciples of Lord Gautama Buddha, the author of the *Abhidharma Jnana Prasthâna* Shastra, who is expected to reappear as a Buddha. (See "Abhayagiri ", etc.) All these schools are highly mystical. Lit., *Stâviranikaya* is translated the "School of the Chairman" or "President" (Chohan).

**Sthirâtman** (*Sk.*). Eternal, supreme, applied to the Universal Soul.

**Sthiti** (*Sk.*). The attribute of preservation; stability.

**Sthûla** (*Sk.*). Differentiated and conditioned matter.

**Sthûla Sarîram** (*Sk.*). In metaphysics, the gross physical body.

**Sthûlopadhi** (*Sk.*). A "principle" answering to the lower triad in man, i.e., body, astral form, and life, in the Târaka Râja Yoga system, which names only three chief principles in man. *Sthûlopadhi* corresponds to the *jagrata,* or waking conscious *state.*

**Stûpa** (*Sk.*). A conical monument, in India and Ceylon, erected over relics of Buddha, Arhats, or other great men.

**Subhâva** (*Sk.*). Being; the self-forming substance, or that "substance which gives substance to itself". (See the *Ekasloha Shâstra* of Nâgârjuna.) Explained paradoxically, as "the nature which has no nature of its own ", and again as that which is *with,* and *without,* action. (See "Svabhâvat".) This is the *Spirit within Substance,* the ideal cause of the potencies acting on the work of formative evolution (not "creation" in the sense usually attached to the word); which potencies become in turn the real causes. In the words used in the Vedânta and Vyâya Philosophies: *nimitta,* the efficient, and *upâdâna,* the material, causes are contained in Subhâva co-eternally. Says a Sanskrit Sloka:

" Worthiest of ascetics, through its potency [that of the "efficient" cause] every created thing *comes by its proper nature*".

**Substance**. Theosophists use the word in a dual sense, qualifying substance as perceptible and imperceptible; and making a distinction between material, psychic and spiritual substances (see "Sudda Satwa"), into *ideal* (i.e., existing on higher planes) and real substance.

**Suchi** (*Sk.*). A name of Indra; also of the third son of Abhimânin, son of Agni; i.e., one of the primordial *forty-nine fires.*

**Su-darshana** (*Sk.*). The Discus of Krishna; a flaming weapon that plays a great part in Krishna's biographies.

**Sudda Satwa** (*Sk.*). A substance not subject to the qualities of matter; a luminiferous and (to us) invisible substance, of which the bodies of the Gods and highest Dhyânis are formed. Philosophically, *Suddha Satwa* is a conscious state of spiritual Ego-ship rather than any essence.

**Suddhodana** (*Sk.*). The King of Kapilavastu; the father of Gautama Lord Buddha.

**Sudhâ** (*Sk.*). The food of the gods, akin to *amrita* the substance that gives immortality.

**S'udra** (*Sk.*). The last of the four castes that sprang from Brahmâ's body. The "servile caste" that issued from the foot of the deity.

**Sudyumna** (*Sk.*). An epithet of Ila (or Ida), the offspring of Vaivasvata Manu and his fair daughter who sprang from his sacrifice when he was left alone after the flood. Sudyumna was an androgynous creature, one month a male and the other a female.

**Suffism** (*Gr.*). From the root of *Sophia*, "Wisdom ". A mystical sect in Persia something like the Vedantins; though very strong in numbers, none but very intelligent men join it. They claim, and very justly, the possession of the esoteric philosophy and doctrine of *true* Mohammedanism. The Suffi (or Sofi) doctrine is a good deal in touch with Theosophy, inasmuch as it preaches one universal creed, and outward respect and tolerance for every popular *exoteric* faith. It is also in touch with Masonry. The Suffis have four degrees and four stages of initiation:1st, probationary, with a strict outward observance of Mussulman rites, the hidden meaning of each ceremony and dogma being explained to the candidate; 2nd, metaphysical training; 3rd, the "Wisdom" degree, when the candidate is initiated into the innermost nature of things; and 4th final Truth, when the Adept attains divine powers, and complete union with the One Universal Deity in *ecstacy* or *Samâdhi*.

**Sugata** (*Sk.*). One of the Lord Buddha's titles, having many meanings.

**Sukhab** (*Chald.*). One of the seven Babylonian gods.

**Sukhâvati** (*Sk.*). The Western Paradise of the uneducated rabble. The popular notion is that there is a Western Paradise of Amitâbha, wherein good men and saints revel in physical delights until they are carried once more by Karma into the circle of rebirth. This is an exaggerated and mistaken notion of Devâchân.

**Suki** (*Sk.*). A daughter of Rishi Kashyapa, wife of Garuda, the king of the birds, the vehicle of Vishnu; the mother of parrots, owls and crows.

**Sukra** (*Sk.*). A name of the planet Venus, called also Usanas. In this impersonation Usanas is the Guru and preceptor of the Daityas—the giants of the earth—in the Purânas.

**Sûkshma Sarîra** (*Sk.*). The dream-like, illusive body akin to *Mânasarûpa* or "thought-body". It is the vesture of the gods, or the Dhyânis and the Devas. Written also *Sukshama Sharîra* and called *Sukshmopadhi* by the Târaka Râja Yogis. (*S. D.*, Vol. I, p. 157)

**Sûkshmopadhi** (*Sk.*). In Târaka Râja Yoga the "principle" containing both the higher and the lower Manas and Kâma. It corresponds to the *Manomaya Kosha* of the Vedantic classification and to the *Svapna* state. (See "Svapna ".)

**Su-Mêru** (*Sk.*). The same as Meru, the world-mountain. The prefix **Su** implies the laudation and exaltation of the object or personal name which follows it.

**Summerland**. The name given by the American Spiritualists and Phenomenalists to the land or region inhabited after death by their "Spirits". It is situated, says Andrew Jackson Davis, either within or beyond the Milky Way. It is described as having cities and beautiful buildings, a Congress Hall, museums and libraries for the instruction of the growing generations of young "Spirits".

We are not told whether the latter are subject to disease, decay and death; but unless they are, the claim that the disembodied "Spirit" of a child and even still-born babe grows and develops as an adult is hardly consistent with logic. But that which we are distinctly told is, that in the Summerland Spirits are given in marriage, beget spiritual (?) children, and are even concerned with politics. All this is no satire or exaggeration of ours, since the numerous works by Mr. A. Jackson Davis are there to prove it, e.g., the *International Congress of Spirits* by that author, as well as we remember the title. It is this grossly materialistic way of viewing a disembodied spirit that has turned many of the present Theosophists away from Spiritualism and its "philosophy". The majesty of death is thus desecrated, and its awful and solemn mystery becomes no better than a farce.

**Sunasepha** (*Sk.*). The Purânic "Isaac"; the son of the sage Rishika who sold him for one hundred cows to King Ambarisha, for a sacrifice and "burnt offering" to Varuna, as a substitute for the king's son Rohita, devoted by his father to the god. When already stretched on the altar Sunasepha is saved by Rishi Visvâmitra, who calls upon his own hundred sons to take the place of the victim, and upon their refusal degrades them to the condition of Chândâlas. After which the Sage teaches the victim a *mantram* the repetition of which brings the gods to his rescue; he then adopts Sunasepha for his elder son. (See Râmâyana.) There are different versions of this story.

**Sung-Ming-Shu** (*Chin.*). The Chinese tree of knowledge and tree of life.

**Sûnya** (*Sk.*). Illusion, in the sense that all existence is but a phantom, a dream, or a shadow.

**Sunyatâ** (*Sk.*). Void, space, nothingness. The name of our objective universe in the sense of its unreality and illusiveness.

**Suoyator** (*Fin.*). In the epic poem of the Finns, the *Kalevala*, the name for the primordial Spirit of Evil, from whose saliva the serpent of sin was born.

**Surabhi** (*Sk.*). The "cow of plenty"; a fabulous creation, one of the fourteen precious things yielded by the ocean of milk when churned by the gods. A "cow" which yields every desire to its possessor.

**Surarânî** (*Sk.*). A title of Aditi, the mother of the gods or *suras*.

**Suras** (*Sk.*). A general term for gods, the same as devas; the contrary to asuras or "no-gods".

**Su-rasâ** (*Sk.*). A daughter of Daksha, Kashyapa's wife, and the mother of a thousand many-headed serpents and dragons.

**Surpa** (*Sk.*). "Winnower."

**Surtur** (*Scand.*). The leader of the fiery sons of Muspel in the *Eddas*.

**Surukâya** (*Sk*). One of the "Seven Buddhas", or *Sapta Tathâgata*.

**Sûryâ** (*Sk.*). The Sun, worshipped in the *Vedas*. The offspring of Aditi (Space), the mother of the gods. The husband of Sanjnâ, or spiritual consciousness. The great god whom Visvakârman, his father-in-law, the creator of the gods and men, and their "carpenter", crucifies on a lathe, and cutting off the eighth part of his rays, deprives his head of its effulgency, creating round it a dark aureole. A mystery of the last initiation, and an allegorical representation of it.

**Sûryasiddhânta** (*Sk.*). A Sanskrit treatise on astronomy.

**Sûryavansa** (*Sk*). The solar race. A *Sûrayavansee* is one who claims descent from the lineage headed by *Ikshvâku*. Thus, while Râma belonged to the Ayodhyâ Dynasty of the Sûryavansa, Krishna belonged to the line of Yadu of the lunar race, or the Chandravansa, as did Gautama Buddha.

**Sûryâvarta** (*Sk.*). A degree or stage of Samâdhi.

**Sushumnâ** (*Sk.*). The solar ray—the first of the seven rays. Also the name of a spinal nerve which connects the heart with the Brahmarandra, and plays a most important part in Yoga practices.

**Sushupti Avasthâ** (*Sk.*). Deep sleep; one of the four aspects of Prânava.

**Sûtra** (*Sk.*). The second division of the sacred writings, addressed to the Buddhist laity.

**Sûtra Period** (*Sk.*). One of the periods into which Vedic literature is divided.

**Sûtrâtman** (*Sk.*). Lit., "the thread of spirit"; the immortal Ego, the Individuality which incarnates in men one life after the other, and upon which are strung, like beads on a string, his countless Personalities. The universal life-supporting air, *Samashti prau*; universal energy.

**Svabhâvat** (*Sk.*). Explained by the Orientalists as "plastic substance", which is an inadequate definition. Svabhâvat is the world-substance and stuff, or rather that which is behind it — the spirit and essence of substance. The name comes from *Subhâva* and is composed of three words — *su*, good, perfect, fair, handsome; *sva*, self; and *bkâva*, being, or *state of being*. From it all nature proceeds and into it all returns at the end of the life-cycles. In Esotericism it is called "Father-Mother". It is the plastic essence of matter.

**Svâbhâvika** (*Sk.*). The oldest existing school of Buddhism. They assigned the manifestation of the universe and physical phenomena to Svabhâva or respective nature of things. According to Wilson the Svabhâvas of things are "the inherent properties of the qualities by which they act, as soothing, terrific or stupefying, and the forms *Swarûpas* are the distinction of biped, quadruped, brute, fish, animal and the like ".

**Svadhâ** (*Sk.*). Oblation; allegorically called "the wife of the Pitris", the Agnishwattas and Barhishads.

**Svâhâ** (*Sk*). A customary exclamation meaning "May it be perpetuated" or rather, "so be it". When used at ancestral sacrifices (Brahmanic), it means "May the race be perpetuated!"

**Svapada** (*Sk.*). Protoplasm, cells, or microscopic organisms.

**Svapna** (*Sk*). A trance or dreamy condition. Clairvoyance.

**Svapna Avasthâ** (*Sk.*). A dreaming state; one of the four aspects of *Prânava*; a Yoga practice.

**Svarâj** (*Sk.*). The last or seventh (synthetical) ray of the seven solar rays; the same as Brahmâ. These seven rays are the entire gamut of the seven occult forces (or gods) of nature, as their respective names well prove. These are: Sushumnâ (the ray which transmits sunlight to the moon);

*Harikesha, Visvakarman, Visvatryarchas, Sannadhas, Sarvâvasu,* and *Svarâj.* As each stands for one of the creative gods or Forces, it is easy to see how important were the functions of the sun in the eyes of antiquity, and why it was deified by the profane.

**Svarga** (*Sk.*). A heavenly abode, the same as Indra-loka; a paradise. It is the same as—

**Svar-loka** (*Sk.*). The paradise on Mount Meru.

**Svasam Vedanâ** (*Sk.*). Lit., "the reflection which analyses itself"; a synonym of Paramârtha.

**Svastika** (*Sk.*). In popular notions, it is the Jaina cross, or the "four-footed" cross (*croix cramponnée*). In Masonic teachings, "the most ancient Order of the Brotherhood of the Mystic Cross" is said to have been founded by Fohi, 1,027 B.C., and introduced into China fifty-two years later, consisting of the three degrees. In Esoteric Philosophy, the most mystic and ancient diagram. It is "the originator of the fire by friction, and of the ' Forty-nine Fires'." Its symbol was stamped on Buddha's heart, and therefore called the "Heart's Seal". It is laid on the breasts of departed Initiates after their death; and it is mentioned with the greatest respect in the *Râmâyana.* Engraved on every rock, temple and prehistoric building of India, and wherever Buddhists have left their landmarks; it is also found in China, Tibet and Siam, and among the ancient Germanic nations as Thor's Hammer. As described by Eitel in his *Hand-Book of Chinese Buddhism.* . (1) it is "found among Bonpas and Buddhists"; (2) it is "one of the sixty-five figures of the Sripâda"; (3) it is "the symbol of esoteric Buddhism"; (4) "the special mark of all deities worshipped by the Lotus School of China". Finally, and in Occultism, it is as sacred to us as the Pythagorean *Tetraktys,* of which it is indeed the double symbol.

**Svastikâsana** (*Sk.*). The second of the four principal postures of the eighty-four prescribed in Hatha Yoga practices.

**Svayambhû** (*Sk.*). A metaphysical and philosophical term, meaning "the spontaneously self-produced" or the "self-existent being". An epithet of Brahmâ. Svâyambhuva is also the name of the first Manu.

**Svayambhû Sûnyatâ** (*Sk.*). Spontaneous self-evolution; self-existence of the *real in the unreal,* i.e., of the Eternal Sat in the periodical *Asat.*

**Sveta** (*Sk.*). A serpent-dragon; a son of Kashyapa.

**Sveta-dwîpa** (*Sk.*). Lit., the White Island or Continent; one of the Sapta-dwipa. Colonel Wilford sought to identify it with Great Britain, but failed.

**Sveta-lohita** (*Sk.*). The name of Siva when he appears in the 29th Kalpa as "a moon-coloured Kumâra".

**Swedenborg, Emmanuel.** The great Swedish seer and mystic. He was born on the 29th January, 1688, and was the son of Dr. Jasper Swedberg, bishop of Skara, in West Gothland; and died in London, in Great Bath Street, Clerkenwell, on March 29th, 1772. Of all mystics, Swedenborg has certainly influenced "Theosophy" the most, yet he left a far more profound impress on official science. For while as an astronomer, mathematician, physiologist, naturalist, and philosopher he had no rival, in psychology and metaphysics he was certainly behind his time. When forty-six years of age, he became a "Theosophist", and a "seer"; but, although his life had been at all times blameless and respectable, he was never a true philanthropist or an ascetic. His clairvoyant powers, however, were very remarkable; but they did not go beyond this plane of matter; all that he says of subjective worlds and spiritual beings is evidently far more the outcome of his exuberant fancy, than of his spiritual insight. He left behind him numerous works, which are sadly misinterpreted by his followers.

**Sylphs.** The Rosicrucian name for the elementals of the air.

**Symbolism.** The pictorial expression of an idea or a thought. Primordial writing had at first no characters, but a symbol generally stood for a whole phrase or sentence. A symbol is thus a recorded parable, and a parable a spoken symbol. The Chinese written language is nothing more than symbolical writing, each of its several thousand letters being-a symbol.

**Syzygy** (*Gr.*). A Gnostic term, meaning a pair or couple, one active, the other passive. Used especially of Æons.

# T

**T.**—The twentieth letter of the alphabet. In the Latin Alphabet its value was 160, and, with a dash over it (T) signified 160,000. It is the last letter of the Hebrew alphabet, the Tau whose equivalents are T, TH, and numerical value 400. Its symbols are as a *tau*, a cross +, the foundation framework of construction; and as a *teth* (T), the ninth letter, a snake and the basket of the Eleusinian mysteries.

**Taaroa** (*Tah.*). The creative power and chief god of the Tahitians.

**Tab-nooth** (*Heb.*). Form; a Kabbalist term.

**Tad-aikya** (*Sk.*). "Oneness"; identification or unity with the Absolute. The universal, unknowable Essence (Parahrahm) has no name in the *Vedas* but is referred to generally as Tad, "That".

**Tafne** (*Eg.*). A goddess; daughter of the sun, represented with the head of a lioness.

**Tahmurath** (*Pers.*). The Iranian Adam, whose steed was Simorgh Anke, the griffin-phœnix or infinite cycle. A repetition or reminiscence of Vishnu and Garuda.

**Tahor** (*Heb.*). Lit., *Mundus,* the world; a name given to the Deity, which identification indicates a belief in Pantheism.

**Taht Esmun** (*Eg.*). The Egyptian Adam; the first human ancestor.

**Taijasi** (*Sk.*). The radiant, flaming—from *Tejas* "fire"; used sometimes to designate the *Mânasa-rûpa*, the "thought-body", and also the stars.

**Tairyagyonya** (*Sk.*). The fifth creation, or rather the fifth stage of creation, that of the lower animals, reptiles, etc. (See "Tiryaksrotas ".)

**Taittrîya** (*Sk.*). A *Brâhmana* of the *Yajur Veda*.

**Talapoin** (*Siam.*). A Buddhist monk and ascetic in Siam; some of these ascetics are credited with great magic powers.

**Talisman.** From the Arabic *tilism* or *tilsam*, a "magic image". An object, whether in stone, metal, or sacred wood; often a piece of parchment filled with characters and images traced under certain planetary influences in magical formulæ given by one versed in occult sciences to one unversed, either with the object of preserving him from evil, or for the accomplishment of certain desires. The greatest virtue and efficacy of the talisman, however, resides in the faith of its possessor; not because of the credulity of the latter, or that it possesses no virtue, but because faith is a quality *endowed with a most potent creative power*; and therefore—unconsciously to the believer—intensifies a hundredfold the power originally imparted to the talisman by its maker.

**Talmidai Hakhameem** (*Heb.*). A class of mystics and Kabbalists whom the *Zohar* calls "Disciples of the Wise", and who were *Sârisim* or voluntary *eunuchs,* becoming such for spiritual motives. (See *Matthew* xix., 11-12, a passage implying the laudation of such an act.)

**Talmud** (*Heb.*). Rabbinic Commentaries on the Jewish faith. It is composed of two parts, the older *Mishnah*, and the more modern *Gemara*. Hebrews, who call the *Pentateuch* the written law, call the *Talmud* the unwritten or oral law. [w.w.w.]

The *Talmud* contains the civil and canonical laws of the Jews, who claim a great sanctity for it. For, save the above-stated difference between the *Pentateuch* and the *Talmud*, the former, they say, can claim no priority over the latter, as both were received simultaneously by Moses on Mount Sinai from Jehovah, *who wrote the one and delivered the other orally.*

**Tamâla Pattra** (*Sk.*). Stainless, pure, sage-like. Also the name of a leaf of the *Laurus Cassia,* a tree regarded as having various very occult and magical properties.

**Tamarisk,** or *Erica.* A sacred tree in Egypt of great occult virtues. Many of the temples were surrounded with such trees, pre-eminently one at Philæ, sacred among the sacred, as the body of Osiris was s to lie buried under it.

**Tamas** (*Sk.*). The quality of darkness, "foulness" and inertia; also of ignorance, as matter is blind. A term used in metaphysical philosophy. It is the lowest of the three *gunas* or fundamental qualities.

**Tammuz** (*Syr.*). A Syrian deity worshipped by idolatrous Hebrews as well as by Syrians. The women of Israel held annual lamentations over Adonis (that beautiful youth being identical with Tammuz). The feast held in his honour was solstitial, and began with the new moon, in the month of Tammuz (July), taking place chiefly at Byblos in Phœnicia; but it was also celebrated as late as the fourth century of our era at Bethlehem, as we find St. Jerome writing (*Epistles* p. 9) his lamentations in these words: "Over Bethlehem, the grove of Tammuz, that is of Adonis, was casting its shadow! And in the grotto where formerly the infant Jesus cried, the lover of Venus was being mourned." Indeed, in the Mysteries of Tammuz or Adonis a whole week was spent in lamentations and mourning. The funereal processions were succeeded by a fast, and later by rejoicings; for after the fast Adonis-Tammuz was regarded as raised from the dead, and wild orgies of joy, of eating and drinking, as now in Easter week, went on uninterruptedly for several days.

**Tamra-Parna** (*Sk.*). Ceylon, the ancient Taprobana.

**Tamti** (*Chald.*). A goddess, the same as Belita. Tamti-Belita is the personified Sea, the mother of the *City of Erech,* the Chaldean Necropolis. Astronomically, Tamti is Astoreth or Istar, Venus.

**Tanaim** (*Heb.*). Jewish Initiates, very learned Kabbalists in ancient times. The *Talmud* contains sundry legends about them and gives the chief names among them.

**Tanga-Tango** (*Peruv.*). An idol much reverenced by the Peruvians. It is the symbol of the Triune or the Trinity, "One in three, and three in One", and existed before our era.

**Tanha** (*Pali*). The thirst for life. Desire to live and clinging to life on this earth. This clinging is that which causes rebirth or reincarnation.

**Tanjur** (*Tib.*). A collection of Buddhist works translated from the Sanskrit into Tibetan and Mongolian. It is the more voluminous canon, comprising 225 large volumes on miscellaneous subjects. The *Kanjur*, which contains the commandments or the "Word of the Buddha", has only 108 volumes.

**Tanmâtras** (*Sk.*). The types or rudiments of the five Elements; the subtile essence of these, devoid of all qualities and identical with the properties of the five basic Elements—earth, water, fire, air and ether; i.e., the *tanmâtras* are, in one of their aspects, smell, taste, touch, sight, and hearing.

**Tantra** (*Sk.*). Lit., "rule or ritual". Certain mystical and magical works, whose chief peculiarity is the worship of the *female* power, personified in Sakti. Devî or Durgâ (Kâlî, Siva's wife) is the special energy connected with sexual rites and magical powers—*The worst form of black magic or sorcery*.

**Tântrika** (*Sk*) Ceremonies connected with the above worship. Sakti having a two-fold nature, white and black, good and bad, the Saktas are divided into two classes, the Dakshinâchâris and Vâmâchâris, or the right-hand and the left-hand Saktas, i.e., "white" and "black" magicians. The worship of the latter is most licentious and immoral.

**Tao** (*Chin.*). The name of the philosophy of Lao-tze.

**Taöer** (*Eg.*). The female Typhon, the hippopotamus, called also *Ta-ur, Ta-op-oer*, etc.; she is the *Thoueris* of the Greeks. This wife of Typhon was represented as a monstrous hippopotamus, sitting on her hind legs with a knife in one hand and the sacred knot in the other the *pâsa* of Siva). Her back was covered with the scales of a crocodile, and she had a crocodile's tail. She is also called *Teb*, whence the name of Typhon is also, sometimes, *Tebh*. On a monument of the sixth dynasty she is called "the nurse of the gods". She was feared in Egypt even more than Typhon. (See "Typhon".)

**Tao-teh-king** (*Chin.*). Lit., "The Book of the Perfectibility of Nature" written by the great philosopher Lao-tze. It is a kind of cosmogony which contains all the fundamental tenets of Esoteric Cosmo genesis. Thus he says that in the beginning there was naught but limitless and boundless Space. All that lives and is, was born in it, from the "Principle which exists by Itself, developing Itself from Itself", i.e., *Swabhâvat*. As its name is unknown and it essence is unfathomable, philosophers have called it Tao (*Anima Mundi*), the uncreate, unborn and eternal energy of nature, manifesting periodically. Nature as well as man when it reaches purity will reach rest, and then all become one with Tao, which is the source of all bliss and felicity. As in the Hindu and Buddhistic philosophies, such purity and bliss and immortality can only be reached through the exercise of virtue and the perfect quietude of our worldly spirit; the human mind has to control and finally subdue and even crush the turbulent action of man's physical nature; and the sooner he reaches the required degree of moral purification, the happier he will feel. (See *Annales du Musée Guimet*, Vols. XI. and XII.; *Etudes sur lie Religion des Chinois*, by Dr. Groot.) As the famous Sinologist, Pauthier, remarked: "Human Wisdom can never use language more holy and profound".

**Tapas** (*Sk.*). "Abstraction", "meditation". "To perform *tapas*" is to sit for *contemplation*. Therefore ascetics are often called Tâpasas.

**Tâpasâ-tarû** (*Sk.*). The *Sesamum Orientate*, a tree very sacred among the ancient ascetics of China and Tibet.

**Tapasvî** (*Sk.*). Ascetics and anchorites of every religion, whether Buddhist, Brahman, or Taoist.

**Taphos** (*Gr.*). Tomb, the sarcophagus placed in the Adytum and used for purposes of initiation.

**Tapo-loka** (*Sk.*). The domain of the fire-devas named Vairâjas. It is known as the "world of the seven sages", and also "the realm of penance". One of the Shashta-loka (Six worlds) above our own, which is the seventh.

**Târâ** (*Sk.*). The wife of Brihaspati (Jupiter), carried away by King Soma, the Moon, an act which led to the war of the Gods with the Asuras. Târâ personifies mystic knowledge as opposed to ritualistic faith. She is the mother (by Soma) of Buddha, "Wisdom".

**Târakâ** (*Sk*) Described as Dânava or Daitya, i.e., a "Giant-Demon", whose superhuman austerities as a yogi made the gods tremble for their power and supremacy. Said to have been killed by Kârttikeya. (See *S. D.*, Vol. II, p. 382.)

**Târakâmaya** (*Sk.*). The first war in Heaven through Târâ.

**Târakâ Râja Yoga** (*Sk.*). One of the Brahminical Yoga systems for the development of purely spiritual powers and knowledge which lead to Nirvâna.

**Targum** (*Chald.*). Lit., "Interpretation", from the root *targem* to interpret. Paraphrases of Hebrew Scriptures. Some of the Targums are very mystical, the Aramaic (or Targumatic) language being used all through the *Zohar* and other Kabbalistic works. To distinguish this language from the

Hebrew, called the "face" of the sacred tongue, it is referred to as *ahorayim*, the "back part", the real meaning of which must be read between the lines, according to certain methods given to students. The Latin word *tergum*, "back", is derived from the Hebrew or rather Aramaic and Chaldean *targum*. The Book of *Daniel* begins in Hebrew, and is fully comprehensible till chap. ii., V. 4, when the Chaldees (the Magician-Initiates) begin speaking to the king in Aramaic—not in Syriac, as mistranslated in the Protestant Bible. Daniel speaks in Hebrew before interpreting the king's dream to him; but explains the dream itself (chap. vii.) in Aramaic. "So in Ezra iv., v. and vi., the words of the kings being there literally quoted, all matters connected therewith are in Aramaic", says Isaac Myer in his Qabbalah. The Targumim are of different ages, the latest already showing signs of the Massoretic or vowel-system, which made them still more full of intentional blinds. The precept of the *Pirke Aboth* (c. i., i), "Make a fence to the Thorah" (law), has indeed been faithfully followed in the Bible as in the Targumim; and wise is he who would interpret either correctly, unless he is an old Occultist-Kabbalist.

**Tashilhûmpa** (*Tib.*). The great centre of monasteries and colleges, three hours' walk from Tchigadze, the residence of the Teshu Lama for details of whom see "Panchen Rimboche". It was built in 1445 by the order of Tson-kha-pa.

**Tassissudun** (*Tib.*). Lit., "the holy city of the doctrine" inhabited, nevertheless, by more Dugpas than Saints. It is the residential capital in Bhutan of the ecclesiastical Head of the Bhons—the Dharma Râjâ. The latter, though professedly a Northern Buddhist, is simply a worshipper of the old demon-gods of the aborigines, the nature-sprites or elementals, worshipped in the land before the introduction of Buddhism. All strangers are prevented from penetrating into Eastern or Great Tibet, and the few scholars who venture on their travels into those forbidden regions, are permitted to penetrate no further than the border-lands of the land of Bod. They journey about Bhutan, Sikkhim, and elsewhere on the frontiers of the country, but can learn or know nothing of true Tibet; hence, nothing of the true Northern Buddhism or Lamaism of Tsong-kha-pa. And yet, while describing no more than the rites and beliefs of the Bhons and the travelling Shamans, they assure the world they are giving it the pure Northern Buddhism, and comment on its great fall from its pristine purity.

**Tat** (*Eg.*). An Egyptian symbol: an upright round standard tapering toward the summit, with four cross-pieces placed on the top. It was used as an amulet. The top part is a regular equilateral cross. This, on its phallic basis, represented the two principles of creation, the male and the female, and related to nature and cosmos; but when the tat stood by itself, crowned with the *atf* ( or *atef* ), the triple crown of Horus—two feathers with the uræus in front—it represented the *septenary* man; the cross, or the two cross-pieces, standing for the lower quaternary, and the *atf* for the higher triad. As Dr. Birch well remarks: "The four horizontal bars . . . represent the four foundations of all things, the tat being an emblem of stability".

**Tathâgata** (*Sk.*). "One who is like the coming"; he who is, like his predecessors (the Buddhas) and successors, the coming future Buddha or World-Saviour. One of the titles of Gautama Buddha, and the highest epithet, since the *first* and the *last* Buddhas were the direct immediate avatars of the One Deity.

**Tathâgatagupta** (*Sk.*). Secret or concealed Tathâgata, or the "guardian" protecting Buddhas: used of the Nirmânakayas.

**Tattwa** (*Sk.*). Eternally existing "That"; also, the different principles in Nature, in their occult meaning. *Tattwa Samâsa* is a work of Sânkhya philosophy attributed to Kapila himself.

Also the abstract principles of existence or categories, physical and metaphysical. The subtle elements—five exoterically, seven in esoteric philosophy—which are correlative to the five and the seven senses on the physical plane; the last two senses are as yet latent in man, but will be developed in the two last root-races.

**Tau** (*Heb.*). That which has now become the square Hebrew letter tau, but was ages before the invention of the Jewish alphabet, the Egyptian handled cross, the *crux ansata* of the Latins, and identical with the Egyptian *ankh*. This mark belonged exclusively, and still belongs, to the Adepts of every country. As Kenneth R. F. Mackenzie shows, "It was a symbol of salvation and consecration, and as such has been adopted as a Masonic symbol in the Royal Arch Degree". It is also called the astronomical cross, and was used by the ancient Mexicans—as its presence on one of the palaces at Palenque shows—as well as by the Hindus, who placed the **tau** as a mark on the brows of their Chelas.

**Taurus** (*Lat.*). A most mysterious constellation of the Zodiac, one connected with all the "First-born" solar gods. Taurus is under the asterisk A, which is its figure in the Hebrew alphabet, that of *Aleph*; and therefore that constellation is called the "One", the "First", after the said letter. Hence, the "First-born" to all of whom it was made sacred. The Bull is the symbol of force and procreative power—the Logos; hence, also, the horns on the head of Isis, the female aspect of Osiris and Horus. Ancient mystics saw the ansated cross, in the horns of Taurus (the upper portion of the Hebrew *Aleph*) pushing away the Dragon, and Christians connected the sign and constellation with Christ. St. Augustine calls it "the great City of God", and the Egyptians called it the "interpreter of the divine voice", the *Apis-Pacis* of Hermonthis. (See "Zodiac".)

**Taygete** (*Gr.*). One of the seven daughters of Atlas third, who became later one of the Pleiades. These seven daughters are said to typify the seven sub-races of the fourth root-race, that of the Atlanteans.

[*Sanskrit words commencing with the letters* Tch *are, owing to faulty transliteration, misplaced, but can also be found under* 'C'.]

**Tchaitya** (*Sk.*). Any locality made sacred through some event in the life of Buddha; a term signifying the same in relation to gods, and any kind of place or object of worship.

**Tchakchur** (*Sk.*). The first *Vidjnâna* (*q.v.*). Lit., "the eye", meaning the faculty of sight, or rather, an occult perception of spiritual and subjective realities (*Chakshur*).

**Tchakra**, or *Chakra* (*Sk.*). A spell. The disk of Vishnu, which served as a weapon; the wheel of the Zodiac, also the wheel of time, etc. With Vishnu, it was a symbol of divine authority. One of the sixty-five figures of the *Sripâda*, or the mystic foot-print of Buddha which contains that number of symbolical figures. The Tchakra is used in mesmeric phenomena and other abnormal practices.

**Tchandâlas**, or *Chhandâlas* (*Sk.*). Outcasts, or people without caste, a name now given to all the lower classes of the Hindus; but in antiquity it was applied to a certain class of men, who, having forfeited their right to any of the four castes-—Brâhmans, Kshatriyas, Vaisyas and Sûdras—were expelled from cities and sought refuge in the forests. Then they became "bricklayers", until finally expelled they left the country, some 4,000 years before our era. Some see in them the ancestors of the earlier Jews, whose tribes began with A-brahm or "No Brahm". To this day it is the class most despised by the Brahmins in India.

**Tchandragupta**, or *Chandragupta* (*Sk.*). The son of Nanda, the first Buddhist King of the Morya Dynasty, the grandfather of King Asoka, "the beloved of the gods" (*Piyadasi*).

**Tchatur Mahârâja** (*Sk.*). The "four kings", Devas, who guard the four quarters of the universe, and are connected with Karma.

**Tcherno-Bog** (*Slavon.*). Lit., "black god"; the chief deity of the ancient Slavonian nations.

**Tchertchen.** An oasis in Central Asia, situated about 4,000 feet above the river Tchertchen Darya; the very hot-bed and centre of ancient civilization, surrounded on all sides by numberless ruins, above and below ground, of cities, towns, and burial-places of every description. As the late Colonel Prjevalski reported, the oasis is inhabited by some 3,000 people "representing the relics of about a hundred nations and races now extinct, the very names of which are at present unknown to ethnologists".

**Tchhanda Riddhi Pâda** (*Sk.*). "The step of desire", a term used in Râja Yoga. It is the final renunciation of all desire as a *sine quânon* condition of phenomenal powers, and entrance on the direct path of Nirvâna.

**Tchikitsa Vidyâ Shâstra** (*Sk.*). A treatise on occult medicine, which contains a number of "magic" prescriptions. It is one of the *Pancha Vidyâ Shâstra*s or Scriptures.

**Tchîna** (*Sk*) The name of China in Buddhist works, the land being so called since the Tsin dynasty, which was established in the year 349 before our era.

**Tchitta Riddhi Pâda** (*Sk*) "The step of memory." The third condition of the mystic series which leads to the acquirement of adept-ship; i.e., the renunciation of physical memory, and of all thoughts connected with worldly or personal events in one's life—benefits, personal pleasures or associations. physical memory has to be sacrificed, and recalled by will power only when absolutely needed. The *Riddhi Pâda*, lit., the four "Steps to Riddhi", are the four modes of controlling and finally of annihilating desire, memory, and finally meditation itself—so far as these are connected with any effort of the physical brain—meditation then becomes absolutely spiritual.

**Tchitta Smriti Upasthâna** (*Sk.*). One of the four aims of *Smriti Upasthâna*, i.e., the keeping ever in mind the transitory character of man's life, and the incessant revolution of the wheel of existence.

**Tebah** (*Heb.*). Nature; which mystically and esoterically is the same as its personified Elohim, the numerical value of both words—Tebah and Elohim (or Aleim) being the same, namely 86.

**Tefnant** (*Eg.*). One of the three deities who inhabit "the land of the rebirth of gods" and good men, i.e., *Aamroo* (Devâchân) The three deities are Scheo, Tefnant, and Seb.

**Telugu**. One of the Dravidian languages spoken in Southern India.

**Temura** (*Heb.*). Lit., "Change". The title of one division of the practical Kabalah, treating of the analogies between words, the relationship of which is indicated by certain changes in position of the letters, or changes by substituting one letter for another.

**Ten Pythagorean Virtues**. Virtues of Initiation, &c., necessary before admission. (See "Pythagoras".) They are identical with those prescribed by Manu, and the Buddhist Pâramitâs of Perfection.

**Teraphim** (*Heb.*). The same as Seraphim, or the Kabeiri Gods; serpent-images. The first Teraphim, according to legend, were received by Dardanus as a dowry, and brought by him to Samothrace and Troy. The idol-oracles of the ancient Jews. Rebecca stole them from her father Laban.

**Teratology**. A Greek name coined by Geoffroi St. Hilaire to denote the pre-natal formation of monsters, both human and animal.

**Tetragrammaton**. The four-lettered name of God, its Greek title: the four letters are in Hebrew "yod, hé vau, hé" ,or in English capitals, IHVH. The true ancient pronunciation is now unknown; the sincere Hebrew considered this name too sacred for speech, and in reading the sacred writings he substituted the title "Adonai", meaning Lord. In the *Kabbalah*, I is associated with Chokmah, H with Binah, V with Tiphereth, and H final with Malkuth. Christians in general call IHVH Jehovah, and many modern Biblical scholars write it Yahveh. In the *Secret Doctrine*, the name Jehovah is assigned to Sephira Binah alone, but this attribution is not recognised by the Rosicrucian school of Kabbalists, nor by Mathers in his translation of Knorr Von Rbsenroth's *Kabbalah Denudata*: certain Kabbalistic authorities have referred Binah alone to IHVH, but only in reference to the Jehovah of the exoteric Judaism. The IHVH of the *Kabbalah* has but a faint resemblance to the God of the Old Testament. [w.w.w.]

The *Kabbalah* of Knorr von Rosenroth is no authority to the Eastern Kabbalists; because it is well known that in writing his *Kabbalah Denudata* he followed the modern rather than the ancient (Chaldean) MSS.; and it is equally well known that those MSS. and writings of the *Zohar* that are classified as "ancient", mention, and some even use, the Hebrew vowel or Massoretic points. This alone would make these would-be Zoharic books spurious, as there are no direct traces of the Massorah scheme before the tenth century of our era, nor any remote trace of it before the seventh. (See "Tetraktys".)

**Tetraktys** (*Gr.*) or the *Tetrad*. The sacred "Four" by which the Pythagoreans swore, this being their most binding oath. It has a very mystic and varied signification, being the same as the Tetragrammaton. First of all it is Unity, or the "One" under four different aspects; then it is the fundamental number Four, the Tetrad containing the Decad, or Ten, the number of perfection; finally it signifies the primeval Triad (or Triangle) merged in the divine Monad. Kircher, the learned Kabbalist. Jesuit, in his *Œdipus - Ægvpticus* (II p. 267), gives the Ineffable Name IHVH—one of the Kabbalistic formulæ of the 72 names—arranged in the shape of the Pythagorean Tetrad. Mr. I. Myer gives it in this wise:

| | | | |
|---|---|---:|---|
| . | 1 | y = | 10 |
| . . | 2 | The Ineffable hy = | 15 |
| . . . | 3 | Name thus w hy = | 21 |
| . . . . | 4 . | hw hy = | 26 . |
| | 10 | | 72 |

He also shows that "the sacred Tetrad of the Pythagoreans appears to have been known to the ancient Chinese". As explained in *Isis Unveiled* (I, xvi.): The mystic Decad, the resultant of the Tetraktys, or the 1+2+3+4=10, is a way of expressing this idea. The One is the impersonal principle 'God'; the Two, matter; the Three, combining Monad and Duad and partaking of the nature of both, is the phenomenal world; the Tetrad, or form of perfection, expresses the emptiness of all; and the Decad, or sum of all, involves the entire Kosmos.

**Thalassa** (*Gr.*). The sea. (See "Thallath".)

**Thales** (*Gr.*). The Greek philosopher of Miletus (circa 600 years B.C.) who taught that the whole universe was produced from water, while Heraclitus of Ephesus maintained that it was produced by fire, and Anaximenes by air. Thales, whose real name is unknown, took his name from Thallath, in accordance with the philosophy he taught.

**Thallath** (*Chald.*). The same as Thalassa. The goddess personifying the sea, identical with Tiamat and connected with Tamti and Belita. The goddess who gave birth to every variety of primordial monster in Berosus' account of cosmogony.

**Tharana** (*Sk.*). "Mesmerism", or rather self.induced trance or self-hypnotisation; an action in India, which is of magical character and a kind of exorcism. Lit., "to brush or sweep away" (evil influences, thârnhan meaning a broom, and *thârnhan*, a duster); driving away the bad bhûts (bad aura and bad spirits) through the mesmeriser's beneficent will.

**Thaumaturgy**. Wonder or "miracle-working"; the power of working wonders with the help of gods. From the Greek words *thauma*, "wonder", and *theurgia*, "divine work".

**Theanthropism**. A state of being both god and man; a divine *Avatar* (*q.v.*).

**Theiohel** (*Heb.*). The man-producing habitable globe, our earth in the *Zohar*.

**Theli** (*Chald.*). The great Dragon said to environ the universe symbolically. In Hebrew letters it is TLI= 400+30+10 = 440 when "its crest [letter] is repressed", said the Rabbis, 40 remains, or the equivalent of Mem; M=Water, the waters above the firmament. Evidently the same idea as symbolised by Shesha—the Serpent of Vishnu.

**Theocrasy**. Lit., "mixing of gods". The worship of various gods, as that of Jehovah and the gods of the Gentiles in the case of the idolatrous Jews.

**Theodicy**. "Divine right", *i.e* , the privilege of an all-merciful and just God to afflict the innocent, and damn those predestined, and still remain a loving and just Deity theologically—a mystery.

**Theodidaktos** (*Gr.*). Lit., "God-taught". Used of Ammonius Saccas, the founder of the Neo-Platonic Eclectic School of the Philalethæ in the fourth century at Alexandria.

**Theogony**. The genesis of the gods; that branch of all non-Christian theologies which teaches the genealogy of the various deities. An ancient Greek name for that which was translated later as the "genealogy of the generation of Adam and the Patriarchs"—the latter being all "gods and planets and zodiacal signs".

**Theomachy**. Fighting with, or against the gods, such, as the "War of the Titans", the "War in Heaven" and the Battle of the Archangels (gods) against their brothers the Arch-fiends (ex-gods, Asuras, etc.).

**Theomancy**. Divination through oracles, from *theos*, a god, and *manteia*, divination.

**Theopathy**. Suffering for one's god. Religious fanaticism.

**Theophilanthropism** (*Gr.*). Love to God and man, or rather, in the philosophical sense, love of God through love of Humanity. Certain persons who during the first revolution in France sought to replace Christianity by pure philanthropy and reason, called themselves *theophilanthropists*.

**Theophilosophy**. Theism and philosophy combined.

**Theopneusty**. Revelation; something given or inspired by a god or divine being. Divine inspiration.

**Theopœa** (*Gr.*). A magic art of endowing inanimate figures, statues, and other objects, with life, speech, or locomotion.

**Theosophia** (*Gr.*). Wisdom-religion, or "Divine Wisdom". The substratum and basis of all the world-religions and philosophies, taught and practised by a few elect ever since man became a thinking being. In its practical bearing, Theosophy is purely divine ethics; the definitions in dictionaries are pure nonsense, based on religious prejudice and ignorance of the true spirit of the early Rosicrucians and mediæval philosophers who called themselves Theosophists.

**Theosophical Society**, or "Universal Brotherhood". Founded in 1875 at New York, by Colonel H. S. Olcott and H. P. Blavatsky, helped by W. Q. Judge and several others. Its avowed object was at first the scientific investigation of psychic or so-called "spiritualistic" phenomena, after which its three chief objects were declared, namely (1) Brotherhood of man, without distinction of race, colour, religion, or social position; (2) the serious study of the ancient world-religions for purposes of comparison and the selection therefrom of universal ethics; (3) the study and development of the latent divine powers in man. At the present moment it has over 250 Branches scattered all over the world, most of which are in India, where also its chief Headquarters are established. It is composed of several large Sections—the Indian, the American, the Australian, and the European Sections.

**Theosophists**. A name by which many mystics at various periods of history have called themselves. The Neo-Platonists of Alexandria were Theosophists; the Alchemists and Kabbalists during the mediæval ages were likewise so called, also the Martinists, the Quietists, and other kinds of mystics, whether acting independently or incorporated in a brotherhood or society. All real lovers of divine Wisdom and Truth had, and have, a right to the name, rather than those who, appropriating the qualification, live lives or perform actions opposed to the principles of Theosophy. As described by Brother Kenneth R. Mackenzie, the Theosophists of the past centuries—" entirely speculative, and founding no schools, have still exercised a silent influence upon philosophy; and, no doubt, when the time arrives, many ideas thus silently propounded may yet give new directions to human thought. One of the ways in which these doctrines have obtained not only authority, but power, has been among certain enthusiasts in the higher degrees of Masonry. This power has, however, to a great degree died with the founders, and modern Freemasonry contains few traces of theosophic influence. However accurate and beautiful some of the ideas of Swedenborg, Pernetty, Paschalis, Saint Martin, Marconis, Ragon, and Chastanier may have been, they have but little direct influence on society." This is true of the Theosophists of the last three centuries, but not of the later ones. For the Theosophists of the current century have already visibly impressed themselves on modern literature, and introduced the desire and craving for some philosophy in place of the blind dogmatic faith of yore, among the most intelligent portions of human-kind. Such is the difference between past and modern THEOSOPHY.

**Therapeutæ** (*Gr.*) or *Therapeutes*. A school of Esotericists, which was an inner group within Alexandrian Judaism and not, as generally believed, a "sect". They were "healers" in the sense that some "Christian" and "Mental" Scientists, members of the T.S., are healers, while they are at the same time good Theosophists and students of the esoteric sciences. Philo Judæus calls them "servants of god". As justly shown in *A Dictionary of . . . Literature, Sects,* and *Doctrines* (Vol. IV., art. "Philo Judmus") in mentioning the Therapeutes—"There appears no reason to think of a special "sect", but rather of an esoteric circle of *illuminati*, of 'wise men' . . . They were contemplative Hellenistic Jews."

**Thermutis** (*Eg.*). The asp-crown of the goddess Isis; also the name of the legendary daughter of Pharaoh who is alleged to have saved Moses from the Nile.

**Thero** (*Pali*). A priest of Buddha. *Therunnanse,* also.

**Theurgia,** or *Theurgy(Gr.)*. A communication with, and means of bringing down to earth, planetary spirits and angels—the "gods of Light". Knowledge of the inner meaning of their hierarchies, and purity of life alone can lead to the acquisition of the powers necessary for communion with them. To; arrive at such an exalted goal the aspirant must be absolutely worthy and unselfish.

**Theurgist.** The first school of practical theurgy (from **qeod,** god, and **ergon** work,) in the Christian period, was founded by Iamblichus among certain Alexandrian Platonists. The priests, however, who were attached to the temples of Egypt, Assyria, Babylonia and Greece, and whose business it was to evoke the gods during the celebration of the Mysteries, were known by this name, or its equivalent in other tongues, from the earliest archaic period. Spirits (but not those of the dead, the evocation of which was called *Necromancy*) were made visible to the eyes of mortals. Thus a theurgist had to be a hierophant and an expert in the esoteric learning of the Sanctuaries of all great countries. The Neo-platonists of the school of Iamblichus were called theurgists, for they performed the so-called "ceremonial magic", and evoked the *simulacra* or the images of the ancient heroes, "gods", and daimonia (**daimovia**, divine, spiritual entities). In the rare cases when the presence of a *tangible* and *visible* "spirit" was required, the theurgist had to furnish the weird apparition with a portion of his own flesh and blood—he had to perform the *thepœa* or the "creation of gods", by a mysterious process well known to the old, and perhaps some of the modern, *Tântrikas* and initiated Brahmans of India. Such is what is said in the *Book of Evocations* of the pagodas. It shows the perfect identity of rites and ceremonial between the oldest Brahmanic theurgy and that of the Alexandrian Platonists.

The following is from *Isis Unveiled*: "The Brahman Grihasta (the evocator) must be in a state of complete purity before he ventures to call forth the Pitris. After having prepared a lamp, some sandal-incense, etc., and having traced the magic circles taught him by the superior Guru, in order to keep away bad spirits, he ceases to breathe, and calls *the fire (Kundalini)* to his help to disperse his body." He pronounces a certain number of times the sacred word, and "his soul (astral body) escapes from its prison, his body disappears, and the soul (image) of the evoked spirit descends into the *double* body and animates it". Then "his (the theurgist's) soul (astral) re-enters its body, whose subtle particles have again been aggregating (to the objective sense), after having formed from themselves an aerial body for the deva (god or spirit) he evoked And then, the operator propounds to the latter questions "on the mysteries of Being and the transformation of the imperishable". The popular prevailing idea is that the theurgists, as well as the magicians, worked wonders, such as evoking the souls or shadows of the heroes and gods, and other thaumaturgic works, by *super natural powers*. But this never was the fact. They did it simply by the liberation of their own astral body, which, taking the form of a god or hero, served as a *medium* or vehicle through which the special current preserving the ideas and knowledge of that hero or god could be reached and manifested. (See "Iamblichus".)

**Thirty-two Ways of Wisdom** (*Kab.*). The *Zohar* says that Chochmah or Hokhmah (wisdom) generates all things "by means of (these) thirty-two paths". (*Zohar* iii., 290a The full account of them is found in the *Sepher Yezirah*, wherein letters and numbers constitute as entities the Thirty-two Paths of Wisdom, by which the Elohim built the whole Universe. For, as said elsewhere, the brain "hath an outlet from Zeir Anpin, and therefore it is spread and goes out to thirty-two ways". Zeir Anpin, the "Short Face" or the "Lesser Countenance", is the Heavenly Adam, Adam Kadmon, or Man. Man in the *Zohar* is looked upon as the twenty-two letters of the Hebrew alphabet to which the decad is added and hence the thirty-two symbols of his faculties or paths.

**Thohu-Bohu** (*Heb.*). From *Tohoo*—"the Deep" and *Bohu* "primeval Space"—or the Deep of Primeval Space, loosely rendered as "Chaos" "Confusion" and so on. Also spelt and pronounced "*tohu-bohu*".

**Thomei** (*Eg.*). The Goddess of Justice, with eyes bandaged and holding a cross. The same as the Greek Themis.

**Thor** (*Scand.*). From *Thonar* to "thunder". The son of Odin and Freya, and the chief of all Elemental Spirits. The god of thunder, *Jupiter Tonans*. The word Thursday is named after Thor. Among the Romans Thursday was the day of Jupiter, *Jovis dies, Jeudi* in French—the fifth day of the week, sacred also to the planet Jupiter.

**Thorah** (*Heb.*). "Law", written down from the transposition of the letters of the Hebrew alphabet. Of the "hidden Thorah" it is said that before At-tee-k-ah (the "Ancient of all the Ancients") had arranged Itself into limbs (or members) preparing Itself to manifest, It willed to create a Thorah; the latter upon being produced addressed It in these words: "It, that wishes to arrange and to appoint other things, should first of all, arrange Itself in Its proper Forms". In other words, Thorah, the Law, snubbed its Creator from the moment of its birth, according to the above, which is an interpolation of some later Talmudist. As it grew and developed, the mystic Law of the primitive Kabbalist was transformed and made by the Rabbins to supersede in its dead letter every metaphysical conception; and thus the Rabbinical and Talmudistic Law makes Ain Soph and every divine Principle subservient to itself, and turns its back upon the true esoteric interpretations.

**Thor's Hammer**. A weapon which had the form of the Svastika; called by European Mystics and Masons the "Hermetic Cross", and also "Jaina Cross", *croix cramponnée;* the most archaic, as the most sacred and universally respected symbol. (See "Svastika".)

**Thoth** (*Eg.*). The most mysterious and the least understood of gods, whose personal character is entirely distinct from all other ancient deities. While the permutations of Osiris, Isis, Horus, and the rest, are so numberless that their individuality is all but lost, Thoth remains changeless from the first to the last Dynasty. He is the god of wisdom and of authority over all other gods. He is the recorder and the judge. His ibis-head, the pen and tablet of the celestial scribe, who records the thoughts, words and deeds of men and weighs them in the balance, liken him to the type of the esoteric Lipikas. His name is one of the first that appears on the oldest monuments. He is the lunar god of the first dynasties, the master of Cynocephalus—the dog-headed ape who stood in Egypt as a living symbol and remembrance of the Third Root-Race. (*S. D., Vol.* II, pp. 184 and 185). He is the "Lord of Hermopolis" —Janus, Hermes and Mercury combined. He is crowned with an *atef* and the lunar disk, and bears the "Eye of Horus", the third eye, in his hand. He is the Greek Hermes, the god of learning, and Hermes Trismegistus, the "Thrice-great Hermes", the patron of physical sciences and the patron and very soul of the occult esoteric knowledge. As Mr. J. Bonwick, F.R.G.S., beautifully expresses it: "Thoth has a powerful effect on the imagination . . . in this intricate yet beautiful phantasmagoria of thought and moral sentiment of that shadowy past. It is in vain we ask ourselves however man, in the infancy of this world of humanity, in the rudeness of supposed incipient civilization, could have dreamed of such a heavenly being as Thoth. The lines are so delicately drawn, so intimately and tastefully interwoven, that we seem to regard a picture designed by the genius of a Milton, and executed with the skill of a Raphael." Verily, there was some truth in that old saying, "The wisdom of the Egyptians".When it is shown that the wife of Cephren, builder of the second Pyramid, was a priestess of Thoth, one sees that the ideas comprehended in him were fixed 6,000 years ago". According to Plato, "Thoth-Hermes was the discoverer and inventor of numbers, geometry, astronomy and letters". Proclus, the disciple of Plotinus, speaking of this mysterious deity, says: "He presides over every species of condition, leading us to an intelligible essence from this mortal abode, governing the different herds of souls".

In other words Thoth, as the Registrar and Recorder of Osiris in Amenti, the Judgment Hall of the Dead was a psychopompic deity; while Iamblichus hints that "the cross with a handle (the *thau* or *tau*) which Tot holds in his hand, was none other than the monogram of his name". Besides the Tau, as the prototype of Mercury, Thoth carries the serpent-rod, emblem of Wisdom, the rod that became the Caduceus. Says Mr.

Bonwick, "Hermes was the serpent itself in a mystical sense. He glides like that creature, noiselessly, without apparent exertion, along the course of ages. He is . . . a representative of the spangled heavens. But he is the foe of the bad serpent, for the ibis devoured the snakes of Egypt."

**Thothori Nyan Tsan** (*Tib.*) A King of Tibet in the fourth century. It is narrated that during his reign he was visited by five mysterious strangers, who revealed to him how he might use for his country's welfare *four precious things* which had fallen down from heaven, in 331 A.D., in a golden casket and "the use of which no one knew". These were (1) hands folded as the Buddhist ascetics fold them; (2) a be-jewelled *Shorten* (a Stupa built over a receptacle for relics); (3) a gem inscribed with the "Aum mani padme hum"; and ( the *Zamotog*, a religious work on ethics, a part of the Kanjur. A voice from heaven then told the King that after a certain number of generations everyone would learn how precious these four things were. The number of generations stated carried the world to the seventh century, when Buddhism became the accepted religion of Tibet. Making an allowance for legendary licence, the four things fallen from heaven, the voice, and the five mysterious strangers, may be easily seen to have been historical facts. They were without any doubt five Arhats or Bhikshus from India, on their proselytising tour. Many were the Indian. sages who, persecuted in India for their new faith, betook themselves to Tibet and China.

**Thrætaona** (*Mazd.*) The Persian Michael, who contended with Zohak or Azhi-Dahaka, the destroying serpent. In the *Avesta* Azhi-Dahaka is a three-headed monster, one of whose heads is human, and the two others Ophidian. Dahaka, who is shown in the Zoroastrian Scriptures as coming from Babylonia, stands as the allegorical symbol of the Assyrian dynasty of King Dahaka (Az-Dahaka) which ruled Asia with an iron hand, and whose banners bore the purple sign of the dragon, *Purpureum signum draconis*. Metaphysically, however, the human head denotes the physical man, and the two serpent heads the dual manasic principles — the dragon and serpent both standing as symbols of wisdom and occult powers.

**Thread Soul**. The same as *Sutrâtmâ* (*q.v.*).

**Three Degrees** (of Initiation). Every nation had its exoteric and esoteric religion, the one for the masses, the other for the learned and elect. For example, the Hindus had three degrees with several sub-degrees. The Egyptians had also three preliminary degrees, personified under the "three guardians of the fire "in the Mysteries. The Chinese had their most ancient *Triad* Society: and the Tibetans have to this day their "triple step"; which was symbolized in the *Vedas* by the three strides of Vishnu. Everywhere antiquity shows an unbounded reverence for the Triad and Triangle—the first geometrical figure. The old Babylonians had their three stages of initiation into the priesthood (which was then esoteric knowledge); the Jews, the Kabbalists and mystics borrowed them from the Chaldees, and the Christian Church from the Jews. "There are Two", says Rabbi Simon ben Jochai, "in conjunction with One; hence they are Three, and if they are Three, then they are One."

**Three Faces.** The *Trimûrti* of the Indian Pantheon; the three persons of the one godhead. Says the Book of Precepts: "There are two Faces, one in *Tushita* (Devâchân) and one in *Myalba* (earth); and the Highest Holy unites them and finally absorbs both."

**Three Fires** (Occult). The name given to Atmâ-Buddhi-Manas, which when united become one.

**Thsang Thisrong tsan** (*Tib.*). A king who flourished between the years 728 and 787, and who invited from Bengal Pandit Rakshit, called for his great learning Bodhisattva, to come and settle in Tibet, in order to teach Buddhist philosophy to his priests.

**Thûmi Sambhota** (*Sk.*). An Indian mystic and man of erudition, the inventor of the Tibetan alphabet.

**Thummim** (*Heb.*). "Perfections." An ornament on the breastplates of the ancient High Priests of Judaism. Modern Rabbins and Hebraists may well pretend they do not know the joint purposes of the *Thummim* and the *Urim*; but the Kabbalists do and likewise the Occultists. They were the instruments of *magic* divination and oracular communication—theurgic and astrological. This is shown in the following well-known facts — (1) upon each of the twelve precious stones was engraved the name of one of the twelve sons of Jacob, each of these "sons" personating one of the signs of the zodiac; (2) both were oracular images, like the *teraphim*, and uttered oracles by a voice, and both were agents for hypnotisation and throwing the priests who wore them into an ecstatic condition. The *Urim* and *Thummim* were not original with the Hebrews, but had been borrowed, like most of their other religious rites, from the Egyptians, with whom the mystic scarabæus worn on the breast by the Hierophants, had the same functions. They were thus purely *heathen and magical* modes of divination; and when the Jewish "Lord God" was called upon to manifest his presence and speak out his will through the *Urim* by preliminary incantations, the *modus operandi* was the same as that used by all the Gentile priests the world over.

**Thumos** (*Gr.*). The astral, animal soul; the *Kâmas-Manas; Thumos* means passion, desire and confusion and is so used by Homer. The word is probably derived from the Sanskit *Tamas*, which has the same meaning.

**Tia-Huanaco** (*Peruv.*). Most magnificent ruins of a pre-historic city in Peru.

**Tiamat** (*Chald.*). A female dragon personifying the ocean; the "great mother" or the living principle of chaos. Tiamat wanted to swallow Bel, but Bel sent a wind which entered her open mouth and killed Tiamat.

**Tiaou** (*Eg.*). A kind of Devachanic *post mortem* state.

**Tien-Hoang** (*Chin.*). The twelve hierarchies of Dhyânis.

**Tien-Sin** (*Chin.*). Lit., "the heaven of mind", or abstract, subjective, ideal heaven. A metaphysical term applied to the Absolute.

**Tikkun** (*Chald.*). Manifested Man or Adam Kadmon, the first ray from the manifested *Logos*.

**Tiphereth** (*Heb.*). Beauty; the sixth of the ten Sephiroth, a masculine active potency, corresponding to the Vau, V, of the Tetragrammaton IHVH; also called Melekh or King; and the Son. It is the central Sephira of the six which compose Zauir Anpin, the Microprosopus, or Lesser Countenance. It is translated "Beauty" and "Mildness".

**Tîrthakas**, or Tîrthika and Tîrthyas (*Sk.*). "Heretical teachers." An epithet applied by the Buddhist ascetics to the Brahmans and certain Yogis of India.

**Tirthankâra** (*Sk.*). Jaina saints and chiefs, of which there are twenty-four. It is claimed that one of them was the spiritual Guru of Gautama Buddha. Tirthankâra is a synonym of Jaina.

**Tiryakarota** (*Sk.*). From *tiryak* "crooked", and *srotas* (digestive) "canal". The name of the "creation" by Brahmâ of men or beings, whose stomachs were, on account of their erect position as bipeds, in a horizontal position. This is a Purânic invention, absent in Occultism.

**Tishya** (*Sk.*). The same as Kaliyuga, the Fourth Age.

**Titans** (*Gr.*). Giants of divine origin in Greek mythology who made war against the gods. Prometheus was one of them.

**Titikshâ** (*Sk.*). Lit., "long-suffering, patience". Titikshâ, daughter of Daksha and wife of Dharma (divine law) is its personification.

**To On** (*Gr.*). The "Being", the "Ineffable All" of Plato. He" whom no person has seen except the Son".

**Tobo** (*Gnost.*). In the *Codex Nazaræus,* a mysterious being which bears the soul of Adam from Orcus to the place of life, and thence is called "the liberator of the soul of Adam".

**Todas.** A mysterious people of India found in the unexplored fastnesses of Nilgiri (Blue) Hills in the Madras Presidency, whose origin, language and religion are to this day unknown. They are entirely distinct, ethnically, philologically, and in every other way, from the *Badagas* and the *Mulakurumbas*, two other races found on the same hills.

**Toom** (*Eg.*). A god issued from Osiris in his character of the Great Deep *Noot*. He is the Protean god who generates other gods, "assuming the form he likes". He is Fohat. (*S. D.*, Vol. I., p. 673.)

**Tope.** An artificial mound covering relics of Buddha or some other great Arhat. The Topes are also called Dâgobas.

**Tophet** (*Heb.*). A place in the valley of Gehenna, near Jerusalem, where a constant fire was kept burning, in which children were immolated to Baal. The locality is thus the prototype of the Christian Hell, the fiery Gehenna of endless woe.

**Toralva**, *Dr. Eugene.* A physician who lived in the fourteenth century, and who received as a gift from Friar Pietro, a great magician and a Dominican monk, a demon named Zequiel to be his faithful servant. (See *Isis Unveiled*, II., 60.)

**Toyâmbudhi** (*Sk.*). A country in the northern part of which lay the "White Island"—*Shveta Dwîpa* of the seven Purânic islands or continents.

**Trailokya**, or *Trilokya* (*Sk.*). Lit., the "three regions" or worlds; the complementary triad to the Brahmanical quaternary of worlds named *Bhuvanatraya*.A Buddhist profane layman will mention only three divisions of every world, while a non-initiated Brahman will maintain that there are four. The four divisions of the latter are purely physical and sensuous, the *Trailokya* of the Buddhist are purely spiritual and ethical. The Brahmanical division may be found fully described under the heading of *Vyahritis*, the difference being for the present sufficiently shown in the following parallel:

| Brahmanical Division of the Worlds. | Buddhist Division of the Regions. |
|---|---|
| 1. *Bhur*, earth. | 1. World of desire, *Kâmadhâtu* or *Kâmadôka*. |
| 2. *Bhuvah*, heaven, firmament. | |
| 3. *Swar* atmosphere the sky. | 2. World of form, *Rûpadhûtu*. |
| 4. *Mahar*, eternal luminous essence. | 3.The formless world *Arûpadhâtu*. |

All these are the worlds of *post mortem* states. For instance, Kâmalôka or Kâmadhâtu, the region of Mâra, is that which mediæval and modern Kabalists call the world of astral light, and the "world of shells Kâmalôka has, like every other region, its seven divisions, the lowest of which begins on earth or invisibly in its atmosphere; the six others ascend gradually, the highest being the abode of those who have died owing to accident, or suicide in a fit of temporary insanity, or were otherwise victims of external forces. It is a place where all those who have died before the end of the term allotted to them, and whose higher principles do not, therefore, go at once into Devachanic state—sleep a dreamless sweet sleep of oblivion, at the termination of which they are either reborn immediately, or pass gradually into the Devachanic state. Rûpadhâtu is the celestial world of *form*, or what we call *Devâchân*. With the uninitiated Brahmans, Chinese and other Buddhists, the Rûpadhâtu is divided into eighteen *Brahmâ* or *Devalokas*; the life of a soul therein lasts from half a Yuga up to 16,000 Yugas or Kalpas, and the height of the "Shades" is from half a Yojana up to 16,000 Yojanas (a *Yojana* measuring from five and a half to ten miles !), and such-like theological twaddle evolved from priestly brains. But the Esoteric Philosophy teaches that though for the Egos for the time being, everything or everyone preserves its form (as in a dream), yet as Rûpadhâtu is a *purely mental region*, and a state, the Egos themselves have *no form* outside their own consciousness. Esotericism divides this "region" into seven Dhyânas, "regions", or states of contemplation, which are not localities but mental representations of these. *Arûpadhâtu*: this "region" is again divided into seven Dhyânas, still more abstract and formless, for this "World" is without any form or desire whatever. It is the highest region of the *post mortem* Trailokya; and as it is the abode of those who are almost ready for Nirvâna and is, in fact, the very threshold of the Nirvânic state, it stands to reason that in Arûpadhâtu (or Arûpavachara) there can be neither form nor sensation, nor any feeling connected with our three dimensional Universe.

**Trees of Life.** From the highest antiquity trees were connected with the gods and mystical forces in nature. Every nation had its sacred tree, with its peculiar characteristics and attributes based on natural, and also occasionally on occult properties, as expounded in the esoteric teachings. Thus the peepul or *Âshvattha* of India, the abode of Pitris (elementals in fact) of a lower order, became the Bo-tree or *ficus religiosa* of the Buddhists the world over, since Gautama Buddha reached the highest knowledge and Nirvâna under such a tree. The ash tree, Yggdrasil, is the world-tree of the Norsemen or Scandinavians. The banyan tree is the symbol of spirit and matter, descending to the earth, striking root, and then re-ascending heavenward again. The triple-leaved palâsa is a symbol of the triple essence in the Universe—Spirit, Soul, Matter. The dark cypress was the world-tree of Mexico, and is now with the Christians and Mahomedans the emblem of death, of peace and rest. The fir was held sacred in Egypt, and its cone was carried in religious processions, though now it has almost disappeared from the land of the mummies; so also was the sycamore, the tamarisk, the palm and the vine. The sycamore was *the* Tree of Life in Egypt, and also in Assyria. It was sacred to Hathor at Heliopolis; and is now sacred in the same place to the Virgin Mary. Its juice was precious by virtue of its occult powers, as the Soma is with Brahmans, and Haoma with the Parsis. "The fruit and sap of the Tree of Life bestow immortality." A large volume might be written upon these sacred trees of antiquity, the reverence for some of which has survived to this day, without exhausting the subject.

**Trefoil**. Like the Irish shamrock, it has a symbolic meaning, "the three-in-one mystery" as an author calls it. It crowned the head of Osiris, and the wreath fell off when Typhon killed the radiant god. Some see in it a phallic significance, but we deny this idea in Occultism. It was the plant of Spirit, Soul, and Life.

**Tretâ Yuga** (*Sk.*). The second age of the world, a period of 1,296,000 years.

**Triad,** or *the Three*. The ten Sephiroth are contemplated as a group of three triads: Kether, Chochmah and Binah form the supernal triad; Chesed, Geburah and Tiphereth, the second; and Netzach, Hod and Yesod, the inferior triad. The tenth Sephira, Malkuth, is beyond the three triads. [w.w.w.]

The above is orthodox Western Kabalah. Eastern Occultists recognise but one triad—the upper one (corresponding to Atmâ-Buddhi and the "Envelope" which reflects their light, the three in one)—and count seven lower Sephiroth, everyone of which stands for a "principle", beginning with the Higher Manas and ending with the Physical Body—of which Malkuth is the representative in the Microcosm and the Earth in the Macrocosm.

**Tri-bhuvana**, or *Tri-loka* (*Sk.*). The three worlds—Swarga, Bhûmi, Pâtâla, or Heaven, Earth, and Hell in popular beliefs; esoterically, these are the Spiritual and Psychic (or Astral) regions, and the Terrestrial sphere.

**Tridandî** (*Sk.*). The name generally given to a class or sect of Sanyâsis who constantly keep in the hand a kind of club (*danda*) branching off into three rods at the top. The word is variously etymologized, and some give the name to the triple Brahmanical thread.

**Tri-dasha** (*Sk.*). Three times ten or "thirty". This is in round numbers the sum of the Indian Pantheon—the thirty-three *crores* of deities—the twelve Âdityas, the eight Vasus, the eleven Rudras and the two Ashvins, or *thirty-three kotis*, or 330 millions of gods.

**Trigunas** (*Sk.*). The three divisions of the inherent qualities of differentiated matter—i.e., of pure quiescence (*satva*), of activity and desire (*rajas*), of stagnation and decay (*tamas*) They correspond with Vishnu, Brahmâ, and Shiva. (See "Trimûrti".)

**Trijnâna,** (*Sk.*). Lit., "triple knowledge". This consists of three degrees (1) belief on faith; (2) belief on theoretical knowledge; and (3) belief through personal and practical knowledge.

**Trikâya** (Sk) Lit., three bodies, or forms. This is a most abstruse teaching which, however, once understood, explains the mystery of every triad or trinity, and is a true key to every three-fold metaphysical symbol. In its most simple and comprehensive form it is found in the human Entity in its triple division into spirit, soul, and body, and in the universe, regarded pantheistically, as a unity composed of a Deific, purely spiritual Principle, Supernal Beings—its direct rays —and Humanity. The origin of this is found in the teachings of the pre historic Wisdom Religion, or Esoteric Philosophy. The grand Pantheistic ideal, of the unknown and unknowable Essence being transformed first into subjective, and then into objective matter, is at the root of all these triads and triplets. Thus we find in philosophical Northern Buddhism (1) Âdi-Buddha (or Primordial Universal Wisdom); ( 2) the Dhyâni-Buddhas (or Bodhisattvas); (3) the Mânushi (Human) Buddhas. In European conceptions we find the same: God, Angels and Humanity symbolized theologically by the God-Man. The Brahmanical *Trimûrti* and also the three-fold body of Shiva, in Shaivism, have both been conceived on the same basis, if not altogether running on the lines of Esoteric teachings. Hence, no wonder if one finds this conception of the triple body—or the vestures of Nirmânakâya, Sambhogakâya and Dharmakâya, the grandest of the doctrines of Esoteric Philosophy—accepted in a more or less disfigured form by every religious sect, and explained quite incorrectly by the Orientalists. Thus, in its general application, the three-fold body symbolizes Buddha's statue, his teachings and his stûpas; in the priestly conceptions it applies to the Buddhist profession of faith called the *Triratna*, which is the formula of taking "refuge in Buddha, Dharma, and Sangha". Popular fancy makes Buddha ubiquitous, placing him thereby on a par with an anthropomorphic god, and lowering him to the level of a tribal deity; and, as a result, it falls into flat contradictions, as in Tibet and China. Thus the exoteric doctrine seems to teach that while in his Nirmâ kâya body (which passed through 100,000 *kotis* of transformations on earth), he, Buddha, is at the same time a Lochana (a heavenly Dhyâni-Bodhisattva), in his Sambhogakâya "robe of absolute completeness", and in Dhyâna, or a state which must cut him off from the world and all its connections; and finally and lastly he is, besides being a Nirmânakâya and a Sambhogakâya, also a Dharmakâya "of absolute purity", a Vairotchana or Dhyâni-Buddha in full Nirvâna! (See Eitel's *Sanskrit-Chinese Dictionary.*) This is the jumble of contradictions, impossible to reconcile, which is given out by missionaries and certain Orientalists as the philosophical dogmas of Northern Buddhism. If not an intentional confusion of a philosophy dreaded by the upholders of a religion based on inextricable contradictions and guarded "mysteries", then it is the product of ignorance. As the Trailokya, the Trikâya, and the Triratna are the three aspects of the same conceptions, and have to be, so to say, blended in one, the subject is further explained under each of these terms. (See also in this relation the term "Trisharana".)

**Tri-kûta** (*Sk.*). Lit., "three peaks". The mountain on which Lanka (modern Ceylon) and its city were built. It is said, allegorically, to be a mountain range running south from Meru. And so no doubt it was before Lankâ was submerged, leaving now but the highest summits of that range out of the waters. Submarine topography and geological formation must have considerably changed since the Miocene period. There is a legend to the effect that Vâyu, the god of the wind, broke the summit off Meru and cast it into the sea, where it forthwith became Lankâ.

**Trilcohana** (*Sk.*). Lit., "three-eyed", an epithet of Shiva. It is narrated that while the god was engaged one day on a Himalayan summit in rigid austerities, his wife placed her hand lovingly on his third eye, which burst from Shiva's forehead with a great flame. This is the eye which reduced Kâma, the god of love (as Mârâ, the tempter), to ashes, for trying to inspire him during his devotional meditation with thoughts of his wife.

**Trimûrti** (Sk). Lit., "three faces", or "triple form"—the Trinity. In the modern Pantheon these three persons are Brahmâ, the creator, Vishnu, the preserver, and Shiva, the destroyer. But this is an after thought, as in the *Vedas* neither Brahmâ nor Shiva is known, and the Vedic trinity consists of Agni, Vâyu and Sûrya; or as the *Nirukta* explains it, the terrestrial fire, the atmospheric (or aërial) and the heavenly fire, since Agni is the god of fire, Vâyu of the air, and Sûrya is the sun. As the *Padma Purâna* has it: "In the beginning, the great Vishnu, desirous of creating the whole world, became threefold: creator, preserver, destroyer. In order to produce this world, the Supreme Spirit emanated from the right side of his body, himself, as Brahmâ then, in order to preserve the universe, he produced from the left side of his body Vishnu; and in order to destroy the world he produced from the middle of his body the eternal Shiva. Some worship Brahmâ, some Vishnu, others Shiva; but Vishnu, one yet threefold, creates, preserves, and destroys, therefore let the pious make no difference between the three." The fact is, that all the three "persons" of the Trimûrti are simply the three qualificative *gunas* or attributes of the universe of differentiated Spirit-Matter, self-formative, self-preserving and self-destroying, for purposes of regeneration and perfectibility. This is the correct meaning; and it is shown in Brahmâ being made the personified embodiment of *Rajoguna*, the attribute or quality of activity, of desire for procreation, that desire owing to which the universe and everything in it is called into being. Vishnu is the embodied *Sattvaguna*, that property of preservation arising from quietude and restful enjoyment, which characterizes the intermediate period between the full growth and the beginning of decay; while Shiva, being embodied *Tamoguna*—which is the attribute of stagnancy and final decay—becomes of course the destroyer. This is as highly philosophical under its mask of anthropomorphism, as it is unphilosophical and absurd to hold to and enforce on the world the dead letter of the original conception.

**Trinity.** Everyone knows the Christian dogma of the "three in one" and "one in three"; therefore it is useless to repeat that which may he found in every catechism. Athanasius, the Church Father who defined the Trinity as a dogma, had little necessity of drawing upon inspiration or his own brain power; he had but to turn to one of the innumerable trinities of the heathen creeds, or to the Egyptian priests, in whose country he had lived all his life. He modified slightly only one of the three "persons". All the triads of the Gentiles were composed of the Father, Mother, and the Son. By making it "Father, Son, and Holy Ghost", he changed the dogma only outwardly, as the Holy Ghost had always been feminine, and Jesus is made to address the Holy Ghost as his "mother" in every Gnostic Gospel.

**Tripada** (*Sk.*). "Three-footed", fever, personified as having three feet or stages of development—cold, heat and sweat.

**Tripitaka** (*Sk.*). Lit., "the three baskets"; the name of the Buddhist canon. It is composed of three divisions: (1) the doctrine; (2) the rules and laws for the priesthood and ascetics; (3) the philosophical dissertations and metaphysics: to wit, the Abhidharma, defined by Buddhaghosa as that law (*dharma*) which goes beyond (*abhi*) the law. The Abhidharma contains the most profoundly metaphysical and philosophical teachings, and is the store-house whence the Mahâyâna and Hînayâna Schools got their fundamental doctrines. There is a fourth division—the *Samyakta Pitaka*. But as it is a later addition by the Chinese Buddhists, it is not accepted by the Southern Church of Siam and Ceylon.

**Triratna**, or *Ratnatraya* (*Sk*) The Three Jewels, the technical term for the well-known formula "Buddha, Dharma and Sangha" (or Samgha), the two latter terms meaning, in modern interpretation, "religious law" (Dharma), and the "priesthood" (Sangha). Esoteric Philosophy, however, would regard this as a very loose rendering. The words "Buddha, Dharma and Sangha", ought to be pronounced as in the days of Gautama, the Lord Buddha, namely "Bodhi, Dharma and Sangha and interpreted to mean "Wisdom, its laws and priests", the latter in the sense of "spiritual exponents", or adepts. Buddha, however, being regarded as personified "Bodhi" on earth, a true *avatar* of Âdi-Buddha, Dharma gradually came to be regarded as his own particular law, and Sangha as his own special priesthood. Nevertheless, it is the profane of the later (now modern) teachings who have shown a greater degree of natural intuition than the actual interpreters of Dharma, the Buddhist priests. The people see the Triratna in the three statues of Amitâbha, Avalokiteshvara and Maitreya Buddha; i.e., in Boundless Light" or Universal Wisdom, an impersonal principle which is the correct meaning of Âdi-Buddha; in the "Supreme Lord" of the Bodhisattvas, or Avalokiteshvara; and in Maitreya Buddha, the symbol of the terrestrial and human Buddha, the "Mânushi Buddha". Thus, even though the uninitiated do call these three statues "the Buddhas of the Past, the Present and the Future", still every follower of true *philosophical* Buddhism—called "atheistical" by Mr. Eitel—would explain the term Triratna correctly. The philosopher of the Yogachârya School would say—as well he could—"Dharma is not a person but an unconditioned and underived entity, combining in itself the spiritual and material principles of the universe, whilst from Dharma proceeded, by emanation, Buddha [Bodhi rather], as the creative energy which produced, in conjunction with Dharma, the third factor in the trinity, viz., 'Samgha', which is the comprehensive sum total of all real life." Samgha, then, is not and cannot be that which it is now understood to be, namely, the actual "priesthood"; for the latter is not the sum total of all *real* life, but only of religious life. The real primitive significance of the word Samgha or "Sangha" applies to the Arhats or Bhikshus, or the "initiates", alone, that is to say to the real exponents of Dharma—the divine law and wisdom, coming to them as a reflex light from the one "boundless light". Such is its *philosophical* meaning. And yet, far from satisfying the scholars of the Western races, this seems only to irritate them; for E. J. Eitel, of Hongkong, remarks, as to the above: "Thus the dogma of a Triratna, originating from three primitive articles of faith, and at one time culminating in the conception of three persons, a trinity in unity, *has degenerated into a metaphysical theory of the evolution of three abstract principles*"! And if one of the ablest European scholars will sacrifice every philosophical ideal to gross anthropomorphism, then what can Buddhism with its subtle metaphysics expect at the hands of ignorant missionaries?

**Trisharana** (*Sk.*). The same as "Triratna" and accepted by both the Northern and Southern Churches of Buddhism. After the death of the Buddha it was adopted by the councils as a mere kind of *formula fidei*, enjoining "to take refuge in Buddha", "to take refuge in Dharma", and "to take refuge in Sangha", or his Church, in the sense in which it is now interpreted; but it is not in this sense that the "Light of Asia" would have taught the formula. Of Trikâya, Mr. E. J. Eitel, of Hongkong, tells us in his *Handbook of Chinese Buddhism* that this "trichotomism was taught with regard to the nature of all Buddhas. Bodhi being the characteristic of a Buddha"—a distinction was made between "essential Bodhi" as the attribute of the Dharmakâya, i.e., "essential body"; "reflected Bodhi" as the attribute of Sambhogakâya; and "practical Bodhi" as the attribute of Nirmânakâya. Buddha combining in himself these three conditions of existence, was said to be living at the same time in three different spheres. Now, this shows how greatly misunderstood is the purely pantheistical and philosophical teaching. Without stopping to enquire how even a Dharmakâya vesture can have any "attribute" in Nirvâna, which state is shown, in philosophical Brahmanism as much as in Buddhism, to be absolutely devoid of any attribute as conceived by human finite thought— it will be sufficient to point to the following —(1) the Nirmânakâya vesture is preferred by the "Buddhas of Compassion" to that of the Dharmakâya state, precisely because the latter precludes him who attains it from any communication or relation with the finite, i.e., with humanity; (2) it is not Buddha (Gautama, the mortal man, or any other personal Buddha) who lives ubiquitously in "three different spheres, at the same time", but Bodhi, the universal and abstract principle of divine wisdom, symbolised in philosophy by Âdi-Buddha. It is the latter that is ubiquitous because it is the universal essence or principle. It is Bodhi, or the spirit of Buddhaship, which, having resolved itself into its primordial homogeneous essence and merged into it, as Brahmâ (the universe) merges into Parabrahm, the ABSOLUTENESS—that is meant under the name of "essential Bodhi". For the Nirvânee, or Dhyâni Buddha, must be supposed—by living in Arûpadhâtu, the *formless* state, and in Dharmakâya—to be that "essential Bodhi" itself. It is the Dhyâni Bodhisattvas, the primordial rays of the universal Bodhi, who live in "reflected Bodhi" in Râpadhâtu, or the world of subjective "forms"; and it is the Nirmânakâyas (plural) who upon ceasing their lives of "practical Bodhi", in the "enlightened" or Buddha forms, remain voluntarily in the Kâmadhâtu (the world of desire), whether in objective forms on earth or in subjective states in its sphere (the second Buddhakshetra). This they do in order to watch over, protect and help mankind. Thus, it is neither *one* Buddha who is meant, nor any particular avatar of the collective Dhyâni Buddhas, but verily Âdi-Bodhi—the first Logos, whose primordial ray is Mahâbuddhi, the Universal Soul, ALAYA, whose flame is ubiquitous, and whose influence has a different sphere in each of the three forms of existence, because, once again, *it is Universal Being itself* or the reflex of the *Absolute*. Hence, if it is philosophical to speak of Bodhi, which "as Dhyâni Buddha rules in the domain of the spiritual" (fourth Buddhakshetra or region of Buddha); and of the Dhyâni Bodhisattvas "ruling in the third Buddhakshetra"or the domain of ideation; and even of the Mânushi Buddhas, who are in the second Buddhakshetra as Nirmanakâyas—to apply the "idea of a unity in trinity" to three *personalities*—is highly unphilosophical.

**Trishnâ** (*Sk.*). The fourth Nidâna; spiritual love.

**Trishûla** (*Sk.*). The trident of Shiva.

**Trisuparna** (*Sk.*). A certain portion of the Veda, after thoroughly studying which a Brâhman is also called a Trisuparna.

**Trithemius**. An abbot of the Spanheim Benedictines, a very learned Kabbalist and adept in the Secret Sciences, the friend and instructor of Cornelius Agrippa.

**Triton** (*Gr.*). The san of Poseidon and Amphitrite, whose body from the waist upwards was that of a man and whose lower limbs were those of a dolphin. Triton belongs in esoteric interpretation to the group of fish symbols—such as *Oannes* (Dagon), the Matsya or Fish-avatar, and the *Pisces*, as adopted in the Christian symbolism. The dolphin is a constellation called by the Greeks *Capricornus*, and the latter is the Indian *Makâra*. It has thus an anagrammatical significance, and its interpretation is entirely occult and mystical, and is known only to the advanced students of Esoteric Philosophy. Suffice to say that it is as physiological as it is spiritual and mystical. (See *S. D.*, Vol. II, pp. 578 and 579.)

**Trividha Dvâra** (*Sk.*). Lit., the "three gates", which are body, mouth, and mind; or purity of body, purity of speech, purity of thought—the three virtues requisite for becoming a Buddha.

**Trividyâ** (*Sk.*). Lit., "the three knowledges" or sciences". These are the three fundamental axioms in mysticism —(a) the impermanency of all existence, or *Anitya*; (b) suffering and misery of all that lives and is, or *Dukha*; and (c) all physical, objective existence as evanescent and unreal as a water-bubble in a dream, or *Anâtmâ*.

**Trivikrama** (*Sk.*).An epithet of Vishnu used in the *Rig Veda* in relation to the "three steps of Vishnu". The first step he took on earth, in the form of Agni; the second in the atmosphere, in the form of Vâyu, god of the air; and the third in the sky, in the shape of Sûrya, the sun.

**Triyâna** (*Sk.*). "The three vehicles" across Sansâra—the ocean of births, deaths, and rebirths—are the vehicles called *Sravaka*, *Pratyeka Buddha* and *Bodhisattva*, or the three degrees of Yogaship. The term Triyâna is also used to denote the three schools of mysticism—the Mahâyâna, Madhyimâyâna and Hînayâna schools; of which the first is the "Greater", the second the "Middle", and the last the "Lesser" Vehicle. All and every system between the Greater and the Lesser Vehicles are considered "useless". Therefore the Pratyeka Buddha is made to correspond with the Madhyimâyâna. For, as explained, "this (the Pratyeka Buddha state) refers to him who lives all for himself and very little for others, occupying the middle of the vehicle, filling it all and leaving no room for others". Such is the selfish candidate for Nirvâna.

**Tsanagi-Tsanami** (*Jap.*). A kind of creative god in Japan.

**Tsien-Sin** (*Chin.*). The "Heaven of Mind", Universal Ideation and Mahat, when applied to the plane of differentiation, "Tien-Sin" (*q.v.*) when referring to the Absolute.

**Tsien-Tchan** (*Ch.*). The universe of form and matter.

**Tsi-tsai** (*Chin.*). The "Self-Existent" or the "Unknown Darkness", the root of *Wuliang Sheu*, "Boundless Age", all Kabbalistic terms, which were used in

China ages before the Hebrew Kabbalists adopted them, borrowing them from Chaldea and Egypt.

**Tubal-Cain** (*Heb.*). The Biblical Kabir, "an instructor of every artificer in brass and iron", the son of Zillah and Lamech; one with the Greek Hephæstos or Vulcan. His brother Jabal, the son of Adah and the co-uterine brother of Jabal, one the father of those "who handle the harp and organ", and the other the father "of such as have cattle", are also Kabiri: for, as shown by Strabo, it is the Kabiri (or Cyclopes in one sense) who made the harp for Kronos and the trident for Poseidon, while some of their other brothers were instructors in agriculture. Tubal-Cain (or Thubal-Cain) is a word used in the Master-Mason's degree in the ritual and ceremonies of the Freemasons.

**Tullia** (*Lat.*). A daughter of Cicero, in whose tomb, as claimed by several alchemists, was found burning a perpetual lamp, placed there more than a thousand years previously.

**Tum**, or *Toóm* The "Brothers of the Tum", a very ancient school of Initiation in Northern India in the days of Buddhist persecution. The "Turn B'hai" have now become the "Aum B'hai", spelt, however, differently at present, both schools having merged into one. The first was composed of Kshatriyas, the second of Brahmans. The word "Tum" has a double meaning, that of darkness (absolute darkness), which as absolute is higher than the highest and purest of lights, and a sense resting on the mystical greeting among Initiates, "Thou art thou, thyself", equivalent to saying "Thou art one with the Infinite and the All".

**Turîya** (*Sk.*). A state of the deepest trance—the fourth state of the Târaka Râja Yoga, one that corresponds with Âtmâ, and on this earth with *dreamless* sleep—a causal condition.

**Turîya Avasthâ** (*Sk.*). Almost a Nirvânic state in Samâdhi, which is itself a beatific state of the contemplative Yoga beyond this plane. A condition of the higher Triad, quite distinct (though still inseparable) from the conditions of *Jagrat* (waking), *Svapna* (dreaming), and *Sushupti* (sleeping).

**Tushita** (*Sk.*). A class of gods of great purity in the Hindu Pantheon. In exoteric or popular Northern Buddhism, it is a Deva-loka, a celestial region on the material plane, where all the Bodhisattvas are *reborn*, before they descend on this earth as future Buddhas.

**Tyndarus** (*Gr.*). King of Lacedæmon the fabled husband of Leda, the mother of Castor and Pollux and of Helen of Troy.

**Typhæus** (*Gr.*). A famous giant, who had a hundred heads like those of a serpent or dragon, and who was the reputed father of the Winds, as Siva was that of the Maruts—also "winds". He made war against the gods, and is identical with the Egyptian Typhon.

**Typhon** (*Eg.*). An aspect or shadow of Osiris. Typhon is not, as Plutarch asserts, the distinct "Evil Principle" or the Satan of the Jews; but rather the lower cosmic "principles" of the divine body of Osiris, the god in them— Osiris being the personified universe as an ideation, and Typhon as that same universe in its material realization. The two in one are Vishnu-Siva. The true meaning of the Egyptian myth is that Typhon is the terrestrial and material envelope of Osiris, who is the indwelling spirit thereof. In chapter 42 of the *Ritual* (" Book of the Dead"), Typhon is described as "Set, formerly called Thoth". Orientalists find themselves greatly perplexed by discovering Set-Typhon addressed in some papyri as "a great and good god", and in others as the embodiment of evil. But is not Siva, one of the Hindu *Trimûrti*, described in some places as "the best and most bountiful of gods", and at other times, "a dark, black, destroying, terrible" and "fierce god"? Did not Loki, the Scandinavian Typhon, after having been described in earlier times as a beneficent being, as the god of fire, the presiding genius of the peaceful domestic hearth, suddenly lose caste and become forthwith a power of evil, a cold-hell Satan and a demon of the worst kind? There is a good reason for such an invariable transformation. So long as these dual gods, symbols of good and necessary evil, of light and darkness, keep closely allied, i.e., stand for a combination of differentiated human qualities, or of the element they represent—they are simply an embodiment of the average *personal* god. No sooner, however, are they separated into two entities, each with its two characteristics, than they become respectively the two opposite poles of good and evil, of light and darkness; they become in short, two independent and distinct entities or rather *personalities*. It is only by dint of sophistry that the Churches have succeeded to this day in preserving in the minds of the few the Jewish deity in his primeval integrity. Had they been logical they would have separated Christ from Jehovah, light and goodness from darkness and badness. And this was what happened to Osiris Typhon;but no Orientalist has understood it, and thus their perplexity goes on increasing. Once accepted—as in the case of the Occultists—as an integral part of Osiris, just as Ahriman is an inseparable part of Ahura Mazda, and the Serpent of Genesis the dark aspect of the Elohim, blended into our "Lord God"— every difficulty in the nature of Typhon disappears. Typhon is a later name of Set, later but ancient—as early in fact as the fourth Dynasty; for in the *Ritual* one reads: "O Typhon-Set ! I invoke thee, terrible, invisible, all-powerful god of gods, thou who destroyest and renderest desert". Typhon belongs most decidedly to the same symbolical category as Siva the Destroyer, and Saturn—the "dark god". In the *Book of the Dead,* Set, in his battle with Thoth (wisdom)_who is his spiritual counterpart —is emasculated as Saturn-Kronos was and Ouranos before him. As Siva is closely connected with the bull Nandi—an aspect of Brahmâ-Vishnu, the creative and preserving powers—so is Set-Typhon allied with the bull Apis, both bulls being sacred to, and allied with, their respective deities. As Typhon was originally worshipped as an *upright stone*, the phallus, so is Siva to this day represented and worshipped as a lingham. Siva is Saturn. Indeed, Typhon-Set seems to have served as a prototype for more than one god of the later ritualistic cycle, including even the god of the Jews, some of his ritualistic observances having passed bodily into the code of laws and the canon of religious rites of the "chosen people". Who of the Bible-worshippers knows the origin of the scape-goat (*ez* or *aza*) sent into the wilderness as an atonement ? Do they know that ages before the exodus of Moses the goat was sacred to Typhon, and that it is over the head of that Typhonic goat that the Egyptians confessed their sins, after which the animal was turned into the desert? "And Aaron shall take the scapegoat (Azâzel) and lay his hands upon the head of the live goat, *and confess over him all the iniquities* of the children of Israel . . . and shall send him away . . . into the wilderness" (*Levit.*, xvi.). And as the goat of the Egyptians made an atonement with Typhon, so the goat of the Israelites "made an atonement before the Lord" (*Ibid.*, v. 10). Thus, if one only remembers that every anthropomorphic creative god was with the philosophical ancients the "Life-giver" and the "Death-dealer"—Osiris and Typhon, Ahura Mazda and Ahriman, etc., etc.—it will be easy for him to comprehend the assertion made by the Occultists, that Typhon was but a symbol for the lower quaternary, the ever conflicting and turbulent principles of differentiated chaotic matter, whether in the Universe or in Man, while Osiris symbolized the higher spiritual triad. Typhon is accused in the Ritual of being one who "steals reason from the soul". Hence, he is shown fighting with Osiris and cutting him into fourteen (twice seven) pieces, after which, left without his counterbalancing power of good and light, he remains steeped in evil and darkness. In this way the fable told by Plutarch becomes comprehensible as an allegory. He asserts that, overcome in his fight with Horus, Typhon "fled seven days on an ass, and escaping begat the boys Ierosolumos and Ioudaios". Now as Typhon was worshipped at a later period under the form of an ass, and as the name of the ass is AO, or (phonetically) IAO, the vowels mimicking the braying of the animal, it becomes evident that Typhon was purposely blended with the name of the Jewish God, as the two names of Judea and Jerusalem, begotten by Typhon—sufficiently imply.

**Twashtri** (*Sk.*). The same as Vishwakarman, "the divine artist", the carpenter and weapon-maker of the gods. (See "Vishwakarman".)

**Tzaila** (*Heb.*). A rib; see Genesis for the myth of the creation of the first woman from a rib of Adam, the first man. It is curious that no other myth describes anything like this "rib" process, except the Hebrew Bible. Other similar Hebrew words are" Tzela, a "fall", and Tzelem, "the image of God". Inman remarks that the ancient Jews were fond of punning conceits, and sees one here—that Adam *fell*, on account of a *woman*, whom God made in his *image*, from a fall in the man's side. [w.w.w.]

**Tzelem** (*Heb.*). An image, a shadow. The shadow of the physical body of a man, also the astral body—*Linga Sharira*. (See "Tzool-mah".)

**Tzim-tzum** (*Kab.*). Expansion and contraction, or, as some Kabbalists explain it—"the centrifugal and centripetal energy".

**Tziruph** (*Heb*)A set of combinations and permutations of the Hebrew letters designed to shew analogies and preserve secrets. For example, in the form called Atbash, A and T were substitutes, B and Sh, G and R, etc. [w.w.w.]

**Tzool-mah** (*Kab.*). Lit., "shadow". It is stated in the *Zohar* (I., 218 a, i. fol. 117 a, col. 466.), that during the last seven nights of a mans life, the *Neshczmah*, his spirit, leaves him and the shadow, *tzool-mah*, acts no longer, his body casting no shadow; and when the *tzool-mah* disappears entirely, then *Ruach* and *Nephesh*—the soul and life—go with it. It has been often urged that in Kabbalistic philosophy there were but three, and, with the Body, *Guff*, four "principles". It can be easily shown there are seven, and several subdivisions more, for there are the "upper" and the "lower" *Neshamah* (the dual Manas); *Ruach*, Spirit or Buddhi; *Nephesh* (Kâma) which "has no light from her own substance", but is associated with the *Guff*, Body; *Tzelem*, "Phantom of the Image" and *D'yooknah*, Shadow of the Phantom Image, or *Mâyâvi Rûpa*. Then come the *Zurath*, Prototypes, and *Tab-nooth*, Form; and finally, *Tzurah*, ' highest Principle (Âtman) which remains above", etc., etc. (See Myer's *Qabbalah*, pp. 400 *et. seq.*)

**Tzuphon** (*Heb.*). A name for Boreas, the Northern Wind, which some of the old Israelites deified and worshipped.

**Tzurah** (*Heb.*). The divine prototype in the *Kabbalah*. In Occultism it embraces Âtmâ-Buddhi-Manas, the Highest Triad; the eternal divine *Individual*. The plural is *tzurath*.

**Tzure** (*Heb.*). Almost the same as the above: the prototype of the "Image" *tzelem*; a Kabbalistic term used in reference to the so-called creation of the divine and the human Adam, of which the *Kabala* (or *Kabbalah*) has four types, agreeing with the root-races of men. The Jewish Occultists knew of no Adam and, refusing to recognise in the first human race Humanity with Its Adam, spoke only of "primordial sparks".

# U

**U** . — The twenty-first letter of the Latin alphabet, which has no equivalent in Hebrew. As a number, however, it is considered very mystical both by the Pythagoreans and the Kabbalists, as it is the product of 3 x 7. The latter consider it the most sacred of the odd numbers, as 21 is the sum of the numerical value of the Divine Name *aeie*, or *eiea*, or again *aheihe*—thus (read backward, *aheihe*)

$$he \quad i \quad he \quad a$$
$$5 + 10 + 5 + 1 = 21$$

In Alchemy it symbolizes the twenty-one days necessary for the transmutation of baser metals into silver.

**Uasar** (*Eg.*). The same as Osiris, the latter name being Greek. Uasar is described as the "Egg-born", like Brahmâ. "He is the egg-sprung Eros of Aristophanes, whose creative energy brings all things into existence; the demiurge who made and animates the world, a being who is a sort of personification of Amen, the invisible god, as Dionysos is a link between mankind and the Zeus Hypsistos" (The *Great Dionysiak Myth*, Brown). Isis is called *Uasi*, as she is the *Sakti* of Osiris, his female aspect, both symbolizing the creating, energising, vital forces of nature in its aspect of male and female deity.

**Uchchaih-Sravas** (*Sk.*). The model-horse; one of the fourteen precious things or Jewels produced at the Churning of the Ocean by the gods. The white horse of Indra, called the Râjâ of horses.

**Uchnîcha**, also *Buddhôchnîcha* (*Sk.*). Explained as "a protuberance on Buddha's cranium, forming a hair-tuft". This curious description is given by the Orientalists, varied by another which states that Uchnîcha was "originally a conical or flame-shaped hair tuft on the crown of a Buddha, in later ages represented as a fleshy excrescence on the skull itself". This ought to read quite the reverse; for esoteric philosophy would say: Originally an orb with the *third eye* in it, which degenerated later in the human race into a fleshy protuberance, to disappear gradually, leaving in its place but an occasional flame-coloured aura, perceived only through clairvoyance, and when the exuberance of spiritual energy causes the (now concealed) "third eye to radiate its superfluous magnetic power. At this period of our racial development, it is of course the "Buddhas" or Initiates alone who enjoy in full the faculty of the "third eye" , as it is more or less atrophied in everyone else.

**Udâna** (*Sk*) Extemporaneous speeches; also Sûtras. In philosophy the term applies to the physical organs of speech, such as tongue, mouth, voice, etc. In sacred literature in general, it is the name of those Sûtras which contain extemporaneous discourses, in distinction to the Sûtras that contain only that subject matter which is introduced by questions put to Gautama the Buddha and his replies.

**Udayana** (*Sk.*). Modern Peshawer. "The classic *land of sorcery*" according to Hiouen-Thsang.

**Udayana Râjâ** (*Sk.*). A king of Kausâmbî, called Vatsarâjâ, who was the first to have a statue of Buddha made before his death; in consequence of which, say the Roman Catholics, who build statues of Madonnas and Saints at every street corner—he "became the originator of Buddhist IDOLATRY".

**Udra Ramaputra** (*Sk.*). Udra, the son of Râma. A Brahman ascetic, who was for some years the Guru of Gautama Buddha.

**Udumbara** (*Sk.*). A lotus of gigantic size, sacred to Buddha: the *Nila Udumbara* or "blue lotus", regarded as a supernatural omen when ever it blossoms, for it flowers but once every three thousand years. One such, it is said, burst forth before the birth of Gautama, another, near a lake at the foot of the Himalayas, in the fourteenth century, just before the birth of Tsong-kha-pa, etc., etc. The same is said of the Udumbara tree (*ficus glomerata*) because it flowers at intervals of long centuries, as does also a kind of cactus, which blossoms only at extra ordinary altitudes and opens at midnight.

**Ullambana** (*Sk.*). The festival of "all souls", the prototype of All Souls' Day in Christian lands. It is held in China on the seventh moon annually, when both "Buddhist and Tauist priests read masses, to release the souls of those who died on land or sea from purgatory, scatter rice to feed Prêtas [classes of demons ever hungry and thirsty], consecrate domestic ancestral shrines,

. . . . recite Tantras . . . accompanied by magic finger-play (mûdra) to comfort the ancestral spirits of seven generations in Nâraka" (a kind of purgatory or *Kama Loka*) The author of the *Sanskrit-Chinese Dictionary* thinks that this is the old Tibetan (Bhon) "Gtorma ritual engrafted upon Confucian ancestral worship," owing to Dhamaraksha translating the *Ullambana Sûtra* and introducing it into China. The said Sûtra is certainly a forgery, as it gives these rites on the authority of Sâkyamuni Buddha, and "supports it by the alleged experiences of his principal disciples, Ânanda being said to have appeased Prêtas by food offerings". But as correctly stated by Mr. Eitel, "the whole theory, with the ideas of intercessory prayers, priestly litanies and requiems, and ancestral worship, is entirely foreign to ancient and Southern Buddhism". And to the Northern too, if we except the sects of Bhootan and Sikkim, of the Bhon or Dugpa persuasion—the *red caps*, in short. As the ceremonies of All Saints' Day, or days, are known to have been introduced into China in the third century (265-292), and as the same Roman Catholic ceremonial and ritual for the dead, held on November 2nd, did not exist in those early days of Christianity, it cannot be the Chinese who borrowed this religious custom from the Latins, but rather the latter who imitated the Mongolians and Chinese.

**Uller** (*Scand.*). The god of archery, who "journeys over the silvery ice-ways on skates". He is the patron of the chase during that period when the Sun passes over the constellation of Sagittarius; and lives in the "Home of the Light-Elves" which is in the Sun and outside of Asgard.

**Ulom** (*Pœnic.*) The intelligible deity. The objective or material Universe, in the theogony of Mochus. The reflection of the ever-concealed deity; the Plerôma of the Gnostics.

**Ulphilas** (*Scand.*). A schoolman who made a new alphabet for the Goths in the fourth century—a union of Greek letters with the form of the runic alphabet, since which time the runes began to die out and their secret was gradually lost. (See "Runes".) He translated the Bible into Gothic, preserved in the *Codex Argenteus.*

**Ulûpî** (*Sk.*). A daughter of Kauravya, King of the *Nâgas* in Pâtâla (the nether world, or more correctly, the Antipodes, America). Exoterically, she was the daughter of a king or chief of an aboriginal tribe of the Nâgas, or Nagals (ancient adepts) in pre-historic America—Mexico most likely, or Uruguay. She was married to Arjuna, the disciple of Krishna, whom every tradition, oral and written, shows travelling five thousand years ago to Pâtâla (the Antipodes). The Purânic tale is based on a historical fact.

Moreover, Ulûpi, as a name, has a Mexican ring in it, like "Atlan", "Aclo", etc.

**Umâ-Kanyâ** *(Sk.)*. Lit., "Virgin of Light"; a title ill-befitting its possessor, as it was that of Durgâ Kâli, the goddess or female aspect of Siva. Human flesh was offered to her every autumn; and, as Durgâ, she was the patroness of the once murderous Thugs of India, and the special goddess of Tântrika sorcery. But in days of old it was not as it is now. The earliest mention of the title "Umâ-Kanyâ is found in the *Kena-Upanishad*; in it the now blood-thirsty Kâlî, was a benevolent goddess, a being of light and goodness, who brings about reconciliation between Brahmâ and the gods. She is Saraswati and she is Vâch. In esoteric symbology, Kâlî is the dual type of the dual soul—the divine and the human, the light and the dark soul of man,

**Umbra** *(Lat.)*. The shadow of an earth-bound spook. The ancient Latin races divided man (in esoteric teachings) into seven principles, as did every old system, and as Theosophists do now. They believed that after death *Anima*, the pure divine soul, ascended to heaven, a place of bliss; *Manes* (the Kâma Rûpa) descended into Hades (Kâma Loka); and Umbra (or astral double, the *Linga Sharîra*) remained on earth hovering about its tomb, because the attraction of physical, objective matter and affinity to its earthly body kept it within the places which that body had impressed with its emanations. Therefore, they said that nothing but the astral image of the defunct could be seen on earth, and even that faded out with the disintegration of the last particle of the body which had been so long its dwelling.

**Una** *(Sk.)*. Something underlying; subordinate; secondary also, and material.

**Undines** *(Lat.)*. Water nymphs and spooks. One of the four principal kinds of elemental spirits, 'which are Salamanders (fire), Sylphs (air), Gnomes (earth), and Undines (water).

**Upâdâna** *(Sk.)*. Material Cause; as flax is the cause of linen.

**Upâdâna Kâranam** *(Sk.)*. The material cause of an effect.

**Upâdhi** *(Sk.)*. Basis; the vehicle, carrier or bearer of something less material than itself: as the human body is the *upâdhi* of its spirit, ether the *upâdhi* of light, etc., etc.; a mould; a defining or limiting substance.

**Upadvîpas** *(Sk.)*. The root (underlying) of islands; dry land.

**Upanishad** *(Sk.)*. Translated as "esoteric doctrine", or interpretation of the

*Vedas* by the *Vedânta* methods. The third division of the *Vedas* appended to the *Brâhmanas* and regarded as a portion of *Sruti* or "revealed" word. They are, however, as records, far older than the *Brâhmanas* the exception of the two, still extant, attached to the *Rig -Veda* of the Aitareyins. The term *Upanishad* is explained by the Hindu pundits as "that which destroys ignorance, and thus produces liberation" of the spirit, through the knowledge of the supreme though *hidden* truth; the same, therefore, as that which was hinted at by Jesus, when he is made to say, "And ye shall know the truth, and the truth shall make you free" (*John* viii. 32). It is from these treatises of the *Upanishads*—themselves the echo of the primeval Wisdom-Religion—that the Vedânta system of philosophy has been developed. (See "Vedânta".) Yet old as the *Upanishads* may be, the Orientalists will not assign to the oldest of them more than an antiquity of 600 years B.C. The accepted number of these treatises is 150, though now no more than about twenty are left unadulterated. They treat of very abstruse, metaphysical questions, such as the origin of the Universe; the nature and the essence of the Unmanifested Deity and the manifested gods the connection, primal and ultimate, of spirit and matter; the universality of mind and the nature of the human Soul and Ego.

The *Upanishads* must be far more ancient than the days of Buddhism, as they show no preference for, nor do they uphold, the superiority of the Brahmans as a caste. On the contrary, it is the (now) second caste, the Kshatriya, or warrior class, who are exalted in the oldest of them. As stated by Professor Cowell in Elphinstone's *History of India*—"they breathe a freedom of spirit unknown to any earlier work except the *Rig Veda*. . . The great teachers of the higher knowledge and Brahmans are continually represented as *going to Kshatriya Kings to become their pupils*." The "Kshatriya Kings" were in the olden times, like the King Hierophants of Egypt, the receptacles of the highest divine knowledge and wisdom, the *Elect* and the incarnations of the primordial divine Instructors—the Dhyâni Buddhas or Kumâras. There was a time, æons before the Brahmans became a caste, or even the *Upanishads* were written, when there was on earth but one "lip", one religion and one science, namely, the speech of the gods, the Wisdom-Religion and Truth. This was before the fair fields of the latter, overrun by nations of many languages, became overgrown with the weeds of intentional deception, and national creeds invented by ambition, cruelty and selfishness, broke the one sacred Truth into thousands of fragments.

**Upanita.**(*Sk.*). One who is invested with the Brahmanical thread; lit., "brought to a spiritual teacher or Guru".

**Uparati** (*Sk*) Absence of outgoing desires; a Yoga state.

**Upâsaka** (*Sk.*). Male chelas or rather devotees. Those who without entering the priesthood vow to preserve the principal commandments.

**Upâsikâ** (*Sk.*). Female chelas or devotees.

**Upasruti** (*Sk.*). According to Orientahists a "supernatural voice which is heard at night revealing the secrets of the future". According to the explanation of Occultism, the voice of any person at a distance—generally one versed in the mysteries of esoteric teachings or an adept—endowed with the gift of projecting both his voice and astral image to any person whatsoever, regardless of distance. The *upasruti* may "reveal the secrets of the future", or may only inform the person it addresses of some prosaic fact of the present; yet it will still be an *upasruti*—the "double" or the echo of the voice of a living man or woman.

**Upekshâ** (*Sk.*). Lit., Renunciation. In Yoga a state of absolute indifference attained by self-control, the complete mastery over one's mental and physical feelings and sensations.

**Ur** (*Chald.*). The chief seat of lunar worship; the Babylonian city where the moon was the chief deity, and whence Abram brought the Jewish god, who is so inextricably connected with the moon as a creative and generative deity.

**Uræus** (*Gr.*). In Egyptian *Urhek*, a serpent and a sacred symbol. Some see in it a cobra, while others say it is an asp. Cooper explains that "the asp is not a uræus but a cerastes, or kind of viper, i.e., a two-horned viper. It is the royal serpent, wearing the *pschent* . . . the *naya hâje*." The uræus is "round the disk of Horus and forms the ornament of the cap of Osiris, besides overhanging the brows of other divinities" (Bonwick). Occultism explains that the uræus is the symbol of initiation and also of hidden wisdom, as the serpent always is. The gods were all patrons of the hierophants and their instructors.

**Uragas** (*Sk.*). The Nâgas (serpents) dwelling in Pâtâla the nether world or hell, in popular thought; the Adepts, High Priests and Initiates of Central and South America, known to the ancient Aryans; where Arjuna wedded the daughter of the king of the Nâgas—Ulûpî. *Nagalism* or Nâga-worship prevails to this day in Cuba and Hayti, and Voodooism, the chief branch of the former, has found its way into New Orleans. In Mexico the chief "sorcerers", the "medicine men", are called *Nagals* to this day; just as thousands of years ago the Chaldean and Assyrian High Priests were called *Nargals*, they being chiefs of the Magi (Rab.Mag), the office held at one time by the prophet Daniel. The word Nâga, "wise serpent", has become universal, because it is one of the few words that have survived the wreck of the first universal language. In South as well as in Central and North America, the aborigines use the word, from Behring Straits down to Uruguay, where it means a "chief", a "teacher and a "serpent". The very word *Uraga* may have reached India and been adopted through its connection, in prehistoric times, with South America and Uruguay itself, for the name belongs to the American Indian vernacular. The origin of the Uragas, for all that the Orientalists know, may have been in Uruguai, as there are legends about them which locate their ancestors the Nâgas in Pâtâla, the antipodes, or America.

**Uranides** (*Gr.*). One of the names of the *divine* Titans, those who rebelled against Kronos, the prototypes of the Christian "fallen" angels.

**Urim** (*Heb.*). See" Thummim". The" Urim and Thummim "originated in Egypt, and symbolized the Two *Truths*, the two figures of **Ra** and *Thmei* being engraved on the breastplate of the Hierophant and worn by him during the initiation ceremonies. Diodorus adds that this necklace of gold and precious stones was worn by the High Priest when delivering judgment. *Thme* (plural *Thmin*) means "Truth" in Hebrew. "The Septuagint translates thummim, as *Truth*" (Bonwick). The late Mr. Proctor, the astronomer, shows the Jewish idea "derived directly from the Egyptians". But Philo Judæus affirms that Urim and Thummim were "the two small images of Revelation and Truth, put between the double folds of the breastplate", and passes over the latter, with its twelve stones typifying the twelve signs of the Zodiac, without explanation.

**Urlak** (*Scand.*). The same as "Orlog" (*q.v.*). Fate; an impersonal power bestowing gifts "blindly" on mortals; a kind of Nemesis.

**Urvasî**(*Sk.*). A divine nymph, mentioned in the *Rig-Veda*, whose beauty set the whole heaven ablaze. Cursed by the gods she descended to earth and settled there. The loves of Purûravas (the Vikrama), and the nymph Urvasî are the subject of Kâlidâsa's world-famous drama, the *Vikramorvasî*.

**Usanas** (*Sk.*). The planet Venus or Sukra; or rather the ruler and governor of that planet.

**Ushas** (*Sk.*). The dawn, the daughter of heaven; the same as the Aurora of the Latins and the hjwvd of the Greeks. She is first mentioned in the *Vedas*, wherein her name is also *Ahanâ* and *Dyotanâ* (the illuminator), and is a most poetical and fascinating image. She is the ever-faithful friend of men, of rich and poor, though she is believed to prefer the latter. She smiles upon and visits the dwelling of every living mortal. She is the immortal, ever-youthful virgin, the light of the poor, and the destroyer of darkness.

**Uttara Mîmânsâ** (*Sk.*). The second of the two Mîmânsâs—the first being *Pûrva* (first) Mîmânsâ, which form respectively the fifth and sixth of the *Darshanas* or schools of philosophy. The Mîmânsâ are included in the generic name of *Vedânta*, though it is the *Uttara* (by Vyâsa) which is really the *Vedânta*.

**Uzza** (*Heb.*). The name of an angel who, together with Azrael, opposed, as the *Zohar* teaches, the creation of man by the Elohim, for which the latter annihilated both.

# V

**V.**—The twenty-second letter of the Latin alphabet. Numerically it stands for 5; hence the Roman V (with a dash) stands for 5,000. The Western Kabbalists have connected it with the divine Hebrew name IHVH. The Hebrew *Vau*, however, being number 6, it is only by being identical with the W, that it can ever become a proper symbol for the male-female, and spirit-matter. The equivalent for the Hebrew Vau is YO, and in numerals 6.

**Vâch** (*Sk.*). To call Vâch "speech" simply, is deficient in clearness. Vâch is the mystic personification of speech, and the female *Logos*, being one with Brahmâ, who created her out of one-half of his body, which he divided into two portions; she is also one with Virâj (called the "female" Virâj) who was created in her by Brahmâ. In one sense Vâch is "speech" by which knowledge was taught to man; in another she is the "mystic, secret speech" which descends upon and enters into the primeval Rishis, as the "tongues of fire" are said to have "sat upon" the apostles. For, she is called "the female creator", the "mother of the Vedas", etc., etc. Esoterically, she is the subjective Creative Force which, emanating from the Creative Deity (the subjective Universe, its "privation", or *ideation*) becomes the manifested "world of speech", i.e., the *concrete expression of ideation*, hence the "Word" or Logos. Vâch is "the male and female" Adam of the first chapter of *Genesis*, and thus called "Vâch-Virâj" by the sages. (See *Atharva Veda*.) She is also "the celestial Saraswatî produced from the heavens", a "voice derived from *speechless* Brahmâ" (*Mahâbhârata*); the goddess of wisdom and eloquence. She is called *Sata-rûpa*, the goddess of *a hundred forms*.

**Vacuum** (*Lat.*). The symbol of the absolute Deity or Boundless Space, esoterically.

**Vâhana** (*Sk.*). A vehicle, the carrier of something immaterial and formless. All the gods and goddesses are, therefore, represented as using vâhanas to manifest themselves, which vehicles are ever symbolical. So, for instance, Vishnu has during Pralayas, *Ânanta* the infinite" (Space), symbolized by the serpent Sesha, and during the Manvantaras—*Garuda* the gigantic half-eagle, half-man, the symbol of the great cycle; Brahma appears as Brahmâ, descending into the planes of manifestations on *Kâlahamsa*, the "swan in time or finite eternity"; Siva (phonet, Shiva) appears as the bull *Nandi*; Osiris as the sacred bull *Apis*; Indra travels on an elephant; Kârttikeya, on a peacock; Kâmadeva on *Makâra*, at other times a parrot; Agni, the universal (and also solar) Fire-god, who is, as all of them are, "a consuming Fire", manifests itself as a ram and a lamb, *Ajâ*, "the unborn"; Varuna, as a fish; etc., etc., while the vehicle of MAN is his body.

**Vaibhâchikas** (*Sk.*). The followers of the *Vibhâcha Shâstra*, an ancient school of materialism; a philosophy that held that no mental concept can be formed except through direct contact between the mind, *via* the senses, such as sight, touch, taste, etc., and external objects. There are Vaibhâchikas, to this day, in India.

**Vaidhâtra** (*Sk.*). The same as the Kumâras.

**Vaidyuta** (*Sk.*). Electric fire, the same as *Pâvaka*, one of the three fires which, divided, produce forty-nine mystic fires.

**Vaihara** (*Sk.*). The name of a cave-temple near Râjagriha, whereinto the Lord Buddha usually retired for meditation.

**Vaijayantî** (*Sk.*). The magic necklace of Vishnu, imitated by certain Initiates among the temple Brahmans. It is made of five precious stones, each symbolizing one of the five elements of our Round; namely, the pearl, ruby, emerald, sapphire and diamond, or water, fire, earth, air and ether, called "the aggregate of the five elemental rudiments"—the word "powers" being, perhaps, more correct than "rudiments".

**Vaikhari Vâch** (*Sk.*). 'That which is uttered; one of the four forms of speech.

**Vaikuntha** (*Sk.*). One of the names of the twelve great gods, whence *Vaikunthaloka*, the abode of Vishnu.

**Vairâjas** (*Sk.*). In the popular belief, semi-divine beings, shades of saints, inconsumable by fire, impervious to water, who dwell in Tapo loka with the hope of being translated into Satya-loka—a more purified state which answers to Nirvâna. The term is explained as the aerial bodies or astral shades of "ascetics, mendicants, anchorites, and penitents, who have completed their course of rigorous austerities". Now in esoteric philosophy they are called *Nirmânakâyas*, Tapo-loka being on the sixth plane (upward) but in direct communication with the *mental* plane. The Vairâjas are referred to as the *first gods* because the *Mânasa putras* and the *Kumâras* are the oldest in theogony, as it is said that even the gods worshipped them (*Matsya Purâna*); those whom Brahmâ "with the eye of Yoga beheld in the eternal spheres, and who are the *gods of gods*" (*Vâyu Purâna*).

**Vairochana** (*Sk.*). "All-enlightening". A mystic symbol, or rather a generic personification of a class of spiritual beings described as the embodiment of essential wisdom (*bodhi*) and absolute purity.

They dwell in the fourth *Arûpa Dhâtu* (formless world) or *Buddhakshetra*, and are the first or the highest hierarchy of the five orthodox Dhyâni Buddhas. There was a *Sramana* (an Arhat) of this name (see Eitel's *SanSk. Chin. Dict.*) a native of Kashmir, "who introduced Buddhism into Kustan and lahoured in Tibet" (in the seventh century of our era). He was the best translator of the semi-esoteric Canon of Northern Buddhism, and a contemporary of the great Samantabhadra (*q.v.*).

**Vaisâkha** (*Sk.*). A celebrated female ascetic, born at Srâvastî, and called *Sudatta*, "virtuous donor". She was the mother-abbess of a Vihâra, or convent of female Upâsikâs, and is known as the builder of a Vihâra for Sâkyamuni Buddha. She is regarded as the patroness of all the Buddhist female ascetics.

**Vaisheshika** (*Sk.*). One of the six *Darshanas* or schools of philosophy, founded by Kanâda. It is called the Atomistic School, as it teaches the existence of a universe of atoms of a transient character, an endless number of souls and a fixed number of material principles, by the correlation and interaction of which periodical cosmic evolutions take place without any directing Force, save a kind of mechanical law inherent in the atoms; a very materialistic school.

**Vaishnava** (*Sk.*). A follower of any sect recognising and worshipping Vishnu as the one supreme God. The worshippers of Siva are called *Saivas*.

**Vaivaswata** (*Sk.*). The name of the Seventh Manu, the forefather of the post-diluvian race, or our own fifth humankind. A reputed son of Sûrya (the Sun), he became, after having been saved in an ark (built by the order of Vishnu) from the Deluge, the father of Ikshwâku, the founder of the solar race of kings. (See "*Sûryavansa*".)

**Vajra** (*Sk.*). Lit., "diamond club" or sceptre. In the Hindu works, the sceptre of Indra, similar to the thunderbolts of Zeus, with which this deity, as the god of thunder, slays his enemies. But in mystical Buddhism, the *magic* sceptre of Priest-Initiates, exorcists and adepts—the symbol of the possession of *Siddhis* or superhuman powers, wielded during certain ceremonies by the priests and theurgists. It is also the symbol of Buddha's power over evil spirits or elementals. The possessors of this wand are called *Vajrapâni (q.v.)*.

**Vajrâchârya** (*Sk.*). The spiritual *achârya* (*guru, teacher*) of the Yogâchâryas, The "Supreme Master of the Vajra".

**Vajradhara** (*Sk.*). The Supreme Buddha with the Northern Buddhists.

**Vajrapâni** (*Sk.*), or *Manjushrî*, the Dhyâni-Bodhisattva (as the spiritual reflex, or the son of the Dhyâni.Buddhas, on earth) born directly from the subjective form of existence; a deity worshipped by the profane as a god, and by Initiates as a subjective Force, the real nature of which is known only to, and explained by, the highest Initiates of the Yogâchârya School.

**Vajrasattva** (*Sk.*). The name of the sixth Dhyani-Buddha (of whom there are but *five* in the popular Northern Buddhism)—in the Yogâchârya school, the latter counting seven Dhyâni-Buddhas and as many Bodhisattvas—the "mind-sons" of the former. Hence, the Orientalists refer to Vajrasattva as "a *fictitious* Bodhisattva".

**Vallabâchârya** (*Sk.*). The name of a mystic who was the *chela* (disciple) of Vishnu Swâmi, and the founder of a sect of *Vaishnavas*. His descendants are called Goswâmi Mahârâj, and have much landed property and numerous *mandirs* (temples) in Bombay. They have degenerated into a shamefully licentious sect.

**Vâmana** (*Sk.*). The fifth avatar of Vishnu, hence the name of the Dwarf whose form was assumed by that god.

**Vara** (*Mazd.*). A term used in the *Vendîdâd*, where Ahura-mazda commands Yima to build *Vara*. It also signifies an enclosure or *vehicle*, an ark *(argha)*, and at the same time MAN (verse 30). *Vara* is the vehicle of our informing Egos, i.e. the human body, the soul in which is typified by the expression a "window self-shining within".

**Varâha** (*Sk.*). The boar-avatar of Vishnu; the third in number.

**Varna** (*Sk.*). Caste; lit., "colour". The four chief castes named by Manu—the Brahmin, Kshatriya, Vaisya and Sûdra—are called *Chatur-varna*.

**Varsha** (*Sk.*). A region, a plain; any stretch of country situated between the great mountain-ranges of the earth.

**Varuna** (*Sk*). The god of water, or marine god, but far different from Neptune, for in the case of this oldest of the Vedic deities, Water means the "Waters of Space", or the all-investing sky, Akâsa, in one sense. Varuna or *Ooaroona* (phonetically), is certainly the prototype of the *Ouranos* of the Greeks. As Muir says: "The grandest cosmical functions are ascribed to Varuna. Possessed of illimitable knowledge he upholds heaven and earth, he dwells in all worlds as sovereign ruler. . . He made the golden . . . sun to shine in the firmament. The wind which resounds through the atmosphere is his breath. . . . Through the operation of his laws the moon walks in brightness and the stars . . . mysteriously vanish in daylight. He knows the flight of birds in the sky, the paths of ships on the ocean, the course of the far travelling wind, and beholds all the things that have been or shall be done. . . . He witnesses men's truth and false hood. He instructs the Rishi Vasishta in mysteries; but his secrets and those of Mitra are not to be revealed to the foolish." . . "The attributes and functions ascribed to Varuna impart to his character a moral elevation and sanctity far surpassing that attributed to any other Vedic deity."

**Vasishta** (*Sk.*). One of the primitive seven great Rishis, and a most celebrated Vedic sage.

**Vasudeva** (*Sk.*). The father of Krishna. He belonged to the Yâdava branch of the *Somavansa*, or lunar race.

**Vasus** (*Sk.*). The eight evil deities attendant upon Indra. Personified cosmic phenomena, as their names show.

**Vâyu** (*Sk.*). Air: the god and sovereign of the air; one of the five states of matter, namely the *gaseous*; one of the five elements, called, as wind, *Vâta*. The *Vishnu Purâna* makes Vâyu King of the Gandharvas. He is the father of Hanumân, in the *Râmâyana*. The trinity of the mystic gods in Kosmos closely related to each other, are "Agni (fire) whose place is on earth; Vâyu (air, or one of the forms of Indra), whose place is in the air; and Sûrya (the sun) whose place is in the air (*Nirukta*.) In esoteric interpretation, these three cosmic principles, correspond with the three human principles, Kâma, Kâma-Manas and Manas, the sun of the intellect.

**Vedanâ** (*Sk.*). The second of the five *Shandhas* (perceptions, senses). The sixth Nidâna.

**Vedânta** (*Sk.*). A mystic system of philosophy which has developed from the efforts of generations of sages to interpret the secret meaning of the

*Upanishads (q.v.).* It is called in the *Shad-Darshanas* (six schools or systems of demonstration), *Uttara Mîmânsâ,* attributed to *Vyâsa,* the compiler of the *Vedas,* who is thus referred to as the founder of the Vedânta. The orthodox Hindus call Vedânta_a term meaning literally the "end of all (Vedic) knowledge"—*Brahmâ-jnâna,* or pure and spiritual knowledge of Brahmâ. Even if we accept the late dates assigned to various Sanskrit schools and treatises by our Orientalists, the Vedânta must be 3,300 years old, as Vyâsa is said to have lived I,400 years B.C. If, as Elphinstone has it in his *History of India,* the *Brahmanas* are the *Talmud* of the Hindus, and the *Vedas* the Mosaic books, then the *Vedânta* may be correctly called the *Kabalah* of India. But how vastly more grand! Sankarâchârya, who was the popularizer of the Vedântic system, and the founder of the *Adwaita* philosophy, is sometimes called the founder of the modern schools of the Vedânta.

**Vedas** (*Sk.*). The "revelation". the scriptures of the Hindus, from the root *vid,* "to know", or "divine knowledge". They are the most ancient as well as the most sacred of the Sanskrit works. The *Vedas* on the date and antiquity of which no two Orientalists can agree, are claimed by the Hindus themselves, whose Brahmans and Pundits ought to know best about their own religious works, to have been first taught orally for thousands of years and then compiled on the shores of Lake Mânasa-Sarovara (phonetically, *Mansarovara*) beyond the Himalayas, in Tibet. When was this done? While their religious teachers, such as Swami Dayanand Saraswati, claim for them an antiquity of many decades of ages, our modern Orientalists will grant them no greater antiquity in their present form than about between 1,000 and 2,000 B.C. As compiled in their final form by Veda-Vyâsa, however, the Brahmans themselves unanimously assign 3,100 years before the Christian era, the date when Vyâsa flourished. Therefore the *Vedas* must be as old as this date. But their antiquity is sufficiently proven by the fact that they are written in such an ancient form, of Sanskrit, so different from the Sanskrit now used, that there is no other, work like them in the literature of this eldest sister of all the known languages, as Prof. Max Muller calls it. Only the most learned of the Brahman Pundits can read the Vedas in their original. It is urged that Colebrooke found the date 1400 B.C. corroborated absolutely by a passage which he discovered, and which is based on astronomical data. But if, as shown unanimously by all the Orientalists and the Hindu Pundits also, that (a) the *Vedas* are not a single work, nor yet any one of the separate *Vedas;* but that each *Veda,* and almost every hymn and division of the latter, is the production of various authors; and that (b) these have been written (whether as *sruti*, "revelation", or not) at various periods of the ethnological evolution of the Indo-Aryan race, then—what does Mr. Colebrooke's discovery prove? Simply that the *Vedas* were *finally* arranged and compiled fourteen centuries before our era; but this interferes in no way with their antiquity. Quite the reverse; for, as an offset to Mr. Colebrooke's passage, there is a learned article, written on purely astronomical data by Krishna Shâstri Godbole (of Bombay), which proves as absolutely and on the same evidence that the *Vedas* must have been taught at least 25,000 years ago. (See *Theosophist*, Vol. II., p. 238 *et seq.*, Aug., 1881.) This statement is, if not supported, at any rate not contradicted by what Prof. Cowell says in Appendix VII., of Elphinstone' *History of India:* "There is a difference in age between the various hymns, which are now united in their present form as the Sanhitâ of the *Rig Veda*; but *we have no data to determine their relative antiquity*, and purely subjective criticism, apart from solid data, has so often failed in other instances, that we can trust but little to any of its inferences in such a recently opened field of research as Sanskrit literature. [a fourth part of the Vaidik literature is as yet in print, and very little of it has been translated into English (1866).] The still unsettled controversies about the Homeric poems may well warn us of being too confident in our judgments regarding *the yet earlier hymns of the Rig -Veda. . . .* When we examine these hymns . . . they are deeply interesting for the history of the human mind, belonging as they do to a much older phase than the poems of Homer or Hesiod." The Vedic writings are all classified in two great divisions, exoteric and esoteric, the former being called *Karma-Kânda,* "division of actions or works", and the *Jnâna Kânda,* "division of (divine) knowledge", the Upanishads (*q.v.*) coming under this last classification. Both departments are regarded as *Sruti* or revelation. To each hymn of the *Rig -Veda*, the name of the Seer or Rishi to whom it was revealed is prefixed. It, thus, becomes evident on the authority of these very names (such as Vasishta, Viswâmitra, Nârada, etc.), all of which belong to men born in various manvantaras and even ages, that centuries, and perhaps millenniums, must have elapsed between the dates of their composition.

**Veda-Vyâsa** (*Sk.*). The compiler of the *Vedas* (*q.v.*).

**Veddhas** (*Sing.*). The name of a wild race of men living in the forests of Ceylon. They are very difficult to find.

**Vehicle of Life** (*Mystic*). The "Septeriary" Man among the Pythagoreans, "number seven" among the profane. The former "explained it by saying, that the human body consisted of four principal elements (principles), and that the soul is triple (the higher triad)" . (See *Isis Unveiled*, Vol. II., p. 418, New York, 1877.) It has been often remarked that in the earlier works of the Theosophists no septenary division of man was mentioned. The above quotation is sufficient warrant that, although with every caution, the subject was more than once approached, and is not a new-fangled theory or invention.

**Vendîdâd** (*Pahlavi*). The first book (*Nosk*) in the collection of Zend fragments usually known as the *Zend-Avesta*. The *Vendidâd* is a corruption of the compound-word "Vidaêvo-dâtern", meaning "the anti-demoniac law", and is full of teachings how to avoid sin and defilement by purification, moral and physical—each of which teachings is based on Occult laws. It is a pre-eminently occult treatise, full of symbolism and often of meaning quite the reverse of that which is expressed in its dead-letter text. The *Vendîdâd,* as claimed by tradition, is the only one of the twenty-one Nosks (works) that has escaped the *auto-da-fé* at the hands of the drunken Iskander the Rûmi, he whom posterity calls Alexander the Great—though the epithet is justifiable only when applied to the brutality, vices and cruelty of this conqueror. It is through the vandalism of this Greek that literature and knowledge have lost much priceless lore in the Nosks burnt by him. Even the Vendidâd has reached us in only a fragmentary state. The first chapters are very mystical, and therefore called "mythical" in the renderings of European Orientalists. The two "creators" of "spirit-matter" or the world of differentiation—Ahura-Mazda and Angra-Mainyu (Ahriman)—are introduced in them, and also Yima (the first man, or mankind personified). The work is divided into *Fargards* or chapters, and a portion of these is devoted to the formation of our globe, or terrestrial evolution. (See *Zend-Avesta*.)

**Vetâla** (*Sk.*). An elemental, a spook, which haunts burial grounds and animates corpses.

**Vetâla Siddhi** (*Sk.*). A practice of sorcery; means of obtaining power over the living by black magic, incantations, and ceremonies performed over a dead human body, during which process the corpse is desecrated. (See "Vetâla".)

**Vibhâvasu** (*Sk.*). A mystic fire connected with the beginning of *pralaya,* or the dissolution of the universe.

**Vibhûtayah** (*Sk.*). The same as *Siddhis* or magic powers.

**Vidyâ** (*Sk.*). Knowledge, Occult Science.

**Vidyâ-dhara** (*Sk.*). And Vidyâ-dharî, male and female deities. Lit., "possessors of knowledge". They are also called *Nabhas-chara*, "moving in the air", flying, and *Priyam-vada,* "sweet-spoken". They are the Sylphs of the Rosicrucians; inferior deities inhabiting the astral sphere between the earth and ether; believed in popular folk-lore to be beneficent, but in reality they are cunning and mischievous, and intelligent Elementals, or "Powers of the air". They are represented in the East, and in the West, as having intercourse with men (" intermarrying ", as it is called in Rosicrucian parlance; see *Count de Gabalis*). In India they are also called *Kâma-rûpins, as they take shapes at will.* It is among these creatures that the "spirit-wives" and "spirit-husbands" of certain modern spiritualistic mediums and hysteriacs are recruited. These boast with pride of having such pernicious connexions (*e.g.,* the American "Lily", the spirit-wife of a well-known head of a now scattered community of Spiritualists, of a great poet and well-known writer), and call them angel-guides, maintaining that they are the spirits of famous disembodied mortals. These "spirit-husbands" and "wives" have not originated with the modern Spiritists and Spiritualists, but have been known in the East for thousands of years, in the Occult philosophy, under the names above given, and among the profane as—Pishâthas.

**Vihâra (***Sk.***).** Any place inhabited by Buddhist priests or ascetics; a Buddhist temple, generally a rock-temple or cave. A monastery, or a nunnery also. One finds in these days Vihâras built in the enclosures of monasteries and academies for Buddhist training in towns and cities; but in days of yore they were to be met with only in unfrequented wild jungles, on mountain tops, and in the most deserted places.

**Vihâraswâmin** (*Sk.*). The superior (whether male or female) of a monastery or convent, Vihâra. Also called *Karmadâna,* as every teacher or guru, having authority, takes upon himself the responsibility of certain actions, good or bad, committed by his pupils or the flock entrusted to him.

**Vijnânam (***Sk.***).** The Vedântic name for the principle which dwells in the *Vijnânamaya Kosha* (the sheath of intellect) and corresponds to the faculties of the Higher Manas.

**Vikârttana** (*Sk.*). Lit., "shorn of his rags"; a name of the Sun, and the type of the initiated neophyte. (See *S. D.,* Vol. I, p. 322, n.)

**Vimoksha** (*Sk.*). The same as Nirvâna.

**Vînâ** (*Sk.*). A kind of large guitar used in India and Tibet, whose invention is attributed variously to Siva, Nârada, and others.

**Vinatâ** (*Sk.*). A daughter of Daksha and wife of Kashyapa (one of the "seven orators" of the world). She brought forth the egg from which Garuda the seer was born.

**Viprachitti** (*Sk.*). The chief of the Dânavas—the giants that warred with the gods: the Titans of India.

**Vîrabhadra** (*Sk.*). A thousand-headed and thousand-armed monster, "born of the breath" of Siva Rudra, a symbol having reference to the "sweat-born", the second race of mankind (*S. D.*, Vol. II., p. 182).

**Virâj** (*Sk.*). The Hindu Logos in the *Purânas*; the male Manu, created in the female portion of Brahmâ's body (Vâch) by that god. Says Manu: "Having divided his body into two parts, the lord (Brahmâ) became with the one half a male and with the other half a female; and in her he created Virâj". The *Rig -Veda* makes Virâj spring from Purusha, and Purusha spring from Virâj. The latter is the type of all male beings, and Vâch, Sata-rûpa (she of the hundred forms), the type of all female forms.

**Vishnu** (*Sk.*). The second person of the Hindu Trimûrti (trinity), composed of Brahmâ, Vishnu and Siva. From the root vish, "to pervade". in the *Rig -Veda*, Vishnu is no high god, but simply a manifestation of the solar energy, described as "striding through the seven regions of the Universe in *three* steps and enveloping all things with the dust (of his beams".) Whatever may be the six other occult significances of the statement, this is related to the same class of types as the seven and ten Sephiroth, as the *seven* and *three* orifices of the perfect Adam Kadmon, as the seven "principles" and the higher triad in man, etc., etc. Later on this mystic type becomes a great god, the preserver and the renovator, he "of a thousand names—Sahasranâma".

**Vishwakarman** (*Sk.*). The "Omnificent". A Vedic god, a personification of the creative Force, described as the One "all-seeing god, . . . the generator, disposer, who . . . is beyond the comprehension of (uninitiated) mortals". In the two hymns of the *Rig -Veda* specially devoted to him, he is said "to sacrifice *himself* to *himself*". The names of his mother, "the lovely and virtuous Yoga-Siddha" (*Purânas*) and of his daughter *Sanjnâ* (spiritual consciousness), show his mystic character. (See *Secret Doctrine, sub voc.*) As the artificer of the gods and maker of their weapons, he is called Karu, "workman", *Takshaka* "carpenter", or "wood-cutter", etc., etc.

**Vishwatryarchas** (*Sk.*) The fourth solar (mystic) ray of the seven. (See *S. D.*, Vol. I., p. 515, n.)

**Vivaswat** (*Sk.*). The "bright One", the Sun.

**Viwan** (*Sk.*). Some kind "of air-vehicle", like a balloon, mentioned but not described in the old Sanskrit works, which the Atlanteans and the ancient Aryas seem to have known and used.

**Voluspa** (*Scand.*). A poem called "The Song of the Prophetess", or "Song of Wala".

**Voodooism,** or *Voodoos.* A system of African sorcery; a sect of black magicians, to which the New Orleans negroes are much addicted. It flourishes likewise in Cuba and South America.

**Voordalak** (*Slav.*). A vampire; a corpse informed by its lower principles, and maintaining a kind of semi-life in itself by raising itself during the night from the grave, fascinating its living victims and sucking out their blood. Roumanians, Moldavians, Servians, and all the Slavonian tribes dwelling in the Balkans, and also the Tchechs (Bohemians), Moravians, and others, firmly believe in the existence of such ghosts and dread them accordingly.

**Votan** (*Mex.*). The deified hero of the Mexicans, and probably the same as Quetzal-Coatl; a "son of the snakes", one admitted "to the snake's hole", which means an Adept admitted to the Initiation in the secret chamber of the Temple. The missionary Brasseur de Bourbourg, seeks to prove him a descendant of Ham, the accursed son of Noah. (See *Isis Unveiled*, I., pp. 545 *et seq.*)

**Vrata** (*Sk*) Law, or power of the gods.

**Vratâni** (*Sk.*). Varuna's "active laws", courses of natural action. (See *Rig - Vedic* Hymns, X., 90-1.

**Vriddha Garga** (*Sk.*). From *Vriddha*, "old", and *Garga*, an ancient sage, one of the oldest writers on astronomy.

**Vriddha Mânava** (*Sk.*) The laws of Manu.

**Vritra** (*Sk.*). The demon of drought in the *Vedas*, a great foe of Indra, with whom he is constantly at war. The allegory of a cosmic phenomenon.

**Vritra-han** (*Sk.*) An epithet or title of Indra, meaning "the slayer of Vritra".

**Vyahritis** (*Slav.*). Lit., "fiery", *words lit by and born of fire.* The three mystical, creative words, said by Manu to have been milked by the Prajâpati from the *Vedas*: bhûr, from the *Rig -Veda*; bhuvah, from the *Vajur-Veda*; and Swar, from the *Sama-Veda* (*Manu* II., 76). All three are said to possess creative powers. The *Satapatha Brâhmana* explains that they are "the three luminous essences" extracted from the *Vedas* by Prajâpati ("lords of creation", progenitors), through heat. "He (Brahmâ) uttered the word *bhûr* and it became the earth; *bhuvah,* and it became the firmament; and *swar,* which became heaven". *Mahar* is the fourth "luminous essence", and was taken from the *Atharva-Veda.* But, as this word is purely *mantric* and magical, it is one, so to say, kept apart.

**Vyâsa** (*Sk.*).. Lit., *one who expands or amplifies;* an interpreter, or rather a *revealer;* for that which he explains, interprets and amplifies is a mystery to the profane. This term was applied in days of old to the highest Gurus in India. There were many Vyâsas in Aryavarta; one was the compiler and arranger of the Vedas; another, the author of the *Mahâbhârata*—the *twenty-eighth Vyâsa or revealer in the order of succession*—and the last one of note was the author of *Uttara Mîmânsâ,* the sixth school or system of Indian philosophy. He was also the founder of the Vedânta system. His date, as assigned by Orientalists (see Elphinstone, Cowell, etc.), is 1,400 B.C., but this date is certainly too recent. The Purânas mention only twenty-eight Vyâsas, who at various ages descended to the earth to promulgate Vedic truths—but there were many more.

# W

**W.**—The 23rd letter. Has no equivalent in Hebrew. In Western Occultism some take it as the symbol for celestial water, whereas M stands for terrestrial water.

**Wala** (*Scand.*). A prophetess in the songs of the *Edda* (Norse mythology). Through the incantations of Odin she was raised from her grave, and made to prophesy the death of Baldur.

**Walhalla** (*Scand.*). A kind of paradise (Devachan) for slaughtered warriors, called by the Norsemen "the hall of the blessed heroes"; it has five hundred doors.

**Wali** (*Scand.*). The son of Odin who avenges the death of Baldur, "the well-beloved".

**Walkyries** (*Scand.*). Called the "choosers of the dead". In the popular poetry of the Scandinavians, these goddesses consecrate the fallen heroes with a kiss, and bearing them from the battle-field carry them to the halls of bliss and to the gods in Walhalla.

**Wanes** (*Scand.*). A race of gods of great antiquity, worshipped at the dawn of time by the Norsemen, and later by the Teutonic races.

**Wara** (*Scand.*). One of the maidens of Northern Freya; "the wise Wara", who watches the desires of each human heart, and avenges every breach of faith.

**Water.** The first principle of things, according to Thales and other ancient philosophers. Of course this is not water on the material plane, but in a figurative sense for the potential fluid contained in boundless space. This was symbolised in ancient Egypt by *Kneph*, the "unrevealed" god, who was represented as the serpent—the emblem of eternity—encircling a water-urn, with his head hovering over the waters, which he incubates with his breath. "And the Spirit of God moved upon the face of the waters." (*Gen.* i.) The honey-dew, the food of the gods and of the *creative bees* on the Yggdrasil, falls during the night upon the tree of life from the "divine waters, the birth-place of the gods". Alchemists claim that when pre-Adamic earth is reduced by the Alkahest to its first substance, it is like clear water. The Alkahest is "the one and the invisible, the water, the first principle, in the *second* transformation".

**We** (*Scand.*). One of the three gods—Odin, Wili and We—who kill the giant Ymir (chaotic force), and create the world out of his body, the primordial substance.

**Werdandi** (*Scand.*). See "Nörns", the three sister-goddesses who represent the Past, the Present and the Future. Werdandi represents the ever-present time.

**Whip of Osiris.** The scourge which symbolises Osiris as the "judge of the dead". It is called the *nekhekh*, in the papyri, or the flagellum. Dr. Pritchard sees in it a fan or *van*, the winnowing instrument. Osiris, "whose fan is in his hand and who purges the Amenti of sinful hearts as a winnower sweeps his floor of the fallen grains and locks the good wheat into his garner". (Compare *Matthew*, 12.)

**White Fire** (*Kab.*). The *Zohar* treating of the "Long Face" and Short Face", the symbols of *Macrocosm* and *Microcosm*, speaks of the hidden White Fire, radiating from these night and day and yet never seen. It answers to vital force (beyond luminiferous ether), and electricity on the higher and lower planes. But the mystic "White Fire" is a name given to Ain-Soph. And this is the difference between the Aryan and the Semitic philosophies. The Occultists of the former speak of the Black Fire, which is the symbol of the unknown and unthinkable Brahm, and declare any speculation on the" Black Fire" impossible. But the Kabbalists who, owing to a subtle permutation of meaning, endow even Ain-Soph with a kind of indirect will and attributes, call its "fire" white, thus dragging the Absolute into the world of relation and finiteness.

**White Head.** In Hebrew *Resha Hivra*, an epithet given to Sephira, the highest of the Sephiroth, whose cranium "distils the dew which will call the dead again to life".

**White Stone**. The sign of initiation mentioned in St. John's *Revelation*. It had the word *prize* engraved on it, and was the symbol of that word given to the neophyte who, in his initiation, had successfully passed through all the trials in the MYSTERIES, it was the potent white cornelian of the mediæval Rosicrucians, who took it from the Gnostics. ' To him that overcometh will I give to eat of the *hidden* manna (the occult knowledge which descends as *divine* wisdom from heaven), and will give him a *white stone*, and in the stone a new name written (the 'mystery name' of the inner man or the EGO of the new Initiate), which no man knoweth saving him that receiveth it." (*Revelation*, ii. 17.)

**Widow's Son**. A name given to the French Masons, because the Masonic ceremonies are principally based on the adventures and death of Hiram Abif, "the widow's son", who is supposed to have helped to build the mythical Solomon's Temple.

**Wili** (*Scand*.). See "We".

**Will.** In metaphysics and occult philosophy, Will is that which governs the manifested universes in eternity. *Will* is the one and sole principle of abstract eternal MOTION, or its ensouling essence. "The will", says Van Helmont, "is the first of all powers. . . . The will is the property of all spiritual beings and displays itself in them the more actively the more they are freed from matter." And Paracelsus teaches that "determined will is the beginning of all magical operations. It is because men do not perfectly imagine and believe the result, that the (occult) arts are so uncertain, while they might he perfectly certain." Like all the rest, the Will is *septenary* in its degrees of manifestation. Emanating from the one, eternal, abstract and purely quiescent Will (Âtmâ in Layam), it becomes Buddhi in its Alaya state, descends lower as Mahat (Manas), and runs down the ladder of degrees until the divine Eros becomes, in its lower, animal manifestation, erotic desire. Will as an eternal principle is neither spirit nor substance but everlasting ideation. As well expressed by Schopenhauer in his *Parerga*, "in sober reality there is neither *matter* nor *spirit*. The tendency to gravitation in a stone is as unexplainable as thought in the human brain. . . If matter can—no one knows why—fall to the ground, then it can also—no one knows why—-think. . . . As soon, even in mechanics, as we trespass beyond the purely mathematical, as soon as we reach the inscrutable adhesion, gravitation, and so on, we are faced by phenomena which are to our senses as mysterious as the WILL."

**Wisdom.** The "very essence of wisdom is contained in the Non-Being". say the Kabbalists; but they also apply the term to the WORD or Logos, the Demiurge, by which the universe was called into existence. "The one Wisdom is in the Sound", say the Occultists; the Logos again being meant by Sound, which is the substratum of Âkâsa. Says the *Zohar*, the "Book of Splendour" "It is the Principle of all the Principles, the mysterious Wisdom, the crown of all that which there is of the most High". (*Zohar*, iii., fol. 288, Myers *Qabbalah*.) And it is explained, "Above Kether is the Ayin, or Ens, i.e., Ain, the NOTHING". "It is so named because we do not know, and it is impossible to know, *that which there is in that Principle*, because . . . it is above Wisdom itself." (iii., fol. 288.) This shows that the real Kabbalists agree with the Occultists that the essence, or that which is in the principle of Wisdom, is still above that highest Wisdom.

**Wisdom Religion**. The one religion which underlies all the now-existing creeds. That "faith" which, being primordial, and revealed directly to human kind by their *progenitors* and informing EGOS (though the Church regards them as the "fallen angels"), required no "grace", nor *blind* faith to believe, for it was *knowledge*. (See "Gupta Vidyâ", Hidden Knowledge.) It is on this Wisdom Religion that *Theosophy is based.*

**Witch.** From the Anglo-Saxon word *wicce*, German *wissen*, "to know", and wikken, "to divine". The witches were at first called "wise women", until the day when the Church took it unto herself to follow the law of Moses, which put every "witch" or enchantress to death.

**Witchcraft. Sorcery**, enchantment, the art of throwing spells and using black magic.

**Witches' Sabbath**. The supposed festival and gathering of witches in some lonely spot, where the witches were accused of conferring directly with the Devil. Every race and people believed in it, and some believe in it still. Thus the chief headquarters and place of meeting of all the witches in Russia is said to be the Bald Mountain (*Lyssaya Gorâ*), near Kief, and in Germany the Brocken, in the Harz Mountains. In old Boston, U.S.A., they met near the "Devil's Pond", in a large forest which has now disappeared. At Salem, they were put to death almost at the will of the Church Elders, and in South Carolina a witch was burnt as late as 1865. In Germany and England they were murdered by Church and State in thousands, being forced to lie and confess under torture their participation in the "Witches' Sabbath".

**Wittoba** (*Sk.*). A form of Vishnu. Moor gives in his *Hindu Pantheon* the picture of Wittoba *crucified in Space*; and the Rev. Dr. Lundy maintains (*Monumental Christianity*) that this engraving is *anterior to* Christianity and is the crucified Krishna, a Saviour, hence a concrete prophecy of Christ. (See *Isis Unveiled*, II., 557,

**Wizard.** A wise man. An enchanter, or sorcerer.

**Wodan** (*Saxon*). The Scandinavian Odin, Votan, or Wuotan.

**World**. As a prefix to mountains, trees, and so on, it denotes a universal belief. Thus the "World-Mountain" of the Hindus was Meru. As said in *Isis Unveiled*: "All the world-mountains and mundane eggs, the mundane trees, and the mundane snakes and pillars, may be shown to embody scientifically demonstrated truths of natural philosophy. All of these mountains contain, with very trifling variations, the allegorically-expressed description of primal cosmogony; the mundane trees, that of subsequent evolution of spirit and matter; the mundane snakes and pillars, symbolical memorials of the various attributes of this double evolution in its endless correlation of cosmic forces. Within the mysterious recesses of the mountain—the matrix of the universe—the gods (powers) prepare the atomic germs of organic life, and at the same time the life-drink, which, when tasted, awakens in man-matter the man-*spirit*.

The Soma, the sacrificial drink of the Hindus, is that sacred beverage. For, at the creation of the *prima materia*, while the grossest portions of it were used for the physical embryo-world, its more divine essence pervaded the universe, invisibly permeating and enclosing within its ethereal waves the newly-born infant, developing and stimulating it to activity as it slowly evolved out of the eternal chaos. From the poetry of abstract conception, these mundane myths gradually passed into the concrete images of cosmic symbols, as archæology now finds them." Another and still more usual prefix to all these objects is "Mundane". (See "Mundane Egg", "Mundane Tree", and "Yggdrasil".)

**Worlds**, *the Four*. The Kabbalists recognise Four Worlds of Existence: viz., Atziluth or archetypal; Briah or creative, the first reflection of the highest; Yetzirah or formative; and Assiah, the 'World of Shells or Klippoth, and the material universe. The essence of Deity concentrating into the Sephiroth is first manifested in the Atziluthic World, and their reflections are produced in succession in each of the four planes, with gradually lessening radiance and purity, until the material universe is arrived at. Some authors call these four planes the intellectual, Moral, Sensuous, and Material Worlds. [w.w.w.]

**Worlds**, Inferior and Superior. The Occultists and the Kabbalists agree in dividing the universe into superior and inferior worlds, the worlds of Idea and the worlds of Matter. "As above, so below", states the Hermetic philosophy. This lower world is formed on its prototype—the higher world; and "everything in the lower is but an image (a reflection) of the higher". (*Zohar*, ii., fol. 2oa.)

# X

X.—This letter is one of the important symbols in the Occult philosophy. As a numeral **X** stands, in mathematics, for the unknown quantity; in occult numerals, for the perfect number 10; when placed horizontally, thus ✕, it means 1,000; the same with a dash over it ✕̄ for 10,000; and by itself, in occult symbolism, it is Plato's *logos* (man as a microcosm) decussated in space in the form of the letter **X**. The ⊗, or cross within the circle, has moreover a still clearer significance in Eastern occult philosophy: it is MAN within his own *spherical* envelope.

**Xenophilus.** A Pythagorean adept and philosopher, credited by Lucian (*de Macrob.*), Pliny and others with having lived to his 170th year, preserving all his faculties to the last. He wrote on music and was surnamed the "Musician".

**Xisusthrus** (*Gr.*). The Chaldean Noah, on the Assyrian tablets, who is thus described in the history of the ten kings by Berosus, according to Alexander Polyhistor: "After the death of (the ninth) Ardates, his son Xisusthrus reigned eighteen sari. In his time happened a great deluge." Warned by his deity in a vision of the forthcoming cataclysm, Xisusthrus was ordered by that deity to build an ark, to convey into it his relations, together with all the different animals, bird etc., and trust himself to the rising waters. Obeying the divine admonition, Xisusthrus is shown to do precisely what Noah did many thousand years after him. He sent out birds from the vessel which returned to him again; then a few days after he sent them again, and they returned with their feet coated with mud; but the third time they came back to him no more. Stranded on a high mountain of Armenia, Xisusthrus descends and builds an altar to the gods. Here only, comes a divergence between the polytheistic and monotheistic legends. Xisusthrus, having worshipped and rendered thanks to the gods for his salvation, disappeared, and his companions "saw him no more". The story informs us that on account of his great piety Xisusthrus and his family were translated *to live with the gods*, as he himself told the survivors. For though his body was gone, his voice was heard in the air, which, after apprising them of the occurrence, admonished them to return to Babylon, and pay due regard to virtue, religion, and the gods. This is more meritorious than to plant vines, get drunk on the juice of the grape, and curse one's own son.

# Y

**Y.**—The twenty-fifth letter of the English alphabet, and the tenth of the Hebrew—the *Yod*. It is the *litera Pythagoræ* the Pythagorean letter and symbol, signifying the two branches, or *paths of virtue and vice* respectively, the right leading to virtue, the left to vice. In Hebrew Kabbalistic mysticism it is the phallic male member, and also as number ten, the perfect number. Symbolically, it is represented by a hand with bent forefinger. Its numerical equivalent is ten.

**Yâdaya** (*Sk.*). A descendant of Yadu; of the great race in which Krishna was born. The founder of this line was Yadu, the son of King Yayâti of the Somavansa or Lunar Race.It was under Krishna—certainly no *mythical* personage—that the kingdom of Dwârakâ in Guzerat was established; and also after the death of Krishna (3102 B.C.) that all the Yâdavas present in the city perished, when it was submerged by the ocean. Only a few of the Yâdavas, who were absent from the town at the time of the catastrophe, escaped to perpetuate this great race. The Râjâs of Vijaya-Nâgara are now among the small number of its representatives.

**Yah** (*Heb.*). The word, as claimed in the *Zohar*, through which the Elohim formed the worlds. The syllable is a national adaptation and one of the many forms of the "Mystery name"IAO. (See "Iaho" and "Yâho".)

**Yâho** (*Heb.*). Fürst shows this to be the same as the Greek Iao. Yâho is an old Semitic and very mystic name of the supreme deity, while Yah (*q.v.*) is a later abbreviation which, from containing an abstract ideal, became finally applied to, and connected with, a phallic symbol—the lingham of creation. Both Yah and Yâho were Hebrew "mystery names" derived from Iao, but the Chaldeans had a Yâho before the Jews adopted it, and with them, as explained by some Gnostics and Neo-Platonists, it was the highest conceivable deity *enthroned above the seven heavens* and representing *Spiritual* Light (Âtman, the universal), whose ray was Nous, standing both for the intelligent Demiurge of the Universe of Matter and the *Divine* Manas in man, both being Spirit. The true key of this, communicated to the Initiates only, was that the name of IAO was "triliteral and its nature secret", as explained by the Hierophants. The Phœnicians too had a supreme deity whose name was triliteral, and its meanings secret, this was also Iao; and *Y-ha-ho* was a sacred word in the Egyptian mysteries, which signified "the one eternal and concealed deity" in nature and in man; i.e., the "universal Divine Ideation", and the human Manas, or the higher Ego.

**Yajna** (*Sk.*). "Sacrifice", whose symbol or representation is now the constellation Mriga-shiras (deer-head), and also a form of Vishnu. "The Yajna", say the Brahmans, "exists from eternity, for it proceeded from the Supreme, in whom it lay dormant from *no beginning*". It is the key to the *Trai-Vidyâ* , the thrice sacred science contained in the *Rig -Veda* verses, which teaches the Yajna or sacrificial mysteries. As Haug states in his *Introduction* to the *Aitareya Brâhmana*—the Yajna exists as an invisible presence at all times, extending from the *Âhavanîya* or sacrificial fire to the heavens, forming a bridge or ladder by means of which the sacrificer can communicate with the world of devas, "and even ascend when alive to their abodes". It is one of the forms of Akâsa, within which the mystic WORD (or its underlying "Sound") calls it into existence. Pronounced by the Priest-Initiate or Yogi, this WORD receives creative powers, and is communicated as an impulse on the terrestrial plane through a trained *Will-power.*

**Yakin and Boaz** (*Heb.*). A Kabbalistic and Masonic symbol. The two pillars of bronze (Yakin, male and white; Boaz, female and red), cast by Hiram Abif of Tyre, called "the Widow's Son , for Solomon's supposed (Masonic) Temple. Yakin was the symbol of Wisdom (*Chokmah*), the second Sephira; and Boaz, that of Intelligence (*Binah*); the temple between the two being regarded as *Kether*, the crown, Father-Mother.

**Yaksha** (*Sk.*). A class of demons, who, in popular Indian folk-lore, devour men. In esoteric science they are simply evil (elemental) influences, who in the sight of seers and clairvoyants descend on men, when open to the reception of such influences, like a fiery comet or a shooting star.

**Yama** (*Heb.*). The personified third root-race in Occultism. In the Indian Pantheon Yama is the subject of two distinct versions of the myth. In the *Vedas* he is the *god of the dead*, a Pluto or a Minos, with whom the shades of the departed dwell (the Kâmarûpas in Kâmaloka). A hymn speaks of

Yama as the first of men that died, and the first that departed to the world of bliss (Devachan). This, because Yama is the embodiment of the race which was the first to be endowed with *consciousness* (Manas), without which there is neither Heaven nor Hades. Yama is represented as the son of Vivaswat (the Sun). *He had a twin-sister named Yami,* who was ever urging him, according to another hymn, to take her for his wife, in order to perpetuate the species. The above has a very suggestive symbolical meaning, which is explained in Occultism. As Dr. Muir truly remarks, the *Rig-Veda*—the greatest authority on the primeval myths which strike the original key-note of the themes that underlie all the subsequent variations—nowhere shows Yama "as having anything to do with the punishment of the wicked". As king and judge of the dead, a Pluto in short, Yama is a far later creation. One has to study the true character of Yama-Yamî throughout more than one hymn and epic poem, and collect the various accounts scattered in dozens of ancient works, and then he will obtain a consensus of allegorical statements which will be found to corroborate and justify the Esoteric teaching, that Yama-Yamî is the symbol of the *dual Manas,* in one of its mystical meanings. For instance, Yama-Yamî is always represented of a *green* colour and clothed with *red,* and as dwelling in a palace of *copper* and *iron.* Students of Occultism know to which of the human "principles" the green and the red colours, and by correspondence the *iron* and *copper,*' are to be applied. The "twofold-ruler"—the epithet of Yama Yamî—is regarded in the exoteric teachings of the Chino-Buddhists as both judge and criminal, the restrainer of *his own* evil doings and the evil-doer himself. In the Hindu epic poems Yama-Yami is the twin-child of the Sun (the deity) by Sanjnâ (spiritual consciousness); but while Yama is the Aryan "lord of the day", appearing as the symbol of spirit in the East, Yamî is the queen of the night (darkness, ignorance) "who opens to mortals the path to the West"—the emblem of evil and matter. In the *Purânas* Yama has many wives (many Yamis) who force him to dwell in the lower world (Pâtâla, Myalba, etc., etc.); and an allegory represents him with his foot lifted, to kick Chhâyâ, the hand maiden of his father (the astral body of his mother, Sanjnâ, a metaphysical aspect of Buddhi or Alaya). As stated in the Hindu Scriptures, a soul when it quits its mortal frame, repairs to its abode in the lower regions (Kâmaloka or Hades). Once there, the Recorder, the Karmic messenger called *Chitragupta* (hidden or concealed brightness), reads out his account from the Great Register, wherein during the life of the human being, every deed and thought are indelibly impressed-—and, according to the sentence pronounced, the "soul" either ascends to the abode of the Pitris (Devachan), descends to a "hell" (Kâmaloka), or is reborn on earth in another human form. The student of Esoteric philosophy will easily recognise the bearings of the allegories.

**Yamabooshee**, or *Yamabusi (Jap.)*. A sect in Japan of very ancient and revered mystics. They are monks "militant" and warriors, if needed, as are certain Yogis in Rajputana and the Lamas in Tibet. This Mystic brotherhood dwell chiefly near Kioto, and are renowned for their healing powers, says the *Encyclopœdia*, which translates the name "Hermit Brothers": "They pretend to magical arts, and live in the recesses of mountains and craggy steeps, whence they come forth to tell *fortunes* (?), write charms and sell amulets. They lead a mysterious life and admit no one to their secrets, except after a tedious and difficult preparation by *fasting* and a species of severe *gymnastic exercise* !")

**Yasna**, or *Yacna (Pahl.)*. The third portion of the first of the two parts of the Avesta, the Scripture of the Zoroastrian Parsis. The Yasna is composed of litanies of the same kind as the *Vispêrad* (the second portion) and of five hymns or *gâthas*. These *gâthas* are the oldest fragments of Zoroastrian literature known to the Parsis, for they are written "in a special dialect, older than the general language of the *Avesta*" (Darmesteter). (See "Zend".)

**Yati** *(Sk)* A measure of three feet.

**Yâtus**, or *Yâtudhânas (Sk.)*. A kind of animal-formed demons. Esoterically, human animal passions.

**Yazathas** *(Zend)*. Pure celestial spirits, whom the *Vendidâd* shows once upon a time sharing their food with mortals, who thus participate in their existence.

**Years of Brahmâ**. The whole period of "Brahma's Age" (100 Years). Equals 311,040,000,000,000 years. (See "Yuga".)

**Yeheedah** *(Heb.)*. Lit., "Individuality"; esoterically, the highest individuality or Âtmâ-Buddhi-Manas, when united in one. This doctrine is in the *Chaldean Book of Numbers,* which teaches a septenary division of human "principles", so-called, as does the *Kabalah* in the *Zohar,* according to the *Book of Solomon* (iii.,Io4a so as translated in I. Myer's *Qabbalah*). At the time of the conception, the Holy "sends a *d'yook-nah*, or the *phantom* of a shadow image" like the *face of a man*. it is designed and sculptured in the divine *tzelem,* i.e., the shadow image of the Elohim. "Elohim created man in his (their) *tzelem*" or image, says *Genesis* (i. 27). It is the *tzelem* that awaits the child and receives it at the moment of its conception, and this *tzelem* is our *linga sharira.* "The *Rua'h* forms with the *Nephesh* the actual personality of the man", and also his *individuality,* or, as expressed by the Kabbalist, the combination of the two is called, if he (man) deserves it*, Yeheedah.* This combination is that which the Theosophist calls the *dual* Manas, the *Higher* and the Lower Ego, united to Âtmâ-Buddhi and become one. For as explained in the *Zohar* (i., 205b, 206a, Brody Ed.): "*Neshamah,* soul (Buddhi), comprises three degrees, and therefore she has three names, like the mystery above: that is, *Nephesh, Rua'h, Neshamah*", or the Lower Manas, the Higher Ego, and Buddhi, the Divine Soul. "It is also to be noted that the *Neshamah* has three divisions;" says Myer's Qabbalah, "the highest is the *Ye-hee-dah*"—or Âtmâ-Buddhi-Manas, the latter once more as a unit; "the middle principle is *Hay-yak*"—or Buddhi and the dual Manas; "and the last and third, the *Neshamah,* properly speaking"—or Soul in general. "They manifest themselves in *Ma'hshabah,* thought, *Tzelem,* phantom of the image, *Zurath,* prototypes (mâyâvic forms, or *rûpas*), and the *D'yooknah,* shadow of the phantom image. The *D'mooth,* likeness or similitude (physical body), is a lower manifestation" (p. 392). Here then, we find the faithful echo of Esoteric science in the *Zohar* and other Kabbalistic works, a perfect Esoteric *septenary* division. Every Theosophist who has studied the doctrine sketched out first in Mr. Sinnett's *Occult World and Esoteric Buddhism,* and later in the *Theosophist, Lucifer,* and other writings, will recognise them in the *Zohar.* Compare for instance what is taught in Theosophical works about the *pre-*and *post-mortem* states of the three higher and the four lower human principles, with the following from the *Zohar:* "Because all these three are one knot like the above, in the mystery of *Nephesh, Rua'h, Neshamah,* they are all one, and bound in one. *Nephesh* (Kâma-Manas) has no light from her own substance; and it is for this reason that she is associated with the mystery of *guff,* the body, to procure enjoyment and food and everything which it needs.

*Rua'h* (the Spirit) is that which rides on that *Nephesh* (the lower soul) and rules over her and lights (supplies) her with everything she needs [with the light of reason], and the *Nephesh* is the throne [of that *Ru'ah. Neshamah* (Divine Soul) goes over to that *Rua'h,* and she rules over that *Rua'h* and lights to him with that Light of Life, and that *Rua'h* depends on the *Neshamah* and receives light from her, which illuminates him. . . When the 'upper' *Neshamah* ascends (after the death of the body), she goes to . . . the Ancient of the Ancient, the Hidden of all the Hidden, to receive Eternity. The *Rua'h* does not [go to *Gan Eden* [because he is [up with] *Nephesh* the *Rua'h* goes up to Eden, but not so high as the soul, and *Nephesh* [animal principle, lower soul] remains in the grave below [Kâmaloka] (*Zohar*, ii., 142a, Cremona Ed., ii., fol. 63b col. 252). It would be difficult not to recognise in the above our Âtmâ (or the "upper" *Neshamah*), Buddhi (*Neshamah*),. Manas (*Rua'h*), and Kâma-Manas (*Nephesh*) or the lower animal soul; the first of which goes after the death of man to join its integral whole, the second and the third proceeding to Devachan, and the last, or the Kâmarûpa, "remaining in its grave", called other wise the Kâmaloka or Hades.

**Yênê, Angânta**. The meaning of the *Angânta Yênê* is known to all India. It is the action of an *elemental (bhût)*, who, drawn into the sensitive and passive body of a medium, takes possession of it. In other words, *angânta vênê* means literally "obsession". The Hindus dread such a calamity now as strongly as they did thousands of years ago. "No Hindu, Tibetan, or Sinhalese, unless of the lowest caste and intelligence, can see, without a shudder of horror, the signs of 'mediumship' manifest themselves in a member of his family, or without saying, as a Christian would do now, ' he hath the devil'. This 'gift, blessing, and holy mission', so called in England and America. is, among the older peoples, in the cradle-lands of our race, where longer experience than ours has taught them more spiritual wisdom, regarded as a dire misfortune."

**Yesod** (*Heb.*). The ninth Sephira; meaning Basis or Foundation.

**Yetzirah** (*Heb.*). The third of the Four Kabbalistic Worlds, referred to the Angels; the "World of Formation", or *Olam Yetzirah*. It is also called Malahayah, or "of the Angels". It is the abode of all the ruling Genii (or Angels) who control and rule planets, worlds and spheres.

**Yeu** (*Chin.*). "Being", a synonym of *Subhâva;* or "the Substance giving substance to itself".

**Yggdrasil** (*Scand.*). The "World Tree of the Norse Cosmogony; the ash Yggdrasil; the tree of the Universe, of time and of life". It has three roots, which reach down to cold Hel, and spread thence to Jotun heim, the land of the Hrimthurses, or "Frost Giants", and to Midgard, the earth and dwelling of the children of men. Its upper boughs stretch out into heaven, and its highest branch overshadows Waihalla, the Devachan of the fallen heroes. The Yggdrasil is ever fresh and green, as it is daily sprinkled by the Norns, the three fateful sisters, the Past, the Present, and the Future, with the waters of life from the fountain of Urd that flows on our earth. It will wither and disappear only on the day when the last battle between good and evil is fought; when, the former prevailing, life, time and space pass out of life and space and time. Every ancient people had their world-tree. The Babylonians had their "tree of life", which was the world-tree, whose roots penetrated into the great lower deep or Hades, whose trunk was on the earth, and whose upper boughs reached *Zikum*, the highest heaven above. Instead of in Walhalla, they placed its upper foliage in the holy house of Davkina, the "great mother" of Tammuz, the Saviour of the world—the Sun-god put to death by the enemies of light.

**Yi-King.** (*Chin.*). An ancient Chinese work, written by generations of sages.

**Yima** (*Zend*). In the *Vendîdâd*, the first man, and, from his aspect of *spiritual* progenitor of mankind, the same as Yama *(q.v.)*. His further functions are not given in the Zend books, because so many of these ancient fragments have been lost, made away with, or otherwise prevented from falling into the hands of the profane. Yima was not born, for he represents the first three human Root-races, the first of which is "not born"; but he is the "first man *who dies*", because the third race, the one which was informed by the rational *Higher Egos*, was the first one whose men separated into male and female, and "man lived and died, and was reborn". (See *S. D.*, Vol. II., pp. 60 *et seq.*)

**Ymir** (*Scand.*). The personified matter of our globe in a seething condition. The cosmic monster in the form of a giant, who is killed in the cosmogonical allegories of the *Eddas* by the three creators, the sons of Bör, Odin, Wili and We, who are said to have conquered Ymir and created the world out of his body. This allegory shows the three principal forces of nature—separation, formation and growth (or evolution) conquering the unruly, raging "giant" matter, and forcing it to become a world, or an inhabited globe. it is curious that an ancient, primitive and uncultured pagan people, so philosophical and scientifically correct in their views about the origin and formation of the earth, should, in order to be regarded as civilized, have to accept the dogma that *the world was created out of nothing!*

**Yod** (*Heb.*). The tenth letter of the alphabet, the first in the four fold symbol of the compound name Jah-hovah (Jehovah) or *Jah-Eve*, the hermaphrodite force and existence in nature. Without the later vowels, the word Jehovah is written IHVH (the letter Yod standing for all the three English letters y, i, or j, as the case may require), and is male-female. The letter Yod is the symbol of the *lingham*, or male organ, in its natural triple form, as the *Kabalah* shows. The second letter He, has for its symbol the *yoni*, the womb or "window-opening" as the *Kabalah* has it; the symbol of the third letter, the Vau, is a crook or a nail (the bishop's crook having its origin in this), another male letter, and the fourth is the same as the second—the whole meaning to be or to *exist* under one of these forms or both. Thus the word or name is pre-eminently *phallic*, it is that of the fighting god of the Jews, "Lord of Hosts"; of the "aggressive Yod" or Zodh, Cain (by permutation), who slew his *female brother*, Abel, and spilt his (her) blood. This name, selected out of many by the early Christian writers, was an unfortunate one for their religion on account of its associations and original significance; it is a *number at best*, an organ in reality. This letter *Yod* has passed into *God* and *Gott*.

**Yoga** (*Sk.*). (1) One of the six Darshanas or schools of India; a school of philosophy founded by Patanjali, though the real Yoga doctrine, the one that is said to have helped to prepare the world for the preaching of Buddha, is attributed with good reasons to the more ancient sage Yâjnawalkya, the writer of the *Shatapatha Brâhmana*, of *Yajur Veda*, the *Brihad Âranyaka*, and other famous works. (2) The practice of meditation as a means of leading to spiritual liberation. Psycho-spiritual powers are obtained thereby, and induced ecstatic states lead to the clear and correct perception of the eternal truths, in both the visible and invisible universe.

**Yogâchârya** (*Sk.*). (1) A mystic school. (2) Lit., a teacher (*âchârya*) of Yoga, one who has mastered the doctrines and practices of ecstatic meditation— the culmination of which are the *Mahâsiddhis*. It is incorrect to confuse this school with the Tantra, or Mahâtantra school founded by Samantabhadra, for there are two Yogâchârya Schools, one esoteric, the other popular. The doctrines of the latter were compiled and glossed by Asamgha in the sixth century of our era, and his mystic tantras and mantras, his formularies, litanies, spells and mudrâ would certainly, if attempted without a Guru, serve rather purposes of sorcery and black magic than real Yoga. Those who undertake to write upon the subject are generally learned missionaries and haters of Eastern philosophy in general. From these no unbiassed views can be expected. Thus when we read in the *Sanskrit - Chinese Dictionary* of Eitel, that the reciting of mantras (which he calls "spells"!) "should he accompanied by music and distortions of the fingers (mudrâ), that a state of mental fixity (*Samâdhi*} might he reached '—one acquainted, however slightly,. with the real practice of Yoga can only shrug his shoulders. These distortions of the fingers or ,mudrâ are necessary, the author thinks, for the reaching of Samâdhi, "characterized by there being neither thought nor annihilation of thought, and consisting of six-fold bodily (*sic*) and mental happiness (*yogi*) *whence would result endowment with supernatural miracle-working power*". Theosophists cannot be too much warned against such fantastic and prejudiced explanations.

**Yogi** (*Sk.*). (1) Not "a state of six-fold bodily and mental happiness as the result, of ecstatic meditation" (Eitel) but a state which, when reached, makes the practitioner thereof absolute master of his six principles", *he now being merged in the seventh*. It gives him full control, owing to his knowledge of SELF and Self, over his bodily, intellectual and mental states, which, unable any longer to interfere with, or act upon, his Higher Ego, leave it free to exist in its original, pure, and divine state. (2) Also the name of the devotee who practises Yoga.

**Yong-Grüb** (*Tib.*). A state of absolute rest, the same as Paranirvâna.

**Yoni** (*Sk.*). The womb, the female principle.

**Yudishthira** (*Sk.*). One of the heroes of the *Mahâbharata*. The eldest brother of the Pândavas, or the five Pându princes who fought against their next of kin, the Kauravas, the sons of their maternal uncle. Arjuna, the disciple of Krishna, was his younger brother. The *Bhagavad Gîtâ* gives mystical particulars of this war. Kunti was the mother of the Pândavas, and Draupadî the wife in common of the five brothers—an allegory. But Yudishthira is also, as well as Krishna, Arjuna, and so many other heroes, an historical character, who lived some 5,000 years ago, at the period when the Kali Yuga set in.

**Yuga** (*Sk.*). A 1,000th part of a Kalpa. An age of the World of which there are four, and the series of which proceed in succession during the manvantaric cycle. Each Yuga is preceded by a period called in the *Purânas* Sandhyâ, twilight, or transition period, and is followed by another period of like duration called Sandhyânsa, "portion of twilight". Each is equal to one-tenth of the Yuga. The group of four Yugas is first computed by the *divine* years, or "years of the gods"—each such year being equal to 360 years of mortal men. Thus we have, in "divine" years:

| | | | | | |
|---|---|---|---|---|---|
| 1. | Krita or Satya Yuga | - | - | 4,000 |
| | Sandhyâ - | - | - | - | 400 |
| | Sandhyansa- | - | - | - | 400 |
| | | | | | 4,800 |
| 2. | Tretâ Yuga | - | - | - | 3,000 |
| | Sandhyâ | - | - | - | 300 |
| | Sandhyânsa | - | - | - | 300 |
| | | | | | 3,600 |

| 3. | Dwâpara Yuga | - | - | - | 2,000 |
| | Sandhya | - | - | - | 200 |
| | Sandhyânsa | - | - | - | 200 |
| | | | | | 2,400 |
| 4. | Kali Yuga | - | - | - | 1,000 |
| | Sandhyâ | - | - | - | 100 |
| | Sandhyânsa | - | - | - | 100 |
| | | | | | 1,200 |
| | | | | Total | 12,000 |

This rendered in years of mortals equals:

| 4800 | X 360 | = | 1,728,000 |
| 3600 | X 360 | = | 1,296,000 |
| 2400 | X 360 | = | 864,000 |
| 1200 | X 360 | = | 432,000 |
| | | Total | 4,320,000 |

The above is called a Mahâyuga or Manvantara. 2,000 such Mahâyugas, or a period of 8,640,000 years, make a Kalpa the latter being only a "day and a night", or twenty-four hours, of Brahmâ. Thus an "age of Brahmâ", or one hundred of his divine years, must equal 311,040,000,000,000 of our mortal years. The old Mazdeans or Magi (the modern Parsis) had the same calculation, though the Orientalists do not seem to perceive it, for even the Parsi Moheds themselves have forgotten it. But their "Sovereign time of the Long Period" (*Zervan Dareghâ Hvadâta*) lasts 12,000 years, and these are the 12,000 *divine* years of a Mahâyuga as shown above, whereas the *Zervan Akarana* (Limitless Time), mentioned by Zarathustra, is the *Kâla*, out of space and time, of Parabrahm.

**Yurbo Adonai.** A contemptuous epithet given by the followers of the *Nazarene Codex*, the St. John Gnostics, to the Jehovah of the Jews.

**Yürmungander** (*Scand.*). A name of the Midgard snake in the *Edda*, whose brother is Wolf Fenris, and whose sister is the horrible monster Hel—the three children of wicked Loki and Angurboda (carrier of anguish), a dreaded giantess. The mundane snake of the Norsemen, the monster created by Loki but fashioned by the constant putrid emanations from the body of the slain giant Ymir (the matter of our globe), and producing in its turn a constant emanation, which serves as a veil between heaven and earth, *i.e.*, the Astral Light.

# Z

**Z.**—The 26th letter of the English alphabet. It stands as a numeral for 2,000, and with a dash over it thus, Z̄, equals 2,000,000. It is the seventh letter in the Hebrew alphabet—*zayin*, its symbol being a kind of Egyptian sceptre, a weapon. The *zayin* is equivalent to number seven. The number twenty-six is held most sacred by the Kabbalists, being equal to the numerical value of the letters of the Tetragrammaton —thus:

$$he \ vau \ he \ yod$$
$$5 + 6 + 5 + 10 = 26$$

**Zabulon** (*Heb.*). The abode of God, the tenth Devachan in degree. Hence Zabulon, the tenth son of Jacob.

**Zacchai** (*Heb.*). One of the deity-names.

**Zadok** (*Heb.*). According to Josephus (see *Antiquities*, x., 8, § 6), Zadok was the first High-Priest Hierophant of Solomon's High Temple. Masons connect him with some of their degrees.

**Zalmat Gaguadi** (*Akkad.*). Lit., "the dark race", the first that fell into generation in the Babylonian legends. The Adamic race, one of the two principal races that existed at the time of the ' Fall of Man (hence our third Root-race), the other being called *Sarku*, or the "light race". (*S. D.*, II, p. 5.)

**Zampun** (*Tib.*). The sacred tree of life, having many mystic meanings.

**Zarathustra** (*Zend*). The great lawgiver, and the founder of the religion variously called Mazdaism, Magism, Parseeïsm, Fire-Worship, and Zoroastrianism. The age of the last Zoroaster (for it is a generic name) is not known, and perhaps for that very reason. Xanthus of Lydia, the earliest Greek writer who mentions this great lawgiver and religious reformer, places him about six hundred years before the Trojan War. But where is the historian who can now tell when the latter took place? Aristotle and also Eudoxus assign him a date of no less than 6,000 years before the days of Plato, and Aristotle was not one to make a statement without a good reason for it. Berosus makes him a king of Babylon some 2,200 years B.C.; but then, how can one tell what were the original figures of Berosus, before his MSS. passed through the hands of Eusebius, whose fingers were so deft at altering figures, whether in Egyptian synchronistic tables or in Chaldean chronology? Haug refers Zoroaster to at least 1,000 years B.C.; and Bunsen (*God in History*, Vol. I., Book iii., ch. vi., p. 276) finds that Zarathustra Spitama lived under the King Vistaspa about 3,000 years B.C., and describes him as "one of the mightiest intellects and one of the greatest men of all time". It is with such exact dates in hand, and with the utterly extinct language of the Zend, whose teachings are rendered, probably in the most desultory manner, by the Pahlavi translation—a tongue, as shown by Darmsteter, which was itself growing obsolete so far back as the Sassanides—that our scholars and Orientalists have presumed to monopolise to themselves the right of assigning hypothetical dates for the age of the holy prophet Zurthust. But the Occult records claim to have the correct dates of each of the thirteen Zoroasters mentioned in the Dabistan. Their doctrines, and especially those of the last (divine) Zoroaster, spread from Bactria to the Medes; thence, under the name of Magism, incorporated by the Adept-Astronomers in Chaldea, they greatly influenced the mystic teachings of the Mosaic doctrines, even before, perhaps, they had culminated into what is now known as the modern religion of the Parsis. Like Manu and Vyâsa in India, Zarathustra is a generic name for great reformers and law-givers. The hierarchy began with the divine Zarathustra in the *Vendîdâd*, and ended with the great, but mortal man, bearing that title, and now lost to history. There were, as shown by the *Dabistan*, many Zoroasters or Zarathustras. As related in the *Secret Doctrine*, Vol. II., the last Zoroaster was the founder of the Fire-temple of Azareksh, many ages before the historical era. Had not Alexander destroyed so many sacred and precious works of the Mazdeans, truth and philosophy would have been more inclined to agree with history, in bestowing upon that Greek Vandal the title of "the Great".

**Zarpanitu** (*Akkad*) The goddess who was the supposed mother, by Merodach, of *Nebo*, god of Wisdom. One of the female "Serpents of Wisdom".

**Zelator**. The lowest degree in the exoteric Rosicrucian system; a kind of probationer or low chelâ.

**Zend-Avesta** (*Pahl.*). The general name for the sacred books of the Parsis, fire or sun worshippers, as they are ignorantly called. So little is understood of the grand doctrines which are still found in the various fragments that compose all that is now left of that collection of religious works, that Zoroastrianism is called indifferently Fire-worship, Mazdaism, or Magism, Dualism, Sun-worship, and what not. The *Avesta* has two parts as now collected together, the first portion containing the *Vendîdâd*, the *Vispêrad* and the *Yasna*; and the second portion, called the *Khorda Avesta* (Small Avesta), being composed of short prayers called Gâh, Nyâyish, etc.

*Zend* means "a commentary or explanation", and *Avesta* (from the old Persian *âbashtâ,* "the law". (See Darmsteter.) As the translator of the Vendîdâd remarks in a foot note (see int. xxx.): "what it is customary to call 'the Zend language', ought to be named 'the Avesta language', the Zend being no language at all and if the word be used as the designation of one, it can be rightly applied only to the Pahlavi". But then, the Pahlavi itself is only the language into which certain original portions of the *Avesta* are translated. What name should be given to the old *Avesta* language, and particularly to the "special dialect, older than the general language of the *Avesta*" (Darmst.), in which the five Ghthas in the *Yasna* are written? To this day the Orientalists are mute upon the subject. Why should not the Zend be of the same family, if not identical with the Zen-sar, meaning also the speech explaining the abstract symbol, or the "mystery language," used by Initiates?

**Zervana Akarna,** or *Zrvana Akarna (Pahl.).* As translated from the *Vendîdâd* (Fargard xix), lit., "Boundless", or "Limitless Time", or "Duration in a Circle". Mystically, the Beginningless and the Endless One Principle in Nature; the *Sat* of the Vedânta and esoterically, the Universal Abstract Space synonymous with the Unknowable Deity. It is the Ain-Soph of the Zoroastrians, out of which radiates Ahura Mazda, the eternal Light or Logos, from which, in its turn, emanates everything that has being, existence and form.

**Zeus** (*Gr.*). The "Father of the gods". *Zeus-Zen* is Æther, there fore Jupiter was called Pater Æther by some Latin races.

**Zicu** (*Akkad.*). Primordial matter, from **Zi**, spirit-substance, *Zikum* and *Zigarum.*

**Zio** (*Scand.*). Also Tyr and Tius, A god in the *Eddas* who conquers and chains Fenris-Wolf, when the latter threatened the gods themselves in Asgard, and lost a hand in the battle with the monster. He is the god of war, and was greatly worshipped by the ancient Germans.

**Zipporah** (*Heb.*). Lit., the shining, the radiant. In the Biblical allegory of *Genesis,* Zipporah is one of the *seven* daughters of Jethro, the Midianite priest, the Initiator of Moses, who meets Zipporah (or spiritual light) near the "well" (of occult knowledge) and marries her.

**Zirat-banit** (*Chald.*). The wife of the great, divine hero of the Assyrian tablets, Merodach. She is identified with the Succoth Benoth of the Bible.

**Ziruph** (*Heb.*). More properly Tziruph, a mode of divination by Temura, or permutation of letters, taught by the mediæval Kabbalists. The school of

Rabbis Abulafia and Gikatilla laid the most stress on the value of this process of the Practical *Kabalah*. [w.w.w.]

**Zodiac** (*Gr.*). From the word *zodion*, a diminutive of *zoon*, animal. This word is used in a dual meaning; it may refer to the fixed and intellectual Zodiac, or to the movable and natural Zodiac. "In astronomy", says Science, "it is an imaginary belt in the heavens 16° or 18° broad, through the middle of which passes the sun's path (the ecliptic) ."It contains the twelve constellations which constitute the twelve signs of the Zodiac, and from which they are named. As the nature of the *zodiacal light*—that elongated, luminous, triangular figure which, lying almost in the ecliptic, with its base on the horizon and its apex at greater and smaller altitudes, is to be seen only during the morning and evening twilights—is entirely unknown to science, the origin and real significance and occult meaning of the Zodiac were, and are still, a mystery, to all save the Initiates. The latter preserved their secrets well. Between the Chaldean star-gazer and the modern astrologer there lies to this day a wide gulf indeed; and they wander, in the words of Albumazar, "'twixt the poles, and heavenly hinges, 'mongst eccentricals, centres, concentricks, circles and epicycles", with vain pretence to more than *profane* human skill. Yet, some of the astrologers, from Tycho Braire and Kepler of astrological memory, down to the modern Zadkiels and Raphaels, have contrived to make a wonderful science from such scanty occult materials as they have had in hand from Ptolemy downwards. (See "Astrology".) To return to the astrological Zodiac proper, however, it is an imaginary circle passing round the earth in the plane of the equator, its first point being called Aries 0°. It is divided into twelve equal parts called "Signs of the Zodiac", each containing 30° of space, and on it is measured the right ascension of celestial bodies. The movable or natural Zodiac is a succession of constellations forming a belt of in width, lying north and south of the plane of the ecliptic. The precession of the Equinoxes is caused by the "motion" of the sun through space, which makes the constellations appear to move forward against the order of the signs at the rate of 501/3 seconds per year. A simple calculation will show that at this rate the constellation Taurus (*Heb. Aleph*) was in the first sign of the Zodiac at the beginning of the Kali Yuga, and consequently the Equinoctial point fell therein. At this time, also, Leo was in the summer solstice, Scorpio in the autumnal Equinox, and Aquarius in the winter solstice; and these facts form the astronomical key to half the religious mysteries of the world—the Christian scheme included. The Zodiac was known in India and Egypt for incalculable ages, and the knowledge of the sages (magi) of these countries, with regard to the occult influence of the stars and heavenly bodies on our earth, was far greater than profane astronomy can ever hope to reach to. If, even now, when most of the secrets of the Asuramayas and the Zoroasters are lost, it is still amply shown that horoscopes and judiciary astrology are far from being based on fiction, and if such men as Kepler and even Sir Isaac Newton believed that stars and constellations influenced the destiny of our globe and its humanities, it requires no great stretch of faith to believe that men who were initiated into all the mysteries of nature, as well as into astronomy and astrology, knew precisely in what way nations and mankind, whole races as well as individuals, would be affected by the so-called "signs of the Zodiac".

**Zohak**, or *Azhi Dâhaka*. The personification of the Evil One or Satan under the shape of a serpent, in the *Zend Avesta*. This serpent is three-headed, one of the heads being human. The Avesta describes it as dwelling in the region of Bauri or Babylonia. In reality Zohak is the allegorical symbol of the Assyrian dynasty, whose banner had on it the purple sign of the dragon. (*Isis Unveiled*, Vol. II., p. 486, n.)

**Zohar**, or *Sohar*. A compendium of Kabbalistic Theosophy, which shares with the *Sepher Yetzirah* the reputation of being the oldest extant treatise on the Hebrew esoteric religious doctrines. Tradition assigns its authorship to Rabbi Simeon ben Jochai, AD. 80, but modern criticism is inclined to believe that a very large portion of the volume is no older than 1280, when it was certainly edited and published by Rabbi Moses de Leon, of Guadalaxara in Spain. The reader should consult the references to these two names. In *Lucifer* (Vol. I., p. 141) will be found also notes on this subject: further discussion will be attainable in the works of Zunz, Graetz, Jost, Steinschneider, Frankel and Ginsburg. The work of Franck (in French) upon the *Kabalah* may be referred to with advantage. The truth seems to lie in a middle path, viz., that while Moses de Leon was the first to produce the volume as a whole, yet a large part of some of its constituent tracts consists of traditional dogmas and illustrations, which have come down from the time of Simeon ben Jochai and the Second Temple. There are portions of the doctrines of the Zohar which bear the impress of Chaldee thought and civilization, to which the Jewish race had been exposed in the Babylonish captivity. Yet on the other hand, to condemn the theory that it is ancient in its entirety, it is noticed that the Crusades are mentioned; that a quotation is made from a hymn by Ibn Gebirol, A,D. 1050; that the asserted author, Simeon ben Jochai, is spoken of as more eminent than

Moses; that it mentions the vowel-points, which did not come into use until Rabbi Mocha (AD. 570) introduced them to fix the pronunciation of words as a help to his pupils, and lastly, that it mentions -a comet which can be proved by the evidence of the context to have appeared in 1264. There is no English translation of the *Zohar* as a whole, nor even a Latin one. The Hebrew editions obtainable are those of Mantua, 1558; Cremona, 1560; and Lublin, 1623. The work of Knorr von Rosenroth called *Kabbala Denudata* includes several of the treatises of the *Zohar*, but not all of them, both in Hebrew and Latin. MacGregor Mathers has published an English translation of three of these treatises, the *Book of Concealed Mystery*, the *Greater* and the *Lesser Holy Assembly*, and his work includes an original introduction to the subject.

The principal tracts included in the *Zohar* are:—" The Hidden Midrash", "The Mysteries of the Pentateuch", "The Mansions and Abodes of Paradise and Gaihinnom", "The Faithful Shepherd", "The Secret of Secrets", "Discourse of the Aged in Mishpatim" (punishment of souls), "The Januka or Discourse of the Young Man", and "The Tosephta and Mathanithan", which are additional essays on Emanation and the Sephiroth, in addition to the three important treatises mentioned above. In this storehouse may be found the origin of all the later developments of Kabbalistic teaching. [w.w.w.]

**Zoroaster.** Greek form of Zarathustra (*q.v.*).

**Zumyad Yasht** (*Zend*). Or *Zamyad Yasht* as some spell it. One of the preserved Mazdean fragments. It treats of metaphysical questions and beings, especially of the *Amshaspends* or the *Amesha Spenta*—the Dhyân Chohans of the *Avesta* books.

**Zuñi.** The name of a certain tribe of Western American Indians, a very ancient remnant of a still more ancient race. (*S. D.*, Vol. II, p. 628.)